FOUR-STROKE PERFORMANCE TUNING

FOUR-STROKE
PERFORMANCE
TUNING
Third edition

A. GRAHAM BELL

Haynes Publishing

First published by G.T. Foulis & Company February 1981
Reprinted March 1982
Reprinted August 1983
Revised and reprinted February 1985
Reprinted January 1986
Reprinted February 1988
Reprinted October 1989
Reprinted January 1991
Reprinted October 1993
Reprinted June 1995
Reprinted March 1997
2nd edition published by Haynes Publishing August 1998
Revised and reprinted January 2001
Reprinted May and December 2002
Reprinted September 2003
Reprinted November 2004
Reprinted January 2006
3rd edition published by Haynes Publishing July 2006

British Library Cataloguing in Publication Data
A catalogue record for this book is available from the British Library

ISBN 1 84425 314 7

Library of Congress catalog card no. 2006921754

Haynes Publishing, Sparkford,
Yeovil, Somerset BA22 7JJ, UK

Tel: 01963 442030 Fax: 01963 440001
Int. tel: +44 1963 442030 Int. fax: +44 1963 440001

E-mail: sales@haynes.co.uk
Website: www.haynes.co.uk

Haynes North America, Inc.
861 Lawrence Drive, Newbury Park,
California 91320 USA

Typeset by G&M, Raunds, Northamptonshire
Printed and bound in Great Britain by J. H. Haynes & Co., Ltd

Jurisdictions which have strict emission control laws may consider any modification to a
vehicle to be an infringement of those laws. You are advised to check with the appropriate
body or authority whether your proposed modification complies fully with the law. The
publishers accept no liability in this regard.

Contents

Preface

Practically no private owners, and only a few workshops where race engines are prepared, possess dynamometers. Consequently experiments in tuning usually must be conducted on a trial and error basis, which may have unfortunate results if the work has been wrongly conceived or executed. This book represents an endeavour to fill the gaps in the enthusiast's and race engine builder's knowledge, or to extend an acquaintance with the subject considerably further.

The range of performance equipment available for almost any car or motorcycle is staggering and often the claims made in advertising various items of equipment are equally staggering. Obviously there must be certain principles, applying to almost any engine, that will, if closely followed, bring good results. I believe that this type of information should be available to the tuner, to enable him to choose the best equipment and the best combination of modifications to suit his needs. With this in mind I have attempted to relate these principles in non-technical English and to illustrate them using many diagrams.

While I have endeavoured to make this work as complete and as comprehensive as possible, undoubtedly there will be questions that I will have overlooked and left unanswered. On the other hand there are certain to be times when the reader may feel that I have dwelt far too long on a particular point. I apologise for this. However, in spite of these possible failings I am sure this book will be found both instructive and informative by all who are involved in developing either high output or maximum effort competition engines.

A. Graham Bell
Maitland
New South Wales

Chapter 1

An Introduction to Four-stroke Engine Tuning Principles

Most people hate the idea of getting into involved physics and associated maths. Like it or loathe it we are surrounded by physical laws that affect us from day to day. Some of those laws we can pretty much ignore but others constantly remind us of their presence. Take the law of gravity or the day/night cycle as the earth rotates around the sun. Now we don't need to know the science behind those things to live but it sure helps when you have some knowledge that establishes a pattern which enables you to work with and use these things to your advantage.

For example, you make decisions, perhaps not consciously, that the sun is high in the sky at the middle of the day. Likewise you make decisions based on the pattern that it is cold in winter and daylight hours are short. Therefore, if you must venture into the mountains at that time, you know what to expect and you plan accordingly to ensure your survival. On the other hand you may plan to take advantage of the low temperature and explore the desert at a most favourable time.

Engine modification and tuning is no different. If we can train ourselves to "see" those patterns established by physical laws we should wisely choose to make our plans to let them work to our advantage. However, if for some reason we have to work against a natural law we can plan accordingly and make provision to ensure that our engine survives.

UNDERSTANDING AIR DENSITY

The very first principle that we have to come to grips with is that air density is not constant. At sea level air is 35% more dense than at 10,000 feet altitude. Therefore it is often said that the air is thinner at high altitude as the gas molecules are spaced further apart. Consequently air weighs less at altitude. The figures are 0.0765lb/ft³ at sea level and 0.0565lb/ft³ at 10,000ft.

Taking this principle a step further it should follow that a 2-litre engine will fill its cylinders with 2 litres of air at 10,000ft just as it does at sea level. However, at 7

Standard Atmosphere Chart

Altitude		Air Pressure			Temperature		Density		Relative Density
ft	m	in Hg	psi	mB	°F	°C	lb/ft³	kg/m³	
Sea level		29.92	14.7	1013	59.0	15.0	0.00765	1.225	1.000
1,000	305	28.86	14.2	977	55.4	13.0	0.00742	1.189	0.997
2,000	610	27.82	13.7	942	51.9	11.1	0.00722	1.156	0.993
3,000	914	26.81	13.2	908	48.3	9.1	0.00714	1.144	0.989
4,000	1219	25.84	12.7	875	44.7	7.1	0.00680	1.090	0.986
5,000	1524	24.90	12.2	843	41.2	5.1	0.00660	1.058	0.982
6,000	1829	23.98	11.8	812	37.6	3.1	0.00639	1.024	0.979
7,000	2134	23.09	11.3	782	34.1	1.2	0.00682	1.093	0.975
8,000	2438	22.23	10.9	753	30.5	-0.8	0.00601	0.962	0.972
9,000	2743	21.39	10.5	724	26.9	-2.8	0.00582	0.933	0.969
10,000	3048	20.58	10.1	697	23.4	-4.8	0.00565	0.905	0.965
11,000	3353	19.80	9.7	670	19.8	-6.8	0.00547	0.876	0.962
12,000	3658	19.03	9.3	644	16.2	-8.8	0.00530	0.849	0.958
13,000	3962	18.30	9.0	620	12.7	-10.7	0.00513	0.822	0.954
14,000	4267	17.58	8.6	595	9.1	-12.7	0.00498	0.797	0.951
15,000	4572	16.89	8.3	572	5.6	-14.7	0.00483	0.773	0.947

Pressure Exerted by Humidity (millibar)

Temperature		Relative humidity %									
°C	°F	10	20	30	40	50	60	70	80	90	100
10	50	1	2	4	5	6	7	9	10	11	12
20	68	2	5	7	9	12	14	15	19	21	23
25	77	3	6	10	13	16	19	22	25	29	32
30	86	4	8	13	17	21	25	30	34	38	42
35	95	6	11	17	22	28	34	39	45	51	56
40	104	7	15	22	30	37	44	52	59	56	74
45	113	10	19	29	38	48	57	67	77	86	96
50	122	12	25	37	49	62	74	86	99	111	123

altitude because those 2 litres of air contain less oxygen (about 26% less) the engine will produce substantially less power. In fact, a rule of thumb is that hp will decrease 3% for each 1,000ft.

However, altitude is not the only factor influencing air density. Heat also expands air, consequently at sea level 40°C air is less dense than air at 5°C. Therefore our 2-litre engine will make less power on hot air than cold air. Another rule of thumb; you lose 1% hp for each 7°C increase in air temperature.

Humidity affects air differently. High humidity, high moisture content in the air causes a barometer to read higher. However, rather than being more dense the air actually has less density – it is simply the combined weight of the air plus the water that appears to make the air more dense. Generally this is not a large consideration, however high humidity at elevated temperatures does reduce the oxygen content enough to reduce power. For example, 65% humidity and 35°C at sea level reduces the oxygen content to a similar level to that at 1,000ft elevation.

Do you see a pattern emerging from the preceding four paragraphs? That is an engine will make more power at sea level on dense air which is cold and dry. Conversely, power decreases with increases in altitude, air temperature and humidity.

AIR DENSITY WITHIN THE ENGINE

The next principle that we need to establish is that two 2-litre engines operating at the same atmospheric conditions can have different hp outputs because the air is more dense in the cylinders of one than the other. Even though air quality started out at the same level things change on the passage into the cylinders. One engine has everything working against it. It is drawing in air which has been heated by the radiator and exhaust manifold. Its inlet manifold receives no cooling air flow, but rather hot air that has passed through the radiator. Internally this engine is very hot. The water temperature is regulated at 95°C so the air flowing into the cylinders collects heat

Right: This engine features an impressive-to-the-eye inlet system featuring what appears to be a tuned length inlet manifold with rolled entry bellmouths. Unfortunately the engine will now be breathing hot low-density air, especially as the uninsulated exhaust headers and the hot engine are only inches away from the air intakes.

Below: Melted ceramic core in CAT blocks exhaust flow.

from the inlet port walls and expands on its way through. The ignition timing is retarded (in itself this reduces power) which raises the temperature of the exhaust valve and that area of the combustion chamber, as well as the piston crown. Consequently as the intake air discharges into the cylinders it expands rapidly and the cylinder volume is quickly filled by what is now 'thin' air.

However, this engine's problem areas don't stop here. The exhaust system is quite restrictive in itself, but additionally the CAT has overheated and the internal honeycomb-like ceramic material has melted blocking many of the gas flow passages. This is causing exhaust back pressure which is not allowing the cylinders to completely empty of exhaust gas. These remaining gases mingle with the fresh inlet fuel/air mixture and upset combustion, but prior to that event because their temperature can easily exceed 800°C they quickly heat the inlet mixture causing it to rapidly expand and block further inlet flow. Consequently the cylinders are filled with a thin, low density, inlet charge.

On the inlet side the story isn't good either. The air filter is blocked with dust and the air filter box doesn't flow well. It has been designed to keep induction noise very low by using various ribs, baffles, resonators and tortuous passages. The final outcome

Right: Carbon build-up on inlet valves blocks air flow and massively lowers air density in the cylinders.

Below: Stock valves backcut to help cylinder filling and lightly polished to slow carbon build-up.

at full throttle is that the engine has a vacuum reading of 2in Hg (mercury), measured just before the throttle body. The vacuum reading ideally should be zero, so that we can take advantage of a full 14.7psi air pressure to push air into the cylinders. A vacuum reading of 2in Hg is almost 1psi, therefore this engine has only 13.7psi working for it to fill the cylinders.

Further on in the inlet tract there are more restrictions. Gaskets overlap a number of inlet passages, but the main concern is the massive build-up of carbon on the back of the inlet valves. This is blocking flow into the cylinders until the valves are lifted nearly 50% off their seats. Obviously all these restrictions work to further lower air density in the cylinders.

The other engine by comparison has everything working in its favour to ensure maximum charge density in the cylinders and maximum hp. The inlet system is free of restrictions. The air intake is at the front of the car collecting air at ambient temperature. The water temperature is regulated so as not to exceed 85°C, thus minimising the amount of heat the air will gather in the inlet passages. The exhaust is a free flow item with zero back pressure to minimise the amount of exhaust gas left behind in the cylinders. The ignition timing has been optimised for best power. As a side benefit this lowers exhaust gas temperature so any residual gas puts less heat into the inlet change. Also the exhaust valve and piston run cooler which helps mixture density as well.

The pattern here is that cylinder charge density is influenced by numerous factors which the engine builder or tuner can control. If the engine is 'plugged up' on the inlet side and/or the exhaust side, cylinder charge density will be lowered. Also if the engine or individual components are excessively hot due to high coolant temperatures or incorrect spark timing (excessive advance will also overheat the piston and combustion chamber, not just retarded ignition) cylinder charge density will be lowered. On the other hand an engine which breathes freely on both the inlet and exhaust side, plus is operating at the ideal coolant temperature and ignition advance, will have a cylinder charge density closer to atmospheric air density.

A cold air intake constructed of polished aluminium to reflect heat from the engine and ceramic coated headers help keep cylinder charge density high.

BEWARE OF CRUTCHES

However, there is another factor to be considered. At this point we have two 2-litre engines, one filled with thin air the other filled with air closer to atmospheric density. Is it possible that at the point of ignition the charge densities could be almost equal? Obviously if we squeeze the low density charge into a small combustion space using a high compression ratio the density can be increased, but remember this will be limited by available fuel octane and the low density charge is much hotter, (this is not always the case) so more likely to detonate anyway. Perhaps if we were extremely conservative and set the compression ratio way too low on the good engine at certain engine rpm the compressed charge densities could possibly be almost equalised; but the problem really hasn't changed – fiddling the compression ratio, using some crutch, usually does not compensate for low charge density.

In other words we must do all we can to avoid low charge density. Otherwise adding any type of tuning modification could become just another crutch. Sure the engine may run much better, but nothing close to its true potential will be realised.

By now it should be clear that it is high charge density that makes power, and apart from poor engine breathing characteristics the big enemy of charge density is heat. Any time heat is added to the air, charge density goes down.

Ensuring the cylinders are packed full, however, is only half the battle. Next we have to ignite that fuel air charge and control the rate at which it burns so as to progressively release all the heat energy locked up in the fuel. That heat energy in turn produces the pressure we need to force the pistons down to turn the crankshaft and make power.

PLAN CAREFULLY

On the surface that may appear fairly simple, however from the outset let me caution you on the need to plan your intended modifications carefully. Avoid over-enthusiasm and keep in mind that seldom, if ever, is the biggest or most expensive the best. Compatibility of the intended modifications cannot be over-stressed. Most enthusiasts realise that it is useless to install a full race cam in a standard motor, yet it is amazing how many will hang very expensive and impressive-looking carburettors off that same standard motor. Then we have the enthusiast who plans his performance modifications carefully. He has a head, cam, carbs and exhaust that work nicely together, but in so doing the motor now produces maximum power at 7,800rpm, whereas the crankshaft, rods and pistons have a safe limit of 6,800rpm. Less enthusiasm with the cam and carburettor size would have produced a motor that was much nicer to drive, and less likely to blow up.

Race engine builders can also fall for many traps in their enthusiasm to find that winning edge. If you have loads of money and/or heaps of engineering talent and time on your hands, go ahead and chase after every 'trick' part or smart idea at the end of the 'horsepower rainbow'. Basically my message is 'don't build oddball engines', but rather within reason try to retain as many stock parts, or heavy-duty parts with stock dimensions, as possible and stick to well-proven, conservative tuning methods.

Additionally have a look around at what other tuners and racers are doing in the way of modifications, and see what kinds of engines are competitive in the particular class where you plan to run. When you notice a lightweight all-alloy 2-litre eight-valve engine with a 30hp power deficit consistently thrash a 2-litre 16-valver with an iron block, and a good number of people race with both engine brands, see what lesson you can learn. Obviously the class demands not more power, but less overall engine weight and less weight in the top of the engine. Hence if you want to be competitive you are going to have to opt for the less sophisticated eight-valve engine, even if it is a brand for which you do not have a passion.

On the other hand, if you fancy yourself an innovator able to change the course of history you might reckon that an all-alloy 16-valve flat four is the way to go; it is light and powerful and has a low centre of gravity. If that is the case, ask yourself why no one else has come up with such a brilliant idea. Could it be that this engine will not fit the conventional chassis too well; is it unreliable; does it require the replacement of virtually every internal part, which makes it twice as expensive to run; is tuning knowledge of this engine limited where you live; are tuning parts hard to obtain, etc?

The idea is to learn from the experience and mistakes of others rather than repeat the whole sorry saga yourself. Hence be prepared to listen and learn, but don't be gullible. For example, if some 'expert' tells you that you must use stronger rod bolts in a Pinto engine to run at 8,500rpm, but no tuning house sells heavy-duty bolts, what conclusion should you reach? Either Pinto rod bolts are very strong so they do not need to be replaced, or else the rods will break before the bolts, so it would be fraudulent to sell anyone a set of stronger bolts. To find which conclusion is correct the next question should be 'what is the safe rpm limit of stock Pinto rods?'

As personal computers become more a part of everyday life, some enthusiasts are turning to the 'web' or to computer discs in the search for tuning information. However, there is a need for caution as it is not without good reason that the so-called information superhighway has been dubbed the 'misinformation superhighway'. Always question if real facts or just hearsay are being presented. When it comes to 'cyber-tuning' from a computer disc, remember that the information presented is only as good as the programme originator and his knowledge of engines. From what I hear, some of the stuff getting on to computer screens is pretty questionable; on the other hand there is information that is quite accurate, providing you are tuning a small-block Chev V8!

Another decision an enthusiast must face is whether he will purchase a fully built engine, a kit of parts that he will assemble himself, or will he plan his modifications himself, then go out and independently purchase all the necessary parts from various sources and finally put everything together? Obviously the first option has the highest initial cost and you miss out on any fun bolting it all together, but if the engine is on the pace at the track and you enjoy racing rather than experimenting, this could be a good option. Option number two gives you the best of both worlds in that it allows you to tap into a professional engine builder's knowledge for the price of a kit of parts that has been proven in competition, but you get to save some money and at the same time gain some enjoyment assembling all the goodies. The last option can appear to be the cheapest, but if you get the wrong mix of parts you could finish up very disappointed. There is a lot of satisfaction in going it alone with an engine and succeeding in your chosen form of competition, but you may go through a lot of money finding just what parts it takes to gain the required performance. I guess it probably gets down to what you want out of the deal. If time is limited and you really   13 enjoy being behind the wheel a lot more than proving yourself as a tuner, opt for a built-up or kit engine. However, if you are really a tuner at heart and you are convinced that long hours in the workshop and dyno room are much more enjoyable than time behind the wheel, you are probably a candidate for option three.

A good engine tuner is in many respects akin to the conductor of a symphony orchestra in that he must work to get everything playing in harmony off the same sheet of music. First he must choose the 'music' – is the engine for road, rally, race circuit or drag strip use? Then he must know and accurately assess his chosen engine. He must dispassionately determine what its good and weak points are and estimate what improvements in performance the rectification of each weak point will bring about in relation to the amount of money it is going to cost to rectify that problem area. However, if one section of the orchestra is tuned to work at 8,000rpm and the other section is only capable of 7,500rpm, we are in trouble.

Another example: if the stock cast iron crank is good for 230hp and 8,500rpm and you are planning a cylinder head that flows only enough air for 200hp at 8,000rpm, why throw out the stock crank for a long-stroke steel crank that will give a 3% power increase and cost an arm and a leg? In similar vein, if the stock block and cast crank work fine with a bore of 84.8mm and a stroke of 88mm, why go to the expensive big-bore block and short-stroke steel crank used by the factory team to obtain an 87mm bore and 84mm stroke? Will knocking 4mm off the stroke and taking the bore out 2mm really make so much difference, or would all that money be better used elsewhere?

However, this is not to say that a large sum of money should not be expended on something like a steel crank. It may in fact be very sound economics to spend that sort of money. If you do a lot of race miles and the cast crank requires replacement every 300 miles due to cracking, it makes good sense to use a steel crank that costs, say, four times the amount but has a 'life' of 5,000 race miles.

Another area for consideration when you set out to plan engine modifications is always to relate the engine to the vehicle in which it is going to be used, and plan your modifications accordingly.

The first influence is the size of the motor. Obviously a heavy vehicle with a small motor will require a power curve biased towards low and mid-range power, rather than to all-out power, if it is to remain driveable. A larger engine in the same car could be more extensively modified and it would produce as much, or even more, power at lower engine speeds.

The engine capacity/vehicle weight relationship must also be reckoned along with gearbox ratios, the number of gears and steps between gears, and also the final drive ratio. This is explained more fully later, but it should be clear that it would be useless to modify a motor to produce maximum power at 7,500rpm if the weight of the car, its air resistance and axle ratio are such that it could only pull 5,500rpm in top gear. To take this hypothetical case a step further we will assume that the gearbox is a five-speed unit, but that the gear spread is such that the motor will drop 3,000rpm between gears. This motor has a 2,000rpm power band, therefore the motor will bog down between gear changes and be slower than the standard unit.

As you plan your modifications, tend to be conservative. A slightly larger carburettor or a cam with a little more duration may give you 5–10hp more at maximum rpm, but you could be losing something like 25hp a couple of thousand revs below maximum. I would trade 5hp at 7,000rpm for an extra 25hp at 5,000rpm any day. Any vehicle, regardless of whether it is used on the road or the race track, will spend more time running at 5,000rpm than it will at 7,000rpm. The message is to modify your engine to produce the best power in the range at which you are going to be running it.

HUMBLY ASSESS DRIVER SKILLS

Another very important aspect is your skill as a driver. You must honestly appraise whether you have the skill and are able to maintain the level of concentration necessary to control a powerful engine with a narrow power band, which comes on to power with a sudden rush. Also will you enjoy working at that level of skill and concentration for an extended period of time? You may feel that you have what it takes, but it is worth noting the results of track testing with a number of drivers and engines in two basic levels of tune.

On one occasion we were getting 270–280hp from 2 litres, and that seemed to be the sort of power everyone was aiming for to keep on the pace. The same engine in rally spec was making about 30–35hp less. Then, without the drivers' knowledge, the team's circuit cars were set up with the two different engines: one in circuit spec and one in rally spec. The regular team drivers were both quicker in the car with the more powerful engine, but interestingly both thought the car with the rally engine felt more powerful and they were surprised that they were off the pace by 0.5–0.7 seconds per lap. However, when experienced second-level drivers took their turn behind the wheel the situation changed quite markedly. Of the three drivers involved only one really came to grips with the circuit spec engine. He was generally less than 0.5 slower than the regular drivers, but the other two were erratic, with some laps okay and others over 2 seconds slower. But on switching to the racer with the rally engine, all three were able to pull more consistent and faster lap times than they were able to put down with the circuit spec engine.

On the day that this testing was done the weather was warm and the track surface was dry and in fair condition. On another day with the track damp, or with race traffic and the temperature down a bit, the difference in speed and consistency of the second string drivers as they switched from the circuit spec engine to the rally spec engine would probably have been even more dramatic.

ENGINE TUNE DEFINITIONS

Throughout the book I make regular reference to an engine's state of tune: standard, sports, semi-race and full race. These terms mean virtually nothing (with the possible exception of the first) without some standard against which to measure them.

Basically, I would define a sports modification as one that results in a moderate power improvement without much loss of low-speed tractability. This is the degree of modification that I would recommend for any road-going vehicle.

Semi-race tune would be recommended only for high-speed road or club rally work. The engine would have very little low-speed power and consequently the gearing and vehicle weight would be an important consideration. An engine in this state of tune would almost always require modifications to strengthen the bottom end.   15

Full race tune is just that – for competition only. An engine in a lesser degree of full race tune would be used in international rallies, quarter-mile dirt speedway and other competitions requiring reasonable mid-range power. A less experienced driver or rider, on the lower-speed road circuits, would be better able to cope with the power characteristics of an engine in this stage of modification rather than be continually battling to keep within the power band of a more highly modified motor.

However, there are so many degrees of full race tune that it is not possible properly to define them. I might add that modifications of this type must be carefully planned to keep the power band compatible with driver ability, circuit layout, race length, engine endurance level and even fuel consumption.

THE FOUR-STROKE CYCLE

It may appear a trifle laughable, especially in a book on high-performance four-stroke tuning, to include an explanation of four-cycle engine operation. However, I have found that many enthusiasts do not really know what happens inside a four-stroke engine, or for that matter why it is called a four-cycle engine in the first place. Therefore I think it would be appropriate to discuss this, so that there is no misunderstanding when we progress into a consideration of the actual modification of an engine of this design.

The following is the sequence of operations in each cylinder, every two revolutions of the crankshaft.

1: induction stroke – As the piston goes down, the inlet valve opens fully and the cylinder is filled with air and vaporised fuel.

2: compression stroke – The piston rises, and part way up the inlet valve closes, allowing the piston to compress the fuel/air mixture. As the piston approaches top dead centre (TDC), the spark plug ignites the mixture.

3: power stroke – The rapid expansion of the burning mixture produces pressure which drives the piston down. Part way down the exhaust valve begins to open.

4: exhaust stroke – As the piston rises to TDC again, the burned gases are expelled from the exhaust port. Before the piston actually reaches TDC, the inlet valve starts to lift off its seat, to allow the fuel/air mixture into the engine when the piston descends on the next induction stroke. (Figure 1.1)

By the time you read to the end of this book you will have a better understanding of how your engine works, and how you can work with and use some of the basic laws of physics to improve its performance.

However, this knowledge is not enough to ensure that the modifications you carry out will be a success. Successful tuning depends also on careful and thoughtful planning, then skilful execution of that plan. Do not let over-enthusiasm cause you to rush through the job. Take your time and make absolutely certain that it has been done correctly.

Engine assembly work should be carried out under ideal conditions. You need good lighting and a clean, tidy, dust-free workshop. Every effort must be made to keep dirt out of the motor. Wash all parts in clean solvent, then immediately cover them with plastic sheeting (not cotton) to keep out the dust. Keep your tools and your hands clean.

Remember that the time you spend on initial preparation and cleanliness contributes immensely to the success of all engine work, in terms of both horsepower and reliability.

Figure 1.1 The four-stroke cycle.

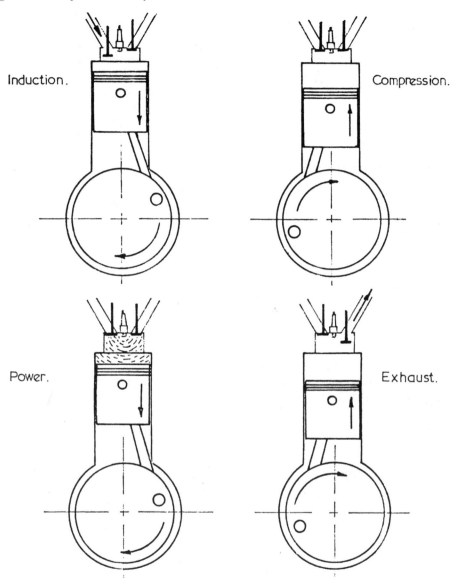

Induction.

Compression.

Power.

Exhaust.

Chapter 2

The Air Inlet System

Logic dictates that we begin our engine tuning journey where air begins its path into the engine. So in this chapter we want to look at everything affecting gas flow from the point where the inlet air enters the air intake right the way through to the point where the inlet manifold terminates at the face of the cylinder head. Thus, with a couple of exceptions – namely carburettor engines and those with throttle body fuel injection – we will be examining, with a critical eye aimed at maximising performance, the whole inlet system up to that point. As we progress through the entire flow path keep in clear focus that anything that will impede gas flow in a naturally aspirated street engine will present an even greater flow restriction in a high performance or race engine because the gas volumes involved are so much bigger. Don't ever think that you can beat flow restrictions simply by going bigger with cams and carburettors, or bumping the compression ratio sky high. You may be forced to follow this route by the sports rule makers in some types of competition, but don't ever voluntarily resort to using such crutches. Getting rid of flow restrictions will have a positive effect on any engine, by significantly increasing charge density in the cylinders.

CHECKING AIR FILTER AND AIR BOX FLOW

Many see the air filter as a major impediment to flow, but in a road car before tossing the filter element and replacing it with something that is supposed to flow better it is wise to do a little investigation. If the stock element isn't blocked by dirt, insects and other rubbish, changing to a so-called high performance element probably won't do much. Frequently it is found that it is the air box, or other sound muffling devices in the inlet duct that are the real culprits in strangling air flow.

The easy way to evaluate the inlet system is by means of a flow bench, but an inexpensive and viable alternative is to use a water manometer (Figure 2.1). While this test can be a bit of a fiddle it will help you to discover a good deal about the science of

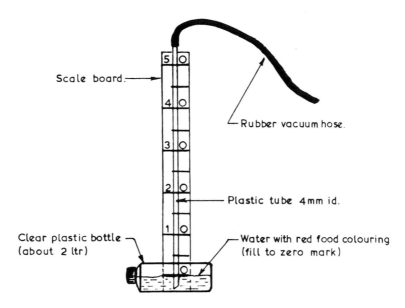

Scale board.

Rubber vacuum hose.

Plastic tube 4mm id.

Clear plastic bottle
(about 2 ltr)

Water with red food colouring
(fill to zero mark)

Figure 2.1 A water manometer can be employed to find where flow restrictions exist.

Figure 2.2 Naturally aspirated and nitrous oxide assisted engines should be tested with a water manometer at all five test points to determine what parts of the intake system are causing flow resistance. Supercharged engines cannot be checked with a water manometer on the pressure side of the inlet system.

Test point 1 – before the air filter element but after any inlet silencers.
Test point 2 – after the air filter element but before the air flow meter.
Test point 3 – after the air flow meter but before the resonator.
Test point 4 – after the resonator but before the throttle plate.
Test point 5 – after the throttle plate.

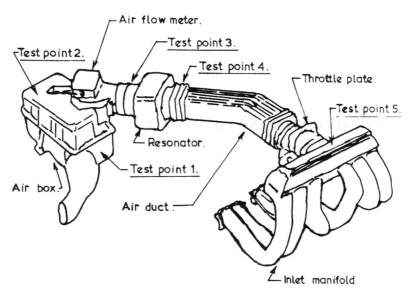

Air flow meter.

Test point 3.

Test point 2.

Test point 4.

Throttle plate.

Test point 5.

Resonator.

Test point 1.

Air box.

Air duct.

Inlet manifold

engine breathing, and you will feel challenged to consider flow restrictions possibly existing in the whole inlet system and not just the air filter element itself.

All the areas we want to check are shown in Figure 2.2. In naturally aspirated and nitrous assisted engines we can use the manometer to test all the way through to the inlet manifold. Remember, however, that when a blower or turbocharger is fitted you cannot check out the pressure side of the inlet tract using this method.

Ideally test while running on a wheel dyno using a 72in water manometer. The pressure drop, which can also be referred to as the vacuum or the depression, is measured by recording how far the water rises in the manometer. When you do this test in a car on the road you will be limited to about 42in column height, so past 5,000rpm the reading could be off the scale if the system is very restrictive.

When testing on the road, you will need an assistant set up with all the gear in the back seat. Using full throttle accelerate from 4,000 to 7,000rpm in 3rd, or preferably 4th, gear up a hill. As you approach each thousand rpm call out to your rear seat passenger. He will mentally record the depression at each call and write the figures down at the end of the run. Extreme accuracy isn't important. For example, if the water level was less than halfway between 20in and 30in, record it as 23in. Preferably, do three runs at each test point to check for errors. Note that a video camera can be used to record this test, but unless you have another tacho that can be duct-taped close to the manometer you may have problems getting both the manometer and tacho in focus.

Now what do these figures that you have written down mean? Standard air pressure at sea level is 14.7psi which equals 29.92in mercury or 406.9in water. Thus 1in mercury equals about 0.5psi and 1in water equals about 0.036psi. If for example at 7,000rpm the reading at Test point 1 is 36in water, it means we have a pressure drop, a flow restriction, of 1.3psi even before we get to the filter! Still at 7,000rpm and this time Test point 2, if the gauge reads 44in then we can calculate that filter restriction is only 8in water (44 − 36 = 8) or 0.29psi, so obviously this car has a problem which won't be solved by replacing the air filter element. Continue on to each test point and calculate the flow restriction in the proceeding section of the tract. By the time we reach Test point 5 we may find a total drop as high as 61in water, or even more, that is 2.2psi, so instead of air pressure of 14.7psi forcing air into the cylinders this car is working with only 12.5psi. Is that costing horsepower? Well, let's put it this way, by getting rid of that flow restriction it's like getting 2.2psi of free supercharging without adding any heat to the air! In hp terms it means that a 200hp engine when restricted like this is going to be limited to around 175–180hp.

The situation is little different with older motorcycles prior to ram-air, and even some ram-air models leave a bit to be desired. The air box fitted to these older bikes has a devastating effect on their performance. Frequently enthusiasts are fooled into thinking that they have gained many horsepower by fitting larger carburettors to their bikes. Usually the improvement in power is the result of the removal of the air filter and box, as many of these kits will not hook up to the standard factory filter and air box. In fact more often than not, the larger carburettors actually cause a decrease in power if the bike is in otherwise near standard tune.

Quite often air filter boxes are so restrictive that it is a complete waste of time modifying the engine in any way without first freeing up the air flow path into the air

box. Generally, I have been able to pick up 3–5% more power by cutting a few simple holes in the air box. Some boxes also have muffling ribs and baffles inside, which should also be cut out.

Table 2.1 shows what happened when a brace of 36mm flat slide carburettors were hooked up to a stock Kawasaki 900. The test was a disaster with virtually nothing happening until the tacho hit 6,000 rpm, and some people believe this engine really needs even larger 39mm carbs! My opinion is that for many riders the factory 34mm CV carbs are too big for the street. Kawasaki obviously fitted these large carburettors to ensure maximum top end hp so that this bike would be a winner in boxstock racing and assumed that street riders would accept mediocre performance below 6,000 rpm. The bike is just so much sweeter when the stock 34mm CVs are binned and smaller 32mm CV carbs installed. Even at low rpm you can be in the wrong gear and grab a fistful of throttle and get instant response, no stumble, no snatching, just a surge of power.

Table 2.1   Kawasaki 900R dyno test

rpm	Test 1 (hp)	Test 2 (hp)	Test 3 (hp)	Test 4 (hp)	Test 5 (hp)
3,500	25.5			25.7	28.6
4,000	33.6			33.4	35.2
4,500	38.2			38.7	39.5
5,000	42.4	31.5	28.9	42.8	43.7
5,500	46.6	39.7	34.3	46.7	48.3
6,000	56.8	50.1	47.2	57.7	58.4
6,500	65.1	61.3	59.6	65.4	67.4
7,000	68.7	63.8	92.9	69.5	71.6
7,500	74.8	71.4	70.5	76.7	80.1
8,000	83.2	82.0	81.6	85.1	86.3
8,500	89.1	87.6	88.2	90.8	89.4
9,000	93.6	93.7	94.5	93.9	93.5
9,500	94.2	95.6	96.8	95.8	94.8
10,000	93.7	95.5	97.6	96.4	93.9
10,500	93.6	95.9	97.1	96.6	93.2
11,000	91.8	93.2	98.4	95.2	89.1

Note: Where dyno would not hold a steady load hp figures have been omitted.
Test 1 – Standard 34mm CV carburettors with stock air filter and box connected.
Test 2 – As above with 36mm flat slide carburettors fitted.
Test 3 – As above with four K & N air filters fitted.
Test 4 – As above with standard 34mm CV carburettors fitted.
Test 5 – As above with 32mm CV carburettors fitted.

POTENTIAL HOT SPOTS

Some say toss out the intake muffler, the air box and filter, and fit a high flow performance pod type filter with tapered neck to attach to the air flow meter to rectify this type of problem. This would be a bad move unless the pod filter is boxed in to prevent hot underbonnet air from entering the intake. The underbonnet air temperature can easily rise by about 30°C (54°F). You can reckon on a power decrease of at least 1%

The stock air box has been replaced by an aftermarket air filter featuring an impressive bellmouth fitted onto the inlet duct. Unfortunately the engine will now be breathing hot, low-density air.

for every 7°C (13°F) the intake air temperature rises. Thus, if the outside air temperature is 25°C (77°F) and the intake air temperature is 55°C (131°F) you are giving away 13hp in a 300hp engine. This illustrates why a cold air intake, drawing air in from outside the hot engine bay, is so important for maximum power. However, at lower engine speeds, particularly during cooler weather, fuel economy in street machines may be poorer as a result of inferior fuel atomisation, even with fuel injection.

There are several areas in the induction system where the inlet charge is being heated. On carburetted car engines most stock inlet manifolds are heated by the engine's exhaust gases or by hot engine coolant. This is done to assist in fuel vaporisation at low rpm. As very high performance engines are operated only in a relatively narrow power band in the higher rpm range, heating of the manifold is not necessary for good atomisation of the fuel. The heating system can be rendered inoperative by blocking the exhaust heat passages, or if water heating is employed, by disconnecting the water hoses.

The inlet manifold may also be heated by radiation from the exhaust headers. Therefore a heat shield made of unpainted aluminium should be fitted between the inlet and the exhaust manifolds. Also, the inlet manifold should be left silver coloured, so that it reflects heat rather than absorbing it.

On 'V-type' engines the inlet manifold is heated by hot oil splashing up from the valley area. The modification required is to fit a shield to keep the oil, and heat being radiated from the valley, away from the manifold.

HIGH PERFORMANCE AIR FILTERS

With carburetted engines some tuners favour a forward-opening bonnet scoop to direct cool air straight into the inlet system. This isn't a problem when a filter with a water resistant element, and water resistant filter oil also for filters requiring to be oiled, is fitted. However, if you disregard my advice and operate without an air filter, air turbulence and buffeting in the carburettor throat may lead to serious fuel metering problems which cause hp losses as bad as, and at times far worse than, drawing in hot air. A better solution if you do not have the resources to properly design and fabricate a suitable ram-air scoop is to turn the thing around to bring in air from the high pressure area just in front of the windscreen.

Table 2.2   Air filter air flow comparison

Holley 850cfm carburettor tested at 1.5in Hg

Remarks	cfm air flow
Carburettor without air filter	823
Carburettor fitted with air horn	839
Standard totally enclosed element with single snorkel air intake	554
As above but with snorkel cut off filter body	594
Standard totally enclosed element with two snorkel air intakes	608
As above but with both snorkels cut off filter body	665
As above but with filter body cut down flush with base	743
As above but with two filter elements fitted	818
High performance speed shop foam type air cleaner	780
K & N cotton filter with stub stack	853

Looking at the example in Table 2.2 it is clear that the stock air filter case was a major impediment to good flow into the engine. Opening up the stock filter case by cutting the top cover down to the base increased flow from 554cfm to 743cfm; a rise of 34%, and not too far short of what the bare carby flowed. Adding a second stock paper element cut flow resistance even more, increasing flow another 10%, so that overall flow was close to equalling that of the open carburettor. Although not shown in Table 2.2, a single K & N filter outflowed all of the other filters when it was fitted to the standard cut-down filter body. Fitted to a well-designed filter case with a properly radiused entry base, it would have flowed even better. When used in conjunction with a K & N stub stack, flow went up to 853cfm, which is more than the carburettor flowed with just an air horn fitted.

It is obvious from these figures that there is no good reason not to run an air filter. A properly sized air filter will not reduce hp so don't ever run without one. Unfortunately in some scenes it isn't cool to use an air filter. Some of these fools claim that they lose power with a filter, but in reality they ditch the filter purely for aesthetics. For those more concerned about under-bonnet beauty than component life I would suggest they have a good look inside of engines that have been ingesting a steady diet of dust, sand and grit. And as they do so it would be wise for them to contemplate just how much sooner everything was ground away, and just how much the engine was down on power because of all the additional leakage past piston rings and valve seats.

This is not meant to imply that all after-market filters will keep dirt out of your engine. You must choose carefully if you ditch the stock element. I am regularly shocked at the very poor design of many replacement air filters. In general, the foam used is too porous to remove abrasive dust from the air. Added to this, the foam 23 element is often poorly retained by the filter body, which in turn allows a huge amount of abrasive material to be sucked into the motor around the edge of the filter and filter case. Also to my mind foam filters that are run unoiled probably aren't very efficient at dust removal.

For these reasons only air filters of good design should be used. Personally, I prefer K & N cotton gauze filters; however, paper-type filters with sufficient filtration area are acceptable if they are renewed frequently. K & N filters flow well, even with a good coating of dust, but paper filters will not. All types of filtering materials restrict air flow, but not to the extent that many would suppose. As pointed out in the earlier examples much of the restriction is often caused by the air filter body design, or perhaps by the filter element being too small.

RAM-AIR INDUCTION

The basic idea behind ram-air is that a car or motorcycle moving at speed will force air into a forward-facing scoop connected to the induction system, and ultimately into the cylinders. In effect, free supercharging. With an increase in speed the pressure rises, so more air is forced in, so the engine makes more power. The idea, called ram-charging, ram-air and forced-air, has been around for decades, but when Kawasaki introduced the concept to the masses upon the release of their potent ZX-11 in 1992 the impression many went away with was one of ram-air giving big inlet pressures and massive power gains.

Table 2.3 Ram-air pressure rise

Speed (kph)	Pressure rise (%)	Water (in)	Mercury (in)	Millibars
100	0.5	2	0.15	5
150	1.0	4	0.30	10
200	1.9	8	0.57	19
250	2.9	12	0.87	29
300	4.0	16	1.20	41
350	5.7	23	1.71	58
400	7.8	32	2.33	79

As Table 2.3 shows the pressure increases are relatively small, but none the less not to be ignored when pursuing the highest levels of performance. While a pressure rise of a bit less than 2% at 200kph may appear small – even in a close to perfect system designed to recover maximum pressure – remember that prior to adding ram-air a free flowing induction tract may well have been operating at a depression of 2–3% at wide open throttle. Therefore the real-world gain may be more like 4–5% at 200kph.

Just sticking any old scoop into the airstream does not qualify as a ram-air inlet. Formula 1 teams and sports motorcycle manufacturers expend a lot of time and money developing their packages. If not done correctly, a scoop can actually block flow by creating turbulent eddies within the airbox and/or a pressure area right in front of the air scoop inlet. Race teams test the effectiveness of their creations in the wind tunnel with a brace of instrumentation to record actual atmospheric conditions in the wind

tunnel, at several points within the airbox, and within every inlet tract. What they are

Properly designed ram-air induction can add power at higher speeds by lightly pressurising the inlet system. Even at low speeds it helps hp by ensuring an unrestricted flow of cool air into the engine.

aiming for is maximum pressure recovery, meaning that pressure within the airbox should equal the theoretical pressure for that particular car speed, plus pressure and velocity conditions at each inlet tract must be uniform. Then on the engine dyno the airbox will be pressurised to simulate a variety of vehicle speeds and the output of each cylinder will be checked to fully assess the effectiveness of the design.

Few engineers have such extensive resources available so must improvise. Unless it is a motorcycle, at the very least we can test using our basic water manometer. With two or three strategic test points built into our airbox we can do a series of runs with the manometer connected in turn to each test point. The water pressure at each test point should be fairly uniform, and if you record a pressure rise close to those in Table 2.3 then you have possibly fabricated a reasonably effective ram-air intake. I say possibly because to really investigate if your design is fully effective you must next check and verify that the pressures in each inlet tract are fairly close.

A more sophisticated method is to use a number of pressure sensors, sited as for the water manometer, connected to a data logger. With just one pressure sensor the test can still tell you what you need to know, it just takes much more time.

Don't worry that atmospheric conditions may change and thus void the validity of your testing. What we are measuring here are relative, not absolute, pressures. As such the water manometer or pressure probe is measuring the air pressure relative to the present air pressure. If the air pressure is different when you test a few hours or a few days later that does not matter. If the water manometer rose 8in water when the barometer read 1,000 millibars (14.7psi) air pressure then it will still rise 8in on another occasion when the pressure is 990mb (14.37psi).

So much for the theory, what is an effective ram-air setup worth in hp terms? Sorry, but I really can't give a definitive answer except to say that if the pressures are uniform from cylinder to cylinder then you should get the same percentage power improvement as the pressures rise. When the pressure goes up 4% then you should see a 4% hp jump. If you don't then you should start searching for answers. If it's a fuel injected engine maybe the air is very turbulent and this is adversely affecting mixture quality. If you find that more spark advance and/or a very rich mixture comes close to 25 giving the power expected then turbulence would be a chief suspect. If you are on carburettors then it is more likely to be a carb metering problem. Turbulence could be upsetting the metering signal, or more likely, the extra pressure acting on fuel in the float bowl is sending mixture richness sky high with fuel simply spilling from the float bowl into the air stream.

Keep in mind if you operate a ram-air sports bike that not all systems were created equal. Some work much better than others at pressure recovery at all speeds, and some leak pressure worse than others. Consequently, if you are after every last little bit of performance measure, the pressure in your system and compare the results with Table 2.3. If you find that it's a lot lower, set about sealing the system more effectively, but don't block the water drain unless you can get it opened quickly in the rain as you could drown your engine. Worse still it could lock up (water doesn't compress), and if your clutch skills are sluggish you will be dumped from your bike pretty quickly.

AIR FLOW METER FLOW RESTRICTIONS

Immediately after the air filter many fuel injected cars have some type of air flow meter. The hot wire type does not present very much impediment to flow, but the vane type with its swinging flap and the Karmen vortex type used on Mitsubishis certainly do. How you deal with each type of flow meter will to a large extent be dictated by what you intend to do with the stock engine management system. If you switch to an aftermarket ECU then you will most likely scrap the air flow meter and go to a speed-

Below left: The vane air flow meter, still attached to part of the air box, illustrates the characteristic shape of air flow meters of this type.

Below right: Hot wire air flow meter has fairly clear air flow path. Removing the mesh screen from both ends cuts flow impediment and may give a 1½–2% power improvement at maximum revs. Main benefit in stock and near stock engines is that removing screens may fool the system to send a marginally lower air flow signal to the ECU, thus shifting stock rich mixture and retarded spark programming closer to what the engine really needs.

density MAP sensor based system. However, if you want to stick with the factory ECU, and there are many good reasons to pursue that course if the car is for mainly street use, then you will have to investigate an alternative path to free up air flow because it is often impractical to convert an ECU from being air flow based to MAP sensor based, and vice versa.

With both hot wire and vane type systems you can swap to larger air flow meters and reprogramme the ECU to accurately sense the true air flow. However, with the vane type there will always be some flow resistance. Personally, that doesn't worry me, I am much more interested in reliability and minimal cost in a road vehicle, so I prefer to stick with the ultra-reliable vane type over the less reliable and expensive hot wire unit. For some, such matters do not enter the equation, so they swap to the more modern hot wire arrangement.

When a vane type meter is utilised it is possible to ease flow resistance by reducing spring tension on the swinging flap. Sometimes this is okay (eg a large flow meter on a small engine), but caution is in order. First, and this is the least important point, easing the spring tension allows the door to swing open further. The ECU will read this as more air flow and richen up the mixture. Consequently any flow gains will be well and truly wiped out by excessive richness unless the ECU is reprogrammed. Second, remember the ECU calculates fuel flow based on how far the flap moves. Therefore with spring tension wound off the flap may swing wide open long before air flow into the engine peaks. In this scenario the ECU would not sense the increase in flow when air flow does actually peak, so there will not be any increase in injector pulse width, the engine will go lean, detonate, and be damaged. Never should the flap swing wide open until air flow into the engine is at its maximum.

DEALING WITH THE KARMEN AIR FLOW METER

There is no easy way around the Mitsubishi air flow meter. I have seen crude arrangements that simply bypass air around the air flow meter, but such a scheme is pretty much hopeless for a road engine because if the bypass is an effective size there will be close on zero flow through the air flow meter at idle and cruise, so the ECU will have little chance of getting the fuelling right.

Because of such difficulties some simply give up and resign themselves to losing a lot of power. When tested with a water manometer a Mitsubishi Lancer turbo was recording a pressure drop at the turbo inlet of 56in water at 6,000 rpm. With all the inlet ducting and air filter removed this decreased to 43in water (about 1.6psi) vacuum; thus showing that 77% of the inlet flow loss was due to the air flow meter. However, that was for a completely stock engine. When modifications were carried out the losses grew. Simply adding a big exhaust saw the pressure drop grow to almost 50in water, and when a bigger turbo was fitted the water gauge went off the scale. Clearly such inlet flow losses are unacceptable, but remember we are talking a powerful turbo engine here (380hp from 1.8 litres), so the losses will be much lower in the naturally aspirated engines we are discussing in this book.

The best Karmen vortex meter bypass arrangement, which I call the T-bone system, is not inexpensive but it does endow the car with perfect road manners even in very high states of tune. As illustrated in Figure 2.3 in normal use at low speeds all air flows through the stock air flow meter and then takes a 90° turn into the inlet 27

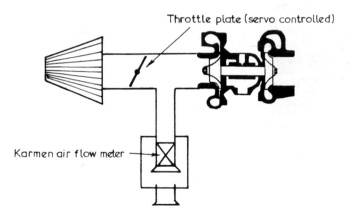

Figure 2.3 T-bone system bypasses restrictive air flow meter.

manifold. With the servo-controlled throttle plate in the secondary inlet closed the stock ECU fully controls fuelling and spark on the factory maps. However, as air flow increases a pressure switch signals a solenoid to open the secondary throttle plate. Simultaneously, a MAP sensor controlled fuel only ECU begins to drive a second set of injectors to provide the engine's increased fuelling requirements. Ideally these secondary injectors should be part of a dual fuel system so that only when operating at high engine loads will expensive high octane fuel be injected.

THROTTLE PLATE SIZE AND UPGRADING

The next potential point of flow restriction is the throttle plate/s. In most road car applications a single throttle body will be used, attached to the inlet manifold plenum. Table 2.4 sets out the size of throttle plate required. If your stock throttle plate is too small look for a suitable replacement at wrecking yards, keeping in mind that you need to find a throttle body with compatible idle air control and throttle pot. Alternatively the stock throttle body may have sufficient wall thickness to permit machining to a larger size, thus alleviating any compatibility worries. Most will bore at least 2mm, and many will allow 5–7mm. Try to go to a size which will allow you to cannibalise a throttle plate off another throttle body. This will save a lot of time and money machining up a larger plate of the correct shape, with the correct angles around the edges.

Table 2.4 Throttle plate requirements

Throttle plate (mm)	Maximum Horsepower
50	170
56	210
62	260
70	330
75	380
85	490
90	550
100	675

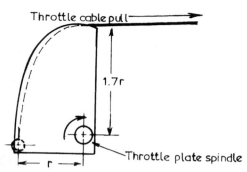

Throttle cable pull

1.7r

r

Throttle plate spindle

Figure 2.4 Progressive throttle cam.

Left: Multiple butterfly progressive opening throttle body can make low speed throttle control much easier.

Remember when you opt for a larger throttle plate that the car will not be so easy to drive around town. With a smaller throttle body, just cracking open the throttle may have given a steady increase in power, but with a big plate a whole lot more air rushes into the engine with just small movements of the accelerator. This may make the car quite jerky and wheelspin on wet roads can be a problem. There are a couple of ways around this problem, apart from resorting to electronic throttle control. We can opt for a multi-plate progressive throttle body with the small plate/s opening about 40° before the large plates/s begin to open, or we can fabricate a progressive throttle cam (Figure 2.4).

Regardless of the size of the throttle body we should be concerned that it is well streamlined. Many are not, so take a look at what can be done to grind out lips and ridges in the flow passage. Also attempt to streamline the throttle spindle and fixing screws without weakening the spindle.

The lip in this throttle body should be tapered into the throttle bore on both the entry and exit side, and the throttle shaft should be thinned as shown. Alternatively the throttle body could be machined out and have a larger throttle plate fitted.

INLET MANIFOLD PLENUM DESIGN

Of much greater importance is the inlet manifold itself. Whether this is a single casting or several bits bolted together the inlet manifold is in fact two distinct parts. First there is the plenum – an air chamber from which the individual cylinders draw air. Then there are the runners which are really an extension of the inlet ports and join the ports to the plenum.

The three things we are interested in with regard to the plenum are its volume, how equally it distributes air to the individual cylinders, and how the openings to the individual runners are formed so as to maximise flow. Some tuners claim that the plenum volume must be carefully monitored, and that volumes of between two and three times the engine size work best. I disagree, having found that anything in the range of 0.8 to 1.5 times engine capacity works well in 3 to 6 cylinder engines, while 8, 10 and 12 cylinder engines are usually happy with considerably less volume.

The most important role of the plenum is to equalise air flow to the individual cylinders. Unfortunately car makers are much more concerned with a neat powertrain package so instead of air entering the plenum about in the middle it is more usual to find that the air enters at one end. This isn't a problem when the plenum is carefully designed with high performance in mind, but once we massively increase the air flow large imbalances begin to show up. Usually it will be found that the cylinder closest to the plenum inlet is down on average air flow to the tune of 3–5%, while the cylinder at the blocked off end of the plenum will be enjoying 5–7% more flow. Obviously this hurts power but of more concern is the danger of engine damage if the engine is not tuned cylinder by cylinder. Unfortunately, instead of tuning each cylinder many simply tune the engine as a whole. If the engine is close to stock that is okay but as we move further away from stock and closer to the engine's limits we have to be more precise. Clearly the cylinder receiving more air will want more fuel and also less spark advance unless the compression ratio has been lowered to compensate. Such is only possible if the ECU facilitates individual cylinder trim for both fuel and spark. If the engine management system is more basic then to prevent detonation in the cylinder receiving the extra air, the mixture and ignition advance will have to be adjusted to suit that one cylinder. This means all other cylinders will be running rich and retarded, and will be down on power.

The way around such a mess is to modify the plenum to balance the flows as much as possible. There are different ways to tackle this depending on the layout of the engine and the extent of modifications planned. For most applications we will have to fabricate the plenum like those illustrated in Figure 2.5. The idea is to slow the air as it

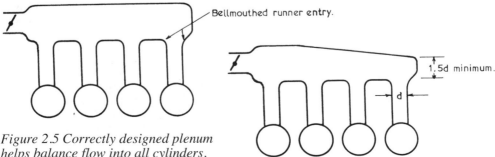

Figure 2.5 Correctly designed plenum helps balance flow into all cylinders.

enters the plenum and to then shape the plenum wall so that it isn't steering the air into the far end cylinder. Deflector ribs can help here, but the main requirement is that the plenum must rapidly grow in size well before the first cylinder and it must also extend well beyond the far end inlet port. If there is insufficient space it is quite acceptable to use a tapering wedge style plenum, but take care not to bring the wall in too close over the opening of the end runner. Preferably the air should not have to make a sharp turn from the plenum into the runners, and in turn the runners should have a nicely formed bellmouth to help flow. Ideally we don't want the plenum wall closer than 1.5 times the runner diameter from the bellmouth, and if possible 2 times the diameter is better.

If you are working with the stock manifold it may be hard to form a proper bellmouth entry into each runner as they are often not spaced far enough apart. However, if the runners are more than a 1/2in apart, it can be worthwhile cutting the plenum in half and welding 1/2in half-round bar stock formed into a circle around each opening. Aluminium epoxy can also be used to form a rolled lip, but be careful that the epoxy's temperature rating is well above what the inlet manifold is ever likely to reach.

The Walkinshaw Holden Commodore provides a lesson in good inlet design. Air enters from a bonnet scoop and air filter, then through a twin butterfly progressive throttle into the plenum. Inside the plenum, tuned length trumpets connect to each inlet port.

INLET RUNNER DESIGN AND SIZE

The runners are a real tuning tool. Both their diameter and length have an influence on the shape of the power curve. The diameter basically fixes the rpm at which the engine makes best hp, so while a big fat runner will let the engine breath freely at high revs, it will be down on power at low rpm. Obviously something to be avoided with all engines, but especially small highly tuned engines in heavy road cars. Runner length tends to 'rock' the power curve around the point fixed by the runner diameter. Thus long runners will push up bottom end power, but once past peak torque rpm the engine will fall on its face. Short runners do the opposite – they kill the bottom end and help the engine maintain power way past the peak (Figure 2.6).

Looking at Table 2.5 you can see how this works out in practice. A street engine is going to be quite sluggish if you choose a fairly racy cam so if the stock manifold is shorter than indicated in the table and the runners are larger in diameter this should warn you that the inlet manifold is not going to help you get back lost bottom end power. Conversely if the runners are longer and smaller in diameter than shown, then you know that you may be able to get a reasonable balance of performance with this particular manifold, even with a barely streetable cam.

Table 2.5 Runner Size

Street/Hillclimb/Rally		Circuit/Drags	
2-valve head	*4-valve head*	*2-valve head*	*4-valve head*
350–400mm	350–400mm	300–330mm	280–330mm
x 0.82–0.9	x 1.08–1.18	x 0.9–1.0	x 1.18–1.31

Note: runner length is measured from valve seat to bellmouth face in plenum;
runner diameter is inlet valve diameter multiplied by the number indicated.

The other way to use the table is to consider the left to right progression of engine specification. Thus a street engine will always work better with longer, smaller diameter runners than a hillclimb or rally engine, while a circuit race engine requires runners just a touch shorter and fatter than either a hillclimb or rally engine. To gain full benefit from this basic principle, back in 1996 Honda's World Superbike Championship engines used variable length intake trumpets. During the recent 3ltr

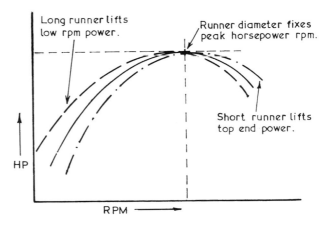

Figure 2.6 This graph illustrates how runner diameter and length influence the power curve.

The Chev Gen III has inlet ports and manifold runners that are too big for good mid-range performance. This can be corrected by filling the bottom of the ports in the head. However, filling the runners as shown here is a specialist operation due to bonding difficulties.

V10 era Formula 1 engine designers followed a similar path to claw back low rpm grunt to enable the engines to pull well all the way from 6,000rpm in low gear corners at Monaco all the way to over 19,000rpm. The Peugeot engine being able to increase trumpet length 20mm, while at Ferrari it was 50mm with the overall length of the induction tract being extendable from 170mm to 220mm. Some went the simpler on-off route with the ECU signalling the actuators to move the trumpets to either their short or long configuration. Other designers chose to programme the ECU to provide infinitely variable length – within the maximum and minimum limits, so that any dips in the torque curve could be addressed, at least partly, by changing the induction tract length. Additionally, if track conditions were wet, it could be added to the tools available for traction control, shortening the tract length to take away engine torque. The principles sound fairly basic but its complexity can be better understood when it is appreciated that even Cosworth dropped the system in 2001 after failing to get it properly sorted on the CK model they raced in 2000.

HOW TO MODIFY THE STOCK MANIFOLD

If the standard manifold has runners which are too long and/or too small in the port diameter you may be able to purchase a more suitable performance manifold, but unfortunately these are only available for a few of the more popular engines. Some companies offer a service called extrude honing, where they pump an abrasive mixture through the runners to increase the port diameter. Obviously this is limited by the casting thickness; go too far and the manifold will fall to pieces from engine vibrations.

    The alternative is to cut up the stock manifold and fit appropriately sized runners. Before cutting the manifold talk to someone well versed in welding aluminium to give you some guidance on where you should cut. If it is a one piece manifold I prefer to make just three cuts; the first just back from the injector mounting bosses, the second just off from the plenum, and the third through the plenum itself.

    The first and second cuts get rid of a major portion of the runners which will be replaced by 3mm wall aluminium tube, mandrel bent to the required shape. Before welding these new runners in place grind out the ports on the part of the stock manifold which bolts to the head. After welding, grind or file any welding 'dags' out of the runners. Finally, do whatever you can to add bellmouths in each runner entry.   33

Chapter 3

The Cylinder Head

The cylinder head is the most important area to be considered by the serious tuner. Its design has more bearing on the end result, performance-wise, than any other component of the high-performance engine. There is no way in which high horsepower can be obtained if the head won't flow efficiently, and in turn burn that air/fuel mixture efficiently.

Many tuners go to extremes, cramming as much air into the cylinder as possible, only to have a combustion chamber that won't burn the mixture efficiently. Personally, I am unimpressed by air-flow figures; they tell very little about how well a head has been modified. There is no point in getting a lot of mixture into an engine unless you can manage to burn it at the right time, and if you try too hard to get high flow figures, you can easily end up with a combustion chamber that won't burn effectively. While I believe a gas flow rig is an aid in head development, I also believe that it is possible to look at a port and decide whether or not air would like to flow through it. A port that is nice and straight and has no projections will generally flow well. Until recent times many engines had a head design so horrible that to create an improvement was relatively simple.

It has always been thought that there is a direct relationship between high air-flow numbers and high power output. In principle this theory sounds correct, but in practice it does not always work out that way. At one time a factory racing department picked the best high-performance heads off the production line for modification. After being ported, each head was flow checked. The heads that recorded the best results were kept for the factory racing team, and the supposedly inferior heads were sold to selected privateers. The interesting thing is that on the dyno, the engines with the heads that produced the best air-flow figures actually recorded power outputs no better than engines with average flow heads. After this discovery the factory tested all their heads for power output, before any were released to the private teams, and they found that some of the 'average' heads they had been selling produced the best power.

INLET VALVE SIZE

If the valves are enlarged and the ports are hogged out to the limit, you will get big power. It is amazing how many people are trapped by this fallacy. Tables 3.1a and 3.1b indicate the valve sizes that you should be aiming for. Valves of this size in an engine in racing tune will yield maximum power at 7,000 to 8,000rpm. Some motors can, because of their over-square short stroke design, benefit from the bigger valves listed, and on these maximum power will be gained at 8,500 to 9,000rpm.

Table 3.1a   Valve sizes for two-valve motors

Cylinder volume (cc)	Inlet valve diameter (in)	Exhaust valve diameter (in)
125	1.16	1.0
200	1.25–1.31	1.06–1.12
250	1.31–1.37	1.16–1.20
275	1.37–1.45	1.20–1.25
325	1.45–1.53	1.25–1.32
375	1.56–1.60	1.32–1.37
400	1.62–1.68	1.37–1.42
450	1.70–1.75	1.42–1.50
500	1.75–1.85	1.50–1.56
600	2.00	1.65
700	2.10	1.75
800	2.25	1.85
900	2.40	1.93

Table 3.1b   Valve sizes for four-valve motors

Cylinder volume (cc)	Inlet valve diameter (in)	Exhaust valve diameter (in)
250	1.16	1.00
325	1.25	1.06
400	1.31	1.12
450	1.35	1.16
500	1.38	1.20
600	1.50	1.28
700	1.60	1.35
800	1.65	1.40

Using the following formula we can estimate at what speed maximum power will occur for a given inlet valve area:

$$rpm = \frac{GS \times K \times Va}{CV}$$

GS is the mean gas speed in feet per second. From Table 3.2 you will be able to determine the approximate gas speed by estimating whether the camshaft is standard, sports, semi-race or full race. Keep in mind that many standard factory high-performance road motors employ sports cams.

K is a constant, 5,900 for two-valve motors and 5,400 for three- and four-valve motors.
Va is the valve area in square inches. This is found using the formula $\pi r2$ where π equals 3.1416 and r is half the valve diameter in inches.
CV is the cylinder volume in cc.

Table 3.2 Estimated gas speed at inlet valve (ft/sec)

Camshaft Profile	Combustion chamber type			
	Pent roof & hemi	*45° twisted*	**Wedge*	*Bath-tub*
Standard	200	200	190	175
Sports	215	215	210	210
Semi-race	235	230	225	220
Full race	260–280	245–260	240–255	230–240

*Note: motorcycles with pent roof and hemi chambers, but non-inclined inlet ports, flow very similarly to wedge chamber heads.

If the engine just cannot physically accommodate valves of the size suggested by this formula, or if the rules preclude the use of oversize valves, you will have to take extraordinary measures to obtain the desired level of performance. Usually this involves the use of extra-long-duration camming and larger-than-recommended carburation. Top-end power will increase, but the mid-range could fall away completely. Restricted to 1.81in inlet valves in one class of historic competition, the old single cam 3.5-litre BMW straight six highlights the problem. It will work only in a narrow 1,800rpm range – from 6,000 to 7,800rpm.

Some engines, however, leave the factory or may be modified and fitted with valves much larger than the formula shows to be necessary. This usually does not create any problems; in fact, it can be of benefit by permitting the use of shorter-duration cams. This has the desirable effect of broadening the power band, providing the inlet ports are kept deliberately small. If the ports are too big, low-speed performance will be poor. At times, though, big valves can suppress high rpm performance. This occurs when the valves are masked due to being too close to the edge of the combustion chamber or the cylinder wall. Porsche for example initially built their 3.6ltr 911 GT3-RSR race engines with 1.654in inlet and 1.417in exhaust valves. These sizes appeared excessive for an engine with a bore diameter of 100mm. Even in Formula 1 it was pretty well established that valve sizes for the inlet and exhaust should not exceed 42% and 34.5% respectively of the bore. Such sizes had been shown to provide the best compromise for gas flow from low valve lifts to fully open in a modern shallow chamber four-valve race engine. Subsequently, after further testing in 2003, Porsche reduced the sizes in 2004 to 1.614in and 1.339in – 41% and 34% of the bore size respectively – and found a performance gain.

INLET PORT SIZE

What Ford did in 1969 when it introduced its Trans-Am Championship challenger, the Boss 302, typifies the thinking of many when it comes to valve and port sizing. Ford engineers equated high flow rig readings with high horsepower, so they gave the 302 massive 2.23in inlet valves and inlet ports 2.5in tall by 1.75in wide. The engine just wouldn't work on the slower tracks, so the next year the inlet valve was reduced to 2.19in. These revised heads were used also on the Boss 351, but were still useless until the floor of the port was filled 3/4in to improve gas velocity. Interestingly, when Ford introduced its aluminium high-performance heads for the Boss 302 and 351 in 1983, they reduced the inlet port volume by 12%. However, they retained the very nice quick-burn combustion chamber of the early head.

Honda had a similar problem in the early '80s with the V6 Formula 2 engine supplied to the Brabham team. They were very peaky and lacked mid-range power in spite of making around 15–20hp less than the Hart and BMW 4-cylinder engines. After a season of frustration Honda invited the Brabham camp to take a look inside the engines themselves. It was noted that the inlet ports were way too big. Simply welding sleeves in gave an immediate 5% gain at the top-end to equal the rival engines, and in the mid-range the improvement was nearer 20%. That single simple change instantly transformed the engine into a winner.

To show that history seems to repeat itself GM made what I believe is a similar error with their 5.7ltr Gen III V8, released in 1996. Depending on the application the factory engines made around 350hp, yet the inlet port needs very little work to easily flow enough air for an output of 600hp. With a 20% reduction in port size an engine with these heads has no trouble giving 520hp, and with the port floors filled that mid-range grunt that big V8s are renowned for, but is sadly lacking in the Gen III, returns. Perhaps GM deliberately tuned out the strong mid-range with big ports to keep ordinary drivers out of trouble, did it somehow help in meeting emissions standards, or was it to relieve stress on the drivetrain and tyres, or to avoid a traction control response that was too obvious and aggressive?

A round port will flow best and basically it should be 0.81 to 0.83 of the inlet valve diameter for best performance on road or track. I have found this figure to give the best compromise for high air flow and high gas velocity, which is important to achieve an acceptable power band and good fuel vaporisation at low revs. The port entry can go much larger than 0.81–0.83 and then taper down without hurting port flow. However, this adds more volume to the port and the power curve is changed, increasing top end hp and engine peak rpm potential, but robbing from the mid-range. The longer the port is maintained at 0.81–0.83 valve diameter the stronger the bottom end and mid-range power.

When the inlet valves are theoretically too large, the port diameter will have to be made smaller than 0.82 of valve diameter – often it would be closer to 0.77–0.80. For example, the Triumph 650 twin should have theoretically 1.5in inlet valves, which would mean a 1.22in to 1.25in port when worked to the 0.81–0.83 ratio. Hence, this is the port size we use with the 1.595in valves fitted at the factory.

Most American heads have rectangular ports, which do not flow so well as round ports, due to the increased surface drag and turbulence. With this type of inlet port I have obtained the best results using a port area of 0.67 of the valve area measured at the push rods, where the port truly begins, and maintaining that area up to the turn into the valve pocket.

A fairly uncommon head layout these days is the 'siamesed' inlet port, where one port serves two cylinders. This is the arrangement used by Austin for the 'A' and 'B' series engines. This type of head has come in for much criticism over the years, but if carefully modified it will yield very good power. The port area must be at least equal to the area of one inlet valve; preferably it should be 2–3% larger.

EXHAUST VALVE SIZE

The size of the exhaust valve and port is currently being scrutinised by engine tuners all around the world. For many years it was believed that racing engines required an exhaust valve at least 85% of the inlet valve diameter for optimum gas flow. A valve of this size enables the exhaust valve and port to flow around 80–85% as much air, on a flow bench, as the inlet tract.

Now it is being questioned if the exhaust flow really has to be so high to make good horsepower. A few years ago it did not really matter if the exhaust valve was too large, but presently we are finding ways of keeping racing machines reliable at higher and higher engine speeds, which makes the use of very large inlet valves a necessity. When all the available combustion chamber space is already taken up, the only way that larger inlets can be accommodated is by reducing the exhaust valve size. This move does not appear to choke the motor with unscavenged exhaust gases; in fact, it could be beneficial to use smaller exhaust valves than usually recommended as some engines have actually shown an increase in mid-range power as a result.

Some tuners maintain that there is no power improvement when the exhaust flow is increased to more than 60% of intake flow, while others claim that a loss in power occurs when exhaust flow drops to 80–83%. I take a middle-of-the-road position. I prefer about 65–70% flow for road and rally engines, and 72–75% for racing motors.

To get this sort of flow balance between exhaust and intake, the exhaust valve need only be 0.78 to 0.82 times the inlet valve diameter in wedge and bath-tub heads. Hemi and pent-roof heads with steeply inclined inlet ports (eg Cosworth BDA and Lotus Twin Cam) require a valve 0.81 to 0.85 times the inlet size because the flat exhaust port does not flow as well, comparatively, as the inclined inlet port. Motorcycles with either hemi or pent-roof heads, and all wedge and bath-tub chambered heads with semi-downdraught inlet ports (see Figure 3.13), should use an exhaust valve 0.79 to 0.83 of the inlet valve size.

EXHAUST PORT SIZE

Generally, exhaust ports should be 95 to 100% of the exhaust valve diameter or area. Siamesed ports need to be considerably larger, but in most instances there just is not enough metal in the port to achieve this.

When the exhaust port area is being enlarged, gas flow increases dramatically if the port roof is raised, as this serves to reduce flow restriction. It has been proved that 'D'-shaped exhaust ports outflow round ports of the same area. Therefore square and rectangular ports can be left with a flat floor, and the port roof should be ground round to give the finished shape of a 'D' turned on to its flat.

I must point out that it is an incorrect practice to match the exhaust port to the header pipe. This is definitely one sure way of losing power, particularly in the mid-range. There must be a sharp step between the exhaust port and the entrance to the header pipe, to reduce exhaust gas backflow into the cylinder. Exhaust backflow is always a problem at lower engine speeds, and unfortunately long-duration camshafts just worsen the situation.

Valve sizes in two-valve engines

	Cylinder volume (cc)	Inlet valve (in)	Exhaust valve (in)
Alfa Romeo 2.0	500	1.73	1.58
Austin Mini 1.3	250–325	*1.48	*1.14
BMW V12 5.0	416	1.65	1.34
K1000	250	1.34	1.18
Buick V6 Series II 3.8	633	1.8	1.52
Stage II heads	750	*2.08	*1.65
Chevrolet Gen II V6 2.8	465	1.72	1.42
small block V8 5.7	715	1.94	1.5
small block 18° heads	625–730	*2.12	*1.62
Brodix 23° heads	625–730	*2.08	*1.62
small block Gen III V8 5.7	715	2.0	1.55
C5R Le Mans/Bathurst 24hr	873	2.18	1.62
big block 454/502	925/1025	2.19	1.88
Dart Big Chief heads	1000–1350	2.4	1.9
Chrysler 'A' block 340	700	2.02	1.6
W-2 heads	625–730	*2.05	*1.6
Cosworth SCA race	250	1.45	1.25
Ducati 600 TT race	300	1.61	1.38
Ferrari Dino V6	400	1.67	1.45
Ford Crossflow 1.6	325–425	*1.63	*1.35
CVH 1.6	400	1.65	1.34
Pinto 2.0	500	*1.8	*1.5
Pinto 2.3	575	*1.89	*1.59
Lotus Twin Cam 1.6	325–440	*1.69	*1.38
Windsor V8 5.0	625	1.85	1.54
SVO N351 heads	625–730	*2.05	*1.6
Cleveland V8	625–865	*2.19	*1.71
SOHC V8 4.6	575	1.75	1.34
429 Boss V8	875–1015	*2.4	*1.9
Harley-Davidson XR750 race	375	1.73	1.38
Kawasaki GPz 1100	275	1.5	1.28
Mercedes (Ilmor) push-rod Indy	429	2.07	1.56
Nissan 1.2/1.4	300–375	*1.5	*1.26
1.8/2.0	450/500	*1.77	1.38
2.4–2.8	400–465	*1.72	1.38
Opel Family II 1.8/2.0	450/500	1.65	1.44
Porsche 911 Carrera 2.0	333	1.77	1.53
2.2–2.8	365–465	1.81	1.57
RSR 2.8/3.0	465/500	1.93	1.63
928 4.5/4.7	559/583	1.77	1.58
Triumph 500	250	1.53	1.31
650/750	325/375	1.6	1.44
VW Golf 1.6	400	*1.61	*1.34
Golf Mk 2 1.8	445	1.58	1.3
Type IV dual carb 1.8	450	1.61	1.34
Yamaha FJ 1100	275	1.5	1.26

*Non-standard valve size

Valve sizes in four-valve engines

	Cylinder volume (cc)	Inlet valve (in)	Exhaust valve (in)
BMW M5 3.5	583	1.46	1.26
K1100	275	1.04	.904
Chev ZR-1 5.7	715	1.54	1.39
Weslake heads	625–875	1.5	1.31
Cosworth DFY/DFR Formula 1	375/437	1.44	1.26
XB Indy/AC F3000/HB F1	331/375/437	1.50	1.26
DFX Indy/DFV Formula 1	331/375	1.33	1.15
GAA Gp A	569	1.46	1.26
GAA F5000	569	*1.52	*1.29
BDB rally	425	1.28	1.08
BDG	500	•1.36/1.4†	•1.15/1.2†
BDH	325	1.28	1.0
BDM	400	1.33	1.15
Ducati 850 sports/race	425	1.26/1.34	1.1/1.18
748R	375	1.42	1.18
Ferrari V10 Formula 1	300	1.59	1.30
Ford Cosworth BDA RS1600	400	1.22	1.0
RS 1800	459	1.32	1.15
YB Turbo	500	1.38	1.22
Zetec 2.0	500	*1.34	*1.18
Cobra V8 4.6/5.4	575/675	1.46	1.18
Honda NS750 race	375	1.28	1.12
VF1000R/VF1100	250/275	1.18	1.04
XR500/600	500/589	1.42	1.22
Kawasaki ZZR-1100	263	1.10	.945
ZX-12R	300	1.31	1.11
KLR600	564	1.5	1.3
Lancia Beta turbo rally	356	1.34	1.06
Mercedes 2.3–16	575	1.5	1.3
500 V8 AMG heads	625	1.46	1.26
Nissan SR20	500	1.34	1.18
Opel XE 2.0	500	*1.38	*1.18
Ecotec 1.8–2.2•	450–550	1.26	1.14
Ecotec 1.6/1.8†	400/450	1.22	1.08
Peugeot V10 Formula 1	300	1.57	1.18
Rover K 1.8/1.8VVC	450	1.09/1.24	.95/1.14
Suzuki TL1000	500	*1.57	*1.3
GS 1150	284	1.10	.906
GS 1300	325	1.3	1.08
Triumph 750 Weslake race	375	1.15	1.0
Vauxhall HS2300	575	1.4	1.18
Lotus head	575	*1.44	1.22
VW Golf 1.8	450	1.26	1.10
Weslake speedway	500	1.38	1.13
Yamaha V-Max 1200	300	1.20	1.02
FJ 1100	275	1.14	.984
TT 550/600	550/600	1.42	1.18/1.22

*Non-standard valve size   •Early model   †Later model

How much power you will pick up because of the mismatch between the port and header pipe will depend on how large the step is, but it seems that the larger the difference in sizes, the greater the power gain. This is not to say that you should choke the engine with an exhaust port that is too small, or build the header with a pipe size that is larger than required, merely to create a big step, but on the other hand do not enlarge the exhaust port to match the header.

For instance, you may have a 1600cc racing engine with 1.43in exhaust valves and ports of the same diameter. The header pipes for this particular unit will have an inside diameter of 1.654in, which gives quite a good step to impede the backflow of gases. From my testing I have determined that a mismatch of this degree can increase maximum power as much as 2–3%, and mid-range power by around 5%.

It seems that the best arrangement is to have the headers built such that the bottom of the pipe almost lines up with the exhaust port floor, leaving most of the mismatch to occur at the port roof. I am not sure exactly why this is so, but it could be that concentrating the obstruction on one side of the pipe creates a strong pulse wave to bounce back down the headers and reduce backflow, whereas a small lip right the way around the pipe may act as a constriction and not produce a pulse wave of any magnitude.

MODIFYING THE INLET PORT

The next aspect of the cylinder head at which we wish to take a look is swirl. Swirl is defined as the directional effect imparted to the inflowing gas by the shape of the inlet port or its angle of entry into the combustion chamber. Swirl assists eventual combustion by causing the mixture to be evenly and homogenously distributed in the cylinder. At the end of every exhaust cycle there is always a certain amount of exhaust gas that is left unscavenged in the cylinder. If this exhaust gas is allowed to collect into a pocket, it will retard the ignition flame travel, even preventing quite an amount of the fuel/air mixture from burning. Good swirl will prevent this pocket of exhaust gas from forming by evenly mixing the fresh mixture coming into the cylinder with the unscavenged exhaust gas. All the time this action is taking place the fuel droplets are being broken down into smaller more readily combustible particles and charge temperatures are being evened out. With hot and cold pockets minimised combustion is more complete, so power rises. Also, with less potential for violent combustion from hot spots or hot gas pockets, the way may be opened to run a little more spark advance or a few points higher compression ratio. This could add power, particularly in the midrange, and widen the engine's effective power band.

Generally, swirl is created by the engine manufacturer offsetting the port from the valve centre. Figure 3.1 illustrates an inlet port in plan view. Any tendency of the port to curve and produce swirl should be encouraged, as shown by the port on the left. The port on the right shows a common mistake made by tuners, who grind away metal at the easiest place. The port-straightening reduces swirl, causing poor mixture distribution, with poor combustion being the end result.

Offsetting the inlet port improves gas flow by causing the mixture to turn as it flows past the valve. This assists in directing flow along the combustion chamber wall and into the cylinder (Figure 3.10). Also the section of valve that is completely unshrouded (ie on the side adjacent to the exhaust valve) will flow more mixture. 41

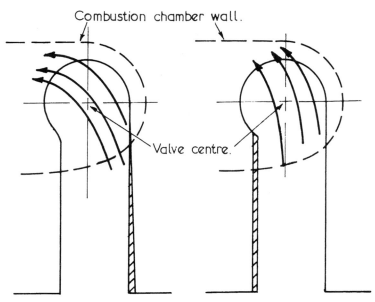

Correct. Incorrect.

Combustion chamber wall.

Valve centre.

Figure 3.1 A correctly modified inlet port promotes swirl.

If you take a look at Figure 3.11, you will note that this extreme example of port offset is the reason why the siamese-port Austin Mini head flows so well.

To improve flow and discourage charge robbing, the Mini inlet port is modified as in Figure 3.2. The port cannot be made much wider because of the location of the push rod holes, but this restriction has little effect on gas flow, provided that the peak between the two inlet pockets is cut back to open up the flow path. The peak deters charge robbing, therefore it should not be cut back further than the port wall alignment, as shown.

Looking at Figure 3.3, you can see that there will be better flow on one side of the valve because of the bend in the inlet port. This is another aspect of flow that we must consider, as gas flow along the floor of the port, and around the short radius into the combustion chamber, can be as little as 25% of the flow on the other side of the valve. The majority of mixture flows along the roof of the port and around the more gentle radius into the engine.

The initial flow into the cylinder at low valve lifts is along the floor of the port. As the inertia generated by this initial flow contributes much toward the total flow of the port at full lift, the lower side of the port must be very carefully modified to assist in cylinder filling.

Obviously the mixture must be encouraged to flow better on the lower side of the inlet tract. Sure enough, the improperly modified port in Figure 3.3 will flow more air, but not with the valve fitted. The mixture flowing down the inside wall merely bangs into the valve and, having lost much of its energy, relies on the underhead shape of the valve to direct it into the combustion chamber.

It is an interesting phenomenon, but an improperly modified port will usually flow more air with the valve removed, while a correctly shaped port actually flows

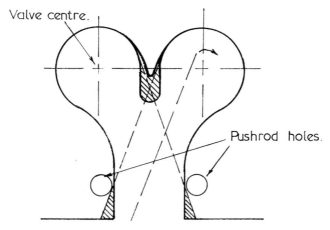

Figure 3.2 This modified siamese inlet port improves gas flow but deters charge robbing.

slightly less air when the valve is removed. This is assuming that a valve with the correct underhead shape is fitted. If a valve of the wrong shape is used, air flow will always increase when the valve is removed completely out of the head.

The correct thing to do is to remove metal in such a way that a progressive radius is retained on the inside wall. This will cause the air mixture to turn progressively as it remains attached to the port wall. Little energy will be lost as the mixture spills into the cylinder. This contributes to more mixture being introduced.

Figure 3.3 The inlet port should be modified to improve gas flow around the back of the valve.

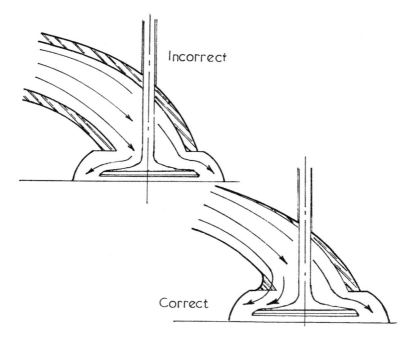

The 3 angle inlet seat and bowl from the combustion chamber side.

INLET VALVE THROAT AND VALVE SEAT

The valve seat and the area immediately under the seat, called the valve throat, is the most important section of the inlet port. As shown in Figure 3.4 the actual seat angle should be 45°, and 0.050in wide. The outside diameter of the seat is cut 0.015–0.020in less than the valve head diameter. The top cut to blend the seat into the combustion chamber has traditionally been a 30° angle, but flow bench tests often show a 38–39° cut is superior, and a 60° throat cut blends the seat into the inlet port. However, in some applications, an additional 70–75° throat cut improves flow.

The bottom cut is blended into a venturi 0.85–0.88 valve diameter, and in some applications it may be benefical to go as large as 0.9 where maximum hp is more important. The venturi then blends into an enlarged throat section that is 0.95–0.97 the

Figure 3.4 The inlet valve seat and throat area.

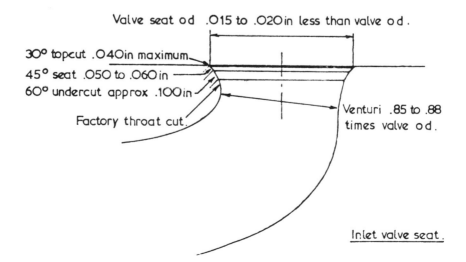

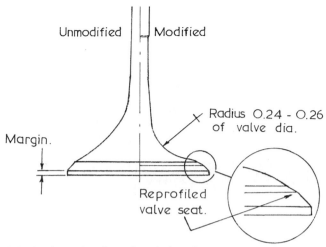

Unmodified | Modified

Margin.

Radius 0.24 - 0.26
of valve dia.

Reprofiled
valve seat.

Figure 3.5 Modified tulip valve for a hemi chamber.

valve diameter. In turn the enlarged throat tapers down to the 0.81–0.83 diameter of the inlet port proper. The science of port modification is in determining the length of port that each of these transitions occupies. As well as affecting port volume and the shape of the power graph, these changes in the inlet port cross-section and the distance over which they occur produce a venturi effect to aid gas flow around the valve and into the cylinder.

INLET VALVE SHAPE

The inlet valves in many motors are tulip shape. This is the preferred valve shape in heads with symmetrical port flow. However, a lot of heads do not lend themselves to this type of flow. The ones that do are purposely designed for high power output and as such have fairly steeply inclined inlet ports patterned after those pioneered by the Ford Lotus Twin Cam and Cosworth 4-valve motors of 40 years ago. These are in the happy position of having the right relationship between port, valve and combustion chamber angle, to eliminate any sharp bend by the port into the combustion chamber. This promotes good gas flow around the entire face of the inlet valve. As shown in Figure 3.5, the underhead radius is 0.24–0.26 of the valve diameter.

Until more recent times the majority of heads had a valve/port arrangement like the bath-tub chamber illustrated in Figure 3.12. Here the inlet port is only just above the valve seat. This style lends itself to a valve shape with an underhead radius 0.19–0.21 of the valve diameter. Flow on the lower side of the port is improved with this valve shape and this is what we are aiming for. Comparison of the two valves in Figure 3.6 shows the improved flow path. You will notice with all inlet valve designs the improvement brought about by recontouring the valve seating area to eliminate any projections.

The inlet valve seat should be cut at 45° and be 0.075in wide. Often a 25°–35° backcut is used to reduce the seat width to the required 0.075in. The backcut angle will vary from engine to engine, as the angle chosen is the one that best blends the valve head contour into the 45° seat cut. The valve margin should be 0.040–0.065in wide, with a sharp edge to discourage backflow of the mixture into the inlet port.

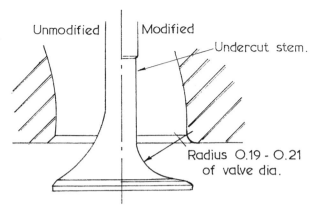

Figure 3.6 Valve modified for a flat-roof chamber.

The stem diameter should be the thinnest you can reliably get by with. A thinner stem means a lighter valve and better air flow, but the downside is more rapid valve guide wear, and as a consequence increased seat wear and a poorer gas seal. In endurance engines guide wear means also increased oil consumption. Also a narrow stem that is reliable in sprint engines may fatigue and drop the valve head if expected to last for 1,000km. The way to get some of the benefit of a narrow stem and of the wider stem is for it to be undercut to reduce its diameter by 0.035in, immediately below the valve head. This improves the flow by about 10% at valve lifts up to 0.360in. As the valve opens further, and the thicker section of stem enters deeper into the port, the improvement in flow tapers off. The valve stem is undercut in the area between the head of the valve and the end of the valve guide, with the valve on the seat.

Figure 3.7 Simple inlet valve modifications can produce as much flow increase as work in the ports. The 30° backcut blends the seat into the underhead radius. Undercutting the stem will help flow but can be dangerous. A square corner between the valve margin and valve face reduces inlet backflow.

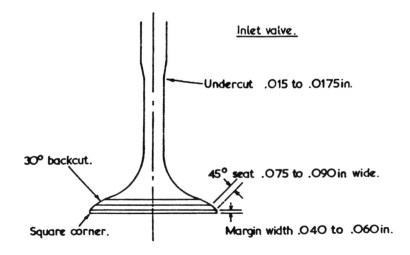

If your stock valves are properly made and are of suitable material they could be quite OK in mildly modified engines. Figure 3.7 shows what can be done to greatly improve the underhead shape to benefit air flow. Polishing them with emery paper will also help slow down carbon build-up and aids the detergents in modern premium unleaded fuel to get rid of stuff that has started to form.

EXHAUST VALVE THROAT AND SEAT

The exhaust valve seat is the exhaust valve's main point of contact with the engine coolant. In this instance the seat should be cut at 45° and be of 0.070in width (Figure 3.8). The exhaust valve reaches a temperature of 1500°–1800°F each combustion cycle, consequently adequate cooling must be maintained through the valve seat and valve guide. The overall diameter of the seat should be the same as or up to 0.010in less than the valve head diameter. (The heat will normally cause the exhaust valve to grow 0.010–0.020in). To finish the seat, a 38° chamber cut should generally be used. The width of the top chamber cut is usually not critical. In fact sinking the exhaust valve a little can help reduce mixture draw through and exhaust gas reversion. However, this increases the combustion chamber volume and lowers the compression ratio. Below the seat a 55–75° throat cut, depending on what the flow bench may indicate is best, would be added. This bottom cut would then blend into a venturi 0.85–0.86 the valve diameter. After that the port would taper out to 95–100% of valve diameter.

EXHAUST VALVE SHAPE

Exhaust valves can also do with some reshaping to improve flow out of the cylinder. The valve face seat should be 0.085in wide, and radiused back to the stem. I add a 30° backcut to bring the seat down to this width. The margin width for best flow is 0.060–0.100in, depending on the valve diameter. The lower edge of the margin should be lightly radiused into the valve face, as a square edge disrupts flow out of the cylinder.

Figure 3.8 The exhaust valve seat and throat area.

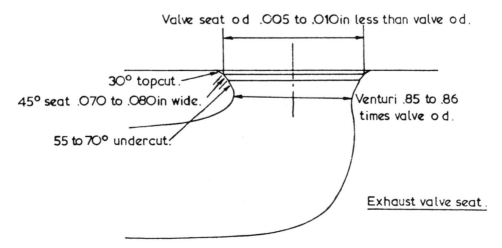

47

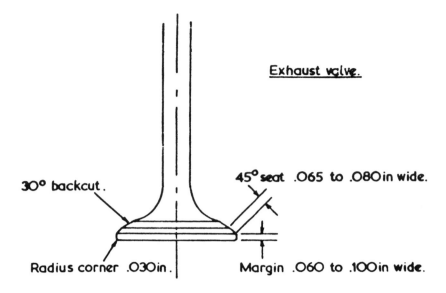

Figure 3.9 A standard exhaust valve can be modified as shown. If high strength austenitic stainless steel valves are used, the stems may be undercut to reduce their diameter by 0.035in.

The comments regarding inlet stem width also apply to the exhaust valve. The only difference is that the underhead stem area is subjected to a significant heat blast so it has to be mechanically stronger. Otherwise, as the valve head is banged continuously onto the seat, the valve head will be pulled off. Consequently the valve material choice is critical if it is intended to run with narrow stems, or if the stem is to be undercut 0.035in.

If you plan on running stock exhaust valves they can be modified in line with what is illustrated in Figure 3.9 to help flow. Sometimes the stems of unwelded stock valves can be undercut, but because the valves are often sourced from a number of different manufacturers there is no certainty that because one set of undercut valves was reliable that the same will be true of another set.

At one time a popular fad in American drag racing circles was to modify the back of the exhaust valve by cutting a ditch into it, hence the term 'ditch cutting'. The ditch is usually cut to a depth of 0.050in all the way around the valve tulip, from the valve stem right to the back of the valve seat. This creates a lip 0.050in high which is intended to impede exhaust backflow. In theory it sounds good, and on the air flow bench there was a reduction in backflow of about 20% at 0.100in valve lift, but in practice I have never been able to pick up any power on the dyno. It is probably just as well that this modification doesn't work, because I don't really think a valve weakened by ditching would stay in shape for too long.

THE SQUISH OR QUENCH AREA AND VALVE SHROUDING

The combustion chamber in most push-rod overhead valve motors is either bath-tub or wedge shape. Figure 3.10 shows a Ford Anglia 105E bath-tub chamber with the swirl

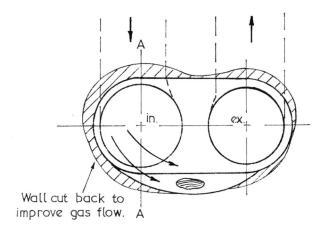

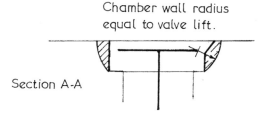

Figure 3.10 Bath-tub chamber modifications.

condition described earlier. It is not possible to get the intake mixture to curl around more than a certain amount, so the first obvious modification is to cut away the chamber wall opposite the port. The correct way to achieve this unshrouding is to grind the chamber wall in a concave curve. This will allow the mixture to flow unimpeded outward from the valve and down the cylinder, still swirling. This is essential to maintain a homogenous mixture in the cylinder.

The flat head surface between the wall of the combustion chamber and the cylinder wall is the 'squish' area, which plays a very important part in the combustion process. As the piston travels up to top dead centre it comes into close proximity with the squish area of the head. This squish action actually drives mixture from this area towards the spark plug, for ignition. Obviously the squish area is important for good combustion, so a compromise has to be made when cutting away the chamber wall to improve gas flow. In combustion chambers 10–13mm deep it is generally beneficial to relieve the chamber wall on the high flow side so that the passage between it and the valve edge is about equal to maximum valve lift (Figure 3.10). Some heads work best with a slightly larger passage but may show only minimal flow gains once the passage width exceeds 85% valve lift. On the low flow side a flow path about 70–75% of valve lift is required for twisted chambers and 60–65% for bath-tub chambers.

The squish area is also called the quench area, or quench band, as it increases the surface area of the combustion area and actually cools or quenches the burning mixture around the edges of the combustion chamber. This assists in maintaining a steady (not violent) burn rate, and offsets any tendency for high-speed detonation or pre-ignition to occur.

Horsepower by the numbers

During the late 1970s air-flow test benches became available from the Superflow company to race engine workshops. Along with the popular and economical Superflow 110 flow bench came a user's instruction manual, which suggested that an engine's horsepower potential could be estimated from the intake port air-flow numbers. The formula for a well-developed race engine was: hp = 0.43 x number of cylinders x air flow (cubic feet per minute (cfm) at 10in water).

Thus, if a four-cylinder engine flowed 100cfm at 0.420in valve lift and it was fitted with a cam lifting the valves at least 0.420in, the potential power output would be 172hp. This idea got many tuners into thinking that air flow was all important when it came to making power; more air flow means more hp. True, an engine will not make good power if the head does not flow well, but a good deal more is involved, such as the quality of the fuel/air mix entering the combustion chamber and the quality of the burn within the combustion chamber during the ignition process.

To illustrate, take an average 2-litre Ford Pinto race engine. It will make only about 200hp with a wild race cam lifting the 1.8in inlet valves in the vicinity of 0.500in, with a compression ratio of 12:1. The inlet flow will be about 117cfm, with the best heads flowing 120cfm. On the other hand an Opel Ecotec 2-litre will also make 200hp, but it will make this power on a completely standard head with a pair of tiny 1.26in inlet valves and a 10.8:1 compression ratio, running very mild hydraulic lifter road cams with only 0.410in valve lift and a duration of 232° at 0.050in lift. Inlet port flow at 0.410in valve lift is 113cfm.

Why does the Opel make similar power with slightly less air flow, less compression and baby road cams? Put simply, the fuel/air mixture entering the cylinder is better homogenised and the combustion chamber shape and spark plug location ensure a uniform, rapid and complete combustion of that inducted mixture.

The story is similar with the 350 Chevy. In speedway classes that demand the use of unported cast iron cylinder heads, those who can afford them seek out the expensive and often difficult-to-find high-performance '034' Bow Tie items. At 0.550in valve lift these heads flow around 144cfm using standard 2.02in Chev inlet valves. This equates to a 350 Chev producing 435hp using a dirt short-track cam with 252° duration at 0.050in and 0.545in lift on the inlet valve.

In my view a better head is that off the L31 Vortec pick-up truck engine, identified by its casting number '906'. When compared with the '034' Bow Tie head, the '906', when fitted with 2.02in Chev inlet valves, flows about 3–5% less air at all valve lifts except at 0.550in, where it is about level at 143cfm. However, in spite of this apparent numerical deficiency it manages to produce around 457hp on the same cam, manifold, carb, compression ratio, etc, and down around 4,000rpm at the bottom of the power band it maintains a consistent 5–6% horsepower advantage.

Where does the '906' gain this sort of advantage? Certainly it's not in air-flow capacity. However, whereas the '034' has a traditional wedge combustion chamber, the '906' has a heart-shaped chamber more like the Austin Mini. Obviously this additional squish area opposite the spark plug improves mixture homogenisation and encourages good flame propagation. Additionally the spark plug has been moved deeper into the centre of the chamber and closer to the chamber roof to assist a more complete burn. This is borne out in the amount of spark advance required with each head. The '034' made best power with 34–35° ignition advance, while the '906' heads only wanted 30°.

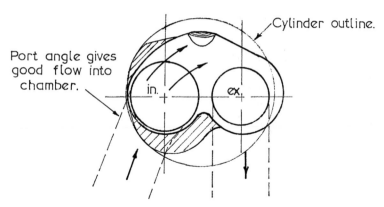

Figure 3.11 Austin Mini chamber modifications.

Under certain conditions it is possible for the combustion flame to pre-heat the fuel charge directly in front of the flame to the point of self-ignition. When this flame collides with the spark-ignited combustion flame, explosion-like combustion results (detonation). The quench area normally prevents this by removing excess heat from the outer gases. With the temperature lowered, the end gases do not self-ignite to initiate a dangerous detonation condition.

The quench area also lowers the piston crown temperature by momentarily restricting the combustion flame to just the area of the combustion chamber. This increases piston and ring life, and helps prevent the piston from becoming a hot spot, able to pre-ignite the fuel/air charge.

The exhaust valve requires very little unshrouding at all. I generally work to a figure of 60% of valve lift for the radius between the valve head and chamber wall. It is a mistake to exceed this figure as the exhaust valve flows very well partially shrouded; in fact, it seems to enjoy being shrouded. I well remember an occasion where I was able to pick up 6hp on a VW 1600 by shrouding the exhaust valve a little. Power went up from 163 to 169hp, which represented a 4% gain.

The heart-shaped chamber of the Mini (Figure 3.11) is an easy one to modify. It yields high power due to the inlet port offset producing a good swirl effect. The valves should be unshrouded as with a bath-tub chamber.

THE TWISTED BATH-TUB CHAMBER

A later development of the bath-tub chamber, which also borrows from the Austin Mini in that the inlet port enters the chamber at a similarly favourable angle, is what is called the 'twisted bath-tub' chamber. This chamber is found in the Isuzu-designed Opel/Holden/Vauxhall Family I and Family II OHC engines. As you will notice from the photograph, the combustion chamber is turned, or 'twisted', through 45°, producing a head with inlet ports on one side and exhaust ports down the other side. With the chamber twisted like this a much greater area around the periphery of both the inlet and exhaust valves is unmasked, so flows into and out of the engine are improved. Also there is a good squish area opposite the spark plug, which is itself located deep into the chamber, giving a good quick burn. For even better inlet flow

Twisting the combustion chambers opens up the inlet and exhaust flow path while maintaining generous squish areas.

some of the squish area near the spark plug can be cut back toward the cylinder outline, but take care not to overdo this.

Remember that we were talking before about squish and its importance in the combustion process. The primary or major squish area should be somewhere about opposite the spark plug, to squish the bulk of the fuel/air mixture over into the combustion area. Now behind the spark plug we have a secondary squish area. Its effect is also to squish and create a pressure wave. As the spark plug ignites the mixture, this wave assists the flame front to travel through and ignite the mixture that the major squish area has pushed towards the spark plug.

If the combustion chamber is cut back right to the bore wall, what is the result? Gas flow may improve, but remember that I said right at the outset that gas flow has to be balanced against good combustion. With no secondary squish to assist the flame front and impede the mixture rushing across from the major squish area, you may lose power. This is what can happen: the mixture being purged across to the spark plug bangs into the chamber wall and spark plug and devaporises, wetting the chamber wall and possibly the spark plug too, depending on its temperature. Try holding your hand in front of an aerosol spray pack when you are spraying and you will see what I am getting at.

At the very least, a head modified in this way will waste fuel and dilute your engine oil. Some of that lovely fuel mixture you have managed to cram into the cylinder will end up going out of the exhaust or, at low revs and/or with a cold motor, it will end up in the sump, wrecking your super-good oil.

One problem with many of these Opel heads is that the inlet ports are way oversize, so keep the grinder away from them or these engines become even more sluggish at lower rpm. Fortunately a number of models have good-size valve seat inserts and the valve spacing is such that larger valves can be easily fitted. Bigger valves will provide a good hp increase at higher rpm without taking anything away from the bottom end. In the later Gen II high port heads GM got it right with smaller, but much superior flow inlet ports. This change boosted midrange power and also maximum power even though a much milder cam with less lift and duration was used.

Canting the valves improves flow because the head of the opening valve moves away from the wall of the combustion chamber and provides a wider flow path.

The 2- and 2.3-litre Ford Pinto head appears to be the same as the twisted bath-tub but it is in fact slightly different in that the inlet and exhaust valves are not vertical. As you can see from the photograph, both valves are tilted, or 'canted', a few degrees. While this gives rise to all sorts of valve gear problems, as anyone who competes with these engines is only too well aware, splaying or canting the valves does have several benefits. First, as the valve opens it moves away from the combustion chamber wall, thus opening up the flow path. This also opens up the way to fit larger valves, which would otherwise be severely masked if arranged vertically. Additionally, as we will discuss in depth later, reducing the port-to-valve angle improves flow around the valve head into the combustion chamber.

As with the early Gen I Opel, these heads also have overly generous inlet ports relative to the standard-size inlet valves. Only when larger valves are fitted should the ports be touched.

THE WEDGE CHAMBER

The wedge chamber in its most basic form is in reality just a bath-tub chamber inclined, usually at around 15°. This is the type of chamber found in almost every American V8 and it presents the serious tuner with many problems, particularly when the chamber is tilted steeply, as it is in the small-block Chev, at 23°.

Why use the wedge chamber then, you may ask? Figure 3.12 illustrates the most obvious benefit from this design, namely the reduction of the bend in the inlet port, allowing the valve to flow better, particularly on the lower side. A straight (non-inclined) port flowing into a bath-tub chamber flows only about 20% of the mixture on the lower or 'dead' side of the valve, but the wedge chamber can flow 25–30% of the mixture on this side.

The other obvious benefit is the concentration of fuel/air mixture close to the spark plug in the deepest part of the chamber. This effectively shortens the flame travel, allowing for more complete combustion if a flat-top piston is used.

53

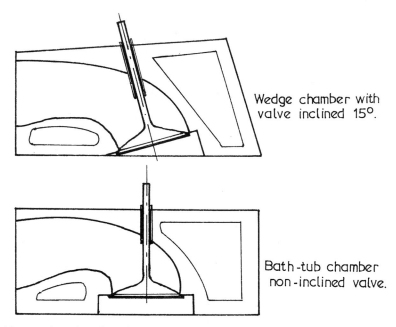

Wedge chamber with
valve inclined 15°.

Bath-tub chamber
non-inclined valve.

Figure 3.12 A wedge chamber decreases the port entry angle.

However, and this again highlights the importance of balancing good air flow with good combustion, in performance and competition applications we soon run into a situation where with many wedge chambers we just cannot get better than a 9.5:1 compression ratio without resorting to high-top pistons. Any piston becomes in effect the 'floor' of the combustion chamber, so the shape of the crown can either promote or retard mixture homogenisation and combustion flame propagation. A high-top piston obviously masks the spark plug and disrupts flame travel across the combustion chamber. Also, of course, there is a mechanical penalty; high-top pistons weigh more, so loads on bearings and connecting rods increase. This could mean that heavier, more expensive rods and crank, or a lower rpm limit, are necessary.

This has led to a serious rethink in Detroit. First in 1989 Chevrolet introduced its 18° Bow Tie range of heads for competition engines. These heads feature smaller, shallower combustion chambers, which in themselves promote a better burn and less detonation trouble. This has meant less piston crown protruding into the combustion chamber while allowing the compression ratio to climb to 15:1 on 112 octane race fuel.

Then at the end of 1996 Chev introduced their revised small-block engine, dubbed the Gen III. While still retaining wedge chambers, the valve inclination is further reduced to 15° to produce a more compact combustion chamber and, like the L31 Vortec '906' heads mentioned previously, the combustion chamber is now heart-shaped.

Ford SVO has done something similar with their N351 cast iron competition heads. In these the valves are inclined at only 10° as opposed to the standard 22°. This effectively makes the combustion chamber more compact and means that only a small protrusion is needed on the pistons to achieve a high compression ratio. To restore air flow the valves were repositioned within the combustion chamber and the inlet ports were raised 0.3in.

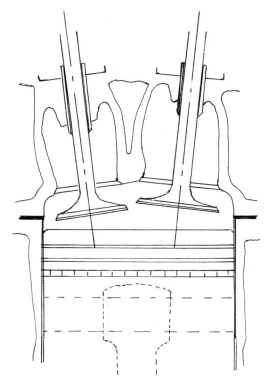

Figure 3.13 Big-block Chev head design.

CANTED-VALVE WEDGE CHAMBER

Canted-valve wedge heads first appeared on the Mark IV Chev big block in 1965. As well as having the inlet and exhaust valves inclined at 26° and 17° respectively to give a wedge-shaped chamber, both valves are also canted 4°. Such a small angle may seem insignificant with regard to the distance the valve head will move away from the combustion chamber wall and cylinder wall as it opens and so present a wider air-flow path. However, consider that in many big blocks we are looking at valve lifts in the 0.800–0.950in range, which means a much wider flow path around the 'dead' portion of the valve periphery at the two ends of the combustion chamber (Figure 3.13). Another feature of these heads that encourages superior air flow is the 'twisting' of the combustion chamber through 20°, although full advantage could not be taken of this because of 'good' and 'bad' inlet ports. When compared with the Ford Cleveland Boss 302/351 wedge chamber, which is twisted around 25° and has symmetrical inlet ports, you can see why the Chev inlet ports are dubbed as being either 'good' or 'bad' (Figure 3.14).

Like the early design wedge heads, the Chev big-block canted-valve wedge chamber also requires a big lump on the piston crown to achieve a suitable compression ratio. Such a large compression lump causes all kinds of combustion problems. Even with a fairly decent cam, high-performance road engines run into detonation problems over 9:1 on 98 octane (Research octane) petrol, and even race engines will not handle anything over 12:1 on 110 octane race fuel. This is not to say that the canted-valve

55

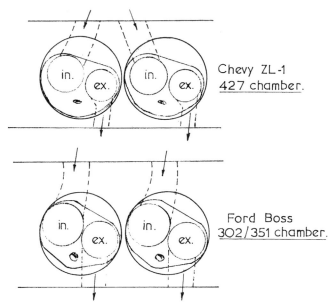

Figure 3.14 Two high-performance 'twisted wedge' chambers.

wedge chamber cannot be made to work; it can, as Chev demonstrated when they produced competition heads for both their small-block V8 and 90° V6 with new-style compact canted-valve wedge chambers. Like the Ford Cleveland these later heads have all 'good' symmetrical inlet ports, and while the inlet and exhaust valves are still canted at 4° as in the Mark IV big-block, the wedge angle has been reduced considerably to provide an inlet valve inclination of 16° and an exhaust valve inclination of 11° to provide a compact combustion chamber with a volume of about 48cc as opposed to the open chamber Mark IV volume of nearly 120cc.

THE HERON DESIGN

This leads us to what I regard as the most horrible design of all time, the Heron head. It works just fine on 2,000rpm diesels, but used on a petrol engine it is nothing like so good. The design utilises a flat-face head without a combustion chamber. Instead, combustion takes place in a combustion chamber cast into the piston crown. Ford used this design in their so-called 'Crossflow' Escort and Cortina and 3-litre V6 Capri motor. Chrysler also used it in their Avenger motors.

Having no effective squish area, this design suffers chronic ignition problems. The Avenger, for example, is only happy with 46–47° spark advance. If you must stick with this design rather than using a head with combustion chambers machined into it (very expensive), there are a few principles to keep in mind. The first is to keep the inlet system on the small side. Use a small carburettor venturi and reduced port diameter to keep gas speed high. Profile grind the inlet port but leave it reasonably rough. Machine the top of the cylinder block to bring the pistons to around 0.005–0.007in from the deck. This will induce some squish effect. I have found that recessing the valves about 0.060in into the head (Figure 3.15) improves not only the

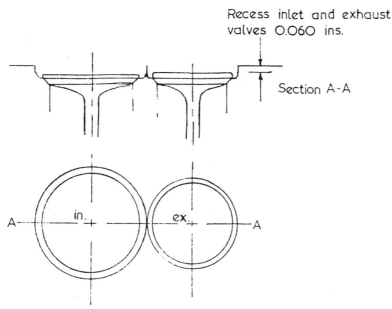

Figure 3.15 Heron head modification.

gas flow but also, I suspect, the combustion. The shrouding of the valves possibly causes some sort of venturi effect, which aids vaporisation and homogenisation of the mixture. The early Ford 1600GT had small combustion chambers machined into the head. This head is best pensioned off and replaced with a counter-bored flat head, which will improve the compression as well.

Besides the combustion problem, a basic mechanical problem exists with the Heron design. Because the combustion chamber is in the crown of the piston, the heat path is made longer, which increases the piston crown temperature. With thermal distortion thrown in for good measure, piston seizure is commonplace. In fact, for this reason some tuners build their 1,700cc Crossflow Ford race engines with flat-top pistons, which finish up about 0.280in down the bore and accept that they will have to run with 10° more spark advance. Note that this is not a viable option for road engines as fuel consumption rises dramatically, and unless 3D electronic ignition is employed throttle response at lower rpm is not good.

Now, I do not deny that Cosworth used this design on their very successful 1-litre SCA engine, finally extracting 140hp from it with a 49° spark advance. However, keep this in mind: a 250cc cylinder running a 12.5:1 compression ratio has a very small combustion chamber, and as half of the combustion chamber on this motor is in the head, the heat path across the piston crown is not much longer than that across a flat-top piston. Furthermore, a racing engine can be run with very big piston clearances and rattle all it likes, so piston distortion and/or seizure would not be such a problem.

HEMI AND SEMI-HEMI CHAMBER

Decreasing the valve-to-port angle is really what high power outputs are all about. By coaxing the 'dead' side of the port and valve to flow better, we can cram more mixture 57

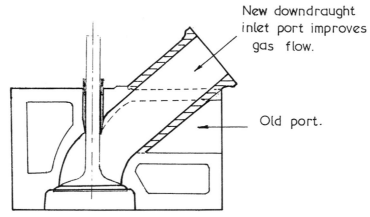

Figure 3.16 Downdraught conversion.

into the cylinder in any given time. Figure 3.16 shows the Ford Anglia 105E head modified with downdraught inlet ports. On the 1,300cc Ford Escort, I have seen 143hp with this head on carburettors, which is all of 15hp, or 12%, more power than the same motor would produce on a 105E sidedraught head.

During the late 1970s many performance engines began to use what is known as the hemispherical chamber for this very reason. The inlet tract is straightened out and a large valve area is possible. This design, too, has had its problems. Back in the early 1950s the hemispherical chamber was being pioneered by such manufacturers as Jaguar, Chrysler and Norton. The design suffered a basic mixture burn problem, so 50° spark advance was commonplace. In Figure 3.17 you will note the valve angle (usually around 70–90° included angle), creating a huge combustion chamber. This large chamber surface area allows heat loss from the compressed mixture, reducing efficiency. Also, because of the large chamber area, the ignition flame must travel an extreme distance. Consequently two spark plugs were used in racing engines to aid combustion. Even today, after years of development, the Chrysler hemi and the air-cooled flat-six Porsche still work better with two plugs.

Figure 3.17 Early Jaguar head design.

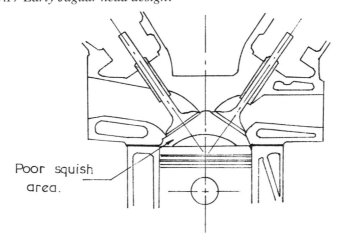

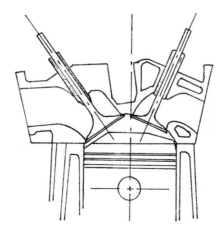

Figure 3.18 The later Chrysler Hemi has improved squish control.

Remember our friend squish? Well, he is also lacking with this design. In Figure 3.17 you will notice that some squish does occur due to the radius of the combustion chamber being smaller than that of the piston dome, but this isn't enough to promote good combustion.

Later, the piston dome design was changed to that shown in Figure 3.18. This modification was adopted by both Chrysler and Jaguar. The piston dome in this design is supplemented by a flat section running right round the crown, which comes into

Figure 3.19 Lotus/Ford Twin Cam head arrangement.

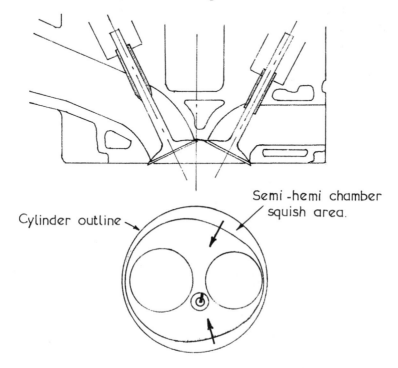

Cylinder outline

Semi-hemi chamber
squish area.

Judged purely from an hp perspective, the cylinder head Colin Chapman had Harry Mundy design for the Ford Cortina 116E engine was the best production 2-valve head ever made. It was let down in competition by a single row timing chain and a central water outlet that upset exhaust valve cooling; both compromises being forced on Mundy by the need to make the engine fit ordinary production cars.

close contact with the lower reaches of the combustion chamber. Squish is improved, bringing an improvement in combustion. This has resulted in higher power outputs and a reduction in spark advance.

In 1963 the brilliant Harry Mundy designed Lotus/Ford Twin Cam was introduced. Not a true hemi but a semi-hemi, this motor set the pace in head design, in the car world at any rate, for many years. In 1.6-litre form this motor will produce 210hp on carburettors, and will run quite happily with just a 30–34° spark lead. In fact, the motor I ran on the road in my Ford Anglia for many years operated with only 25° total advance. It was no slouch either, producing 156hp at 6,800rpm.

The semi-hemi combustion chamber (Figure 3.19) has two distinct squish areas that drive the fuel mixture towards the spark plug. The valve angle has been closed up (54° on Lotus/Ford Twin Cam), allowing the use of a flat-top piston. Consequently this design enjoys a more compact combustion chamber than the true hemi, and this feature, combined with good squish control, makes for high power outputs while still allowing a large valve area and a relatively straight inlet port.

You will also note that with this design, as with the hemi, the inlet valve, and also generally the exhaust valve, are completely unshrouded. This allows for fairly even mixture flow right round the valve head. Instead of the valve flowing 80% on one side and 20% on the other, as with the bath-tub chamber, it will probably be flowing something more like 57% and 43% in this instance. Therefore the available area is being used more effectively so that air flow and horsepower go up.

FOUR-VALVE PENT-ROOF CHAMBER

The next development of this type of head is what we call the pent-roof chamber (Figure 3.20). This design is immediately associated with Cosworth because of the pioneering done by Keith Duckworth in developing firstly the 1.6ltr 225hp Ford FVA Formula 2 and

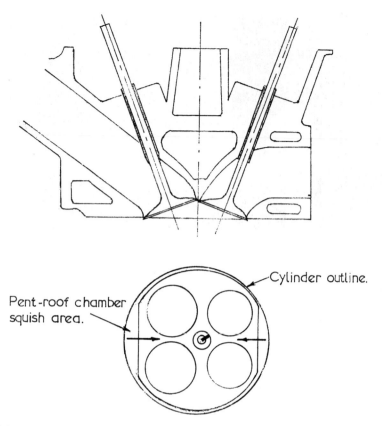

Figure 3.20 Cosworth Chevy Vega four-valve head.

later the 3ltr 470hp Ford DFV Formula 1 engine, proving the advantages of the four-valve pent-roof chamber. However, from the outset, the advantages of the design were not so obvious.

Prior to World War I, Peugeot went racing with twin cam four-valve engines with great success. Henri Peugeot's race engine designer Ernest Henry chose an included valve angle of 60° with the two 1.575in inlet, and identically sized exhaust valves, lifted a maximum of 0.354in to provide breathing for each of the engine's four 746cc cylinders. Considering that the cylinders were only 78mm diameter the valve sizes were massive even by today's Formula 1 standards. Other great racing marques Mercedes, and later Maserati, at times also built four-valve race engines.

Both Coventry Climax and BRM also tried this layout in their Grand Prix engines but without much improvement over the more conventional semi-hemi. BRM, in its typical enthusiasm, even tried a four-valve with diametrically opposed inlet and exhaust valves. Can you imagine designing the intake and exhaust system for a V12 so equipped?

It was the motorcycle world that brought the four-valve design again to the attention of race engine designers. Back in the early 1960s Honda was using the four-valve principle on its Grand Prix bikes. At that time they were running a five-cylinder 125, a six-cylinder 250 and 297 and a four-cylinder 500, all with four-valve pent-roof

For 40 years the Duckworth designed 4-valve head for the Ford Cosworth DFV Formula 1 engine has been the basis for all other high performance cylinder head development.

chambers. The 250 produced 60hp at 17,000rpm. Honda then carried the design on to the car Grand Prix circuit with their 160hp 1ltr Formula 2 engine. The two-valve 140hp Cosworth SCA was no match, so when the Formula 2 capacity limit was lifted to 1.6 litres, Keith Duckworth designed his new motor, the Ford FVA, around the four-valve pent-roof chamber. He got his design right; for the first time the FVA rode the dyno it pushed out 202hp at 9,000rpm; over 10% more than comparable two-valve engines.

Initially Honda used a fairly wide valve angle of 63°, which required the use of high-top pistons. Cosworth, however, closed the valve angle up to 40° (32° on DFV, DFX Indy turbo and stroked DFL sports racer), producing a very shallow combustion chamber which allows the use of flat-top pistons. Squish is good and from opposite sides of a single, central, spark plug.

Now virtually every designer utilising the pent-roof four-valve arrangement follows the design refined by Keith Duckworth. Over the years since then the valve angle has been closed up even more, sacrificing valve area, to produce a flatter, more combustion friendly chamber. In 1983 Cosworth, now with Mario Illien heading design, produced a new Formula 1 engine dubbed the DFY. This had the inlet valves inclined at 10° and the exhausts at 12^1/$_2$° for an included angle of 22^1/$_2$°. In 2000 the Ferrari Tipo 049 Formula 1 engine had valves set at 25°, but at the same time for their big 6ltr V12 550 sports car Ferrari engineers chose 20°; 11° inlet and 9° exhaust. It appears that around 20° included angle is now pretty much the accepted norm for purpose designed race engines, but that obviously is not the case for other high power applications. When designing the V12 6ltr Aston Martin DB9 engine, Cosworth decided on a relatively wide 50° (25° for both inlet and exhaust), and the Porsche GT3 has its valves at a more conventional 27.4° (14.7° inlet and 12.7° exhaust). Like the Porsche GT3 many sports bikes have an included angle around 25–27°; and comparably, usually a degree or two more inclination on the inlet valve.

Honda radial valve dirt bike head has valves tilted in two directions to move valve head away from cylinder wall and improve air flow.

RADIAL OR COMPOUND FOUR-VALVE CHAMBER

In 1984, Honda released a number of single-cylinder dirt bikes in 250, 350 and 500 sizes with what they termed 'radial four-valve' cylinder heads; what today is more commonly called 'compound four-valve'. This development of the basic four-valve pent-roof design involved moving the two inlet valves so that their valve stems were no longer parallel to each other, but were canted several degrees. The stems of the exhaust valves were similarly canted. As for the big block Mark IV Chev this arrangement permitted a small increase in valve size for any given cylinder bore diameter. More importantly, canting moves the opening valve heads away from the cylinder wall to provide a superior air-flow path that aids cylinder filling, mixture agitation and homogenisation.

Because the Honda was a single overhead cam engine they employed a complex dual rocker arrangement for valve activation. Later when Formula 1 engineers first adopted this style of head an inverted bucket tappet, pinned to prevent rotation and with a tapered lobe contact surface, transferred cam lobe motion to the valves. The Peugeot V10 for example followed this design, but with the valves tipped just 3° from vertical there were cam lobe to cam follower friction and wear issues even with diamond like coating (DLC) of the working surfaces. Later when F1 engine builders moved to finger followers they chose to stay at around 3° valve canting even though there was freedom, from a mechanical standpoint, to go much more aggressive. However, extensive testing has shown that while flow may be superior with more radical canting we lose out in other areas. Combustion chamber surface area increases, so there are larger heat losses and because the chamber is slightly deeper we also lose compression. Likewise when we apply deeper valve cut-outs to the piston crown; necessary for the more steeply canted valve to avoid contact with the piston as it approaches and descends from top dead centre.

THE FOUR-VALVE ADVANTAGE

The arrangement of two inlet and two exhaust valves in the combustion chamber allows for an increase in valve area over that possible with a two-valve hemi, but contrary to what many believe, this is not the real reason for the superior performance of a four-valve engine. To give you an example of this, consider a 1,700cc Cosworth rally engine when compared to a 1,700cc Lotus/Ford Twin Cam rally engine. The Cosworth BDA has two 1.22in inlet valves, giving an area of 2.34sq in, while the Lotus/Ford Twin Cam has one 1.69in inlet valve with an almost identical valve area of 2.24sq in. Both engines develop maximum power at 8,000rpm; 190hp for the Cosworth, 170hp for the Lotus/Ford. The Cosworth is always much faster on any rally surface due to having a 1000rpm wider power band and far superior top-end and bottom-end power. This occurs because the Cosworth, although having a similar valve area, has 44% more valve flow area than the Lotus/Ford at all valve lifts. Remember the air does not flow through the valve but rather around the periphery of the valve, thus flow area is equal to valve circumference multiplied by valve lift. Therefore a four-valver can use short duration cams, which improve mid-range power without sacrificing maximum power.

THE FIVE-VALVE CHAMBER

A later development of the four-valve pent-roof chamber is the five-valve design brought to us by Yamaha. When the FZ 750 motorcycle appeared in 1985 it produced a true 86hp at 11,500rpm in standard road trim. Caring for the breathing of each of its 187cc cylinders were three tiny 0.827in inlet valves and two 0.906in exhaust valves. By comparison the then radical Suzuki GSX-R750 from the same era used two 0.984in inlets and two 0.945in exhaust valves.

In time a number of manufacturers tested the design but all struggled with excessive fuel consumption brought about by poor charge homogenisation and

The Yamaha R7 5-valve chamber has good squish areas and inlet flow but the raised middle valve seat effectively divides the combustion chamber and hurts combustion.

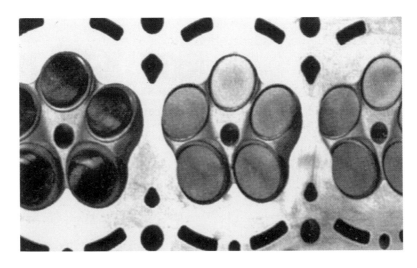

sluggish combustion. Sure the extra valve improves air flow into the engine, but a lot more fuel is needed to get power levels on a par with a four-valver. A couple of manufacturers have stuck with the five-valve arrangement, most likely as a marketing tool to give themselves a distinctive identity, but at this time even with the benefit of something like five redesigns by Yamaha, the five-valve head should be seen as a performance handicap relative to an average four-valve configuration.

The basic problems with this layout all stem from adding that fifth valve. First up, the inlet porting is a mess and as a consequence the port isn't able to properly control air flow direction and motion into the cylinder, badly hurting mixture quality. This was further exacerbated by an inadequate amount of squish, although Yamaha did address this with generous squish areas in later versions. The biggest problem though is the lump of metal in the combustion chamber running from the seat of the extra valve out across the spark plug area. Because of that lump the spark plug has to be recessed. Consequently when the piston approaches top dead centre and the plug fires the flame is masked, isolated in that recess, delaying flame propagation throughout the combustion space until the piston reverses, moving away from the head. Additionally, like the dome on high compression pistons, the lump basically divides the combustion chamber into two. Thus when the piston rises on compression mixture homogenisation

The 5-valve Ferrari 360 chamber illustrates limited squish and serious spark plug masking. In the inlet port the design doesn't provide good control of mixture flow direction as it enters the cylinder.

is lessened; meaning that not only have the air and fuel molecules not been fully stirred up and mixed uniformly, but that two cool pockets of mixture have been allowed to form near the two outer inlet valves. In turn, those two cool pockets burn much more slowly, so following ignition, combustion is incomplete and power output is hurt relative to the amount of fuel consumed.

MODIFYING SEMI-HEMI AND FOUR-VALVE HEADS

The design of semi-hemi (eg Lotus Twin Cam) and four-valve pent-roof heads is usually quite good so not much can be done to easily improve upon them and pick up the big hp increases that are possible with low tech push-rod heads. The combustion chamber sometimes requires mild reshaping, particularly if larger valves are fitted. However, there are quite basic things you can do to improve flow in the inlet and exhaust ports. The main point to keep in mind is to keep your grinding tools away from the ports. You can clean out the 'dingle berries' but apart from that there isn't much else you should attempt without the aid of a flow bench. Really the part to focus your efforts on is the valve seat proper and the area immediately under the valve seat in the throat area. Usually there are sharp ridges around where the valve seat meets the port that can be quite easily ground out It is always difficult and expensive to get sizeable power increases from a head that is a good design to begin with.

Unfortunately, many motorcycle engines do not gain full benefit from inclined valves and hemi or pent-roof chambers, as the inlet port often has a sharp bend in it. On cars it is usually no big problem to fit the inlet manifold on downdraught or semi-downdraught inlet ports, but on bikes the ports often have to be kept as low as possible so that the carburettors or fuel injection clears the frame and fuel tank.

Main flow improvement comes from work in the inlet port valve bowl area. Valve seat insert overhanging the valve throat, the sharp lip where the machining meets the rough cast and port 'dingle berries' all upset flow.

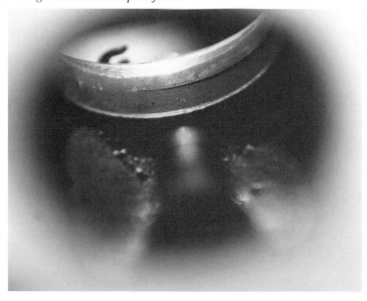

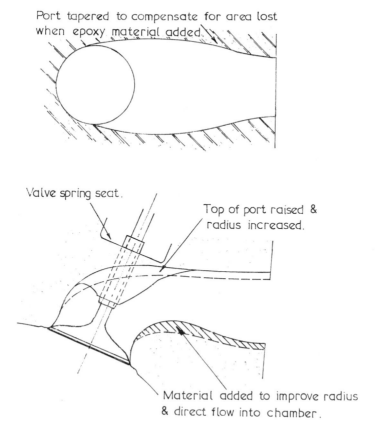

Port tapered to compensate for area lost when epoxy material added.

Valve spring seat.

Top of port raised & radius increased.

Material added to improve radius & direct flow into chamber.

Figure 3.21 Motorcycle inlet port modification.

This presents quite a problem as the inlet ports can usually be raised no more than about one-eighth of an inch, and this small amount does little to straighten out the bend into the combustion chamber. Usually all that can be done is to increase the radius of the bend. By grinding the top curve of the port, the top radius can be increased, but the amount of grinding is limited by the close proximity of the valve spring seat. The bottom side of the port is built up with epoxy or aluminium weld, and this effectively increases its radius. To further aid air flow, the port should be made gradually wider, so that at the bend it is no longer round, but oval.

A typical 1.2in round port would narrow down at the bend to a height of perhaps 0.9in (due to the small radius being welded up), and widen out to a width of around 1.45in (Figure 3.21).

VOLUMETRIC EFFICIENCY AND COMPRESSION RATIO

The next aspect to consider is the compression ratio, which is the relationship between the total volume of the cylinder, head gasket and combustion chamber, with the piston at bottom dead centre (BDC), and the volume contained in the space between the piston crown, head gasket and combustion chamber at top dead centre (TDC). 67

Changes in the compression ratio have a considerable effect on power output, because the higher the ratio, the higher the compression pressure at any given engine speed. As is true at all times, you cannot get something for nothing, which applies equally in this instance. An increase in compression ratio brings a corresponding increase in combustion temperature, so will the valves stand it? Bearing loads increase, as does the load on the ignition system, so do not rush in without considering the consequences. As a general rule, a road engine running on 95 to 98 octane petrol will be quite happy on a 9.5–10.5:1 ratio, while racing engines using 100 octane petrol usually run an 11–12.5:1 ratio and up to 13.5:1 on 100/130 Avgas fuel. With methanol, this can be increased to 14:1 or 15:1.

Above a true compression ratio of 14:1 no power is gained. However, if the engine has exceptional anti-detonation characteristics, a theoretical compression ratio of 15:1 may pick up a little power due to the fact that unsupercharged engines seldom, if ever, attain a volumetric efficiency of 100%. Simply stated, volumetric efficiency is the ability of an engine to fill its cylinders with mixture expressed as a percentage of the actual volume of the cylinders. Therefore a motor with cylinders of 100cc will be operating at 50% volumetric efficiency if it manages to get only 50cc of mixture into its cylinders. Obviously, such a motor, while operating on a theoretical compression ratio of 14:1, will, in fact, have a true compression ratio of only 7:1. As the average racing motor operates at approximately 93% volumetric efficiency, the theoretical compression ratio of 15:1 will actually be a true compression ratio of 14:1.

RELYING ON THE KNOCK SENSOR KILLS POWER

Some have got the mistaken idea that you can push the compression ratio way up, then just back off the spark advance, or let the knock sensor take care of it when the engine goes into detonation. The reasoning is that more compression means more hp, hence more must be better, and anyway isn't this what many car manufacturers do on their road cars? Don't they run the compression up high, then, when detonation is detected by the knock sensor, electronically retard the spark until knocking ceases? Yes, this is the way manufacturers design a number of their road cars, but remember they are chasing maximum performance, not necessarily maximum power. It all gets back to the volumetric efficiency. A road engine may spend much of its life cruising at 2,000–3,000rpm with the throttle just cracked open, so the cylinders are only being partially filled. Ideally, to obtain maximum cruise power and fuel economy the compression ratio needs to be pushed up, say, from 8.5:1 to 11:1, but here's the catch: all of these engines do not spend their entire time cruising. Hence when the accelerator is floored and more air gets into the cylinders, increasing the VE, the compression will now be too high and the engine will detonate.

Perhaps you are wondering why don't we have a variable compression engine that gives us an ideal compression ratio to suit various engine operating conditions. Yes, a bright idea, but we do not currently have those for passenger cars, so the manufacturers came up with a compromise. Instead of an 8.5:1 compression ratio that will not detonate on 92 octane fuel, they have pushed it up to say 9.3–9.8:1, not the best for cruise power and economy, but better than 8.5:1. However, this higher compression ratio will be destroying the engine by detonation at wide-open throttle when the VE will be up around 87%. To avoid this a knock sensor is stuck on the engine, and when internal hammering is detected the spark timing is backed off a few degrees. If the knocking does not stop the computer backs off the spark lead some more until it does.

However, this engine with a higher-than-ideal compression ratio running with retarded spark will not be making as much power at wide-open throttle as an engine that has a compression ratio more compatible with available fuel octane and optimum spark advance. Manufacturers accept this trade-off, usually of about 4% in maximum power, for improved part-throttle performance and reduced fuel consumption.

Performance and race engines spend much of their time not cruising at 2,000–3,000rpm with the throttle barely cracked open, but at wide-open throttle. Therefore that 4% trade-off (and I've seen over 6% at times) in maximum power because the compression ratio is too high is not acceptable. Obviously when you start out you do not know the ideal compression ratio. The idea is to start conservatively. Remember that an engine with a low compression ratio and lots of spark timing will make much better power than one that has to have the timing backed right off because the compression ratio is too high.

FIGURING THE IDEAL COMPRESSION RATIO

Getting back to volumetric efficiency again, it should be obvious that an engine that breathes well at high rpm, filling its cylinders completely, will have to run a lower compression ratio than an engine that has a lower VE. A practical example of this is the small-block Chev V8 when modified for various types of competition. In 5-litre road-race trim it will be limited to a compression ratio of around 13.5:1 on 100/130 Avgas fuel and breathing through throttle-body fuel injection. When the capacity is increased to the small block's practical maximum of 6.6 litres, the compression ratio can be raised to 14.4:1 because the average VE will be poorer even though the bigger engine, by virtue of its larger bore, can accommodate larger 2.2in inlet valves as opposed to 2.1in, and it can run a wilder cam because the additional cylinder volume improves mid-range power. However, this improved breathing capability does not keep pace with the increased cylinder size, so the VE decreases.

Another aspect of how far we can go with compression ratios is vehicle weight and gearing. A lightweight racer in a low gear can accelerate rapidly through the 'detonation zone' and avoid trouble. However, lug the engine in that danger area often enough or for sufficient time and you will destroy it. This should tell you that any engine that has to operate through a wide power band in high gears will require a lower compression ratio than one operating through a narrow power band and a super-close-ratio gearbox.

What then is the 'correct' compression ratio? Obviously this varies with engine design and available fuel, but, as we have seen, where the engine will be used and the driver's skill in keeping it out of the danger zone also have some bearing on this. Race engine tuners spend a lot of time pondering this very problem.

On the dyno an 11.8:1 engine with 36° spark advance and an identical 12.3:1 engine with, say, 31° advance may give seemingly similar performances, but on the race circuit one may be superior to the other, or it may be superior on certain types of circuits (eg long, fast circuits). However, I have yet to see an engine give good hp that runs a compression ratio so high that it had to have the spark backed off more than a   69

The most suitable compression ratio is not solely reliant on fuel octane ratings. While Shell Racing 100 (MON 100) and VP C-23 (MON 119) both permit very high compression ratios, many other factors also influence what is best for performance and reliability.

few degrees less than stock to keep it out of detonation. Thus if the standard item in the showroom worked with 32° spark timing we would expect a modified unit to tolerate 28° or more advance.

Another indicator that the compression ratio may be too high is when the engine will not make good power with the camshaft running in an advanced timing position, but prefers to run with the cam in a split timing, or perhaps even in a retarded timing position. The net effect of this, along with the need for reduced spark advance, is to compress the engine's power band and reduce hp at many points along the power curve.

When calculating compression ratios a conservative rule of thumb is to start with a figure of 0.115 multiplied by the Motor Octane Number (MON) of the petrol permitted in that particular class of competition. Thus, if you are running Avgas 100/130 (usually 100 MON), you would start out with a compression ratio of 11.5:1, which would be a good starting point for an engine with carburettors requiring a broad power band. To begin our testing on electronic fuel injection we would use a factor of 0.118 multiplied by the MON. At the other end of the scale, an engine with very sophisticated electronic engine management, operating on a relatively narrow power band, and which has seen a huge amount of developmental work and testing, may be operating at a factor as high as 0.146, ie 13.3:1 compression ratio with 91 MON fuel.

MEASURING THE COMPRESSION RATIO

It should be noted at this stage that quoted compression ratio figures are always theoretical compression ratios and are expressed by the following formula:

$$CR = \frac{CV + CCV}{CCV}$$

CV is the cylinder volume, and is easily found by dividing the engine capacity by the number of cylinders. Therefore a 2,000cc four-cylinder motor has a cylinder volume (or swept volume) of 500cc.

CCV is the combustion chamber volume, and is not so easy to calculate. It is made up of the combustion chamber volume, plus the volume that remains above the piston when the piston is at TDC, plus the volume caused by the thickness of the head gasket, plus the volume of the dish if dished pistons are used, or minus the amount displaced if high-top pistons are used.

Assuming that the pistons are flat tops, the formula for finding the volume of the head gasket or the volume above the piston is:

$$V = \frac{\pi D^2 \times H}{4000}$$

where π = 3.1416, D = the diameter of the bore in mm, and H = the compressed thickness of the head gasket or the clearance between the piston crown and the block deck in mm.

The volume of the combustion chamber is measured as shown in Figure 3.22, using a burette filled with liquid paraffin. If the head has been modified by a tuner, he should

Figure 3.22 Measuring combustion chamber volume.

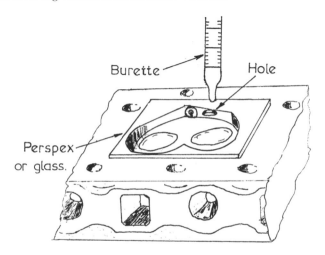

have told you the chamber volumes when you purchased it. Incidently, the combustion chambers should have been equalised in volume so that the volume of the largest is no more than 0.2cc larger than that of the smallest.

If you are running dished or high-top pistons you can find what increase or decrease in combustion chamber volume they are causing by using the method shown in Figure 3.23. In this instance let us assume that the cylinder bore is 102mm in diameter and the piston crown is 13mm from the block deck, therefore using the formula

$$V = \frac{\pi D^2 \times H}{4000}$$

this volume should be

$$V = \frac{\pi \times 102^2 \times 13}{4000}$$

which is 106.2cc.

However, measuring the volume with a burette we find it to be only 74.7cc. Therefore the lump on top of the piston occupies 106.2 – 74.7 = 31.5cc. Having found these volumes we must go back to the original formula to calculate the compression ratio.

VALVE MATERIALS AND CONSTRUCTION

Today's engines make extremely taxing demands on the valves. Let us just look at a typical exhaust valve during a single cycle. At the beginning of the intake stroke, during the overlap period, it is subjected to a chilling blast of fuel mixture. Then it is slammed against the valve seat and blasted with a hot flame that will raise its temperature to perhaps 1,800°F, before it is suddenly hit by another chilling intake charge. In an average racing engine this can be happening 3,500–5,000 times a minute, during which time it is expected to form a gas seal that successfully contains a pressure of around 1,500 pounds per square inch (psi).

Figure 3.23 Measuring high-top piston displacement.

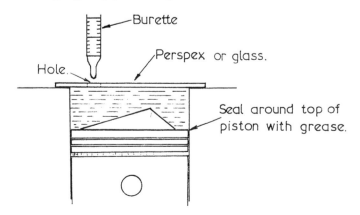

To exist under such conditions, a valve has to be made of pretty good material, but here we have a problem. Racing valves are made of austenitic stainless steel, which, while being able to withstand high combustion temperatures, has very poor scuff resistance. Therefore they should be used only with valve guides made of silicon aluminium bronze, which is more compatible with austenitic steel as far as anti-scuffing is concerned, and of course bronze aids with heat transfer. The type of material we want to use in the valves is something like KE965, EN54, 21/4N or Nimonic 80a steel.

Most current production valves are of bi-metal or tri-metal construction, ie the valve head and stem are of different materials, welded together, in order to overcome the scuffing problem mentioned earlier. The result is that we have a head made of quality austenitic steel such as 21/4N and a stem made of something like EN8, which is perfectly happy running in a cast iron valve guide. A valve made of such material is suitable for a high-performance or budget racing engine.

The way to test if the valve is of austenitic steel is to see if it is magnetic. This applies to all valves: if they are magnetic they are no good. If the stem is magnetic and the head is non-magnetic, it is a welded valve, which is all right. Check before you buy any worked-over heads or valves to see that you are getting good examples. Generally, production inlet valves use a head of EN52 steel welded to a stem of EN8, which is not quite good enough, unless you don't plan on more than a modest power increase; this type of valve has a magnetic head and stem.

If the budget and race regs allow them then we want to do all we can to reduce valve weight by using either hollow stem or titanium valves. Titanium is preferable, dropping valve weight by about 35%. However, if the rules insist on stainless steel, going the hollow stem route may be a viable alternative. This can save up to 20% weight in valves with thicker stems over about 8mm.

In addition to the valve's mechanical durability we have to do everything possible to preserve the integrity of the valve seat. As the seat wears power drops off due to a poorer gas seal and poorer air flow over the resculpted seat surface. Typically this amounts to around a 1% hp reduction after 1,000km. And because of that wear expensive valves that may be mechanically sound will be tossed so as to maintain performance. To get longer valve life and keep the seat in good shape, application of a DLC makes good sense. Anatech's Casidiam coating is an extremely hard and flexible carbon coating that won't chip and will cut seat wear to a quarter of that of an uncoated valve. Applied to steel it cuts the coefficient of friction by 45% and on titanium it's down by 75%.

VALVE GUIDE MATERIAL AND CLEARANCE

A little earlier we mentioned the valve guide's role of transferring heat, from the exhaust valve in particular, to the engine coolant. An equally important aspect of the valve guide is its role with reference to engine performance. As its name implies, the guide is responsible for guiding the valve accurately on to the seat, to effect a gas seal. A worn guide cannot do this, so power is lost. If the inlet guide is worn, it will allow oil into the engine, upsetting combustion and perhaps cause detonation.

Just as too much clearance between the valve stem and guide is to be avoided, so is too little clearance. In this situation the exhaust valve can seize in the guide and 73

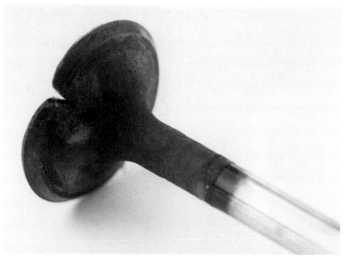

Sloppy valve guides add up to an overheated exhaust valve. Once the hot gases begin eroding the seat area this soon happens.

knock a hole in the piston crown. Air-cooled and supercharged engines are prone to this problem, so be sure to measure the clearance – do not just rely on your sense of feel. Generally, the clearance should be from 0.0015–0.003in for inlet valves and 0.002–0.0045in for exhaust valves.

However, naturally aspirated water-cooled engines with high-oil-retention valve guide materials like silicon aluminium bronze and silicon copper nickel (Colsibro) should run much tighter clearances: 0.0007–0.0012in for the inlets and 0.0012–0.0017in for the exhaust valves.

VALVE STEM SEALS

In the past, when valve guide materials were not so good, I seldom ran competition engines with valve stem seals on the exhausts so as to ensure good stem-to-guide lubrication. However, in most instances I now recommend the use of seals on both the inlet and exhaust valves in naturally aspirated engines. To some extent the type of seal used will depend on how much space there is for a seal between the valve stem and inner valve spring, and how much oil consumption and carbon build-up on the back of the valve heads is tolerable. Obviously in an endurance engine or one that will be rebuilt only every couple of thousand miles, we want as little carbon build-up on the valve heads as possible. Carbon deposits not only cut gas flow into and out of the engine, but such deposits on the valve stem also accelerate guide wear, particularly on the exhaust valve, which is operating at very high temperature.

Neoprene seals as fitted by many car manufacturers can be suitable but are not ideal. On the inlets I find that they tend to either allow the valve guide to run too wet, with the resulting problem of carbon on the valve head and exhaust smoke on starting up the engine, or too dry, which leads to premature stem/guide wear and possible seizure. Fitted to the exhausts they do not seem to handle the heat too well, so they quickly harden and fail to provide good oil control.

It is important to ensure that there is sufficient clearance for valve stem oil seals between the valve cap and valve guide at maximum valve lift.

Perfect Circle-type teflon seals are preferred for competition engines. Like neoprene seals they slip over the top of the valve guide, but in race engines that always have minimum valve-stem-to-guide clearance, and hence no valve stem wobble, they do a more consistent job of controlling valve stem oil flow. However, when the clearance increases they work quite poorly, so if you allow your engines to run down like this you may be better off with another type of seal. When fitting these seals over exhaust valve guides it is a good idea to lightly ream them, using a reamer the same size as the valve stem diameter to allow a little more oil flow to the guide.

A less hi-tech solution is to fit an 'O' ring seal up under the valve collets (valve locks) and an oil splash shield under the spring retainer. The 'O' ring prevents much of the oil flowing from the camshaft and/or rocker arms from travelling down the valve

Oil splash shields can be fitted under the valve caps to direct oil away from the valve stems. 'O' rings are also installed under the valve locks to stop oil flowing through the collet gaps.

stem in the gaps between the collets. Instead, most of the oil has to flow out over the valve cap and the oil splash shield fitted under it, then down over the valve spring. This doesn't work on the inlet valve as well as a neoprene or Perfect Circle teflon seal, but it does increase oil flow over the valve springs. Without a good flow of oil to carry away heat, valve springs begin to fatigue and lose pressure.

Another solution that works in the same manner as an 'O' ring, but more effectively, is to seal the gaps between the valve collets with Silastic RTV when the engine is being assembled. Note that for this to work properly the top of the valve stem, the collets and retainer must be carefully degreased with solvent and allowed to dry before applying the Silastic silicone sealant. Using this method I have seen oil consumption halved and carbon build-up on the valves almost eliminated in endurance-type engines.

In engines with large-diameter inner springs, the old 'umbrella'-type seal can possibly be fitted. However, as is also true when the neoprene and Perfect Circle types are used, there must be sufficient space for it between the bottom of the valve spring retainer and the top of the valve guide at full valve lift.

A point not to be overlooked when it comes to valve stem oil control is that some engines, either by design or negligence, allow a lot of oil to 'puddle' around the valve springs with the result that the top of the valve guide may become submerged in oil. Obviously if all of that oil is needed to cool the valve springs, as may be the situation in some overhead-cam engines with inverted bucket tappets, only neoprene or Perfect Circle-type seals will be of any use. However, it is also possible for valve guides to become submerged in oil due to oil drain back holes or dry sump scavenge pick-ups being in the wrong place because consideration has not been given to G forces being imposed by long high-speed turns. Obviously the drain back problem should be rectified, then any appropriate valve stem oil control system can be chosen.

HOW TO CHOOSE WISELY

Armed with all this information on cylinder heads you are in a good position to make a sensible choice when you go shopping for a modified head. There are, however, just a few more points worth mentioning at this time. Do not allow yourself to be tempted by all the dazzle and shine of the ports and chambers. You are wasting money; the finish should be good and fine, but it certainly does not need to be polished. Some cars have such poor carburettors that fuel will actually collect on a polished port wall. This point must be kept in mind particularly if you are running a competition motor where alcohol fuel is permitted. Alcohol, being less volatile, separates from the air easily, and as the inlet tract is pretty well refrigerated, especially so when running on alcohol, it remains clinging to the port, causing a flat spot and power loss.

Also don't be fooled into thinking that a CNC ported head is better than a hand ported item, or vice versa. Remember that all CNC ported heads were hand ported with a die grinder during the development and testing stages. Only when porting that was proved to work was finally settled upon was the expensive task undertaken of transferring the trace and machining sequence to a multi-axis CNC machine. Then following that operation the programming would have been tweaked, perhaps several times, to match the CNC ported head to the hand ported original. Yes, CNC porting is great. If the porter knew his stuff and the hand ported head worked very well, then the CNC clone will be just as good, and it will be consistently to the same standard in every

The tool marks in the valve bowl area indicate that this is a CNC ported head. How well it performs is dependent on many factors.

port and every combustion chamber. The CNC machine doesn't produce any Friday or Monday heads. It doesn't make any major or minor slip-ups. However, if the original hand ported head was a dud or not suited to your application then the CNC clone of that head can only deliver the very same unsatisfactory result. The situation is the same if the CNC head wasn't a true clone of the good hand ported original, it simply won't work as well as the original. The latter occurs for a number of reasons: perhaps the CNC programming is poor or incorrect, maybe corners have been cut to reduce the number and/or complexity of machining operations, or it could simply be that an old worn out machine or a new less sophisticated machine is performing the work.

Before you take delivery of the ported head it should be matched to the inlet manifold. At the same time studs or dowels should be fitted so that each time the manifold is removed, it will, on being replaced, align perfectly with the ports in the head. These dowels need only be one-eighth of an inch diameter silver steel.

The inlet ports are scribed to match the inlet manifold. As well as machining to eliminate the lip either dowels or studs are required to ensure the ports always align.

While the head porting work is being done, other specialised work should also be carried out such as re-cutting the valve spring pads. Therefore the head modifier will have to be given specific instructions by you regarding such things as what valve springs, retainers and collets to fit, what the valve spring fitted height should be, and what rocker stud modifications are required.

CYLINDER BLOCK PREPARATION

At the same time you should find out if you need to do any grinding of the cylinder block so that your nice big valves do not bang into the top of it. Figure 3.24 illustrates the modification required on the Mini when oversize exhaust valves are fitted. To prevent any damage being done to the piston, rings or bore if this grinding has to be done on an assembled engine, I would suggest that plenty of grease be applied to the piston crown to seal it in the bore. The grease will trap the iron dust and prevent it going down the side of the piston.

The deck of the block needs to be perfectly flat and completely free of any foreign material such as rust, grit, or the remains of the head gasket and sealants before we fit the cylinder head. The way to get rid of such rubbish is by very deliberate use of a flat scraper. If the block has dowels or studs still in place be extremely careful to cut in close to the base of these. Personally I do a better job using a bootmaker's knife in this area. When undertaking a clean up of the deck take care that dislodged material doesn't find its way into oilways, the sump etc. Do not under any circumstances use emery paper or wet-and-dry paper as abrasive particles will undoubtedly end up in the cylinders, and in push-rod engines you can add the cam and lifters too. Don't think that compressed air will help – most likely it will spread the grit deeper into the engine.

HEAD GASKET SELECTION

Obviously all this preparation is intended to provide a nice flat bed for the head and head gasket to seal against. In a race engine the head gasket has to withstand pressure of up to 1,800psi, so obviously we may require something better than the stock gasket.

Figure 3.24 Austin Mini exhaust valve cut-out.

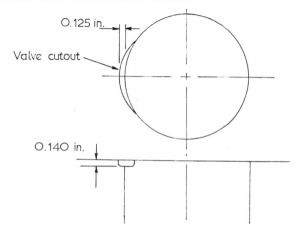

However, it isn't high cylinder pressures as such that gives head gaskets a hard time. The real culprit is detonation, so if we keep the engine free of detonation blown head gaskets generally will not be a problem.

Copper asbestos gaskets are definitely out as the thin annealed copper sheet is just too soft to hold up. On the other hand, stainless steel sheet gaskets are too hard to deform into minute surface imperfections, so give trouble too. Steel/copper/asbestos head gaskets at times work better than stock composite gaskets. This type has a mild steel face and cylinder fire ring, with copper sheet on the other face, and asbestos in between. Some high performance composite gaskets use a special cylinder fire ring which is better able to withstand detonation than a sheet mild steel or sheet stainless steel fire ring. A round wire steel ring is okay with cast iron heads but is too aggressive with aluminium, so a pre-flattened steel ring gasket or a round wire hard copper ring gasket may work better. Another type that works well in many engines with cast iron block and aluminium head, plus four studs per cylinder clamping, is the multi-layer steel gasket.

After this we get into more specialised sealing methods, sometimes in conjunction with a stock type composite head gasket and sometimes with a full copper head gasket. In addition to the gasket some type of 'O' ring may be fitted around each bore to exert a greater compressive load on the gasket. With the softer stock type composite gaskets the first choice is the stainless steel 'W' ring followed by the copper 'O' ring, but the mild steel round wire 'O' ring may also be suitable. However, the latter is more likely to be used with a solid copper type gasket. The usual procedure with steel 'O' rings is to machine the block to accept 0.041in mild steel wire, such that it stands proud of the deck about 0.006–0.008in. As such it exerts a considerable compressive force against the gasket and head.

HEAD GASKET CLAMPING FORCE

Apart from detonation the other big destroyer of head gaskets is insufficient clamping force between the head and block, allowing the gasket fire ring to flap about in response to the violent fire storm going on in the combustion chamber. We have already discussed the need for a perfectly clean and flat deck surface on both the head and block, and later we will cover correct head tension and tensioning technique. That leaves us with a mechanical clamping problem caused by poor design of the block and/or head and also insufficient and/or inefficient clamping devices – read head studs or bolts – around each cylinder bore.

The most common cure for blown head gaskets is to fit head studs if the manufacturer is relying on bolts to clamp the head to the block. Studs clamp better than bolts and they cause less distortion and pulling of the bock deck (which is none too solid in some engines), so that sealing is improved. When initially fitting the studs, torque them to 30lb ft. Remember that when studs are fitted to Vee-style engines it will often be impossible to remove the heads, due to a lack of clearance, unless the engine is first lifted out of the vehicle.

With some engines the factory has deleted bolts where they were too difficult to fit in a normal assembly line situation. However, for a high performance or race engine we may be able to devise a method of adding those missing bolts and it is amazing just how four additional $^5/_{16}$in NC bolts tensioned to 18–20ft lb cures the sealing problems of powerful big-block Chevys.

After this we have to consider the integrity of the deck of the cylinder head and block. If we find the deck of the head is so thin and lacking in internal bracing that it is bowing under pressure and not clamping tight against the head gasket we have to come up with a solution. If an aftermarket head is available it may have a thicker, stronger deck. When there is no alternative but to stick with the stock head investigate what you can do to strengthen it. This may involve tapping some holes into the water jacket in the top of the head and screwing long $^5/_{16}$in NC bolts into those holes to push up against the water jacket side of the deck so as to reinforce and brace it against bowing.

If the trouble is the deck of the block bowing we may be able to reinforce it by converting to a dry deck arrangement. All water passages and oil return passages in the block have to be plugged with threaded plugs and any holes that cannot be plugged must be welded closed. This serves to strengthen and brace the deck. The deck is then ground perfectly flat. Naturally when a dry deck is used an external water tube must be devised to carry coolant from the block into the head and if a wet sump lube system is used an oil return from the head to the crankcase will be required.

Another way to reinforce the block deck is by means of an 8–12mm thick steel plate screwed and glued, using a high tech sealant, to the deck. After bonding and curing is complete thin-wall dry liners are pressed in, then the deck plate is surface ground and the cylinder bores honed. The additional deck height also allows for the use of longer con rods and/or more crank stroke. If we prefer to not use liners we have to use a piston design which keeps the top ring from travelling into the deck plate.

HEAD BOLTS AND TENSIONING

Even if an engine does not have a history of head gasket sealing problems we can easily bring problems on ourselves. For some time now a number of manufacturers have utilised stretch-to-yield type head bolts. These are a use once and then throw away item. If reused they will continue to stretch and so not provide the clamping force necessary for the head gasket to do its job. Consequently if you stick with this type of stock bolt follow the factory recommendation and use them only once. The same applies if the factory has what appears as a non-conventional head tensioning method. If they say warm the engine and apply additional bolt tension, then do it.

Now that we have sorted out the head gasket/sealant situation, it is time to fit the head. The head bolts should have their threads buffed and oiled and be tightened in the sequence recommended by the manufacturer. A typical sequence is shown in Figure 3.25. This sequence must be reversed when the bolts are being loosened to remove the head. I always tension the head in four or five progressive steps, to prevent head warpage. Therefore if the head tension is 80lbf ft you would take it down to 30, 50, 60, 70 then 80. After the gasket has had time to set (usually 10–15 minutes), go over the bolts again. That's about it if the head is alloy. If the head is cast iron, the motor should be started and brought to normal operating temperature and the bolts re-tensioned. Final gasket set should take place by the time you have done 300 miles, when the head (alloy or cast iron) should be tensioned again.

One thing to keep in mind when tensioning head studs or bolts on an engine that has short studs along one side of the head and longer studs down the other side is that long studs stretch more than short ones. Therefore the head gasket will not be clamped

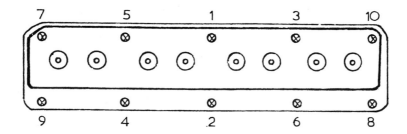

Figure 3.25 Cylinder head bolt tightening sequence.

as tightly down one side of the head. To overcome this, tension on the longer studs should be increased by approximately 10%. For example, if the recommended tension is 65lbf ft, torque the short studs to this figure and the long studs to 72lbf ft.

CYLINDER HEAD HEAT TREATMENT FAILURE

Many head gasket failures, however, are not due to inappropriate head gaskets being fitted, incorrect tensioning, or a block deck that is not perfectly flat. The problem, if it is an aluminium alloy head, could be that the head has been annealed when it was previously overheated and blew a head gasket. What happens is that the hot gases destroy the heat treatment and the head goes soft. Consequently it will no longer hold a head gasket and it has probably lost its crush on the valve seats as well. In this state the head also changes shape; it will be shorter and narrower. Hence a head that does not easily drop down on the block dowels or is jamming on the head studs is probably annealed. If you use head bolts rather than studs and you find trouble getting the bolts started into the block, it means the same thing; the head has gone soft.

This can be checked with a Brinell or Rockwell hardness tester. On the Brinell scale a good head will read in the 95-plus range, and anything under 75 is too soft. When testing on the Rockwell B scale this translates to a hardness in the 48 to 60 range being ideal, while anything under 38 is soft. Obviously the place to test is in an area where the gasket has blown. Do not be content with a hardness test in just a couple of places. A casting flaw could throw the reading way off, so over an area of about a square inch test in at least 10–12 spots.

If the head is soft and you have a lot of money invested in it, it may be worthwhile to have it heat-treated afresh. This is not cheap and it may not be possible in heads where the cam runs directly on the aluminium. Ask around to find what specialists can do, or if it is a head from an aftermarket supplier, get them to give you a price. Basically the seats and guides are knocked out and it is then heated in an oven at 520°C for around 5 hours (some manufacturers specify up to 20 hours). Then it is quenched in 80°C water and tempered (reheated) at 200°C for another 4 hours (up to 20 hours), then allowed to cool slowly in the air. Following this the head will be machined for oversize guides and seats and the deck will have to be resurfaced. This all costs a lot, but if the head is a good one with lots of fancy port and chamber work you will not want to throw it away. Note also that any time a head is welded close to a head gasket fire ring line or valve seat it will also require a fresh heat treatment. 81

Chapter 4

Carburation

The fuel mixing system is looked upon as the most obvious place at which performance modifications should begin. A certain amount of glamour and fascination has always surrounded large or multiple carburettors, and as a result unwary enthusiasts can often be caught out with mixing devices that are either too large or totally unsuited to their particular engine. This results in sluggish performance and excessive fuel consumption.

The basic requirement of a performance carburettor is that it mixes the fuel and air in combustible proportions to produce the best horsepower. Usually the mixture we want is around 1:12 or 1:13, ie 1 pound of petrol for every 12 or 13 pounds of air. However, for other conditions such as starting or light load operation, the fuel–air requirement is different (see Table 4.1), so the carburettor has to be able to sense the engine's operating conditions and adjust the fuel–air mix accordingly. If the carburettor is not able to do this, flat spots and engine surging will result. For this reason we have to be very selective as to the type and size of carburettor that we choose for our particular engine.

Table 4.1   High-performance engine fuel–air requirements

Running condition	Mixing ratio (by weight)
	Fuel : air
Starting	1:1–3
Idling	1:6–10
Low-speed running	1:10–13
Light-load ordinary running	1:14–16
Heavy-load running	1:12–14

To understand more fully what we should be looking for in a high-performance carburettor, we need to go back to the basics and get to know how a carburettor works.

Nearly all carburettors employ a fuel inlet system, an idle system, a main running system, and also an acceleration-pump system and a power system.

FUEL INLET SYSTEM

The inlet system consists of the fuel bowl, the float, and the needle and seat.

The fuel passing to the other metering systems is stored in the fuel bowl and is maintained at the correct level by the float and the needle and seat. If the fuel is not at the correct level in the fuel bowl, the fuel metering systems will not be able to mix the fuel and air in the correct proportions, particularly when accelerating, cornering and stopping.

A high fuel level will cause high fuel consumption and erratic running. Due to fuel spill-over through the carburettor discharge nozzle and/or vent during cornering or braking, it could cause the engine to falter or stop. The high level may be the result of an incorrectly adjusted float, or a needle that is not seating properly and shutting off the fuel supply when the float reaches the correct level. This may be due to excessive wear of the needle and/or seat, or it may be caused by a weak bumper spring (Holley carburettors). High fuel pressure will also raise the fuel level, each 1psi increase in fuel pressure raising it by about 0.020in.

A low fuel level causes flat spots because of lean-out in turns and when accelerating. Even more serious is the possibility of a full power lean-out due to reduced fuel flow capacity, resulting in melted pistons. The low fuel level may be due to an improperly adjusted float, low fuel pressure, an excessively strong bumper spring (Holley carbs), or a needle and seat too small to flow sufficient fuel to keep the fuel bowl full.

The fuel bowl is always vented so that the fuel is being mixed according to the outside air pressure. Once the fuel passes through the needle and seat it is no longer under pressure. Any fuel vapour is released through the vent, so at all times the metering systems respond to the prevailing atmospheric conditions.

The float is hinged in such a way that it operates the opening and closing of the fuel inlet valve (needle and seat). As the fuel drops, the float drops and opens the valve, allowing fuel to enter the bowl. When the engine is running with a constant load, the float moves the needle to a position where it restricts fuel flow, allowing in only enough fuel to replace that being used.

The float may be made of brass stampings soldered together into an airtight assembly, or of a closed cellular material. Brass floats are resistant to attack from all types of fuel, except nitromethane. Generally, the cellular floats are not damaged by most of the common fuels, but it is always wise to check with the carburettor manufacturer if you are using a fuel other than petrol or methanol.

The needle and seat fuel inlet valve controls the flow of fuel into the bowl. The seat is usually steel and the needle may be steel or steel with a Viton coating on the tip. The latter provides good sealing, but it should not be used with alcohol or nitro fuels.

The needle and seat are usually available in a number of sizes to give the required rate of fuel flow into the bowl. The seat size is selected to allow reasonably quick filling of the bowl so as to be able to meet the demands of wide-open throttle and high rpm operation. A seat that is too large is a definite hindrance, as it may give rise to flooding. For this reason use an inlet assembly only marginally larger than the fuel flow requirement of the engine.

CALCULATING FUEL FLOW REQUIREMENTS

How much fuel does your engine need? Remember we said that the best power is produced with a fuel-air ratio of 1 pound of fuel to every 12½ pounds of air (only if the fuel is petrol). Therefore if we calculate how much air the engine is pumping we can also work out our engine's maximum fuel flow requirement.

The formula we use to find the airflow in lb/hr is

$$4.38 \times \frac{D}{32.8} \times \frac{rpm}{1,728} \times \frac{VE}{100}$$

where D = displacement in cc, rpm = engine speed, and VE = volumetric efficiency.

At maximum torque rpm the volumetric efficiency (VE) would be 90–100% in a racing engine, and this would fall, relative to the engine's torque curve, at higher and lower rpm. If an engine produced maximum torque of 100lbf ft at 5,750rpm and 74lbf ft at 6,800rpm (maximum power rpm), the VE at 5,750rpm is, say, 95%; therefore the VE at 6,800rpm will be

$$\frac{74}{100} \times 95 = 70.3\%$$

Obviously the engine speed at which the most air is passing through the engine is at maximum horsepower rpm (Tables 4.2 and 4.3), so calculate your air flow at this engine speed.

To find the fuel flow (lb/hr), multiply the air flow by the fuel–air ratio. If the ratio is 1:12.5, multiply by ¹/₁₂.₅, or 0.08. Petrol weighs 7.5lb per gallon, so to find the fuel flow in gallons per hour (gph) divide by 7.5.

TESTING FUEL FLOW CAPABILITY

How are you going to know how much fuel a needle and seat will flow? Some manufacturers have published information available, but if you are not able to uncover the particulars from the carburettor maker, you will have to measure the fuel flow yourself.

This may seem to be something of a hassle but it is a very important consideration, particularly in regard to motorcycles, as these seem to be the worst affected by fuel flow restrictions. Actually it is very easy to measure the flow to a bike's fuel bowl as you do not have to worry about fuel pump pressure.

Fill the fuel tank, and after removing the fuel bowl from one carburettor, time how long it takes to drain down to reserve. Now accurately measure how many gallons you have drained off and calculate your fuel flow in gph. Multiply this figure by the number of carburettors on the engine, and compare the answer with the fuel flow requirement for your engine. You are probably in for a surprise; many motorcycles cannot be held wide open for too long on the dyno without fuel starvation problems.

Even if you find that the needle and seat can flow sufficient fuel, you will probably find that the fuel tap will not, so repeat the test with the fuel lines removed from every carburettor, and determine the tap's fuel-flow capabilities.

Generally, it is not possible to obtain larger needle and seat assemblies (or fuel taps) for motorcycles, so it will be necessary to modify these by very carefully drilling oversize the fuel delivery holes. I would recommend that you use a pin vice when you drill the fuel inlet seat's fuel discharge holes.

COLD START SYSTEM

The cold starting system provides mixture enrichment to allow starting when either the engine or the weather is cold. The system used on Weber DCOE, SU and some motorcycle carburettors does not affect the air flow capabilities of the carburettor. However, the choke plate and shaft fitted to most carburettors does reduce air flow and creates unwanted turbulence through the carburettor throat. Racing engines should therefore have the choke assembly removed if the regulations allow this modification.

If you live in a warm climate, the choke assembly can be removed from road machines, but it may be necessary to floor the accelerator a few times to provide a rich starting mixture via the accelerator pump. You will have to allow the engine to warm up before driving off, but this is really a good thing as engine wear and oil dilution will be reduced.

IDLE AND PROGRESSION SYSTEM

The idle system provides a rich mixture at idle and low speeds, when not enough air is being drawn through the venturi to cause the main system to operate (Figure 4.1).

When the throttle plate (butterfly) is nearly closed, the restriction to air flow causes a high vacuum on the engine side of the throttle plate. This high vacuum

Figure 4.1 Idle system operation.

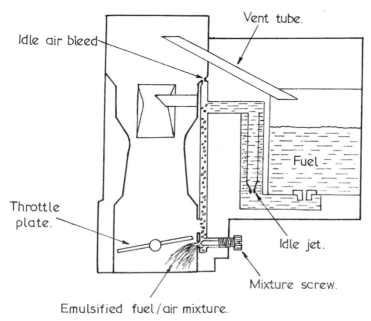

Idle air bleed

Vent tube.

Throttle plate.

Fuel

Idle jet.

Mixture screw.

Emulsified fuel/air mixture.

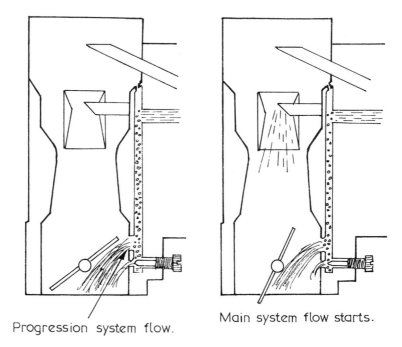

Progression system flow.

Main system flow starts.

Figure 4.2 Progression system operation.

provides the pressure differential for the idle system to operate. The normal air pressure (14.7psi) acts on the fuel in the float bowl, forcing it through the idle jet, and past the idle mixture screw into the manifold.

To emulsify the fuel before it reaches the mixture screw, an air bleed is included in the system. Increasing the size of the air bleed leans the idle mixture, if the size of the idle jet remains constant. Conversely, decreasing the air bleed diameter richens the idle mixture.

The progression or transfer holes are a part of the idle system (Figure 4.2) and allow a smooth transition from the idle fuel circuit to the main fuel system without 'flat spots', provided that the carburettor size has been correctly matched to the engine displacement.

As the throttle is opened wider, the progression holes are uncovered, and begin to flow fuel metered and emulsified by the idle jet. At this time fuel flow past the mixture screw decreases and gradually tapers off as the next progression hole is opened by the throttle plate.

When the throttle is opened further, the pressure differential between the idle progression holes and the air pressure acting on the fuel in the fuel bowl decreases, causing fuel flow in the idle system to taper off. Finally, the pressure is not great enough to push the fuel up to the idle jet, and the idle system ceases to supply fuel.

Fuel flow through the main metering system begins before the flow through the idle circuit is reduced, if a carburettor of the right size is being used. The main system meters fuel for cruising and high-speed operation.

As the throttle is opened and the engine speed increases, air flow through the venturi is increased so that the main system comes into operation, discharging fuel through the discharge hole in the auxiliary venturi (boost venturi).

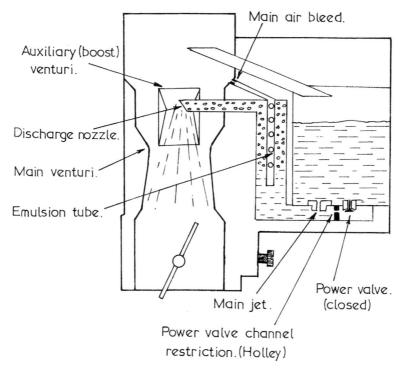

Main air bleed.

Auxiliary (boost) venturi.

Discharge nozzle.

Main venturi.

Emulsion tube.

Main jet.

Power valve. (closed)

Power valve channel restriction. (Holley)

Figure 4.3 Main and power system operation.

THE VENTURI

The heart of the carburettor is the main venturi, as it produces the pressure differential necessary for the fuel to be pushed from the fuel well, through the main jet, to the discharge nozzle (Figure 4.3).

In the internal combustion engine, a partial vacuum is created in the cylinder by the downward stroke of the piston. Because atmospheric pressure is then higher than the pressure in the cylinder, air rushes in through the carburettor to equalise the pressure within the cylinder. On its way through the carburettor, the air passes through the venturi, a restriction designed by Italian physicist G. B. Venturi about 200 years ago.

The venturi necks down the inrushing air, then allows it to widen out to the throttle bore. To get through the venturi, the air must speed up, thus reducing the pressure inside the venturi to below atmospheric pressure. This pressure differential allows the main system to discharge fuel, and is commonly referred to as the 'signal' of the main metering system. No fuel issues from the discharge nozzle until the air flow through the venturi produces a pressure drop or signal sufficiently strong for the atmospheric pressure, acting on the fuel in the fuel bowl, to push the fuel up through the main jet to the discharge nozzle.

Pressure drop (or vacuum) within the venturi varies with the engine speed and throttle opening. A wide-open throttle and peak rpm will give the highest air flow, and consequently the highest pressure difference between the fuel bowl and the discharge nozzle. This in turn gives the highest fuel flow into the engine. 87

To compensate for various engine displacements, carburettors with a variety of venturi diameters are available to create the necessary pressure drop to bring the main fuel circuit into operation. A small venturi will provide a higher pressure difference at any given rpm and throttle opening than a large-diameter venturi. This is a very important aspect of carburation, which partly explains why the biggest is seldom the best. If the signal being applied by the venturi is too weak (due to the venturi being too large), this could delay fuel discharge in the main system, causing a flat spot. If you must err when buying a carburettor, err on the small side.

The auxiliary venturi acts as a signal amplifier for the main venturi, allowing for more accurate and quicker fuel flow responses. This is important in a performance engine as it allows the use of a larger, less restrictive main venturi than would normally be possible, without sacrificing throttle response.

The tail of the boost venturi discharges at the lowest pressure point in the main venturi. Thus the air flow is accelerated through the boost venturi, and because of this, the air and fuel emerging are travelling faster than the surrounding air passing through the main venturi. This has the effect of assisting fuel atomisation, and subsequently improves combustion.

MAIN METERING SYSTEM

The actual fuel metering is controlled by the main jet, the air bleed jet, and the emulsion tube.

The main jet controls fuel flow from the fuel well. An increase in diameter richens the mixture, but more is involved. The shape of the jet entry and exit, as well as the bore finish, also affect fuel flow. Carburettor manufacturers measure the flow of every jet, for high-performance and low-exhaust emission applications, and number the jet according to its flow characteristics, not according to its nominal bore diameter. For this reason jets used to meter petrol should not be drilled to change their size, if you desire accurate fuel metering. An engine burning alcohol does not require such accurate metering, unless fuel consumption is a consideration, so jet drilling may be in order if large jets are not available.

The air bleed reduces the signal from the discharge nozzle, so there is a less effective pressure difference to cause fuel flow through the main jet. This allows for more fine tuning of the main metering system. A large air bleed leans the mixture, particularly at higher engine rpm.

The air bleed also introduces air into the emulsion tube, to emulsify the fuel into a lighter, frothy mixture of fuel and air. This is done to improve atomisation when the fuel is released from the discharge nozzle. Also it serves to lower the viscosity of the fuel, making it lighter, and able to respond faster to signal changes from the auxiliary venturi. This enables the main system to keep more in step with the fuel requirements of the engine.

The emulsion tube has the task of emulsifying the previously metered air issuing from the air bleed jet with the fuel coming from the main jet. Its influence is more marked at less than full throttle and during acceleration. The diameter of the emulsion tube and the size and location of holes to emulsify the fuel all affect and influence its operation. Usually, a change in emulsion tube will require a change in main jet and air bleed size.

POWER SYSTEM

Many carburettors also have a power system for mixture enrichment at heavy load operation. This system supplies additional fuel to complement the main metering system at above normal cruising loads. The added fuel supplied by the power system is controlled by manifold vacuum, which accurately indicates the load on the engine. As the load increases, the throttle must be opened wider to maintain a given speed. This lessens the restriction to air entering the engine, which in turn reduces the manifold vacuum.

The system usually employed (Figure 4.3) relies on a high manifold vacuum to hold the power valve closed. As the manifold vacuum drops (usually to around 4–6in of mercury) the power valve spring overcomes manifold vacuum and opens the valve, allowing fuel to flow from the fuel bowl through a power valve jet and into the main metering system. This increases fuel flow in the main system, effectively richening the mixture.

ACCELERATOR PUMP

The accelerator pump system complements all of the other systems and fills in for them, so as to eliminate flat spots. It does this by injecting raw fuel for a sufficient length of time to allow the other systems to catch up to the fuel demands of the engine.

If the throttle is opened quickly, the manifold vacuum instantly drops to a pressure approaching atmospheric, allowing the fuel to drop out of vapour and wet the manifold and port walls. (A high manifold vacuum helps to keep the fuel vaporised. Remember that an increase in altitude, resulting in a lower atmospheric pressure, lowers the boiling point of water. Likewise with fuel: lower the atmospheric pressure and it vaporises more easily.) To make up for the lean condition caused by the fuel clinging to the manifold and port walls and to avoid a flat spot, it is necessary instantly to make up the deficiency by injecting more fuel into the air stream.

The accelerator pump also has to supply fuel if the throttle is opened quickly to a point past the idle-progression system supply period. With gentle acceleration there is an overlap of fuel being supplied by both the idle and the main system, but if the throttle is opened quickly, the main system has not started to supply fuel when the idle system has already shut off supply. To eliminate a lean-out, the accelerator pump injects fuel for a time, to allow the main system flow and metering to be established.

FACTORS IN CHOOSING A CARBURETTOR

Having discussed the various carburettor systems, it should be obvious that not all carburettors are suitable for performance applications. Some are just too small; others do not have metering systems with changeable jets or, if they do, the jets are not readily obtainable; and others have metering systems that allow acceptable performance in stock machines, but are too crude to provide the correct fuel–air mixture in a high-performance engine. For these reasons I usually limit myself to the use of Holley, SU and Weber carburettors for cars, and Mikuni carburettors for motorcycles. Don't get me wrong – there are other good carburettors available (eg Dellorto DHLA sidedraught), but I have found those listed to be the most easily 89 obtainable, and there is no problem obtaining jets, etc. It is pointless to use a good carburettor if it cannot be tuned correctly due to the unavailability of alternative jets.

Obviously the choice is yours when it comes to selecting a carburettor, but give heed to my advice regarding the size to use. Always remember that the carburettor meters the fuel according to the signal being received in the fuel well. A carburettor too large for the engine produces a weak signal; consequently the metering system cannot function correctly.

To illustrate the problem, let us assume that we are cruising with a light throttle, then we step on the gas. The accelerator pump delivers a shot of fuel to make up for the lag in fuel delivery through the main circuit. At the same time air velocity through the venturis picks up a little because of the reduced resistance of flow – only a little because the car has not yet started to gain speed. All we have done is to go from a high manifold vacuum on closed throttle, to a low vacuum when the throttles were cracked wide open.

If the carburettor has huge venturis, there will not be enough air speed to create the depression necessary for the main system to flow fuel, so you will end up with a big flat spot. Conversely, if the venturis are small, the slight increase in air velocity when the throttles are opened will give the necessary pressure differential necessary to get fuel discharging through the main system. This in turn allows the engine to produce more power, which gets the vehicle moving faster. With the vehicle moving faster, air flow through the venturis continues to increase, as does the fuel delivery rate. The result: crisp acceleration and good throttle response.

If you are still not convinced of the need for a strong signal to get the fuel metering systems working, try this simple experiment. Fill a container with water and

The brace of 48 IDA Webers on this Ford GT40 is visually impressive, but more important good basic design of the metering circuits, and a ready supply of alternative jets means that they can be tuned to provide good engine performance over a wide power range.

draw it up first through a straw, then a piece of ⅝in heater hose. Did you notice the difference? How much more sucking you had to do to get the water flowing up the heater hose! That very same principle applies to fuel flow through a carburettor's metering system. The small venturi being sucked on by the engine (like you sucking on the straw) gets the fuel responding quickly to the needs of the engine.

The other benefit of using a carburettor with venturis of the right size is this. A high air velocity through the venturi lowers the air pressure (creates a partial vacuum), which makes the fuel more volatile and easily atomised. Additionally, the high air speed itself assists in the vaporisation of the fuel. Properly atomised fuel improves fuel distribution from cylinder to cylinder, and power goes up because the quality of combustion is improved; raw fuel will not burn at the correct rate to produce power.

DUAL-STAGE CARBURETTORS

Carburettor engineers have worked with these problems for quite some time, and their solution is simple: use a dual-stage carburettor. One stage (primary) is for low speed and fuel economy operation, and the secondary stage is for maximum air flow. The latter may be opened mechanically by linkages operating from the primary barrel, such that the secondary throttle plate begins to open when the primary throttle plate is about 40° open. This type is said to be a progressive, mechanical secondary carburettor.

The vacuum-operated secondary carburettor does not have a throttle linkage connected to the throttle shaft. Instead, the air demand of the engine at higher engine speeds creates a vacuum that operates on a diaphragm to control the secondary opening. The diaphragm, if correctly adjusted, automatically opens the secondary by the correct amount to meet the air flow needs of the engine. Some feel that this feature gives them licence to go ahead and fit the largest available vacuum secondary carburettor. They reason that if the carburettor is too large it does not matter, as the secondary will not open fully anyway. This is false reasoning; maybe the performance will not suffer too much, but fuel consumption could easily increase by 12–15%.

Do not be confused into thinking that all two- and four-barrel carburettors are designed to give a small venturi area with just the primaries open at lower engine speeds and when cruising. This is not so; some have simultaneous throttle action, meaning that all the throttle plates open together. These carburettors are really two, three or four individual carburettors sharing a single carburettor body and a single fuel bowl, in the case of the two-barrel versions. Carburettors of this type include the Weber DCOE and IDA, the Dellorto DHLA, and the Holley 4500 Dominator (Nos 6464 and 6214) and 4160 (No 4224). Carburettors of this type will give excellent performance on the correct engine and manifold. The Weber and Dellorto carburettors have very special metering systems enabling them to be used even on small high-performance road engines without sacrificing much low-speed performance. The Holley carburettors with simultaneous throttle action are for racing use only.

CARBURETTOR MODIFICATION

A popular fad is the modification of American four-barrel carburettors to 'improve' them. The 'improvement' is usually said to be in air flow, due to the throttle bores and the venturi bores being bored out to a larger size. Some may flow more air, but more air is of no value unless fuel has been mixed with it in the correct proportions, to say nothing of throttle response and metering signals. A carburettor modified along these lines will be useless in a vehicle requiring any sort of power range. It would work in a racing boat or in a stick-shift drag car with a 7,500–9,000rpm power band, but in any other application it would prove a hindrance.

The only type of modification for Holley four-barrel carburettors of which I approve involves re-calibration of the fuel metering circuits to provide more accurate metering. This modification serves to broaden the power range on a racing engine when a large carburettor is being used, by precise fuel metering right from part-open to wide-open throttle.

The problem is that racing engines produce a weaker vacuum signal due to their need for very large carburettors to provide good power at high rpm. Camshaft design also affects fuel metering, because the fuel delivery signal is weakened as the inlet valve is opened earlier and earlier, and as the valve overlap period is increased. As a result the carburettor requires more sensitivity to weaker signals, or it will excessively lean the mixture and reduce the power output at lower engine speeds.

Some feel that this problem can be solved by using a more sensitive booster venturi, but I have found the converse to be true. In a racing engine the carburettor is subject to severe reversion pulses ('spit back') and during this reverse flow period more fuel is added to the air; then as the air flows back into the engine the booster senses its flow and further fuel is added. This means that during its three passes through the carburettor, fuel has been added to the air; consequently the mixture becomes extremely rich. A booster that is more sensitive will aggravate this situation at certain engine speeds, and do little to richen the mixture at lower engine speeds where the lean condition is being experienced.

The low-speed lean condition is not, in fact, due to any insensitivity in the main metering system, but generally due to the signal being too weak to activate the idle-progression system. Changes to the accelerator pump circuit will help, but the way around the problem is to add an intermediate fuel circuit. This will fill in gaps in the Holley's fuel metering circuits and allow it to perform well at lower engine speeds, to produce a power band almost as wide as that possible when using Weber carburettors.

If you use a Holley carburettor and need a wide power range for road racing or short speedway, take your carburettor to someone who will re-calibrate it as outlined; forget about those firms who rebore the venturis.

Regardless of the type of carburettor you use, it should not be modified (except the SU) by boring the venturi or by radiusing the corners at the air entry.

If you take a careful look at the venturi you will find that it has a radiused inlet and diverging tail section. Designers work the venturi shape to create the maximum pressure drop with minimum flow losses. Frequently, when the venturi is re-bored, the basic internal shape is not changed to suit the larger internal diameter. Reboring really requires that both the entry radius and the divergent angle of the tail be changed, otherwise the increase in bore size will not increase air flow, but that will result in a less effective metering signal.

Radiusing the corners of the air entry can reduce the auxiliary venturi signal, since the inflowing air tends to turn into the main venturi sooner and take away flow from the centre of the venturi where the auxiliary venturi (booster) is located. This reduces the signal at the booster and results in main circuit fuel lean-out.

Another bad modification involves cutting down the divider wall between the primary and secondary side of a four-barrel carburettor for clearance under the hood or for improved air flow. Removing just one-quarter of an inch could upset booster sensitivity to the extent that main jets three or four sizes richer would be required, and this will not fully solve the problem.

The message is to keep your fingers, your files and your grinders right away from the carburettor, particularly its mouth. Any modification in this area will almost always deaden booster sensitivity, which will generally affect fuel flow into the engine adversely.

THROTTLE SHAFT MODIFICATION

This is not to say that all modifications to improve the air flow through the carburettor are to be avoided. As I have already pointed out, you should get rid of the choke plate and shaft. That simple modification will improve the flow of a Holley by about 50cfm.

The next area that you should take a look at is the throttle shaft and throttle plate screws. Most shafts are 5/16–3/8in diameter and the butterflies are attached by two screws. Some carburettors use countersunk screws, carefully trimmed so that they do not project through the shaft. However, most screws have a flat head and they usually protrude through the shaft by 1/16–3/32in. Together the shaft and screws disrupt air flow by causing turbulence and by partly blocking the carburettor bore.

In racing applications, particularly if the carburettor size is limited by the rules, a useful increase in air flow (10–12%) can be gained by removing the screws and cutting down the shaft width (Figure 4.4) One half of the shaft should be cut away completely, and the other half slabbed so that it is no more than 1/16in thick, then ground with a radiused edge. The butterflies are attached by heliarc welding through the existing screw holes.

This modification should be carried out only by a competent machine shop, taking special care not to bend or twist the very thin and weak throttle shaft. If it is twisted, the butterflies will not be synchronised. The heliarc welding is also a delicate operation; again special care is necessary to ensure that the butterflies are going to open together.

Figure 4.4 Modified throttle shaft.

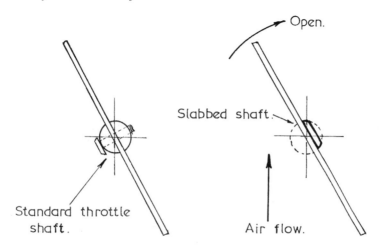

When a carburettor modified as described is being fitted, be sure to attach the throttle return spring to the same end of the throttle shaft as the throttle linkage. If the spring is attached to the opposite end, the shaft will twist due to the opposing forces on each end.

FLOAT MODIFICATION

If you race on a speedway and use a Holley carburettor, you are probably aware of the problem of fuel surge and starvation caused by the constant side forces that push the

---

Wide-open throttle

Probably all tuners have experienced an engine that seems to be under-performing. Then, during the search to find the problem, they discover that something is holding the carburettor back from getting full throttle; it could be a linkage jamming, a frayed throttle cable, even new sound-deadening material under the carpet! With the snag removed and an extra quarter-inch of pedal travel available, the expectation is that the car will be faster, but it isn't. In fact I've seen engines lose performance when that last little bit of throttle has been gained. Why does this occur and what can we learn from the experience?

First it indicates that in the real world, when we attach a carburettor to a manifold and cylinder head, the last few degrees of throttle plate movement do not necessarily bring any increase in air flow. Actually the converse can be true; the last few degrees of opening may reduce air flow in the order of 2–3%. When this comes about it indicates that the inlet tract works better with flow biased to a particular side or area of the port. A throttle plate can provide just such a bias by imparting a directional effect to the air/fuel mixture as it flows over its surface.

This is easy to test on the flow bench. There is no need to concern yourself with throttle plate angle; just check flow with feeler strips of differing thicknesses inserted at the throttle stop, and when the best flow is realised adjust the stops accordingly. The same sort of test can also be carried out with the engine running on the dyno. When downdraught carburettors like Weber IDAs are fitted I also modify the inlet manifold with two sets of carb-fixing lugs so that I can swing the carburettors around 180° on the manifold (equivalent to mounting downdraught carbs upside down) and test which way the engine works best.

The second way that less than fully open throttle plates may at times contribute to improved performance is attributable to their effect on the quality of the fuel/air mixture. A mixture of small, evenly distributed fuel particles burns to produce more power than larger, poorly dispersed droplets. As an engine accelerates on to the straight at full throttle, going from, say, 6,000rpm to 8,500rpm in each gear, there will be points in that rev range where mixture homogenisation and droplet size will be found to be wanting. Air speed in the inlet tract could be a little slow, or there may be reversion pulses or other undesirable harmonics upsetting fuel metering. However, a throttle plate tipped slightly in the air stream will get the fuel/air mixture swirling around. Some larger fuel droplets will smash into the plate and be broken down to a combustible size. Also the throttle plate being tilted a little off full-open may act to dampen unwelcome pulses in the inlet tract, thus enabling the carburettors to receive a 'purer' metering signal, which in turn means that the quantity of fuel being introduced into the air stream is closer to what the engine properly requires for best hp.

fuel to the right-hand side of the float chamber, at times at a 45° angle. So steep an angle can easily uncover a main jet and allow air into the main well.

To overcome the problem remove the brass float and replace it with a modified cellular float. By cutting the end of the float at 45° it can be tricked into staying down and admitting extra fuel to keep the main jets covered. After cutting, it is necessary to re-seal the float using a fuel resistant epoxy, otherwise the float, being porous inside, will sink and flood the engine.

CHOOSING THE RIGHT SIZE

Earlier it was established that the carburettor has to rely on the signal produced in its venturi by the inflowing air to meter fuel correctly into the engine. Then it has to wait for the atmospheric pressure to act on the fuel in the fuel bowl to force it through a series of jets and passages, then into the air stream. This takes time, so the engine's fuel requirements are not instantly met, resulting in delayed throttle response.

Thus the displacement of the engine, the weight of the vehicle, the axle ratio and the desired power range all have a big influence on the size and type of carburettor that will give the best performance. To add a little extra confusion to the issue, half of the world sizes its carburettors according to the diameter of the throttle bore, while the other half rates them in accordance with how much air they flow. Therefore to know what you are actually buying, you need a little background information to understand what all the numbers mean.

All carburettors made in the UK, Europe and Japan are identified by the diameter of the carburettor bore at the throttle plate. The size may be stated in inches or millimetres. Generally, the stated size tells you very little about the carburettor, as it is the combination of the venturi diameter and the throttle bore diameter that determines the air flow capabilities of the carburettor. For example, the Weber 45 DCOE carburettor is a two-barrel, simultaneous throttle action unit, with throttle bores 45mm in diameter. However, a range of replaceable venturis are available from 30 to 40mm, which allows this carburettor to be used on a wide variety of engines in all stages of tune.

The American system of rating carburettors in cubic feet per minute (cfm) air flow is just as confusing. Enthusiasts have been conditioned to believe that working to the following formula guarantees selection of the correct size of carburettor:

$$\text{cfm} = \frac{D \times \text{rpm} \times VE}{3,456 \times 100}$$

where D = displacement in cu in, rpm = engine speed at maximum horsepower, and VE = volumetric efficiency at maximum horsepower.

Taking as an example the 350cu in Chevy Z-28 engine in Table 4.2, we find its air flow at 5500rpm, at a volumetric efficiency of 75.1, to be 418.3 cubic feet per minute. According to the formula, this engine would work best with a carburettor rated to flow 400–450cfm. In actual practice this particular engine will work best using a 600–650cfm carburettor for street use, and a 750–780cfm carburettor for drag racing.

The Chevy racing engine in Table 4.3 would have a peak air flow of 640.8cfm at 95

Table 4.2   Theoretical fuel flow in the 350 cubic inch Chevy blue-printed Z-28 (1:12.5 fuel–air ratio)

rpm	hp	torque (lbf ft)	VE	air flow (lb/hr)	fuel flow (lb/hr)
3,000	198	346	81.7	1,087.2	87
3,500	237	355	83.8	1,301	104.1
4,000	274	360	85	1,508.2	120.7
4,500	303	354	83.6	1,668.7	133.5
5,000	326	342	80.8	1,792	143.4
5,500	333	318	75.1	1,832.2	146.6
6,000	326	285	67.3	1,791.2	143.3
6,500	295	238	56.2	1,620.4	129.6

Note: the actual fuel flow will be approximately 20–25% more than the theoretical flow due to unequal distribution from cylinder to cylinder and to accelerator pump operation.

Table 4.3   Theoretical fuel flow in the 350 cubic inch Chevy racing engine (1:12.5 fuel–air ratio)

rpm	hp	torque (lbf ft)	VE	air flow (lb/hr)	fuel flow (lb/hr)
4,500	362	423	89.1	1,778.5	142.3
5,000	415	436	91.8	2,036	162.9
5,500	471	450	94.8	2,312.8	185
6,000	515	451	95	2,528.4	202.3
6,500	547	442	93.1	2,684.3	214.7
7,000	572	429	90.4	2,807	224.6
7,500	570	399	84	2,794.5	223.6

Note: the actual fuel flow will be approximately 20–25% more than the theoretical flow due to unequal distribution from cylinder to cylinder and to accelerator pump operation.

7,000rpm with a volumetric efficiency of 90.4%. However, for circle track racing you would use a Holley carburettor of either 850 or 1050cfm.

On paper the air-flow formula looks good, but it is of little use as the actual air flow of the engine and the theoretical laboratory air flow of the carburettor are worlds apart due to a number of factors.

In the test laboratory, carburettor manufacturers measure the air flow of each type of carburettor at a constant vacuum, usually 3 inches of mercury (Hg) for one- and two-barrel carburettors, and 1.5 inches of Hg for three- and four-barrel carburettors. Right away you can see that there is not a true comparison of the theoretical amount of air that two- and four-barrel carburettors will flow. A carburettor subject to a vacuum of 3 inches of Hg at wide-open throttle will naturally flow more air than one tested at 1.5 inches of Hg. A two-barrel Holley rated at 650cfm will not flow as much air as a four-barrel Holley rated at 650cfm.

To relate the two measurements we must use the formula

$$\frac{\text{cfm @ 3in Hg}}{1.414} = \text{cfm @ 1.5in Hg}$$

Therefore the 650cfm two-barrel will flow only 460cfm when tested at 1.5in Hg.

Taking this principle a step further, it will be found that many racing engines have a manifold vacuum of only 0.5 inches of Hg at wide-open throttle, not the 1.5 inches at which the four-barrel carburettors are flow tested. At a depression of 0.5 inches of Hg the flow will equal the cfm at 1.5 inches of Hg divided by 1.735. Therefore a 1,050cfm carburettor will flow approximately 605cfm when fitted to a racing engine with a manifold vacuum of 0.5 inches of Hg.

On the test bench the carburettors are subjected to a constant vacuum for air flow measurement purposes, but in practice a carburettor fitted to an engine has to contend with reverse flow (or reversion) pulses, which also cause the air flow capacity of the carburettor to be reduced. Racing engines produce a stronger reversion pulse than stock units, due to the use of wild camshafts that cause more reverse flow in the inlet tract because of early inlet valve opening and lots of valve overlap. Manifold design also influences the intensity of the reverse pulse.

Another aspect of carburettor air flow not considered in the flow room is the on-and-off-type of flow actually experienced by the carburettor when the inlet valve opens, then closes. If the inlet valve was held wide open for 1 minute, carburettor air flow

Fitted to an isolated runner manifold these 48 DCOE Webers are adequate up to about 240hp. However, used on this two-plane V8 manifold, they can flow enough air to more than double that figure.

would be constant for that minute, but in use the inlet valve may open and close 4,000 times during that minute, serving to reduce air flow. Obviously a tap turned on for a minute will flow more water than one that is turned on and off 4,000 times in a minute.

The more cylinders to which a carburettor venturi is flowing air, the more constant the air flow through the carburettor will be, so air flow per minute goes up. This partly explains why a small engine with one barrel per cylinder may require a huge carburettor to flow enough air for good power. If you take a look at the RS 1800 Escort rally engine, you will find that it breathes through two 48DCOE Webers, each carburettor capable of flowing around 650cfm. The motor had a power output of 240hp from 2,000cc, and a power band compatible with international rally events. Fitted to a V8 Ford Cleveland 351 (5,700cc) racing engine, a pair of Weber 48 DCOE carburettors will flow enough air to produce in excess of 525hp.

ISOLATED RUNNER MANIFOLD

The RS 1800 uses what we call an 'isolated runner' manifold (Figure 4.5), with one carburettor throat directly connected to each cylinder. This means that each cylinder is totally independent of and isolated from all of the other cylinders. Fuel distribution problems and charge robbing is eliminated, improving fuel economy and power output. An induction arrangement of this type is commonly found on road racing engines, European performance cars and all motorcycles.

From the aspect of horsepower output there is not a lot of difference in the peak power output of V8 engines using four Webers on an isolated runner manifold, or two four-barrel Holleys on a plenum ram manifold. If fuel distribution is given proper attention, the latter would produce more power (at times up to 7% more). For this reason Holleys are usually preferred for drag racing, but for road racing, where a wide power band and good throttle response are more important, an isolated runner manifold and Webers are a combination hard to beat.

An important consideration when you go out to buy an isolated runner manifold is to find a design that is not too short; some manifolds are virtually just stubs connecting

Weber chokes (venturis) too small?

Some people think that there is something to be gained by boring Weber carburettor chokes to a size larger than that manufactured by the factory. Thus 40 DCOE chokes are bored to 38mm, 45 DCOE to 42mm and 48 DCOE to 45mm, when the factory's biggest chokes are 36, 40 and 42mm respectively. Are we to assume here that Weber got it wrong? Apparently a number of tuners believe so, judging by the number of Webers I see with chokes bored out or even discarded completely! Obviously the idea is that a bigger hole must flow more air, and more air equals more hp, so it has to be a good thing.

Personally I believe that Weber did get it wrong – some of their chokes are too big! I've yet to see an engine produce more power when running 40 DCOEs on anything larger than a 33 or 34mm choke. Past this size the auxiliary venturi is the major impediment to air flow. Interestingly the 42 DCOE, which is virtually identical, has a maximum choke size of 34mm. Likewise with 45COEs; 38 or 39mm chokes seem to give the same top end as 40s, and these smaller chokes generally give a superior mid-range when compared with 40mm chokes.

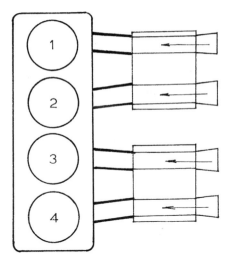

Figure 4.5 Isolated runner manifold.

the carburettor straight on to the head. This can be particularly bad in the case of Weber sidedraught carburettors (or Weber downdraught carbs if you are using a downdraught head). If you reduce the manifold bore from 45mm (1.77in) at the carburettor to 1.3in at the head too quickly, this will over-accelerate the fuel mixture after it leaves the carburettor. The resulting turbulence could effectively reduce the area of the inlet port by as much as 40%. By increasing the length of the manifold, the contraction of the intake gases is more gradual, allowing the manifold and port to flow at 100% efficiency.

TWO-PLANE MANIFOLD

Most V8 engines in production use a two-plane manifold (Figure 4.6). Originally this type was designed to avoid charge robbing, which resulted when all eight cylinders breathed through a single carburettor. By using a two- or four-barrel carburettor, the manifold passages are arranged so that cylinders 1, 4, 6 and 7 draw through half of the carburettor and one plane of the manifold, and cylinders 8, 3, 5 and 2 draw through the other half and the second plane, assuming a 1–8–4–3–6–5–7–2 firing order. This separates the induction pulses by 180° and allows reasonably equal cylinder filling if the manifold is of a good design.

Because there is less air mass to activate on each inlet pulse, throttle response is usually quicker and mid-range power is improved, as compared to a single-plane manifold. The division of the manifold into two planes is, however, a mixed blessing as it causes a flow restriction at high rpm because only half of the carburettor flow capacity is available on any intake stroke.

For this reason the divider can be reduced in height or sometimes removed completely, to make more carburettor flow capacity available; top-end performance is improved but bottom-end power is reduced. With the divider cut down, charge robbing can be a problem, but not to the extent of single-plane designs.

The two-plane manifolds fitted in normal production are generally of very poor design, with many tortuous corners and restrictive passages that retard air flow. For 99 most V8 road vehicles I recommend the use of either an Edelbrock or Weiand two-plane manifold, but before purchasing any manifold inspect it for casting flaws or core shift that could result in port misalignment.

I like this type of manifold for the good throttle response it is able to produce. This is important on the road, particularly if the vehicle weight to engine displacement ratio is not good. Because the two-plane manifold fosters low and mid-range power, a double-pumper mechanical secondary Holley or a pair of 48 DCOE Webers on a Waneford cross-over manifold adapter will work very well. If you use a Holley, pick a 600–650cfm carburettor for a 300–350cu in engine and a 700–750cfm unit for engines in the 380–450cu in class.

SINGLE-PLANE MANIFOLD

Single-plane manifolds (Figure 4.7) are found on nearly all in-line engines, and quite a few V8 manifold manufacturers are marketing replacement high-performance single-plane (360°) manifolds. This is the very simplest layout with all the cylinders drawing from a single chamber. The manifold may be fitted with any combination of carburettors, but in high-performance applications it is more usual to fit two single-barrel carburettors, or a single two- or four-barrel carburettor.

Figure 4.6 Two-plane V8 manifold.

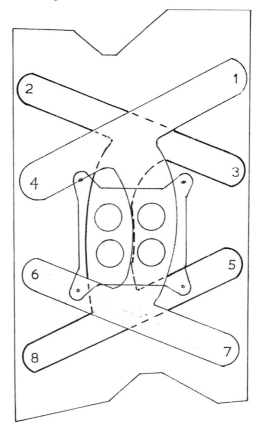

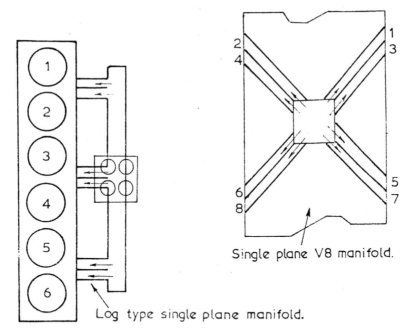

Single plane V8 manifold.

Log type single plane manifold.

Figure 4.7 Single-plane manifolds.

The main problem with the single-plane design is the tendency for one cylinder to rob mixture from another. However, by careful design, this deficiency can, and is, being overcome by manifold manufacturers.

In general I prefer to keep well away from single-plane manifolds for in-line engines as they are ideal for the isolated runner set-up. For sports engines the single-plane manifold will work reasonably well, providing that the manifold is of a 'log' design (Figure 4.7). To the eye this type may not look as racy as a manifold with nice curves, but it will assist in mixture distribution and will also help prevent the fuel dropping out of suspension and wetting the manifold and port walls.

The pockets produced at the ends of the log manifold and beneath the carburettor tend to form a soft air cushion that helps keep the mixture atomised as it makes a change in direction. Also, because the shape of the end ports more closely resemble the shape of the inner ports, mixture distribution is equalised. A good rule to keep in mind if you are using a single-plane manifold and you desire reasonably equal mixture distribution is this: where possible, divide the mixture before a change in direction occurs.

There are a number of good, single-plane V8 manifolds available, but in general I stick to the Holley Street Dominator for all engines in sports tune, and engines up to 320cu in in semi-race tune. The Edelbrock Victor Junior is suitable for motors larger than 320cu in, if in semi-race tune. For race engines, the Holley Strip Dominator and Edelbrock Victor are a good choice.

Because throttle response and low-end power is not so good, it is best to use a vacuum secondary Holley of around 600cfm for street engines up to 350cu in and a vacuum secondary of 780cfm for larger engines. Race engines work well with a 750cfm mechanical secondary double-pumper up to 315cu in, an 800cfm up to 350cu in, and a 1,050cfm above 400cu in.

101

Offenhauser have tackled the problem by offering a dual-port, single-plane manifold. A small-passage and large-passage manifold are stacked one on top of the other in a single casting. The small ports are connected to the primary side of the carburettor, to give a high mixture speed at low rpm; this assists in mixture distribution and gives good throttle response. The larger ports connect to the secondary barrels of the carburettor for high rpm operation.

There are several features that the dual-port manifold can boast. The small primary passages, as well as assisting low rpm operation and contributing to good throttle response, also provide a very effective space to keep engine heat away from the secondary passages. This serves to increase the secondary air density, thus improving high-speed performance.

The small passages also lift mid-range performance in this way. When the secondary mixture gets to the end of its runner, it is accelerated by the high-speed primary fuel/air mixture. This serves to ram the air down the inlet port, and the differences in air speed shears the secondary fuel particles to aid in mixture atomisation. This is a good manifold for the 3.8-litre Buick V6 and the German Capri 2.8-litre V6. Use a Holley vacuum secondary 390cfm carburettor on the Capri and a 465cfm on the Buick.

PLENUM RAM MANIFOLD

All-out drag cars and racing boats commonly use a plenum ram manifold (Figure 4.8) with either one four-barrel, or more commonly dual four-barrel, carburettors. This manifold is very similar to the isolated runner manifold, with a plenum chamber added between the carburettor base and the manifold runners. The plenum helps to dissipate the strong pulsing, common to the isolated runner design, so less pulse enters the carburettor to disrupt air flow. Also it allows the cylinders to share the flow capacity of the carburettor(s) for super-high rpm operation, ie 10,000rpm on a 302 Chevy or 9,000rpm on a 427cu in Chevy. Manifolds of this design are not suitable for use below 5,000–6,000rpm, and some, such as the Edelbrock TR-2Y for the 396-427-454 Chevy, will not work below 7,000rpm.

For Chevrolet engines I prefer the Holley Pro Dominator manifold. This type has a split plenum, which is a real asset when manifold modifications are being tested. All plenum ram manifolds have a removable plenum, but to get inside it to carry out modifications it is frequently necessary to saw the chamber in half. Then, after any grinding and filling, it has to be welded together – all very expensive and time-consuming.

CHOOSING A MANIFOLD

When you go out to buy a manifold there are several things to look for and to keep in mind. First, you want to buy a manifold that will, if possible, fit the carburettor(s) that you wish to use, without an adaptor. Generally, adaptor plates restrict the air flow by creating undue turbulence, because they attempt to change the air flow path too quickly, the plate being only 1/2–1 1/2in thick.

Many of the adaptors made to mount the large Holley 4500 carburettors (1,050 and 1,150cfm) on standard four-barrel-pattern manifolds restrict the air flow potential

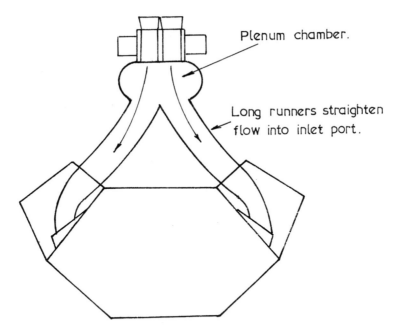

Plenum chamber.

Long runners straighten flow into inlet port.

Figure 4.8 V8 plenum ram manifold.

of the carburettor by 100–250cfm, which effectively takes away any advantage of the larger carburettor.

Take an inlet manifold gasket with you to check how the manifold ports match up. As most stock gaskets have port holes much larger than necessary, to allow for port misalignment, it will be necessary to make up a gasket with the exact port and stud locations of your cylinder head. If your engine is a V6, V8, flat-four, etc, you will need two gaskets; be sure to mark each left or right.

Try to find a manifold that matches as closely as possible to the gasket as this will save some work when the manifold and head are matched. Additionally, look at the ports to check their smoothness; high spots ('dingle berries') can be ground out, but depressions can be a problem if a suitable epoxy filler is not available.

You should also note the 'join' in the manifold, which is where the core boxes were joined when the manifold was cast. At times the core and core boxes are not correctly aligned, resulting in half of the port being offset from the other half. Choose a manifold with little or no evidence of core shift.

MANIFOLD MODIFICATION

After you have bought your manifold, try fitting it to your engine before you modify it in any way, as you may have to return it if it does not fit. Some V6 and V8 manifolds will not fit with non-standard distributors; on the other hand a couple will not fit with the stock distributor. Due to the large variety of exhaust headers available, a few manifolds will not clear the headers on in-line engines.

When you are sure that the manifold will clear everything, match up the manifold runners with the inlet ports and match the carburettor bore to the manifold 103 entrance. The only exception to this is with Edelbrock Streetmaster manifolds, as these have purposely mismatched runner walls that should not be modified. Edelbrock claim that the mismatch serves to reduce reversion pulses, but as I have not had any experience with this manifold (because it is designed for low-performance emission engines), I cannot confirm or deny this.

With the manifold aligned to the ports and the carburettor bore, clean any 'dingle berries' out of the runners with a high-speed grinder, but do not polish the ports. As I have mentioned before, a smooth surface will flow as well as a polished surface, but fuel vaporisation is much better if the ports are left smooth rather than polished. Polished ports can reduce power by 3–4%.

MINIMISING FUEL DISTRIBUTION PROBLEMS

Proper fuel distribution always has and probably will be a major problem as long as we use carburettors and non-isolated-runner-type manifolds. Several factors affect distribution, such as manifold design, carburettor size and type, inlet charge temperature, engine speed and consequently air flow speed. Obviously if port-type fuel injection or an isolated runner manifold is being used, there can not be any variation in the quantity of fuel reaching each cylinder.

Generally, V8 engines using single-plane and low-profile cross-ram manifolds have the worst distribution. The stock two-plane manifold is also affected, but replacement performance manifolds are quite good. So too are the plenum ram manifolds.

In-line engines with one SU (or SU-type) carburettor to each pair of cylinders do not have any distribution deficiencies, but single-plane manifolds with a two- or four-barrel carburettor, or two or three single-throat carburettors, may cause serious fuel variations from cylinder to cylinder.

Before we delve into manifold modifications to assist in achieving equal fuel distribution, there are a couple of principles that should be considered.

The purpose of this exercise is to equalise as closely as possible the quantity of fuel entering each cylinder. Equality of air flow is a different consideration and beyond the scope of a tuner without access to an air flow test bench. Therefore you have to assume that the manifold design engineer has done his job and each cylinder is receiving a reasonably equal quantity of air. Fuel distribution variations have a much more serious effect on engine performance than slight air flow differences. Unfortunately many tuners do not realise this.

Because high-performance engines (or for that matter all engines) operate at less than their ideal engine speed for some of the time, air speed through the carburettor and ports is not high enough to ensure good fuel vaporisation. Some of the fuel separates from the air and falls to the floor of the manifold. When this happens it will be directed partly by the force of gravity to one or more of the inlet ports. If the manifold floor is not horizontal, the wet fuel will flow to cylinders at the low end of the manifold. Therefore the first check should be to ensure that the manifold is horizontal to the ground, not to the angle of the engine. If you have a 'V' or flat engine, the manifold will have to be checked both in-line and across the engine. Obviously braking, cornering and acceleration, as well as ascending and descending hills, will upset wet flow distribution, but there is no way of overcoming these continually varying forces, except on speedway machines where the cornering force may be reasonably constant.

In production engines, exhaust heat or hot engine coolant is circulated through the manifold floor directly below the carburettor. The heat will cause some fuel to vaporise, but we may want to remove the heat in semi-race and full-race engines to improve high rpm air density. In this instance we may have to sacrifice distribution uniformity at lower engine speeds to ensure peak power at maximum rpm.

If hood clearance is not a problem, raising the carburettor using a 1–1 1/2in spacer may assist distribution in two ways. First, because the carburettor is further removed from the floor of the manifold, the fuel/air charge will have less directional effect imparted to it as it leaves the carburettor. This will allow the charge to flow from the carburettor, around the corner of the manifold opening and into the ports. If the carburettor is mounted very close to the manifold (as is often the case) the fuel/air mixture continues straight on after leaving the carburettor, then the air turns abruptly into the manifold and throws the fuel out of suspension and on to the floor of the manifold. The fuel is much heavier than the air so it cannot change direction as quickly, therefore it continues straight on until it hits the manifold floor.

At small throttle openings the spacer also promotes better distribution by reducing the directional effect imparted to the fuel/air mixture by the angle of the throttle plate. This can be a serious problem in the upper plane of two-plane manifolds, causing two cylinders to run very lean. After the spacer (riser) is fitted, distribution will be improved markedly.

After ensuring that the manifold is horizontal, a check must be made on the actual fuel distribution from cylinder to cylinder. The only really accurate way to determine this is by fixing a lambda sensor into each header tube to show which cylinders are rich and which are lean.

As a back-up, the exhaust gas temperature measurement system is also used. It is less sensitive than chemical analysis, as it does not take into account exhaust temperature variations from cylinder to cylinder, due to differences in exhaust scavenging. However, it is a particularly valuable test in the dyno room, to determine the heat level of a given cylinder, so as to avoid engine damage due to an excessively lean mixture condition.

Careful inspection of the spark plug tips will give some indication of mixture distribution problems in engines allowed to run leaded fuel.

Obviously at the race track, or on the road, you are not able to use either system. In this case your eyes become the test instrument as you rely on the appearance and colour of the spark plug electrodes and porcelain to tell the story of fuel distribution equality.

At the very best this system is only a rough guide, but it will provide us with valuable information if approached correctly. The engine must be in good condition; broken or worn rings and worn valve guides will distort the readings very badly. Also the spark plugs must be of the correct heat range for the engine.

Actually, the colour of the porcelain insulator nose is not as important as some would suppose, as it may not be possible to colour the plugs using certain types of fuel unless the mixture is extremely rich. Added to this it can take many, many miles for the insulator nose to colour, so you will appreciate that there is a good deal more to plug-reading than merely examining the colour of the insulator.

It takes practice and a proper magnifier of 4x to 6x power to pinpoint fuel distribution equality. The things to look for that indicate certain operating conditions are indicated in Table 4.4. You will note that all of the plug end actually exposed to the combustion flame is examined and read, not just the insulator nose.

Table 4.4   Checking fuel distribution by spark plug reading

Spark plug mixture condition	Indications
Normal – correct mixture	Insulator nose white or very light tan to rust brown. Little or no cement boil where centre electrode protrudes through insulator nose. Electrodes not discoloured or eroded.
Fuel fouled – rich mixture	Insulator nose dark grey or black. Steel plug shell end covered with dry, black soot deposit that will easily rub off.
Overheated – lean mixture	Insulator nose chalky white or may have satin sheen. Excessive cement boil where centre electrode protrudes through insulator nose. May be milk white or meringue-like. Centre electrode may 'blue' and be rounded off at edges. Earth electrode may be badly eroded or have molten appearance.
Detonation – lean mixture	Insulator nose covered in tiny pepper specks or maybe tiny beads of aluminium leaving piston crown. Excessive cement boil where centre electrode protrudes through insulator nose. Specks on steel plug shell end.

For the plug reading to be accurate it will be necessary to run the engine at full throttle and maximum speed on the track (or road), then immediately cut the engine dead. If you allow the engine to slow down as you bring the vehicle to a stop, the plug reading will be meaningless.

Table 4.5 Checking fuel distribution by combustion chamber, exhaust valve and piston crown colour

Mixture condition	Indication
Normal	Dry, dark, hard carbon in combustion chamber and piston crown. Light tan to rust brown exhaust valve.
Rich	Dark soft carbon in combustion chamber and on piston crown. Carbon may be wet or have wet stains. Dark exhaust valve.
Lean	Grey to white deposit in combustion chamber and on piston crown. Oil may be burned a very dark brown under piston crown. Called 'death ash' if burned to black ash. White chalky colour exhaust valve.

A tuner must use everything at his disposal to check the distribution from cylinder to cylinder. Usually, race engines are frequently stripped for inspection and periodic replacement of parts. This is an ideal time to read the combustion chamber and also the exhaust valves and the top of the piston. Naturally if the engine is burning a lot of oil through being overdue for a rebuild, a reliable reading will not be possible (Table 4.5).

SINGLE-PLANE V8 MANIFOLD 'FIXES'

Having determined which cylinders are rich, normal or lean, we must then set about correcting the problem. Usually, single-plane V8 manifolds cause us the most problems. As this design is very popular in high-performance and racing applications, we will concentrate on 'fixes' to overcome distribution deficiencies in manifolds of this type.

The distribution situation can at times be improved by staggered jetting of the carburettor. If you find two adjacent cylinders (ie 1 and 3, 5 and 7, 2 and 4, or 6 and 8 – or for Ford engines 1 and 2, 3 and 4, 5 and 6, or 7 and 8) that are both either rich or lean, the condition may be corrected by changing the jets in the barrel of the carburettor feeding those cylinders. This will sometimes correct the distribution, but if you find little improvement after several jet changes, you can assume that manifold modifications are necessary.

Before you alter the manifold it is advantageous to determine if the manufacturer has incorporated changes in later versions of that same basic manifold to fix a distribution problem. You will find that manifold manufacturers are continually updating their products, so by studying the refinements made by the manufacturer and incorporating these in your manifold, you can save yourself a lot of time experimenting to find a suitable 'fix'.

Earlier I mentioned that there is always some liquid fuel running around the floor of the manifold. If some of this fuel can be directed into a lean cylinder, or prevented from entering a rich cylinder, the power output of the engine will be improved and the fuel consumption will decrease.

Most racers are after more power, but few are concerned about fuel consumption. However, in reality many long-distance events on road circuits and super speedways have been won and lost on this point. Tuners who work really hard to equalise fuel distribution have been able to get 10–15 more laps out of each tank of fuel on the super speedway than their competitors, on the same number of gallons of fuel.

There are two very simple modifications that will correct the majority of distribution deficiencies: fuel dams and fuel slots (Figure 4.9).

A dam can be constructed of 1/8in rod epoxied to the plenum floor (use a fuel-resistant epoxy). It may be placed across the entry of just one runner or a pair of runners, to reduce the amount of liquid fuel reaching those cylinders. After this modification it is sometimes necessary to fit leaner carburettor jets, as the cylinders without the fuel dams may become too rich.

Fuel slots can be utilised in conjunction with dams or they may be beneficially used just by themselves. Such slots are used to channel liquid fuel to the individual manifold runners that need it. The slots are cut in the floor of the plenum chamber and runner with a high-speed 1/4in spherical cutter to a depth of 1/8–3/16in. To ensure that the fuel reaches the desired cylinder, the slot must extend approximately 1in past the entry of the runner into the plenum chamber, and 1 1/4–1 1/2in down the throat of the runner itself.

You are probably wondering how the directing of liquid fuel to a lean cylinder, or preventing it from entering a rich cylinder, will improve power output. It is true that liquid fuel contributes little in the way of actual power because of its very slow burning characteristics, but more is involved.

Normally, to prevent damage in a lean cylinder it is necessary to increase the carburettor jet sizes so that this cylinder receives sufficient fuel. As a result the power

Figure 4.9 Manifold modified to improve fuel distribution.

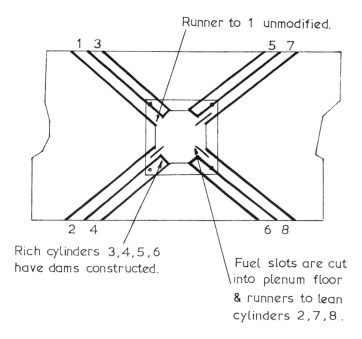

Runner to 1 unmodified.

1 3   5 7

2 4   6 8

Rich cylinders 3,4,5,6
have dams constructed.

Fuel slots are cut
into plenum floor
& runners to lean
cylinders 2,7,8.

output of the engine will be reduced as the rest of the engine will no longer be receiving a fuel/air mixture for best power; the other cylinders will now be too rich.

However, by channelling liquid fuel to a lean cylinder, the fuel/air mixture in the other cylinders will be virtually unchanged. The liquid fuel passing into the lean cylinder will not do much to lift its power output to equal that of the other individual cylinders, but it will slow down the burn rate of the combustion flame to deter piston or valve burning and serious detonation. With the lean cylinder taken care of, it is usually possible to fit smaller jets to slightly lean the rest of the engine, such that they are receiving the best fuel/air mix for maximum power. This results in a power increase and a reduction in fuel consumption. The engine will respond more crisply and be less prone to plug fouling.

Moreover, restricting the flow of liquid fuel to a rich cylinder raises the engine's power potential. An over-rich mixture burns very slowly, and combustion is usually incomplete, due to the lack of oxygen for proper burning. Consequently less heat is being generated to cause the pressure necessary to force the piston down during the power stroke. The result is a loss of power.

ATMOSPHERIC CONDITIONS AFFECT JETTING

You already know that air is less dense at 5,000 feet than it is at sea level, but did you realise that prevailing atmospheric conditions could reduce the air density at sea level to approximately the same density as air at an altitude of 5,000 feet?

Since the temperature, humidity and barometric pressure all affect air density, it is obvious that the ratio of fuel and air being introduced into your engine will vary from hour to hour, and this will influence the power output of the engine. Under normal circumstances the change in air density from hour to hour is of little or no consequence to the average enthusiast, but the racing engine tuner seeking as much power as possible, or wanting to prevent burned pistons and valves, has to take the present air density into consideration before each and every race or during a rally, where large changes in altitude and climatic conditions are experienced.

When the air density decreases, it reduces the amount of oxygen inducted into the cylinders, and the mixture becomes richer. Conversely, an increase in the air density increases the quantity of oxygen entering the motor, so there is a corresponding leaning of the fuel/air mixture. To compensate, it will be necessary to fit richer or leaner carburettor main (and at times idle) jets.

Remember when compensating for a change in air density that the change in density also affects the pressure exerted on the fuel in the float bowl. Therefore a decrease in relative air density (RAD) will automatically lean the fuel/air mixture to a degree, because of the lower air pressure.

This means that you do not fit 5% smaller jets when the RAD drops by 5%. Usually I reckon that a 12% change in RAD requires a 5% change in fuel jet size.

To make sure that the correct change in jet size is made, you first have to know the relative air density at the time when the carburettor was originally jetted to deliver peak power. If the engine was set up on a dyno, the air density will usually be stated on the dyno sheet, so you can work your calculations from that figure.

If the engine was not tuned on the dyno, or the dyno jetting is found to be all wrong (this can happen), you have to set about finding the ideal jet sizes from first

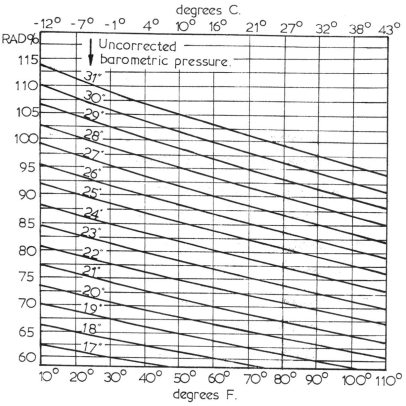

degrees C.

Note - standard sea level pressure at 59°F = 29.92" Hg.
(1013 millibars or 14.706 lb./sq. inch)

Figure 4.10 Relative air density chart.

principles. When you find what jets give the best performance, make a note in your tuning diary of the jet size and the relative air density, for future reference.

The relative air density can be worked out (Figure 4.10) providing that you know the air temperature and the uncorrected barometric pressure. Relative air density meters are available and these give a direct percentage density reading.

There is another factor involved and unfortunately this cannot be read off the relative air density graph or meter, but as its influence affects the true air density, we have to take it into account to be completely accurate.

The effect of the humidity on the density of the air is small except when both the temperature and the relative humidity are high. Water vapour has weight and as such combines with the weight of the air to distort the true weight or density of the air. Think of it in this way: you are the air and your clothing is water vapour. With clothes on you are going to exert more pressure (weight) on the bathroom scales than your true undressed weight. To find your true weight you have to subtract the weight (or pressure) exerted by your clothes. Similarly, when we want to find the true air density, we have to subtract the pressure exerted by the water vapour.

If you look at Table 4.6 you can see that the pressure exerted by water vapour at 100°F is 1.93 inches of Hg. If the barometric pressure at the time is 30 inches of Hg, the true air pressure is only 28.07 inches of Hg, or a drop of 6.4%. Therefore the fuel/air ratio will be 6.4% rich if the jets are changed to suit the uncorrected air density.

Table 4.6   Humidity saturation pressure and percentage

Temperature		Saturation pressure		Saturation percentage of water
(°F)	*(°C)*	*in Hg*	*millibars*	
0	−17.8	0.038	1	0.12
20	−6.7	0.103	3	0.33
40	4.4	0.247	8	0.83
60	15.6	0.521	18	1.7
70	21.1	0.739	25	2.5
80	26.7	1.03	35	3.3
90	32.2	1.42	48	4.7
100	37.8	1.93	65	6.5

Usually, the amount of water vapour is less than the amount indicated in the column headed 'Saturation pressure', as this assumes a relative humidity of 100%. (Relative humidity compares the amount of water vapour present with what the atmosphere is capable of holding.)

To find the true air pressure use the formula

$$CAP = UMP - \left(\frac{SP \times RH}{100}\right) \text{ inches of Hg}$$

where CAP = corrected air pressure; UMP = uncorrected barometric pressure, ie read straight off the barometer; SP = saturation pressure (from Table 4.6); and RH = relative humidity.

Once the corrected air pressure had been calculated, the true relative air density can be read straight off the relative air density graph (Figure 4.10).

If you are using a relative air density meter, the percentage reading must be corrected using the formula

$$\text{corrected RAD} = \text{RAD reading} - S\% \times \frac{RH}{100}$$

where S% = saturation percentage of water (from Table 4.6) and RH = relative humidity.

The one thing that you must be sure to do if you wish to be successful in tuning your motor according to the relative air density is to keep complete and accurate notes. If you find that the engine works best with 150 main jets and 10° initial spark advance   111 when the air density is 90%, be sure that you make a note of the fact in your tuning diary. Then on each occasion that the air density is again 90%, you will know exactly what size jets and how much spark advance to use to obtain peak performance.

At another location the relative air density might be 98%, so armed with the information in your diary you know that you should try the next larger size of main jet. Maybe it will be the correct size, maybe it will not. There are no hard and fast rules here; no two engines respond to air density changes exactly alike. Usually, small-displacement, high-rpm engines, in a high state of tune, are the most affected by a change in air density.

MANIFOLD AIR LEAKS

The mixture ratio is also affected if there are any air leaks, so you must be very careful to seal the manifold to the head, and the carburettor to the manifold, using the correct gasket and the right type of gasket cement. This may seem rather trivial but you would be amazed at the number of tuners who use Silastic to seal the manifold gasket. Silastic is excellent as an oil sealant but it is not petrol resistant, therefore it should not be used anywhere in the induction tract. I recommend the use of Permatex No 3 in this area.

Even when the manifold and carburettor have been correctly installed, this does not guarantee that you do not have an air leak, or that a leak will not start later on. I always check for leaks around the base of the carburettor and along the face of the manifold. The best method is to squirt petrol out of an oil can around the manifold face and carburettor with the engine running. If there is a leak, the engine will run rich or may even stop. If you use this method of leak detection, always have a fire extinguisher at hand. Usually there are no problems, but a backfire could start a serious fire with all that fuel running around.

Some types of carburettor have a tendency to loosen the screws that attach the body to the base. These should be regularly tightened, but do not use Loctite on them as this may cause the soft threads to strip.

Many engines loosen the manifold retaining bolts very quickly, so these should be Loctited. If the same bolts also retain the exhaust manifold, the Loctite will not work too well, so you should tighten them frequently. By paying careful attention to this, most induction air leaks can be avoided.

THROTTLE LINKAGE

When you are setting up the carburettors or fuel injection, spend some time sorting out a good throttle linkage. This is not usually a problem when a single carburettor is used, but with a multiple-unit set-up it is essential that the butterflies open together and that they remain synchronised right through to the full throttle position. If any of the throttle linkages are cranked, it is possible for the butterflies to break open simultaneously, but as full throttle is reached the throttle plates could be opened to differing angles.

While you are attending to the throttle linkage, you should also see that you are indeed getting full throttle. Ask someone to hold the pedal flat to the floor while you check that the butterflies are opening fully (be sure that the engine is not running!).

This old Nissan has been properly set up with an inline fuel filter and pressure regulator to keep fuel pressure limited to 4psi, thus ensuring that excessive pressure does not overfill the fuel bowls and upset metering. The throttle linkage has also been nicely arranged to help when delicate application is necessary.

FUEL PUMP AND FUEL LINE SELECTION

Earlier in this chapter we had a look at the fuel flow requirements of modified engines. As well as considering the flow through the needle and seat, we must also check that the fuel pump and fuel lines will flow the required quantity of fuel so that the fuel bowl remains full at sustained high rpm. If the bowl empties slightly, this will immediately lean the fuel/air mixture, reducing power and possibly causing damage to the pistons and valves.

Most fuel pumps are flow rated in gallons per hour (gph). At first glance it would seem very easy to match a given pump to a particular engine – if the engine requires 37gph of petrol at maximum power rpm, hook up a pump rated at 40gph.

Unfortunately there is a lot more involved than this. First, the output volume of the pump will drop off as you increase the restriction in the fuel lines and needle valve. Many pumps are rated 'free flow' without any inlet or outlet restriction. For instance, the big Holley 110gph electric pump will flow not 110gph but something closer to 65–70gph when used with 3/8in i/d fuel lines.

Whenever a liquid flows through a closed pipe there is bound to be a certain amount of restriction due to friction in the pipe, sharp corners and the needle and seat, and this causes a drop in pressure from one end of the pipe to the other. The pump may have an output pressure of 5psi, but at the other end of the pipe the pressure may read only 2psi due to restriction.

There is always some pressure loss between the fuel tank and the carburettor. 113

It does not matter whether you have the fuel pump mounted on the engine, drawing fuel from the tank at the rear of the car, or whether the pump is mounted near the tank at the back of the car, pushing fuel up to the engine. The pressure drop due to line restrictions is the same in both cases.

The pressure drop increases as the square of the volume of flow through the pipe, so if you double the gph flow the pressure loss would be multiplied four times. Conversely, the pressure drop is inversely proportional to the square of the internal diameter of the pipe. Thus if you were to use a pipe twice the diameter, a given gph flow rate would only have one-quarter the pressure loss. Obviously when large increases in an engine's fuel requirements have been made, larger-diameter fuel lines are in order.

A car's acceleration also effectively causes a flow restriction by tending to pull the fuel back to the tank; this can account for a 2–3psi pressure loss in a drag car.

In view of these factors, the fuel pump selected should be able to produce more than the gph flow requirement of the engine. I use a rule of thumb for a petrol-fired racing engine of 1.5 times the theoretical fuel flow requirement, or 0.08 times the maximum horsepower. Because a high-performance road engine is not usually held at sustained high rpm, the required flow is considerably less.

When selecting a pump, be sure that you know whether it is rated in Imperial or US gallons. If you live outside the US you will run into trouble if you calculate your fuel flow to be, say, 70gph and you fit a 70gph American pump. One US gallon is 0.8 of an Imperial gallon, so the American pump will actually flow 56 Imperial gph. (The above rule of thumb calculates the fuel flow requirement in Imperial gallons per hour when working from the maximum horsepower.)

Most high-flow American fuel pumps have a very high delivery pressure, which may cause English and European carburettors to flood. Holley carburettors are designed to operate at an idle speed pressure of 6–7psi, and 4.5psi at maximum speed. Weber carburettors should not have a delivery pressure (at the carburettor) of more than 4–4^1/2psi at idle, and the pressure at maximum speed should not be less than 3psi.

To regulate the pressure, you will have to use an in-line pressure regulator or a bypass line. Holley make a regulator for use with their high-pressure pumps, which pump at up to 15psi unregulated. The regulator must be fitted close to the carburettor, then adjusted according to the fuel pressure gauge reading at idle.

Some racers prefer to use a bypass line from the pump outlet back to the tank, to reduce the pressure. This system will work very well, but a lot of time can be spent finding what size of restriction plug should be fitted in the bypass line to get the required fuel pressure. I would recommend that you use a ^{1}/4in line and start your testing using a restrictor with a ^{1}/16in hole.

The front-mounted fuel pump is acceptable in most instances for engines in up to medium semi-race tune. Above this degree of modification an electric pump mounted near the fuel tank should be used.

The main weakness of using a front-mounted pump is that it aggravates vapour lock. A high-performance engine requires a lot of fuel so the line from the pump back to the tank will always be subjected to suction or a vacuum. This means that the fuel in the pipe is going to boil at a much lower temperature than it would if at normal atmospheric pressure. The only way around this is to use a rear-mounted electric pump.

In large displacement racing machines it is at times necessary to use two or three electric pumps. These must be connected in parallel, so that each has an inlet line running to the fuel tank. The outlet lines may be left separate until they reach the front of the car, or they may be connected to a single large-bore fuel line.

When installing an electric pump I recommend that a Holley safety switch be included in the electrical circuit, so that the pump will not work unless there is oil pressure. This not only ensures that the engine will not be flooded when it is switched off (a simple isolator switch will also do this), but more importantly, in a crash gallons of fuel could otherwise be pumped over everything before the pump was switched off, if an ordinary switch was used. With the ever-present risk of fire, this would be extremely dangerous.

The fuel line must be protected from possible mechanical damage for the same reason. Flying stones or abrasions between rubbing parts could puncture the line and allow fuel spillage. To avoid this, the line must be carefully routed, and sections exposed to stone damage must be shielded with suitable covering.

The line may also fracture because of vibration. To overcome this, a flexible section of line of sufficient length must be used to connect the fuel line to the engine and also the fuel tank. If an electric pump is used, flexible line must be used on the inlet and outlet as these pumps are subject to considerable vibration.

When routeing the line, be sure to keep it well away from the engine and the exhaust. This will ensure that the fuel remains cool. If the fuel is heated it will flash into vapour upon passing into the fuel bowl, creating an under-bonnet fire hazard and upsetting the carburettor fuel metering.

A fuel filter should be fitted in the system to remove dirt and water from the fuel. In racing applications it may be advisable to use two filters in parallel, to reduce flow restriction. A filter should never be fitted on the suction side of the fuel pump.

WEBER CARBURETTOR

Weber carburettors are known the world over as about the best that money can buy. However, many people do not realise that there are Webers and Webers. Some are simply metering devices for use on baby Fiats; others, such as the DCOE and IDA series, are racing carburettors that can be tuned to work very well, even on mildly modified street engines.

Many people feel that the Weber is difficult to tune; they never seem to be able to get it to work correctly. I would say that the Weber is one of the very easiest of carburettors to tune, and that it holds its tune even when subjected to severe banging on a rally car.

The Weber DCOE is a sidedraught unit available with throttle bore diameters of 40, 42, 45, 48 and 50mm. Because of the large range of venturis (commonly called 'chokes') available, these five basic carburettors can be tuned to suit any engine.

The downdraught Weber IDA is available in sizes of 40, 44, 46 and 48mm. It appears to be a DCOE turned up in the air, but really there is little similarity between the two types.

Table 4.7 indicates the carburettor size and choke size recommended for cylinders of various displacements. There will be exceptions to these recommendations but generally you will find them to be very close.

Table 4.7a   Weber carburettor and choke size for a four-cylinder engine with siamesed inlet ports

Cylinder displacement (cc)	Choke size (mm)				Recommended carburettor
	Sports	*Semi-race*	*Full-race* 7,000rpm	8,000rpm	
200	27	28	30	31	40 DCOE
250		31	32	34	42 DCOE
	28	32	33	35	40 DCOE
325	33	35			42 DCOE
	32	34	36	38	48 IDA or 45 DCOE
400	33	35	37	40	48 IDA or 45 DCOE
450	34	36	38	40	48 IDA or 45 DCOE
500	36	38	40		45 DCOE
			40	42	48 IDA or 48 DCOE

Table 4.7b   Weber carburettor and choke size for a four-cylinder engine with an inlet port per cylinder

Cylinder displacement (cc)	Choke size (mm)					Recommended carburettor
	Sports	*Semi-race*	*Full-race* 7,500rpm	8,500rpm	9,500rpm	
200				29	32	2 x 40 DCOE
250	27	28	29	32	34	2 x 40 DCOE
325	29	32	34	36		2 x 40 DCOE
				35	38	2 x 45 DCOE
400	32	34	36			2 x 40 IDA or 2 x 40 DCOE
			36	40	40	2 x 44 IDA or 2 x 45 DCOE
				40	42	2 x 48 DCOE
450	33	35	36			2 x 40 IDA or 2 x 40 DCOE
			37	40		2 x 45 DCOE
				40	42	2 x 48 DCOE
500	34	36	38	40		2 x 45 DCOE
			38	42	45	2 x 48 IDA or 2 x 48 DCOE
				42	45	2 x 50 DCOE
550	35	37	40			2 x 45 DCOE
	32	35	39	42	45	2 x 48 IDA or 2 x 48 DCOE
				42	45	2 x 50 DCOE
600	34	36	40	43		2 x 48 IDA or 2 x 48 DCOE

Table 4.7c   Weber carburettor and choke size for a six-cylinder engine with an inlet port per cylinder

Cylinder displacement (cc)		Choke size (mm)			Recommended carburettor
			Full-race		
	Sports	*Semi-race*	*6,500rpm*	*7,500rpm*	
330	27	29	30	32	3 x 40 DCOE
400	28	30	33	36	3 x 40 DCOE
450	30	31	34	37	3 x 45 DCOE
500	31	32	36	40	3 x 45 DCOE
				38	3 x 48 DCOE
600	33	34	38	40	3 x 45 DCOE
			37	40	3 x 48 DCOE
700	36	38	40		3 x 45 DCOE
	35	37	39	42	3 x 48 DCOE
800	36	38	42		3 x 48 DCOE

Table 4.7d   Weber carburettor and choke size for a V8 engine with an inlet port per cylinder

Cylinder displacement (cc)		Choke size (mm)				Recommended carburettor
				Full-race		
	Sports	*Semi-race*	*7,000rpm*	*8,000rpm*	*9,000rpm*	
500			38	39	42	4 x 48 DCOE or 4 x 48 IDA
	36	38	42	44		2 x 48 DCOE
600		36	38	40	43	4 x 48 DCOE or 4 x 48 IDA
	36	38	42	44		2 x 48 DCOE
700	36	38	42	44		4 x 48 DCOE or 4 x 48 IDA
	38	40	43	45		2 x 48 DCOE
800	38	42	44	45		4 x 48 DCOE or 4 x 48 IDA
	38	42	45			2 x 48 DCOE
900	40	42	45			4 x 48 DCOE or 4 x 48 IDA
	40	42	45			2 x 48 DCOE
1000	42	42	45			4 x 48 DCOE or 4 x 48 IDA
	40	42	45			2 x 48 DCOE

Note: the twin 48 DCOE set-up uses a Waneford cross-over manifold mounted on a single or two-plane manifold.

The auxiliary (also called the secondary or booster) venturi is located in the throat of the carburettor, in front of the main venturi (choke). The number stamped on this item indicates the size of the fuel spray hole that connects to the main fuel circuit. Usually, a 4.5mm auxiliary venturi is the correct size, but at times a 3.5 or 5mm may be needed. The influence of the flow passage size is felt more markedly at high rpm.   117

Table 4.8 Weber carburettor settings

Engine	Capacity (cc)	Tune	Carburettors	Choke	Main	Air	Emulsion	Pump	Pump bleed	Idle	Auxiliary venturi
Alfa Romeo T/C	1300	Sports	2 x 40 DCOE	29	110	200	F16	35	70	50F11	4.5
T/C	1600	Sports	2 x 40 DCOE	30	125	220	F16	35	50	50F11	4.5
Abarth T/C	1000	Full race	2 x 40 DCOE	33	135	250	F11	40	45	50F8	4.5
Austin	998	Sports	1 x 45 DCOE	32	130	165	F9	50	50	45F9	5.0
	1098	Sports	1 x 45 DCOE	32	140	180	F16	40	50	45F6	5.0
	1098	Full race	1 x 45 DCOE	37	180	200	F2	50	50	50F9	3.5
	1275	Sports	1 x 45 DCOE	34	130	175	F2	50	50	50F9	3.5
	1310	Full race	1 x 45 DCOE	40	195	200	F2	50	50	50F9	3.5
	1366	Full race	1 x 48 IDA	40	195	170	F2	50	closed	120 & 60F10	4.5
Austin Healey	3000	Full race	3 x 45 DCOE	34	130	160	F2	45	closed	50F2	3.5
	3000	Sports	3 x 45 DCOE	32	135	180	F2	45	closed	50F2	4.5
Avenger	1600	Full race	2 x 40 DCOE	34	130	170	F16	40	closed	45F8	4.5
	1800	Rally	2 x 40 DCOE	33	135	170	F15	40	closed	45F8	4.5
Aston Martin T/C	3670	Sports	3 x 45 DCOE	40	155	150	F2	55	closed	50F6	4.5
BMW ohc	2000	Sports	2 x 45 DCOE	38	125	170	F9	40	70	45F8	5.0
Chrysler Slant	3687	Sports	3 x 45 DCOE	36	145	150	F2	40	closed	50F8	3.5
	3687	Full race	3 x 45 DCOE	38	145	155	F2	40	closed	50F8	3.5
Chrysler Hemi 6	4342	Sports	3 x 45 DCOE	38	135	180	F2	50	closed	55F9	4.5
	4342	Semi-race	3 x 45 DCOE	40	145	180	F2	50	closed	55F9	4.5
Chevrolet	4949	Full race	4 x 48 DCOE	40	165	160	F2	50	closed	55F8	4.5
	5735	Semi-race	2 x 48 DCO	42	185	165	F2	60	closed	60F9	4.5
	6096	Full race	4 x 58 DCO	44	190	200	F15	55	closed	55F9	4.5
	5350	Sports	2 x 48 DCOE	38	170	185	F2	60	closed	60F8	4.5
	6490	Semi-race	4 x 48 IDA	42	160	140	F7	50	closed	100 & 65F10	4.5
Coventry Climax	2495	Full race	2 x 58 DCO	47	190	200	F15	55	closed	70F6	4.5
Chevette T/C 4V	2279	Rally	2 x 48 DCOE	42	170	190	F2	50	closed	55F9	4.5
Ford	997	Full race	2 x 40 DCOE	33	125	175	F16	35	closed	40F9	4.5
	1594	Semi-race	2 x 40 DCOE	33	125	170	F16	40	closed	45F9	4.5
	1762	Semi-race	2 x 45 DCOE	34	135	175	F16	40	closed	45F9	4.5
x	1298	Semi-race	2 x 40 DCOE	32	125	180	F16	40	closed	45F9	4.5

T/C	1594	Sports	2 x 40 DCOE	33	120	160	F11	40	closed	45F8	4.5
T/C	1594	Full race	2 x 45 DCOE	39	170	180	F9	45	closed	50F8	4.5
T/C	1720	Semi-race	2 x 42 DCOE	34	135	170	F15	40	closed	45F8	4.5
T/C 4V	1977	Rally	2 x 48 DCOE	42	180	175	F9	50	closed	50F9	4.5
ohc	1993	Sports	2 x 45 DCOE	34	135	170	F16	45	closed	45F9	4.5
T/C 4V	1298	Full race	2 x 45 DCOE	37	140	165	F16	40	closed	45F9	4.5
	4949	Semi-race	2 x 48 DCOE	38	165	150	F2	60	closed	60F9	4.5
	5752	Semi-race	2 x 48 DCOE	42	190	155	F2	60	closed	60F9	4.5
	5752	Full race	4 x 48 IDA	43	170	180	F2	55	closed	120 & 55F10	4.5
	4736	Sports	2 x 48 DCOE	36	155	175	F2	55	closed	60F8	4.5
Hillman ohc	998	Rally	2 x 40 DCOE	32	120	180	F11	35	closed	45F9	4.5
	1725	Sports	2 x 40 DCOE	33	135	170	F15	40	closed	45F8	4.5
Jaguar T/C	4200	Sports	3 x 45 DCOE	38	165	190	F2	40	closed	65F8	3.5
MG	1800	Sports	1 x 45 DCOE	34	145	165	F2	50	50	50F9	3.5
	1800	Full race	1 x 45 DCOE	36	165	160	F16	60	50	50F9	5.0
Nissan	1300	Semi-race	2 x 40 DCOE	30	115	160	F16	40	closed	45F6	4.5
ohc	1600	Sports	2 x 40 DCOE	33	135	160	F15	40	closed	50F8	4.5
ohc	1800	Rally	2 x 45 DCOE	34	145	170	F15	40	closed	50F8	4.5
T/C 4V	2200	Rally	2 x 48 DCOE	40	165	180	F15	50	closed	55F9	4.5
Porsche ohc	2000	Sports	2 x 40 IDA	30	125	180	F26	50	closed	55	4.5
ohc	2000	Semi-race	2 x 40 IDA	32	130	180	F3	50	closed	55	4.5
ohc	2800	Full race	2 x 46 IDA	42	170	145	F24	50	closed	70	4.5
Renault x	1255	Semi-race	2 x 40 DCOE	32	125	200	F15	35	40	45F8	4.5
x	1296	Rally	2 x 40 DCOE	34	125	160	F15	40	closed	45F8	4.5
Triumph	2500	Semi-race	3 x 45 DCOE	33	130	175	F15	40	closed	45F9	4.5
	2188	Sports	2 x 45 DCOE	34	140	150	F15	50	closed	50F8	4.5
4V	1998	Full race	2 x 48 DCOE	40	165	175	F15	50	closed	50F9	4.5
Volvo	2198	Full race	2 x 45 DCOE	35	155	170	F15	50	closed	50F8	4.5
VW	2180	Full race	2 x 48 IDA	40	155	150	F2	50	50	120 & 55F10	4.5
	1850	Semi-race	2 x 44 IDA	35	145	170	F11	45	closed	100 & 50F10	4.5
	1750	Sports	2 x 40 IDA	32	120	160	F11	40	closed	100 & 50F10	4.5

Note: Rally tune indicates an engine tuned for club tarmac rallies.

T/C = Twin-cam, T/C 4V = Twin-cam four-valve, 4V = ohc four-valve, x = push rod crossflow

WEBER MAIN JET

In Weber carburettors the main jet, emulsion tube and air corrector jet are pressed together to form a single assembly. The individual parts may be separated using a pair of pliers, but never grip the emulsion tube with pliers as it may be damaged.

The main jet is pressed into the bottom of the emulsion tube. It is stamped with a number indicating its nominal bore diameter (eg a 175 jet has a 1.75mm bore).

As a starting point, the main jet size can be selected by multiplying the size of the main venturi by 3.9 to 4.3 (eg a 32mm choke will usually have a main jet size of 125 to 135). However, on certain competition engines this rule of thumb can be way off the mark. If you check Table 4.8 you will see that this is usually in the case of racing engines with siamesed inlet ports. In this instance the multiplying factor is 4.6 to 5.0.

The air corrector (or air bleed) jet is pressed into the top of the emulsion tube. Air corrector jets from 1.50 to 2.00mm are more commonly used. By increasing the diameter of this jet the fuel mixture is weakened more at high rpm than at lower rpm. A change in the size of the main jet changes the mixture strength uniformly at both high and low rpm.

With DCOE carburettors, the air corrector jet will usually be 0.30 to 0.50mm larger than the main jet size, eg with a 125 main jet try a 155 to 175 air corrector. In general, road engines will use the larger jets and racing engines the smaller jets.

Engines using IDA carburettors will generally require an air corrector jet around the same size as the main jet. Racing vehicles may need jets 0.20mm, and at times up to 0.50mm, smaller than the main jet.

The emulsion tube emulsifies the fuel previously metered by the main jet. It affects engine performance more at small throttle opening angles and during acceleration.

The fuel well into which the emulsion tube fits in the carburettor is of a fixed size, but the tubes themselves are available with a large variety of air holes and in varying diameters. The F2 and F15 tubes have the same number, size and disposition of holes, but the tubes are of a different diameter.

The amount of fuel available to be drawn into the air stream is governed by the diameter of the emulsion tube and the air hole pattern. This is why the emulsion tube has such an effect on throttle response and mid-range running.

Once we have selected main and air corrector jets to meet the engine's high rpm fuel requirements, we have to set about finding an emulsion tube of the correct diameter, and with suitable air drillings, to satisfy the engine's mid-range fuel needs: a rich tube is one that is thin and with just a row of air holes at the top, while a lean tube is thicker, with holes all the way down. For most applications F2, F15 and F16 tubes are used; F11, F9 and F7 tubes are used in a smaller number of applications.

For the majority of engines with DCOE carburettors using chokes smaller than 36mm, and one barrel per cylinder, either F16 or F15 tubes will be correct. Engines with larger chokes (36–40mm) and using DCOE carburettors with one barrel per cylinder usually require an F2 emulsion tube. Engines with siamesed inlet ports or four-cylinder engines using one DCOE carburettor generally use an F2 tube; however, some may need an F9. When IDA carburettors are fitted, an F2 or F7 will be correct in

the majority of applications.

WEBER ACCELERATOR PUMP JET

As in every carburettor, the accelerator pump circuit in the Weber supplies a shot of fuel to assist in smooth, no-lag acceleration. Additionally, this circuit also serves as a power circuit to supply additional fuel at high speeds.

The size of the pump jet and the pump bleed jet (or exhaust jet), and the length of the pump rod all affect the amount of fuel supplied during acceleration. The size of the pump jet alone determines the fuel metering when the pump circuit serves as a high-speed power circuit. Therefore the pump jet size is selected to supply the correct fuel/air mixture for high-speed operation.

Once the correct pump jet has been chosen, you have to determine if the mixture is too rich or lean during acceleration. If too much fuel is supplied, it may be necessary to use an open pump bleed jet, which is situated in the bottom of the fuel bowl, under the float(s). Usually a closed jet (ie one without a bleed hole) is used in semi-race and racing motors. However, if the mixture is too rich during acceleration, a pump bleed jet will be required. These are available with a bleed hole from 0.35 to 1.5mm. If a bleed jet is required, usually a 40, 45 or 50 will be the correct size. To remove or replace this jet you will need a special screwdriver with a 'screw-grip' attachment.

The length of the pump rod governs the amount of fuel in the pump well; the longer the rod, the bigger the shot of fuel available. Rods of varying lengths are available for the DCOE model carburettor, but with the IDA the pump stroke can be shortened by the use of a collar.

The promptness of fuel delivery is controlled partly by the bleed jet and partly by the strength of the pump spring. A closed bleed jet and a strong spring give a quick shot of fuel of short duration. If a weaker spring is used, there will still be a quick initial delivery of fuel, but the duration of the delivery will be longer. The use of an open bleed jet delays the delivery of the fuel, and reduces the amount delivered.

Seldom is it necessary to change either the length of the pump rod or the strength of the pump spring. However, at times I have found it advantageous to use a strong spring and a 59.5mm rod when a single 45 DCOE is used on the 1300 Mini Cooper 'S' and 1800 MG 'B' engines.

WEBER IDLE JET

Both the DCOE and IDA model carburettors have an idle jet assembly that meters fuel and air into the idle circuit. When the correct jet has been chosen, the mixture adjustment screw should be 1/4 to 1 1/4 turns open to obtain the correct idle mixture.

In DCOE carburettors the idle jet has a fuel hole and an air bleed hole. The fuel hole size is the first number stamped on the jet, eg if the jet is a 45 F9, the fuel hole is 0.45mm; F9 is a code referring to the air bleed hole size. Table 4.9 sets out the 'F' code, from rich to lean. Some jets have two air bleed holes, but this has been taken into consideration when working out the table.

All IDA idle jets are coded F10. The F10 jet does not have an air bleed hole; instead air correction is handled by the idle jet holder. The 1,366cc Mini, for example, uses a 60 F10 idle jet and a 120 jet holder. This indicates that the jet holder has a 1.20mm air bleed. A 100 or 120 jet holder is used in the majority of applications. A larger air bleed hole leans the idle mixture.

Table 4.9   Weber idle jet air bleed characteristics

Air bleed code

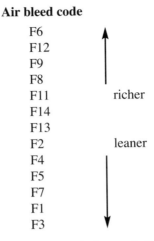

F6	
F12	
F9	
F8	
F11	richer
F14	
F13	
F2	leaner
F4	
F5	
F7	
F1	
F3	

Note: F10 idle jet has no air bleed hole and is for use in IDA carburettors only.

Table 4.10   Weber idle jet fuel hole selection

Cylinder displacement (cc)	Fuel jet size
200	35
250	40
325	45
400	45–50
450	50
500	50
550	55–60
600	55–60
700	65–70
800	70–75
900	75
1000	80

Note: where two cylinders share one carburettor barrel, or where the engine has siamesed inlet ports, the idle jet size should be increased one size larger than indicated. Engines with wild camshafts may require jets two sizes larger due to poor fuel distribution at low rpm when two cylinders share one carburettor barrel.

To determine the approximately correct idle jet refer to Table 4.10, which sets out the sizes of the fuel metering holes. If, for example, the cylinder capacity is 400cc, you will require a 50 F8 or 50 F9 jet with which to begin testing. I have arbitrarily selected an F8 or F9 air bleed hole in this instance as either size is correct in 80% of cases; the other 20% use an F2 or F6 air bleed.

If you were using an IDA carburettor you would select a 50 F10 idle jet in the above example, and you would use either a 100 or 120 jet holder.

After having made your idle jet selection, start the engine and bring it up to normal operating temperature (at this time the float level should have been correctly adjusted). Then carefully adjust the idle mixture and idle speed screws to get the smoothest idle. Remember that if the correct idle jets have been selected, the mixture screws should be 1/4–1 1/4 turns open.

When the mixture has been adjusted, open the throttle to bring the idle speed up to 2,000–2,500rpm (at this speed the main circuit should not be discharging fuel). If the engine is too lean it will be backfiring or popping through the carburettors. On the other hand, if it is too rich it will be backfiring through the exhaust. If you have access to an exhaust gas analyser, the fuel/air ratio should be 1:11.5 or 12.5 (note that many analysers read the other way around to give the air/fuel ratio, ie 11.5 or 12.5:1).

The starting jets in Webers I never worry about as I have never found it necessary to use the choke to get a Weberised engine started, even when the car has been covered in snow. A few pumps on the accelerator to operate the accelerator pump is all that is required.

Usually, you have more trouble starting a Weber-equipped engine when it is hot, due to flooding. If it will not start first hit, slowly push the accelerator right to the floor and turn the motor over until it starts. In most cases the engine will start on the first or second try, but keep the accelerator pedal down until it does. If you pump the pedal you will end up with a real problem.

DCOE FLOAT LEVEL ADJUSTMENT

The float level adjustment is critical on all carburettors and especially so on sidedraught Webers, as engine vibration can cause fuel frothing and flooding. Webers have an additional adjustment to ensure that the float drops enough to open the needle valve completely when fuel demand is high.

Figure 4.11 Weber DCOE float levelling.

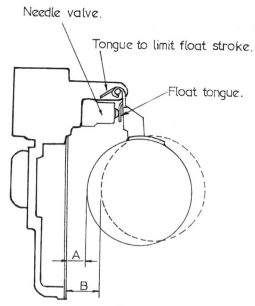

To adjust the float level and float stroke on the DCOE it is necessary to remove the top of the carburettor. The jet inspection cover also has to be removed before the top becomes free. Take care not to damage the floats as they are very delicate, being made of sheet 0.16–0.20mm thick; do not blow them with compressed air.

With the top removed, ensure that the needle valve is tightly screwed into its housing and check that the spring-loaded ball incorporated in the valve is not jammed.

When checking the float level, hold the carburettor top in the vertical position (as shown in Figure 4.11) and, with the float tongue just contacting the spring-loaded needle ball, check the distance between both floats and the carburettor top gasket (measurement A). If the float level is not correct, push out the float pivot pin and remove the float, then carefully bend the float tongue to obtain the correct dimension.

After the float level has been checked and adjusted, hold the float fully open and measure the float stroke (measurement B). If the stroke requires adjustment, bend the tongue to increase or decrease the stroke.

To measure the distances A and B, Weber make a special float gauge, but as these are often difficult to obtain I have made my own set of gauges out of steel or aluminium bar. The gauge should be about 8 inches long, dimension A thick and dimension B wide. Be sure to machine four grooves in the bar (two in each of two faces) so that the gauge clears the soldered joining band of the float halves. Without these clearance grooves you will not be able to adjust the float accurately as you will be measuring between the soldered join and the carburettor top gasket, rather than between the floats proper and the gasket.

The actual measurements A and B will vary from one application to another, depending primarily on the angle at which the carburettor is mounted. Weber DCOE carburettors are designed to be mounted at 0–5° from horizontal, and usually at that angle dimension A is 8.5mm and dimension B 15mm.

In some applications the manifold manufacturer finds it necessary to change the mounting angle, so that the carburettor will clear some part of the body or exhaust system. When this is done, a special float level setting is required. The manifold manufacturer should tell you what setting is required when you buy his manifold.

The majority of Austin Mini manifolds have the Weber mounted at an angle of 7–7 1/2°; in this instance dimension A is 7mm and dimension B 15mm. Some cars (eg Aston Martin DB4, Alfa Romeo 2600) use a high float level with dimension A 5mm and B 13.5mm.

IDA FLOAT LEVEL ADJUSTMENT

To check the float level of IDA model carburettors you will need to make a set of gauges or use Weber gauges Nos 9620.175.1839, 9620.175.1840 and 9620.175.2411 and spring No 9620.175.1329.

Referring to Figure 4.12, the check is carried out as follows:

- Remove the carburettor top and the gasket and insert the spring (No 9620.175.1329) between the float and the side of the bowl.
- Position gauge No 9620.175.1840 on the carburettor body and manipulate the float so that the tongue just contacts the tip of the gauge. (Note that the gauge must first be adjusted to 24.2mm as shown.)

- With the float in this position check using gauge No 9620.175.1839 that the float is 5.5–6mm above the carburettor body. Ensure that the gasket is removed when this is being checked. Should the level be incorrect, bend the float tongue to obtain the correct level.
- Finally, using gauge No 9620.175.2411 check that the needle valve ball is 25mm from the surface of the carburettor top. When carrying out this check, the top must be inverted and the needle valve ball must not be depressed.

Cars equipped with three-barrel IDA, IDAP, IDL, IDS, IDT and IDTP model carburettors have a float level adjustment very similar to the two-barrel IDA. The main change is that gauge No 9620.175.1840 is adjusted to 18mm and that a different float level gauge (No 9620.175.2849 instead of No 9620.175.1839) is used so that the float level is 12.5–13mm. On Lamborghini Miura cars equipped with IDL carburettors, float level gauge No 9620.175.3071 is used, and in this case the float level is 14–14.5mm. All of these three-barrel carburettors have a needle-ball-to-carburettor-top dimension of 18mm.

Figure 3.12 Weber IDA float levelling.

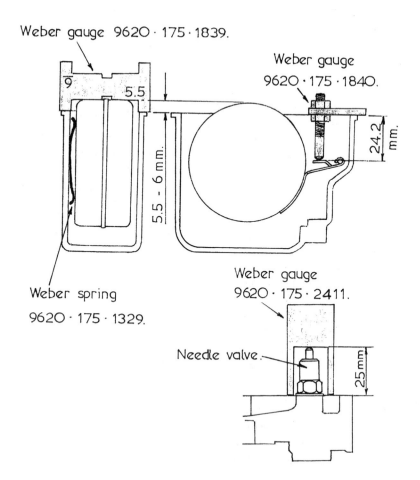

HOW TO MOUNT ON INLET MANIFOLD

There are just a few points to keep in mind when Weber carburettors are fitted. First, I would suggest that you obtain a copy of the *Weber Technical Introduction* 2nd edition (or later) and follow very carefully their installation instructions. Pay careful attention to what they have to say about throttle linkage arrangements so that all the butterflies open together.

DCOE carburettors must never be mounted solidly, but must always have a neoprene insulator block or a light alloy plate with an 'O' ring in both faces fitted between the carburettor and the manifold. This is necessary to reduce carburettor vibration, which causes fuel frothing, flooding and inaccurate metering.

When tightening the carburettor mounting bolts, ensure that they are tensioned just enough to effect a good seal, but not enough to squash the 'O' rings or insulator block. Self-locking nuts and, if possible, light double-wound spring washers should be used, as fitted on the Twin Cam Ford Escort; these are designed to be tightened until there is a gap of 0.040in between the coils.

Various screws on some model Webers are safety wired, and those parts must always be re-wired whenever the wire is removed or broken. The wire is there for a very good reason, for if a screw were to drop out, the engine would stop or run badly. For example, the IDA has the float pivot pin wired; if the pin falls out, the engine floods. The 45 and 48 DCOE have safety-wired grub screws that hold the auxiliary venturis in place. If a screw comes out, the auxiliary venturi can rotate and cut off fuel to the discharge nozzle.

TUNING WEBER CARBURETTORS

Before attempting to tune and synchronise the carburettors, the ignition timing, spark plugs, points and float level, etc, should have been adjusted. Check that the carburettor choke control levers are all back against their stops, then bring the engine up to normal operating temperature and switch off. Carefully screw in each idle mixture adjusting screw until it just contacts its seat, then unscrew it three-quarters of a turn. (If you find that you need more or less than three-quarters of a turn to get your engine running, adjust all the mixture screws by the same amount.)

Synchronising the throttle plates in the majority of twin DCOE applications is very easy when an interconnector linkage, as fitted to the Twin Cam Lotus Fords, four-cylinder Alfa Romeos, Renault Gordinis, etc, is used. In these instances start the engine and turn in the idle speed screw until the idle speed reaches 1200rpm (it may be higher if a lumpy cam is used). For the actual synchronisation of the throttle plates you will need either a carburettor synchroniser or a length of quarter-inch rubber hose and a good ear.

Press the synchroniser over one throat of the carburettor (check the carburettor with the idle speed adjusting screw first), then turn the synchroniser ring so that the indicator float dwells at mid-height in the indicating column. Move the synchroniser to the next carburettor and turn the interconnector linkage screw in or out so that the float again dwells at mid-height.

The second carburettor can also be synchronised with the first by listening to the intensity of the hiss of the first carburettor, then adjusting the other to produce a hiss of equal intensity.

After synchronisation, screw out the idle speed screw slightly to reduce the idle speed to 800–1,000rpm.

At this point it may be necessary to slightly adjust each mixture screw to obtain the smoothest idle. It should not be necessary to adjust any screw more than one-eighth of a turn, either in or out.

On other installations, where throttle control rods operate the carburettor shafts, a similar tuning procedure to that outlined is used. However, in this instance the throttle control rods should generally all be disconnected and each carburettor must be synchronised to the first carburettor, using the idle speed adjustment screw fitted to each one. After the throttles have been synchronised, reconnect and adjust the length of each throttle control rod, then back off all of the idle speed screws and adjust the speed screw on the first carburettor to give the desired idle speed. Now carefully screw in all of the other idle speed screws so that they just contact the throttle stop lug on the throttle lever. To complete the job it may be necessary to adjust each mixture screw to smooth out the idle.

Some Weber models incorporate an adjustable idle air bleed passage to equalise the idle air flow in every barrel. These carburettors can be identified by the idle air bleed screw with lock nut located on the opposite side of the barrel from the idle mixture screw on some IDA models, and located close to the accelerator pump jet on some DCOE models.

Before accurate synchronisation of these models is possible, the air bleed lock nuts must be slackened and the air bleed screws very carefully screwed in until seated. Be careful not to use too much pressure or the seats could be damaged.

With the air bleeds closed, the butterflies of the carburettors can be synchronised as outlined earlier, using a carburettor synchroniser. When this is being carried out ensure that the idle speed is 1,200–1,500rpm. Once the throttle plates are synchronised, the idle speed should be reduced to normal (800–1,000rpm). Then use the carburettor synchroniser to find which barrel causes the float indicator to rise the highest in the tube and adjust the air bleed screws on all the barrels, by screwing them out, to cause the float to rise to the same level. While this is being done, it will usually be necessary to lower the idle speed, as the engine will tend to speed up. When the float rises to the same level on every barrel, the air compensation is correct and the lock nuts should be tightened.

After the carburettors have been synchronised, it will be necessary to determine if the main and air corrector jets, and the pump jets, are correct. This check is best done on the dyno, but follow up with a road or track test to confirm that the correct jets have been chosen. It is not possible to accurately determine the accelerator pump metering on the dyno, so this will have to be checked on the road.

When the most suitable jets are fitted, there should be no hesitation during acceleration or when the throttle is suddenly flattened, nor should there be any black smoke (indicating richness) from the exhaust. After a run at sustained high rpm, the spark plugs should be checked against the indications in Table 3.4.

SU CARBURETTORS

The SU constant depression carburettor has been around for many years and it still has something to offer those interested in better performance. It is a very simple carburettor, but one that can be exceedingly difficult to tune with precision.

The majority of SU carburettors are type H and type HS. A few of the type HD 'diaphragm' carburettors are still around but these are used only in 1³/4 and 2in sizes. The type H and HD can be identified by having a solidly mounted float chamber, while the HS has an external nylon tube connecting the float chamber to the jet. Table 4.11 indicates the throttle bore diameters of these models.

Table 4.11   SU carburettor types

Type	Throttle bore (in)
H2, HS2	1¹/4
H4, HS4	1¹/2
H6, HS6, HD6	1³/4
H8, HD8	2

In Table 4.12 I have outlined the size of carburettor recommended for various engine displacements. You will note that the SU must always be connected to at least two cylinders, otherwise its constant vacuum principles of operation are upset.

SU carburettors are supplied with either a 0.090, 0.100 or 0.125in jet. These rarely need to be changed except for methanol, when 0.187 or 0.250 jets may be necessary.

The volume of fuel introduced into the air stream is controlled by the taper of the needle; needles are made to suit 0.090, 0.100 and 0.125 jets, and there are approximately 300 different needles listed for 0.090 jets alone. When the 0.1870 or 0.250 alcohol jets are fitted, needles intended for use with 0.125 jets may be used, although at times these will be too rich at lower rpm. In this instance you will have to make your own needles from ¹/8in bronze welding wire.

Table 4.13 lists just a few 0.090 jet needles. The numbers refer to the diameter of the needle at 12 or 13 different points along its length, commencing at the shoulder at the top of the needle and then continuing every one-eighth of an inch.

Table 4.12   Recommended SU carburettor sizes

Displacement (cc)	Tune	
Four-cylinder engine	*Sports*	*Semi or full race*
850	2 x 1¹/4in	2 x 1¹/4in
1,000	2 x 1¹/4in	2 x 1¹/2in
1,300	2 x 1¹/4in	2 x 1¹/2in
1,600	2 x 1¹/2in	2 x 1³/4in
1,800	2 x 1³/4in	2 x 1³/4in
2,000	2 x 1³/4in	2 x 2in
2,200 plus	2 x 2in	2 x 2in
Six-cylinder engine	*Sports*	*Semi or full race*
2,000	2 x 1³/4in or 3 x 1¹/2in	3 x 1¹/2in
2,500	2 x 2in or 3 x 1¹/2in	3 x 1³/4in
3,000	2 x 2in or 3 x 1³/4in	3 x 2in
3,500 plus	2 x 2in or 3 x 2in	3 x 2in

Table 4.13   SU carburettor needles

MME	CZ	BC	3	H4
0.089	0.089	0.089	0.089	0.089
0.085	0.085	0 085	0.085	0.085
0.0813	0.0827	0.0815	0.0814	0.081
0.078	0.0806	0.0782	0.0785	0.0778
0.074	0.0785	0.0745	0.0765	0.076
0.0707	0.0745	0.0695	0.0744	0.0741
0.0673	0.0727	0.0647	0.0723	0.072
0.0636	0.071	0.060	0.0703	0.0702
0.060	0.0693	0.0557	0.0683	0.0683
0.0563	0.0675	0.0515	0.0661	0.0663
0.053	0.0657	0.0474	0.064	0.064
0.0495	0.064	0.043	0.063	0.062
0.046	0.0625	0.039	0.062	

There are no rules to determine which needle to try first; about all that you can do is refer to the listing I have given in Table 4.14 (and any other lists you can find) and choose a needle for an engine that is similar to yours. After that, it is a matter of testing to find at what point the needle is rich or lean. Then you will have to consult the complete SU needle tables and find a needle that is richer or leaner at the point where you want it to be.

When going from a weak needle to a richer one, it is better to try one about 0.002 thinner at a time, but when changing from a rich needle to a weaker one try a needle 0.001 thicker, unless there are signs of excessive richness.

PISTON SPRING AND DASHPOT OIL

The mixture strength is also controlled to a degree by the carburettor piston spring and the type of oil in the dashpot. I have seen all grades of oil used in SU carburettors, but for best results I recommend the use of automatic transmission fluid. Unfortunately, the dashpot seldom remains full for long, so check the level frequently as a low level will result in hesitation or spit back when accelerating, due to a lean mixture condition.

The correct oil level for carburettors with a vent hole in the damper piston is 1/2in above the top of the hollow carburettor piston rod. Carburettors with a non-vented damper cap should be filled to 1/2in below the carburettor piston rod.

The effect of the oil (and the spring) is to slow down the rate of rise of the carburettor piston and so momentarily enrich the mixture immediately following a snap opening of the throttle. This serves the same purpose as an accelerator pump.

Piston springs are identified by a colour code painted on the end coils. The range for carburettors up to and including the 13/4in SU is: 21/2oz blue, 41/2oz red, 8oz yellow and 12oz green. The correct strength of spring is one that allows the piston to reach its maximum lift at maximum power rpm. This is assuming that carburettors of the correct size are being used.

Table 4.14   SU tuning specification

Engine		Displacement (cc)	Tune	Carb	Needle	Spring
Austin		997	sports	2 x 1¼in	GZ	Red
		998	sports	2 x 1¼in	GY	Blue
		970	sports	2 x 1¼in	AN	Red
		1070	sports	2 x 1¼in	H6	Red
		1275	sports	2 x 1¼in	M	Red
		970	full-race	2 x 1½in	CP4	Blue
		1070	full-race	2 x 1½in	MME	Blue
		1275	full-race	2 x 1½in	BG	Blue
		1098	sports	2 x 1½in	AM	Blue
		998	semi-race	2 x 1¼in	M	Blue
Austin Healey		2912	full-race	3 x 2in	UH	Blue/Black
		2912	sports	3 x 2in	UH	Red/Green
		2912	sports	3 x 1¾in	BC	Green
		2912	sports	2 x 1¾in	CV	Yellow
Ford		997	sports	2 x 1¼in	A5	Blue
		1198	sports	2 x 1¼in	H6	Red
		1500	sports	2 x 1½in	CZ	Red
		2553	sports	3 x 1½in	3	Red
		2553	sports	3 x 1¼in	ES	Red
		2553	sports	2 x 1½in	7	Yellow
		997	full-race	2 x 1½in	AM	Blue
Hillman	ohc	875	sports	2 x 1¼in	H4	Blue
		1600	sports	2 x 1½in	QA	Red
Jaguar	T/C	3441	sports	2 x 1¾in	TL	Red
	T/C	3781	sports	2 x 1¾in	TU	Red
	T/C	3781	sports	3 x 2in	UM	Blue/Black
	T/C	4235	sports	3 x 2in	UM	Blue/Black
	T/C	3441	sports	3 x 2in	UE	Blue/Black
MG	T/C	1588	sports	2 x 1¾in	OA6	Red
		1800	sports	2 x 1½in	MB	Red
		1800	full-race	2 x 2in	UVD	Blue/Black
		1098	sports	2 x 1¼in	AN	Blue
		1800	semi-race	2 x 1¾in	KP	Red
Triumph		1147	sports	2 x 1¼in	MO	Red
		1147	full-race	2 x 1½in	DB	Blue

Normally a red spring is used, but if the carburettors are the sizes recommended in Table 4.12 for semi- and full-race engines, a blue spring may be required. Conversely, if a pair of carburettors are fitted to a six-cylinder engine, or if carburettors smaller than indicated are used (eg 2 x 1½in on a 2,000cc four-cylinder), a stronger yellow or green spring will probably be required, to allow for a richer acceleration.

FLOAT CHAMBER AND FLOAT LEVEL

Float chambers are made in three sizes as indicated in Table 4.15. When the carburettor is mounted at an angle (do not exceed 30°) it is necessary to machine the attachment lug to keep the chamber vertical at all times.

Table 4.15   SU float level settings

H and HD series carburettors

T1 float chamber (1^7/$_8$in diameter) – use ^{7}/$_{16}$in test bar.
T2 float chamber (2^1/$_4$in diameter) – use ^{7}/$_{16}$in test bar.
T3 float chamber (3in diameter) – use ^{5}/$_8$in test bar.

HS series carburettors

Brass float – use ^{5}/$_{16}$in test bar.
Nylon float – use ^{1}/$_8$–^{3}/$_{16}$in test bar.
Delrin needle and new type float – use ^{1}/$_8$–^{3}/$_{16}$in test bar.

Whenever SU carburettors are used on high-performance vehicles, the float chamber must always be mounted ahead of the carburettor so that the fuel does not surge away from the jet when accelerating.

The float level should be checked using the appropriate size test bar shown in Table 4.15. With the float chamber lid inverted, and the hinged float lever resting on the needle, it should be possible to slide the test bar between the radius of the hinged lever and the chamber lid lip.

The procedure is a little different on the later model HS series carburettors, which have the float attached to the lid. With the lid inverted and the needle valve held in the closed position by the weight of the float only, it should be possible to slide a ^{1}/$_8$–^{3}/$_{16}$in test bar between the float lever and the rim of the lid.

SU CHECKING AND ADJUSTMENTS

Before attempting to tune and synchronise SU carburettors, several checks are in order, but be very careful not to mismatch any parts from one carburettor to another when these checks are being carried out.

Attempt to wriggle the throttle shaft. If there is more than minimal play, new bearings and shaft will be required, as the carburettor will suck air here and make it impossible to synchronise the butterflies or adjust the idle.

Next, mark the relative location of the suction chamber with the main body of the carburettor, then remove the fixing screws and carefully lift off the chamber. (If you drop or dent the chamber, it could be ruined.) Then lift the piston from the body, taking care not to bend the needle.

When removed, check that the needle is not bent or worn on any side (this indicates that the jet is not centred). Make sure that the shoulder of the needle is flush with the bottom of the piston. If it is not, you will not be able to get the mixture strength right. Now determine that the needle locking screw is tight.

Using clean petrol (or a non-oily solvent), thoroughly clean the piston   131

SU carburettors work well if handled carefully to avoid denting the suction chamber, and if the jet is correctly centralised so that the needle doesn't jam.

(particularly the surface that bears on the wall of the suction chamber) and the inside of the suction chamber. Never use any abrasive or metal polish on these parts.

After being cleaned the piston and suction chamber may be refitted to the carburettor body, but do not oil the inside of the suction chamber or the piston bearing surface – these should remain dry. Be sure to line up the mark that you put on the carburettor body and fully tighten the retaining screws.

Next, lift the piston about one-quarter of an inch and let it drop. There should be a definite click as it hits the carburettor bridge. If it does not click, the jet is not central and is binding on the needle. (Note that this check must be done with the jet screwed into the fully up position. Be sure that the piston is fully raised when the jet is being screwed up.)

To centralise the jet you must slacken the jet locking nut, then insert a thin screwdriver or a pencil through the damper hole in the top of the carburettor and hold the piston down firmly. Re-tighten the jet locking nut while you hold the jet up hard against the adjusting nut. Finally, check that the piston falls freely and that it clicks as it hits the bridge.

After these checks have been carried out, the carburettors are ready to be tuned and synchronised. First bring the engine up to normal operating temperature, then loosen the clamps connecting the carburettor shafts together and back off the idle speed screws such that they just contact the stops when the throttles are fully closed. Next, turn in each idle speed screw three-quarters of a turn to open the throttle plates.

Screw all the jets fully up, then turn each jet adjusting nut down two complete turns. If the choke is connected to more than one carburettor, be sure to loosen the choke connecting clamps before adjusting the jets.

SU TUNING

Now re-start the engine and, using the carburettor synchroniser, adjust all of the idle speed screws in turn, to raise the indicator float to mid-height in the indicator column (see the Weber tuning section above for more information). Re-tighten the throttle shaft interconnecting clamps.

Turn the jet adjusting nuts the same amount on all carburettors, either up to weaken the mixture or down to enrich it, until the fastest idle speed consistent with even running is obtained. Then re-adjust the idle speed screws to give the correct idle speed.

Check for the correct mixture by gently pushing up the piston lifting pin of the front carburettor $1/32$in (after the free travel has been taken up). If the mixture is lean, the engine speed will drop or the engine may even stop. If rich, the engine will speed up and hold that speed. When the mixture is correct, the engine may speed up for just an instant then slow down to just about normal.

Repeat this operation on all the other carburettors, then check again as they are all interdependent, being connected via the manifold balance pipe.

With the throttle plates synchronised and the mixture adjusted, you can check the suitability of the needles fitted. Table 4.16 indicates which segments control which part of the mixture range. You will note that in the smaller carburettors the tip of the needle does not affect the fuel metering; eg with the $1^1/4$in SU the last four segments do not do any metering.

Table 4.16   SU needle metering range

Carburettor		Metering Segments	
Size	*Idle*	*Acceleration and cruising*	*Top speed*
$1^1/4$in	1st, 2nd	3rd, 4th, 5th, 6th	7th, 8th, 9th
$1^1/2$in	1st, 2nd	3rd, 4th, 5th, 6th	7th, 8th, 9th, 10th
$1^3/4$in	1st, 2nd, 3rd	4th, 5th, 6th, 7th	8th, 9th, 10th, 11th
2in	1st, 2nd, 3rd	4th, 5th, 6th, 7th, 8th	9th, 10th, 11th, 12th

HOLLEY CARBURETTORS

A single four-barrel Holley is the simplest performance set-up, from the aspect of carburation, for any V6 or V8 engine. Unless class regulations require the use of a two-barrel carburettor, forget about using the two-barrel Holley on any V8.

The triple two-barrel arrangement used on some of the V8 muscle cars a few decades ago is also a waste of time. A good four-barrel will work better and it is no trouble to tune. The triple two-barrel system is all 'pose', nothing else.

Some enthusiasts like a pair of four-barrel Holleys mounted on a low-profile ram manifold for hot street cars. This is a very nice set-up if you can sort out the grave fuel distribution problems usually associated with manifolds of this design.

Table 4.17 lists the Holley carburettors recommended for engines in varying states of tune. Generally, the engines referred to are fitted in the lightest bodies available, eg the Chevy motors listed are tuned for use in Nova, Camaro or Corvette   133

Table 4.17 Holley carburettor recommendations

Engine	Cubic in	Tune	Manifold type	Carb No	Size CFM
Buick	455	sports	Edelbrock B-4BQJ	R-6979	600
		semi-race	as above	R-4780*	800
	231 V6	semi-race	Offenhauser Dual Port	R-1849	550
Chevrolet	200-229 V6	sports	Holley Street Dominator	O-9694	450
	283-305	sports	Edelbrock Performer	R-6979	600
		semi-race	as above	R-4776*	600
	327-350	sports	Edelbrock Performer or Torker	R-6979	600
		semi-race	as above	R-4778*	700
		semi-race	Edelbrock Victor Jr	R-4778*	700
		full-race	Edelbrock Victor 4 + 4	R-4780*	800
		sports	Holley Street Dominator	R-1850	600
	396-427	sports	Edelbrock Torker	R-6979	600
		semi-race	as above	R-4781*	850
		semi-race	Edelbrock Victor Jr 2R	O-4781	850
		full-race	Edelbrock Victor 2R	R-4781*	850
				or R-4575*	1050
Chrysler	340-360	sports	Edelbrock Torker or Performer	R-7009	600
		semi-race	as above	R-3310	780
		full-race	Holley Strip Dominator	R-4778*	700
	413-440	sports	Edelbrock Torker	R-7009	600
		semi-race	as above	R-4779*	750
		full-race	as above	R-4780*	800
Ford	170 V6	sports	Offenhauser Dual Port	R-6299	390
	289-302W	sports	Holley Street Dominator	R-1850	600
		semi-race	as above	R-4777*	650
	351W	sports	Holley Street Dominator	R-1850	600
		semi-race	as above	R-4777*	650
	351C	sports	Edelbrock Torker	R-7010	780
		semi-race	as above	R-6709*	750
		full-race	Holley Strip Dominator	R-4781*	850
	390-428	sports	Holley Street Dominator	R-6919	600
		semi-race	as above	R-3310	780
	429-460	semi-race	Edelbrock Torker	O-3310	780
		full race	as above	O-4780	800
Oldsmobile	400-455	sports	Edelbrock Torker	R-3310	780
Pontiac	400-455	sports	Edelbrock Torker	R-3310	780
		semi-race	as above	R-4780*	800

*Indicates double-pumper carburettor.

bodies. Engines in semi-race tune would use four-speed manual transmission and a 3.5:1 rear axle.

When you fit your Holley you will usually find the 'out of the box' jetting to be reasonably close to what you want for a road machine. Even on fairly wild racing engines the jetting should be such that you will be able to get the engine running. Once the engine is working, you can decide what to do to get the jetting right.

There are two basic series of Holley main jets. Those with the prefix 122 followed by the jet size number are the standard jets that have been with us for years. With these jets there is a tolerance of 3% flow difference between jets of the same number. From one size of jet to the next there is an average flow increase or decrease of 4.5%.

A development by Holley has seen the introduction of a close-limit series of jets. These were developed primarily for pollution control carburettors, but they are very useful for fine-tuning performance engines. These jets also have the prefix 122 followed by the jet size number, but following the jet number is a suffix, indicating the jets' flow variation from standard. For example, a 662 jet is a size 66 jet flowing within 1.5% of standard, ie 0.75% on the rich or lean side of standard. A 663 jet is a 66 jet flowing up to a maximum of 1.5% more than a 662 jet, while a 661 is a lean 66 jet flowing up to 1.5% less than a 662 jet. Therefore there is a maximum of a 1.5% flow difference between any two jets with the same jet number and the same jet suffix.

These jets are available from Holley in sizes 35 to 74, so if you have a carburettor fitted with the ordinary jets in this size range it would be well worth the trouble to replace them with a set of close-limit jets. At this time only standard jets with a 2 suffix are available, although jets with a 1, 2 or 3 suffix are being fitted to new pollution carburettors at the factory.

All Holley jets are flow rated, but for the benefit of those who may wish to use some exotic fuel blend, I have included Table 4.18 so that you have a means of comparing one jet size with another.

Table 4.18 Holley main jet nominal bore size

Jet No	Drill size (in)	Jet No	Drill size (in)	Jet No	Drill size (in)
40	0.040	41	0.041	42	0.042
43	0.043	44	0.044	45	0.045
46	0.046	47	0.047	48	0.048
49	0.048	50	0.049	51	0.050
52	0.052	53	0.052	54	0.053
55	0.054	56	0.055	57	0.056
58	0.057	59	0.058	60	0.060
61	0.060	62	0.061	63	0.062
64	0.064	65	0.065	66	0.066
67	0.068	68	0.069	69	0.070
70	0.073	71	0.076	72	0.079
73	0.079	74	0.081	75	0.082
76	0.084	77	0.086	78	0.089
79	0.091	80	0.093	81	0.093
82	0.093	83	0.094	84	0.099
85	0.100	86	0.101	87	0.103
88	0.104	89	0.104	90	0.104
91	0.105	92	0.105	93	0.105
94	0.108	95	0.118	96	0.118
97	0.125	98	0.125	99	0.125
100	0.128				

Here a pair of Holleys have been mounted on a tunnel ram manifold. This helps top-end hp but hurts output lower down.

All Holley model 4160 and 4175 carburettors have a metering plate with drilled restrictions rather than removable main jets for fuel control in the secondary half of the carburettor. These metering plates also have idle feed restrictions, so they are identified by a code number. Unfortunately this number is just a code and does not relate to the size of the main or idle feed hole. Table 4.19 indicates the code number stamped on the plate and also the main system and idle hole diameters. For example, plate number 10 has a 0.076in main hole and a 0.026in idle hole.

The main air bleeds are a fixed size and therefore cannot be altered except by re-drilling to a different size. This is not recommended as it is virtually impossible to drill all four bleeds to exactly the same size.

HOLLEY POWER VALVE

Holley carburettors employ the power enrichment system mentioned earlier, illustrated in Figure 4.3. Many tuners mistakenly believe that this system is a waste of time, so they remove the power valve and fit a plug made by Holley for this purpose. I guess some even feel that as Holley makc a plug to stop up the power valve hole, they must propose the removal of the valve in high-performance or racing applications. This could not be further from the truth.

Holley make the plug specifically for those engaged in road racing and circle track racing. In such applications the G forces generated are high enough to move fuel away from the power valve inlet, so air can enter and lean the mixture dangerously. When the secondary power valve is removed, the main jet size must be increased to compensate for the lost fuel flow area of the power valve restriction. Usually, an increase of 4 to 8 numbers in main jet size is about right.

When the power valve is removed, fuel will flood through the main jets and out of the discharge nozzles during braking. In fact, this can be such a problem, even when

Table 4.19   Holley secondary metering plates – metering restrictions

Plate No No	Main feed (in)	Idle feed (in)	Plate No No	Main feed (in)	Idle feed (in)
7	0.052	0.026	34	0.052	0.029
3	0.055	0.026	4	0.059	0.026
32	0.059	0.029	40	0.059	0.035
5	0.063	0.026	18	0.064	0.028
30	0.064	0.029	13	0.064	0.031
33	0.064	0.043	8	0.067	0.026
23	0.067	0.028	16	0.067	0.029
9	0.067	0.031	36	0.067	0.035
6	0.070	0.026	19	0.070	0.028
20	0.070	0.031	41	0.070	0.053
35	0.071	0.029	39	0.073	0.029
37	0.073	0.031	17	0.073	0.040
10	0.076	0.026	22	0.076	0.028
43	0.076	0.029	12	0.076	0.031
3	0.076	0.035	28	0.076	0.040
38	0.078	0.029	11	0.079	0.031
24	0.079	0.035	44	0.081	0.029
21	0.081	0.040	31	0.081	0.052
29	0.081	0.063	46	0.082	0.031
25	0.086	0.043	5	0.089	0.037
27	0.089	0.040	26	0.089	0.043
4	0.093	0.040	15	0.094	0.070
45	0.096	0.040	14	0.098	0.070
42	0.113	0.026	5792	0.059 and 0.076	0.076
10–3	0.063 and 0.073	0.070	5790	0.070 and 0.073	0.070
6221	0.078 and 0.082	0.040	6217	0.089 and 0.093	0.040
4482	0.094 and 0.099	0.070			

the power valve is in place and standard size main jets are used, that some road racers drill out the power valve channel restriction so that smaller main jets can be fitted to reduce the tendency to flood under braking. This is just one problem associated with the use of Holley carburettors on a road racer, which is why I stay well clear of them in this type of application and use Webers instead.

As you can see in Figure 4.3, the power valve does not control the volume of fuel entering the main system; this is done by the size of the power valve channel restriction. If you decide to change the size of this restriction, proceed very carefully in steps of 0.002in. Carburettors using the four- and six-hole power valves should not have the two restriction holes increased to more than 0.062in. The newer window-type power valves can be used with larger restriction holes, but do not exceed 0.090in. The number 125–1 power valve is a special high-flow type, suitable for two restriction holes of up to 0.122in.

The power valve is really a vacuum-operated switch, designed to open and allow extra fuel into the main system when the manifold vacuum drops to a predetermined   137 figure. The vacuum at which the valve opens can be determined by the valve suffix number. For example, all the standard window-type valves have a prefix 125, followed by a suffix number from 25 to 105, in increments of 10. A valve with the number 125–45 will open when the manifold vacuum drops to 4.5 inches of Hg, while a valve numbered 125–105 will open at a vacuum of 10.5 inches of Hg.

Holley also make two-stage power valves, but these should not be used in carburettors fitted to performance vehicles.

To determine what size of power valve you need in the primary side of the carburettor you will have to carry out a series of tests with a vacuum gauge and accurately record the results.

If the engine is fitted with a wild cam, you should note the manifold vacuum at idle. If the gauge reads 6 inches of Hg at idle, you will have to install a 45 (4.5 inches of Hg) power valve so that the valve is not open all of the time; the valve should always open at a lower vacuum pressure than the vacuum at idle.

If the engine has an idle vacuum of more than 10 inches of Hg, the vacuum should be checked when the accelerator is floored, as during an overtaking manoeuvre. Note the lowest vacuum reading then fit a valve that opens at a vacuum 1 to 1.5 inches higher. If the vacuum is a minimum of 7 inches of Hg, use power valve number 85, which will open when the vacuum falls to 8.5 inches.

As a double check to ensure that you have selected the correct power valve, keep an eye on the vacuum gauge for a few days when you are climbing long hills at close to full throttle. If the gauge regularly reads, say, 7–8 inches of Hg, your 85 power valve will provide the needed enrichment in this circumstance. However, if the vacuum stays fairly close to 8–9 inches, you will have to replace the 85 valve with a 95.

If you are involved in drag racing you should check the vacuum during the run, and particularly as you approach the traps at the end. If the valve closes towards the end of the run you could very easily hole a piston because of the resulting lean mixture condition. For example, if the manifold vacuum through the traps is 4 inches of Hg, a 55 or 65 valve should be fitted, but keep in mind that the valve must be closed at idle, as in the first example.

Carburettors with power valves on the secondaries are normally fitted with a valve that opens at a manifold vacuum 2 inches lower than the primary valve. Therefore if the primary valve is an 85, a 65 will be used in the secondary. There are exceptions to this general rule. Holley calibrate a small number of their carburettors with the same number primary and secondary valve or even with a primary valve of a lower number than that of the secondary valve.

HOLLEY ACCELERATOR PUMP

When it comes to tuning the accelerator pump on the Holley there are a number of factors to consider. First, Holley offer two different pumps. The standard pump is a 3cc (or 30cc per 10 shots) unit. They also have available an optional 5cc (50cc per 10 shots) pump, which is fitted as standard on the secondaries of all their double-pumper mechanical secondary carburettors. The 5cc pump should be used in all semi- and full-race applications.

Two other components, the pump cam and the discharge nozzle, actually regulate the pump delivery. The total lift of the cam controls the pump stroke, and the profile of the cam affects the phasing of the pump.

The pump cam can be attached in two positions. In the more usual No 2 position it provides a greater initial delivery of fuel and less final volume; the No 1 position gives a moderate initial delivery and more final volume.

The shape of the pump cam is of little importance in drag racing providing that a cam giving a sufficiently long pump stroke is used. However, on the road or racing circuit the shape of the cam has a great effect on throttle responsiveness. A sharp-nose cam gives a quick pump action while a cam with a more gentle shape delivers a slower action.

Holley pump cams are colour coded. Table 4.20 indicates which cam supplies the most fuel (rich cam) and which supplies the least, in both the No 1 and No 2 positions. In most instances the richest cam supplies about double the volume of fuel of the leanest cam.

Table 4.20   Holley accelerator pump cams

	No 2 position	No 1 position
↑	black	white
	white	blue
leaner	red	red
	blue	orange
richer	orange	black
	green	green
↓	pink	pink
		brown

Note: this chart considers only the volume of fuel delivered, not delivery promptness or duration.

The accelerator pump discharges through the discharge nozzle (shooter), which is available in a number of sizes. The number stamped on the nozzle indicates the bore size in thousandths of an inch, ie a 28 nozzle has a 0.028in discharge hole.

A small discharge nozzle lengthens the delivery duration, while a large nozzle provides a larger initial volume of fuel. Therefore a car fitted with a large motor in relation to its weight and a numerically large axle ratio will need a large discharge nozzle.

When it comes to tuning, find which nozzle gives the crispest throttle response, then try the different cams to see if the response can be improved. If a better cam is found, go through the discharge nozzles a second time to be sure that you have found the combination that will give the best performance.

There are a couple of important points to keep an eye on when working with the Holley accelerator pump. First, the pump over-ride spring must never be adjusted so that it is coil-bound. The spring must always be compressible to avoid damage to the pump or pump diaphragm. Also, be sure to check that there is no clearance between the pump actuating lever and the pump cam. Just changing the idle speed can move the cam away from the lever, which will delay the discharge of fuel from the pump. When you re-adjust the pump lever adjusting screw to make contact with the cam, be sure to check that at wide-open throttle the diaphragm lever can travel an additional 0.015–0.020in by inserting a feeler gauge between the lever and the adjusting screw.

HOLLEY VACUUM SECONDARIES

Holleys with vacuum-operated secondary barrels should not be changed over to mechanical operation. Some people feel that this must improve performance because all of the racing Holleys have mechanically opened secondary throttles, but remember that these are double-pumper carburettors and the secondary pump is able to prevent a lean condition when the secondaries are blasted open.

Other people like the 'kick in the pants' feel that you usually get when you change from vacuum control to mechanical. What you are actually feeling is a flat spot followed by a surge of power as the fuel supply catches up with the air flow into the motor.

To allow you to 'tune in' the secondary opening and the rate of opening, Holley provide a selection of diaphragm springs. A light spring will allow the secondaries to open sooner and more quickly than a heavy spring. A light car with a large powerful motor will use a lighter spring than a heavier car with the same motor and rear axle ratio. Table 4.21 indicates the range of springs available. Most Holleys have a green, purple or red spring fitted at the factory.

Table 4.21   Holley vacuum secondary springs

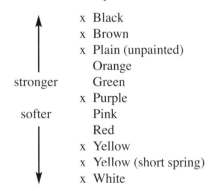

Note: springs marked 'x' are supplied in Holley spring kit No 20–13.

The way to find which spring will give the best performance is to time your acceleration from about 3,000–3,500rpm to maximum engine speed. Obviously the optimum spring is the one that shows the quickest time. To reduce the number of variables to a minimum, carry out the test in top gear and over the same stretch of road.

As mentioned earlier, there is no other modification that you should do to 'improve' the secondary throttle operation. Change the springs by all means, but leave everything else alone.

At times, vacuum-operated secondary throttles can be slow or sticky in operation, due to the accumulation of gum and carbon on the throttle shaft. Regularly, and before you attempt any tuning, you must hold the primary wide open and manually open the secondaries. No stiffness should be encountered and the secondaries should close smoothly, unassisted.

If, after you have manually opened and closed the secondaries several times, resistance is still present, you can be reasonably certain that the binding is due to incorrect or uneven tightening of the carburettor base nuts. This can be a problem when a phenolic heat insulator is used between the carburettor and the manifold. The insulator is necessary to isolate engine heat from the carburettor, but take care to tighten each nut a little at a time so that the carb base tightens down evenly, without distortion. The use of thick or multiple-base gaskets is to be avoided as this can lead to base distortion and shaft binding.

HOLLEY IDLE METERING

The idle metering system on Holleys is non-adjustable, except for the mixture screw. There are pressed-in brass air bleeds in the air horn and fuel flow restrictors in the metering blocks. The only way around the problem is drilling the air bleeds (to lean the mixture) or the idle feed restriction (to richen the mixture). This is definitely not a job for the average enthusiast.

In the majority of road applications no changes to the idle system metering will be necessary, but racing engines will require some change. If you do not have the patience or skill to attempt this very fine work, find someone who can do the modifications, or be prepared to spend a lot of money on ruined metering blocks.

If you find that the engine will not idle, first ensure that there is not something else wrong. Air leaks, loose screws, incorrect float or fuel level, etc, will all cause you some problem and distort the picture. Only after you have thoroughly checked everything should you modify the carburettor in any way.

Keep an accurate and complete record of every move you make from this point. Remove the carburettor from the manifold and, with the throttle lever held against the stop (first wind the screw back to the factory setting), measure the throttle-plate-to-throttle-bore clearance in both primary bores, using a feeler gauge.

Refit the carburettor and start the engine. Note how many turns you have to give the idle speed screw to keep the engine running, then attempt to adjust the mixture screws to improve the idle. (It is important that you first lightly seat both screws, then turn them out an equal amount.) If turning both screws an equal amount does not seem to improve the idle, record that fact.

If you haven't already checked the idle vacuum and fitted a power valve that will stay closed at idle, do so now, and check the idle after the change.

Remove the carburettor if there is little or no improvement and turn it upside down. Then measure how much of the transfer slot is visible above the throttle plate. If there is more than 0.040in visible, drill a 1/16in hole in each throttle plate (primary side only) about midway between the throttle shaft and the edge of the throttle plate. (Drill the hole on the same side of the plate as the transfer slot.)

Some Holleys already have throttle plate holes from the factory so in this instance it will be necessary to enlarge the holes by the equivalent of a 1/16in hole in area; ie if the standard hole is 1/16, increase the hole size to 0.088in (or 3/32in closest equivalent).

Before refitting the carburettor, adjust the idle speed screw to obtain the factory-set clearance between the throttle plate and throttle bore (this is the first measurement you recorded).

Refit the carburettor and start the engine. If after adjusting the mixture the idle speed is right, the holes are of the correct size. If it is too slow, larger holes are required, or if too fast, solder over the holes and redrill them a smaller size.

When you are sure that the throttle plate holes are the correct size, check how much change occurs to the idle speed by turning out the mixture screws to richen the mixture. (Note that on some Holleys you turn the screw *in* to enrich the mixture.) If the engine speed drops and the engine runs rough, the idle feed restriction in the metering block is the correct size.

However, if the mixture screws appear to have little or no control of the idle mixture richness, the idle feed restriction hole will have to be enlarged until turning the mixture screws causes the engine to run rough. The idle feed restriction hole should be enlarged only in steps of 0.002in, using numbered wire drills and a pin vice.

Once the mixture screws have some control of the idle mixture, very slowly turn the idle speed screw to bring the engine speed up to about 3,000rpm, or below the point where the main system comes into operation. Be certain to increase the engine speed very slowly so that fuel will not issue from the accelerator pump and cover up the lean mixture for which we are looking.

If the engine beat becomes splashy, or it seems to stumble as the speed is increased, a lean mixture condition is indicated. Try to correct this by turning out the mixture screws. If the screws have to be backed out more than half a turn from the mixture setting previously established, you will have to continue opening out the idle feed restriction holes by 0.002in at a time until there is no miss up to 3,000rpm.

Once the mixture is correct up to 3,000rpm with no load, you are ready to test the engine at a light load. Accelerate the car as slowly as possible from 15 to 35mph in the highest gear in which it will run without excessive transmission snatch. If it surges, the mixture is lean. As a cross-check, hold the car on a very light throttle at a steady 20mph, then a steady 25mph, and so on up to 35mph, in the highest gear possible, for half a mile at each speed on a smooth and level road. If the engine tends to surge, try turning the mixture screw out half a turn. If more than half a turn is required to fix the problem, then it is back to increasing the idle feed restriction hole size in 0.002in steps to enrich the idle mixture.

When you are carrying out all of the idle mixture testing and light-load running you will have to use fairly warm spark plugs to avoid false results from fuel-fouled plugs.

HOLLEY FUEL SYSTEM

Three types of fuel bowls are used on the four-barrel Holley carburettors. Most high-performance models use a dual inlet, centre-pivot float, with external float level adjustment. This type of float and bowl is best suited to road circuit and speedway racing where high cornering forces are involved.

Many models use the side-hung float and bowl, with external float level adjustment; usually this design is preferred for drag racing. The other type also uses a side-hung float, but it does not have an external float level adjustment. Instead, the float level is set by bending the tongue contacting the needle valve until the proper clearance is obtained between the float and the top inside edge of the bowl (this varies with different models). This measurement must be taken with the bowl inverted so that the weight of the float closes the needle valve.

The bowls with externally adjustable floats have a sight plug in both the primary and secondary fuel bowls. With the plugs removed, fuel should just be visible along the bottom of the threads when the engine is running. The level is adjusted by loosening the external needle valve lock nut and turning the assembly up or down until the fuel level is correct. If the engine idle is very rough, the idle speed will have to be increased when this adjustment is being executed, otherwise the rocking of the engine could give a false fuel level.

As Holley carburettors are used mainly on large-displacement engines requiring a high fuel flow, needle valves with sufficient flow capacity must always be used. In Table 4.22 I have set out the approximate flow capabilities of the various Holley needle valve assemblies.

Table 4.22   Holley needle valves – fuel flow

Valve diameter (in)	Fuel flow at 4psi (lb/hr)	Fuel flow at 6psi (lb/hr)
0.082	155	205
0.097	175	225
0.101	195	255
0.110	230	275
x0.110	235	295
x0.120	240	305
x0.130	244	310

Note: needle valves marked 'x' have discharge windows, while the smaller sizes have
     discharge holes.

Holley market a couple of special devices to aid in fuel control within the float bowl. Some models already incorporate these 'fixes' direct from the factory, but if your particular carburettor does not have them fitted, you should fit them for improved performance.

A vent 'whistle' (Part No 26–40) should be used in the primary fuel bowl to prevent fuel sloshing into the vent and upsetting the mixture during severe acceleration. The vent whistle extends the bowl vent path over and above the fuel, to provide continuous venting of the primary bowl.

Main jet slosh tubes (Part No 26–21) are used in the secondary main jets for racing and very-high-performance engines. On maximum acceleration, fuel moves to the rear of the bowl and away from the secondary main jets. When slosh tubes are fitted, fuel starvation is eliminated.

Some Holley carburettor models have stuffers fitted in the float bowls and metering blocks to reduce the fuel bowl capacity. This is purely an emission device that should be removed when these models are used on modified engines. Serious fuel starvation will result if the stuffers are left in place.

When it comes to bolting up a new Holley on your manifold there are few problems that you are likely to encounter. However, before you slam the hood closed after fitting the new carburettor, ensure that there is sufficient clearance between the hood and the carburettor. Also check that the accelerator pump lever is not fouling the manifold. When the 50cc pump is used, it is often necessary to use a 1/4in spacer to raise the carburettor. Lastly, ask someone to hold the accelerator pedal flat while you check that the throttle plates are opening fully.

MIKUNI CARBURETTORS

In the world of motorcycles the Mikuni carburettor reigns the present king. Other carburettors are able to equal or even surpass the Mikuni in certain respects, but overall the Mikuni has much to offer those interested in a good power range and ease of tuning.

Most Japanese motorcycles leave the factory fitted with Mikuni constant velocity (CV) type carburettors, which work on the same principle as the SU carby. These carburettors are used to reduce exhaust emissions and improve fuel economy. However, they do stifle high rpm breathing and it is very difficult to obtain suitable needles and jets to tune them. Hence it is often advisable to replace these carburettors with slide-type Mikunis on modified engines. However, do not fall into the trap of replacing a CV carburettor with a slide-type of the same size or you will have a badly over-carburated engine. CV carburettors flow considerably less air than slide-throttle carburettors, so in general slide-type Mikunis approximately 4–6mm smaller will be required for road engines. Table 4.23 indicates the sizes required for radically modified engines.

Table 4.23   Recommended slide-type Mikuni carburettor sizes

Cylinder displacement (cc)	Recommended carburettor size (mm)			
	Semi-race		*Full-race*	
		8,500rpm	*10,500rpm*	*12,500rpm*
125–150	24			26
175–200	28		29	31
225–250	32		34	36
275–300	34		36	
325–350	34	36	38	
375–425	36	38		
500–650	35	37		

Mikunis use two types of main jets. The hex-head jets are flow-rated in cc per minute, and jets from size 50 to 195 are available in steps of 5, and size 200 to 500 in steps of 10. The round-head main jets are aperture-sized; the largest jet available is a 250, with an aperture size of 2.50mm.

The needle jet uses a code to identify its size. The first number indicates the jet series; eg a 159 series jet fits a 30–36mm spigot mount Mikuni (Table 4.24). The letter–number combination below the series number shows the fuel hole size. The letter denotes the size in increments of 0.05mm and the number signifies size increments of 0.01mm; eg a P-4 jet would have a hole size of 2.670mm. There is one exception to this: the size –5 needle jet is 0.005mm larger than the –4 jet (Table 4.25).

The needles are identified by a code such as 6DP5. The first number indicates the needle series, while the following letter(s) indicate the needle taper. If there is one

Table 4.24   Mikuni needle jet application

Series No	Type	Main jet	Sizes available	Carb type
159	P	Hex	O-O to R-8	30–36mm spigot
166	P	Hex	O-O to R-8	38mm spigot
171	P	Hex	O-O to Q-8	30mm flange
176	B	Hex	N-O to Q-8	30–36mm spigot
183	B	Hex	N-O to Q-8	38mm spigot
188	P	Hex	O-O to Q-8	32mm flange
193	P	Hex	N-O to Q-8	24mm flange
196	P	Round	O-O to Q-8	30–36mm spigot
205	P	Hex	O-O to Q-8	34mm flange
211	P	Hex	N-O to Q-8	30–36mm spigot

Note: 'P'-type needle jets are intended for use primarily in two-stroke piston port engines. 'B'-type needle jets have bleed holes and are normally used in four-stroke and rotary-valve two-stroke engines.

Table 4.25   Mikuni needle jet sizes

Size	Diameter (mm)	Size	Diameter (mm)	Size	Diameter (mm)
N-0	2.550	N-2	2.560	N-4	2.570
N-5	2.575	N-6	2.580	N-8	2.590
O-0	2.600	O-2	2.610	O-4	2.620
O-5	2.625	O-6	2.630	O-8	2.640
P-0	2.650	P-2	2.660	P-4	2.670
P-5	2.675	P-6	2.680	P-8	2.690
Q-0	2.700	Q-2	2.710	Q-4	2.720
Q-5	2.725	Q-6	2.730	Q-8	2.740
R-0	2.750	R-2	2.760	R-4	2.770
R-5	2.775	R-6	2.780	R-8	2.790

letter, the taper is uniform along the length of the needle, but if there are two letters, this indicates that the taper changes midway along the tapered section; the first letter indicates the upper taper and the second letter the lower taper. Starting with the letter A, which indicates 15 minutes of arc, each letter in sequence denotes an additional 15 minutes to the angle between the two sides of the needle. Therefore a DP taper has an angle of 1°0" on the top and 4°0" on the bottom taper.

The number after the letters is a manufacturing code that indicates how far down the needle the taper starts. For example, needles marked 6DP1 and 6DP5 have the same taper, but 6DP1 is the richer needle as the taper starts 28.9mm from the top of the needle, whereas the taper begins 32.1mm down with the 6DP5. Table 4.26 indicates the dimensions of the more common Mikuni needles. A final number, separated by a dash or in parentheses, indicates the circlip groove position, counting the top groove as number 1 (eg 6DP5-3).

Table 4.26a   Mikuni series 6 needles
To fit all 30–38mm spigot-mount carburettors

Needle	X	Y	10	20	30	40	50	60
6H1	62.3	37.5	2.510	2.510	2.510	2.412	2.041	1.696
6DH2	62.3	28.0	2.511	2.511	2.466	2.295	2.000	1.660
6F9	62.3	28.9	2.516	2.516	2.475	2.210	1.949	1.678
6CF1	61.5	29.5	2.512	2.512	2.429	2.240	1.974	1.710
6FJ6	62.3	35.2	2.505	2.505	2.505	2.376	2.040	1.606
6DH3	62.3	22.0	2.512	2.512	2.458	2.286	1.948	1.607
6J3	62.3	36.7	2.515	2.515	2.515	2.359	1.912	1.456
6L1	62.3	37.0	2.512	2.512	2.512	2.335	1.826	1.313
6DP5	62.3	32.1	2.518	2.518	2.518	2.372	1.834	1.141
6N1	62.3	37.0	2.514	2.514	2.514	2.278	1.672	1.058
6DP1	62.3	28.9	2.511	2.511	2.476	2.312	1.748	1.075
6F3	60.5	34.2	2.512	2.512	2.512	2.313	2.050	
6DH4	62.3	25.5	2.520	2.520	2.440	2.258	1.915	1.575
6J1	64.0	36.2	2.517	2.517	2.517	2.339	1.919	1.495
6DH7	62.2	28.5	2.516	2.516	2.505	2.316	2.009	1.688

Note: X is the overall length of the needle in mm.

Y is the dimension from the top of the needle to the start of the taper.

The numbers 10–60 indicate the needle diameter in mm at points 10–60mm respectively from the top of the needle.

Table 4.26b   Mikuni series 6 needles
To fit all 30–38mm spigot-mount carburettors

Needle	X	Y	Z	10	20	30	40	50	60
6F5	62.3	38.1	19.0	2.515	2.456	2.454	2.364	2.098	1.840
6F4	62.3	32.0	19.4	2.515	2.442	2.436	2.206	1.939	1.678
6F8	62.3	34.0	21.5	2.512	2.512	2.386	2.214	1.945	1.688
6FJ11	62.3	36.0	18.7	2.519	2.481	2.481	2.367	2.030	1.610
6F16	59.1	36.7	18.5	2.519	2.489	2.489	2.372	2.104	
6DH21	52.3	30.1	16.5	2.515	2.470	2.465	2.328	2.024	
6F16	64.6	31.2	18.4	2.520	2.404	2.400	2.201	1.941	1.679

Note: X is the overall length of the needle in mm.

Y is the dimension from the top of the needle to the start of the taper.

Z is the dimension in mm from the top of the needle to the pronounced taper point.

The numbers 10–60 indicate the needle diameter in mm at points 10–60mm respectively from the top of the needle.

Table 4.26c   Mikuni series 5 needles
To fit all 26–32mm spigot-mount and all 28–34mm flange-mount carburettors

Needle	X	Y	10	20	30	40	50	60
5D6	59.3	27.5	2.515	2.515	2.460	2.290	2.120	
5FJ9	59.2	35.0	2.517	2.517	2.517	2.364	2.021	
5D120	59.1	28.2	2.520	2.520	2.479	2.311	1.980	
5F3	58.0	27.4	2.519	2.519	2.419	2.135	1.863	
5EH7	57.6	28.5	2.517	2.517	2.473	2.210	1.848	
5E13	57.5	29.5	2.515	2.515	2.484	2.197	1.803	
5EJ13	57.8	26.5	2.519	2.519	2.431	2.210	1.766	
5DL13	60.2	32.0	2.515	2.515	2.515	2.362	1.922	1.463
5EJ11	60.3	28.5	2.515	2.515	2.515	2.241	1.839	1.420
5EL9	60.3	27.0	2.517	2.517	2.441	2.221	1.780	1.248
5FL11	60.3	28.2	2.518	2.518	2.438	2.175	1.740	1.256
5EP8	60.2	33.0	2.513	2.513	2.513	2.245	1.780	1.120
5FL14	58.0	28.0	2.520	2.520	2.440	2.170	1.735	
5FL7	58.0	28.0	2.518	2.518	2.440	2.170	1.735	
5DP7	57.6	26.4	2.512	2.512	2.440	2.259	1.580	
5J6	58.0	27.5	2.518	2.518	2.340	1.890	1.450	
5L1	58.0	27.0	2.518	2.518	2.330	1.811	1.297	
5C4	55.1	24.0	2.516	2.516	2.448	2.310	2.179	
5F18	58.0	27.0	2.521	2.521	2.515	2.257	2.006	
5J9	58.0	27.0	2.522	2.520	2.432	1.996	1.505	
5F12	51.5	23.3	2.021	2.021	1.882	1.631	1.375	
5D1	53.5	27.6	2.510	2.510	2.496	2.338	2.169	
5DP2	60.3	32.4	2.515	2.514	2.513	2.418	2.067	1.418
514	60.0	27.0	2.514	2.509	2.442	2.071	1.690	1.332
5D5	57.6	30.0	2.513	2.513	2.510	2.366	2.205	

Table 4.26d   Mikuni series 4 needles
To fit all 18mm carburettors and 22 and 24mm flange-mount carburettors

Needle	X	Y	10	20	30	40	50
4D3	50.3	25.3	2.511	2.511	2.421	2.253	2.100
4D8	50.3	22.8	2.519	2.519	2.381	2.211	2.000
4E1	50.3	28.0	2.515	2.515	2.345	2.127	1.924
4DG6	50.3	24.0	2.518	2.518	2.405	2.119	1.850
4DH7	50.3	23.0	2.518	2.518	2.386	2.098	1.790
4F15	50.3	26.5	2.512	2.512	2.400	2.120	1.881
4J13	50.2	24.0	2.513	2.513	2.230	1.800	1.400
4L6	50.3	24.5	2.515	2.515	2.178	1.660	1.190
4F6	50.5	25.3	2.514	2.514	2.406	2.145	1.876
4L13	45.1	25.0	2.518	2.516	2.339	1.842	
4F10	50.2	24.5	2.513	2.513	2.385	2.135	1.877
4J11	41.5	21.3	2.512	2.506	2.188	1.776	
4P3	50.5	25.0	2.510	2.506	2.436	2.284	2.122

The throttle slide cutaway size is indicated by the number stamped on the slide, eg 2.5 signifies a 2.5mm cutaway. The cutaway affects off-idle acceleration up to half-throttle. A large cutaway leans the mixture and a smaller cutaway enriches the mixture.

The idle jet (or pilot jet) is available in sizes 15 to 80 in steps of 5. Fine adjustment of the idle mixture is by means of the idle air screw, which enriches the idle mixture when turned in (clockwise).

The float level is adjusted with the fuel bowl removed and the carburettor inverted (Figure 4.13). With the float tongue contacting the needle valve the distance 'A' should be equal to the specified float level. Usually this will be 25 to 35mm, depending on the carburettor type. Some Mikuni carburettors have the float level adjusted to dimension 'B'; in this instance the level is usually around 9 to 10mm; again this varies from model to model.

MIKUNI TUNING

Many enthusiasts first attempt to tune the Mikuni by trying to determine the correct main jet size. This procedure is correct, but only if the engine has not been extensively modified and the stock carburettor is being used. If you find that large changes in the size of the main jet do not seem to be having very much influence on the half and full throttle mixture strength, you can be fairly certain that the needle jet is too small.

When the engine has been extensively modified I prefer to begin testing (after adjusting the float level) with the main jet removed. If the engine will just run at part throttle, but floods as the throttle is opened, the needle jet is close to the right size. However, if you find that the engine keeps going at three-quarters to full throttle, you can be sure that a larger needle jet is required. This test should be done with the needle lowered to the No 1 (ie lean) position.

After you have found a needle and needle jet combination that is too rich, you can then try various sizes of main jets until you find one that allows the engine to run reasonably well at full throttle; do not worry about throttle response or acceleration for the moment. Carry out this test with the needle raised to the middle position.

Next find what size of idle jet (pilot jet) is required. Start these adjustments by backing out the idle speed screws until the throttle slides are completely closed, then turn the screws back in until the slides just open.

Having done that, close the idle air screws completely and back each one out 1 to

Figure 4.13 Mikuni float levelling.

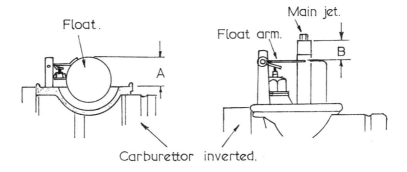

1¹/2 turns. Start the engine and attempt to obtain a smooth 1,000rpm idle by juggling the idle air screws and the idle speed screws in turn. If you can get the engine to settle down to a good idle, synchronise the throttle slides using a set of vacuum gauges or the multiple-column mercury balancer described later.

If the engine will not idle, it is probable that the idle jets are wrong. Jets that are too small are indicated by an increasing idle speed as the air screws are turned in. When the idle jets are of the correct size turning the screws in should cause the engine to run rich at some point (usually 1 to 1¹/2 turns from being fully closed). An idle jet that is too large is indicated by an ever-increasing idle speed as the air screws are backed out further and further. The air screw must not be opened more than 3 turns.

When the correct idle jets have been established, the throttle slides should be synchronised. Once this has been done, you can test that the cutaway is of the correct height. This influences the mixture most up to one-quarter throttle, so if the engine tends to cough and die when the throttles are cracked open, change to slides with less cutaway (ie richer).

When you have settled on the correct slide, re-check the slide synchronisation and determine that the idle jet is still the correct size. Generally, a change in idle jet size is necessary only when a large change in slide cutaway height has been made.

With the idle jets, needle jets and slides finally selected and synchronised, you are ready to begin fine tuning.

First check that the main jet is approximately correct by testing the bike at three-quarters to full throttle. If the engine runs well and the plugs read a good colour, the main jet is close enough to begin finding the correct needle profile and/or position.

The needle taper and position controls the fuel/air mixture between one-quarter and three-quarter throttle. To determine if a change is required, test the bike on a smooth and level road for at least half a mile at one-quarter throttle, then at a half and three-quarter throttle. If the engine snatches and surges at a steady throttle opening, the mixture is too rich, so lower the needle one groove at a time until smooth running is achieved.

Next, try steady accelerations from one-quarter to half throttle and from half to one-quarter throttle, and note whether the engine appears to be rich or lean. Repeat the test but snap the throttle open each time.

Table 4.27   Mikuni metering guide

Throttle-opening position

	1/8	*1/4*	*3/8*	*1/2*	*3/4*	*full*
Slide cutaway	A	A	B	B	C	D
Pilot or idle jet	A	A	B	C	D	D
Pilot air screw	A	A	B	C	D	D
Needle jet	B	A	A	C	D	D
Needle size	C	B	A	A	C	C
Needle position	B	B	A	A	C	D
Main jet	D	D	C	C	B	A

The letters A–D indicate metering effectiveness at various slide openings.

A – most effective; B – fairly effective; C – small influence; D – no influence

You may find that the mixture is lean at one-quarter throttle and changes to rich between half and three-quarter throttle. This would indicate that the needle's taper is too steep, so change to a needle with a smaller angle of taper. Obviously a mixture condition the opposite of this would require a needle with more taper (ie a larger angle).

Once the correct needle has been determined, the bike should be tested at three-quarter to full throttle, to find the right main jet diameter.

The tuning procedure for any carburettor using a needle metering system is always slow and tedious. However, by keeping clear notes and by regularly referring to Table 4.27 to see what controls the metering at various throttle openings, eventually you will be rewarded with smooth and responsive carburation.

MULTI-COLUMN CARBURETTOR BALANCER

Most workshop manuals recommend the use of vacuum gauges to balance multiple motorcycle carburettors. However, I have found these to give less than perfect

Figure 4.14 Four-column motorcycle carburettor balancer.

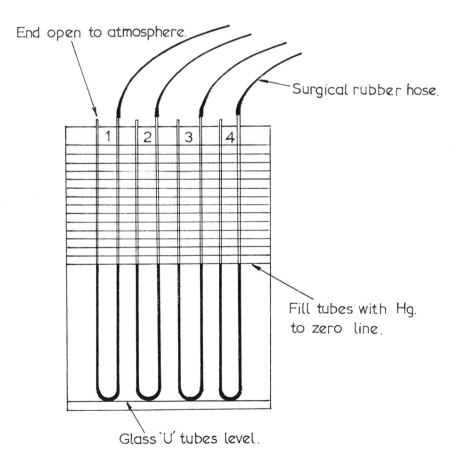

synchronisation. As they cost a lot of money, I feel that it is a better plan to make your own mercury column balancer.

The instrument that I will describe is illustrated in Figure 4.14. If you intend to tune a six-cylinder bike, you will need a six-column rather than a four-column manometer.

The face board should be 18in wide and 36in high, with a matt black background and white scale lines 1cm apart. The board should be permanently fixed to a wall in your workshop or else mounted solidly on a suitable base, so that it will not fall or be blown over.

The glass 'U' tubes should have an inside diameter of 5/32in and be exactly 6ft long. You could buy the tubes already formed or else buy straight 6ft lengths of tube and heat each with a gas torch until the glass becomes plastic enough to bend into a 'U' shape around a piece of 2in pipe.

Mount the tubes on the face board with the tops of each tube protruding approximately 1in past the top of the board, and their bottoms level. The tubes may be mounted by drilling a number of 1/16in holes in the board and inserting copper wire through the holes and around each glass tube.

Once the 'U' tubes are secure, they should be filled to the zero line (the halfway point) with mercury; about 10cc will be required in each column. Mercury is a very dangerous accumulative poison and as such it is not easily obtained in many countries. At times it can be bought from laboratory supply firms, but generally you will have to know someone who has the right contacts, for example a chemistry teacher or an electrician who has access to old mercury switches.

Because mercury is deadly, never handle it or breathe its vapour. It appears to be stable but actually it is very volatile, giving off poisonous vapour continually. Therefore when the balancer is not in use, stop up the ends of the tubes or connect the two ends together with rubber hose, to prevent the escape and build-up of vapour in your workshop. Always keep the balancer locked away from children or pets. Remember the poison is accumulative, which means that it builds up in your body. When the concentration reaches a certain level it will cause blindness, insanity or death.

To connect the 'U' tubes to the inlet manifold you will need 9ft lengths of 1/4in i/d surgical rubber hose. This length and type of hose provides the necessary damping without impairing the accuracy of the readings. Note that the hose is connected to one end of the 'U' tube, the other end being open to the air.

The final connection from the hose to the vacuum test holes in the manifold is made using adaptors produced for this purpose by the manufacturer of your machine, or you may choose to make a set of adaptors yourself.

The balancer is very easy to use. You merely adjust the slide opening of each carburettor to get an even reading in each mercury column. Once the slides have been synchronised, the idle speed and mixture are then adjusted for the best idle.

Bikes with an individual throttle cable to each carburettor can be a problem, so after the initial synchronisation the carburettors should be checked for balance at several rpm levels. Changes in balance indicate sticky slides or uneven cable pulls.

This balancer is not just for bikes. The triple and quad Weber set-ups and those carburettors with air screws are also best tuned using this multi-column manometer.

Chapter 5

Electronic Fuel Injection

Electronic fuel injection (EFI) is a rather frightening concept for tuners who have grown up working with carburettors. However, in practice there are many similarities between a carburettor-type fuel delivery system and an EFI system. Additionally the very same laws of physics work in exactly the same way with either system. Thus, just as large-diameter manifold runners kill low rpm torque while increasing top-end hp with carburettors, we likewise see the very same thing with EFI. In a similar vein, when we increase carburettor throttle plate size, say swapping from a pair of 45DCOE Webers with 45mm throttle bores to 48DCOEs with 48mm throttle bores, we increase both high rpm air flow and maximum power at the expense of a fall in mid-range output. With EFI we see the same sort of thing when we replace a throttle body with 45mm throttle plates with a larger-bore body with 48mm plates. Also, just as finely atomised fuel droplets issuing from a carburettor to be evenly distributed throughout the intake air charge burn more uniformly to produce more power, so likewise with EFI.

Clearly the major difference between the two systems is with regard to fuel metering. The carburettor relies on a series of jets with correctly sized metering orifices to deliver the correct quantity of fuel into the intake air stream. This occurs because of the pressure differential existing, with the inlet tract being subjected to a vacuum, and fuel in the carburettor's float bowl being acted on by normal air pressure, pushing the fuel through the various jets into the intake air. Electronic fuel injection is different in that the central brain or computer, which we call the electronic control unit (ECU), calculates how long it will open the fuel injector nozzles to deliver the correct quantity of fuel into the intake air stream, based on information that it is receiving from various sensors.

The correct length of time that the injectors must spray, called the 'pulse width', is determined during extensive dyno testing of the engine. For example, if at wide-open throttle the engine makes 300hp at 8,000rpm with the injectors open for 8.72 milliseconds, and makes 305hp with a pulse width of 8.64 milliseconds, then drops to

302hp when the pulse width is reduced to 8.58 milliseconds, the ECU will be 'told' that at wide-open throttle and 8,000rpm the engine must be given an 8.64-millisecond injector spray period so as to ensure that the engine makes best hp. This process, which we call 'mapping', is continued under every possible combination of operating conditions that the particular engine is ever likely to experience.

When car manufacturers start such mapping tests the process can take 12 months and cost a couple of million dollars because they have to meet exacting standards of not only engine performance, but also driveability, economy and government emissions requirements. Competition engines, however, are far less demanding, and even when you are working with an engine with which you are not too familiar it is possible to generate a basic fuel map in a couple of hours (Figure 5.1).

The fuel map thus generated in effect becomes a 'library' that is programmed, using a laptop computer, into the ECU's memory. From this information store the ECU 'knows' exactly how long the injectors must remain open, spraying fuel, for literally hundreds of engine operating conditions. Citing our previous example, when sensors relay to the ECU that the engine is spinning at 8,000rpm and the throttle is wide open, the ECU instantly files through its library of stored information and finds that the injectors should spray for 8.64 milliseconds. The ECU immediately sends out an

The ECU receives signals from various sources, then computes the appropriate injector 'pulse width'.

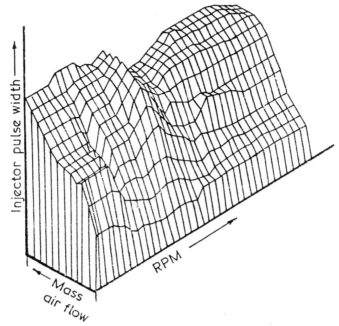

Figure 5.1 An EFI fuel map.

electrical current to pulse the injectors for precisely 8.64 milliseconds. Along with this map reference point the ECU will have anywhere from 120 to 800 other map reference points placed in its memory enabling it to provide the correct injector pulse width for any operating condition the engine is going to encounter.

From this you will appreciate that before the ECU can determine the appropriate injector pulse width it must first be provided with information about what the engine is actually doing, and in particular precisely how much air is flowing into the cylinders at that particular moment. There are a number of methods that we can use to determine air flow into the engine: we can measure it using an air flow meter; we can calculate it based on engine rpm and manifold vacuum levels; or we can calculate air flow from the engine rpm and the throttle plate open angle. As each system has its advantages and disadvantages we will look at each in turn.

MASS AIR FLOW SYSTEM

The first arrangement using an air-flow meter is what we call a 'mass air flow' system. The earliest air-flow meter, often called a vane air-flow meter, is a simple unit that passes the air flowing into the engine through a passage blocked by a spring-loaded flap (Figure 5.2). As the air flows through the meter it 'blows' the flap open to a certain angular position, dependent on the force of the spring and the amount of air flowing in the passage. Connected to the flap pivot is a variable resistor, a potentiometer, which changes the ECU's input voltage according to how wide the flap has been swung open.

Remember that air density changes with the ambient temperature, as well as other factors, so air-flow input in itself is not adequate for accurate fuel metering. Thus

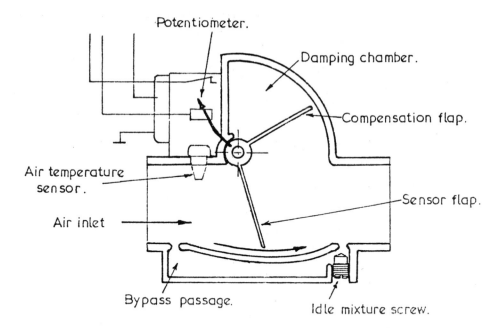

Figure 5.2 Vane-type air-flow meter.

the air-flow meter also houses an air temperature sensor, and this signal, along with the air-flow signal, is used by the ECU to calculate mass air flow. You will note that this air-flow meter also has a bypass passage with a mixture adjusting screw. By varying the amount of air that is permitted to bypass the sensor flap, the air-flow meter signal can be changed to alter the air/fuel ratio at idle.

The other common air-flow meter, originally called a 'mass air flow' (MAF) sensor, or 'hot wire meter', is now usually referred to as a MAF sensor. It is basically a tube in the inlet duct through which the air flows to enter the engine. Stretched across this tube is a very fine platinum wire, which is heated by an electric current to maintain a constant temperature above ambient. An air temperature sensor in the meter signals the ambient temperature to the ECU so that it sends out the correct amount of power to keep the wire at the required temperature. However, air passing into the

The vane air-flow meter has basically been made redundant by the better flowing hot-wire type. This Nissan hot wire unit has a large slotted adjusting screw (top left beside terminals) that permits the voltage signal going back to the ECU to be altered, thus changing the A/F ratio and spark timing. From the factory, cars typically run slightly rich and retarded, so on Nissans with this style of meter a correction can be made by tweaking this screw while running on a chassis dyno.

engine flows over the wire and cools it in direct proportion to mass air flow. Consequently the ECU must increase the current flow in the wire to keep the temperature constant, and it then reads this signal as mass air flow.

A third type of air-flow meter is the vortex flow sensor, which uses an ultrasonic sender and receiver to measure the rate at which vortices pass through a control passage. The signal from the sensor is measured by the ECU, and after being corrected for inlet air temperature and barometric pressure, the mass air flow is calculated and the injector pulse width determined.

Many manufacturers use a mass air flow type system as it provides very accurate fuel metering when air flow into the engine varies over a very wide range. Also, because the air-flow meter is the major source for the ECU in determining the injector pulse width, this type of system can compensate for slight differences in engine specifications and long-term engine wear. However, it does have its drawbacks. Car manufacturers originally looked at other systems because air-flow meters are costly. From the aspect of performance, though, the major negatives are air-flow restriction, particularly of the flap-type meter, and inaccurate metering due to reverse pulsing in the inlet tract when long-duration, high-overlap cams are employed.

SPEED DENSITY SYSTEM

To get around the high cost factor of air-flow meters, manufacturers developed the speed density system. In this system there isn't any air-flow meter to provide information about air flow into the engine to the ECU. Rather the ECU uses manifold vacuum and engine rpm as the central keys to establishing the engine's fuel requirements. In addition the ECU also receives input from the air charge temperature sensor and the barometric pressure sensor (Figure 5.3).

The advantage with this arrangement is that there is no air-flow meter to cause any flow restriction, and the manifold absolute pressure (MAP) sensor will respond to both positive and negative manifold pressures. Thus the system is well suited to turbo and

The main source of input for the speed density system is engine load (measured as vacuum, or boost in the case of supercharged engines, in the inlet manifold) and engine rpm. Either an external MAP sensor like this one, or an internal sensor within the ECU, is connected to the inlet manifold by a hose. The sensor converts that engine load (boost/vacuum) signal to an electrical signal which the ECU uses to adjust fuelling and spark timing.

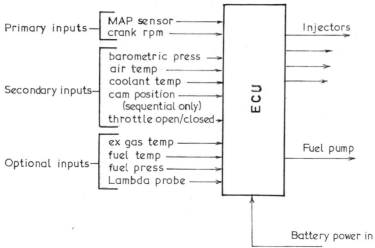

Figure 5.3 Speed density type fuel injection.

supercharged applications. However, wild camshafts that cause strong reversion pulses in the inlet tract can give rise to metering difficulties with the speed density system.

ALPHA-N SYSTEM

The third type, the Alpha-N system, was originally developed for competition engines. The primary ECU inputs for determining inlet air flow come from the engine speed sensor and the throttle position sensor (Figure 5.4).

The advantage with this system is again that there is no air-flow meter involved, so there are no obstructions to air flow. Also, with no manifold pressure sensor being required, the Alpha-N arrangement is immune to metering difficulties caused by either low or wildly fluctuating manifold vacuum levels and massive reversion pulses.

Figure 5.4 Alpha-N type fuel injection.

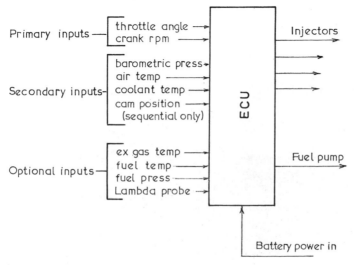

However, this does not mean that it is totally free of metering problems. With this system accurate throttle position input is important because the assumed air flow into the engine is based on the exact throttle plate open angle, and the engine speed. This is not a worry with competition engines, but with road cars the first few degrees of throttle opening are most important for ease of driving. However, it is in these first few degrees of throttle movement, where big changes in inlet air flow are occurring, that potentiometers have their greatest resolution problems.

If the throttle shaft was connected to a pot swinging through a radius of 100mm, a change of $1/2°$ in throttle plate movement could be accurately measured by a voltage change going to the ECU, and the injector pulse width would be adjusted to correspond with the change in air flow. Unfortunately the potentiometer radius is closer to 20mm, so small changes in throttle position may not be accurately sensed. This will not stop the engine from running, but it will take away the low-speed and cruise smoothness that we have come to expect from fuel injection. Rather the engine may feel as though it is not up to temperature and has Weber carbs fitted with overly big chokes.

OTHER ECU INPUTS

Apart from inputs which relate to air flow into the engine, the ECU will also be receiving input from at least one other source, and perhaps several. When the engine is cold more fuel must be delivered to ensure that it will run, and not stumble on acceleration. Thus, according to input from the coolant temperature sensor, the ECU will increase the injector pulse width until the engine comes up to normal operating temperature.

Because today's race engines are being tuned to finer and finer levels in search of more power, the dividing line between engine survival and destruction from detonation is narrowing. Thus in the higher levels of competition it is no longer possible to run a 'safe' rich fuel/air mixture, but rather we are running as close as possible, just a hair's breadth away from detonation, with a full-power lean mixture. This means that more inputs are necessary to keep the ECU fully informed as to just what is going on, not only within but also around the engine.

For example, there are fewer fuel molecules in 1cc of hot petrol than in the same

The signal from the air temperature sensor may be used by the ECU to adjust not only fuelling and spark but also in supercharged applications to activate intercooler water spray and/or intercooler fan, water injection, adjust water-to-air intercooler pump speed etc.

volume of cold fuel. Thus the true fuel/air ratio will become leaner and perhaps send the engine into detonation if the ECU does not adjust the injector pulse width as the fuel temperature increases. Conversely, without compensation a decrease in fuel temperature will increase mixture richness. This will reduce engine hp slightly, and in distance race engines where we may be chilling the fuel to a low temperature prior to dumping it into the car's fuel tank in an effort to stretch the distance between fuel stops, we will not be gaining the full mileage advantage from the cold fuel. Thus when the ECU has input from a fuel temperature sensor it will adjust the pulse width to compensate for the temperature of the fuel being injected.

Another problem about which the ECU needs to know is reduced fuel pressure. Obviously when the fuel pressure drops, less fuel will flow though an injector in a given time than when the pressure is normal. This is not normally a problem because fuel injection systems are designed to provide a reliable and steady fuel pressure. However, if we are running high fuel pressure, or are running distance events, a fuel pressure input to the ECU could save the engine from a meltdown, or in endurance events could help us reach the finish.

For example, if we have mapped our engine on the dyno with 60psi fuel pressure and battery voltage drops off during the race, we could lose the engine because pump speed and fuel pressure will fall, resulting in a lean-out. In distance races the same sort of thing can happen, but a more usual problem is a fuel filter blockage knocking pressure at the fuel rail, or a pump losing speed due to a bearing seize-up and not being able to maintain system pressure.

Another source of input, the exhaust oxygen sensor, or 'lambda probe', was originally developed for road cars expected to meet government emissions requirements. This sensor is fitted in the exhaust header collector, and is a metal-coated ceramic probe that functions like a weak battery, producing about 100 millivolts when oxygen content in the exhaust gas is high, as when the fuel/air mixture is lean. When the oxygen content falls, indicating a rich mixture, the probe's voltage output to the ECU increases. With this input the ECU can check on itself and when necessary make programme adjustments.

With time the O_2 sensor has found a home on many race engines. During dyno

Single wire lambda probe is a narrow range sensor primarily designed to maintain cruise fuelling at an A/F ratio close to 14.7:1. Wide range sensors such as the four wire AC Delco are used in high performance applications and for engine tuning/mapping.

AIR FLOW DETERMINATION	INLET MANIFOLD DESIGN	INJECTOR SPRAY PULSING
Mass Air Flow ↓ air flow meter	Plenum Manifold ↓ air flow into plenum controlled by throttle body with 1,2 or 4 throttle plates	Batch Fire ↓ all injectors spray simultaneously every crank revolution
Speed Density ↓ speed sensor and MAP sensor		
Alpha-N ↓ speed sensor and throttle pot	Isolated Runner Manifold ↓ air flow into each inlet port controlled by separate throttle plates	Sequential ↓ injectors spray in sequence during the inlet valve open period

Figure 5.5 Distinguishing features of electronic fuel injection systems.

mapping sessions an exhaust oxygen input can save a lot of time, and it can help avoid an engine meltdown. For example, you can key in a safe air/fuel ratio of 12.7:1 and quickly build a map at all load sites at that mixture richness. Also, in a race car the tailpipe sensor can perform an engine-saving role by overriding the ECU at any time the exhaust indicates a dangerous lean-out, say leaner than 13.5:1.

However, there are good reasons not to rely on the lambda to tune the fuel injection system for you. At full throttle, for example, the engine may run safe at an air/fuel ratio of 12.7:1, but remember that we are searching for maximum power. Thus at some engine speeds we may make more power at 12.5:1, while at other rpm the magic number may be 13.4:1. Also, in sequential systems we lose the benefit of individual cylinder trim, where we adjust the air/fuel ratio differently for each cylinder to make maximum hp.

Another ECU input in maximum-effort engines is exhaust gas temperature. With a sensor in every header tube, depending on what we found in testing, the ECU would make programme adjustments to keep exhaust gas temperature (EGT) below a certain danger figure. In one engine the safe EGT may be 800°C, but in another we may lose valve seats at 780°C.

PLENUM TYPE MANIFOLD

Apart from differentiating fuel injection systems by looking at the three basic ways of how the ECU determines engine air flow, we also define systems by what type of inlet manifold is fitted to the engine. In multi-point injection, where we have at least one injector supplying fuel to each cylinder, there are two basic types of manifold: the plenum type and the isolated runner throttle body type (Figure 5.5).

The majority of car manufacturers' multi-point injection systems use a plenum-type manifold. These are often referred to as 'tuned port injection' (TPI) because the long manifold runners that join the inlet port and the plenum are of a tuned length to take advantage of pressure pulses generated in the inlet tract to pump up mid-range power and torque. The plenum has a volume typically about 80% of the engine size, and all the manifold runners draw off air from the plenum to the cylinders. Air flow into the plenum is controlled by a throttle body containing either one or two throttle plates.

A plenum manifold with long runners boosts mid-range performance in a road car, but restricts high rpm power on a competition engine.

This arrangement works very well in road cars where strong bottom-end power is needed. However, as power levels rise the long manifold runners begin to restrict air flow and kill top-end hp. Looking at Table 5.1 you can see what happened during the testing of a 5-litre Ford Mustang that was being developed for a club racer wanting a good manageable power spread suitable for a hillclimb and road circuit car. Below 5,200rpm the stock long-runner plenum manifold had a clear advantage over the isolated runner manifold, which was originally designed to accommodate four 48 IDA Weber carburettors. However, past 5,500rpm the isolated runner manifold, with short, large-diameter runners, just walks away from the stock manifold as it struggles to flow sufficient air.

Table 5.1   Ford Mustang 5-litre inlet manifold comparison

rpm	Test 1 hp	Test 1 Torque	Test 2 hp	Test 2 Torque
4,500	298.6	348.5	284.9	332.5
5,000	347.8	365.3	311.5	327.2
5,500	355.7	339.7	396.2	378.3
6,000	357.3	312.8	425.3	372.3
6,500	330.0	266.6	454.5	367.2
7,000	268.2	201.2	439.6	329.8
7,500			424.8	297.5

Test 1 – standard Ford manifold.
Test 2 – Pantera 48mm throttle bodies on 4 x 48 IDA Weber manifold.

Compensation for ram air

On race cars running at high speeds a significant supercharge effect can be induced in the inlet tract by connecting a large forward-facing air scoop to the cold air box. However, unless the ECU is kept informed of this rising level of air flow into the engine, which increases according to car speed, the fuel/air mixture will lean out, resulting in lost hp and most probably engine damage. Additionally, if the car is following in the slipstream of another car this throws another variable into the equation.

Obviously we cannot accurately simulate the ram air effect when we are building up the fuel map on the dyno. The simple alternative is to measure air pressure within the cold air box just as we would for a turbo or supercharged engine, then programme the ECU to adjust the injector duty cycle to compensate for changing air box pressure. To perform this function we would have a MAP sensor relaying air box pressure information to the ECU. Then, when pressure in the air box increased, the ECU would lengthen the injector duty cycle to maintain the correct fuel/air ratio, and it would also retard the spark to avoid detonation.

This sounds simple enough, but it takes a considerable amount of track testing to programme the ECU to adjust correctly the base fuel and ignition maps to compensate for ram air. Clearly, for ram air to deliver the desired power increase it must be done correctly otherwise it could cost hp or even the engine!

To give some indication of where we are heading with this kind of tuning, we really need data acquisition from a lambda probe to show what the engine's air/fuel ratios are on the parts of the circuit where the engine is on full throttle for several seconds, accelerating hard. If we had best hp on the dyno with an average air/fuel of around 13.2:1 at full throttle and now, from our data logging, we find that MAP sensor trim at high speed is richening the air/fuel to 12.5:1, we would then reduce MAP compensation to lean the mixture back closer to 13.2:1.

Note that to save time when tuning from a lambda we usually do not think in terms of air/fuel ratios – we simply work straight from the lambda reading rather than converting back and forth. A lambda number of 1.0 equals an air/fuel ratio of 14.7:1 (lambda x 14.7 = air/fuel ratio). Therefore we would be looking at maintaining the lambda at about 0.895, with a maximum richness around 0.86 and a minimum of 0.93.

Do not get the idea from this that plenum-type manifolds are never capable of decent air flow. If the intake runners are the correct length and diameter, and the throttle body flowing air into the plenum is sufficiently large, plenum-type manifolds will make good power. I do not think anyone could argue that the twin-throttle-body plenum ram manifolds developed by the Walkinshaw team for the Group A Holdens and Rovers were in any way deficient in air-flow capabilities, and the same could be said for the Accel Super-Ram manifold for the small-block Chev.

In similar fashion it is possible to obtain good results by fitting a throttle body, usually with four throttle plates, on a single or dual-plane manifold originally designed to house a big four-barrel carburettor. These manifolds from manufacturers such as Offenhauser, Weiand and Edelbrock are available for many American V6 and V8 engines. Dual-plane manifolds, due to their long, small-size runners, favour low-end power, while single-plane manifolds with their larger, short runners gain top-end power at the expense of the bottom end.

Table 5.2   Comparison of Ford Mustang 5-litre fuel injection versus carburettor

| | Test 1 | | Test 2 | |
rpm	hp	Torque	hp	Torque
4,500	284.2	331.7	284.8	332.4
5,000	315.3	331.2	315.0	330.9
5,500	387.3	369.8	378.4	361.3
6,000	420.5	368.1	421.0	368.5
6,500	439.9	355.4	441.8	357.0
7,000	440.5	330.5	431.3	323.6
7,500	416.0	291.3	400.6	280.5

Test 1 – Edelbrock Victor Jr manifold with Harrop 1,000cfm throttle body.

Test 2 – Edelbrock Victor Jr manifold with Holley 750cfm carburettor.

Table 5.2 illustrates how well an Edelbrock Victor Jr single-plane manifold performed on the 5-litre Mustang discussed earlier. This manifold had a Harrop four-blade 1,000cfm throttle body bolted on in place of a four-barrel carb. Close to where the runners meet the cylinder heads they were milled and eight fuel injector bosses welded in place to ensure that the injectors sprayed at the correct angle down each inlet port. When you compare the results with what was obtained with the isolated runner manifold in Table 5.1 you can see that there is not a great deal in it up to 6,000rpm, but at the power peak the isolated runner manifold, by virtue of its greater air-flow capacity, is about 3.2% stronger, and at maximum engine speed makes 1.9% more hp.

Table 5.2 also shows that in absolute hp terms fuel injection does not make a whole lot more power than a well-sorted carburettor set-up; typically the hp difference at wide-open throttle will be 2–3%. However, when it comes to responsiveness, driveability and part-throttle performance, properly sorted fuel injection on a correctly sized inlet manifold will always be way ahead of any carburettor set-up.

FUEL ATOMISATION AND ISOLATED RUNNER MANIFOLDS

However, making power is not just about air flow, as I have pointed out in earlier chapters. There is also fuel atomisation and distribution to be considered, and here the isolated runner arrangement offers the tuner a good deal more freedom in that he can take the engine closer to the limit of its hp-producing capabilities while still maintaining engine reliability.

Some people have the idea that fuel injection delivers fuel droplets of exactly the correct size into the air stream, and that these droplets perfectly homogenise with that inflowing air and will later burn at exactly the correct rate to produce maximum power. Such a theory is very easily disproved by the fact that injection systems invariably inject more fuel when the engine is cold. This is done because only a percentage is in combustible droplet size and mixed in combustible proportions with the surrounding air at the time that the spark plug fires. When the engine is hot the air and the fuel droplets gather heat from the inlet tract, the cylinder walls, the piston crown, the combustion chamber, the valves and the spark plug. This serves to improve   163

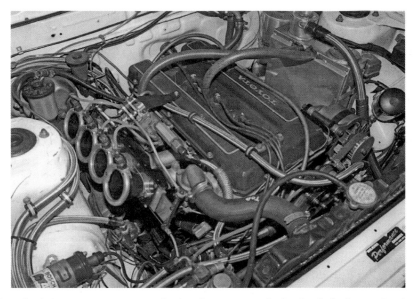

Mounting the injectors way out on the intake trumpets helps both fuel atomisation and volumetric efficiency. This occurs because in pulling heat from the inlet tract to convert from liquid to vapour the fuel cools the intake charge and increases charge density in the cylinders.

fuel atomisation, so with a greater percentage of very fine fuel droplets in contact with oxygen molecules during the combustion phase, the ratio of fuel droplets to oxygen molecules becomes excessive; the mixture is too rich. Therefore to avoid such a waste of fuel, and the loss of power, the injection pulse width is progressively cut back as the engine heats up to normal operating temperature.

What has this got to do with isolated runner manifolds? Well, at high engine speeds the inlet tract of a race engine is not a lot different from the situation I have just described that exists in a cold engine. We have to use big injectors to spray sufficient

Figure 5.6 Isolated runner manifold with outboard injectors.

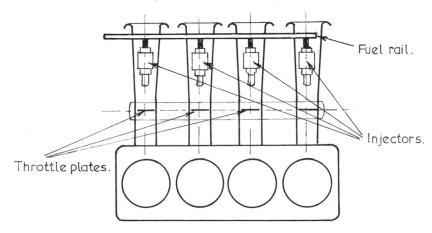

fuel in the short time available. This means that the fuel droplets entering the air stream are larger than those from smaller injectors spraying for a longer period of time in an engine operating at low rpm. The result is a larger portion of non-combustible droplets, which marginally upset the combustion process, with the result of reducing engine performance.

One way that we can improve this situation is to move the injectors further away from the engine, and if we use a sequential system we can even mount them outboard of the throttle plates (Figure 5.6). In stock engines we are used to seeing injectors mounted close to the head and spraying right at the back of the hot inlet valve. This improves atomisation, stopping the fuel dropping out of suspension and not burning at low rpm when air speed in the inlet tract is slow. Also 'inboard' injectors improve low speed and mid-range rpm throttle responsiveness, and in batch fire systems they stop charge robbing.

However, with a race engine running sequential injection we do not have such a problem so we can move the injectors way out to the intake trumpets. From this location some of the fuel droplets entering the air stream will smash into the throttle plate and be broken down in size. Other droplets will collect some heat on their relatively long journey down the inlet tract and this will also aid atomisation. Additionally, introducing the fuel into the inlet stream a long way from the valve allows extra time for the fuel droplets to more evenly mix with the air as it swirls around the throttle plate and down the inlet tract. Thus with improved fuel atomisation and better mixture homogenisation we gain some power, and with improved combustion control the possibility of running more compression or leaning the mixture opens up, with another small power gain probable.

Another way in which we can gain some power with the isolated runner manifold is by turning the throttle body upside down, or rather than turning it through 180° we may turn it through 90° or 270°. Moving the throttle body like this changes the directional effect that the throttle plate imparts to the fuel/air mixture flowing over its surface. This can serve to increase hp in two ways; it may bias air flow to a particular side of the intake tract and increase the quantity of air passing into the cylinder, or it may change the swirl characteristics of the inlet tract, improving fuel and air homogenisation and thus improving the quality of the fuel/air charge entering the cylinder.

DUAL INJECTOR ARRANGEMENT

An isolated runner manifold opens up yet another possibility for increased power due to improved combustion. Earlier we saw how small injectors spraying for a longer period deliver more finely atomised fuel droplets into the inlet air stream. With an isolated runner manifold we can take advantage of this situation by running two small injectors, placed in two different locations along each inlet tract, spraying the same total quantity of finely atomised fuel as one large injector. Obviously a lengthy dyno session is required to determine the ideal 'staging' of the two injectors and the best location for the second one.

With a broad-power-band hillclimb or rally engine it may be found that one injector should be mounted inboard, close to the stock location and be staged to spray at lower rpm. The other injector, mounted outboard of the throttle plate, may be staged

Intake trumpets

Intake trumpets or air stacks are those beautiful shapely things that are supposed to assist air flow into the inlet manifold and throttle body. I suspect that many are designed with gorgeous tapers and rolled bell-mouths for eye pleasure rather than to serve some practical purpose like assisting engine hp. It is quite simple to make a whole load of different designs, but picking a winner from flow bench tests is about as reliable as deciding that the best-looking one obviously has to help the engine make more power.

For example, on the flow bench you may find that a 6in length of parallel-wall tubing flows 100cfm. You can then flow another 6in trumpet that tapers over its entire length by anything from 3° up to about 7° and find the maximum flow increasing to something like 108–115cfm. You then take an ugly-looking stack with parallel walls for say 3in that then taper at 10–12° over the remaining 3in, and find the flow rising to 120–122cfm. You might then add a beautiful 3/4in radius bell-mouth to every trumpet and find that it makes absolutely no difference to the flow on some, and perhaps adds another 1% or 2% to others.

When you get on the dyno it is even more perplexing. You will find that some trumpets give fair gains in some places, but big losses at other rpm. However, after a lot of testing you will find a set of air stacks that add a little bit in a few places on the power curve without pulling the hp down anywhere else.

Frequently the gains come in other very subtle ways. Perhaps the length rather than the taper of the trumpet is more important, in spite of what the flow bench might say, or in spite of the 'look good' factor. Getting the length right could help an adjoining cylinder to run 'cleaner' and make more power simply because there is a fuel stand-off problem. Flow pulses in the air box could have been blowing some of that loose fuel into the wrong cylinder, causing it to run rich and its neighbour to be a bit lean; changing the trumpet length may help to reduce this, or it may ensure that the loose fuel is more evenly distributed between cylinders and thus allow the injector pulse width to be cut back a touch.

With sequential injection, getting the intake trumpet length right can have a big influence on injector phasing, ie when they are timed to begin spraying. If the length is wrong the phasing may have to be delayed until well after the intake valve opens. Then to get the required amount of fuel into the cylinder in the short time remaining while the inlet valve is still open, very big injectors and a short pulse width would be necessary. In this situation fuel atomisation and cylinder cooling will not be so good and hp will be down. However, getting the intake length right may allow the use of small injectors firing early before the intake valves open, with the end result being more power due to better internal cooling of the combustion chamber and piston crown, and better fuel atomisation and homogenisation.

by the ECU to commence spraying as the engine rpm increases and reaches into the lower end of the power band, with the throttle plates open past, say, 80°.

On the other hand a maximum-effort engine may work better with both injectors mounted outboard of the throttle plate (Figure 5.7). The injector mounted in the intake trumpet would be staged to fire first, while the top-up injector mounted on the wall of the air box would spray straight down the throat of the intake trumpet. It would probably be staged to fire as the engine approached peak torque rpm at throttle plate angles greater than 50°, but this could only be established on the dyno.

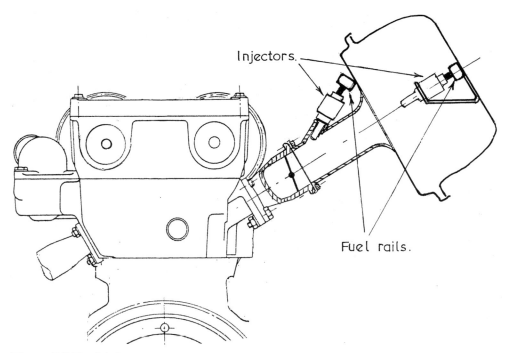

Figure 5.7 Dual injector arrangement.

However, even without a lot of dyno time, if weight isn't a concern, it could be smart to choose the dual injector route, both to save some money and pick up a handy 3–4% power boost. Big competition injectors to supply an engine's needs can carry quite a large price tag. An alternative is to retain your stock injectors in their standard location, and then fit another set of injectors, even a cheap set complete with fuel rail from the wreckers, mounting them further out along the inlet tract. Don't worry about testing to determine the best location. Just mount them at about 45° to the air flow like the stock injectors and as far out on the manifold runners as practicable. A less worrisome alternative, provided the injectors do not have a wide cone spray pattern, is to mount them in the air box so as to spray down the trumpet throats.

Whatever arrangement is used the outer injectors must not be staged to spray until air flow is sufficiently high to ensure that the fuel does not drop out of suspension on its journey into the cylinders. Also with batch fire injection you don't want the injectors firing when wave resonance in the inlet tract, or reverse flow out past the inlet valve, will send fuel back up the runner into the air box. Both scenarios can bring on a big lean stumble, the engine splutters and backfires, with the final result being perhaps a destructive fire in the air box or air filter.

The simple way around these issues is to stage the outer injectors to spray only when the throttle is at least 85% open and the engine is no more than 2,000rpm below maximum hp revs. If you can afford the dyno time do another test with them staged to fire at 75% throttle, and also 95%, starting within about 2,000–3,000rpm of maximum hp. Repeat testing at 75%, 85% and 95% throttle and 1,200rpm below max hp. The lambda meter will give you some indication of problems with fuel falling out of suspension, or reversion issues. However, don't get too excited until you check what 167

On the Yamaha R7 the factory decided to limit power to 106hp by leaving the outer injectors non-operational. Only when the race kit was fitted did the outer injectors work.

works best at the track. Sometimes all the numbers may look good, but throttle response can be disappointing.

The percentage of total fuel supplied by the inner and outer injectors to make best hp can also be sorted out on the dyno. Some tuners don't concern themselves with this and simply activate the outers as soon as the inner units exceed a certain duty cycle; usually somewhere from 80–90%. I don't agree with this practice for two good reasons. First, you are not really gaining very much benefit from the dual set-up. Second, when the outer injectors are first switched on the injection period will be very short, leading to erratic metering and poor atomisation of any fuel these actually spray.

If funds aren't available for a lot of dyno time to test what works best, I prefer to see the inner injectors cut back to 40–60% of total fuel flow. This means that if you decide to drop to 40% the outer units immediately begin supplying 60% of the engine's fuel needs when they commence spraying. Then as the engine's fuel requirements rise the additional fuel will be supplied in that same ratio; 40% from the inners and 60% from the outers. If you have dyno time, test with the inner units held at the initial 40% fuel figure, and send all additional fuel through the outer injectors. Alternatively flow from the inners could be tapered off (don't go lower than 2 milliseconds) and the outers could provide an increasing proportion as rpm and throttle angle increases. Remember that using the outer injectors to supply a larger proportion of the fuel, providing the engine is working at reasonably high revs, helps overall fuel atomisation. Plus this fuel pulls heat out of the inlet tract improving volumetric efficiency and ultimately engine power.

THROTTLE BODY SIZE

All of this concern to ensure that finely atomised fuel and a properly homogenised fuel/air mixture enters the cylinder should help you to understand that just as with a carburettor-type fuel system where we cannot just fit the largest-size carburettor with impunity so likewise with a fuel injection system. Here we must use a correctly sized inlet manifold and throttle body. Smaller-diameter manifold tracts and throttle bores serve to improve cylinder filling at engine speeds lower in the power band. Also they tend to reduce the intensity of reversion pulses, so there is actually less restriction to inlet flow at certain rpm. The other benefit of going small is that the engine will pull more vacuum, and more vacuum also results in improved fuel vaporisation. However, go too small and you will kill the top end of the power band.

Table 5.3 highlights the effect of such tests with 45mm and 48mm throttle bodies on a 16-valve 2-litre Nissan rally engine that was tuned for forest stages. Below 4,500rpm both throttle bodies produced virtually identical power. This was probably due to the size of the ports in the head and in the inlet manifold being flowed to suit the 48mm throttle bodies, and thus they were a bit too big to allow the smaller 45mm throttle bodies to bring the power up right at the bottom of the usable power range. Except for a slump in power at 6,500rpm, which with more development time no doubt could have been rectified, the smaller-bore throttle bodies allow this engine to make more power at nearly every point between 5,000 and 7,500rpm. Down at 5,000 and 5,500rpm the engine is a very useful 20hp stronger, and at the very top of the rev range it only loses 5–10hp to the bigger 48mm throttle bodies.

Table 5.3   Throttle bore comparison on a 16-valve 2-litre Nissan

	Test 1		Test 2	
rpm	hp	Torque	hp	Torque
4,000	93.7	123.0	94.2	123.7
4,500	116.2	135.6	116.5	135.9
5,000	147.9	155.4	128.3	134.8
5,500	166.4	158.9	148.1	141.4
6,000	186.3	163.1	179.6	157.2
6,500	191.7	154.9	202.0	163.2
7,000	209.6	157.2	211.8	158.9
7,500	226.4	158.5	220.5	154.4
8,000	229.8	150.9	235.4	154.5
8,500	218.5	135.0	228.1	140.9

Test 1 – 45mm-bore throttle bodies.

Test 2 – 48mm-bore throttle bodies.

Note: in both tests the same inlet manifold was used, which tapered from a 48mm bore down to match the inlet port.

Suzuki learned the same lesson with their 130hp (155hp in race trim) GSX-750R. It was introduced with huge 46mm throttle bodies, but because of poor throttle response and sluggish mid-range these were replaced by 42mm units. As a further admission of the need for inlet tract air speed Suzuki added a second throttle plate in each inlet tract, progressively opened by the ECU. The throttle bore sizes recommended in Table 5.4 will serve as a reliable guide in enabling you to select throttle bodies with a bore size close to that with which the engine should work best.

Table 5.4   Recommended throttle body sizes

Throttle bore dia (mm)	hp of one cylinder
36	27–37
40	35–46
45	43–56
48	50–65
52	60–77
56	70–87
62	80–98

INLET TRACT LENGTH

Together with the bore of the throttle body we have to consider the length of the inlet tract. Just as the tuned length of exhaust headers can be beneficially used to alter the power characteristics of a competition engine, so also the length of the inlet tract can be adjusted, using various-length intake trumpets, to modify the engine's power curve.

Generally, when we add length to the inlet tract we expect to see an hp increase at the bottom of the power band, along with some reduction in hp at the peak. Conversely, when we take length away we may add power at the peak while knocking something off the bottom end. However, if we go too far in either adding length, or in taking length off, we will probably lose power at full throttle right across the power band.

Table 5.5 shows how taking just 15mm off the length of the intake tract of the Nissan rally engine mentioned earlier lost an average 3–4hp right across the engine's operating rpm range. However, this engine responded in the classic manner when 25mm was added. At 5,500rpm it was 9hp stronger, but peak power was down over 4hp, and at the engine red line it is down 7hp. In a circuit racer or tarmac rally car this sort of loss would not be acceptable except on a very tight track, or perhaps if the car

Table 5.5   Inlet trumpet comparison on a 16-valve 2-litre Nissan

	Test 1		Test 2		Test 3	
rpm	hp	Torque	hp	Torque	hp	Torque
4,500	112.1	130.8	116.2	135.6	118.8	138.7
5,000	143.3	150.5	147.9	155.4	151.2	158.8
5,500	163.2	155.8	166.4	158.9	175.6	167.7
6,000	184.2	161.2	186.3	163.1	190.8	167.0
6,500	187.3	151.3	191.7	154.9	193.3	156.2
7,000	206.6	155.0	209.6	157.2	207.3	155.5
7,500	224.5	157.2	226.4	158.5	223.8	156.7
8,000	227.1	149.1	229.8	150.9	225.3	147.9
8,500	217.2	134.2	218.5	135.0	211.4	130.6

Test 1 – 60mm-long trumpets.

Test 2 – 75mm-long trumpets.

Test 3 – 100mm-long trumpets.

Intake chokes

Tuners usually associate chokes with Weber carburettors having a removable air venturi, which is available in a variety of bore sizes, to tune the carburettor to suit the air-flow characteristics and power requirements of the engine. Before teams had the vast sums of money they have today to enable them to build engines to suit specific race circuits, or in the case of rally cars to build engines to suit specific types of rallies, they had to make do with engines in just one or two levels of tune. However, to change the power characteristics an interesting tuning device was hidden away in the inlet manifold; while the throttle bodies may have had a bore of, say, 48mm, concealed behind the throttle body in the inlet manifold were removable 'chokes' that may have necked the manifold bore down to 45mm on circuits where more low-speed grunt was required. Then on very-high-speed circuits a plain 48mm bore sleeve without a venturi would be fitted.

Intake chokes work very well, but do pattern your chokes after the way Weber and Dellorto shape the venturis in their chokes. You will probably only want to use one or two choke sizes in competition, even though you may check three or four sizes going down in 1.5 or 2mm steps while running on the dyno. Remember that you will require a different map in the ECU for each size; a dash-mounted switch will make programme selection simpler.

was running with less than ideal gearing. However, in the forests this engine with the long trumpets was on average 0.3sec faster per mile.

However, not all engines react in the 'normal' way. The 5-litre Chev circuit engine referred to in Table 5.6 was running in a restricted compression class (10.5:1) with a 7,500rpm rev limit. During the course of testing this engine appeared to be pretty much insensitive to induction tract length, showing virtually identical hp at all rpm points right the way from 3,750 to 7,500rpm running with 75mm, 60mm and 45mm trumpets. However, when trumpets 100mm long were tried the power shot up, not at the bottom of the power band, but right at the peak!

Table 5.6   Inlet trumpet comparison on a 5-litre Chev

| | Test 1 | | Test 2 | |
rpm	hp	Torque	hp	Torque
3,750	255.9	358.4	258.3	361.8
4,000	292.2	383.6	290.9	382.1
4,500	331.8	387.3	335.0	391.0
5,000	403.0	423.3	401.2	421.4
5,500	466.6	445.6	468.1	446.9
6,000	500.0	437.7	505.4	442.4
6,500	553.3	447.1	550.4	444.7
7,000	584.2	438.3	587.9	441.1
7,250	591.4	428.4	604.6	438.0
7,500	588.5	412.1	611.7	428.3

Test 1 – 60mm-long trumpets.

Test 2 – 100mm-long trumpets.

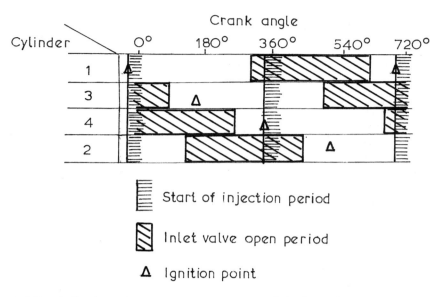

Figure 5.8 Batch fire injection sprays once every crankshaft revolution.

As for the overall inlet tract length, somewhere between 310 and 330mm is a good starting point. This measurement is from the start of the trumpet down to the valve seat, and it seems to work for many engines producing maximum hp at anything from 7,000 to 8,500rpm.

BATCH FIRE

The next area we need to take a look at is the actual timing of the injector spray period. In the batch fire type system all the injectors spray simultaneously once every revolution of the crankshaft, ie each injector sprays twice during each complete engine cycle (Figure 5.8). In a four-cylinder engine the firing of the spark plugs for cylinders 1 and 4 triggers the ECU to commence the spray period for all the injectors, which is why this system is usually called batch fire injection.

Thus while this arrangement results in the injectors sometimes firing when the inlet valve is closed, it does have the benefit of simplicity. Additionally, the fact that they pulse twice allows for the use of smaller injectors. This reduces their cost, but the other benefit is that at lower rpm and light engine loads the injector spray period can be made longer by programming the ECU to skip every second firing, ie the injectors only fire once every two revolutions of the crankshaft. This improves metering precision as most injectors become erratic and lose metering precision when the pulse width is reduced much below about 2 milliseconds.

SEQUENTIAL FIRING

However, in time manufacturers began to switch to sequential fuel injection (SFI), with the injectors being timed to synchronise their spray period with the opening of the inlet valves. With production cars it is usual to time the injectors to commence

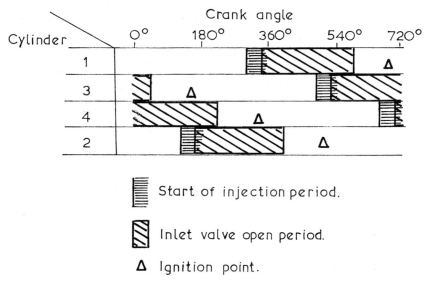

Start of injection period.

Inlet valve open period.

Δ Ignition point.

Figure 5.9 Production car sequential systems typically begin spraying just before inlet valve opening.

spraying about 40–50° before the inlet valves start to open (Figure 5.9). To get around the difficulty caused by using large injectors spraying just when the inlet valve is open, it is quite common for manufacturers to fit small injectors. Thus at cruise rpm and light engine loads the injectors will finish spraying before the inlet valve closes. This lowers emissions, reduces fuel consumption, and improves throttle response.

However, as engine loads and rpm increase these small injectors are not able to flow sufficient fuel in the approximately 240° that the inlet valve is open. Manufacturers solve this problem by extending the injector pulse width, allowing the injectors to continue spraying long after the inlet valves close. This charges the inlet tract with more fuel, which will be inducted during the next inlet cycle. Obviously at high rpm and high engine loads this arrangement is not very different from the batch fire system, which is why in stock road engines not much power difference is seen between the batch fire and sequential systems. It is really only at low rpm and cruise that sequential injection provides an advantage in the stock engine.

In a competition engine we do not have to worry so much about low-speed running and exhaust emissions, so we can use very large injectors that can supply the engine's full throttle fuel requirements in a short period of time. Usually, when sequential injection is applied to competition engines the injectors are timed to stop spraying just before the inlet valve closes. The ECU calculates the injector pulse width in the usual manner, so at lower engine loads the injectors may not commence spraying until mid-stroke of the inlet cycle. As rpm and engine loading increase the injectors spray for a longer portion of the inlet valve open period (Figure 5.10).

Some believe that the injector spray period must not be extended beyond the inlet valve open period. Thus if the cam had an inlet lobe duration of 310°, the injector pulse width – its spray period – would be limited to 310° of the crankshaft rotation. At the bottom of the power band this is true, but as we approach maximum engine speed we usually find a power advantage when the injectors are open for 430–500°. Thus if

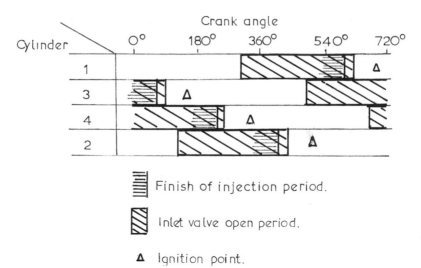

Finish of injection period.

Inlet valve open period.

Δ Ignition point.

Figure 5.10 Race engine sequential systems are often phased to finish spraying just before the inlet valve closes.

we were running a 310° cam the injectors would be timed to commence spraying anywhere from 120 to 190° before the inlet valves commenced opening, and they would shut off just before the valves closed.

When dual injectors are used it is usual for them to be 'staged', or phased, to provide the best throttle response and hp all the way from the bottom of the power band right up to the red-line rpm. Depending on the computing capacity of the ECU we can experiment with the size and the phasing of the inboard and outboard injectors. For example, we may find it advantageous to allow the ECU to work the pulse period of the inboard and outboard injectors in different ways. The inboard injector spray

Table 5.7   Ford Cosworth 'YB' 2-litre fuel injection comparison

rpm	Test 1		Test 2	
	hp	**Torque**	**hp**	**Torque**
5,500	180.0	171.9	189.8	181.2
6,000	204.2	178.7	209.9	183.7
6,500	220.7	178.3	230.4	186.2
7,000	245.2	184.0	251.6	188.8
7,500	260.2	182.2	269.3	188.6
8,000	273.9	179.8	282.6	185.5
8,250	277.1	176.4	293.3	186.7
8,500	286.8	177.2	297.6	183.9
8,750	284.6	170.8	297.2	178.4
9,000	278.8	162.7	294.1	171.6

Test 1 – batch fire injection.

Test 2 – sequential injection with dual 'staged' injector phasing and individual cylinder trim for both fuel and spark.

time may be based on fixing the commencement of injection at, say, 40° ahead of inlet valve opening, then allowing the ECU to determine when injection time would hold at a certain maximum, or be permitted to decay to a shorter duty cycle. The outboard injectors may be staged to begin spraying once the inboard injectors reach a certain pulse width, often well below 80% duty cycle. However, their spray time may be based on a fixed shut-off, timed to correspond with the closing of the inlet valve, and the ECU would be allowed to determine when the spray period should commence.

Again, with sequential injection and a powerful ECU we can exercise individual cylinder trim. This means that we no longer inject the same quantity of fuel into each cylinder, but rather treat each cylinder as an individual unit and vary the amount of fuel injected. The variation, or trim, from cylinder to cylinder is not very much, usually only a maximum difference in pulse width of 1–2% between the richest and leanest cylinders.

As Table 5.7 indicates, there are big power gains to be made when switching a maximum effort engine from batch fire to sequential injection. Some tuners are

Figure 5.11 Speed density type electronic fuel injection for a turbo competition engine. The components illustrated are: 1 injectors; 2 throttle plates; 3 air temperature sensor; 4 throttle position switch; 5 MAP sensor; 6 ECU; 7 exhaust gas temperature sensor; 8 coolant temperature sensor; 9 fuel temperature sensor; 10 fuel pressure sensor; 11 fuel pressure regulator; 12 fuel rail; 13 fuel filter; 14 fuel pump; 15 excess fuel return line; 16 manifold vacuum/boost sensor hoses.

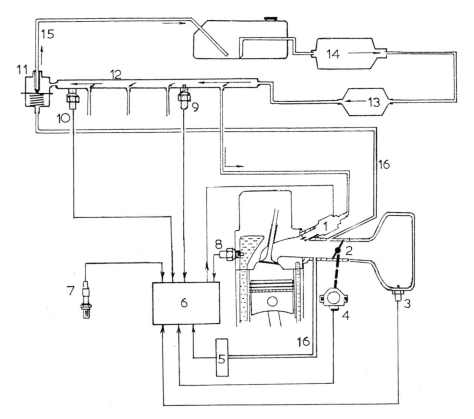

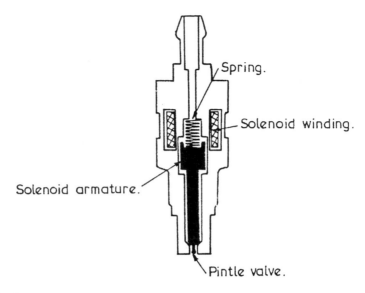

Figure 5.12 Electronic system fuel injector.

claiming rises in peak torque of 5–7% and a peak hp rise of around 5%. I think these claims are fairly optimistic in most cases; it is more typical to see a 3–4% rise in torque, but often not at the peak. Individual cylinder trim of spark and fuel is frequently worth another 1% hp.

FUEL INJECTORS

In Figure 5.11 you can see the various components of a typical competition-type electronic fuel injection system. The basic EFI system can be broken down into three groupings: the air flow and electrical systems, which we have already covered, and the fuel system, comprising the injectors, pressure regulator, fuel pump and fuel filter, which we will now discuss as these parts have to be carefully matched to meet the fuelling needs of the engine. Obviously any deficiency here will cause the engine to be way down on power, or if a severe lean condition occurs the engine will be destroyed.

We cannot just look at an engine's fuel requirements simply from the aspect of injector size. Actual fuel flow into the inlet air stream is a product of the injector's size, the injector pulse width and the fuel pressure (Figure 5.12). Also, as we are considering maximum hp, we have to factor in the injector duty cycle, which is expressed as the maximum percentage of time the injector is spraying fuel to meet the engine's maximum fuel-flow needs. If the injector is open continuously, 100% of the time, it will overheat and either fail to respond accurately to signals from the ECU, or else it will burn out. In road cars I will not run injectors longer than an 85% duty cycle, and in competition cars with batch fire injection I keep the duty cycle below 80%. This means that if the injectors have a factory-rated static fuel flow of 390cc/min at 2.7 bar (39.2psi) fuel pressure, the maximum quantity of fuel that one injector can flow at this pressure and an 80% duty cycle will be 312cc per minute (390 x 80% = 312).

However, it will often be found during dyno testing that an engine will make best power with correctly phased sequential injection when the duty cycle is 60–70%. A shorter duty cycle of around 40–45%, phased to occur while the inlet valve is open, is often too short for best fuel atomisation and engine cooling. This is especially so in turbo and supercharged engines. Note here that these comments apply to sequential injection only; I cannot ever recall seeing any power difference in batch fire systems at duty cycles ranging from 65% right up to 80%.

Taking this matter of injector duty cycle a step further, it should be obvious that if we are using a sequential system and we are desirous of obtaining maximum possible hp output, we should be looking at running injectors large enough, and with a fuel pressure high enough, to permit dyno testing at a 60% duty cycle. There is not much gain, perhaps no gain at all, in running a sequential system in a race engine and using fuel injectors so small, or fuel pressure so low, that you have to run a 75–80% duty cycle to get sufficient fuel into the engine at high engine speeds.

To determine the approximate amount of fuel flow needed per cylinder for engines burning petrol, I use the following formula:

$$\text{Fuel flow (cc per minute)} = \frac{\text{HP x K}}{\text{C}}$$

where HP = maximum horsepower, K = 4.6 for naturally aspirated engines, or 5.6 for turbo/supercharged engines, and C = number of cylinders.

Thus a 280hp non-turbo engine with four cylinders requires about 322cc of petrol per minute per cylinder to produce that hp.

The next step is to take a look at what size injector we require to provide that flow of 322cc/min while keeping the duty cycle down to our required figure, using this formula:

$$\text{Injector static flow (cc per minute)} = \frac{\text{TF x 100}}{\text{N x M}}$$

where TF = theoretical flow, N = number of injectors per cylinder, and M = injector duty cycle.

Assuming that we wish to run sequential injection with one injector per cylinder, and we want to test the hp at duty cycles down to 60%, the required injector static flow would be:

where TF = 322, N = 1 and M = 60,

$$\text{Injector static flow} = \frac{322 \text{ x } 100}{1 \text{ x } 60}$$

$$= 536.7\text{cc/min}.$$

But before we run off to purchase four injectors with a static flow of at least 536.7cc/min, we need to consider that such large injectors cost a considerable amount 177

The pulse width and duty cycle relationship

As engine rpm increases, the time available in which to complete the injection of fuel into the intake air stream becomes shorter and shorter. Obviously an engine running wide-open throttle at 9,000rpm has only two-thirds of the amount of time in which to get injection completed compared with an engine running at 6,000rpm. However, an injector cannot be held open continuously or it will burn out. In a modified road engine it can be active, or on 'duty', up to 85% of any given time period – this is termed its duty cycle. Clearly its 'rest cycle', where there is no electricity passing through the solenoid winding, accounts for 15% of that fixed time period. Because stock road cars seldom see extended high-rpm, wide-open throttle running, some manufacturers allow up to a 93% duty cycle, but in competition engines, which run at reduced throttle opening for only short periods of time, we should not extend the duty cycle beyond 80%.

This necessary 20% rest cycle impacts on the time that the injector has available in which to pulse and spray fuel into the air stream. We can calculate the maximum permissible pulse width using this formula:

$$\text{Maximum pulse width (milliseconds)} = \frac{M \times 60,000}{\text{rpm}}$$

where M = injector duty cycle, and rpm = maximum rpm for batch fire, and half maximum rpm for sequential injection.

If during dyno testing we find from our pulse width meter that the injectors are going beyond an 80% duty cycle at any engine speed, we will have to fit larger injectors or increase the fuel pressure. However, remember that the maximum permissible pulse width increases at lower rpm:

Maximum pulse width (milliseconds)

rpm	*70%	80%	85%
4,500	18.67	10.67	11.33
5,500	15.27	8.73	9.27
6,500	12.92	7.83	7.85
7,500	11.20	6.40	6.80
8,500	9.88	5.65	6.00
9,500	8.84	5.05	5.37

*Indicates sequential injection; the 70% duty cycle is suggested as a maximum for best hp. However, the injectors can stay open for an 80 or 85% duty cycle providing 16ms is not exceeded.

Note, however, that in general injectors will not pulse for longer than 16 milliseconds. This usually is not a concern with naturally aspirated batch fire engines, but turbo and supercharged batch fire engines, which produce very high torque at low rpm, can run into trouble here, as can all engines running sequential injection.

of money, and we can perhaps achieve comparable flow from smaller injectors by increasing the fuel pressure. Most of the manufacturers state the static flow of their injectors at a fuel pressure of either 2.5, 2.7 or 3.0 bar. However, we can get good flow gains by increasing the fuel pressure up to about 4.0 bar. Never push the pressure past 5.0 bar (72.5psi) or injector control will be lost. At any rate I have found that only a few very high flow injectors actually show any flow increase once 4.0 bar fuel pressure is exceeded. Smaller injectors often show no flow increase, or not more than a gain of 2–3%, when the fuel pressure is raised from 4.1 to 4.8 bar.

Note here that I am discussing ordinary fuel injectors. Some very high pressure injectors, fashioned after those designed for diesel engines which operate up around 2000 bar, are in use in applications such as Formula 1 where cost is no impediment and maximum performance is the objective. In these big flow injectors pressure is maintained close to the mandated 100 bar limit, similar to the direct injection Le Mans winning Audi 3.6 and Bentley 4.0 litre V8s, to ensure the best possible atomisation of fuel in the extremely short time available at 19,000rpm.

At lower fuel pressures (ie below 4.0 bar) we can estimate the injector static flow with raised fuel pressure using the formula:

$$\text{Revised static flow} = \text{SF} \times \sqrt{\frac{\text{RP}}{\text{OP}}}$$

where SF = injector static flow at manufacturer's standard pressure, RP = revised fuel system pressure, and OP = manufacturer's standard pressure.

Using this formula we can calculate if the '036' injectors fitted in the 928 Porsche would be close to what is required. Bosch rate these at 480cc/min at 2.5 bar pressure. We will calculate what the flow might increase to at 3.4 bar fuel pressure:

where SF = 480, RP = 3.4, and OP = 2.5,

$$\text{Revised static flow} = 480 \times \sqrt{\frac{3.4}{2.5}}$$

$$= 559.8\text{cc/min.}$$

Obviously the '036' injector should be capable of supplying this engine's fuel needs when operating at a 60% duty cycle. Table 5.8 sets out a list of a wide range of injectors from Bosch, Lucas and ND and provides a flow estimation chart for various fuel pressures using the above formula. Note, however, that these revised fuel flow rates are estimates only and actual flow may be well down, as is illustrated by the results of testing two injectors at various pressures in Table 5.9.

Really, before running injectors in any competition engine we should have them flow tested at a variety of fuel pressures to ensure that they will actually give the sort of flow required. Naturally the injectors should be matched for flow; we do not want more than a maximum of 2% flow difference. Ordinary Bosch injectors, for example, have a flow tolerance of ±3% (6% overall) according to the manufacturer, but if you speak to anyone who does flow testing they will tell you it can be worse than stated. In a sequential system with individual injector trim this is not such a problem, but with a batch fire system our fuel mixtures end up all over the place.

Something to keep in mind is that if overly large injectors are fitted and you wish to keep the injector spray period relatively long, you can lower the fuel pressure to reduce injector flow. However, the pressure must not be reduced below 2.0 bar otherwise fuel atomisation suffers. At this point any possible improvement in atomisation gained by increasing the injector pulse width will be lost due to larger fuel droplets issuing from the injector tip when the fuel pressure is brought below 2.0 bar.

Table 5.8   Fuel injector flow

Injector		Flow cc/bar	Estimated flow at revised pressure				
			2.5	*2.7*	*3.0*	*3.4*	*4.0*
Bosch	150208	145/2.7	139	145	153	163	176
	150205	167/2.5	167	174	183	195	211
	150901		180	187	197	210	228
	150203	195/2.7	188	195	206	219	237
	150157	214/2.5	214	223	235	250	271
	150255		226	235	248	264	286
	150013		304	316	333	355	385
	150009	340/2.7	327	340	358	382	414
	150014		360	374	395	420	456
	150803	390/2.7	375	390	411	438	475
	150024		455	472	498	530	575
	150036	480/2.5	480	499	526	560	607
	150351	560/2.7	539	560	590	628	682
	412911	800/2.5	800	832	876	933	1012
Lucas	5207007	147/2.7	141	147	155	165	179
	5207003	164/3.0	150	156	164	175	189
	5207002	188/2.5	188	196	206	220	238
	5208001	188/2.5	188	196	206	220	238
	5207013	201/2.7	193	201	212	226	245
	5207011	218/3.0	199	207	218	232	252
	5208004	237/2.5	237	247	260	276	300
	5208005	237/2.5	237	247	260	276	300
	5206004	260/2.5	260	270	285	303	329
	5207009	299/2.5	299	311	327	349	378
	5207006	323/2.7	311	323	340	362	393
	5207008	368/2.7	354	368	388	413	448
	5208010	422/2.7	406	422	445	474	514
	5207005	503/2.7	484	503	530	564	612
	5207601	503/2.7	484	503	530	564	612
	5207602	540/2.7	520	540	569	606	657
Nippon Denso	195500–2020		536	557	587	625	678
	195500–830		660	686	723	770	835
	N304132500		806	838	883	940	1020

Table 5.9   Effect of fuel pressure on injector flow

	380/3.0 injector		500/3.0 injector	
Fuel pressure	*Estimated flow*	*Measured flow*	*Estimated flow*	*Measured flow*
2.5	347	353	456	452
2.7	360	364	474	472
3.0	380	389	500	498
3.4	405	401	532	526
4.0	439	423	577	565
4.8	481	429	632	601

FUEL PRESSURE REGULATORS

To ensure precise fuel flow through the injectors it is necessary to maintain a constant fuel pressure in the system, otherwise at higher fuel pressures the engine would run rich and at lower pressure it would be lean. Therefore a fuel pressure regulator is required, and there are three types available: manifold pressure referenced, non-referenced fixed pressure, and non-referenced adjustable pressure.

The advantage of manifold pressure referenced regulators is that they increase the dynamic flow range of the fuel injectors. At lower rpm, and when manifold vacuum levels are high, this allows for a longer injector pulse width, with resultant improvements in fuel atomisation. In turbo or supercharged applications, because this type of regulator increases fuel pressure as manifold pressure rises, smaller injectors are able to flow at a higher rate to meet the engine's fuel needs.

To help you understand how this comes about, consider the situation when a non-referenced fixed pressure regulator is fitted. A road car at idle or cruise may have an inlet manifold vacuum level of around 15 inches of Hg, or 7.4psi below atmospheric pressure. Obviously in this situation, with inboard injectors the effective fuel pressure at the injector tip will be 7.4psi (or about 0.5 bar) higher than the pressure set by the pressure regulator because the high manifold vacuum will actually draw fuel through the injectors during their open cycle. Therefore if the pressure regulator is fixed at 2.5 bar (36.6psi), rather than flowing as if they have a 36.3psi fuel rail pressure, they will flow as if they have 43.7psi fuel pressure (36.3 + 7.4 = 43.7psi). This in effect means that the injectors will be flowing about 10% more fuel. We can overcome this by programming the ECU to reduce the injector pulse width. In a road car this is not a good idea as such a move will reduce the intake charge quality because fuel metering becomes erratic when injector spray time is cut down to around 2 milliseconds.

If the engine is turbo or supercharged the situation regarding injector fuel flow reverses when the manifold is experiencing full boost. For example, if maximum boost is 16psi (1.1 bar) the injectors will now flow as if they have only 20.3psi (36.3 − 16) fuel pressure. In effect, injector flow will decrease about 25% because manifold pressure will be restricting flow out of the injectors. This problem could be overcome by fitting larger injectors, but then we would have to cut back on injector pulse width at idle and cruise, which would really adversely affect intake charge quality.

To avoid this undesirable situation we can choose a manifold pressure referenced regulator. This diaphragm-operated pressure regulator maintains fuel pressure at a fixed figure, as the injectors see it, relative to either manifold depression or manifold boost. One side of the regulator diaphragm senses fuel pressure, while the other side is connected to the inlet manifold to react to the prevailing vacuum level, or prevailing boost level. A spring is fitted in the engine vacuum side to establish a nominal pre-load of pressure. If this pre-loaded pressure is, for example, 2.5 bar and the inlet manifold depression at cruise is 15 inches of Hg, this will draw against the spring and reduce its nominal pre-load from 36.3psi down to 28.9psi (36.3 − 7.4), so fuel rail pressure drops to that figure. Then, when manifold boost increases to 16psi, this pressure works in unison with the spring, increasing its nominal pre-load from 36.3psi up to 52.3psi (36.3 + 16), and fuel pressure in the fuel rail will rise to this figure. With this type of regulator, regardless of whether the inlet manifold is experiencing 20 inches of Hg   181

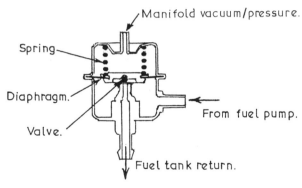

Figure 5.13 Manifold pressure referenced fuel pressure regulator.

vacuum or 30psi boost, the injectors will flow exactly the same quantity of fuel (Figure 5.13).

In a naturally aspirated competition engine we can choose to ignore such considerations and use either a non-referenced fixed pressure regulator, or more usually an adjustable pressure non-referenced regulator. With the latter option we can very quickly increase or decrease engine fuelling without having to reprogramme the ECU. Thus if the track is wet we can back off the pressure a little to lean the mixture and reduce the risk of plug fouling. Conversely, if the humidity takes a dive we might up the pressure to avoid detonation damage.

FUEL PUMP FLOW REQUIREMENTS

Fuel is supplied to the injectors by a high-pressure roller-type electric fuel pump. This pump must be large enough to deliver more fuel than the maximum requirement of the engine so that full fuel pressure is maintained at wide-open throttle and maximum rpm. On leaving the pump the fuel passes through a high-flow fuel filter containing a paper element, which traps anything in the fuel that would otherwise block the injectors. Note that to avoid flow restriction the filter must be replaced regularly; be sure to fit it with the flow direction arrow pointing the correct way. After exiting the filter the fuel continues on through the fuel line up into the fuel rail and to the individual injectors. This all sounds simple enough, but obviously to ensure sufficient flow of fuel at the fuel rail at the correct pressure we have to take care to choose the correct fuel system components, and then correctly instal them.

First we must calculate the engine's maximum expected fuel flow at wide-open throttle and maximum rpm. We want to choose a pump that can over-supply the engine's needs, but we have to be careful not to go too big, otherwise if return fuel is routed back to the swirl pot rather than the fuel tank we would have a lot of fuel flowing in a closed loop gaining more and more heat with each pass through the fuel rail (Figure 5.14). With this in mind I work on a 30% theoretical over-supply using the formula:

$$\text{Fuel pump flow (cc per minute)} = HP \times K$$

where HP = maximum horsepower, and K = 6.0 for naturally aspirated engines, or 7.3 for turbo/supercharged engines.

Avoid losing octane

Most racers know that high-octane race fuels, and in particular unleaded fuels, can go 'stale', losing their octane, if allowed to vent their octane-boosting components to the atmosphere. They thus take care to keep all fuel drums, etc, tightly sealed to prevent these additives, often aromatic hydrocarbons, from boiling off their 'light ends'. However, it is easily forgotten that a similar process is occurring in a race car's fuel tank when the fuel is allowed to heat up and vent octane-boost compounds to the atmosphere. Thus as the race progresses the fuel will suffer a deterioration in octane level, and if the ECU has not been programmed to compensate for fuel temperature changes, the engine will experience both a leaning of the fuel/air mixture and a loss of octane. Clearly hp will be lost at least, or worse the engine may be damaged.

The fuel tank must therefore be shielded from heat radiating from the exhaust, brakes, transmission and tyres. Additionally, fuel pump over-capacity must be kept in check otherwise large volumes of fuel heated by its circuit through the engine bay will be dumped back into the tank. Some racers fit a fuel cooler into the fuel return line, but such a cooler must not be installed unless fully protected from stones, track debris, etc, which may puncture it and create a massive fire hazard under the car. Really a better location for the cooler is within the car, close by the fuel tank, and with a meshed-over duct flowing cooling air across the cooler.

Therefore a naturally aspirated engine producing 280hp would require a fuel system capable of flowing 1,680cc (approximately 1.7 litres) per minute. Note here that we are not talking about 1.7 litres free flow into an open container, but rather 1.7 litres flowing from the pump at fuel system pressure. When system pressure is regulated higher, pump flow is reduced because the pump has to work harder to push fuel into the fuel line. Typically a system regulated to 3.0 bar fuel pressure will see the free

Figure 5.14 Fuel system plumbing. The components illustrated are: 1 fuel tank; 2 swirl pot feed pump; 3 swirl pot; 4 pressure pump; 5 fuel filter; 6 fuel rail and injectors; 7 fuel pressure regulator; 8 suction lines; 9 high-pressure fuel supply lines; 10 excess fuel return lines.

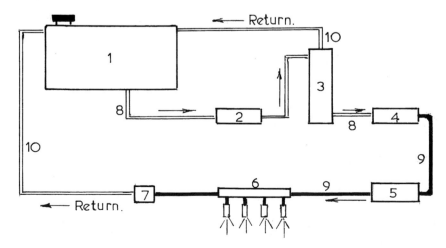

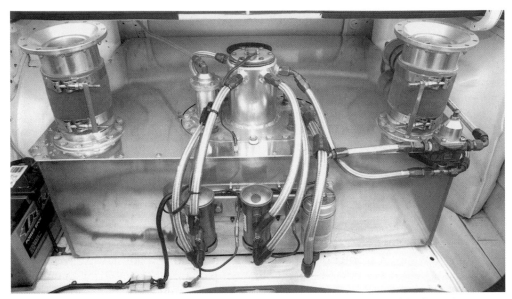

Good fuel injection performance depends on an ample flow of filtered fuel, at the correct pressure, being constantly available at the injectors.

flow figure reduced by about 15–20%. Thus if the pump flows 2.2 litres per minute into an open container, real flow at 3.0 bar fuel pressure will be around 1.76–1.87l/min. However, move the pressure up to 4.0 bar and flow will drop another 10–15% to about 1.5–1.68l/min. Now if we were to add a turbo pumping 1.0 bar boost, and this was referenced to the pressure regulator, we would see fuel rail pressure rising from 4.0 bar to 5.0 bar. At this pressure pump flow would fall another 10–15% to around 1.28–1.51l/min.

Some believe that you have to bundle up your entire fuel system and truck it off with the engine into the dyno room to determine if the pump will flow enough fuel at system pressure. Accordingly the engine is set up with the car's fuel system laid out in the dyno cell to take into account flow restrictions caused by the fuel filter and fuel lines. Next they disconnect the fuel tank return line and run it into a container to see if at full throttle and maximum rpm there is an excess of fuel at the fuel rail, indicated by fuel flowing from the return line. Apart from the danger of all that fuel in the dyno room, such a test is really a waste of time. You can easily do a quick, safe test in your own garage, which will give a good indication of flow at the fuel rail.

For this test you need to have the entire fuel system installed in your car. The engine does not have to be in place, but you will need to have the fuel rail and injectors connected. The fuel pressure regulator must be adjusted to the pressure at which you intend to operate the system. If it is a turbo installation with a manifold pressure referenced regulator, you will need to pressurise the regulator to normal turbo boost. This can easily be done by fitting a 'tee' to the regulator; a pressure gauge is attached to one branch of the tee, and a tyre valve to the other, to enable a tyre pump to apply the appropriate 'boost' to the regulator. Now disconnect the tank return hose and direct it into a graduated measuring container. Energise the fuel pump to fill the fuel system and get it up to pressure, then empty the measuring container and activate the fuel pump for exactly

2 minutes. The quantity of fuel collected divided by 2 is your system's fuel flow per minute. Obviously the flow must not be less than what you have previously calculated.

The only problem with this test arises if the car's electrics are a bit wimpish. Because the only load is what is being drawn by the fuel pump, the pump may be receiving a voltage boost compared with when the system also has to power the ignition, cooling fan, injectors, transmission oil pumps, etc. You can estimate on a reduction in fuel flow of around 12% for every drop of 1 volt at the pump; for example, if voltage at the pump is 10.6 volts rather than 12.6 volts, flow will be down 24%. The way to avoid this unwanted trouble is to ensure that you use good-size wiring, good connections and ample alternator capacity.

SWIRL POT AND FUEL LINES

However, getting fuel to the injectors is only part of the equation – we also have to get fuel to the fuel pump. In a race car with a fuel cell and correctly positioned fuel pick-ups, this is not such a problem, but what if you are running a normal steel fuel tank? As the fuel level falls it may drop below the fuel pick-up when subjected to strong G forces caused by cornering, braking and accelerating. At that time the fuel pump will pump air; fuel pressure will drop and the engine will stumble. Even fuel-injected road cars with well-designed fuel pick-up systems in place in the fuel tank can come up against this sort of trouble when converted for competition use.

The simplest solution is to run a second fuel pump that pumps into a small-capacity swirl pot, which should be large enough to supply the engine's fuel needs for at least half a minute (Figure 5.15); for our 280hp engine, that means about 1 litre.

Figure 5.15 Fuel swirl pot.

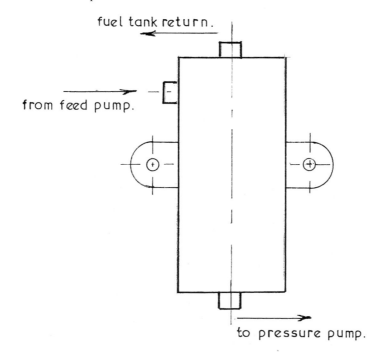

However, I think it is wiser to reckon on 1ltr per 160–180hp, so I would choose a 1.5–1.8ltr collector for this particular engine. As it is not subjected to pressure it can be fabricated quite easily from 3in tube. Exhaust tubing is acceptable, but if it is to look pretty you might prefer stainless steel or aluminium.

I prefer to use the same type of pump to supply the swirl pot as I would run for the pressure pump. Some, however, choose to use a small pump to feed the swirl pot, and run the fuel return line back to the swirl pot rather than to the fuel tank. I do not believe that this is such a good idea for two reasons: first, unless the swirl pot is fairly large it can run dry at high engine loads and high rpm, and second, at lower engine loadings the fuel will get hot circulating in a closed loop and the engine could become dangerously lean.

Both the suction fuel line from the fuel tank to the pressure pump and the pressure line from the pump to the fuel rail must be of adequate size and with bends of sufficiently generous radii to not unduly restrict fuel flow. Table 5.10 sets out the approximate hp levels that various sizes can support. Note that when stainless steel braided hoses are used these will have an id smaller than that indicated in the table, but as only small lengths are involved this should not be a concern. Incidently, these hoses are identified by a dash number representing 1/16in, thus a '–6' hose is for connecting to a 3/8in (6/16) hardline tube. On the pressure side a hose of this size will flow enough fuel for a 500hp engine.

Table 5.10   Fuel line fuel flow

Tube od	Tube id	hp pressure	hp suction*
1/4	.180	165	110
5/16	.243	300	200
3/8	.319	500	335
1/2	.444	1000	675

* These figures can also be used to estimate fuel line size for engines with carbs.

Chapter 6

Fuel and Fuel Boosters

Fuel to a large extent is still a great mystery. Most racers and enthusiasts know a little about petrol (gasoline), methanol and nitromethane. They know that an engine will make more power on methanol than petrol and they understand that a high octane rating will permit a high performance engine to make more power without engine wrecking detonation. However those same individuals would deride anyone who suggested that half a dozen formulations of petrol with the same octane rating could produce an overall variation of 5% in power outputs, or that one formulation gave significantly sharper throttle response.

WHAT FUEL OCTANE RATINGS MEAN

The problem has been over the years we have been unwittingly led to understand that fuel octane ratings are a measure of the fuel's power producing potential. The thought was an engine will make more power on 110 octane petrol than 102 octane, so by inference two formulations measuring 105 octane produce identical outcomes. They do, but only with regard to knock resistance in a standard single cylinder fuel test engine under standard test conditions. In areas such as fuel consumption, throttle response and power output there will be measurable differences.

Since this confusion exists as to what octane ratings really mean it is best to look at the subject before we tackle the tricky field of fuel formulation. As we have already mentioned most people realise that an engine can make more power and pick up fuel economy with a higher octane fuel because such fuel will allow a rise in the compression ratio and/or more spark advance. However many don't seem to appreciate that simply changing from 95 octane unleaded to 100/130 Avgas, which has an octane rating of around 105–110, will not necessarily give any power increase and may even cause a slight power loss if the engine does not have knock sensor engine management controls, or was not retuned in any way to take advantage of the octane increase.

HISTORY OF OCTANE STANDARDS

To better appreciate what octane numbers are all about we have to take a trip back in history to the time of World War I. At that time it was found that aircraft engines would suddenly self-destruct through detonation. An engine might run fine on one load of fuel, but punch holes in the pistons on the next batch. The problem for the fuel refiners was the fuels seemed to be the same, weigh the same, and may perhaps have come from the very same refinery.

The fuel companies tried chemical analysis in an endeavour to achieve parity from one batch of petrol to the next, but in spite of intensive lab programmes they were not able to identify the batches that were prone to promote engine knock. Because of this problem special fuel research engines, with a variable compression feature, were constructed to evaluate and grade fuels. Such a standard heavy-duty, single cylinder test engine would be warmed up to a standard test temperature, run at standard rpm and load, and then have the compression ratio increased until the fuel being tested just produced engine knock. Its anti-knock rating would then be specified as its Highest Usable Compression Ratio (HUCR).

However, even with every fuel lab supplied with the same type of test engine, and using the same standard test procedure, it was discovered that the same fuel could test out with differing HUCR numbers in different laboratories. Obviously some

The standard fuel test engine is a heavy-duty single cylinder unit. Insets show the rod and piston, which take a regular pounding without failure, and the knock meter.

unvarying standard was needed by which to calibrate the lab test engine. Two pure substances were chosen as reference fuels. The high reference fuel was what we commonly call iso-octane (2-2-4 trimethylpentane), while the low reference fuel was normal heptane (n-heptane).

Now it was decided that a fuel under test would be run in the variable compression test engine and its HUCR determined. Then a series of runs would be made with various mixtures of iso-octane and n-heptane until a blend was found which produced knock behaviour identical to the fuel being tested. At this point the quality of the test fuel would be rated in relation to the percentage of iso-octane in the reference fuel mixture which gave identical test results. For example, a fuel that behaved the same as 95% iso-octane/5% n-heptane would be called 95 octane petrol. Using this standard test procedure, fuel of consistent anti-knock quality could be refined and supplied for a variety of applications.

RESEARCH AND MOTOR TESTS

Since that time a number of test procedures have come into use to simulate a variety of engine operating conditions. Motor spirit is rated according to the Research and Motor test methods. Both measuring techniques use the same single cylinder, variable compression test engine, but as indicated in Table 6.1 the Motor method employs a greater engine speed and a higher inlet mixture temperature. Hence the Motor method is a more severe test, and generally yields octane numbers 6 to 12 less than the Research numbers as shown in Table 6.2. This distinction is important as it informs us that the Motor Octane Number (MON) is more relevant in high performance engines than is the Research Octane Number (RON) as such engines usually operate at high temperatures for long periods at full throttle. Fuel technicians often state that the RON gives a better indication of a fuel's part throttle knock resistance, while the MON indicates its full throttle knock resistance.

Table 6.1 Comparison of Motor and Research test procedures

	Motor Octane Test	Research Octane Test
Inlet air temperature	148.9°C	65.6°C
Engine jacket temperature	100°C	100°C
Engine rpm	900	600

Table 6.2 Octane test comparison

Research octane number	Motor octane number	Pump octane number
92	85	88.5
96	88	92
98	90	94
100	91.5	95.8
105	95	100
110	100	105
113	103	108
115	105	110

VP racing C-23 has a very high Motor Octane Number (MON) of 119. It is heavily leaded (7.2gm/gal) and has a specific gravity (SG) of 0.71.

The spread between the RON and MON is known as the fuel's sensitivity and it is quite important to understand what this distinction is exactly. Because intake temperature affects different fuel compounds in various ways it is possible for a refiner to come up with a fuel which has a high RON (or high Pump Octane Number) of say 98, but by the Motor test that same fuel would rate as, say 86 octane. Hence it would perform as an 86 octane fuel in a typical performance engine. However, on another day the fuel company could use a different blend of fuel compounds, depending on what was in storage or the type of crude oil being 'cracked', and produce a fuel with a RON of 98, but with a MON of 91. This is one reason for the frequent complaint among performance enthusiasts of 'bad fuel'. The RON may legally be up where the company say it is, but because of the sensitivity of the blending compounds the fuel could be performing like low octane stuff. In the past when high lead levels were usual this sensitivity problem seldom surfaced as lead tends to 'cushion' fuel sensitivity. However, with today's unleaded and lead replacement fuels, fuel sensitivity will continue to cause us problems for as long as RON figures are used as the industry standard to rate commercially available fuels.

R + M/2 AND SUPERCHARGE NUMBERS

In the USA service station pumps carry a Pump Octane Number (PON) rather than the Research number seen on pumps in other parts of the world. This rating, usually expressed as R + M/2 is the average of the RON plus MON divided by two.

The Supercharge test is applied to aircraft fuels which exceed 100 octane numbers, as the other tests obviously become meaningless at anything over 100 octane. The Supercharge Octane Numbers (SON) are really performance numbers obtained by linearly extending the scale beyond 100. In this test the reference fuel is iso-octane plus lead (1gm of lead added to 4 litres will increase the octane about 6 points). Two tests are involved, the F3 and F4, which explains why aircraft fuels have a dual rating such as 100/130. The first number refers to the F3 test which simulates a supercharged engine running on a chemically correct air/fuel mixture as when

190

cruising. The F4 number gives an indication of the fuel's performance rating with richened mixture and increased boost, as would be supplied during take-off.

FUEL CHEMISTRY AND OTHER TEST STANDARDS

The anti-knock properties of hydrocarbon fuels are related to their molecular properties. When the hydrogen and carbon molecules are tightly bonded together it takes considerable heat and pressure to break those bonds so as to permit complete combustion to take place. The heat energy required for this process actually comes from the combustion flame itself. Therefore when tightly bonded molecules are present in the fuel formulation, heat energy which would otherwise have been used to rapidly increase pressure in the cylinder is partly diverted to fracture and rip apart those tightly bonded fuel components. Naturally enough this process slows down the rate of pressure rise and combustion speed to an orderly controlled process.

Another factor in all of this is the rate at which fuel vaporises, and at what temperature. If the fuel recombined in the inlet tract or cylinder to the liquid state it wouldn't burn. On the other hand if it boiled easily into vapour, controlling combustion speed would be impossible, plus there would be huge problems in storing and handling the stuff. Therefore the challenge facing fuel chemists is to produce a fuel with the right mix of compounds to provide the necessary knock resistance (octane level) and which readily vaporises at specific temperatures.

In the past a lot was made of a fuel's RVP (Reid Vapour Pressure), but relative to fuel performance the numbers are pretty meaningless. Governments regulate the RVP to ensure relatively safe fuel handling (if it boiled too easily fuel tanks and drums would bulge and eventually explode), reduced emissions during fuel transfer operations, and in the case of aircraft they don't want planes falling out of the sky due to the fuel boiling and causing vapour lock in the fuel lines. The European Standard EN228 calls for car fuel from service stations to have RVPs between 5.08 and 10.15psi in summer, and between 7.98 and 13.05 in winter. Formula 1 fuel regulations demand RVPs of from 6.53psi up to 8.7psi. Avgas has to be maintained between 5.5psi and 7psi, and most race fuels fall into the same range.

Leaded 100 racing fuel is often straight Avgas 100/130. This is the high lead green variety, but as the drum states that it is not for aviation use. Other hydrocarbons – most likely benzol and/or toluol, which would have lowered the RVP below the aviation standard – have obviously been blended in.

What gives us much more insight is the distillation curve as it shows us how rapidly and at what temperatures the fuel turns to a readily combustible vapour. The volume which evaporates up to 70°C must be adequate to aid cold starting, but if the proportion is too large fuel will boil in the fuel lines. The amount which vaporises at 100°C establishes the engine's warm-up running qualities, and also its acceleration and throttle response at normal engine temperature. The vapourised volume at 140°C and 180°C should be sufficiently high to minimise dilution of the lube oil, particularly before the engine reaches normal operating temperature.

The European Standard for summer blend states that at 70°C a minimum volume of 15% must evaporate. By 100°C at least 40% has to be boiled off. At 180°C 85% of the fuel must have vaporised, and by 215°C all must have boiled to vapour. By comparison Formula 1 fuel, which is supposed to mirror what you can purchase at European service stations (I kid you not!) has to have lost a minimum of 20% volume to vapourat 70°C, while at 100°C 46% has to be boiled off and at 140°C the minimum which has boiled off is 75%. By 210°C all the fuel must have evaporated, with a 2% residue (tar) allowed to remain. European fuel specification sheets will also state at what temperature 30%, 50%, 90% and 95% of the fuel is vaporised, and the final boiling point (FBP) – the temperature at which all liquid has been converted to gaseous form (Table 6.3).

Table 6.3 European Standard race fuel characteristics

		Elf Avgas 2T	Elf WRF	Elf LMS	Elf Moto 4T-2M
Octane RON		118-120	101.6	101.2	99.5
MON		102	89.4	89.4	86
PON		110-111	95.5	95.3	92.7
Specific gravity		0.784	0.763	0.765	0.765
RVP		3.10	6.96	6.96	7.25
Distillation	30%	95°C	76°C	82°C	70°C
	50%	100°C	99°C	101°C	82°C
	90%	106°C	128°C	134°C	119°C
	95%	108°C	151°C	158°C	
	FBP	120°C	169°C	173°C	140°C
% vol @ 70°C			24	20	
% vol @ 100°C			52	50	
Oxygen content		2.4%	2.6%	2.5%	2.6%
Lead content gm/gal		2.27	0	0	0

Elf Avgas 2T 96.7 – complies with regulations permitting Avgas 100LL fuel
Elf WRF – control fuel for World Rally Championship
Elf LMS – control fuel for Le Mans
Elf Moto 4T-2M – complies with Superbike regulations

In America fuel regulations are different. As such their fuel test sheets will not include details of the volume of fuel vaporised at 70°C and 100°C. They record at what temperature fuel first evaporates; called the IBP (initial boiling point). Then it is recorded at what temperatures 10%, 50% and 90% of the fuel turns to vapour. Finally they record the end point; the temperature at which all the fuel changes to vapour.

Table 6.4 sets out the characteristics of five race fuels for comparison purposes. You will note that Trick Turbo fuel requires 10°C more heat than Trick 108 to evaporate 10% of the fuel, indicating that it will not be brilliant when the engine is cold. However it is going to give good throttle response in spite of the high octane rating as 90% of the fuel is vapour at 113°C. By comparison, two of the VP fuels need a lot more heat initially, but then are completely evaporated at relatively low temperature.

Table 6.4 American Standard race fuel characteristics.

		Trick 108	Trick Turbo	VP MR#9	VP MS 103	VP C-23
Octane	RON	113	119	98.1	107	
	MON	103	109	87	99	119
	PON	108	114	92.5	103	
Specific gravity		0.73	0.73	0.718	0.743	0.71
RVP			6.1	11.22	2.86	4.54
Distillation IBP		36°C	34°C			
	10%	58°C	68°C	44.4°C	87.8°C	77.9°C
	50%	94.5°C	96°C	57.7°C	99.1°C	97.6°C
	90%	117°C	113°C	115.6°C	102.8°C	99.7°C
	end point	146°C	144°C	164.8°C	107.6°C	110.1°C
Oxygen content				2.7%	MTBE	
Leaded		Yes	Yes	Yes	No	Yes

Petrol can be a combination of various amounts of up to about one hundred different components. If the fuel was mainly composed of less volatile anti-knock hydrocarbons the engine would be hard to start and throttle response at normal engine temperatures would be poor. Also when the engine was cold some fuel would remain unburned, washing oil off the cylinder walls and diluting oil in the sump. On the other hand if the main fuel components were extremely volatile there would be very little resistance to engine knock and fuel boil.

Consequently the composition of race fuel and aircraft fuel, and that for street use is quite different. Also street fuel composition changes according to the season. While there are government regulations stipulating how readily the fuel will vapourise in summer and winter, hence the terms 'summer blend' and 'winter blend', fuel companies actually change the formulation each month. In aircraft the throttle is basically set and only altered for take-off and landing, so throttle response isn't a factor in the blending of that fuel. And, because the engine does very little cold running with infrequent start-ups, cylinder lubricant wash and oil dilution isn't an issue. In this regard race fuels are similar, but unlike aircraft race cars must have excellent throttle response, which calls for a different blend of tightly bonded anti-knock fractions and more easily ignited components.

HOW MOLECULAR STRUCTURE AFFECTS KNOCK RESISTANCE

The paraffins, such as normal heptane and kerosene, are long chains of carbon and hydrogen held together by weak molecular bonds, which are easily broken by heat. 193

Methyl benzine, Shell's name for toluol, is an aromatic with extremely high knock resistance. During the Formula 1 turbo era the usual fuel blend was 86% toluol and 14% n-heptane, the latter being added to improve fuel atomisation and aid combustion speed.

Iso-octane is a member of the iso-paraffin family. These have branched chain structures that form stronger bonds to better resist detonation. The cycloparaffins or napthenes also have good anti-detonation properties with their hydrogen and carbon atoms well bonded in a ring shaped molecule. The aromatic fuels, such as toluol, also have a ring-shaped structure with very strong bonds, hence their excellent anti-knock characteristics.

As has already been pointed out, the chemical composition determines just how rapidly and completely the fuel will burn, and whether it will be resistant to detonation at high cylinder pressures and temperatures. The fuels required for ease of starting and throttle response have weak molecular bonds, so break up and burn spontaneously (ie without being ignited by the combustion flame initiated by the firing of the spark plug) at lower temperatures and pressures than fuels with strongly bonded structures. Some fuel additives, such as the aromatics, make good anti-detonants because they burn slowly and don't oxidise or burn completely until combustion chamber temperature and pressure is very high. Such components thus inhibit, or slow down, combustion. Hence a high octane fuel will only increase power in an engine that actually needs a fuel which is chemically stable at high temperature and pressure. Obviously if the engine does not have a compression ratio, boost pressure and spark advance great enough to produce high combustion pressure and temperature, then the high octane fuel may not burn completely during the early phase of the power stroke, resulting in reduced throttle response and perhaps a power loss.

This is one reason for my fondness for the dual-fuel approach in very high performance road cars. With an ordinary, relatively inexpensive street fuel in the main tank you get easy starting, good throttle response and minimal cylinder wash and oil dilution. Then with either toluol, a toluol/Avgas mix, or straight Avgas in the secondary tank, connected to a second injection system, you achieve excellent detonation resistance with inexpensive, easily obtainable fuels. Plus, because these fuels with tightly bonded structures are only being released at higher engine load levels, combustion is rapid and complete, ensuring good power output combined with a high level of knock resistance.

AVGAS-BASED RACE FUELS

In the past a lot of race fuel was simply some grade of Avgas relabelled. Thus 115/145 was sold as 'racing 115', although to be completely accurate some brands of 115 did contain around 20% toluene, not so much to increase its knock resistance but to decrease fuel consumption and to make for easier fuel and oil blending in two stroke engines. This fuel is no longer available, except to the military and operators of old fighter aircraft. Most leaded 'Racing 100' is in fact Avgas 100/130. The old green coloured variety has more lead (4.5–6 gm/gal) than the more recent blue low lead type (2–2.7gm/gal). Tested by the Research method the octane rating of both is generally 108–110, by the Motor method it will be 100 minimum, and up to 102. Both attain their high octane by a high percentage of alkylates plus lead. The blue type though, to get back octane lost due to lower lead levels, also contains a good portion of aromatics, usually toluol.

Avgas 112/160 used to be available in some parts of the USA and is now marketed there as 'Leaded Racing 108', reflecting its Pump Octane Number. It has a Research number in the 112–114 range and a Motor number of 102–104. However, like the old 'Racing 115MB' (for methyl benzine, a Shell trade name for toluol), it also contains a high portion of heavy aromatics which lift its specific gravity (SG) from the 0.69 typical of aircraft fuel to 0.73. This means that there is more energy in every tankful so the mixture has to be leaned off to maintain the correct air/fuel ratio, but it also allows a race car to go another 5–6% distance, an important factor in endurance events.

SOPHISTICATED RACE FUELS

In time though fuel companies recognised the commercial advantages in batching special race fuels which provided not only the detonation resistance possible with Avgas, but also better throttle response and a good power increase. Typically 4–5% at the top of the power curve and even more in the mid-range, which also serves to

Motorsport 103 is a street legal oxygenated RFG unleaded fuel with a high octane rating (103 by R+M/2 method and 99 MON) and SG of 0.728.

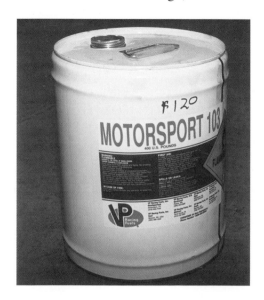

broaden the power band, are seen on the dyno. MR#3 from VP is representative of this class of fuel. It is heavily leaded (7.2gm/gal), contains 2½% oxygen, has a seemingly low MON around 90, but its actual resistance to detonation under race conditions makes it seem 4–6 numbers higher, and costs $US 7.00 per litre!

While this was going on more sanctioning bodies began to ban leaded fuels in the more highly promoted and publicised classes (NASCAR being the exception). The transition has not been too smooth for some racers though. What has caused some confusion is that 'Unleaded Racing 100', which in Europe is rated by the Research method, unlike the old leaded 'Racing 100' which gets its 100 rating with the tougher Motor test. Obviously a switch to the unleaded 100 without suitable engine modifications and retuning would cause the engine to be destroyed by detonation.

Adding to the problem was the fact that many high octane unleaded road and race fuels contain the quite effective octane booster MTBE (methyl tertiary butyl ether) in concentrations usually below 10%, but sometimes up to a maximum of about 15%. MTBE is also an oxygenate, meaning it carries some oxygen, so as well as giving an octane boost it also provides a tiny amount of additional oxygen for the combustion process. So it is important to note that if the race fuel specifications indicate an oxygen content that this is taken into account as it affects fuel/air ratios. MTBE is more dense than petrol, so the SG goes up. Previously a high SG would alert a tuner to lean off the quantity of fuel going into the engine. However because MTBE is an oxygenate the SG is a somewhat misleading measure as to how much the mixture can be leaned off. Some tuners did not understand this and lost engines. In America, VP Motorsport 103 is very popular (99 MON, 107 RON), it contains MTBE but VP do not state the oxygen content (they do on most other fuel). The power king in this class is Power-Mist RFG (reformulated gasoline). It contains 6% oxygen and tests at 105 MON and 111 RON.

By far the most money and resources are devoted to Formula 1 fuel development. F1 must use unleaded with maximum RON of 102 and maximum SG of 0.775. Maximum oxygen content is now 2.7% and benzene allowable is right down to 1%. Even after the turbo era aromatics in F1 fuels were often over 50%, but now have been pegged at a maximum of 35%. Major components in descending order are: toluol, xylene, sopentane, iso-octane, hexene-1, n-butane, 2-methylpentane.

OCTANE BOOSTERS

As you can see toluol and xylene are the main anti-knock agents in F1 fuel. Unfortunately straight xylene is difficult to obtain (paint thinners may contain a considerable portion of xylene and/or toluol but as it also contains other compounds its use is fraught with danger) and while such is not the case with toluol there is a question mark over using it as an octane boosting agent in high octane unleaded pump fuel. In the past a reliable method of increasing the octane rating of petrol was to add up to 33% toluol (bigger percentages were not recommended due to cold weather starting difficulties). This percentage would raise the octane rating of leaded fuel (0.2 gm/ltr) about 6 numbers Research and 2.5 numbers Motor respectively. However, as lead levels have decreased, government regulations permitting, petrol refiners have substituted high-octane hydrocarbons to bring the octane back up, so a reliable octane increase cannot be guaranteed by their addition. A guide as to whether fuels such as toluol, triptane, benzol, xylene etc have been added by the fuel company is to check

Concentrated octane boosters vary considerably in potency and should be used with a high degree of caution.

the specific gravity. If the SG is high and there is no government regulation limiting these products to 5% maximum (they are reported to be cancer causing), the petrol probably contains up to 20% of these products either singularly or in combination.

However if the government limits their use to a maximum of 5% then with the exception of benzol and triptane all will provide a good octane boost of about 1 MON for every 10% added up to a maximum of around 25%. Additionally, in distance racing, by virtue of their high SGs they significantly reduce fuel consumption, and thus the number of pit stops required.

The situation is similar with another very effective octane booster, MMT (methyl cyclopentandienyl maganese tricarbonyl), which is the base product in the most impressive concentrated octane boosters (Australian made NF Racing Formula and Nulon Pro Strength). In low octane unleaded (91 RON) both will provide a consistent 5 RON boost. However when added to 95 RON premium unleaded the results waver between a 2 and 3.5 RON rise, and with super 98 RON unleaded it varies between a 1.5 and 3 RON increase.

Actually concentrated octane boosters vary considerably in potency. You really cannot take much notice of the octane increase claims. If any of the claims were true then they must have been obtained when added to the 83–86 RON stuff which is the staple diet for motor vehicles in some poor parts of the earth. Also be careful of any change in product which you have previously found to be effective. The word 'reformulated', new packaging etc. should get the alarm bells ringing. It probably means the product has had to be changed due to government regulations or steep increases in the price of key ingredients, and that it no longer is as effective as previously. 104+ and Super 104+ are a typical example. The old stuff was about the best of the 'bottle boosters'. Then in 1999 it was changed (identified by the eagle logo on the back) and slumped to being a very ordinary performer giving only about half the octane boost (1 RON for Super 104+ with 95 RON unleaded) as the previous formula. 197

When using these concentrated additives there are two points you must keep in mind. The first is that American concentrates are usually marketed in US quarts which equal 946cc as opposed to the Imperial quart of 1136.5cc. The US gallon is also different (see Appendix), so if you live outside the USA you will have to carefully work out the blending ratio. The second point is with regard to mixing technique. Don't just pour a can of octane booster into your fuel tank and expect it to blend uniformly. What is preferable is to mix the concentrate with about 2–3 gallons of petrol, give the mixing drum a good shake, and then add this mixture to the untreated fuel.

TESTING, PURCHASING AND STORAGE OF PUMP FUEL

Really any time you blend a commercial pump petrol you are at the mercy of the fuel companies, so what worked with one batch of fuel may not work with another. Apart from certified racing fuels the only other fuel that is a known quantity and highly regulated is Avgas. Consequently my advice is don't muck around with fuel blending, it could cost you an engine. If you are in a competition class restricted to 98 RON unleaded test different brands to determine what brand gives the best overall power and throttle response. Do this preferably in summer when fuel turnover is high and when summer blend is being supplied. When you find the 'power king' buy up what you require to do you for the race season. Be sure to store fuel in sealed drums away from sunlight; you don't want vital components evaporating or being destroyed by light (both can happen and high octane unleaded is more prone to this damage). Also remember fuel companies swap fuel between themselves and frequently use a series of common pipe networks so if your dyno testing of fuel is going to be of any value you really have to be quick to buy fuel from the very same service station where you sourced your winning test sample before new, possibly different supplies, are dumped in the storage tanks.

WHY METHANOL RAISES HORSEPOWER

By now it should be obvious that a fuel's octane rating is not a true measure of its power potential. Its octane rating, its knock resistance, is important but it is not the whole story. When we examine an alcohol fuel such as methanol this becomes even more evident. When we look at Table 6.5 we see that methanol has only a very modest Motor octane of about 89–91 and the high Research numbers are only possible with extremely rich mixtures. The problem then is, why does it permit a higher compression ratio (CR) than petrol and provide up to a 20% power increase?

Methanol has a very high latent heat of vaporisation, ie it takes a lot of heat to be converted from liquid into vapour. Petrol has a latent of evaporation of 135Btu/lb, while for methanol it is 472Btu/lb (One British Thermal Unit (Btu) is the amount of energy required to raise the temperature of 1 pound of water 1°F). This heat required for proper atomisation is drawn from the inlet tract, the piston crown, the combustion chamber and the inlet and exhaust valves. An internally cooler engine does not put as much heat into the inlet charge, with the result being that mixture density in the cylinders goes up, and hp rises. Also less initial heat means a slower burn, so the engine may accept more spark lead or higher CR, resulting in more hp or improved throttle response.

Table 6.5 Fuel characteristics

Fuel	Specific gravity	RON	MON	Fuel/air ratio (lb/lb)	Heat energy (Btu/lb)	Latent heat of evap	Weight (lb/gal)
Acetone	0.79			1:10.5	12,500	225	8
Avgas100/130							
'green'	0.69	105-110	100-102	1:12.9			7
'blue'	0.71	105-110	100-102	1:12.7			7
Benzol	0.88	105-110	95-100	1:11.5	17,300	169	8.7
Ethanol	0.79	108-115	90-92	1:6.5	12,500	410	8
Ether(diethyl)	0.71				15,000	153	7
Methanol	0.79	105-115	89-91	1:4.5	9,800	472	8
Nitromethane	1.13			1:2	5,000	258	11.3
Nitropropane	1.05				6,700		10.5
Petrol							
premium unleaded	0.74	*96	*85-86	1:12	19,000	135	7.4
premium leaded	0.73	96	86	1:12.5	19,000	135	7.3
racing leaded (USA)	0.73	112-114	102-104	1:12.7			7.3
racing unleaded (USA)	0.75	104-106	94-96	1:13.2			7.5
racing unleaded 100	0.75	100	90-92	1:13.0			7.5
Propylene oxide	0.83				14,000	220	8.2
Toluol (methyl benzine)	0.87	120-124	110-112	1:9.8			8.7
Triptane	0.69	110-112	100-102				6.9
Xylene	0.86	117-118	115-116				8.5

* Premium unleaded in some lands has a higher rating (often 98 RON, 87 MON)

That's part of the story; the other part relates to the amount of energy available in the fuel burned. Using petrol the air/fuel ratio for the best power in a performance engine will be somewhere between 12.3:1 and 13.1:1, with about 12.7:1 not far from the mark. With methanol the air/fuel ratio increases to somewhere between 4.5:1 and 5.5:1, with about 5.1:1 being pretty close. One pound of petrol has the energy potential of about 19,000 Btu. In comparison, methanol delivers around 9800Btu/lb, which means that it produces less than 52% of the heat energy of 1lb of petrol. However because we are mixing more methanol with each pound of air, we are actually producing more heat energy by burning methanol.

To work out how much more heat energy is produced we have to divide 12.7 by 5.1, which is 2.49. Next we multiply 9,800 by 2.49, which gives 24,402. This tells us that in theory methanol will produce 28% more heat energy than petrol.

$$\left(\frac{24,402 \times 100}{19,000}\right) - 100 = 28.4\%$$

On average this equates to a power increase around half that, or 14%. Some engines will give close to 20% more hp, particularly if they have been prone to overheat burning petrol, while for some others the gain will be closer to 10%.

Are alcohol fuels only for high-compression race engines?

Because alcohol fuels, either methanol or ethanol, burn slowly, the myth has arisen that there is no power gain when switching from petrol unless the engine has a high compression ratio: the figure frequently quoted is anything less than 12:1.

The truth is just the opposite: low-compression race engines will show a much greater percentage hp gain than high-compression race engines when appropriately re-tuned to burn alcohol fuel. Also, restricted classes forced to run small carbs and unported heads pick up more power usually than unrestricted class engines. Thus while a 14:1 engine might deliver 11% more power on methanol than Avgas, a 10:1 engine will probably show more like a 14% gain.

Why is this? Both methanol and ethanol have much lower Motor Octane than Avgas (about midway between premium unleaded and Avgas). Thus these fuels are better suited to engines with more modest compression ratios, and they show the greatest hp improvement in engines with lower compression ratios.

FUEL FLOW INCREASES REQUIRED WITH METHANOL

Right away you can see that an engine running straight alky will burn more than twice as much fuel as one burning petrol. Therefore you must be careful to ensure that the needle valve, fuel pump and fuel lines will flow the required amount of fuel.

This can present some problems as many carburettors will not flow the required amount of fuel through the needle and seat, and others do not have main jets large enough. For this reason fuel injection is preferred for alky and nitro burners.

The SU carburettor can be fitted with two or even three fuel bowls if necessary to get proper flow. Holley and Weber have alcohol size needle valves available. If you have a carburettor that you cannot get larger needle valves for, you will have to enlarge the discharge area of the standard needle and seat, but check the fuel flow into a container before you run the engine. If it is not flowing enough fuel you will melt the pistons.

Some carburettor jets are classified with regard to the fuel flow, the number stamped on the jet representing the ccs of fuel passing through the jet in a given time. For example, the hexagon-head Mikuni carburettor jets follow this pattern. If you are

Shell 'A' racing fuel is 96%
methanol and 3% acetone.

changing from petrol to alky then you will have to start testing with jets 2.2 times as large, eg change a 200 main jet to a 440.

Other manufacturers rate their jets according to their nominal bore diameter in inches or millimetres: eg a Holley 66 jet has a nominal aperture of 0.066in, a Weber 175 jet a nominal aperture of 1.75mm, a Mikini 250 round head main jet a nominal aperture of 2.5mm. When changing from petrol to alcohol you will have to begin testing with jets with an aperture area 2.2 times as large. (Aperture area = πr^2).

Since most engines are relatively insensitive to rich methanol mixtures, the carburettor jets can be drilled out if large jets are not obtainable. Weber have an excellent set of drills for this purpose, but they are expensive.

PROBLEMS AND DANGERS OF METHANOL

There are many problems involved in the use of alcohol, some of which will affect you and some of which will affect your vehicle. Since your well-being and life are more important, we will deal with you first.

Methanol is extremely poisonous, and as it is accumulative enough can build up and oxidise to form formaldehyde, causing blindness and even insanity. It can be absorbed through the skin and lungs, and inhalation of the exhaust gas is also dangerous as vaporised methanol is usually present, and especially so when rich mixtures are being used.

Regarding your car you need to know that methanol is a very effective paint stripper and it may attack some types of fibreglass resin. It has a scouring effect on tanks and fuel lines so these should be soaked in methanol and then drained so that the residue does not find its way into the injectors or carburettor jets when you convert from petrol over to methanol.

Methanol will absorb huge amounts of water, so it must always be kept in an air-tight container. (In fact when using lean mixtures up to 10% water is at times added to the fuel to act as an anti-detonant). Following every race meeting the fuel will have to be drained and the entire fuel system flushed through with petrol. Also run the engine to prevent the formation of water-induced rust and oxidation. This can be particularly damaging to aluminium and zinc parts, and usually results in blocked carburettor metering blocks and injectors. It is preferable to use stainless steel where possible for things like fuel rails.

Caution must also be exercised in other areas of the fuel system. Petrol tends to lubricate so flat slide and barrel type throttles seldom stick. Methanol does not lubricate at all, plus there are the added problems of corrosion and possible ice formation, which may allow the throttle to stick, possibly in the wide-open position. Therefore simple butterfly throttles are preferred. Motorcycles using methanol should have only carburettors with chrome plated brass slides fitted, or you could end up a dead rider due to an aluminium or magnesium slide stuck wide open.

In colder climates, starting difficulties may be encountered when straight alcohol is being used. Some use other more volatile fuels blended with the methanol to help overcome this problem; usually 5% acetone or a maximum of 3% ether. Ether is particularly dangerous because of the possibility of engine damage from detonation so I do not recommend its use, nor do I recommend the use of starting aerosols which also contain a lot of ether. Personally I feel the best method is to spray petrol into the inlet manifold if it can be easily got at. Do not attempt to do this while the engine is being cranked over; if it backfired you could be badly burned. The alternative is, 201

Alcohol fuels absorb water so either a stainless steel or triple marine grade anodised aluminium fuel rail and methanol injectors are essential.

before fitting the warm-up spark plugs, spray about 3–5cc of petrol down each spark plug hole.

Many starting problems can be traced to an inadequate ignition or electrical system. Obviously the system must have enough grunt to spin the engine rapidly to fire. Also the ignition system must be up to firing wet plugs or fuel loaded spark gaps. Methanol burns much more slowly than petrol, so it is necessary to advance the ignition accordingly. As a guide you can reckon on the engine requiring 15–25% more advance than for petrol, right through the rev range.

NITROMETHANE USE AND BLENDING

Nitromethane is different again, and if you look at the fuel characteristics table (Table 6.5) you will see that it is not even assigned an octane number (because there are too many variables), yet it can easily double the power of an engine burning petrol. Compared to methanol, for every 20% nitro added it increases hp by 10%. This is possible due to nitro's very special chemical composition, and also due to the fact that extremely rich mixtures can be burned satisfactorily. In itself, nitromethane is a very poor fuel, but because it contains approximately 53% oxygen by weight it permits the induction of large quantities of fuel into the engine for conversion to heat energy. Also because it burns so slowly it continues to apply force to the pistons almost to the bottom of the power stroke.

In the past nitromethane was burned in the most powerful drag machines in ratios of 80–98% nitro and 2–20% methanol. Today Top Fuel rails are limited by the rules to 85% nitro in an attempt to restrict engine power and trap speed. On the speedway scene and hill climbs nitro is used, often illegally, in smaller percentages (usually 10–20%) as a power booster. Methanol is the base fuel, and acetone plus other 'doping' agents may also be added (plus about 0.5% castor oil as an odour masking agent).

To deter detonation or other engine damage, it is always necessary to reduce the compression ratio when nitro is used. At all times the air/fuel ratio must be very rich. With an 80–90% blend of nitro it may be as rich as two parts fuel to one part air, or as lean as two parts air to one part fuel. Using 20% nitro this would change to three or four parts air to one part fuel (Table 6.6).

Table 6.6 Fuel flow increase for nitromethane

% nitro in methanol (by volume)	Flow increase over straight methanol
10	25%
20	50%
30	75%
40	100%
50	125%
60	150%
70	175%
80	200–230%
90	225–260%
98	250–290%

When blending nitro with other fuels the safest method to avoid error is to mix according to volume. Thus for a 20% nitro blend you would add one litre of nitro to four litres of methanol. Some people also blend using a hydrometer calibrated for this purpose. The problem with this method is that the hydrometer will only give a true nitro content percentage reading when the fuel temperature is 20°C/68°F. From Table 6.7 you can see that with a fuel temperature of 38°C/100°F, a fuel with a true nitro content of 80% will read 73% nitro on the hydrometer. Consequently you should always measure the temperature of the fuels before attempting any mixing.

Many don't seem to understand that a nitro hydrometer is calibrated to give a true reading only when straight methanol and nitro are being blended. When a methanol/acetone/nitro mix is used the hydrometer will still give an accurate reading because methanol and acetone share the same specific gravity. However if any other doping agents were added, such as propylene oxide, the hydrometer reading would be of no value at all.

Table 6.7 Nitro hydrometer temperature correction chart

True Nitro (%)	Hydrometer reading at fuel temperature °C/°F										
	4/40°	10/50°	16/60°	20/68°	24/75°	27/80°	29/85°	32/90°	38/100°	43/110°	49/120°
100	106	104	102	100	98	97	95	94	92	90	87
90	97	94	92	90	88	87	86	85	83	80	78
80	86	83	82	80	78	77	76	75	73	70	68
70	75	73	71	70	69	68	66	65	63	61	59
60	66	63	61	60	59	58	57	56	54	52	50
50	55	53	51	50	49	48	47	46	44	42	40
40	45	43	41	40	38	37	36	35	33	31	30
30	35	33	31	30	28	27	26	25	23	22	20
20	27	25	22	20	19	18	17	16	15	13	11
10	20	16	13	10	9	9	8	7	5	3	1

Igniting high percentage nitro fuel is always a problem. Top Fuel dragsters run the equivalent of a mini welder delivering 1.2 amps to each spark plug. As higher percentages of nitro are burned the combustion rate is reduced (unless a fuel ignition accelerator such as propylene oxide is added). Therefore the spark advance must be increased, with Top Fuel engines typically running a system locked on about 50° advance.

NITROMETHANE DANGERS

There is considerable risk to yourself and others associated with the use of nitro. After combustion relatively large amounts of vaporised nitric acid are exhausted. The higher the nitro dose, the more acid vapour is released. When inhaled, nitric acid vapours cause a muscle reaction, making it impossible to breathe. Therefore the use of the correct gas mask is essential if the driver is in a position to inhale the exhaust gases. Certainly mechanics working around the car and those in the starting area will require masks.

Some people have the idea that nitromethane is explosive. It isn't, but like any fuel it can be made shock sensitive. The following are the main causes of nitro becoming dangerous:

- The addition of hydrazine in fuel blending. Hydrazine is banned in many countries because of the danger.
- The use of caustic soda or any other alkaline for cleaning fuel tanks or lines.
- The use of 'unpickled' anodised aluminium fuel tanks. After anodising the tank must be allowed to stand for a few days filled with a solution of 90% water and 10% vinegar. This serves to remove any deposits remaining in the tank after anodising.
- The use of excessive fuel pump pressure. Nitro is liable to become unstable when confined and subjected to shock. Even though some Top Fuel dragsters routinely run 500psi fuel pressure anything over 100psi should be considered dangerous.

When using more than 20% nitro, there is always the danger of a sump fire or explosion due to the large amount of fuel that finds its way past the rings and into the sump. The first signs of such a fire are yellowish flames appearing at any of the breathers. Therefore it is important to keep an eye on the engine for at least 2–3 minutes after shut-down.

OTHER FUEL COMPOUNDS

All the base fuels – petrol, methanol and nitromethane – may have other compounds added for a variety of reasons.

Propylene oxide (epoxy propane) is used in high-percentage nitro fuel to increase the combustion flame speed. The amount used should never exceed 15% of the amount of nitro in the fuel as the combustion rate could rapidly increase to the point of severe detonation and engine destruction. For example, if you are using 80% nitro you could use up to 12% propylene oxide.

Propylene oxide can also be used with Avgas or heavily leaded race fuels, and also methanol up to a maximum of about 5% to give a modest 2–3% power gain. Of much greater benefit though is the greatly improved throttle response which makes the engine feel much sharper, as though with less flywheel weight to accelerate. However, caution is in order to get the mixture a little rich and the timing backed off, otherwise expensive engine damage will result.

Once blended with other fuels, propylene oxide is relatively stable, but it can become explosive in its pure state if allowed to come into contact with copper, copper alloys, or rust particles. Therefore it must be stored in aluminium or plastic containers.

Nitropropane is listed in Table 6.5, but I would recommend its use, with extreme caution, only in sprint type engines, either naturally aspirated or else operating at relatively modest boost levels. Be mindful of the fact that it is an oxygen bearing fuel and will cause a severe lean-out unless fuelling is enriched. As a starting point, increase the fuelling by three times the percentage of nitropropane added, (ie for 10% nitropropane increase fuelling by 30%) and take out some spark lead too as combustion speed with this stuff can quickly get out of hand.

Like propylene oxide, acetone and peric acid, nitropropane is a member of the nitroparaffin family. It can be used with heavily leaded race fuel or Avgas up to a maximum concentration of about 12%, to produce a power gain in the order of 5–6%. It can also be blended with methanol in like percentages to provide a similar power boost as that when added to Avgas. However, if more than about 3% acetone (propanone) is present in the methanol then concentrations over 5–6% should not be used. Be aware that many fuel companies do not supply pure methanol. Often they blend in 2–3% acetone to improve methanol's ability to be mixed with other fuel compounds. Actually up to 10% acetone will improve the combustion rate of methanol, improve cold weather starting, and in like vein to water reduce the tendency for lean mixtures to detonate.

ASSESSING OCTANE REQUIREMENTS

Some have stated that an engine requires an octane increase of 5.0 for every 1.0 increase in the compression ratio. At best this is a gross oversimplification of a very complex matter, at worst such a 'rule' could easily lead to serious engine damage. I would prefer to state the matter in quite different and non-specific terms.

The first 'truism' is that anytime we significantly increase the intake air temperature, and place the engine under load we need increased fuel octane to ward off detonation. Increases in ambient temperature obviously produce similar increases in intake air temperature. Unscavenged exhaust gas does the same thing, but actually inside the cylinders. Increased water and oil temperatures also add heat to the inlet charge. The latter can be the product of higher ambient temperature, but it can also be as a result of a very dense, cool inlet charge producing a massive increase in heat energy as a result of all the fuel added to that dense charge to provide the correct air/fuel ratio.

Now I have to make what may appear to be a reversal of my first truism, that is: anytime we significantly increase charge density, and place the engine under load, we need additional fuel octane to fend off detonation. Thus cool dense atmospheric conditions could produce engine knock. In similar vein adding an efficient 'cold air' or

Here the combustion chamber volume is about to be measured so that the compression ratio can be calculated. While the compression ratio is important in assessing octane requirements, other factors such as engine temperature, cam lobe characteristics and cam advance, combustion chamber shape, exhaust efficiency, vehicle weight and gearing, engine rpm, etc. all have some influence.

'ram air' system could produce engine knock. As indicated in the sidebar a big drop in humidity could lead to the engine detonating. And, yes, a more efficient exhaust could cause knock. Less unscavenged exhaust gas increases charge density, but less exhaust gas means less corruption of the combustion flame through the mixture. More flame speed can lead to an excessively rapid cylinder pressure rise, out of control combustion – detonation.

As I stated this is quite complex. It is all very much a delicate balance: a slight increase in charge temperatures or charge density isn't a problem, but a big increase in either will call for more octane. Likewise a small increase in both charge density and charge temperature will likely require more octane.

PERFORMANCE INCREASES WITH RACE FUELS

Finally let's consider in real terms how much specialised race fuel can be worth even when an engine can't be re-tuned to take much advantage of the increased knock resistance and superior combustion characteristics. The test mule was a stock Honda VTR-1000 SP-1 from a race series restricted to strictly standard 1,000cc V-twin bikes. The engines and electronics were sealed to prevent any tampering, control tyres were supplied and only brake pads, dampers and springs were free. Consequently with large starting grids on some relatively short circuits regular podium finishes were going to be hard to achieve. The series controllers encouraged the use of 98 RON premium unleaded, and to prevent cheating with special 'home brews' any runners electing not

Humidity – a natural octane booster

We do not tend to think much about humidity until our clothes begin to stick to us and perspiration drips from us. This indicates that the air is saturated with water vapour. However, not only are there a lower number of oxygen atoms being dragged into the cylinders when the humidity rises, but there is also a much larger number than usual of water molecules interspersed between the oxygen and fuel molecules. The effect is that the space between the two increases, which slows combustion flame speed within the combustion chamber because rather than progressing rapidly from fuel molecule to fuel molecule, the flame front comes up against water molecules that do not contribute to the combustion process. Thus the water suppresses violent combustion – detonation – just as an octane booster does by chemical means. This means that increases in humidity will often compensate for increases in ambient air temperature, which typically demands a 1.0 octane increase for every 13°C that the mercury rises. Conversely a big decrease in humidity and an increase in intake charge temperature or air temperature could see a race engine being destroyed by detonation if octane levels are not increased, or boost pressure reduced and fuel mixture richness increased. A rise in barometric pressure of 1 inch of Hg calls for an octane boost of 1.0 octane, which alternatively can be compensated for by enriching the mixture or reducing the spark lead. However, a steep rise in the humidity level decreases the degree of compensation required. As indicated in the accompanying table, we determine humidity levels by taking temperature readings from two thermometers, one with a dry bulb and one with a wet bulb covered by a water-soaked cotton wick. When both thermometers read the same temperature the humidity is 100%. However, if the dry one reads 25°C and the wet bulb reads 24°C, a depression of 1°, then the humidity is 92%.

Percentage humidity

Dry bulb °C	Wet bulb depression °C					
	-1	-3	-5	-8	-12	-18
5	86	58	35			
15	90	71	52	30		
25	92	77	64	45	22	
35	94	80	70	55	37	15

to source their fuel from the circuit pumps were required to use only race fuels not containing any alcohol or nitro. The race fuel had to be decanted directly from a sealed drum into the bike's fuel tank, and fuel samples taken at any time from the bike had to match a fuel sample that the organisers had drawn from a sealed drum prior to the race season commencing. A further disincentive was that all fuel testing costs were charged to the competitor.

Given the series promoter's tight fuel policy and the bike's stock tune requirement many competitors simply resigned themselves to the vagaries of circuit pump fuel. The reasoning being 'how much can race fuel be worth in a stock road engine that cannot even have an ignition advance adjustment?' A few though saw the fuel rule as a big hole in the series regulations and feared that they could lose out if they didn't at least investigate if there were any gains to be made. My feeling was that as these engines were operating at up to 11,000rpm and cylinder diameter was close on 100mm there was a real possibility of finding a fuel with superior characteristics that enabled it to firstly, vaporise and blend better with the inlet air charge, and secondly, to burn more completely. Thus providing a power boost and better throttle response.

With a bore of 100mm and a relatively short stroke of 63.6mm the Honda could have been at a disadvantage in the mid-range compared to other manufacturers. Its 54mm throttle body was larger than the rest, possibly giving rise to sluggish throttle response. At 10.8:1 its compression ratio was 0.6–1.0 lower too, so there was a real need to find gains in engine performance.

Table 6.8 Race fuel test

rpm	Test 1(hp)	Test 2(hp)	Test 3(hp)	Test 4(hp)	Test 5(hp)	Test 6(hp)
4,500	58.6	55.4	59.7	58.3	63.2	58.9
5,000	61.3	59.5	62.1	61.4	65.8	61.5
5,500	62.9	61.2	64.0	62.8	66.7	63.8
6,000	76.8	74.5	76.7	76.8	78.2	76.8
6,500	85.4	83.9	85.2	85.6	88.1	85.5
7,000	93.0	92.6	93.3	92.9	96.3	93.4
7,500	102.4	102.5	102.6	102.3	106.0	102.7
8,000	110.5	110.6	110.3	110.8	114.9	112.1
8,500	115.3	114.9	115.9	115.6	119.7	116.8
9,000	118.1	118.2	118.9	118.4	122.6	121.8
9,500	116.6	116.8	117.0	116.9	120.9	119.5
10,000	113.9	113.9	114.4	114.2	118.9	116.3
10,250	107.3	107.4	107.8	107.6	112.1	111.6

Test 1 – Pump 98 RON summer blend unleaded
Test 2 – Racing 100 leaded (Avgas 100/130LL)
Test 3 – Racing unleaded 100 MON
Test 4 – Racing leaded 108 MON
Test 5 – Racing leaded 90 MON oxygenated
Test 6 – Racing unleaded 105 MON heavily oxygenated

Table 6.8 shows the results from some of the fuels tested. As expected Avgas 100/130 was the poorest performer in hp terms, and throttle response on the dyno felt pretty 'doughy'. What was a real surprise was that the majority of expensive specialty race fuels, sourced from Japan, USA and Europe, were only marginally better, both in outright power and throttle response. Obviously the outcome would have been quite different if ignition advance and fuel curve tweaks had been permitted to take advantage of the higher octane. However one fuel did stand out (Test fuel No. 5) and a couple of others also worked well (Test fuel No 3 at the bottom of the power curve and Test fuel No. 6 at the top of the power curve).

When testing was transferred to the race circuit Test fuel No 5 proved clearly superior. No 3 was only better than 98 RON pump fuel on a fast track where full throttle was held for a major part of the lap. Fuel No. 6 was on equal terms with Test fuel No 5 on the fast track, probably because its higher octane was better managing combustion as piston and combustion chamber temperatures climbed on the two very long uphill straights. However on a shorter circuit similar to those much of the series was to be fought out, lap times were slower.

Chapter 7

Combustion and
The Ignition System

When engine performance is discussed the main thread of the conversation invariably revolves around such things as the size of the engine, cylinder head flow potential, camshaft timing and lift etc. While all these aspects of performance are relevant they are in fact only one half of the performance equation. The other half of the equation is equally, if not more, important for it focuses on releasing every drop of energy from the fuel/air charge which has been drawn into the engine. It is relatively easy to come to an understanding and give numbers to the things to which the performance industry tends to divert our attention. However, the process of igniting the fuel/air mixture and ultimately totally consuming it by means of the process of combustion is not so easy to quantify; it is considerably more abstract. Possibly it is for this reason that this most important facet of performance is so seldom discussed by enthusiasts and club racers, nor elevated to its rightful position of importance.

Most of the people involved in engine development appear to understand the importance of filling the cylinders with fuel/air charge, but unless we take proper steps to release the energy locked up in that mixture we have pretty much wasted our effort in getting it into the cylinders in the first place. Consequently if we are to have our engine operating at its true potential we have to ensure that the fuel charge is ignited at the correct time with a spark of sufficient intensity to initiate combustion. Then we have to utilise a number of 'tools' to keep the flame started at the spark plug moving through the entire combustion space at the correct speed. If flame travel is slow, cylinder pressure will rise too slowly to give the crankshaft a good sustained shove. On the other hand if combustion is too rapid, it can run away and become violent, and like a nuclear reactor meltdown eventually destroys the engine.

FACTORS INFLUENCING THE COMBUSTION PROCESS

From earlier chapters you will have gathered that there is a lot more involved with combustion than the ignition system. In reality the ignition system's true function is to   209

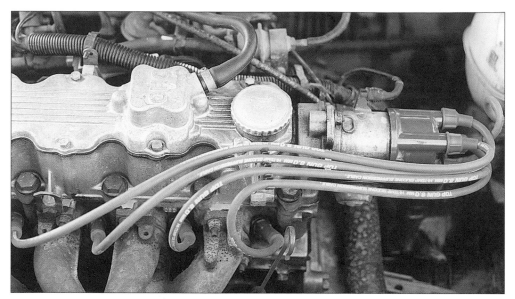

Manufacturers of aftermarket ignition components would prefer us believe that combustion involves nothing more than the actual ignition system hardware. The reality is that these parts only start the fire.

initiate combustion. To that end it must be robust enough to get the flame started. Today, unlike earlier times when some mechanical arrangement was employed, an electronic engine management system controls when the spark plug fires to start that flame off. However there are a whole host of factors which influence the manner and speed at which that flame then proceeds through the whole combustion space. When we come to understand these factors we are in a much better position to extract the maximum potential from our engine.

The major factors are mixture quality, mixture movement or turbulence within the combustion space, and the design of the combustion space. These appear to be relatively simple concepts, but unfortunately each is extremely complex due to the fact that internal combustion engines operate over a broad range of rpm and load conditions. Therefore what is optimal under one set of conditions will be less than optimal at other rpm and throttle open angles.

MIXTURE QUALITY AND TURBULENCE

Mixture quality involves filling the cylinder with fuel particles of the correct size, evenly dispersed throughout the air. During the preparatory stage prior to combustion we have to break the liquid fuel down to a vapour, increasing its surface area to the maximum. That means that outside of the cylinder we have to choose the correct type of fuel and fuel injector, plus we need to inject that fuel into the airstream at the optimal location and angle. Following that we have to rely on the physical shape of the inlet port and valve, and their angle to the cylinder to impart a swirling or tumbling motion to this fairly poorly blended mixture of fuel and air as it enters the cylinder.

Once in the cylinder we want this action to continue. The shape of the combustion chamber and piston crown then become a major controlling influence. Four-valve combustion chambers and flat top or dish top pistons are superior in this regard as they do not impede the tumbling or swirling action of the mixture. All of us have observed the swirls and eddies in a flooded river, and no doubt you have marvelled at how peaceful the flow can be in one area while right alongside being so turbulent. A similar action is in progress in many two-valve combustion chambers, and also in those engines with high-top pistons. Even very minor redesigns of shallow valve cutouts in the crown of flat-top pistons fitted in 4-valve engines has resulted in power increase in the range of 2–3%. Therefore the impact of the shape of the combustion space on mixture motion and combustion flame propagation should not be underestimated as the possible gains are much greater in engines with less favourable designs.

The purpose of this mixture motion is often said to be to homogenise the mixture – to have an even distribution of fuel molecules and air throughout the cylinder. However this agitation also serves to further break down the fuel into smaller more readily combustible particles. An equally important aspect, and at times an even more important consideration, is the fact that this motion tends to even out the temperature of the mixture. Cool pockets tend to burn slowly and so contribute nothing to power production. The real danger though are hot pockets. These may self ignite the main body of mixture before the spark plug fires. This is what is termed pre-ignition. Another more common scenario is for a hot pocket to self ignite after the spark plug fires. This flame front and the one initiated by the spark plug collide and set off violent combustion of the remaining fuel charge. This is called detonation.

THE SHAPE OF THE COMBUSTION SPACE

We have already touched on how the shape of the combustion space influences mixture motion prior to ignition. Following ignition this area continues to exert its influence. Its design can help the combustion flame spread through the moving fuel mixture at the desired speed. Additionally in the area furthest away from the spark plug the combustion chamber will be pulling some heat out of the mixture, so stalling ignition in these areas where the pressure is rapidly rising, until they are reached by the spark plug initiated flame.

Apart from causing mechanical problems the high-top piston seriously disrupts the combustion process.

Radial 4-valve piston is almost flat, but minor work to smooth valve cut-outs and modify the crown shape has given good power gains.

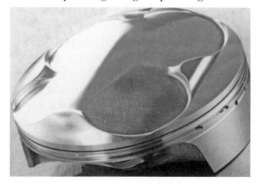

In both respects the four-valve chamber is superior. First off the spark plug is in the middle of the combustion space. Hence the combustion flame does not have to travel further to get to one end of the combustion chamber. An added bonus with respect to this design is that the deepest area of the combustion space, and thus the area where there is the greatest concentration of fuel/air mixture, is across the centre of the combustion chamber. The outer areas further away from the spark plug are shallower and in contact with a relatively large surface area. Consequently the mixture here is less inclined to bring on detonation.

Actually the radial four-valve chamber is even better in this respect. As the combustion chamber is shaped like a saucer turned upside down, rather than like a pentroof as in the traditional four-valver, the entire outer perimeter of the chamber is shallow. Unfortunately arranging the valves at a compound angle makes for a more complex valve actuation arrangement which introduces its own set of problems.

OTHER ASPECTS OF MIXTURE MOTION

In any engine, coming to grips with the complexities of mixture motion and combustion are extremely difficult. These matters are always a compromise. Thus a road engine intended to provide acceptable cruise performance, coupled with good fuel economy and low exhaust emissions, will favour a design which provides a high level of mixture motion and rapid combustion at very small throttle open angles, most likely in the 2,500 to 4,500rpm rev range. However at full throttle and high revs the situation changes. The mixture motion will now be excessive, limiting the air flow potential of the engine, and it may even throw some fuel into the liquid state in extreme cases due to centrifugal action. Then during the combustion phase, even though the engine is not detonating, flame speed may none the less be so high as to limit hp output and induce engine harshness.

In high performance road and competition engines we would eliminate these problems by changing the porting and/or the shape of the combustion chamber so as to reduce swirl or tumble. Then to control flame speed we would perhaps reduce the combustion chamber squish area, open up the clearance between the piston crown and the combustion chamber wall and change the shape of the piston crown, depending on what gave the most favourable outcome. Naturally enough these changes would all contribute to a road engine being less efficient at cruise.

Spark ignition internal combustion engines rely on an electric spark to start combustion of the fuel charge in each cylinder. If these engines are to run efficiently, that spark must be delivered at precisely the right moment in relation to the position of the piston and the rotational speed of the crankshaft. Also, the spark must be of sufficient intensity to fire the fuel/air mixture even at high compression pressure and high rpm.

POINTS-TYPE IGNITION

The most simple ignition system relies on a points-type distributor to time and distribute the spark, and a coil to provide the spark (Figure 7.1).

The distributor has two switches, the contact breaker points and the rotor, and also an advance mechanism to vary the time at which the points open and close.

The switching of the primary (low-tension) circuit is accomplished by the contact breaker points, which are opened and closed by the distributor cam. When the points

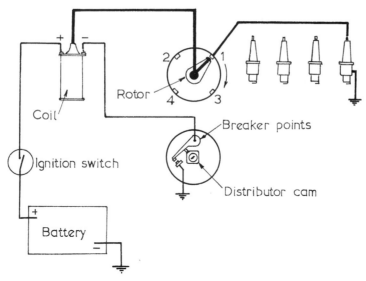

Figure 7.1 Conventional negative earth ignition system.

are closed, electric current flows through the coil primary winding, then through the points, to earth. The current in the low-tension winding produces a magnetic field that surrounds the secondary or high-tension winding. As soon as the points open, current flow through the primary stops and the magnetic field collapses, causing a current to be induced in the secondary winding. This creates a high-voltage current (up to 25,000 volts) capable of jumping across the spark plug gap, to fire the fuel mixture.

The high-voltage current flows from the coil to the centre of the distributor cap and through the carbon brush to the rotor button. The turning rotor then directs the current back to the distributor cap and to the individual cylinders.

At normal engine speeds and low-compression pressures, this conventional system works very reliably, with just periodic maintenance required to replace the points. However, when an engine is modified the ignition system has to work much more efficiently under adverse conditions.

For example, the very first problem we see with points-type ignition is that as engine rpm increased the time that the points are closed between each plug firing is decreased. This means that the coil has less time to build up a full magnetic field between each plug firing, so the ignition energy available to fire the plugs is reduced and a high-speed misfire occurs.

HIGH ENERGY ELECTRONIC IGNITION

The common electronic transistorised ignition is similar to the contact breaker system in that it is also an inductive storage-type ignition system. However, rather than using mechanical contact points to open and close the low-voltage circuit it relies instead on magnetic pulses and electronic circuitry to perform this function (Figure 7.2).

A number of different designs are in use, but the basic mode of operation is similar. The distributor shaft turns a pulse generator rotor inside a stationary permanent magnet. Functioning like a mini-alternator, this induces a signal in the pick-

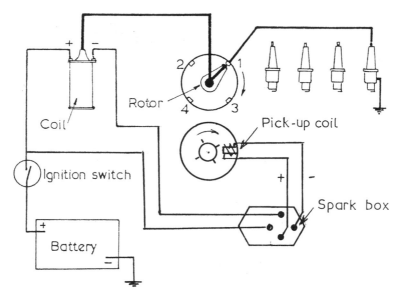

Figure 7.2 Transistor HEI ignition.

up coil located within the distributor. This electric signal flows through the electronic control module (also called the ignition module, amplifier or igniter) causing the electronic circuit to switch 'on' or 'off'. When the circuit is switched on, current flows through the primary windings of the ignition coil. When it is switched off, the magnetic field collapses, inducing a high voltage in the coil's secondary winding. As in the points-type system, the high-voltage current then flows to the centre of the distributor cap, through the carbon brush and rotor button out to the individual spark plugs. Because the transistor ignition system does not contain tungsten contact points that pit and burn, a substantially higher primary circuit current and voltage can be utilised to saturate the coil fully, even in the short time available at higher engine speed. Thus a high-intensity, or high-energy, spark is provided, which has led some manufacturers to call this 'high-energy ignition', or HEI.

The HEI ignition Bosch in Australia supplied Ford and General Motors during the 1980s for their base domestic engines is a good example of just how well a good stock electronic system can perform in a competition environment. These units were designed to fire across huge plug gaps of up to 0.065in when new spark plugs were first fitted, in a combustion chamber filled with poorly atomised fuel from a carburettor, that was contaminated by lots of exhaust gas intended to keep exhaust emission levels down. Obviously to start a fire and keep it burning, with a gale blowing in the combustion area, the ignition system had to produce a spark that was not only intense, but also of very long duration to put considerable heat into the fuel/air mix close to the spark plug tip. As indicated in Table 7.1 when compared with CD ignition, current output is only 40%, but at 8,000rpm on a V8 the Bosch HEI had a spark duration of 0.4 millisecond, meaning that there was a continuous flame between the spark plug electrodes for 19.2° of crank rotation. So long, in fact, that the ignition module cuts it short to keep the entire spark duration within the combustion cycle, and give the coil adequate time to be recharged with energy to fire the next spark plug.

If you look carefully at the distributor in this big block 440 Mopar, you will see the word 'ICE'. IC & E in Melbourne, rebuild the Bosch HEI distributor, used by Ford and General Motors on their Australian models during the 1980s, to fit a large variety of engines producing up to 1000hp. Because it was designed to get a fire started across huge plug gaps of up to 0.065in, in a combustion chamber filled with poorly atomised fuel from a carburettor and contaminated by big quantities of exhaust gas intended to keep emissions down, the Bosch HEI ignition had to produce an intense, very long duration spark.

Table 7.1   Ignition characteristics – V8 engine test

	Engine speed (rpm)							
	1,000	**2,000**	**3,000**	**4,000**	**5,000**	**6,000**	**7,000**	**8,000**
Bosch HEI								
Output m amps	50	55	60	60	60	60	60	60
Duration m sec	1.2	1.2	1.2	0.9	0.75	0.6	0.5	0.4
crank°	7.2	14.4	21.6	21.6	22.5	21.6	21	19.2
Capacitor Discharge (multi-spark)								
Output m amps	150	150	150	150	150	150	150	150
Duration m sec	0.13	0.13	0.13	0.13	0.13	0.13	0.13	0.13
crank°	0.8	1.6	2.3	3.1	3.9	4.7	5.5	6.2
Twin-point Conventional*								
Output m amps	30	25	20	15	10	10	7.5	4.5
Duration m sec	1.1	0.8	0.7	0.5	0.35	0.3	0.25	0.1
crank°	6.6	9.6	12.6	12	10.5	10.5	10.5	4.8
Single-point Conventional*								
Output m amps	30	20	10	7.5	5	2.5		
Duration m sec	1.0	0.7	0.5	0.3	0.18	0.11		
crank°	6	8.4	9	7.2	5.4	3.9		

* Competition points with lightweight contacts and high spring tension to increase rpm at which point bounce set in

Note: when comparing the Bosch HEI keep in mind that its output is superior to many stock units, and equal to the best competition HEI systems

Whereas a points-type system can supply about 18,000 sparks per minute, which corresponds to 9,000rpm for a four-cylinder engine, but only 6,000rpm for a six-cylinder and 4,500 for a V8, a stock HEI ignition raises this figure to just over 20,000 strong sparks per minute, and a good competition HEI system should increase this to at least 30,000. This latter figure means that a top-of-the-line race transistor ignition system should enable a good ignition burn with a single coil at engine speeds of 15,000, 10,000 and 7,500rpm in four-, six- and eight-cylinder engines respectively.

MULTI-COIL AND CAPACITOR DISCHARGE IGNITION

However, what if we require the engine to run at higher speeds, or what if we are burning a fuel that requires a very high intensity spark of long duration to effect good combustion? Depending on race regulations we could opt for an HEI multi-coil system, or capacitor discharge (CD) ignition, with either a single ignition coil or multiple coils. With a multi-coil system more time is available to saturate each coil fully because usually individual coils may be firing only one or two spark plugs, although in some V8 and V12 applications each coil may be firing three or four.

When race rules bar the use of multi-coil systems or we wish to avoid such complexity, we can choose capacitor discharge ignition. Unlike the previously discussed inductive storage ignition systems, CD ignition does not store ignition energy in the ignition coil, but rather in a capacitor. Even the best transistor ignition amplifier and coil combination begins to run out of ignition at about 7,500rpm on a V8. At higher speeds a single-coil HEI system runs out of time for the amplifier to 'soak' the coil, discharge all the energy from it to fire the plug, then fully saturate the coil in readiness for the next plug firing. Thus above 7,500rpm, in single-coil V8 applications, race HEI systems yield less and less secondary spark voltage and energy, the end result being a more and more feeble spark and reduced hp at best, or a misfire at worst.

Some tuners, however, believe that CD ignition is inherently superior to transistorised HEI, and it is therefore the logical choice for a competition engine, even if the engine is running at speeds below that at which a transistor HEI system is running out of ignition energy. The reasoning is that a bigger spark must produce a superior burn, therefore it has to be good for power. However, my testing indicates that an excess of ignition energy does not mean that an engine will produce more power. Only when an ignition system is inadequate will a switch to a better system allow the hp to increase.

Table 7.2 shows what I typically find when a good single-coil transistor ignition is tested against a CD system at engine speeds within the capabilities of transistorised HEI-type systems. This V8 Ford Windsor 351 was running in a class that required the use of unported cast iron heads (N351 heads fitted), flat-top pistons (12.2:1 compression ratio), and Avgas 100/130 petrol. Clearly at V8 engine speeds below about 8,000rpm one type of ignition does not show any superiority over the other when burning petrol. Also, opening up the plug gaps did not show any change in hp.

CD ignitions in single-coil V8 applications should not begin to run out of ignition energy to speeds in excess of 10,000rpm because it takes considerably less time to charge and discharge a capacitor than it does to charge and discharge a coil. In CD systems current in the primary circuit powers a mini-oscillator/transformer, which

Table 7.2   Ford 351W ignition system comparison

	Test 1		Test 2		Test 3	
rpm	**hp**	**Torque**	**hp**	**Torque**	**hp**	**Torque**
4,500	386	451	388	453	385	449
5,000	430	452	431	453	430	452
5,500	467	446	466	445	466	445
6,000	502	439	500	438	500	438
6,500	530	428	531	429	530	428
7,000	542	407	544	408	544	408
7,500	540	378	538	377	538	377
8,000	436	286	440	289	439	288

Test 1 – Ford SVO transistorised high energy ignition, 0.040in plug gaps.

Test 2 – Allison (now Crane) capacitor discharge ignition, 0.040in plug gaps.

Test 3 – as above but with 0.060in plug gaps.

in turn charges a capacitor at about 400 volts. The distributor has either a magnetic or LED (light-emitting diode) trigger system. In this latter arrangement a tiny infra-red light beam passes across a gap between an LED and a photo transistor. A slotted distributor rotor interrupts the light beam to produce the triggering signal, which passes to the control module for amplification. This amplified signal then breaks the primary circuit, at which time the capacitor almost instantly dumps its stored energy in the coil's primary winding. The coil, acting as a pulse transformer, steps up the 400 volts or so delivered from the capacitor to something in the order of 30,000 to 40,000 volts, which is directed to individual spark plugs via the rotor button, distributor cap and plug leads in extremely quick time (Figure 7.3).

Figure 7.3 CD-type ignition system.

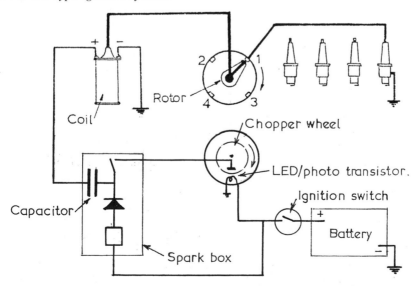

To enable the Cosworth DFV Formula 1 engine to work at over 10,000rpm Lucas developed this CD ignition unit.

Rise time for a conventional ignition is 75–125 microseconds, but CD systems have a rise time of only 20 microseconds. This enables a CD ignition to fire badly fouled or wet plugs, which means that an engine that has been 'loaded up' during a spin and stalled will quickly fire again. With other systems the rise time may be so slow that a wet plug will bleed off voltage across the fouled insulator, and there will be insufficient ignition energy left to heat the plug gap and get the engine running. A CD ignition, however, delivers full energy to the spark gap, because the voltage is produced so quickly that it jumps the plug gap before the spark energy has time to bleed off.

MULTI-SPARK CD IGNITION

A disadvantage of ordinary CD ignition is that it produces a spark of very short duration. What happens is that there is ample ignition energy to bridge the spark plug electrodes, but because the spark is of such short duration, turbulence within the combustion chamber blows out the spark before it gets sufficient heat into the fuel/air mixture to initiate a good combustion flame. This problem led to the development of multi-spark CD systems, which typically produce multiple sparks for up to 20° of crank rotation. In turn, the introduction of multi-spark CD ignition has led to a lot of misunderstanding about CD systems, and this has opened up the floodgates for advertising propaganda to add to the confusion.

First, let us consider the multi-spark aspect. Some advertising seems to indicate that the ignition will supply a sequence of, say, six sparks per plug firing, regardless of engine rpm. This is just not so, except at very low engine speeds when the ignition can get in six quick sparks in the relatively long time it takes the crank to rotate through 20°. Thus in CD systems fitted to V8 engines, by about 3,500rpm the system will have reverted to just one fat spark that may be all over in less than 3° of crank rotation. Obviously in a race engine we want to know how much spark energy is available at high rpm per spark, not per spark sequence. Whether the system gives three or six sparks per firing sequence at idle does not matter too much; what we need to consider is how much ignition energy is available at 8,000rpm. One system that produces, say, six sparks per firing sequence at idle may give a relatively feeble, by CD standards, 85 millijoule (mj) stored energy level at 8,000rpm. By comparison, another system which only produces a three-spark sequence per plug firing at idle, may be banging out 140mj of stored spark energy at 9,000rpm.

To further complicate matters manufacturers often do not specify the energy value per spark. Instead, the multiple sequence of sparks is frequently added together to give a big millijoule energy figure that could lead you to believe that you are reading the spec sheet for a welder, rather than that of an ignition system. When a stored-energy-per-spark-sequence figure is quoted, find out from the manufacturer at what engine speed, on how many cylinders, and at how many sparks per sequence they obtain that figure. It is the stored energy level per spark at high rpm that really counts.

Even then we run up against a problem in that energy losses vary from one ignition system to another. Thus one CD ignition may have a stored energy value for a single spark of 140mj, but only 50% of that energy is actually available to fire the plug. Another CD system may have a stored energy figure of only 100mj, but it is very efficient and delivers 75%, or 75mj of ignition energy, at the plug gap. Clearly there is more involved than merely looking at raw numbers, as these two systems could actually be quite closely matched in real-world performance. Note that, by comparison, race HEI and points-type systems will be hard pressed to deliver better than 50% of their peak stored energy, about 95mj and 28mj respectively, at the spark plug.

IGNITION VOLTAGE REQUIREMENTS

At this point we should consider how an engine's secondary voltage requirements enter the ignition system equation. Some people believe that we should be looking at systems that will deliver, say, 50,000 to 60,000 volts in a race engine. This is wrong thinking, because at anything in excess of 40kV in a distributor cap – regardless of whether the system is a distributor or distributorless type – you will see sparks jumping to earth from plug wires and boots. Every time this sort of thing happens there is no fire at the plug gap, so hp falls off.

Really the engine's voltage requirements depend mainly on the width of the spark plug gap, and the compression ratio. At the bottom end of the scale an engine running 0.028in plug gaps and a compression ratio of 11:1 will require about 20kV to get a spark across the plug electrodes. A 0.040in gap and a 12.5:1 compression ratio will push the voltage requirement to about 27kV, while a 0.060in gap and a 15:1 compression will see this requirement rise to around 35kV.

The effect of this secondary voltage requirement in drawing off stored ignition energy is substantial. In the above three examples, with voltage requirements of 20, 27 219 and 35kV, the stored energy given up just to get a spark started will be in the order of approximately 10mj, 18mj and 31mj respectively.

Obviously, from these figures you can see that if the ignition system is capable of delivering, say, 20mj across the spark plug gap, we would have to run with narrow plug gaps otherwise we would get no spark at all in an engine with a voltage requirement of 35kV. If the voltage requirement was 27kV we would have enough energy to get a spark, but there would only be 2mj of energy left over to keep the spark gap ionised and get the combustion flame started (20mj – 18mj = 2mj); in reality there probably would not be enough heat produced in the plug gap to initiate combustion. However, if we bring the voltage requirement down to 20kV we should have enough ignition energy to bridge the spark plug electrodes in the first instance, and have 10mj left over to pour heat into the gap and get the fuel/air mixture burning (20mj – 10mj = 10mj).

From the above we should understand that the more secondary ignition energy we have left after all of the losses in the ignition system, the better are our chances of starting and sustaining combustion at high engine speeds. Also, we must take note of the fact that as the voltage requirements increase because of big plug gaps and high compression ratios, we must switch to an ignition system with more available spark energy to ensure that we have enough heat energy in the plug gap to initiate and sustain combustion.

Table 7.3 illustrates how we also need more spark energy to burn exotic fuels such as methanol and nitro efficiently. It is much more difficult to get these fuels to burn initially, then to keep them burning for complete combustion. The same V8 Ford 351W with N351 heads was used, but for the tests the fuel was switched from Avgas to methanol. Normally a short-track speedway engine running on alcohol would have a compression ratio closer to 14:1, rather than 12.2:1 like this engine. This would put the ignition system under more pressure, and the performance differences between a good single-coil transistor ignition, when used on a V8, and a CD system would be even more apparent.

Table 7.3   Ford 351W ignition system comparison

	Test 1		Test 2		Test 3	
rpm	hp	Torque	hp	Torque	hp	Torque
4,500	416	485	417	487	418	488
5,000	463	486	466	490	465	488
5,500	511	488	514	491	515	492
6,000	555	486	557	488	560	490
6,500	587	474	593	479	588	475
7,000	601	451	613	460	613	460
7,500	597	418	615	431	614	430
8,000	471	309	490	322	495	325

Test 1 – Ford SVO transistorised high energy ignition, 0.040in plug gaps.

Test 2 – Allison (now Crane) capacitor discharge ignition, 0.040in plug gaps.

Test 3 – as above but with 0.060in plug gaps.

The converse must also be taken into account, ie when race regulations or our budget preclude the use of high-energy ignition systems, we must do something about reducing our engine's ignition energy requirements. The place to start is to reduce the spark plug gap in line with what is discussed later in this chapter. I know a lot of noise has been made about the modest power gains possible with wider plug gaps, but remember that much of this is based on what tuners are discovering when working with the small-block Chev V8 and other American V8s. However, most other race engines do not use high-dome pistons, which block up the combustion chamber and retard flame travel through the fuel/air mixture, so it is not so important to have such a big flame right at the start of the combustion process.

This is borne out by a test on a 350 Chev burning methanol in a class that required the stock HEI to be retained, with only a high-performance coil upgrade allowed. The rules also called for factory cast iron cylinder heads and flat-top pistons, which resulted in a compression ratio of 10.2:1. Many racers claim that 0.045in plug gaps give better performance in this sort of environment, but looking at the results in Table 7.4 it appears to me that around 0.030–0.032in may be a good compromise. Obviously, over 5,500rpm with 0.045in gaps the ignition is producing insufficient spark, and at 7,000rpm it is misfiring.

Table 7.4   Spark plug gap comparison with stock HEI system

	Test 1		Test 2		Test 3	
rpm	hp	Torque	hp	Torque	hp	Torque
3,500	246	369	252	378	245	368
4,000	327	429	330	433	324	426
4,500	412	481	411	480	410	478
5,000	455	478	459	482	456	479
5,500	489	467	487	465	493	471
6,000	498	436	491	430	500	438
6,500	489	395	478	386	494	399
7,000	441	331	423	317	445	334

Test 1 – 0.035in spark plug gap.

Test 2 – 0.045in spark plug gap.

Test 3 – 0.030in spark plug gap.

CHOOSING AN IGNITION

As you have already seen from the example of the Bosch HEI introduced over 25 years ago we shouldn't automatically assume that the factory ignition isn't up to the task. The aftermarket ignition manufacturers might want you to believe the stock ignition is junk, but this usually is not the case. Modern ignitions have to operate reliably without misfires otherwise the manufacturers fail government emissions standards. Such testing is considerably tougher than the environment in which many performance and competition cars operate as the ignition has to ignite very lean mixtures, contaminated by high levels of exhaust gas (usually purposely introduced so as to keep nitrogen oxide emissions low) while firing across extremely wide spark plug gaps. The main area where stock systems have a problem is at very high rpm. However you can reliably assume that as you will invariably be operating on considerably richer mixtures and with smaller spark plug gaps the power differences between the stock system and high performance ignitions will be negligible up to the rev limit set by the car manufacturer. In fact I've seen many aftermarket systems give marginally less power and a few gave a lot less at such rpm. When the revs rose way beyond the factory rev limit though, or when a rich methanol mixture had to be ignited, then some aftermarket ignitions significantly outperformed the stock unit.

Another important factor in choosing an ignition system is its reliability. Therefore ask the manufacturer about their standard 'burn-in' and testing procedures, and about the ease and cost of repair. The ignition amplifier (also called the spark box or black box) contains numerous electronic components, which, if they are going to fail, will do so in the first few hours of operation. With this in mind we should be looking for a unit from a manufacturer where every spark box coming from the factory is given a 4–6 hour burn-in and testing with normal ignition loads before it is packaged for sale. Obviously an amplifier subjected to this type of testing may cost a good deal more than if the manufacturer were to pull one box off the production line out of every hundred, or a random unit every couple of weeks, for a burn-in and test.

The other concern is amplifier repairability. Some manufacturers, after mounting all of the electronic components, fill the spark box with either a rubbery or a hard epoxy compound to keep out air and moisture. However, when the amplifier breaks down all this filler material makes it virtually impossible to replace failed components, so the entire ignition box has to be scrapped. The alternative sealing method used by some other manufacturers involves dipping the mounted amplifier components, but the case is not filled with any epoxy. When any parts break down the sealer can be penetrated, the defective part replaced, then the assembled components all dipped once more to reseal the electronics.

HELPING THE IGNITION LIVE

However, having said all that, most high-energy ignition troubles are caused by the user, not the manufacturer. The basics to keep in mind are that these systems will not tolerate excessive heat, vibration or moisture, and they quickly fail from high voltage build-up within the system. Therefore before fitting the ignition into the car read the installation instructions carefully. If you are not clear on some point, talk to the manufacturer. On the other hand, if the instructions appear to make sense after a quick read through, re-read them; no instructions are that easy to follow, and you may have misread something!

Be sure to mount the spark amplifier and the coil away from the headers, and shield them from heat being radiated or blown off the headers. If it is practical direct a small cool air duct over the spark box. Whenever components mounted on a heat sink are replaced, take care to apply the appropriate heat sink grease when the new components are being fitted. To control vibration use the mounting rubbers provided by the manufacturer, and if the rubber pads are through-bolted do not squash them tighter than specified.

Do not blast any part of the ignition system with a pressure washer. If any sealer or insulator is less than perfect a tiny fraction of moisture could see a high-voltage flash-over and subsequent system failure when the engine is started – even after several days' drying time. Keep in mind also that detergent and degreaser residues are corrosive and conduct electricity.

Heat and water are enemies of electronic components. Therefore whenever components mounted on a heat sink are replaced, be sure to help heat transfer by using the appropriate heat sink grease.

To avoid power overload in any part of the system, never disconnect any wires with the engine running. In similar vein, never crank the engine over with any of the spark plug leads or the coil lead disconnected, without first isolating the ignition system. With many systems the engine can be cranked while the leads are disconnected providing that the low-voltage positive (+) ignition wire is disconnected at the coil, but check this with the manufacturer.

Battery chargers and welders have also taken their fair toll in destroying ignition components. When using a battery charger with the battery still fitted in the car, disconnect both battery cables before hooking up the charger. When welding on the car disconnect both battery cables and disconnect the main harness going to the spark box as well as any earth straps connected to it. Also put the welder earth clamp in a place where it can make a good ground connection close to where you want to weld.

IGNITION ADVANCE REQUIREMENTS

With any type of road ignition system and most types of competition ignition, some arrangement is employed to adjust the ignition timing angle to suit various engine operating conditions. For example, at idle the ignition may be timed to fire the plugs at anything from 5° to 20° before the piston reaches top dead centre (TDC) on the compression stroke. However, at wide-open throttle and at high engine rpm the spark lead needed for best hp may be around 25° to 35° BTDC for engines burning petrol (on alcohol or nitro add about 10° and 20° respectively). Then at cruise on the highway, or under a yellow light at the speedway, an additional 10° to 15° advance may be necessary to give best economy and performance.

These changing ignition advance angles are necessary to give the fuel/air mixture the correct amount of time to burn properly. Most engines produce maximum power when we start ignition so as to reach peak cylinder pressure at around 12–14° after TDC. Clearly at 7,000rpm the combustion flame must have been progressed the same amount as it would have at 3,000rpm, so that maximum energy is available to force the piston down and produce power at the crankshaft. Remembering that most power-producing force has been expended by mid-stroke, it should be obvious that the only way that this time deficit can be made up is to start the burning of the combustion flame earlier.

Apart from the time factor, there are several other reasons why the spark angle must be varied for different engine operating modes, and why the ignition advance   223 changes from one engine to another. The main contributory factors are the fuel/air ratio, mixture density, exhaust gas reversion, engine design and fuel type.

Both very lean and rich fuel/air mixtures burn slowly and require more spark lead. A mixture close to full power lean burns the fastest and requires less advance. At cruise, for example, road engines are usually tuned to be a little lean in the interests of economy, so more advance is necessary. However, mixture density is also a factor, because in this situation, with the throttle just cracked open, the cylinders do not become crammed with fuel/air mixture, so even when compressed as the piston rises to TDC, the oxygen and fuel molecules are separated slightly, which in turn slows the speed at which the combustion flame travels through the combustion chamber.

Understanding this you will appreciate that an increase in the compression ratio has the reverse effect. This increases mixture density, so we have to reduce the spark lead. A cam change also influences mixture density, as do any changes made to the intake or exhaust, which affect the volumetric efficiency of the engine. When cam lobe duration is increased, mixture density will be reduced at lower rpm, while in the mid-range and at maximum rpm it will be greater. To compensate, ignition advance will have to be increased at lower engine speeds, then reduced higher up the rev range. Changes to the intake system have a similar effect on mixture density, but the influence of the exhaust system is different.

When an efficient exhaust system is fitted the amount of exhaust gas left unscavenged in the cylinder, or reverse flowing into it, is reduced. This leaves more room in the cylinder to pack in fuel/air mixture, so mixture density increases and the spark lead must be reduced. The other effect of upgrading the exhaust system is that there are fewer inert exhaust gas molecules to separate the oxygen and fuel molecules, so flame speed through the combustion space is faster, which again calls for less advance.

Engine design also figures in the amount of ignition advance required for efficient combustion. The size of the combustion space and the position of the spark plug(s) obviously influence the amount of spark lead needed. The further the flame has to travel, as in a large combustion chamber with only one spark plug, the longer it will take to burn the mixture. Conversely, the closer the spark plug is to the centre of the chamber, as in four-valve chambers, the faster the combustion time. Cylinder heads with inlet ports and combustion chambers that impart a high degree of swirl to the inlet charge improve mixture homogenisation, and this speeds up flame propagation so less advance is called for. Increasing the amount of squish, by reducing the squish clearance between the piston and head, has a similar effect. The stroke of the crankshaft, and the ratio of the con rod length to the length of the stroke, can also influence the amount of ignition advance necessary because these two factors affect the time it takes the piston to move to, and just past, TDC.

The fuel compounds used also affect combustion speed. Petrol burns fairly rapidly, so requires less advance than other fuel types. Alcohol fuels burn more slowly, and nitro is slower still, which means that these fuels need more spark advance. However, when a flame accelerator compound is added to either alcohol or nitro, spark lead must be reduced.

Obviously in a modified engine some, or perhaps all, of the above factors will have been changed from the stock engine. Therefore the amount of spark advance needed under various engine operating conditions will probably be quite different from that determined by the factory to achieve best power and economy.

MECHANICAL ADVANCE LIMITATIONS

Points-type distributors and early electronic ignition distributors relied on a mechanical system of revolving bob weights and springs, along with a vacuum canister, to provide an appropriate amount of ignition advance to suit various engine operating conditions. We will not discuss how these distributors can be modified to alter the advance curve because high-performance road and competition engines really deserve a better system, which can give an exact ignition firing angle to suit any engine operating condition. With a mechanical system we can achieve a correct spark angle at only some engine speeds, while at other rpm and throttle plate angles we have to make do with a compromise. This means less power and less efficiency, and it can also mean an engine wrecked by detonation.

Looking at Figure 7.4 you can begin to appreciate the sort of problems that are encountered when we are stuck with a mechanical advance system. In a stock situation the engine has, say, 5° initial advance, then at 1,000rpm the revolving bob weights and spring begin to allow the advance angle to increase in a linear fashion all the way up to 4,500rpm, where it reaches 38°. That 38° spark angle is then maintained right up to the engine's rev limit.

As explained previously, when the engine has been modified the advance requirements are different. The second curve illustrates what might be required in a competition engine. Because of the increase in the camshaft lobe duration, the engine now requires a lot more advance early on in the rev range, but with better cylinder filling at higher rpm less ignition lead is required past about 3,000rpm. Thus the initial advance in this example is adjusted to 12° before TDC and the distributor springs and weights are modified so that the distributor advances the timing very quickly to 30° at 3,000rpm. Again note that the spark lead advances in a linear fashion between 1,000 and 3,000rpm, and past 3,000rpm the timing is maintained at 30° even though dyno tests show that this

Figure 7.4 Mechanical distributor advance curves.

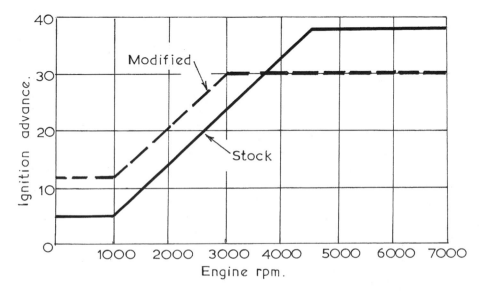

engine would make more power with the advance at 33° at 6,500rpm. Unhappily, because of the mechanical nature of the system we cannot go for this additional spark lead because at lower rpm the engine would detonate and probably split a piston due to excessive advance at an engine speed when cylinder filling is superior.

ELECTRONIC ADVANCE CONTROL

However, fully computerised ignition does not constrain our search for maximum power and performance. The 2D system required under some race rules restricts the electronic control unit (ECU) to adjusting the ignition advance purely on the basis of engine speed, but the preferred 3D system does not impose such a restriction. With this latter system the ECU electronically adjusts the spark plug firing angle to suit both engine rpm and engine load conditions. With road cars the ECU receives signals from a variety of sensors, then, according to its programmed memory, selects the appropriate advance angle to meet performance and emissions requirements. For example, the ECU will adjust the spark timing in response to such things as the electric engine cooling fan switching in while you are stopped at traffic lights. If the car has power steering and you swing on the steering wheel while creeping into a parking bay the ECU will bring engine power up, usually by increasing the spark advance. When the water and oil are cold, this information will be relayed to the ECU and the advance angle will be increased to improve engine smoothness and responsiveness.

With a competition engine the primary inputs are engine rpm and throttle plate angle, and with turbo or supercharged engines boost pressure is also taken into account by the ECU. Thus during dyno testing an ignition map such as that illustrated in Figure 7.5 is built up and programmed, usually via a laptop computer, into the ECU memory. For example, the first series of tests will establish what ignition advance the engine

Figure 7.5 Computerised spark timing ignition map.

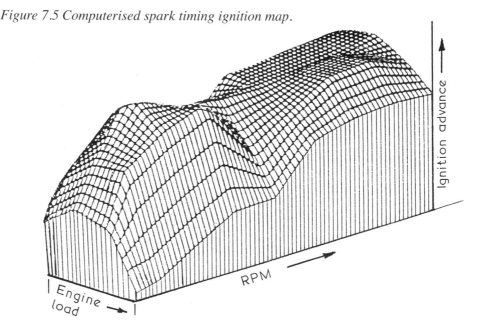

prefers to make best power at wide-open throttle. For a competition engine with a 4,000 to 8,500rpm working range this may be, say, 34° at 4,000rpm, 33° at 4,400rpm, 31° at 4,800rpm, 33° at 5,200rpm, 34° at 5,600rpm, 36° at 6,000rpm, 38° at 6,400rpm, 36° at 6,800rpm, 35° at 7,200rpm, 35° at 7,600rpm, 36° at 8,000rpm, and 38° at 8,400rpm. Clearly this is the sort of advance curve that no mechanical system could achieve. The advance angles would then be stored in the memory and later, whenever the ECU received an input indicating that the engine was operating at wide-open throttle at, say, 6,400rpm, it would give the engine 38° spark advance; if it was running at 8,000rpm this would change to 36° ignition lead, and so on.

This dyno test process would then be repeated at various throttle plate angles. If the engine is to reside in a circuit race car we may choose only a few throttle plate angles and rpm points to actually dyno test, then intermediate points would be estimated. For example, we might test a throttle plate angle of 10° at 4,000, 6,000 and 8,000rpm; 25° throttle at these same rpm; and finally 50° throttle at the same rpm. A forest rally car, however, may require a lot more work, particularly at lower rpm and small throttle openings, so that the engine runs well at legal speeds on non-competitive stages and through towns and villages, etc. The end result will be a car that is much easier to drive, more powerful and more responsive to the throttle than could ever be achieved using mechanical distributor advance.

Just how much power increase can we realistically expect with computerised spark timing? At wide-open throttle it is usual to find a power improvement of around 1¹/₂–2¹/₂% with a circuit race engine that breathes very efficiently and has a fairly narrow power band running from, say, 6,000 up to 8,500rpm. An engine tuned for a wider power range running from, say, 4,500 to 8,500rpm, as would be used in a rally car or endurance racer, has more compromised high-rpm breathing. Hence it benefits much more from the additional spark advance because of its poorer cylinder-filling abilities in the upper rev range, so may show around a 4% hp increase.

Competition engines typically want an additional 3 or 4° spark lead at peak hp revs than that required at peak torque rpm. Then, past peak hp, they may want another couple of degrees of advance up to the rev limit, or some may want another couple of degrees taken off. When a mechanical advance system is used, a tuner will often split the difference, so if the engine calls for 32° at peak torque rpm and 36° at the rev limit, the tuner will set a compromise angle of 34° and hope that the engine does not detonate and break a piston due to excessive advance at the torque peak. Electronic spark timing overcomes this type of problem by giving the tuner the scope to provide the optimum spark advance angle to suit any engine speed or engine load condition.

Table 7.5 sets out the test results of a 1,700cc Lotus Ford Twin Cam rally engine when it was swapped from a mechanical to an electronic advance system. These figures represent the results of tests at wide-open throttle; at part throttle the power improvement was even more impressive.

However, increased power is just one aspect illustrating the worth of electronic advance control. Many categories of competition disallow the use of active traction control systems, but with a little ingenuity we can achieve something similar by fiddling the spark advance curve. For example if we have too much bottom-end torque, which is giving us traction problems off turns at a particular circuit, we can kill some of that wheelspin by taking off spark advance at the bottom of the power band when we run at that track. If we have enough ECU capacity we can run several

Table 7.5   Lotus Ford Twin Cam ignition advance mechanism comparison

	Test 1		Test 2	
rpm	**hp**	**Torque**	**hp**	**Torque**
4,000	89.9	118.1	89.6	117.6
4,500	104.0	121.4	104.3	121.7
5,000	121.6	127.7	119.4	125.4
5,500	138.0	131.8	137.7	131.5
6,000	154.9	135.6	155.1	135.8
6,500	159.8	129.1	159.0	128.5
7,000	165.8	124.4	165.5	124.2
7,500	171.2	119.9	168.4	117.9
8,000	172.4	113.2	168.5	110.6
8,500	166.2	102.7	160.7	99.3

Test 1 – Allison ignition with electronic advance control.

Test 2 – Allison ignition with mechanical advance control.

advance programmes to help with traction. In the basic system we can run one spark curve that kills mid-range torque when in first, second or third gear. Then in fourth, fifth or sixth gear the selector sensor switches to the normal advance curve. A more advanced system would have a gear selector sensor and also a dash control knob with three or perhaps four possible positions. On a circuit racer those positions would be marked 'dry', 'damp' 'wet' and 'yellow'. The first three positions allow the selection of an advance curve to suit track surface conditions, while the 'yellow' position would not normally call up a different advance curve but would rather 'trim' a certain percentage off the fuel injection pulse width when running under a yellow flag. This would lean the fuel right off so as to avoid the risk of fouling the plugs, and in a distance racer it would cut fuel consumption if the yellow was on for a lengthy period.

IMPROVING SPARK TIMING ACCURACY

When we switch to electronic advance control we no longer need a distributor with bob weight, etc, to effect ignition advance. We can now discard the distributor and go to a distributorless system. This move offers many advantages, but the most significant is improved spark timing accuracy. Generally distributors are driven by the camshaft, or else by a jackshaft driven by the timing chain. Either way, harmonics in the valve train play havoc with the motion of the distributor and the problem worsens as valve spring pressures and engine rpm increase.

Added to this, some engines have the cam drive at one end of the camshaft and the distributor drive at the opposite end. This does not present a problem at ordinary engine speeds, cam lobe lifts and valve spring pressures, but in a competition engine the story changes dramatically. Engine speeds rise spectacularly, cam lobe lifts rise and the camshaft diameter may decrease to achieve such a big lift, and valve spring pressure may double or treble. What happens now – particularly in push rod V8 engines – is that the cam tends to screw up, with the distributor drive end of the shaft lagging behind the other end where the timing sprocket is attached.

Multi-coil distributorless ignition eliminates problems with timing accuracy and distributor cap flashover, plus it extends the rpm potential of transistorised HEI ignition.

However, the distributor end of the cam does not trail behind for ever; depending on which valves the cam is pushing open, the camshaft will wind up so far, then instead of the distributor end trailing, it will unwind and spring forward. This means that the triggering signal being intercepted by the ECU to reference TDC, and thus determine the spark firing angle, is unreliable and inaccurate. In reality this means that what should have been a 32° before-TDC firing angle at 8,000rpm may become a 35° angle on cylinder No 1, a 29° angle on No 2, 33° on No 3 and 32° on No 4. Obviously, because in this example No 1 is firing 3° advanced due to camshaft 'spring', we have to retard the timing on all of the other cylinders so as to avoid detonation in the No 1 hole. This costs us power and it may cost us in another way. Those cylinders that are now retarded may 'afterburn' due to late ignition. In turbo engines this could reduce turbo life and limit our boost pressure. In naturally aspirated engines the temperature of exhaust valves and valve seats could tip over the edge and introduce reliability problems.

Distributors driven from the camshaft by a helical gear experience timing error problems in a different manner. Unless the distributor shaft is shimmed to keep end play to a minimum – 0.003in is preferred – the distributor gear will ride up and down on the cam gear and upset timing accuracy. Likewise a camshaft 'walking' backward and forward in the block due to excessive end float also contributes to erratic ignition timing. Cam end float should be 0.003in, controlled either by a thrust plate or, where one is not fitted by the factory, a timing cover incorporating a thrust button and appropriate reinforcement, to keep cam walk to a minimum. However, even when both distributor shaft end float and cam walk are kept to the specified minimum, a measure of ignition timing error still occurs.

When we get rid of the distributor we also rid the engine of another potential trouble spot, namely the distributor cap. With small spark plug gaps and low secondary ignition voltages, ignition flashover, or crossfiring, within the cap is rare. However, the situation changes as plug gaps are opened up and ignition voltages increased. With four- and six-cylinder engines it is possible, by going to a large cap diameter, to put more space, and hence a bigger air gap, between the terminal posts. However, with eight-cylinder engines it can be difficult to find sufficient space to fit such a large distributor cap, and the problem is compounded when we go to 10- and 12-cylinder engines, as the cap diameter grows ever larger.

If we have enough ECU capacity, accurate distributorless ignition also opens up the prospect for ignition with individual cylinder trim, which means that we can adjust

Correcting the distributor

When running a distributor-type ignition we may be able to 'correct' the distributor to achieve exactly the same ignition firing angle on every cylinder. For example, if the distributor has an LED/photo transistor triggering system we can refile the slots on the chopper wheel to correct ignition errors. If it has a reluctor (star wheel) and pick-up coil system it may be possible, if the reluctor 'teeth' are not too short, to bend the teeth to correct the timing. Alternatively a new reluctor can be machined with teeth positioned so as to provide the correct advance angle.

To check just how much the timing varies from cylinder to cylinder you will need a good bright timing light and clear timing check marks on the harmonic balancer or crank pulley. You may have found in dyno tests that the engine makes best hp with 33° spark advance. However, finding that angle for every cylinder on the harmonic balancer is too much of a fiddle, so it is best to adjust the distributor to fire No 1 at 30°, then correct the distributor to ensure that all other cylinders also fire at 30°. Later, after you have corrected the distributor and verified that all cylinders are firing at 30°, you can swing the distributor back to where the engine makes best power. However, after correcting the distributor the optimum timing angle may have changed from what was previously determined on the dyno.

On an even-fire engine, where you put your 30° check marks on the harmonic balancer is easy enough to figure out. The TDC mark is actually 360°, so the No 1 firing mark will be 30°. If it is a four-cylinder engine, No 4 should also fire at 30°, and Nos 2 and 3 at 210°. An even-fire six-cylinder engine has cylinders firing 120° apart, so the check marks will be at 30°, 150° and 270°, while a V8 (with dual-plane crank) has a cylinder firing every 90°, so our check marks will be at 30°, 120°, 210° and 300°.

The rpm at which the ignition timing is checked is important, so make sure that you check every cylinder at exactly the same engine speed. For most engines I would pick an rpm at about the middle of the power band. Thus if the engine was normally run between 5,500 and 8,500rpm, I would do the timing check at 7,000rpm. However, if it is an engine like the push rod Chev V8 with the timing gear at one end of the cam and the distributor drive at the other end, I would check the timing at both the bottom and the top of the power band.

Remember that high rpm timing checks are quite dangerous. Before starting ensure that the harmonic balancer is well bonded and not about to fly apart. Also, if the engine has a mechanical fan, remove it for the duration of the test. Even after these precautions be aware that drive belts can fly off or break, so do not stand in their 'firing line'.

the spark firing angle to suit the characteristics of each cylinder. In this way each cylinder can be tuned as if it was an individual engine. For example, due to engine breathing characteristics, less than perfect coolant flow through the block and head, or fuel distribution problems in single-carburettor installations, one or more cylinders may run hotter or cooler than others. With ignition trim we can get more power out of the cool-running cylinders by giving them more spark advance. Additionally, we may get more power, or at least better reliability, when we cut back on the advance angle for the cylinders that are running hot.

When the distributor is discarded we have to use another means of informing the ECU when each piston reaches TDC. Instead of using a pulse trigger within the distributor, this function is transferred to a pulse trigger that is usually attached to the front of the crankshaft. The alternative is to have 'firing' pins embedded in the circumference of the flywheel. Regardless of their position, as each firing pin moves past the stationary magnetic pick-up a pulse is relayed to the ECU. The ECU in turn calculates the appropriate advance angle and switches the ignition primary (low-voltage) circuit on and off.

Probably the main things to watch with these crank trigger-type systems are that the firing pins are precisely located, that they are of the correct diameter, and that the air gap to the magnetic pick-up is correctly adjusted. The need to have the timing pins precisely located so as to ensure accurate spark timing is obvious enough, but the need to use pins of the correct diameter is less so. The manufacturer of the system should state the minimum pin diameter, but in any case it is a good idea to use a diameter not much smaller than the size of the pick-up. Thus if the pick-up is about 6mm in diameter, use firing pins with a 6mm head. If you use 3mm pins the pick-up may not 'read' them accurately, leading to all kinds of problems. Likewise the air gap where the firing pin passes the pick-up must be adjusted to that recommended by the manufacturer, usually 0.020–0.040in, otherwise you will have trouble getting the engine to fire up.

DETERMINING OPTIMUM IGNITION TIMING

Regardless of the type of ignition system used, it is imperative to get the ignition timing spot on for your engine. Many enthusiasts have a tendency to over-advance the timing in an effort to pick up every last fraction of performance, but my advice is to use the least amount of advance conducive with peak performance. Years ago the advice I regularly heard was to bump up the timing until the engine rattled, then back off the advance 2°. This sort of tuning may get you close with a low-performance, close-to-stock, road engine, but it is not good advice for a competition engine. You do not hear a race engine rattle, and if you do, the damage is already done.

The place to get the timing sorted is on the dyno. Keep adding spark lead while watching the read-out, and when adding additional advance brings no power increase, or even perhaps a drop in hp, back off the timing, as you have gone too far. If the timing is adjusted using a transient 'acceleration' dyno test rather than a 'steady state' step test, the timing could be way too far advanced, depending on the acceleration rate programmed into the dyno. This occurs because the load is not held for sufficient time to get a lot of heat into the combustion chambers and pistons. Therefore the engine will take more advance before it detonates or the power falls off than it would in the real world. Acceleration tests are useful for initial quick setting up, but keep the rate down to 100rpm/sec, and back up the results with steady state dyno pulls.

If you run very close to the maximum total advance that the engine will tolerate without going into high-speed detonation, you must be very careful to compensate for changes in the atmospheric conditions. A 7–10% increase in the relative air density (RAD) could result in a fuel/air mixture lean enough to produce a set of melted pistons, if you do not enrich the mixture accordingly. Also a decrease in the relative humidity could see the engine detonating unless the spark advance, or the amount of cam advance, is reduced.

ABNORMAL COMBUSTION

Detonation and pre-ignition are both engine wreckers. Pre-ignition is self-ignition of the fuel caused by a hot spot within the combustion chamber, or due to the fuel becoming unstable because of excessive pressure or heat. Detonation is a violent burning of the fuel (almost an explosion) caused by colliding flame fronts after the spark plug has fired.

When engine damage results from either condition, the culprit can usually be identified after an examination of the pistons and spark plugs.

Pre-ignition damage is caused by extreme combustion temperatures melting the top of the piston and possibly also the ring lands. If a hole is present in the piston crown, it will appear to have been burned through with a welding torch, and the metal around the hole will have a melted appearance. Spark plugs exposed to sustained pre-ignition quite often have the centre electrode melted away, and in extreme cases the insulator nose may also be fused.

Usually, pre-ignition can be traced to combustion chamber or exhaust valve deposits becoming incandescent, but it may also be due to blocked water jackets creating a hot spot, or a glowing spark plug with a heat range too hot for the engine. In a few cases pre-ignition can be traced to an overheated piston, perhaps due to inadequate lubrication, improper clearance or a broken ring.

Piston erosion almost directly under the spark plug or around the edges is a sure indicator of detonation or pre-ignition.

A piston damaged by detonation will show signs of pitting on the crown; in extreme examples the piston crown may be holed. The hole will appear to have been punched through, with radial cracks and a depressed area around it. A spark plug subjected to detonation will usually show signs of cracking at the insulator nose.

When detonation occurs, a portion of the fuel/air charge will begin to burn spontaneously due to excessive heat and pressure after normal ignition takes place. The two flame fronts ultimately collide and the resulting explosion hammers the engine's internal components. Detonation can be attributed to excessive spark advance and/or lean fuel/air mixtures. In supercharged and turbocharged engines, excessive intake charge temperatures can also lead to this condition.

THE ROLE OF THE KNOCK SENSOR

Many modern engines have one or more knock sensors fitted by the manufacturer. In these cars the sensor alerts the ECU of any abnormal combustion condition. The ECU then takes action, depending on how it has been programmed, to bring combustion back to normal. This may be achieved by retarding the spark, adding more fuel or lowering boost. In practice this usually works reasonably effectively with stock and lightly modified engines. However as we get into higher levels of tune the ECU most likely will not be able to bring combustion back on track due to programming limitations. Consequently the engine may be damaged if we leave it to the knock sensor and ECU to control combustion.

Another problem is that when we modify an engine the knock sensor may begin responding to phantom 'noise', assuming it to be abnormal combustion, and then set about reducing hp to 'protect the engine'. In reality those vibrations detected as knock could be due to increased piston or bearing clearances, wilder cams and increased valve train harshness, or even the fact that the engine is now spinning at more rpm. Some stock engines also generate phantom signals from such sources and manufacturers get around the problem by filtering out signals from the knock sensor above a certain number of rpm, or over a certain rev range. Too bad if the engine actually detonates during those periods!

Consequently I prefer to disconnect the knock sensor from the ECU and instead have it activate a warning light and a buzzer to alert me to knock, either real or phantom. Immediately I can lift off the accelerator to protect the engine and then set about adjusting fuelling and ignition advance, and perhaps lowering engine temperature. If the knock light still came on I would then keep running the engine in that condition for a few seconds. Following that the plugs would be pulled and carefully examined, and likewise for the tops of the pistons using a borescope poked down the spark plug holes. If there was no evidence of detonation, the inference would be that engine harmonics or rough combustion at those rpm and throttle opening were setting the knock sensor off.

SPARK PLUG HEAT RANGE

Due to increased combustion temperatures in a modified engine, consideration must be given to find a spark plug with the correct heat range. A hot plug transfers combustion heat slowly and is used to avoid fouling in engines with relatively low   233

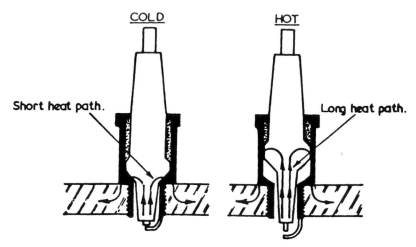

Figure 7.6 The heat rating of a spark plug is dependent on the length of the insulator nose and the electrode material composition.

combustion chamber or cylinder head temperatures, ie in a relatively low-horsepower motor. A cold plug, on the other hand, transfers heat rapidly from the firing end and is used to avoid overheating where temperatures are high, as in a racing engine.

The length of the insulator nose and the electrode alloy composition are the primary factors in establishing the heat rating of a particular plug. Hot plugs have long insulator noses, and therefore a long heat transfer path, while cold plugs have shorter nose lengths to transfer heat more rapidly from the insulator tip to the water jacket via the metal spark plug body. (Figure 7.6).

Motors in sports tune will probably require a standard plug or one not more than a couple of steps colder than standard. Semi-race engines cause us more problems as two plug types may be needed to cope with city driving and high-speed running. A plug two or three grades colder than standard should be tried for everyday street use and short full-throttle bursts; it must also be able to resist low-speed fouling and pre-ignition at a constant 80mph. The second plug type would be used under competition conditions or sustained high-speed driving.

Race engines also require two plug heat ranges, one for engine warm-up and one for racing. If there is sufficient space in the combustion chamber, projected-nose or regular-gap plugs are best used for warm-up, otherwise use the hottest retracted-gap racing plug available. Whenever warm-up plugs are fitted, tag the tacho or steering wheel as the engine could be destroyed if, in the heat of the moment, your memory lets you down and you race with hot plugs fitted.

After you have decided on a plug of the correct heat range, you must test to ensure that your choice is the right one. Providing that the engine is in good condition and the carburettor is correctly tuned, reading the nose of the plug will indicate if it has the correct heat range. To avoid engine damage, it is always advisable to begin testing with plugs that are too cold, or else test the machine at moderate load and speed, then check the plugs before you engage in any full-power running.

For the plug reading to be accurate it will be necessary to run the engine at full throttle and maximum speed on the track (or road), then cut the engine dead. If you allow the engine to keep running as you bring the vehicle to a stop, the plug reading will be useless.

As I pointed out in an earlier chapter, we are not just interested in the colour of the insulator nose. Some fuels will not colour a plug, and it takes miles for many types to colour the insulator. Therefore all of the plug firing end exposed to the combustion flame must be examined and read. The signs to look for are indicated in Table 7.6.

Of course, for those involved in road racing or long and short course speedway racing, the spark plug heat range must be tailored to each race circuit. Tracks with long straights or high-speed banked turns usually require a colder plug than a circuit with short straights and many esses and hairpin corners.

When the fuel blend is changed, the plug heat range will have to be changed accordingly. In unsupercharged applications, the plug will probably have to be one grade colder for each 10–15% of nitro added.

Table 7.6   Spark plug readings for correct heat range and other conditions

Spark plug condition	Indications
Normal – correct heat range.	Insulator nose white or very light tan to rust brown.
	Little or no cement boil where centre electrode protrudes through insulator nose.
	Electrodes not discoloured or eroded.
Too cold – use hotter plug.	Insulator nose dark grey or black.
	Steel plug shell end covered with dry, black soot deposit that will rub off easily.
Too hot – use colder plug.	Insulator nose chalky white or may have satin sheen.
	Excessive cement boil where centre electrode protrudes through insulator nose. Cement may be milk white or meringue-like.
	Centre electrode may 'blue' and be rounded off at edges.
	Earth electrode may be badly eroded or have molten appearance.
Pre-ignition – use colder plug and remove combustion chamber deposits.	Insulator nose blistered.
	Centre electrode and side electrode burned or melted away.
Detonation – retard ignition and richen mixture.	Fractured insulator nose in sustained or extreme cases.
	Insulator nose covered in tiny pepper specks or even tiny beads of aluminium leaving the piston.
	Excessive cement boil where centre electrode protrudes through insulator nose.
	Specks on plug shell end.
Insulator glazing – replace with plugs of same heat range. If condition reoccurs fit plugs one grade colder.	Shiny yellow, green or tan deposit on insulator nose, particularly close to centre electrode.
Ash fouled – clean or replace with plugs of the same heat range.	Thick yellow, white or light brown deposit on insulator, centre and side electrode.

Once you have determined the correct plug heat range, do not swap over to another brand with an 'equivalent' heat range. Heat range conversion charts should be used as a guide only when you swap from one plug brand to another, as different plug manufacturers use different methods of determining the heat range of their plugs. If you cross-referenced the conversion charts from all the plug manufacturers, you would find that they disagree with each other, due to different test procedures.

Even spark plugs with the same number from a particular manufacturer can have a wide heat range tolerance. This is why some mechanics are very particular about the brand of plug that they use in their engines. They claim that one particular brand gives a more consistent heat range, so they do not have to test dozens of plugs with the same number to find a set that has the same heat range.

SPARK PLUG GAP STYLE AND ELECTRODE MATERIALS

As well as the heat range, the gap style of the plug must be considered to obtain the best performance, and in some instances to avoid mechanical engine damage (Figure 7.7).

The best plug to use in most engines, where there is sufficient physical space between the tip of the plug and the valves and piston crown, is the projecting nose, or projecting core, type with copper implants in both electrodes, to increase heat transfer

Figure 7.7 Spark plug gap styles.

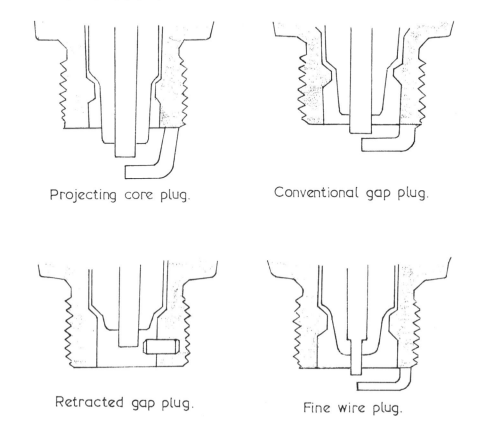

Projecting core plug.

Conventional gap plug.

Retracted gap plug.

Fine wire plug.

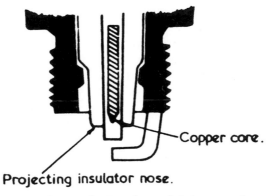

Figure 7.8 Copper implants in the spark plug electrode/s increase heat transfer rates, giving both projecting nose and regular gap designs a wider heat range.

rates (Figure 7.8). It has a very wide heat range to resist both fouling and pre-ignition. At high speeds the long insulator nose is cooled by the incoming fuel charge to increase its cold heat range, while at low speeds the long tip runs hotter, to prevent fouling. Projecting nose plugs are not recommended for highly supercharged engines or those using more than 20% nitro fuel.

If you change from a regular-gap or retracted-gap plug to a projecting nose type it may be necessary to retard the advance slightly. The projecting nose starts the ignition flame burning physically deeper in the combustion chamber and this reduces the length of flame travel within the chamber. Often, projecting nose plugs will raise the power output of the engine right through the power range because of improved combustion.

The conventional-gap plug is next preferred after the projecting nose type, and can be used in engines not able physically to accommodate projecting nose plugs. This style has a wider heat range than a retracted gap plug and provides superior ignition flame propagation.

The retracted-gap racing plug is necessary in highly modified, supercharged or high-percentage nitro-fuelled racing engines. It may also be used in racing engines where there is insufficient clearance between the spark plug and valves or piston to use either a projecting nose or regular-gap design. A plug of this type should be used

Carefully check the tips of all spark plugs for the telltale signs of detonation. Use at least a 4X lighted magnifier.

Filing the earth electrode back to the middle of the centre electrode and tapering the corners has two effects. Reducing the length of electrode exposed to combustion heat makes the plug run cooler by around half a grade. More significantly, because there is less earth electrode in the way, the spark initiated flame kernel moves out through the entire fuel/air charge more uniformly, thus giving faster more complete combustion.

only when absolutely necessary. It has very little resistance to fouling and generates a poor ignition flame front.

The fine wire plug (eg Champion Gold Palladium) has some use in semi- and full race engines. It was originally developed for racing two-stroke engines but can be used in four-stroke applications requiring a wide heat range (similar to projecting nose plugs) in the colder grades. These plugs are expensive, due to the use of a fine semi-precious metal electrode, but they perform very well in high-performance and racing engines requiring a cold plug relatively resistant to low-speed fouling. They are not recommended for highly supercharged or high-percentage nitro-burning engines. Also as many fine wire plugs utilise a platinum electrode care must be exercised when burning methanol. Platinum acts as a catalyst in the presence of methanol and may cause pre-ignition. Some racers have been blissfully unaware of this and not had any problems, but others have not been so fortunate.

SPARK PLUG REACH

Whenever a cylinder head with larger valves, modified combustion chamber, or relocated spark plug is used, or when pistons with a non-standard crown are fitted, always check that the spark plug is of the correct reach and gap style to avoid mechanical damage to the engine.

With the head removed, check that the plug reach (ie the length from the plug seat to the end of the thread) is neither too long nor too short. A plug that does not extend the full threaded length of the plug boss in the head will reduce performance by masking the ignition flame and invite hot spots from carbon build-up in the unused thread. A plug that is too long (ie has exposed threads in the combustion chamber) can cause damage and stripping of the plug boss threads in the head as carbon build-up on the exposed plug threads makes plug removal very difficult. Also the exposed threads can become a hot spot to initiate pre-ignition. In some instances a change to a plug with a different reach may be in order, but in most cases the use of a single solid copper gasket on each plug will ensure the proper depth fit. The range of Champion gaskets is listed in Table 7.7.

Table 7.7   Champion spark plug gaskets

Plug diameter (mm)	Gasket thickness (in)	Part No
10	0.045	Y-674
	0.055/.045	Y-678
12	0.057	P-674
	0.070/.052	P-678
	0.095	P-677
14	0.057	N-675
	0.135	N-677
	0.070/.052	N-678
	0.080	N-673X1
18	0.080	A-675
	0.065/.050	A-676
	0.075/.055	A-678

With the head fitted, check that sufficient clearance exists between the plug and the piston. To allow for rod stretch the normal plug gap should be increased by 0.025in. Turn the engine over by hand, then remove the plugs and inspect them for closed gaps. When carrying out this check remember that a hot projecting nose plug extends further into the combustion chamber than a colder one, so be sure to make the check using the hottest plug that will be used in the engine.

SPARK PLUG GAP

The width of the spark plug gap for best performance depends primarily on the compression pressure of the fuel/air mixture, the engine speed and the coil saturation time. Increasing the first two factors and decreasing the latter calls for a decrease in plug gap. It is safe to say that all modified engines using factory ignition require a plug gap narrower than stock.

Manufacturers stipulate a relatively wide gap as this improves the engine idle and low-speed performance. The ignition spark from a wide gap is larger than that from a narrower gap, so a larger initial combustion flame is generated, assisting low-rpm running. However, at high engine speeds and compression pressures the coil is not able to supply electrical energy of sufficient intensity to jump the spark gap, so the gap must be reduced to avoid a high-speed misfire, or the possible breakdown of the high-voltage system insulation.

From experience I would recommend that no high-performance engine using a conventional high-energy electronic ignition should use a plug gap exceeding 0.035–0.040in. Semi- and full race engines may need a gap as small as 0.028–0.032in with conventional plugs, and down to 0.025in when using retracted-gap racing plugs. Race engines running methanol will require gaps 0.005–0.010in smaller than these figures because it is much more difficult to get methanol burning initially, then keep it burning for complete combustion.

Engines with a capacitor discharge ignition can pick up some power with wider plug gaps as this type of ignition is relatively insensitive to high engine rpm. In this instance the plug gap should be set to the ignition manufacturer's specifications for 239 short-distance events and ordinary road use. However, those involved in long-distance racing and rallying or constant high-speed road driving should not use a gap exceeding 0.045in, as any weakness developed in the CD unit during a race could lead to total ignition failure. A closer plug gap reduces the load on the 'spark box', minimising the chance of any weakness developing, and if some trouble does arise, the system may have just enough reserve to finish the event.

COIL POLARITY

Always ensure that your coil polarity is correct before you try experimenting to determine what plug gap gives the best performance. The equivalent of 40% coil energy is lost when the polarity is reversed.

The spark should always jump from the centre electrode of the plug to the side electrode as this considerably decreases the voltage required for ignition. Due to the centre electrode being at a much higher temperature than the side electrode, less voltage is needed to produce a spark, as electrons will leave the hotter surface at a lower voltage. This is why it can be difficult to get a cold motor started; because the centre electrode is cold, a much higher voltage is required to produce a spark.

The coil polarity can be checked by looking at the coil's low-voltage connections (electricity supply wire from ignition switch to positive; module/amplifier wire to negative), or by using an oscilloscope. The oscilloscope's trace pattern will be upside down if the polarity is not correct. A dished or eroded spark plug side electrode also indicates wrong polarity; the dish is caused by metal leaving the electrode each time a spark jumps across to the centre electrode.

SPARK PLUG MAINTENANCE

The life of a spark plug is not as short as many would suppose. Some drag racers believe that a new set of plugs is required for each quarter-mile trip, but cars involved in 500-mile speedway races and 12- and 24-hour road events go the full distance without a plug

A centre electrode eroded like this indicates correct coil polarity and shows that a good strong spark is being produced. However, with lead deposits on the insulator nose and the gap widened like this, the plug should be replaced.

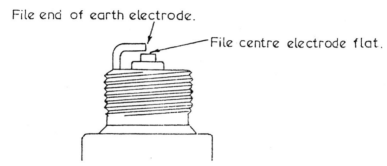

Figure 7.9 Spark plug electrode filing.

change. A road machine should not require a plug replacement more frequently than 10,000–20,000 miles, and racing plugs will easily last 300 miles with proper care, or about 50 trips down the drag strip for unsupercharged petrol or methanol burners.

A road vehicle with electronic ignition should have the plugs filed, gapped and tested every 6,000 miles, and a race machine after each event. Retracted-gap plugs cannot be filed, and fine wire electrode plugs should not be filed.

Projecting nose and conventional-gap plugs should have the earth electrode bent back far enough to permit filing of the sparking surfaces shown in Figure 7.9. A point file can be used to file a flat surface with sharp edges on both the centre and side electrodes. This lowers the voltage requirement to fire the plug, not only because electricity prefers to jump across sharp edges, but also because the electrical conductivity of the electrodes is improved. The heat and pressure of combustion tends to oxidise and break up the electrode firing surfaces, increasing the electrical resistance. Filing removes this 'dead' metal and exposes new highly conductive material.

Spark plugs should never be cleaned with a wire brush as metallic deposits will impregnate the insulator and short out the plug. I also do not recommend cleaning with a plug cleaner, as some abrasive material always seems to become wedged between the insulator and the plug shell. If this cannot be probed out with a scriber, it will drop out in the engine and possibly cause some damage. If you choose to have your plugs abrasive blasted, be sure to remove all abrasive grit from inside the plug nose and from the threads.

Personally, I prefer to leave plugs uncleaned. If they are fouled by fuel or oil I clean them with a toothbrush and ether, or some other non-oily solvent. If the insulation is breaking down due to leaded fuel deposits, I throw the plug away.

SPARK PLUG LEADS

The spark plug leads provide the electrical connection between the distributor cap and spark plugs. Most stock road cars use radio suppression cables with a powdered carbon-impregnated rayon cord to conduct this high-voltage current, which will ultimately jump across the plug gap and initiate combustion. With age, the electrical resistance of this cable increases, so less and less energy is available to provide a big hot spark. Eventually one or more of the plugs will not fire at all. Therefore carbon suppression cables should be discarded and replaced by high-quality induction-type suppression leads. These leads have a metal core to conduct full electrical energy to 241 the plugs, and they have a metal induction spiral wound within the cable to provide both noise and induction suppression. Remember that inadequate suppression could seriously upset the proper functioning of the ECU, and other electronic or radio-type devices, so do not use ordinary solid copper core or stainless steel core cable.

The other good reason for using induction spiral leads is to minimise the incidence of induction crossfire. This is a real problem with today's high-energy ignitions. Basically, due to magnetic induction, whenever high-voltage wires are grouped closely together, or run in parallel for any distance together, one with current flowing through it can induce a corresponding voltage in a neighbouring wire. In fact, this is the way in which your ignition coil works, but it is not what we want going on between plug wires! Induction crossfire in its mildest form causes the engine to run roughly, but in situations of high engine load or high rpm such as are typical under competition conditions, it can result in serious engine damage.

To help you better understand the seriousness of the problem, let us take a look at a typical V8, as these engines most frequently experience a crossfire problem. A crossfire that will destroy cylinder walls, pistons, bearings, cranks, heads or head gaskets is most likely to occur between consecutive firing cylinders when these are located alongside each other in the engine. Taking the most common V8 firing order of 1–8–4–3–6–5–7–2, we see that No 7 cylinder is one likely to suffer crossfire damage, because when No 5 fires at say 35° before TDC, No 7 is trailing only 90° behind, or 125° BTDC, and it is almost full with fuel/air mixture. At this stage No 7 piston is moving up on the compression stroke and, depending on the cam profile, the inlet valve is closed or at least about to close. It is in this setting that No 5 plug wire has a high-voltage current surging through it. If the resulting magnetic pulse induces current flow in the No 7 plug wire, that plug also fires, but as it is 90° early violent combustion occurs. Depending on how often this happens, and under what sort of engine load conditions, engine damage can range from a blown head gasket through to a wrecked block or crankshaft.

The way to avoid this sort of problem is to use induction spiral suppression leads, but this is not the total solution. The plug wires should also be separated preferably by about an inch – 1/2in is the minimum – and in V8 engines consecutive firing cylinders, usually Nos 5 and 7, should have their respective plug leads crossed once. Crossing the problem wires once inverts the magnetic field in the second wire and cuts out any induction. Never tape plug wires together or run them through metal clips or other metal fittings. Not only can this lead to induction crossfiring, but can also open the way for misfiring.

For the plugs to fire the plug wires have to prevent the coil's high-voltage current from tracking to earth. With today's high-energy ignition systems, and tuners insisting on running race engines with big plug gaps, plug wires need all the help you can give them. If you do not keep plug leads separated about half an inch, and if you do not keep them a similar distance away from the engine and other metal parts, you could run into a misfire problem. With most race engines pushing out about 50–80hp per cylinder, that means you lose 50–80hp each time the spark plug fails to light.

The average race engine needs at least 20,000 volts, and anything up to 35,000 volts if the plug gaps are very wide, to get a spark across the spark plug. When you compare the amount of insulation that you have available to prevent all that electrical pressure flashing across to earth with what the power companies use on their overhead power lines, you begin to appreciate what you are up against. To work in this sort of environment you must use only top-quality silicone cable and boots. I recommend 8mm silicone wire for the majority of road applications and race engines that will not see voltages much over 20kV. This means plug gaps down around 0.028in and an 11:1 compression ratio. When we open the gaps up to 0.040in and push the compression ratio to 12.5:1 the voltage to fire the plug rises to about 27kV. At this sort of voltage and higher we have to be careful to choose only the best grades of ignition wire. Some people think that 9mm or even 10mm wire is the solution. However, 8mm Moroso spiral core wire has a dielectric insulation strength of well over 50kV, which is superior to anything else I know of, and it combines the highest levels of electro-magnetic suppression with the least electrical resistance to ensure maximum ignition energy at the spark plug.

DISTRIBUTOR CAP AND ROTOR BUTTON

Besides the plug leads, other potential high-voltage leakage or flashover areas are the distributor cap, rotor button and coil tower. These parts must be free of accumulated dust, moisture, cracks and carbon tracks to ensure that the full voltage is reaching the plugs. Therefore a periodic check must be made to ensure that none of these conditions exist.

Unknowingly, some tuners bring trouble upon themselves by removing carbon from the distributor cap terminals and the rotor button contact. Actually, carbon in these areas assists electrical conduction. The real problem is that quite often the knife or screwdriver being used to scrape the carbon from the terminals slips and scratches the glaze inside the cap. This drastically reduces the dielectric strength and can lead to a carbon track forming during wet conditions. Often a piece of abrasive paper is used to polish the rotor button contact. This cuts straight through the insulating glaze and results in voltage leaking to earth.

When high-voltage ignition systems are used, particular attention must be paid to keeping all the insulating mediums clean, otherwise less voltage will be available to fire the plugs than when the standard ignition system was fitted. Actually, when a high-output ignition is fitted, only top-quality distributor caps and rotors, made of alkyd material, should be used, being resistant to carbon tracking even when cracked.

As mentioned earlier, another thing we have to worry about with high-energy ignition is the problem of crossfiring within the distributor cap. This is usually not a worry with four- and five-cylinder engines, but it begins to surface with six-cylinder engines and becomes a real difficulty once we get to eight or more cylinders because the high-voltage posts are just so close to one another. The first move is to swap to a larger-diameter cap containing well-designed anti-flashover ribs; this will put more space – a larger air gap – between the posts.

However, the location of the rotor button when the ignition fires, and the length of the rotor button's brass tip, also have a bearing on internal flashover. We tend to think of an ideal situation with the rotor button being dead centre with the distributor cap post at the time the ignition fires, but it is not like that at all, which is why there is such a long brass tip on the rotor button to help place it somewhere close to the distributor cap post when the ignition fires. This is not a problem when ignition voltage is low, but as we begin to increase electrical pressure in the system to shoot a spark across a plug gap in a high-pressure environment in the combustion chamber, the situation changes.

243

Now the easiest path to earth – and remember that electricity always takes the easiest path – may not be across to the distributor post to which the rotor button is closest and down the plug wire. Instead, that wide brass tip on the rotor button may be closer – not physically, but from the aspect that the electrical resistance is less – to a distributor cap post either directly in front of, or else directly behind the cylinder that is supposed to be getting ignition energy. When this situation exists the electricity jumps from the tip of the rotor across to a post that may be half an inch or more away, then travels down the plug wire to fire a plug in that empty cylinder. Because it is not that cylinder's turn to fire, there is less pressure in it, so it is easier for the electricity to get to earth via that route, even though it has to jump a much bigger gap to get across to the distributor terminal for that cylinder.

There are a number of ways to minimise this sort of flashover. If it is possible the easiest way is to cut back on the length of the rotor button's brass tip. To check this remove the distributor cap and turn the engine over to 10° before TDC, then accurately scribe a line on the brass tip to correspond with the centre of the plug wire post. Move the crank back to 35° BTDC and again scribe the rotor button to correspond with the distributor cap post. The brass tip extending beyond the boundary of those two scribed lines can now be cut off, thus widening the air gap to the adjacent plug wire terminal in the distributor cap.

When doing this check you may be surprised to find that the rotor button is way off lining up with the plug wire post. Here there are two options: relocate the rotor or relocate the distributor cap. If you choose to relocate the rotor, have a new locating slot cut into the distributor shaft. Some enthusiasts knock out the locating tab of the rotor, then either epoxy or pin the rotor to the distributor shaft, but this is not always successful.

The brass contact on this rotor button has been shortened at both ends to prevent crossfiring within the distributor cap.

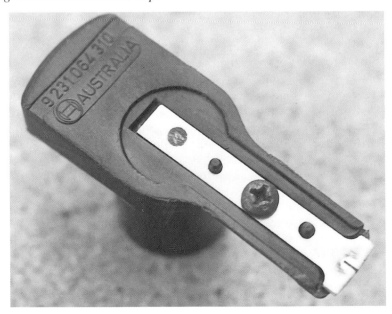

Another way to reduce flashover within the distributor cap is to vent it of ionised air. What is needed is a 10mm hole between each plug wire terminal around the circumference of the distributor cap, and at about the same height in the cap as the rotor.

This brings us to the final solution when we are forced to run a distributor-type ignition system, and that is to narrow the spark plug gaps. When we reduce the plug gap we reduce the electrical resistance to earth, so the high-voltage ignition pulse will choose to take this path of less resistance and fire the plug as it is supposed to, rather than crossfire to another cylinder within the distributor cap.

PRIMARY VOLTAGE INFLUENCES IGNITION PERFORMANCE

Before we finish with the subject of ignition systems, we need to give some consideration to how the power being consumed by today's very-high-energy ignitions can affect the performance of other electrical components on the vehicle. Additionally we should look at the idea that pushing up the primary-side voltage will increase the energy available to fire the plugs.

The electrical energy consumed by high-intensity electronic or capacitor discharge ignitions is not insignificant. Added to this, racers have over the years added more and more electricity-consuming devices to their race cars. When electronic fuel injection, electric fuel pumps, electric cooling fans, etc, became a standard part of the modern race car, loads on the electrical system increased dramatically by comparison with what they were previously. Because some racers have not given proper attention to this aspect of race car engineering, they find that their cars are down on power at best, or they may experience reliability problems, with the car stopping out on the track for apparently no reason.

For example, CD ignition can have a current draw two or three times higher than a transistorised HEI system – up around 8–10 amps. However, while the average power draw of an HEI system is relatively low, the instantaneous amperage draw, when the module first switches the primary circuit to charge the coil, is very high. It is for this reason that a transistor HEI must be wired directly to the ignition switch using heavy 10 gauge wire, and nothing else should be connected in that circuit. Now, when the current begins to surge into the coil, that high instantaneous power drain can, if the electrical system has not been designed properly, cause it to malfunction – lose the plot for an instant. However, it can occasionally cause the ECU to shut down completely – then the engine stops. Incidentally, I have seen the same sort of thing happen when the electric cooling fan cuts in and sends a surge through the electronics.

Also, the idea that increasing the system voltage from, say, 12 volts to 16 volts, to achieve a bigger output from CD ignition, is a fable. All the CD systems I know give a constant output regardless of whether the feed voltage is 10 volts or 16 volts. If you see increased ignition output with CD systems when the supply voltage is increased, you can be certain that you have a problem in the primary feed circuit. Either the cable is too small or too long, or you have 'hot' joints with cables poorly crimped to connectors, or connectors not making perfect contact and cutting supply voltage at the amplifier to less than 10 volts.

Transistor HEI systems, however, are very different in this respect. Any reduction in supply voltage will cause a corresponding reduction in coil output.

Conversely, any increase in system supply voltage will provide an increase in secondary coil energy. As a minimum we should be expecting the ignition supply voltage at the coil positive (+) terminal to be the same as the battery voltage. Thus if the battery measures out at 12.6 volts, we should see the same voltage at the positive coil terminal with the engine running and all of the car's electrical equipment turned on. If the voltage is less than the battery voltage, you are losing out on maximum spark energy, so increase the size of the ignition circuit wiring and ensure that nothing else except the ignition is connected in this circuit. Note that you must take care when carrying out this test as there could be 350 volts at the coil negative (−) terminal.

To give you some idea of how low voltage affects transistor HEI ignition spark intensity, and consequently engine hp, note what happened during the testing of a 350 Chev. The engine had been rebuilt with new exotic CNC ported hand-finished cylinder heads which it was hoped would lift power output to around 650hp. However, after being run-in the first few pulls were showing nothing better than 570hp. With some fiddling during an entire day this finally rose to a disappointing 582hp, 40hp less than the previous pair of heads with minimal CNC porting.

The following day started out even worse with the engine sounding sick, and the printout proved it. After a lot of checking the problem was isolated to a faulty new race battery which was almost 4 volts down on the rated output voltage. With a new up to spec battery connected the engine note immediately changed to a healthy crisp sound. After a few pulls to optimise the fuel and spark the engine made 646hp. Based on these figures you can see the low battery voltage – and the available peak current flow would have been way down too – was costing something like 10% hp.

Many transistor HEI systems will accept higher supply voltages and thus provide more secondary spark energy to fire the plugs at higher engine speeds, or else fire bigger plug gaps or exotic fuel. For example, a V8 system that works at 7,500rpm on a six-cell battery (up to 12.6 volts) will work up to about 8,200rpm with a seven-cell battery (up to 14.7 volts), and up around 8,800rpm when connected to an eight-cell battery (up to 16.8 volts). Remember to check with the ignition manufacturer before you increase the input voltage, otherwise you may overload some part of the system and 'blow' the electronics.

When purchasing a higher-voltage battery obtain one with extra terminals that allow you to tap the correct voltage supply for various electrical items on the car. Thus while the ignition may work adequately at 16.8 volts, or even up to 18 volts, with the exception of the starter motor nothing else will survive for any time at this level. The fuel injection pump also pumps more fuel and at higher pressure at higher voltage, but most become unreliable at more than 14 volts. The remainder of the electrics, however, should not be operated at more than 13 volts.

Chapter 8

The Engine Management System

The modern engine management systems available to the engine tuner can provide services far beyond basic control of the fuel and ignition requirements of the engine. With today's very specialised engine management systems you can almost specify anything you want, money permitting! The optional features available include: spark and fuel trim to permit ignition timing and mixture adjustments to each individual cylinder; injector phasing to control when during the inlet valve open period primary, secondary and tertiary injectors fire; traction control; data logging of engine, suspension, transmission and chassis; secondary fuel system control, or water injection control, etc.

In road cars, and sometimes in competition cars too, there are some other features we may require or perhaps find highly desirable. This would include: radiator cooling fan control; idle air stepper motor control; closed loop Lambda control; muffler bypass control; inlet tract switching control; cam phasing control.

While it is obviously very necessary to focus on engine management features that are absolutely vital we have to be cautious that we do not become so dogmatic in demanding a particular feature that we back ourselves into a corner and ultimately lose anything which we had hoped to gain with that particular engine management system. What can very easily happen is that we are virtually forced to purchase a particular unit because it is the only one with a feature that we feel we must have. The problem could be that that particular system demands a huge investment of time both on the dyno and on the track to get it set up, and if that input isn't given it will cause the engine to run worse than a more basic system. Another problem can be that the management system is just so specialised that there are only a handful of people about who actually understand how to properly programme the thing. If you can't find someone who knows both the engine management system and your engine you may never realise your dreams. In fact it is more probable that your dreams will quickly become a nightmare! In similar vein keep in mind that some systems are well known and understood in one country or one branch of motor sport but are unknown 247 elsewhere. If you are outside that circle of knowledge then it could be risky to set your focus on such a unit.

Another thing you may need to plan for is upgradeability. If you are in a very competitive league where progress is constant you will most likely want an engine management system backed by a manufacturer who will provide regular inexpensive upgrades and extensive technical backup. If you are not in such an area of motorsport keep on the lookout for the 'junk' from the upper echelons of the sport. The stuff that they are tossing out for peanuts could well be a high-end system that is more than adequate at your level of competition.

THE FACTORY COMPUTER

Very often stock engine management systems are rubbished and then replaced by inferior aftermarket systems from a 'name' manufacturer. Obviously there is nothing wrong with getting rid of an ECU which is either impossible to reprogramme or else does not have many of the necessary control features required to allow the engine and car to perform at an acceptable level. However, I question why you would want to toss an easy to programme ECU with everything you need to make street driving as pleasant as possible, and fit an expensive computer which can't properly control basic things such as the idle air stepper motor or the radiator cooling fan.

Also when you decide that it is necessary to replace the factory computer don't automatically think of purchasing an aftermarket unit as you could find a number of good inexpensive ECUs at your local wrecking yards from an earlier model of your car, or another model from the same manufacturer, or even from another brand of car. I know it goes against the grain for some people to do this, but it doesn't make much sense to reject a part on such grounds.

For example where I operate you can find any number of GM Delco '808' (so called because these are the last digits of the part number) computers for about the same price as 5 litres of Mobil 1. Using Kalmaker software they can be reprogrammed

The Delco 808 ECU can be reprogrammed to provide excellent performance for minimal cash outlay.

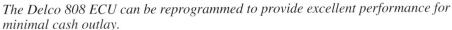

to work wonderfully in many applications. Most though snigger at such an idea, which is great for those in the know as there will be a ready supply of such ECUs and matching wiring harnesses around for next to nothing for a long time. These units may be only 16KB and not provide sequential injection but they are considerably more sophisticated than many low spec aftermarket ECUs. Also because they have a removable EPROM 'chip' it is simple and inexpensive to have one chip burned with a programme suitable for everyday road use on pump fuel, and another chip for weekend competition on an exotic brew.

In the early '90s GM began using a 32KB ECU which supported semi-sequential injection on 4- and 6-cylinder engines. These units are more expensive than the Delco 808, but are a steal in comparison with the price of an equivalent aftermarket ECU. The semi-sequential injection capability isn't a bonus, but the improved computing ability greatly improves idle control and cruise fuel economy in road cars. Also these units have a high speed serial data link which enables you to read out in real time, using Kalmaker software and a laptop, exactly what is going on with regard to ignition timing, injector pulse width etc. Actually the early Delco 808 can be upgraded very simply by fitting the later 32KB MemCal (GM speak for the EPROM chip).

Soon after this GM switched to a 64KB Delco unit which also incorporates auto trans control. They called this a powertrain control module (PCM). It also did not support sequential injection. This feature came later when GM adopted the 128KB three plug Delco unit in the mid '90s. These dropped MAP sensing and instead used mass air flow sensing, but can be switched back to MAP sensing.

With Nissans it is sometimes possible to change back to an earlier reprogrammable ECU. The R32 Skyline models could handle an extensive power upgrade with relative ease due to the stock computer's design. When the next model, the R33, came along that all ended – the ECU was now a 'no go' zone. However, for about an eighth of the price of the 'brand' Japanese computers you can obtain secondhand units out of R32s that will plug straight into the R33.

The Nissan R32 computer is programmable. This one, sourced from a 2ltr 6-cylinder model, is destined to replace the 'locked up' ECU in an R33.

Clearly when it comes to selecting an engine management system there are a huge number of factors to consider. Unfortunately many base their decisions on hardware specifications. For example, looking at the above mentioned Delco units it could be easy to conclude that the 16KB 808 was useless even as a boat anchor and that the 128KB hardware would be the obvious choice. However, hardware specifications are only a small part of the equation. I've already mentioned that you require a system that can be easily programmed, but on top of that requirement there are other factors which will influence our decision.

CHOOSING AN AFTERMARKET COMPUTER

Rather than hardware we should perhaps focus more on software. Unfortunately engine tuners don't know much about software. If they did they would be in that industry making a lot more money. Consequently manufacturers of engine management equipment can't appeal to them to make purchasing decisions based on impressive software capability. Rather they have to talk to us in language we understand, so we are bombarded with hardware sell. How many million calculations

MoTeC engine management system has great flexibility.

The Autronic replacement board that fits in the stock ECU case has all the features of the high spec Autronic SMC unit. The hose connects from the internal MAP sensor to the inlet manifold.

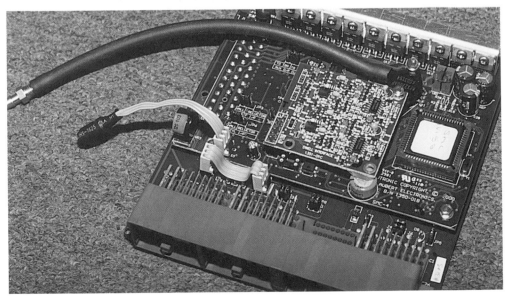

it will make per second, how it still functions in adverse environments (heat and vibration), and so forth. However as engine tuners we have to question: 'So what if the hardware can make a million calculations per second? If the software is flawed the instructions issued will be useless anyway!' Really, we must never look at the hardware in isolation but rather the entire package.

In addition we need to remember that the engine management system has to integrate with other areas of the vehicle. The Australian MoTeC system is a good example of the kind of features we would be looking for in a high-end competition management system. The MoTeC accepts a huge range of sensor inputs and will drive a diverse range of fuel injectors. It has multiple injector and ignition outputs, so can batch fire, group fire, sequentially fire or phase fire injectors, and it can trigger single coil or multi-coil ignition systems directly from the ECU. Modern race cars rely very heavily on data acquisition and complex LCD dash displays. The MoTeC interfaces with such systems from companies like Pi Research and CIC.

If we were looking at engine management purely from the aspect of engine performance, as in the numbers we see on the dyno, then the Autronic ECU will provide performance equal to, and some would say superior to, MoTeC units. The Autronic has numerous impressive features such as a full three-dimensional cold-start feature which doesn't simply add a percentage increase to the injector open time but rather operates on a load versus coolant temperature map. In supercharged engines the boost pressure can be controlled as a function of coolant temperature (low boost when the engine is cold) and as a function of what gear has been selected (less boost in lower gears to control wheelspin or transmission damage). Programmable outputs can switch such things as the water pump in the water-to-air intercooler system when the inlet air temperature reaches a certain temperature. Like numerous stock type ECUs the Autronic also has a limp home mode and it will flash out fault codes to inform you of problems without having to be connected to a laptop. However unlike the MoTeC computer there is very little flexibility in terms of sensor configuration, especially in the area of ignition pick-ups where only a few specific ignition triggers can be deciphered. Some tuners though consider this as a positive as the Autronic does not suffer signal 'noise' problems like other ECUs designed to function with a broad range of sensor types. Additionally for popular vehicles the Autronic can be supplied as a board which slips into the factory ECU case and connects to the stock harness, to retain a totally stock appearance.

Unfortunately Richard Aubert, the man behind Autronic and previously the software expert at MoTeC, has devoted all his energy to producing and constantly refining a brilliant ECU. Consequently supplied documentation isn't slick, nor easy to follow. Don't let this put you off the Autronic units though. I understand Richard is in the process of correcting this matter, but there are alternative sources. A couple of enthusiastic Autronic users, Steve Cox (www.quickfitmotorsport.com.au) and Ray Hall (www.turbofast.com.au), both with a lot of experience wiring and mapping the unit in a wide variety of applications, decided to take matters into their own hands and produce their own manuals.

A mid-range engine management system, with the unlikely brand name EMS (also from Oz) has one interesting feature which adds to its user friendliness. I usually don't like, nor do I recommend units which are programmed from a hand controller. Tuning is too much a fiddly hassle for my liking. Fortunately the latest EMS brand 251

The EMS brand electronic control unit has a number of useful features including live-data while you drive. This can make mapping glitches easier to identify and rectify. In spite of what the label seems to indicate this is not a fuel only control.

units give you the option of calibrating the ECU using either their hand controller or a laptop. I would choose the laptop route every time. However, having said that, the hand controller does have one appealing function – it can provide live-data as you drive. As such it can save you fitting extra gauges that you would otherwise need to obtain to provide you with such information as charge air temperature and the air/fuel ratio. For this latter function to operate a wide-band lambda sensor must be fitted to replace the stock exhaust oxygen sensor.

Having the air/fuel ratio meter function built into the hardware is unique and enables the vehicle owner to report back to the tuner any fuelling problems after the system has been initially mapped on the rolling road. Car manufacturers have a powertrain team spend months, at a cost of many millions, in an effort to get the programming correct. Obviously a tuner in a few hours on the dyno can't duplicate every conceivable engine operating condition to achieve similar results. With the EMS computer providing an air/fuel ratio readout, any tuning glitches can be fairly quickly identified as being either a fuelling problem or an ignition advance problem during normal operation on the street.

The Haltech ECU is supplied with excellent documentation to simplify installation.

Idle speed stepper motor control is required in street vehicles. It prevents stalling by compensating for increased engine loads when air con or electric cooling fan cycles, or when using power steering while idling into a tight parking space.

There are other aspects to a computer being user friendly. As mentioned, if you want to wire the thing up yourself, or call on the local auto electrician with no knowledge of this sort of stuff, then you will want extensive, totally accurate and easy to understand documentation supplied with the ECU. This is where a mid-range unit such as the Haltech has no peers. The Haltech as far as I know is also the only unit capable of operating the idle speed stepper motor in GM and Toyota vehicles. In addition for those modifying turbo engines it has pulse modulation boost control and turbo anti-lag control as standard features.

In spite of all the advances that have been make with aftermarket ECUs we have to realise that none will do all the things that the standard ECU fitted in today's cars will do. In general the aftermarket ECU is designed mainly with ease of programming and engine management as the priority. So in a road car how do we keep the security system functioning and the air con climate control working, while at the same time achieving the injector and spark timing that our modified engine demands? Basically the answer is you can't unless the stock ECU is retained.

REPROGRAMMING THE STOCK ECU

The very first option we should always carefully examine is the possibility of reprogramming the stock ECU. In the past it was popular to re-chip the ECU; either swapping the EPROM chip for a chip with a different programme or else by soldering a new chip onto the stock ECU circuit board for those computers which didn't have a plug-in chip. Usually these replacement chips were supplied by mail order, and at huge expense. As such they didn't do much for performance, not to mention engine life and fuel economy, in spite of very impressive advertising claims. The truth is that tuning of this sort can only be done on the dyno. Even a dozen precision-assembled race engines of the same specifications, put together by a top engine builder, will require slightly different ECU calibration to deliver optimum performance, so how can a programmer burn a perfect chip for an engine he has never seen? The truth is that he can't, he is only guessing.

The EPROM chip can be reprogrammed to adjust many parameters affecting engine performance.

The chip plugs into ECU socket as shown.

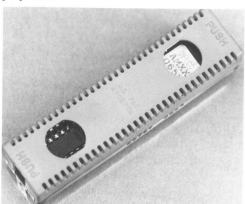

However, if done properly on a dyno, using good software which enables the tuner to access the manufacturer's original programme codes and correctly modify those codes, so called chip tuning is very successful and has much in its favour. First of all it ensures that everything in the car will keep functioning as the manufacturer originally intended. Depending on car specification that can include stuff like the sound system, navigation system, anti-theft devices, climate control, electric seats and mirrors etc. Also if the manufacturer's cruise mode and idle mode maps aren't fiddled very much the car should idle well and cruise nicely without surging and flat spots, plus it should pass emissions tests.

RUNNING TWO COMPUTERS OR A PIGGY-BACK SYSTEM

What though if the stock ECU cannot be reprogrammed either because nobody has been able to crack the programming codes or because the reprogramming options available are either too limited or too complex? There are two alternatives which both retain the stock ECU: either we can run two ECUs together or we can use an interceptor piggy-back ECU arrangement. What path we ultimately take will depend on how far we have gone with our modifications.

Personally I prefer to use two ECUs as it allows considerably more flexibility. For example we are not limited in how far we can go with our modifications, and when we bring the car back to stock, or if we resell it, it is very easy to remove the second ECU and have everything working normally again. When we go with this setup the new ECU will control only the engine management side of things, ie fuel injection, ignition timing, boost etc. The stock ECU will retain control of all the other functions.

There can be problems though with the two ECU system when there is a connection between engine management and other vehicle operations. Traction control is one problem area, as is electronic throttle control and electronic clutch arrangements. Frequently it is difficult, if not impossible, to achieve the required degree of cross-talk between two ECUs to get these sophisticated systems working satisfactorily and so the only alternative is to opt for an interceptor piggy-back ECU arrangement. These things aren't actually an ECU, nor are they a chip even though one very capable unit would appear to infer that by its name – Unichip.

The Unichip piggy-back interceptor manufactured in South Africa is only sold through distributors as part of an install and map package.

An interceptor is cut into, or plugged into, the wiring harness to receive and then modify signals prior to the stock ECU receiving them. (Some systems modify the signals going out from the ECU, while others modify a few of the incoming signals as well as some outbound signals.) As a result of receiving input that has been tampered with, the stock ECU will then send out a different set of fuelling and ignition advance instructions. And if the stock installation features a pulse modulation boost control valve that setting can also be modified. Cars with speed limiters and over-boost cut out can also have those functions disabled.

However, the interceptor has its limitations which is why if it is possible to reprogramme the stock ECU or run twin ECUs that would be the way I always prefer to go with road cars. What has to be understood is that the interceptor is limited by what the manufacturer has put on the stock maps. It can only replace one set of tuning codes with another bundle that are already available on that particular map. Consequently an interceptor is only suitable for reasonably moderate engine modifications. Usually ignition timing isn't a worry as most allow ±12–15° from the stock settings, but fuelling is a problem as you will often be limited to not more than a 15–20% increase and it usually isn't possible to change fuel pressure or fit larger injectors as many stock maps don't have sufficient latitude to permit the interceptor to lean the fuelling off the required amount when the engine isn't at wide open throttle and full boost.

However, if there is no alternative but to employ an interceptor then we have to accept the limitations that go along with that course. This means choosing the best interceptor for the job at hand and then taking care to keep our tuning efforts within the bounds of what the interceptor can comfortably accommodate. Very often the reverse occurs with the enthusiast modifying the engine and then being disappointed by the final result because the engine spec is way beyond what any interceptor can handle.

PROGRAMMING THE COMPUTER

Regardless of the path we have chosen the end result will only be as good as the steps we have taken to ensure that our engine management system is correctly programmed. Thus enabling our engine to produce maximum power along with good reliability, and also good fuel economy if that is of importance. In essence we have to be prepared to put in the time running on a dyno to get the right setup. That might sound simple enough but it is anything but. The big problem is that there are lots of tuners around who don't have a clue about mapping, and equally there are many dynos about that are completely unsuited for mapping.

A new ECU and the mapping of it represent a huge investment for most people, and I'm not just talking in terms of the cash outlay involved. Really it doesn't matter how much money and effort you have put into the engine and the rest of the car, if the engine management system isn't spot on the whole exercise has been pretty much wasted effort. Therefore it is imperative that you choose carefully. Don't just think in terms of buying an ECU, or a chip, or an interceptor. Rather plan on buying a package that includes suitable hardware and software, plus a tuner who understands and can get the best out of that hardware and software, and who is working on a dyno suited to mapping.

So often I see enthusiasts pay good money for rubbish results. They buy the ECU they think they need and then try to find someone who can map the thing. I realise that it is very much a catch twenty-two situation, we are dealing with relatively new and constantly evolving technology here, and every tuner has to learn somewhere. That is okay if he is learning in his time and at his expense, but when you are paying the bill it is not such a great idea especially as you will invariably find that the exercise is repeated several times with you going from one tuner to another before you actually have the car running satisfactorily, much less the way you know it should.

CHOOSE THE RIGHT DYNO

When it comes to developing engines the engine dyno is always the way to go, however mapping is different. Generally it is preferable for mapping to be done on a chassis dyno – a rolling road. This is especially so in the case of turbo engines as under-bonnet heat has a large influence on engine tune. Obviously you will gather from this statement that the bonnet should be closed for final map fine tuning to most closely replicate the actual environment that will exist on the road or track.

However, not just any rolling road is suitable. What we need is a modern, eddy current electronic dyno that allows the operator to hold the roller speed. Many newer dynos are the much cheaper inertia type, with the Dynojet perhaps the most well known. Instead of having an electric brake or a water brake these have a very heavy roller ($2^1/2$ tons in the case of the Dynojet) which the tyres accelerate. Calculating the rate at which the roller accelerates, the dyno computer can then do a print-out of the vehicle's hp at the wheels. That's fine if your only concern is determining the engine's

Any engine management system is only as good as the time and effort put into careful mapping. This is best done by an operator who knows his stuff using a modern eddy current dyno.

power while accelerating at full throttle as the test is very fast and the likelihood of engine damage is minimal. However, when properly tuning an engine, we are not just interested in how it runs from low rpm to maximum revs at wide-open throttle. We want to get it accelerating well without a stumble and without detonation over a broad range of engine speeds and a wide range of throttle openings. Additionally we want the engine to be capable of holding maximum engine revs at full throttle for several seconds just as it will be called upon to do lap after lap on a race circuit. (In acceleration mode the engine doesn't get time to heat up fully internally so it is very easy to go overboard with excessive boost and spark advance, or a too lean fuel mixture that looks fine on the dyno but will destroy the engine on the track.)

The eddy current dyno, when switched to closed loop mode, has this ability as an electric brake holds roller rpm regardless of load. Thus when mapping the operator can calibrate the ECU with the engine held at a fixed engine speed. Having dialled in the rpm he wants the dyno to hold, he can then set about tapping in different fuel and ignition settings and the engine speed will not change – only the torque readout will change, indicating whether the new settings are to the engine's liking. When happy with the result at that rpm point and throttle angle the operator can move on to the next site until the map has been completed.

A similar thing can also be accomplished with a water brake type chassis dyno, but it is more of a fiddle and takes longer. Like the eddy current type the water brake can be used to map at any throttle opening, but the problem is that as the spark or fuel is altered and power output goes up or down engine revs will rise or fall in response to those changes, moving the engine to a different rpm and load site on the map. The operator then has to adjust the water brake to alter the load on the engine to get back to the map target site. Naturally this takes time and costs you money. Plus there is always the risk of the operator becoming frustrated at the engine revs constantly jumping about and simply giving up before the best setting has been established. This matter of the engine rpm changing is especially troublesome at the instant high output turbo engines come on boost, and of all engines they are probably the ones we need to be extra careful with to ensure that the mapping is spot on.

ENGINE MANAGEMENT SYSTEM INSTALLATION

Dyno operators are only human, so if they see sloppy component installation, bodged up wiring etc you are not likely to leave with a satisfactory mapping result. Either he will lose heart and give up pretty quickly, or he will reason 'this bloke doesn't care, so why should I?' Consequently do all you can to do the job correctly. The finished result should look neat and tidy.

All joints should be properly soldered and insulated. All wires should be tied to something solid to prevent them fracturing from vibration. The plastic insulation may appear okay, but inside the conductors can break, making contact sometimes and not at other times. Make sure connectors can't pull apart and are waterproof so as to avoid problems later. Remember we are dealing with tiny electrical flows in many parts of this system, so we want to prevent corrosion or poor contact at all connectors and terminals. For this very same reason we need to very carefully route all cables. If the instruction manual says to keep certain wires apart then do so even if the job doesn't look as neat. We don't want electrical current in one wire producing current, or

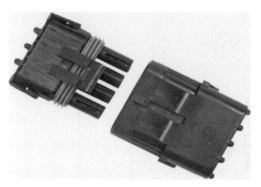

Use good quality waterproof connectors when wiring in the ECU and any associated sensors.

This system clearly states that additional wires should not be routed close to the distributor. Doing so could alter the triggering/speed sensor signal.

electrical 'noise' in a neighbouring wire that the ECU may read as an instruction from a sensor.

Take care to correctly earth shielded cable too. The shielding, a braided layer of copper or aluminium wire between the inner and outer plastic insulation, can only shield the conductor in the middle of the cable from induction or noise if it is actually earthed. That means paring back the outer insulation, twisting up the braided shielding wires, soldering on an earth connector, and then attaching that connector to a true earth. A big lump of metal, if it doesn't connect back to the battery earth, is not a true earth. Needless to say neither is plastic, fibreglass, or carbon fibre. Even major car manufacturers can get this wrong. A friend is a Philips technician. Their radios are fitted by many different car manufacturers, but in one particular brand reception and station range were terrible in certain cars. The radios worked fine on the bench, back in the car was a different story. Technical experts tried all sorts of things and finally concluded that some cars were producing some type of 'rogue' electrical signal. Ordinary tradesmen in one workshop couldn't accept this intellectual drivel and went searching for the real rogue. It turned out to be a false earth. Up under the dash there was a sheet of plastic insulating material with a silver finish that gave the appearance of being metal; the radios were being earthed there!

The major sources of electrical noise are the spark plug wires and spark plugs. If you are from the old school it is hard to accept that tossing away perfectly good, highly conductive solid copper leads, and spark plugs without resistors or resistor gaps, can be a good thing. However, believe me they have no place in an electronically managed vehicle. Fit high quality suppressor leads and resistor plugs and don't fret. Your new, powerful ignition system will give a fatter spark – even with these seeming impediments – than anything possible from old systems.

Many problems can be avoided if you first carefully read the manual supplied with the ECU. If the instructions are not clear, talk to the maker. As I have previously mentioned, if the instructions seem to make sense on a quick read-through, re-read them as no instructions are that easy.

Some things are pretty obvious but should not be taken for granted. The ECU doesn't like heat, water or excessive vibration, so mount it appropriately. Remember

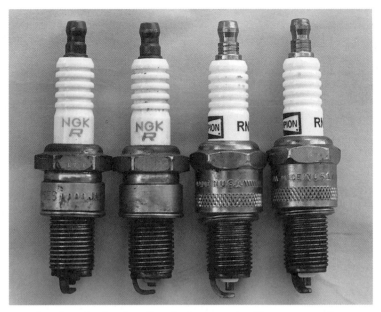

ECUs are upset by electrical noise. Spark plugs and cables are a major source of this sort of interference, so resistor plugs, identified by the 'R' in both NGK and Champion brands, should be used.

an area may be cool at cruise but turn into a stove-top at continuous full throttle. If the ECU has to be insulated from vibration by mounting on rubber pads then don't tighten the screws down so that the pads become solid.

SPEED/CRANK ANGLE SENSOR

If you are sticking with the original electronic distributor you only need a few simple checks. Firstly, make sure the new ECU can read the type of signal the distributor delivers. Some ECUs can handle many different signal forms, others are quite specific. Secondly, check the mechanical integrity. If the shaft and/or bearings are worn, allowing the shaft to wobble, this needs to be fixed. Or if the distributor has a helical drive gear ensure that thrust washers of the correct thickness are fitted to keep end float down to about 0.003in. Remember the ECU is taking its cue from here regarding crankshaft angle and piston position in the cylinder, so if the distributor shaft is allowed to ride up and down or wobble then that information will be incorrect. Thirdly, if there is oil in the distributor cap, fit a new distributor oil seal; or if crankcase blow-by pressure is forcing oil into the distributor spend your money reconditioning the engine first!

When converting from a mechanical distributor with bob weights and vacuum advance mechanism, be it an electronic or points type, you should first check if a later model of your engine utilised electronic engine management and a distributor that can be easily adapted to your engine. If so, and your new ECU can decipher its signal, then get a distributor from a wreck and follow the three steps in the previous paragraph to get it into top condition.

If there is no easy alternative but to stick with the bob weight distributor there are a number of other things to take care of, in addition to the above three. Obviously the bob weights can be removed and the shaft welded. Likewise for the vacuum advance mechanism. Next, if it was a points type, you will need some type of pick-up to signal crank rpm and angle. Rather than fitting this into the distributor you will probably find it simpler to use a toothed triggering wheel and pick-up from a later distributorless engine and use the distributor only to direct the spark to the correct cylinder.

Even in electronic bob weight distributors it can be easier to go the toothed wheel route and forget about using the inbuilt pick-up. The problem is rotor alignment. With a helical drive gear this generally isn't an issue, but if the drive is via a pin or slot, you will almost certainly wind up with the rotor arm pointing at the wrong angle. Moving the plug wires around the distributor cap won't fix it. Under load the rotor may be close enough to the correct terminal to fire the correct plug. However at cruise when a lot of advance is added-in the rotor could be closer, electrically not necessarily physically, to the adjoining distributor cap terminal, and so fire the wrong plug.

The way around the problem obviously is to reposition the rotor button on the distributor shaft. How much it needs to be moved, and in which direction is another problem. Ask around; if it's a distributor that is commonly used for engines with electronic engine management, some kind tuner may let you in on his secret, or you may be able to find the answer on the internet.

If you can't you will have to leave sorting it out until you tackle mapping the system. Before that you can save time and ensure better accuracy if you remove the distributor cap, and after carefully noting where the internal high voltage posts are located, paint corresponding marks on the distributor body. Later the dyno operator/mapper should check, with a timing light, that the timing at the crank pulley is the same as that indicated on the ignition timing map. If they are different the distributor should be moved until both coincide. This doesn't affect engine tune, it just ensures that the on-screen ignition advance numbers reflect the actual amount of advance when the plugs fire.

Following that remove the distributor cap, and with No 1 cylinder on the compression stroke, slowly rotate the engine. Particularly in the range of 10–60° before TDC, the rotor arm should be opposite one of the marks you previously painted on the distributor body. Most likely it won't be, so the rotor will have to be moved. If it is fixed with two screws you may be able to elongate the existing holes, or drill a pair of new ones; either way be careful to keep the rotor central so that it isn't going to scrape the distributor cap around one side. If it is located by a slot in the shaft lift the rotor button and turn it to the most suitable position, about 180° around, and facing a painted mark. Scribe or paint a reference mark on the shaft and cut a new locating slot. If you use a hacksaw you shouldn't have any trouble identifying the correct slot to use. If you are more fussy and mill the slot be sure to file a 'V' or put a hacksaw cut in the bottom to make it distinctive. Now move all the plug wires to their correct place on the cap and put a paint mark at No 1.

TRIGGER WHEEL SYSTEM

The alternative, as explained in the previous chapter, is to run a triggering wheel on the crankshaft along with a fixed pick-up. Here we can choose to use an expensive

Locating the trigger wheel on the drive end of the crankshaft improves timing accuracy even more than that possible with it on the pulley end. Plus, being located in the bellhousing, the pick-up is not exposed to damage from flying track debris or drive belts. However, in the event of sensor failure this can make replacement more difficult.

triggering arrangement such as that made by MSD for all-out race engines. Their system features an aluminium wheel with a number of rare-earth magnets that rotate past a non-magnetic fixed pick-up to send a triggering signal. Another arrangement suitable for high rpm running is to use magnetic studs in the crank pulley or flywheel. As these pass a magnetic pick-up a triggering signal is transmitted.

The relatively inexpensive way is to utilise something from one of the car makers. When scrounging for a trigger wheel also get a pick-up, but prior to doing so be sure you know what wheel and pick-up you need to communicate with your ECU. Most of these systems are reliable, and obviously will get the job done at normal engine rpm. However the 35 tooth (36–1) pressed trigger wheel Ford use on some models can be prone to shedding or bending teeth at continuous high rpm. Shortening the teeth will help, but cut off no more than 2mm and take care when straightening the teeth that you don't set-off the fracturing process yourself. The Ford wheel should now live at up to a regular 7,500rpm. The 58 tooth(60–2) Bosch trigger wheel is more robust and quite easy to find in wrecking yards.

Before deciding on a location for the pick-up get a good idea of how you are going to fix the tooth wheel to the crankshaft. Don't mount it at this time, just have a look at where and how you will fit it up. With that figured out find the best location for the pick-up sensor. You want it in a position where it won't be vulnerable to damage and where it is not going to make normal service jobs a lot more difficult. Mount it solidly and allow for adjustability. If the ECU has no provision for a few degrees misalignment of sensor and trigger wheel you will have to use slotted mounting holes to get the TDC reference correct. Also it is a good idea to provide for air-gap adjustment between the teeth and pick-up sensor. If the signal is a bit weak or suffering 261 from noise, moving the sensor closer can sometimes help. Conversely if you are running the Ford wheel at very high rpm you may want to make the gap wider to ease the risk of centrifugal force spreading the teeth and taking out the sensor.

After this the tooth wheel can be properly fixed in position. Here you will require some information from your ECU manual as to the triggering angle before TDC. If it states 120° before TDC then you will have to very carefully move the crank to that angle on cylinder No 1, and lock it there. Then fix the trigger wheel so that the first tooth immediately after the gap is lined up with the pick-up. How this works is that the ECU receives regular pulses as each tooth passes the sensor. Then when it misses a pulse because of a missing tooth it knows the crank angle before TDC. The tooth immediately after the gap is its reference point. If that reference angle isn't spot on then all of the ECU's calculations will be erroneous by that angle of error too.

Some people are confused about how many teeth work best when just one magnetic stud per two cylinders seems to be fine on many competition systems. Basically more teeth keep the ECU more regularly updated as to crankshaft speed, nothing more. Nissan chose to inform their ECU of crank rpm every 1°; Bosch with their 60–2 wheel decided on letting the ECU know engine rpm every 6°; most makers have gone with a 36–1 tooth wheel, meaning the ECU gets a new crank rpm figure every 10° of crank rotation. Many competition systems get the latest crank speed info to the ECU as infrequently as every 180° (4-cylinder engines), 120° (even fire 6-cylinder), 90° (V8 engines). The claim by some is that more frequent updates make for a sharper, more responsive engine. I must be missing something, but then I chose to be a tuner rather than a racer, so what would I know?

THROTTLE POT SENSOR

Along with some fuel injection systems, carburetted engines with electronic engine management also require a throttle pot to inform the computer of how wide the throttle

The throttle position sensor informs the ECU how far the throttle is open so must be carefully adjusted prior to any attempt at mapping the ECU.

is open. For the pot to properly inform the ECU of the throttle position you have to set it up properly. First, ensure that the throttle is opening fully. Get someone in the car holding the pedal to the floor and have a look. This is important, because if you get half-way through mapping and find you can't fully open the throttle and you then set about rectifying the problem all the mapping up to that point is lost!

With full throttle taken care of, back off the throttle screws to allow the throttle to fully close. If there is any oil, carbon, dust, or grit in the throttle body or on the butterfly/s, get it cleaned out. The throttle must be allowed to close fully before you set the throttle pot closed position. Now fit the pot over the 'D' on the end of the throttle shaft. Don't force it into the fully closed position; you want the pot just fractionally open. When all is as it should be tighten the mounting screws.

PRELIMINARIES TO MAPPING THE ECU

This section is included to assist those tuners who have access to a dyno and would like to learn the noble art of ECU mapping. As previously stated you need an electronic eddy current dyno – either engine dyno or rolling road. Don't even momentarily entertain the idea of mapping on anything else. Start out learning with an engine that's already run-in and that isn't turbocharged, supercharged or has wild valve timing. An engine in good mechanical order, running nicely on Weber carbs and some type of mechanical ignition, either points or electronic, and is now being converted to fuel injection and electronic ignition, would be a good practice tool.

Before you even attempt to start the engine there are a number of basic checks that are necessary. Don't fool yourself, mapping isn't easy, so anything you can do to minimise frustration along the way will help you to achieve a good outcome. The battery must have plenty of cranking capacity to spin the engine fast, and have sufficient voltage to give a good fat spark so that you have some sort of sporting chance of firing a fuel mixture that is likely to be excessively rich or massively lean.

If the car didn't come from the factory with fuel injection, your first check should be to ensure the fuel supply system is working. Connect a fuel pressure gauge into the fuel rail and turn the ignition on. You should be able to hear the pump whirring for a few seconds getting the system up to pressure, and then stop. In-tank pumps have their noise muffled pretty well so this may not be so obvious. Take a look at the pressure reading. It should be holding steady, and in the case of a fixed pressure regulator, be fairly close to its preset pressure. If not and the pressure is very high have a look to ensure that fuel hoses into and out of the pressure regulator are connected to the correct ports and have not been reversed. A low reading could indicate that the regulator has dirt or grit in it, so blow it out with high pressure air in the direction of flow, and try again.

With that done it's time to link your laptop to the ECU. Select the live mapping tab (it may also be called live adjustment mode, live communication mode etc), and take a look at the screen. Here common sense comes into play. If some readings don't look right then it's probable that there is a problem somewhere, so don't ignore it and assume that it will go away. For example the engine isn't running as yet so the rpm should be 0; the engine water temp and air temp readings should be pretty much the same etc. Any readings outside of what you consider normal must be followed through by checking that your connections and wiring are correct, or that sensors are working properly; yes even new ones can be faulty.

If the engine has a throttle pot you most likely will have to adjust it in accordance with the instructions provided with the ECU. Correctly adjusted, the screen should read 'load site 0' when the throttle is fully closed and rise smoothly to the maximum stated in the manual when fully open.

Now it's time to begin cranking the engine over. Murphy's Law dictates that it won't fire and that over the next few hours your resolve to be an engine mapper will be fully tested, but don't be discouraged, don't get flustered, don't think you are a completely hopeless individual. If, as the engine cranks over, the screen gives an rpm reading you know the ECU is getting a signal from the speed/crank angle sensor, so that is one problem out of the way. The battery voltage should preferably be reading higher than 9 volts while cranking. Anything lower and the spark could be pretty feeble, the injectors may not open, and the ECU may not compute.

Next determine if the lack of fire in the cylinders is ignition – either advance angle, or in the case of converted bob weight distributors, wrong plug wire positions – or is it fuel – too lean or too rich. There are two easy methods to check this. One is to spray a starting aerosol into the inlet tract – not the air filter – as the engine is cranked over. Alternatively, if you have pulled the plugs to see if they are wet, you can spray about 3–5cc of petrol down each plug hole, or if the engine has an isolated runner type inlet manifold squirt the fuel down each inlet tract.

If the engine now runs, even if only for a few seconds, you know the ignition is okay to at least get it running, so obviously the engine needs more fuel. Depending on the software you may be able to trim the fuel richer as you crank the engine. If not, you will have to add more fuel in the base fuel map. If the engine is running roughly try to get it idling at 1,700–2,000rpm. Now move the fuelling to give the most stable smooth idle. When it is reasonably smooth set it at 1,150–1,300rpm.

If the engine doesn't run when the aerosol or fuel is sprayed in, instead just coughing and blowing back through the inlet tract, then the problem is ignition. Assuming a distributor-based trigger system, slowly move the distributor while cranking the engine. When it fires keep moving it to achieve the best idle, if necessary backing off the idle screw to bring it down around 1,150–1,300rpm.

Before you go any further you now have to carry out an ignition advance alignment. Your management system manual will explain this operation, but usually it means using a timing light to determine the ignition advance angle and confirming that the timing figure stated onscreen matches. If it doesn't, the software may allow the reference angle to be corrected, or it may be necessary to physically move the distributor, or pick-up in the case of tooth, or magnet, wheel arrangements.

SORTING IDLE MAPPING

With the preliminaries taken care of we can get into the serious business of getting the spark and fuelling right at idle. Start with the ignition advance. For a road engine you don't want more than about 10° at idle. Sure the engine will rev a lot faster with anything up to perhaps 40°, but don't do it. This will only make it an absolute pain, if not impossible, to get the fuel map right. With stacks of idle advance the throttle plate/s need to be almost totally closed to keep idle speed down to 1,000rpm. Consequently with very little air going into the engine it only requires a correspondingly small amount of fuel. Injector flow is pretty erratic at low flow so mapping gets quite tedious and idle quality will suffer.

If you are getting spit-back in the inlet system it probably means the mixture is lean. What happens is that as the fuel is leaned to provide the correct idle mixture any slight decrease in injector flow causes a big, sudden drop in idle speed as well. Now with low air speed in the inlet tract a lot of that fuel will drop out of suspension, the engine will go lean and may even stall. Another scenario is that even if you manage to get idle fuelling half decent the engine will experience a massive off-idle flat spot that will make the car a big problem to get off the line unless lots of throttle and clutch slipping are brought into play. These hassles are avoidable; just use 10° idle advance for a street engine.

Below idle though the story changes. At the 500rpm speed site you can give the engine a heap of advance; often up around 30–40°. With all this advance below the 1,000rpm idle speed site, any time the engine speed drops below 1,000rpm more advance is added, nudging the idle speed back up. This provides for a smoother idle and virtually eliminates any chance of the engine stalling when the air conditioner or radiator fan cuts in while you are stopped at traffic lights.

The situation is similar with regard to fuelling. Below idle the fuel number has to get bigger simply because if the engine begins to lose revs air speed falls and a lot of fuel will fall out of suspension, causing mixture leanness. Therefore if the fuel number at 1,000rpm is 30, then make it around 40–45 at 500rpm and 55–60 at 0rpm to ensure the mixture is actually combustible.

IGNITION MAPPING

With the idle sorted we can move on to roughing out a base map for both the spark and injectors. If the engine was previously running well on a bob weight distributor then those ignition advance numbers will be a good starting point. If you don't have any idea where to start then it pays to be conservative to begin with; you can always give a working engine more advance later.

Table 8.1 will provide a starting point, but remember that I don't know what engine you are running, nor its state of tune. Nor do I have any control of how lean you have gone with the fuel mixture. Consequently if you don't have a warning light or alarm connected to a knock sensor to alert you to detonation take care to listen out for it and don't focus completely on how the engine is performing! Conversely don't fool yourself into thinking that grossly retarded ignition advance won't cause any harm. Late ignition means a lot more heat in the exhaust passage. That means hotter exhaust valves and seats, and exhaust header/s. Excessive heat here could see the valve seats cracking, distorting, or dropping out of the head. The exhaust valve head could begin to melt, distort, or even fracture and fall into the cylinder. An exhaust glowing red is a warning; it may look spectacular, but don't ignore this sign. Additionally, mapping while retarded, it will be a lot more trouble to get the fuelling correct. With retarded ignition the engine may respond favourably when an excess of fuel is available. Later when you realise the advance is way too retarded, you will have to waste a stack of time rewriting the heavy load fuelling a good deal leaner.

Table 8.1 Generic ignition advance map

		Ignition Advance°	
	Bore dia (mm)	**2,500rpm**	**4,000rpm**
2 valve full throttle	100	25	32
	84	22	28
	68	20	25
2 valve quarter throttle	100	30	42
	84	26	34
	68	23	30
4 valve full throttle	100	20	28
	84	18	25
	68	15	22
4 valve quarter throttle	100	28	37
	84	24	33
	68	21	29

Note: use the suggestions in this table only if you do not have more specific ignition advance information for your particular engine. These figures are a good starting point only for engines with alloy cylinder head, compression ratio of 10:1 or less, water temperature 80°C or less, burning 98 RON summer blend unleaded fuel.

Autronic A/F ratio meter connected to a wide-range Lambda probe will accurately measure A/F ratios from as rich as 9.4:1 to as lean as 36.0:1. Mapping the mixture for around 12.7:1 is a safe ballpark figure for naturally aspirated engines; supercharged engines frequently prefer a little more fuel.

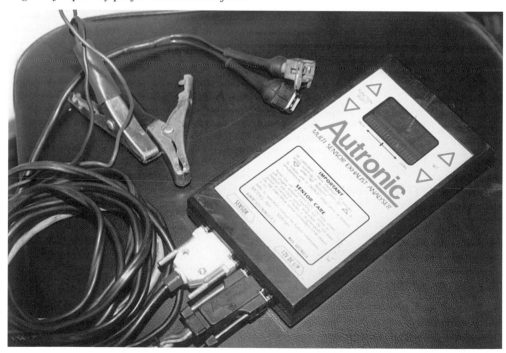

FUEL MAPPING

With a base ignition map written, have a 'feel' for how the engine is running. The idle should be stable and the engine shouldn't be thrashing about. Now blip the throttle and at the same time watch the lambda number. Probably the engine will splutter and die. If the lambda shows you need more fuel, then add this to the load sites just above and below idle. Keep this routine going until you are able to get the engine to cleanly rev up when the throttle is blipped. It should now be possible to drive off from idle and run up over 2,000rpm.

Now we can move to the more serious fuel mapping. On light throttle, at around 2,500–3,000rpm, adjust the fuelling until the engine runs crisply. Then move through the load sites until you are about midway between quarter and half throttle, aiming to get the engine feeling smooth and crisp.

With that done we need to take a deep breath and have a careful look at our map. The fuel figures shouldn't be jumping about all over the shop. When we look at the numbers they should be all heading in the same direction, either progressively increasing or progressively decreasing. Any number out of line with this trend should be tweaked a bit to 'smooth' the map. For example if a number at one site is bigger than its neighbours, lower it and perhaps raise the neighbouring numbers a little.

When the engine is for road use then you have to be concerned with fuel consumption at legal speed limits. You don't want the mixture so lean that the engine is surging or popping through the exhaust. Operating like that, like running rich, also wastes fuel. On the other hand don't get too concerned that going lean you will cook the engine, melt the pistons etc. At small throttle openings you won't get into this sort of trouble. Just get sufficient fuel in to avoid surging and exhaust popping, and enjoy the smaller fuel bill!

Competition engines are different in this regard. Usually we simply want them to run well at lower rpm so as to get on the cam as quick as possible. However, if fuel consumption when behind the safety car is an issue then we need to factor that in.

At these lower engine speeds and smaller throttle open angles, don't be too concerned with lambda numbers; simply aim to get the engine running nicely. As we move past half throttle though the situation changes. Now we have to pay a lot of attention to the lambda. Quickly blip the throttle and note how the engine responds. If it stumbles and the lambda went lean, add fuel to those parts of the map. Conversely if it reads rich take fuel out. There is no point in taking the engine to max rpm at this stage. Most engines need the biggest fuel number at peak torque revs. Therefore if you know the engine makes best torque at 6,000rpm don't waste time now mapping at higher rpm.

Keep at this until you are happy with how the engine feels. When you reckon the fuelling is close and that you won't damage the engine when doing more severe testing, it's time for you to take another look at your fuel map. Again search for numbers that are out of line with their neighbours. When such are found then smooth the fuelling by changing the target number, and follow up with a mild tweak of the neighbour on either side. Also at this time fill in the blank sites above the guesstimated peak torque speed. From peak torque right up to the rev limit simply put the same fuel numbers in and leave tweaking top-end fuelling until we do a full power curve.

Run the engine again and double-check that at each site above about half throttle the fuel number is safe with an air/fuel ratio around 12.5:1–12.7:1. Don't get too   267 carried away striving for a particular number, anything in that range will be safe. Just be sure to keep a close eye on the lambda and don't hold the power on and make fuelling changes. This is hard on the engine, particularly at anything past 90% throttle and at rpm past peak torque. Always get off the throttle and only then adjust the fuel number. When you are absolutely sure that all is in order we can proceed to the exciting stuff – producing a power curve!

The idea of course is to produce the highest power at each rpm/load site. What further complicates things is that several fuel numbers will give the same hp. Remember the dyno is an artificial environment. In a real environment an engine accelerates through a number of speeds; engine loads change as tyres grip up and lose traction; the vehicle is moving, so air flows around the engine are in a state of constant flux etc. These factors, and many others, affect the temperature of the combustion chamber and piston crown. So in the real world what fuel number should we choose? There is no simple answer to this, but as a general rule I would go for the low number at 50% up to about 80% throttle. Above that I incrementally increase fuelling so that I'm about midway between the high number and the low number by the time I get to 100% throttle. If I'm tuning for endurance racing and the track has only a relatively short straight and no steep climbs, the fuel number may possibly be safely trimmed without risk of engine damage, and incur only marginal power losses. However, if there are big climbs and/or long straights I am more inclined to go closer to the top fuel number above 95% throttle. This will help the pistons live and will keep the hp up for the full length of the climb or the straight; hopefully compensating for less track mileage between fuel stops.

With the oil and water at operating temperature, do your first acceleration power run. Don't take your eye off the lambda meter for an instant. If at any point the lambda goes lean abort the run, add more fuel, and try again. When you manage to do a full acceleration run with good lambda numbers stop and take time to examine the power curve. Find at what rpm peak torque occurs. Remember previously we only guessed this. Now add a little fuel at rpm past true peak torque up to the rev limit and do another full acceleration run. Did top-end power rise? If so, it tells you that you may be losing fuel out the exhaust during the cam overlap period and/or the exhaust tuned length could be a problem. Then again there may be no clear answer; some engines just demand more fuel. If adding fuel wasn't to the engine's liking try pulling a little out and do another power run.

Now overlay the three power curves. You may find that a dip in one curve didn't exist, or wasn't as severe, in another curve. If that's the case then change the fuelling at that site/s and do another acceleration run and again overlay the curves to confirm that you are heading the right way.

IGNITION MAP

With the base fuel map in place we can set about constructing a proper ignition map. This is fairly straightforward. Just remember that as for fuelling a range of spark advance numbers will give the same hp. However, unlike when building the fuel map this time we always use the lowest advance number. Additional advance over what gives max hp never helps. In fact, on-track testing may reveal that you need to knock off a couple of degrees at a few sites when the piston crown and combustion chamber are fully heated up. This, along with a touch more fuel, could be necessary on circuits where you are at 100% throttle for a lot of the lap.

Start out with mapping at light loads, and then progress through 50%, 75% and perhaps also 85% throttle open following a similar procedure as for developing the fuel map. When you have an adequate number of sites filled in you can guesstimate some of the gaps and then smooth any numbers that are high or low when compared with their neighbours.

When you are happy with the result proceed to a full throttle acceleration run. If there was no warning from the knock sensor indicating excessive advance in some parts of the map, you can then simply pull 2° advance out of the entire map and do another 100% throttle acceleration run. Overlay the two curves and compare the result. If on the retarded run you lost power everywhere, try adding 2° advance. If the engine didn't pick up power don't waste time and add to engine wear with another power test. Rather go back and this time look at the torque curve. Generally, engines like more advance right at the top of the power band, so at sites above peak torque rpm begin adding more spark advance. If the engine breathes very well high in the rev range – indicated by a torque curve that very gradually falls past max torque rpm – and is artificially rev limited to reduce the frequency of rebuilds, avoid component failure, comply with race regulations etc, then you may only need 3–4° more spark lead at the rev limit and slightly less, perhaps 1–3° at max power rpm. On the other hand, an engine that runs out of breath pretty rapidly at the top of the power range – indicated by a torque curve that drops away steeply – may want 5–8° more advance at the rev limit and a fairly similar amount, or maybe just 1–3° less at maximum hp revs. Don't be greedy and think adding more and more advance will help. It won't. Much more likely the outcome will be reduced performance and engine damage, plus the engine may not want to over-rev very much past max hp revs. Always strive for the highest hp with the least ignition lead.

SIMULTANEOUS RUNNING-IN AND MAPPING

It isn't a great idea to map a newly built engine until you have gained some experience. Eventually though the day will arrive when you will have to actually get the engine management sufficiently sorted for an engine to run reasonably well in a short time, and then get down to the serious business of bedding the rings etc.

The basic procedure to begin with is the same as for a used engine. Follow what was written under the IGNITION MAPPING subheading, page 265, and then quickly get into fuel mapping. Don't muck about with the idle and low rpm fuelling. Go straight to 2,500–3,000rpm, or higher if the cams are pretty wild. You don't want the engine running under 2,000rpm. Low rpm lubrication is poor, particularly to the valve train, so keep engine speed up.

The idea is to set the dyno load for the engine to run at 2,500–3,000rpm with the throttle on the first load site and adjust the fuelling so that the engine smooths out. Next, with the throttle angle unchanged, reduce the dyno load so as to allow the engine revs to increase up to the next rpm site. Adjust the fuel number to get the engine running sweetly. Keep repeating this routine of reducing dyno load, moving to the next speed site and adjusting the fuel. Eventually you will reach a point where the engine won't rev any faster. From then on right up to the rev limit simply fill in the last fuel number at all of the remaining speed sites.

Now repeat the procedure with the throttle moved a bit wider open and with enough dyno load to hold 2,500–3,000rpm. Adjust the fuel, then reduce dyno load to move to the next rpm site, adjust the fuel and so on. Repeat this until you reach 50% throttle, by which stage the engine should be nicely run-in to allow you to map the high load sites and perform full acceleration runs as previously outlined under the FUEL MAPPING subheading, page 267. Alternatively you could do the idle mapping next, and then map the fuelling for high loads above 50% throttle.

When the fuelling has been sorted you can then move on to finalising the base ignition map. Previously the map was pretty much an educated guess based on the figures in Table 8.1 and the knowledge you have of your particular engine; purely aimed at getting the engine running well enough, without damaging it, to enable the fuel map to be written. Now with correct fuelling we have to get the spark timing spot-on as discussed under the subheading IGNITION MAP, page 268.

ACCELERATION ENRICHMENT

With a carburetted engine an accelerator pump squirts extra fuel into the airstream when the throttle is rapidly opened. This arrangement is in place to make up for the time lag between when the throttle is floored, and all the additional air rushes into the cylinders, and when the carb is able to provide more fuel through the normal metering channels and jets to compensate for that increased air. Without the extra fuel the mixture would go lean; the engine may die momentarily and stumble with a big flat-spot.

Fuel injection basically doesn't change this scenario. The main difference is we don't have to introduce as much additional fuel into the airstream because fuel atomisation is superior with fuel injection. Plus with the injector shooting at the back of the inlet valve in the majority of engines, there is less likelihood of the fuel dropping out of suspension and remaining behind clinging to the port walls.

The main thing to watch with acceleration enrichment is that we don't fiddle about adding enrichment where it isn't needed, or doesn't work very well. I think even the major motorcycle manufacturers have been caught out here. A number of bikes were plain horrible to ride around the street at small throttle openings, constantly snapping and surging. Some of this was due to throttle bodies sized more for racing than for the street, but another culprit was improper light throttle mapping and a desire to add acceleration enrichment right from idle. In normal use you don't cruise with the engine running at idle speed and then snap the throttle open, but it seemed to me that bike makers were mapping like this. There is no point in adding acceleration enrichment lower in the rev range than the engine is ever going to be accelerated from. At higher revs the increase in air flow when the throttle is quickly opened is nowhere near as dramatic as at low rpm. Consequently the engine management and injection systems have adequate time, without adding acceleration enrichment, to get the extra fuel into the air stream before the mixture leans out.

Before you begin working on acceleration enrichment be absolutely sure that your mapping is spot-on in the light throttle load sites at engine speeds from idle up to about 2,000rpm. If the engine feels dead and unresponsive in this area the mixture is probably lean, and/or the spark may be retarded. If it's hunting and shaking it's very rich. Don't blame the cam in an attempt to excuse poor mapping. A fuel injected engine can run quite nicely with a pretty mean cam if mapped properly.

The management system manual will inform you of how the ECU handles acceleration enrichment. Some provide for you to select a percentage increase of fuel for a time period, or for a number of injector pulses. Also there may be provision for 'decay' – how long the extra injection tapers off for, either in time or number of pulses, rather than simply switching off and returning to the base number.

Don't try to do this sort of tuning on the dyno; the road or track is where you need to be. Drive as you normally would and add acceleration fuel until there is no hesitation when you hit the throttle. Please don't expect a race engine to accelerate cleanly from ridiculously low revs when it's off the cam. And don't expect a road engine to get up and go from low rpm when the throttle bodies are way too big and you are in a high gear. The idea is to be realistic and attempt to anticipate at what rpm, in what gear, and how rapidly the throttle will be opened when accelerating in the engine's regular environment. You don't want to waste fuel adding more enrichment than the engine and your driving style demands. Also if the engine is very powerful, and traction is limited, why exacerbate the issue with perfect acceleration enrichment that leads to perfect plumes of tyre smoke and slower lap times? In many motorsport situations a big number of competitors have major problems with delicate throttle control, particularly on wet surfaces. Thoughtful limiting of acceleration enrichment can assist.

AIR TEMPERATURE COMPENSATION

There are two angles to consider here – as air temp increases the amount of air going into the cylinders decreases, so less fuel is required. You can generally figure that for every 3–4° temperature increase air density goes down 1%. Therefore the amount of fuel the engine requires will decrease by a similar amount; about 1%. However as the temperature continues to rise the engine may become more sensitive to abnormal, or even out-of-control combustion. This situation calls for less spark advance and perhaps more, rather than less fuel.

Basically the reverse occurs at low air temp. More air density calls for more fuel, but what happens with ignition advance can be a bit of a lucky dip. Some engines will happily give more power with extra advance and display incredible resistance to detonation. Others though demand less advance because the more tightly packed air and fuel molecules transfer the combustion flame faster and faster through the combustion space, until the rate is too high and the mixture explodes.

Engine management software is usually written around a standard temp of 20°C. So to protect the engine and ensure best hp, on the air temperature correction screen, there will be provision to adjust both ignition advance and fuelling to compensate for temperature changes. Unlike a few sophisticated ECUs that give full three dimensional control, most management systems offer more basic correction. Thus there will be a coarse compensation for fuelling and spark based purely on air temperature without consideration of engine rpm or throttle position. Hence if you enter 5% enrichment when the air temp falls to 5°C, then that amount of additional fuel will be added to all of the base fuel figures even though the engine may only really benefit from that extra fuel at wider throttle openings.

COOLANT TEMPERATURE COMPENSATION & CRANKING ENRICHMENT

At first glance these topics appear to be pretty similar. Provide lots of fuel when the cold engine is cranking over, and then progressively reduce fuel flow back to the base number when the engine reaches normal water temp. However, cranking enrichment is also a significant issue with hot engines, even very hot engines. Many of the problems you see, and perhaps will later experience, of hot engines failing to fire up can be traced back to cranking enrichment. Sluggish cranking rpm with race engines due to weak battery power, high compression etc can be part of the problem too. Frequently though it will be found that with wild camming, monster throttle bodies and so forth, a competition engine, even a hot one, will only fire with 20–30% cranking enrichment. The idea here is to keep adding fuel until it comes to life easily. An excess of fuel generally won't hurt provided you don't wet the plugs. Also be aware that because of the decay feature cranking enrichment is only available for a specific number of seconds. If the fire hasn't started in that time frame, don't just keep cranking; the enrichment will by now have ceased. Rather get off the starter, wait a moment, then spin the engine over again. If the plugs are getting wet you need to take fuel away, otherwise keep adding fuel until the engine consistently comes to life easily. We are assuming here that the starter motor, battery and ignition system are up to the task. Be aware though that not all hot engines want a lot of enrichment. In fact some will refuse to fire with more than 4–5% added. The idea is to commence at 10%, then go to 15%, then 20% etc. Don't waste time, 5% steps will get you close to feeling what the engine wants. With a cold engine at 15°C start out adding 60% enrichment, and don't be frightened to go past 100% if the temp is close to freezing. Depending on the software, cranking enrichment is usually halved the moment the engine starts.

After the engine begins running, injection duration and spark timing will be compensated for via the coolant temp adjustments. This can consume a lot of time as the engine quickly comes up to temperature before you have time to actually test how nicely the engine operates while cold. Mind you, this isn't such a bad thing for competition engines; purposely keeping cold running horrible so that impatient drivers don't work the engine hard until it is fairly well up to operating temperature can cut maintenance bills! For road engines you don't want the engine spluttering and dying as you enter a busy motorway. So even though running hard when cold will kill the rings and upper cylinder region the engine has to be able to take a boot-full of throttle from almost the moment it fires. To achieve this you will need long cool-down periods, even overnight, to retest your latest cold enrichment. As a guide, if you found the engine wanted 60% cranking enrichment at 10–15°C, start out with 30% at 20°C, 20% at 40°C and 8% at 60°C. If the engine feels sluggish and there is no sign of black smoke the engine is probably lean, so add fuel and try again. If it's still sluggish, pull the spark plugs; black sooty tips indicate too much fuel, nice clean plugs likely mean the engine wants more enrichment.

Many cold engines respond nicely to a few degrees more spark lead. At times though, due to emissions laws, road engines may be purposely retarded to get an unheated CAT up to temperature more rapidly. When this isn't a consideration you may like to start out testing with an additional 5° advance with the coolant at 20°C, tapering down to 1–2° extra at 50°C.

MAPPING ROAD VS RACE ENGINES

A non-turbo track engine isn't difficult to map. You basically want it to start easily, cold or hot, idle without spluttering and dying, and then pull cleanly until it's on-cam. After that it has to make maximum power over as wide a rev band as possible at throttle angles of 60–100% open.

With road engines we have to have all the above, plus a whole lot more. There has to be minimal fuel burn at cruise without surging or popping through the exhaust. The engine has to work just as well at all temperatures between freezing and 100°C. Then to really make a tuner's life difficult, the thing must be crisp and rearing to race at every conceivable throttle position and engine speed, even when in a gear that's one or two cogs higher than what the engine really should be pulling! To achieve this state of tune takes the big manufacturers months and millions of dollars. All we can do is an honest job and help the enthusiast understand that we need accurate input from him over perhaps several weeks to massage away every tiny hesitation. Also if the cold engine fuelling was tackled in summer you will probably need to tweak the enrichment as the mercury heads downwards in winter. Realistically if it takes half a day to map a race engine don't be disappointed if a road engine takes another day longer. And the sad thing is after that extra day the engine probably won't be any stronger on the dyno; it will just be a much nicer drive!

Even without a lambda meter, customers can give you good mapping feedback from on-road testing. A digital voltmeter connected to the lambda sensor will give a rough idea of where the mixture is heading. If the customer reports surging or hesitation at cruise or gentle acceleration and the voltage is very low (below about 200–300 millivolts) this would indicate excessive leanness. At full throttle any reading under about 930–950 millivolts should be considered lean, ie approximately 13:1.

TEST DRIVE MAPPING REFINEMENTS

Regardless of how carefully and conscientiously you work on the dyno there is no substitute for actually driving on the road or race circuit. A great drive on the dyno seldom translates to a great drive under real-world conditions. As I have previously alluded to, you are bound to find flat spots. Pinpoint where they are occurring and fix them with minor fuel and spark tweaks. If the exhaust is popping on over-run the mixture is lean on mid-range and high rpm sites at small throttle openings, so add fuel until the popping goes away. Alternatively, if the management system has provision for cutting the fuel on over-run put that feature to use and ignore any tales that you may have heard that this causes a flat spot when you get back onto the throttle. Just make sure the fuel comes back on well before the engine stalls and you won't notice any hesitation.

Before you quit mapping and pack up it is a good idea to either follow the vehicle or get someone to follow you. Look for black exhaust smoke under heavy acceleration and at steady full throttle, indicating a very rich mixture. Note that if the sun is getting low in the sky and you are looking toward it exhaust smoke appears far worse than it actually is, so if you can't see smoke with the sun behind you the fuelling is probably okay.

MAP RESOLUTION

Before we move on from the topic of mapping we need to spend some time on the subject of resolution, ie the number of rpm and load sites on a map. I am not sure as to the reason but in recent times more individuals are requesting – some are demanding – finer and finer resolutions. Unfortunately the manufacturers of engine management systems have to a large degree gone along with this nonsense to such an extent that some maps have hundreds of sites waiting to be filled in. Regardless of what you have perhaps read elsewhere, or been told, you need only eight load sites for a naturally aspirated engine, and up to double that number with forced induction. Many competition engines really don't require that number. Anything more is overkill and a total waste of time. For rpm sites some people are fooling around with 100 and 200rpm steps. With a competition engine you don't want more than about 11 or 12rpm sites. In a road car most people stick to sites at every 500rpm step. This is okay but really isn't necessary. There is nothing wrong with 1,000rpm steps as soon as you get into the area where the engine spends the least time. For competition engines that means the bottom half of the rev range and for road cars the top end. Hence even if the ECU can be taken down to extremely fine resolutions, don't do it. That 'feature' is only there to accommodate those who don't mind wasting their time or think they know more than the best tuners.

For those really into this sort of thing they really should try the Autronic ECU – it has sensitivity fine enough to allow map sites as close as 1kpa (0.145psi) on the load axis and 1rpm on the other axis! However, all those sites are provided for a very good purpose. Some ECUs demand that all sites be filled in (the Haltech for example) but the Autronic simply makes the provision to enable very precise engine management during those areas of the rpm/load range where the engine suddenly gets very busy. A turbo engine may rapidly make loads of boost in unison with the variable cam

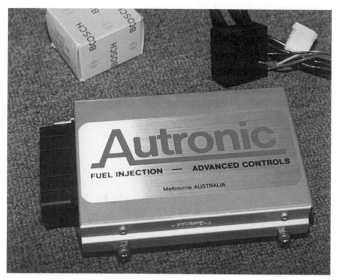

The very fine resolution possible on the Autronic engine management system makes it much easier to map on very temperamental high output rotary and turbo engines. Again the labelling is misleading; it is not a fuel only unit.

mechanism performing a big cam swing. With a rotary engine the porting and exhaust can fully sync in an instant. Consequently over a very limited rpm range the engine may require major fuelling and spark advance refinements which may not be adequately met by sites at say, 3,500rpm and 4,000rpm. In fact it may be a waste of time having sites at those two points because the big influences are all occurring between 3,680 and 3,930rpm. Therefore it may be more effective to have a three site cluster in that rpm span, with the closest site either side perhaps 600–800rpm away.

Chapter 9

The
Exhaust System

In the case of the exhaust system, appearances can be misleading. It may be visually impressive because of its shape, but to many it is still just a bundle of pipes that direct hot gas from the cylinders. Informed modifiers, however, realise full well the importance of tuning the exhaust plumbing to improve performance. As with all other areas of the high-performance engine, the exhaust system cannot be regarded as an individual entity; it is influenced by, and in turn affects, other areas, so it must be considered as a part of the whole. The aim is that the cylinders are completely scavenged of exhaust gas. On all-out racing engines the exhaust system is tuned so that the exhaust gas momentum and pressure waves actually 'suck' the intake charge into the cylinder; in this way the cylinder can actually be overfilled, ie a volumetric efficiency of 101–105%. Camshaft valve overlap and the induction system both have a part to play to make this possible.

INERTIA TUNING

Before we discuss the 'black art' of pulse tuning we will look at what can be done to efficiently scavenge the cylinder of exhaust gas by gas momentum or inertia tuning.

Figure 9.1 Exhaust valve overlap between cylinders 1 and 3.

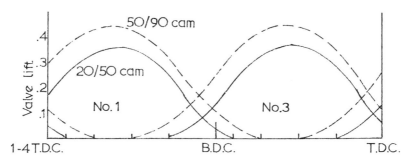

The principle of inertia tuning is that exhaust gases have weight, so once we get the gas 'rolling' it will continue to flow even after the exhaust valve has closed. This creates a partial vacuum with a resultant suction action that we can use to scavenge the cylinder. As engine speeds increase, the time available for effective cylinder exhausting will decrease, hence the need to use this suction action to empty the cylinder of exhaust gas more quickly.

Obviously if we have a gas pressure of 20psi in the exhaust manifold when the exhaust valve opens, this will restrict gas flow out of that cylinder. On the other hand, if manifold pressure is –5 to 0psi the flow restriction will be much less. For this reason we use the extractor-type header with individual pipes, rather than a common manifold. The basic idea is to arrange the pipes so that the exhaust gas of one cylinder will not pressurise another. For example, look at what occurs in a four-cylinder engine where all cylinders share a common manifold (Figure 9.1). The firing order we will assume to be 1–3–4–2. At the end of its exhaust stroke No 2 tends to be pressurised by No 1; No 4 will pressurise No 3 and so on. For this reason modified cams are a waste of time if this type of manifold is retained.

Figure 9.2a Four-cylinder exhaust headers.

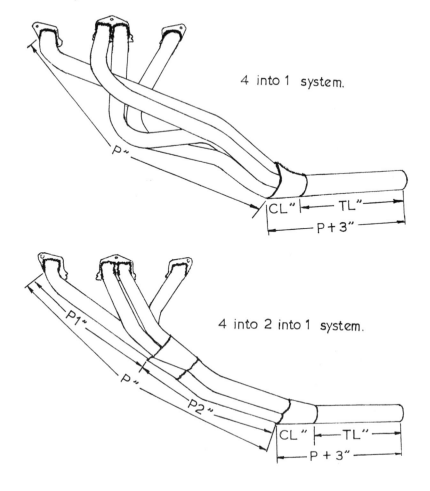

4 into 1 system.

4 into 2 into 1 system.

For many years racing engines used individual pipes for each cylinder, but it is now a well-established fact that in most instances it is more beneficial to join these individual pipes together, using a collector to which we attach either a straight tailpipe or a megaphone. This arrangement picks up power and, as an added bonus, improves the power range. Figures 9.2a–d show the various header designs for four-, six- and eight-cylinder engines. The six- and eight-cylinder exhaust would usually be split into two separate systems, while the four-cylinder engine, whether in-line, vee or flat, works best with the individual pipes collected into one.

Looking at the drawings you will note there are two basic header designs for four-cylinder engines. The system giving the best power is the '4 into 1' arrangement, where the four primary pipes collect into one tailpipe. However, there are disadvantages: this type weighs more and there are usually clearance problems when trying to fit four exhaust tubes between the side of the motor and the steering gear. Another factor to be considered, particularly where four-cylinder engines are involved, is the effect of the 4 into 1 system restricting the power band. If good mid-range power is required, the '4 into 2 into 1' system is the one to adopt, although maximum power can be down by as much as 5–7% in comparison to that obtainable when using a 4 into 1 system.

The other two four-cylinder designs (Figure 9.2b) are for Austin-type engines with a siamesed centre port. The header with the long centre branch is the one to use, as the increase in volume tends to keep the pulse frequency of the centre pipe in tune with the other two branches. The second design is really only suitable if a mild cam is used.

Figure 9.2b Austin four-cylinder headers.

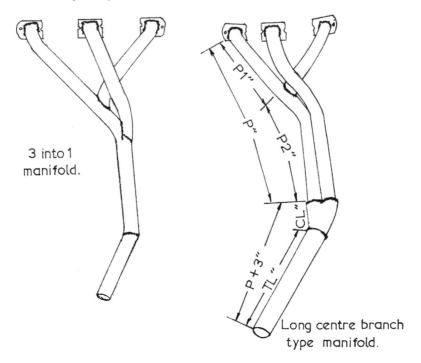

3 into 1 manifold.

Long centre branch type manifold.

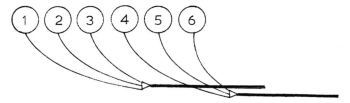

Figure 9.2c Six-cylinder exhaust header.

V8 engines pose a problem in that most use a 90° two-plane crankshaft. 180° cross-over headers will give the best power, but how you fit them under the hood of the average car is beyond me. For this reason the 4 into 1 system for single-plane 180° cranks is generally used. However, as for the four-cylinder header, with a few exceptions, this design isn't the best solution for most applications. If you are operating in a class where you are constantly battling a lack of traction, and where

Figure 9.2d V8 exhaust headers.

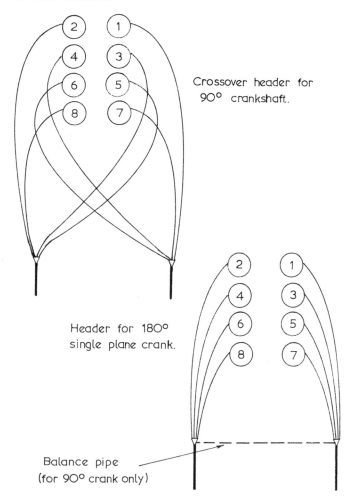

Crossover header for 90° crankshaft.

Header for 180° single plane crank.

Balance pipe
(for 90° crank only)

279

F3000 engines used 4–2–1 headers to improve mid-range power. Note the comparative length of the primary and secondary pipes.

outright power is all important, then opt for the crossover or the 4 into 1 style as these will reduce mid-range hp and sometimes give a bit more at the top-end. For all other situations choose the less popular 4 into 2 into 1 tri-Y type which for many years was treated as inferior, or at best as being only suitable for street use. For tuners who had rubbished this design it was quite a surprise to see them being utilised on Formula 3000 open wheelers running with a 9,000rpm limit. And it probably came as an even greater surprise to see them on the big NASCAR sedans, running at times in excess of 9,500rpm, in a class where squeezing out the maximum outright power is so important. V8 engines with a two-plane crank require a pipe connection order like that shown in Figure 9.7.

Something not to be overlooked with V8s is that the exhaust pipes from the left and right banks should be joined together as one pipe over a length of approximately 10–12in. Alongside the gearbox is about the earliest you can do this. If you find that it is simply impossible to get the two pipes running side by side so as to be joined as one then you should use a balance pipe to connect between them. This should be of the same diameter as the main exhaust pipes. Unfortunately a balance pipe doesn't give anything like the power increase and it usually only works in the lower half of the rev range. On the other hand, a 10–12in sleeve will often give double the hp increase possible with a balance pipe, and this is over the entire power band. Additionally the sleeve approach will lower exhaust noise even more than a balance pipe.

ACOUSTICAL TUNING

Now that we have had a look at the basic header pipe designs to take advantage of exhaust gas inertia, we next must determine the individual pipe length and diameter.

This is where pulse tuning or acoustical tuning enters the scene. The exhaust gas is expelled from the cylinder at a velocity of between 200 and 300ft per second, but pulses or pressure waves are moving through that gas at around 1,500 to 1,700ft per second. By understanding the behaviour of these waves, we can use them to improve cylinder scavenging and to increase cylinder filling with fuel/air mixture.

As the initial charge of burnt gas bursts from the cylinder into the exhaust system, it creates a wave of positive pressure that travels at the speed of sound through the gas to the end of the pipe. As it surges into the atmosphere, the positive wave dissipates and produces a negative pressure wave (suction wave), which returns along the exhaust pipe into the cylinder. It arrives with a certain amount of evacuation power because its pressure is much lower than the cylinder pressure. The art of exhaust tuning is to determine the length and size of the exhaust pipe for this suction wave to arrive back at the cylinder during the valve overlap period.

DETERMINING HEADER DIMENSIONS

When cam timing and valve overlap periods increase so the need to be more specific with exhaust header dimensions becomes a necessity. Part of the reason for this is that at certain rpm the cam will be causing a number of undesirable things to happen, and we can use good exhaust design to reverse, or at least minimise those problems. In addition to that, we can call on the exhaust to work in harmony with the cam, particularly at higher engine speeds, to maximise both the scavenging of exhaust gas from the cylinders and their being refilled with high density air/fuel charge in the very short time frame open to us.

This means not only do we have to connect the exhaust side of the cylinders in the correct order, but we also have to select exhaust tubes of the appropriate diameter and length. Obviously the best place to do this type of experimentation is on an engine dyno. However it is possible to achieve reasonable results if we understand the principles of exhaust tuning and then make choices in accord with those basic rules.

Header pipe diameter fixes the velocity of exhaust gas through the pipe. A large diameter pipe, relative to the size of the cylinder, will reduce gas velocity. Because engines typically produce peak torque at a mean gas velocity of around 250ft/sec the header pipe diameter in turn influences at what rpm peak torque will occur. Thus a large pipe size moves the rpm at which peak torque is produced further up the rev range.

Changing the length of the pipes tends to 'rock' the power curve of the engine around the point of maximum torque. Adding length to the pipes will increase low speed and mid-range power, with a reduction in power at maximum rpm. Shorter pipes give an increase in high-speed power, at the expense of a reduction in the mid-range. However there will be little change in the peak torque number or the engine speed at which it occurs (Figure 9.3).

With these factors in mind a good starting point, whether selecting an off-the-shelf header or you set out to design your own, can be found by referring to Table 9.1. For a 4-cylinder road engine or a competition engine operating at less than 9,000rpm I would always choose a 4 into 2 into 1 interference header style. Keep in mind that the length of the secondary pipe also includes the length of the first collector. All street engines regardless of the number of cylinders or the type of header would use the 281

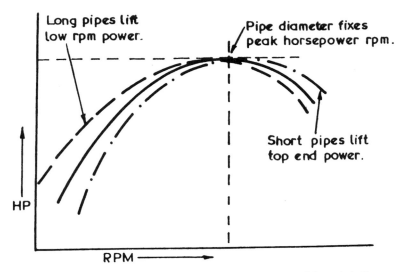

Figure 9.3 This graph illustrates how header tube diameter and length influence the shape of the power curve.

smallest pipe diameters listed. Engines used for hillclimb or ski boat events would generally use an intermediate pipe diameter. In most instances, only high rpm, maximum output engines would benefit from headers using tubes anything larger than an intermediate size.

Table 9.1 Header pipe sizes for engines with competition cams

Cylinder Size (cc)	4–2–1 interference header		4–1 header 3–1 header
	Primary pipe (in)	*Secondary pipe (in)*	*Primary pipe (in)*
250	1.375 to 1.5 dia x 20 to 30 long	1.625 to 1.75 dia x 8 to 18 long	1.625 to 2.0 dia x 29 to 38 long
325	1.5 to 1.625 dia	1.75 to 1.875 dia	1.625 to 2.0 dia
400	1.625 to 1.75 dia	1.875 to 2.125 dia	1.75 to 2.125 dia
500	1.75 to 2.125 dia	2.0 to 2.25 dia	1.875 to 2.125 dia
600	1.875 to 2.125 dia	2.0 to 2.5 dia	*1.75 to 2.0 dia
700	1.875 to 2.125 dia	2.0 to 2.5 dia	*1.875 to 2.125 dia
800	1.875 to 2.25 dia	2.0 to 2.5 dia	1.875 to 2.25 dia
900	2.0 to 2.375 dia	2.25 to 2.5 dia	2.0 to 2.375 dia
1000	2.0 to 2.375 dia	2.25 to 2.75 dia	2.125 to 2.5 dia

* 4-cylinder engines would use pipe sizes 0.125 to 0.25in larger.

Note: all pipe lengths are as shown for 250cc cylinder and include the length from the exhaust valve to the end of the exhaust port.
The secondary pipe length also includes the length of the first collector.
All pipe diameters are outside diameters.

As mentioned previously, engines with street cams rely more on exhaust flow characteristics rather than pulse tuning. Therefore pipe diameters which provide adequate flow are chosen, while tube length should be such that there should not be any back flow of exhaust gas from one cylinder to another. As you can see from Table 9.2 this leaves header choice quite open. However for street engines I would tend toward choosing headers of the smallest diameter listed, particularly if the engine was small relative to vehicle weight.

Table 9.2 Header pipe sizes for engines with street cams

Cylinder size (cc)	4– 2–1 interference header		4–1 header 3–1 header
	Primary pipe (in)	*Secondary pipe (in)*	*Primary pipe (in)*
250	1.25 to 1.375 dia x 12 to 18 long	1.5 to 1.625 dia x 15 to 24 long	1.25 to 1.375 dia x 15 to 30 long
325	1.375 to 1.5 dia	1.625 to 1.75 dia	1.375 to 1.5 dia
400	1.5 to 1.625 dia	1.75 to 1.875 dia	1.5 to 1.625 dia
500	1.625 to 1.75 dia	1.875 to 2.0 dia	1.625 to 1.75 dia
600	1.75 to 1.875 dia	1.875 to 2.125 dia	+*1.625 to 1.75 dia
700	1.875 to 2.0 dia	2.0 to 2.125 dia	*1.75 to 1.875 dia
800	1.875 to 2.0 dia	2.0 to 2.125 dia	1.75 to 1.875 dia
900	1.875 to 2.125 dia	2.0 to 2.25 dia	1.875 to 2.0 dia
1000	1.875 to 2.125 dia	2.0 to 2.25 dia	1.875 to 2.0 dia

*4-cylinder engines would use pipe sizes 0.125 larger.
+ V6 engines would use pipe sizes 0.125 larger

Note: all pipe lengths are as shown for 250cc cylinder.
The secondary pipe length also includes the length of the first collector.
All pipe diameters are outside diameters.

Rather than simply choosing a header from a simple table I prefer to do some calculations using formulae that I know from experience to work reasonably well in a wide variety of applications.

The formula to work out the primary pipe length is:

$$P = \frac{850 \times ED}{rpm} - 3$$

where rpm = the engine speed to which the exhaust is being tuned, and ED = 180° plus the number of degrees the exhaust valve opens before BDC.

To make the task simpler I have prepared Table 9.3, so that the primary length can be read straight off. Generally, road motors will require a manifold tuned to work at maximum torque rpm. Racing motors, on the other hand, use a header tuned to work at either maximum horsepower rpm or at a speed midway between maximum torque and maximum hp revs.

Table 9.3   Exhaust primary pipe length (in)

Tuned rpm	Exhaust valve opening degrees before BDC								
	50°	*55°*	*60°*	*65°*	*70°*	*75°*	*80°*	*85°*	*90°*
4,000	46.0	46.9	48.0	49.0	50.2	51.2	52.1	53.3	54.4
4,500	40.5	41.3	42.3	43.2	44.3	45.1	46.1	47.1	48.1
5,000	36.2	36.9	37.7	38.6	39.5	40.4	41.1	42.0	43.0
5,500	32.6	33.2	34.1	34.8	35.7	36.4	37.1	38.0	38.8
6,000	29.6	30.3	31.9	31.7	32.5	33.1	33.8	34.5	35.4
6,500	27.2	27.7	28.4	29.0	29.8	30.4	31.0	31.7	32.4
7,000	25.0	25.5	26.1	26.7	27.4	28.0	28.6	29.2	29.8
7,500	23.1	23.6	24.2	24.7	25.4	25.9	26.5	27.0	27.6
8,000	21.5	21.9	22.5	23.0	23.6	24.1	24.6	25.2	25.8
8,500	20.0	20.5	21.0	21.5	22.1	22.5	23.0	23.5	24.0
9,000	18.7	19.2	19.6	20.1	20.6	21.1	21.5	22.0	22.5
9,500	17.6	18.0	18.4	18.9	19.4	19.8	20.2	20.7	21.2
10,000	16.5	16.9	17.4	17.8	18.3	18.6	19.1	19.6	20.0
10,500	15.6	16.0	16.4	16.8	17.2	17.6	18.0	18.4	18.8
11,000	14.8	15.1	15.5	15.9	16.3	16.7	17.0	17.4	17.8
11,500	14.0	14.3	14.7	15.1	15.5	15.8	16.2	16.6	17.0
12,000	13.3	13.6	14.0	14.3	14.7	15.0	15.4	15.8	16.1

Once the primary pipe length has been determined, we can then work out the inside diameter using the following formula:

$$ID = \sqrt{\frac{cc}{(P+3) \times 25}} \ \times 2.1$$

where cc = cylinder volume in cc, and P = primary length in inches.

Headers for road engines usually work well enough if the pipes are of the same diameter as the exhaust valve, but racing engines demand more exactness than this if we are to achieve ultimate performance. In using the above formula, sizes will have to be worked to suit exhaust tubes that are available commercially.

If a '4 into 2 into 1' system is preferred, we use the same formula or Table 9.3 to work out the total length (P) of the header pipes, which will be the combined length of the primary pipe (P1) plus the length of the secondary pipe (P2). The inside diameter can then be determined for the four primary pipes (P1) using the same formula:

$$ID = \sqrt{\frac{cc}{(P+3) \times 25}} \ \times 2.1$$

Once the inside diameter of the primary pipes is calculated, we can then work out the inside diameter of the two secondary pipes (P2) by the formula:

$$IDS = \sqrt{ID^2 \times 2} \ \times 0.93$$

where ID = the calculated inside diameter of the primary pipes (P1).

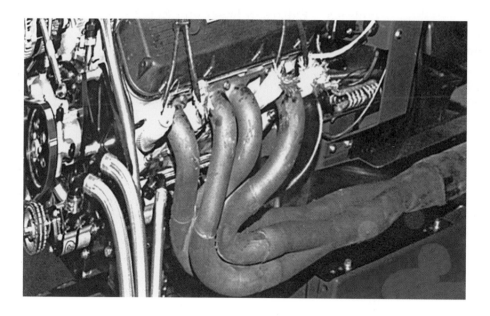

This 5ltr V8 Supercar engine has very short secondary pipes which helps top-end hp. In this class the cars are traction limited by relatively narrow tyres, so for most circuits more top-end power is of greater benefit than is a stronger bottom-end. Note that as well as being of 4–2–1 design these headers are also stepped and use a venturi merge-type collector.

The length of the primary pipes (P1) should always be at least 15in. Adding length to the primaries will favour top-end power, while adding it to the secondaries helps the mid-range. The length of the secondary pipes (P2) can be found by simple subtraction: P2 = P – P1.

The calculations for the '4 into 2 into 1' system are also used to determine the pipe sizes for the long centre branch type Austin header; the only difference is that the centre branch is the same diameter as the secondary pipe (IDS) for the full length (P).

PRACTICAL HEADER TUNING

In theory it looks very simple to arrive at a header design with pipes of precisely the right length and diameter; unfortunately in practice it does not often work out that way. A header constructed to the formulae outlined will work reasonably well and provide a good basis for further experimentation on the dyno or at the race track. However, due to variables in the design of cams, inlet manifolds, cylinder head porting, etc, the length and diameter of the header pipes will have to be changed about to arrive at the ideal size for your engine.

If you find that the engine's torque peak is at 7,000rpm and you want maximum torque at 6,000rpm, reduce the pipe diameter. Generally, a reduction in primary pipe diameter of 0.125in will move the torque peak down by 500–600rpm in larger engines, and by 650–800rpm in motors smaller than 2 litres. Conversely an increase in the diameter of the headers will raise the engine speed at which maximum torque occurs by approximately the same rpm for each 0.125in increase.

Table 9.4 shows the results of testing headers of various sizes on an Opel 2-litre race engine. As can be clearly seen, the 2¹/₈in headers really only worked very high up in the rpm range, but as this engine would be competing in a class with an enforced 8,500rpm limit, the power loss in the lower ranges would not be compensated for by the modest power increase seen above 7,750rpm. The 2in pipes provided a much superior power spread while losing out to the 1⁷/₈in headers below 7,000rpm.

Table 9.4　2-litre XE Opel header comparison

rpm	Test 1		Test 2		Test 3	
	hp	Torque	hp	Torque	hp	Torque
5,250	164.8	164.9			169.9	170.0
5,500	172.5	164.7			182.5	174.3
6,000	204.0	178.6	196.7	172.2	202.8	177.5
6,500	221.3	178.8	212.5	171.7	224.3	181.2
6,750	231.5	180.1	225.7	175.6	234.9	182.8
7,000	243.1	182.4	235.1	176.4	241.1	180.9
7,250	249.3	180.6	245.2	177.6	245.8	178.1
7,500	253.9	177.8	255.8	179.1	253.8	177.7
7,750	256.5	173.8	258.5	175.2	259.3	175.7
8,000	264.9	173.9	267.2	175.4	268.7	176.4
8,250	275.2	175.2	276.2	175.8	270.3	172.1
8,500	273.0	168.7	276.9	171.1	264.9	163.7
8,750	268.7	161.3	273.2	164.0	260.4	156.3
9,000	264.2	154.2	269.9	157.5		

Test 1 – 2in race headers, 4 into 1.

Test 2 – 2¹/₈in race headers, 4 into 1.

Test 3 – 1⁷/₈in race headers, 4 into 1.

　Note: in all tests the same primary pipe length was used and the tailpipe length and diameter was not changed.

Previously I stated that changing the length of the pipes tends to 'rock' the power curve of the engine around the point of maximum torque. Adding length to the primary pipes will increase low-speed and mid-range power, with a corresponding reduction in power at maximum rpm. Some race engines, however, do not conform to this general rule and will show a good increase in mid-range power with very little loss at the top end even with substantial increases in primary pipe length. Usually we expect to see an engine respond in a similar way to a 4in increase in primary pipe length as it would to 0.125in decrease in pipe diameter. Thus a 350 Chev race engine would work pretty much the same with 1⁷/₈in primaries 34in long as with 1³/₄in pipes 30in long. However, the V6 Buick (and some others) keeps gaining bottom-end power without knocking the top end with primaries lengthened to around 44in, about 12in longer than comparable competition engines.

　　Unfortunately many racers only concern themselves with developing an exhaust that gives the best power over the largest rpm range without ever understanding that they can use a number of different headers to alter the power characteristics of the engine to better suit different tracks and surface conditions, etc. When traction is not a problem, lots of mid-range grunt will help drive the car out of corners more rapidly. However, that power, which was so desirable at one circuit, may actually slow the car or overwhelm the driver at another circuit, or under different track conditions. A relatively quick fix for a problem like this is to swap the headers to a set that takes away a rush of power in the mid-range. Note, however, that engines utilising computerised ignition and fuel injection may require a 'chip' change when the header is changed.

The dirt speedway is a typical example of a track with quickly changing surface conditions. Early in the night the track might be very heavy, calling for a header that will 'tune' the engine for maximum bottom-end power. For a 350 Chev this probably means a header with 1⁵/₈in primaries 30in long going into a 3in tailpipe. After a few hours of racing the track may dry out and the surface could harden like concrete. Such conditions may call for a shift to more top-end power. A suitable header may have 'stepped' primaries 1³/₄in for the first 13in, stepping up to 1⁷/₈in for 15in, terminating in a 3¹/₂in tailpipe. On the other hand, the track surface may break up badly as racing progresses, so to kill bottom-end power headers with 2in tubes 30in long leading into a 3in tailpipe may be fitted.

A similar situation exists in club-type rallying. Some events may be smooth, dry tarmac. Here an Escort with a 1700 BDA Cosworth may benefit from a stepped header that starts out at 1³/₄in for 10in, then steps up to 1⁷/₈in for 18in, then into a 2¹/₂in tailpipe so as to lift power in the upper range. However, such power characteristics could prove to be a handful to a novice when that same tarmac is snow covered. Under such conditions we want the engine to respond very gently to delicate throttle movements – we do not want sudden surges of power. The approach here may be to use unequal-length stepped headers.

UNEQUAL LENGTH PIPES

Why unequal length primary pipes? Well, this tunes the torque peak in each cylinder to a different rpm, thus flattening and smoothing the torque curve. It tunes out that sudden rush of power, so instead of the engine coming on song at, say, 6,250rpm, the torque peak will be lowered slightly but may go all the way from, say, 5,500 to 6,500rpm. Hence one cylinder may peak at 6,000rpm, another at 5,750, another at 5,500 and still another at 6,250.

To achieve this the primary length would be adjusted to minus 2in plus 4in from the ideal length. Therefore if the 'correct' length was found to be 29in, the four pipes would vary in length from 27in to 33in. In reality I prefer unequal-length headers in most applications. For a long time it was thought that equal-length tuned headers were the best way to go, but when it was discovered in installations where equal-length pipes just would not fit that the package often became more drivable, some tuners slowly came around to acknowledge the advantages of unequal-length pipes.

In restricted classes equal-length primaries are more important, as here the chassis, tyres or driver are less likely to be overwhelmed by an excess of power. In these categories of competition the breathing may be impeded by a single small carburettor, or power may be pegged by a low compression ratio of 9:1 and perhaps the use of lower-octane pump fuel rather than race fuel. Such imposts rule out a sudden rush of power, so every cylinder must be tuned to make maximum hp at every point in the usable power band. This calls for carefully designed equal-length headers.

STEPPED HEADERS

Earlier mention was made of stepped headers, ie primary pipes with 'steps' or changing pipe diameters. Those who follow any form of two-stroke competition know that the two-stroke exhaust is formed from a series of cones. The first part, also known as the header pipe, usually tapers at somewhere between 1.25 and 2.2°. This is because in terms of physics a cone provides the best exhaust flow, and when the angle is shallow it preserves gas momentum while keeping flow restriction and turbulence to a minimum. Obviously a stepped header more closely approximates this ideal than a tube of constant diameter.

A typical stepped header would have just one or, in a few cases, two steps, with the header diameter increasing 0.125in at each step. At times engines that like very long primaries work best with a quarter-inch step. An example is the V6 Buick, which usually works well on road courses with primary tubes of 1⁷/₈in diameter for the first 11 or 12in, stepping up to 2¹/₈in tubes 34in long.

Table 9.5   2-litre XE Opel stepped header comparison

	Test 1		Test 2	
rpm	**hp**	**Torque**	**hp**	**Torque**
5,500	172.5	164.7	179.5	171.4
6,000	204.0	178.6	206.5	180.8
6,500	221.3	178.8	224.9	181.7
6,750	231.5	180.1	234.3	182.3
7,000	243.1	182.4	243.5	182.7
7,250	249.3	180.6	251.4	182.1
7,500	253.9	177.8	257.3	180.2
7,750	256.5	173.8	263.8	178.8
8,000	264.9	173.9	268.7	176.4
8,250	275.2	175.2	277.4	176.6
8,500	273.0	168.7	276.3	170.7
8,750	268.7	161.3	275.2	165.2
9,000	264.2	154.2		

Test 1 – 2in race headers, 4 into 1.

Test 2 – 1⁷/₈in to 2 to 2¹/₈in stepped race headers, 4 into 1.

Note: in addition to being stepped, the headers in Test 2 had primary pipes 3in longer than those used in Test 1.

In Test 2, phasing of both inlet and exhaust cams was altered slightly to optimise improved exhaust scavenging.

Because of improved engine efficiency, the ignition curve had to be modified with about 1° less advance up to 7,250rpm and 2° less from 7,500rpm up to the rev limit in Test 2.

A lot of time can be spent figuring out where to step the primaries, but you can usually reckon on the first step being about 10 to 14in from the exhaust port. In theory, if the first section of pipe is relatively small to improve bottom-end power, exhaust reversion will occur at around the 10 or 11in mark, so that is where the first step should go. On the other hand, if the pipe size is quite generous, favouring more the top-end of the power range, the first step will probably want to be closer to the 14in point to avoid losing bottom-end power.

Where should the second step be located? That takes even more dyno time to get right. Some say that if the primary length is 30in, the steps should be set at equal intervals, ie with the first step at 10in and the second at 20in. If only a tuner's life were so simple! To give you some guidance in this I feel it makes more sense to figure how far back from the collector the second step should be.

When the overall primary length is reasonably short, ie 24 to 28in, I would begin testing with the second step around 0.2 times the primary length back from the collector. Thus a 25in primary would have the second step marked off 5in from the collector. However, as the primary length increases to around 36–40in, the second step will be located closer to 0.25 times the primary length before the collector.

Depending on which way you step, a carefully developed step header can add around 500rpm to either the bottom or the top of the power band. Therefore if your current header has 1⁷/₈in tubes and you want more bottom end, step down at the exhaust port to 1³/₄in. However, if the bottom end is already acceptable and you want more top end, you would continue to come off the head in 1⁷/₈in tube, then step up to

Stepped headers can bring a power gain and broaden the power band of most types of engines. Originally it was thought that stepping wasn't applicable to very high rpm engines, or those with cylinders smaller than about 450cc.

2in at the first step. Assuming that the bottom end is still intact after this change, you may like to try introducing a second step and go up to 2¹/₈in pipe at that point.

When the 2-litre Opel mentioned earlier was re-tested with a stepped header, it produced the figures shown in Table 9.5. Clearly the engine responded very well to a header that stepped from 1⁷/₈ to 2 to 2¹/₈in. Previous dips in the power curve have been smoothed out, and in addition there is a little more power right on the limiter and also down at 5,500 and 6,000rpm.

Don't assume that stepped headers are the way to go on all engines – they are not. To gain the theoretical benefits can involve a lot of dyno time; perhaps time and money that may reap richer rewards elsewhere. Also if your style of competition doesn't demand a broad power range stepping will most likely be a waste of time, or perhaps even a handicap if you are already struggling for traction in the middle of the power band. On the other hand, if you have a good size budget, don't be quick to conclude that stepping won't work on your engine. I started out thinking that it wasn't worth the effort and expense in engines operating at very high rpm, or with small cylinders. Now of course you would be hard pressed to find factory racers from the bike manufacturers that don't have tapered header tubes, or Formula 1 engines that don't run stepped headers.

THE COLLECTOR'S INFLUENCE

The next part of the header, the collector, is where the individual primary tubes come together as one. Again this is an area where the serious tuner has the option of choosing from a number of collector styles to 'tune' the characteristics of the header. Remember that, regardless of the style chosen, the collector can only boost torque at engine rpm below the torque peak, the shape of the power curve above the torque peak being determined by the primary pipe diameter and length.

Generally we want to boost engine torque whenever possible. However, as I've previously stated, in some circumstances excessive torque at lower rpm may be a hindrance, actually reducing overall performance. Consequently in some classes of drag racing the pipes from individual cylinders are not brought together with a collector as any increase in mid-range torque just makes traction problems more difficult. You may have witnessed the same sort of thing with sprint cars on dirt speedways. When there are no noise rules and when traction is limited you will see these cars racing without collectors so as to get rid of unwanted torque.

Going back to the introduction to this chapter, you will recall that exhaust theory revolves around using exhaust gas momentum or inertia and pressure waves to scavenge exhaust gas from the cylinder in the first instance, then, during the valve overlap period, the waves begin to move the intake charge down the inlet tract and into the cylinder. When the exhaust valve closes any vacuum 'energy' left remaining in that particular primary pipe will be lost if that pipe is not connected to another primary pipe. Using a collector to connect the primary pipes together allows this unused, left-over vacuum to lower the pressure in all of the other primary pipes, thus assisting exhaust flow out of those cylinders that have open exhaust valves.

However, once past the torque peak rpm there is not enough time for the primary tube to 'empty' of exhaust gas after the valve closes, so it is unable to 'pull' a vacuum on any of the other primary pipes to which it is connected. Obviously if the primary pipe was made very short, vacuum would reach down to the collector at higher rpm and draw on the other primaries, but shortening the primaries has the undesirable effect of killing bottom-end power, so this action would only work on tracks where a narrow power band was acceptable.

BAFFLE COLLECTOR DESIGN

Figure 9.4 illustrates an ordinary collector that I personally prefer to call a 'baffle' collector. With this arrangement the primary tubes terminate abruptly into an open tapering chamber that feeds into the tailpipe. When the primaries terminate abruptly like this a pressure wave returns up the primary. Now if a negative pressure wave (suction wave) arrives back at the exhaust port during the time when the exhaust valve is next open, it will work in harmony with any vacuum created by exhaust gas momentum to aid in efficient evacuation of that cylinder of exhaust gas, also pulling in fresh air/fuel charge. Additionally, depending on primary pipe length, at certain engine rpm a positive pressure wave will arrive just as the exhaust valve is about to close to reduce the amount of fuel/air charge that 'spills over' (called over-scavenging) into the exhaust during the valve overlap period due to the effect of exhaust gas momentum.

That is the positive aspect of what this type of exhaust collector will accomplish. The negative side is that at certain rpm a positive pressure wave will arrive back at the exhaust port during the early phase of the exhaust valve opening period and actually impede exhaust flow out of the cylinder. Likewise, in other parts of the rev range a negative pressure wave will arrive just as the exhaust valve is closing and draw even more air/fuel mixture out into the exhaust. Obviously both scenarios lead to reduced hp and increased fuel consumption.

Consequently this type of collector is better suited to road engines and competition engines utilising milder race cams with a duration of up to about 260° measured at 0.050in lobe lift, and lobe centres in the range of 105–110°. In this kind of application the baffle collector works very well.

Some competition headers using a baffle collector have a 'spear' welded to the centre of the baffle where all the primaries terminate. This is supposed to reduce flow turbulence, but I believe that devices like this are really just a marketing gimmick. The main thing to watch with any collector is the angle at which it tapers. In general terms

Figure 9.4 Baffle-type collector.

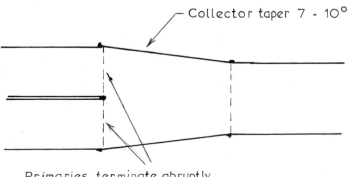

Collector taper 7 - 10°

Primaries terminate abruptly.

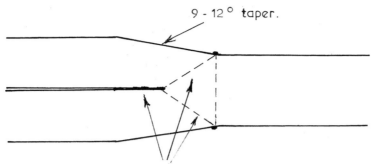

9 - 12° taper.

Primaries blend into each other.

Figure 9.5 Merge-type collector.

I have found the best angle to be 7 or 8° (14 or 16° included angle). However, some engines will work best with a steeper taper of 9°, or even up to 10°. Very shallow tapers of less than 7° do not seem to work too well, probably due to excessive collector volume allowing massive flow turbulence.

MERGE COLLECTOR DESIGN

The collector that is better suited to maximum-effort race engines with long-duration, big-overlap cams is known as a 'merge' collector (Figure 9.5). With this type the primary pipes do not terminate abruptly, but 'merge' or blend into the tailpipe. This has the effect of reducing the intensity of reflected pressure pulse waves in the primaries, which in effect tunes out of the header the negative aspects of pulse tuning mentioned previously. Of course, using this type of collector means that the headers lose out on the positive aspects of pulse tuning. However, as we are talking about maximum-effort engines, operating over a very narrow rev range, this gives the exhaust tuner more scope to build the headers to scavenge the cylinders effectively, relying on exhaust gas momentum or inertia alone.

With the merge design the primaries must generally come together fairly abruptly to give a collector taper of about 10°, and I would always begin testing at this angle. Some very peaky high-rpm engines respond well to even steeper angles of around 12°, and a number also work best with slightly shallower tapers around 8¹/2 to 9°.

VENTURI MERGE COLLECTOR

Another collector, which many also refer to as a merge collector, is what I prefer to call a 'venturi merge' collector. Referring to Figure 9.6 you will see that this design necks down, then flares out into a cone to meet the tailpipe. This has the effect of picking up gas speed to boost the scavenging power of the header, which serves to extend the rpm range over which inertia tuning works. Venturi merge collectors seem to work best when the tailpipe diameter is very large relative to the primary tube diameter, so I suspect forcing the gas to accelerate through a relatively small venturi further serves to diminish the amplitude of pressure waves travelling within the primaries, thus ensuring that the header is working more in concert with exhaust gas momentum and is less influenced by pressure pulse waves.

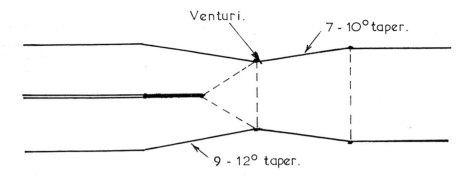

Figure 9.6 Venturi merge-type collector.

Whereas a typical race header with a merge-style collector may have, say, 2in primaries exhausting into a 2¹/₂in tailpipe, a venturi merge collector would be used if a large tailpipe of around 3 or 3¹/₂in was necessary in V6 and V8 race engines with cylinder capacities up around 700 to 800cc exhausting into primaries around 1⁷/₈in to 2¹/₈in. As with the ordinary merge collector, the venturi type has the primaries converging at around 10°. That is where I would begin testing, and I would then set the diffuser cone taper at 8°. This may not be the ideal taper, but it will be close. Anything in the range of 7–10° will work – it is just a matter of dyno time and track time to determine what works best.

While these two angles are important, what is equally important is the actual diameter of the venturi. A rough rule of thumb is to make the venturi half an inch larger in diameter than the size of the primary tubes; thus with 2in primaries the venturi becomes 2¹/₂in. The final size may end up anywhere from 2³/₈in to 2³/₄in, but what I have suggested is a good starting point.

SPLIT INTERFERENCE COLLECTOR

The fourth style of collector, which I call a 'split interference' collector, has a number of virtues, one of which is that it hides from prying eyes just what style of header you are running! Figure 9.7 illustrates how this collector connects the primaries to a 4–2–1-type configuration. However, whereas the conventional '4 into 2 into 1' header uses fairly short primaries and (usually) comparatively longer secondary tubes, this split interference style collector provides an arrangement of long primaries and short secondaries that may give a useful increase in mid-range power without drastically killing off the top end. This occurs because any vacuum created in a primary tube by exhaust gas momentum will not be 'diluted' by what is taking place in the other three tubes to which it is connected. Instead, with this collector only one other pipe is involved, so at lower gas speeds, when vacuum levels are fairly poor, the full influence of that vacuum will be felt by the other primary to which it is connected. This is what serves to pull up mid-range power. Then at high rpm, because this design does not have long secondaries to restrict exhaust flow, there is only minimal hp loss at the upper end of the power band.

4 cylinder.

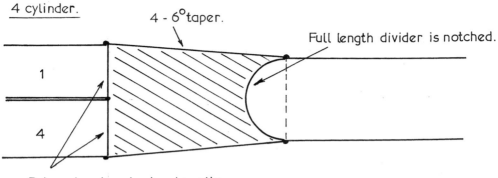

4 - 6°taper.

Full length divider is notched.

1

4

Primaries terminate abruptly.

V8.

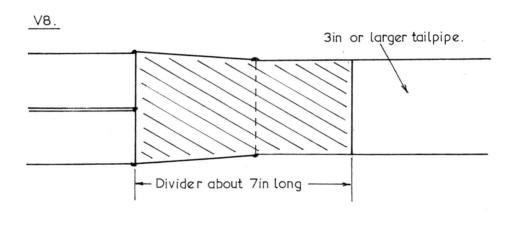

3in or larger tailpipe.

Divider about 7in long

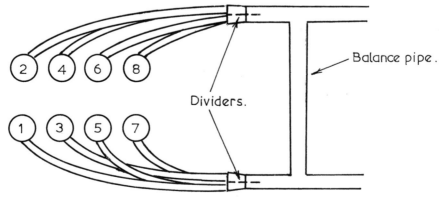

Balance pipe.

Dividers.

Header connections for 1 8 4 3 6 5 7 2 firing order.

Figure 9.7 Split baffle collectors.

With this collector attached to a four-cylinder engine, primary pipes of cylinders firing 360° apart are connected. However, with V8 engines primaries alternatively firing 270° and 450° apart are joined, which tends to produce a torque peak at different rpm in each cylinder, thus flattening the torque curve much like unequal-length headers. Additionally, because with this style the collector volume is halved, there is reduced flow turbulence at this point, which tends to help the torque curve at a number of places.

Some people run this type of collector at all times, but I feel that the time to resort to the split interference collector is when there is no time to change the headers to suit changes in track conditions. When you need more bottom-end power quickly it only takes a few minutes to swap over from another collector type to a split interference type. My suggestion to get the best from this is to build your headers with the primaries about 3–4in shorter than what is required. When you want a true '4 into 1' header, slip on a collector that includes primary extensions 3–4in long to give the correct tuned length. Then when you want more bottom-end grunt, it is a simple thing to remove that collector and attach a split interference type, which in effect will add something like 6–8in as a secondary to the header. However, because the primaries are 3–4in short anyway by design, the actual tuned length will increase by 2–4in, which helps the mid-range without knocking the top end by very much.

A collector fashioned like this will not benefit all engines. Mid-size V8s seem to be the most inconsistent, with some responding favourably, some indifferent and a few losing out everywhere. V8s under about 5 litres mostly work well, as do monsters over 8 litres, but in between results are patchy. Four-cylinder engines, however, almost always respond nicely to the split interference collector.

When building a collector for a V8 I would begin with a divider 7in long, which means that it will extend into the tailpipe. Four-cylinder engines, which usually work best with a relatively small-diameter tailpipe, will suffer power losses if this approach is followed, so it is preferable to use a long, shallow collector with a $4^1/2$ to $5^1/2°$ taper. The divider can run the full length of the collector, but it must be notched so that gas flow into the tailpipe is not unduly restricted. A short notch increases the venturi effect and serves to broaden the power band, while a longer notch reduces this effect but improves higher rpm gas flow.

Using the following formula we can work out the length of the collector:

$$\text{Collector length} = \frac{\text{ID2} - \text{ID3}}{2} \times \text{Cot A}$$

where ID2 = diameter of the collector inlet, ID3 = diameter of the collector outlet, and Cot A = cotangent of angle of taper ($4^1/2° = 12.7$, $5^1/2° = 10.4$, $7° = 8.15$, $8^1/2° = 6.7$, $10° = 5.7$, $12° = 4.7$, $15° = 3.7$).

TAILPIPE DIMENSIONS

When it comes to the tailpipe there are a couple of ways in which we can establish a baseline size to begin dyno testing. When an open unsilenced exhaust is used, the combined length of the collector and tailpipe will be the same as the length of the primary pipe plus 3in. Then the tailpipe inside diameter is calculated using the following formula:

$$ID3 = \sqrt{\frac{cc \times 2}{(P + 3) \times 25}} \quad \times 2$$

where ID3 = tailpipe id in inches, cc = volume of one cylinder in cc, and P = primary length in inches.

The alternative is to set the combined collector and tailpipe length the same as the primary length, then from Table 9.6 read off the tailpipe outside diameter based on engine hp output.

Table 9.6   Tailpipe size

hp	pipe od (in)
80–120	1$7/8$
110–140	2
130–150	2$1/8$
140–185	2$1/4$
180–220	2$1/2$
210–265	2$3/4$
250–320	3
280–360	3$1/2$
400–500	4
480–630	4$1/2$
580–750	5

Note: when two exhausts are used divide engine hp by two.

Establishing a suitable tailpipe size is becoming more complex with road cars because of the addition of the catalytic converter to reduce tailpipe emissions. Because CATs typically add considerable heat to the exhaust gas, it is not unusual to find that an increase in exhaust diameter of 0.125in to 0.375in over the size indicated in Table 9.6 from the CAT back, will show some power increase.

CUTTING DOWN ON NOISE

Likewise more and more classes of competition now make the use of CATs mandatory, and noise limits have caused tuners to consider mufflers and a number of other measures to avoid pushing noise meters past the regulated level, leading to possible disqualification.

Conventional thinking among some is to build a maximum-hp unsilenced exhaust, then add to it what is required to meet noise regulations and accept the inevitable large power losses. Approached from this level of thinking it is obvious that a lot of hp will be knocked off, perhaps up around 10%. Some shrug this off, saying that everyone else has to meet the same noise limit so they must be hurting the same amount. The truth is that some will not be losing even 5% because they have invested dyno and track time to see what works and what does not.

The very first requirement is to read carefully the regulations and see what the rules are; if the rules do not say that you cannot do something, then assume that you can legally. Hence if the rules do not state that the tailpipe must terminate at the rear of the car, do not run it out the back unless doing so helps you gain hp or lower noise. Likewise, do not run the exhaust out of the side where it points at the noise gun just because everyone else does; the idea is to aim the tailpipe away from the sound meter. So if you run anti-clockwise on speedways and the noise meter is on the infield, aim the tailpipe out of the right side with a turn-down tip, so the maximum amount of sound is absorbed by the track rather than being reflected back to the meter by concrete walls or empty seating shelters. On road courses, where meter locations vary from track to track, it is usually possible on sedan cars to design the exhaust so that it can be swapped to exit on either the left or the right.

To avoid using a muffler, or to permit a small, low-restriction resonator to pass noise tests, some tuners have tried all sorts of exhaust tricks. Their reasoning is; keep away from mufflers at all costs, they just kill power. Therefore even when the rules do not call for a rear-exit exhaust, they will run a full-length pipe, and perhaps step it down a couple of sizes hoping to get the noise down. The thinking is that since there is no measurable back pressure in the system, there cannot be any loss of power. Well, let me assure you that I have seen $2^1/2\%$ losses in both hp and torque in systems like this. The relationship between back pressure and hp is not at all clear at the lower end of the pressure scale.

Table 9.7 details the results of tests on a 223hp race engine with various exhaust and muffler combinations. Clearly there is a fairly fuzzy relationship between back pressure and power, and for that matter between noise and power. Also note that both purpose-made race mufflers, which I have numbered 1 and 7, failed the noise tests, and

Table 9.7   Exhaust and muffler tests

Description	hp	%loss	back pressure	comments
open tuned tailpipe	223.2		0	tailpipe 26in x 2¹/₂in
side exit extension (A)	221.8	0.6	0	plus 42in extension
rear exit exhaust (B)	217.3	2.6	0	2¹/₂in tailpipe, 129in overall
big-bore rear exit (C)	220.4	1.2	0	3in system
exhaust (C) fitted with:				
muffler 1	220.2	1.3	0	failed noise test
muffler 2	216.0	3.3	2.04	passed noise test
muffler 3	215.5	3.5	0.4	failed noise test
muffler 4	216.7	2.9	1.1	easily passed noise test
muffler 5	217.3	2.7	1.37	easily passed noise test
muffler 6	218.4	2.2	1.45	just failed noise test
muffler 7	210.4	5.8	1.2	failed noise test
exhaust (A) fitted with:				
muffler 4	218.4	2.1	0.9	easily passed noise test
muffler 5	218.8	2.0	1.23	passed noise test
muffler 6	219.7	1.6	1.3	just passed noise test with exit away from sound gun

in addition muffler 7 was way down on power in spite of some impressive claims being made by its manufacturer. Mufflers 4, 5 and 6 were all high-performance road mufflers; 6 was constructed of stainless steel with welded seams and no packing, so it would hold up well in race applications. Numbers 4 and 5, however, were 'S'-flow glass packs with rolled seams. These usually have a short life in race environments, but they can be cut open and duplicated in stainless with stainless packing, with good results.

Some tuners are surprised when they find that certain mufflers actually seem to give a power increase. However, be assured that mufflers do not increase power! When such a situation arises it is an indication that at certain places in the power band the engine is being over-scavenged, but the addition of a silencer is changing the engine's flow characteristics so less fuel/air mixture is being lost into the exhaust during the cam overlap period, hence power now goes up. When I see something like this, at the first opportunity I aim to test with a shorter-duration exhaust lobe or slightly less overlap. Alternatively, if it is a push rod engine I will change the exhaust rockers from, say, 1.6:1 to 1.5:1 and check the result.

Another benefit of reducing over-scavenging is that it can reduce exhaust noise levels, which if you are just over the limit may help you get through noise tests. Also, in endurance-type competition a reduction in over-scavenging will help lower fuel consumption, which could mean fewer fuel stops or a lighter fuel load.

CAT PROBLEMS AND MODIFICATION

When it comes to CAT converters the advice is to have a look at what is available, check the rules to see where it must be located and, if there is no specific placement rule, move it around while testing on the dyno. Note that in high-performance and competition environments CAT flow performance must regularly be checked as many do not hold up well to extended wide-open throttle running. A collapsed CAT can easily rob a 300hp engine in excess of 20hp.

If the core of the CAT looks like this on the inlet side it is probably okay. A more reliable method of checking the CAT for blockage is to measure the backpressure before the CAT when it is brand new, and then at regular intervals afterwards. Do the check preferably on the dyno, but out on the road at full throttle in 3rd gear holding the car on the brakes at 5,000rpm is also a valid test.

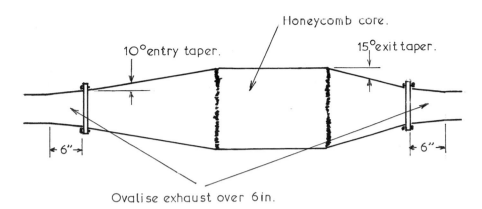

Figure 9.8 CAT modifications improve flow.

However, it is not just the honeycomb innards of the CAT that cause an exhaust flow problem. Even when the honeycomb is in good condition a poorly designed CAT will impede gas flow due to turbulence caused by the exhaust diverging at anything from 35° to 60° into the honeycomb, then converging again into the tailpipe at a similarly steep angle. To overcome this problem the CAT must have a gentle entry and exit taper. On the inlet side a taper of around 10–12° allows the exhaust gas to expand gradually to the full size of the honeycomb with minimal turbulence. Similarly, on the exit a taper of 12–15° forces the gases to converge into the tailpipe without unduly disturbing the exhaust flow. When modified in this manner ordinary street CATs will double their flow rate (Figure 9.8).

HEADER FINISH AND FABRICATION

When it comes to header design and fabrication I regularly see many errors, and very basic errors at that. Enthusiasts waste hours polishing the inlet tract to a mirror finish, then throw on a header with welding 'dags' hanging into each tube where they are welded to the flange. A few minutes with a grinder or round file would rid the header of such impediments to good gas flow.

Header tubes overlapping the exhaust flange like this seriously limit gas flow.

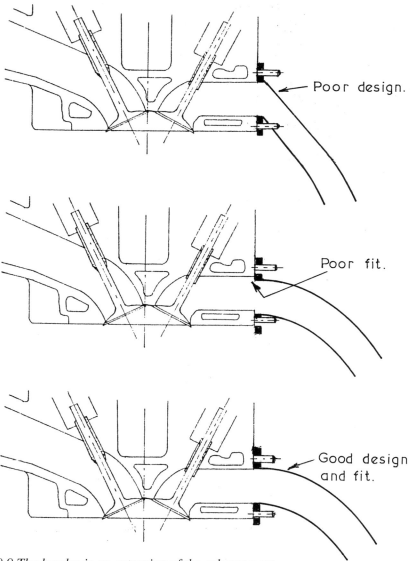

Figure 9.9 The header is an extension of the exhaust port.

Another factor that many do not seem to understand is that the header is an extension of the exhaust port, so any abrupt change in direction as gas flows from the port into the header is to be avoided. Many headers leave much to be desired in this area. Often tubes bend through a full 90° right at the flange, and in the very worst examples I have seen pipes cut off at around 50°, then welded directly to the flange so as to avoid the time and expense of actually bending the tube (Figure 9.9).

To compensate for sloppy manufacturing and to ease fitting problems, grossly oversized flange holes are common, possibly allowing the header to overlap the exhaust port, thus restricting gas flow. This can be rectified by pushing sleeves into the oversize holes, then checking for overlap using the manifold gasket as a template.

At times I do use slotted flange holes to check the effect of moving the header up or down relative to the exhaust port, usually a maximum of 0.125in. These slots are sized so that when the header is lifted to its limit, the floor of the exhaust port and header tube match. (This may improve peak hp a little.) Conversely, when the header is lowered the roof of the exhaust port lines up with the top of the header tube. (This can reduce exhaust reversion and improve mid-range hp.) I generally use this technique when doing header design work on the dyno, but on engines that show a liking for this sort of tuning it is a trick that can be used to 'tune' the engine to a particular circuit or surface (Figure 9.10).

Another problem area that has arisen since mandrel pipe-benders have become more commonly available to general exhaust workshops is a real lack of design planning in the placement and severity of bends in the header pipes, and indeed in the entire exhaust system. Years ago when most pipe-benders noticeably reduced the tube diameter at bends, a real effort was made to limit the number of bends and their severity. Just a quick glance at the exhaust told you that any sort of bend was bad news for gas flow. However, when mandrel benders came along the resulting bends looked so much better that many forgot that bends do impede gas flow. Also be aware that few so-called mandrel benders produce a perfect constant-diameter bend; many in fact reduce the pipe size by about 1mm.

Figure 9.10 Slotted dyno headers.

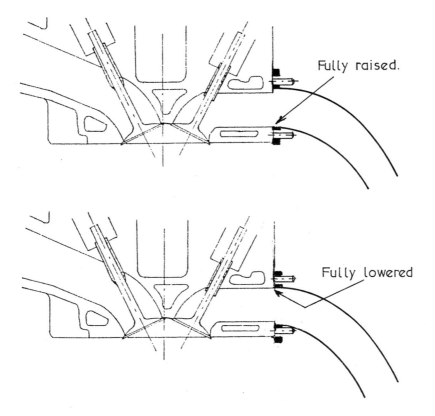

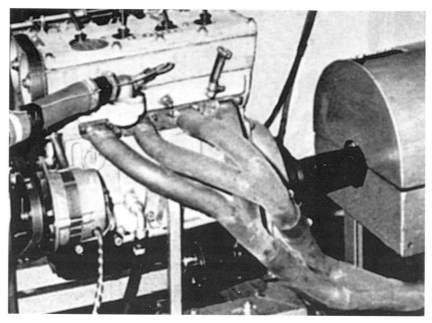

With wilder cams, testing of headers on the dyno is critical. Subtle changes can gain or lose a lot of hp anywhere in the rev range.

THE CAM'S INFLUENCE

In some applications small tube headers are called for, but there is confusion over what to do when the exhaust port is larger than the header id. Obviously the lip formed when a 1.6in diameter port meets with a 1.375in id header tube will cause massive flow turbulence, but this is exactly what some small tube headers are like. Some try grinding out the flange to get rid of such a lip, but this does not really help very much. In a situation like this I prefer to flare the tubes gently over a length of at least 1in, and preferably 1 1/2in. However, if the pipes have to bend very close to the exhaust port, this may not be practical so it may be necessary to come off the ports in larger diameter tube for, say, 5–10in, then step down to the smaller tube size. However, again flare the small tube up to the size of the larger over a length of 1–1 1/2in to avoid a lip.

In conclusion, let me make one final point that may save you a good deal of money and frustration. While we have had an in-depth look at header tuning, do not get too carried away applying this science to a mild street engine. Any reasonable header will work well with a road cam as pulse tuning is limited due to the short valve overlap period of this type of cam. A 3% power difference between an 'in tune' and an 'out of tune' header is typical. However, when the valve overlap increases past about 65° measured at 0.050in lobe lift, the header-tuned length becomes critical, to the point that a slightly out of tune header can easily knock the power by 10%.

I came across a dramatic example of this when setting up a 1600 VW Golf rally engine that was supposed to have been an ex-works unit. It made good power at the top end, peaking at close on 160hp at 7,250rpm, but there was a massive hole in the mid-range; at 5,000rpm it showed only a little over 90hp when it should have been at

Table 9.8   1.6 litre VW Golf header comparison

	Test 1		Test 2	
rpm	**hp**	**Torque**	**hp**	**Torque**
4,000	77.8	102.2	89.6	117.7
4,500	86.4	100.8	102.0	119.1
5,000	90.4	95.0	114.9	120.7
5,500	118.0	112.7	136.6	130.4
6,000	137.2	120.1	147.0	128.7
6,500	153.5	124.0	151.7	122.6
7,000	156.1	117.1	153.3	115.0
7,250	159.8	115.8	151.6	109.8
7,500	149.4	104.6	142.9	100.1
8,000	123.4	81.0	126.0	82.7

Test 1 – 4–1 Group A headers.

Test 2 – 4–2–1 headers.

least 105–110hp (Table 9.8). The owner was not overly concerned as he was regularly setting the pace in his class out in the forests. However, I was not convinced that the 4–1 Group A header was working, so we bolted on a 4–2–1 pipe, which I knew worked with the cam I regularly fitted in Golf rally engines. Power immediately rose to just under 115hp at 5,000rpm, while at the top end the engine was now peaking at 153hp at 7,000rpm. If the owner had had the money to outlay on further header development I am confident that we could have regained most of what had been lost at the top end while retaining the strong mid-range.

Chapter 10

Camshaft
and Valve Train

Among the most important components in any performance or racing engine are the camshaft and valve train assembly. Basically, the camshaft is designed to open valves before the piston starts a stroke and to close them after the completion of the stroke, in order to utilise the inertia or momentum of the fast-moving gases to fill and empty the cylinder efficiently.

The intake valve is opened before top dead centre (TDC) on the induction stroke, to get the valve moving off the seat before the piston starts down. It is then kept open well after bottom dead centre (BDC) to let the inertia of the high-velocity fuel/air mixture to literally ram in additional mixture while the piston is starting up on the compression stroke.

The exhaust valve begins to open long before the end of the combustion stroke. Most of the effective expansion power of combustion is over by mid-stroke and opening the exhaust valve early lets the cylinder pressure 'blow down' before the piston starts up on the exhaust stroke. By leaving the valve open after TDC the momentum of the exhaust gases is used to scavenge the cylinder efficiently. As the inlet valve is also open during this overlap period, the exhaust gas inertia will actually assist cylinder filling by creating a partial vacuum in the cylinder and inlet tract.

However, this theory is not going to work from idle to full engine rpm. At low engine speeds the fuel mixture coming into the cylinder has little velocity and consequently little momentum. In fact, the piston will start to push the mixture out of the cylinder back up the inlet port as it comes up on the compression stroke. A similar situation occurs with the late closing of the exhaust valve. When the outgoing exhaust gases have low inertia at low rpm, the piston travelling down on the intake stroke will cause the burned gases to turn around and be sucked back into the cylinder. The other possibility is the fuel/air mixture flowing straight past the exhaust valve during the overlap period. This can be particularly troublesome with hemi and pent-roof combustion chambers. It is obvious that a compromise must be made to favour either low or high engine speeds. One cam cannot give you both with maximum efficiency.

CAM LOBE LIFT AND DURATION

Today, with the advances that have been made to improve the breathing ability of engines, it is not always necessary or desirable to employ a long-duration, high-lift cam to improve performance. In fact, such a cam can very easily spoil an otherwise well-thought-out engine modification. As we will discuss later, the valve timing and duration figures reveal very little about the power characteristics of a cam. The numbers game is played in the cam-grinding industry, too, so beware.

The science of camshaft design and operation is very complex, but our understanding of the basics will assist us to choose and correctly install a high-performance cam.

The base circle is the part of the cam that should, at all times, be at a constant radius from the centre of the cam core. The ramp (or clearance ramp) is the part that takes up the valve clearance and begins lifting the valve in a gentle manner, while the flank is the part that initiates the valve opening (Figure 10.1).

When designing a performance cam, the base circle must remain in the area of 140–160° (280–320 crankshaft degrees). This is necessary to allow the valves to dissipate heat and to give the whole valve train time to recover from the shock through which it has just gone. The ramp will, on a production cam, have 30–40° duration, while the flank will on average be 60–70°. To increase the duration of a cam we increase the flank angle to 70–80°, and to do this we must cut the ramp angle back to 20–30°.

All production engine designers like to use fairly long ramps in order to lift and seat the valve gently. This has the effect of cutting down on mechanical noise and increasing camshaft life. However, when designing a performance cam we cannot reduce the base circle angle so we have to shorten the ramp.

The average production engine timing is 10°–50°/50°–10°, ie the inlet valve opens 10° before TDC and closes 50° after BDC, and the exhaust valve opens 50°

Figure 10.1 Camshaft lobe.

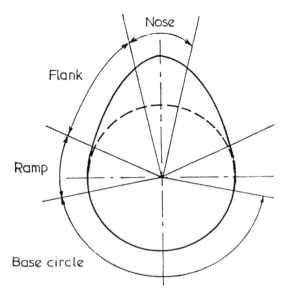

before BDC and closes 10° after TDC. This type of cam will give good low-speed performance. A sports cam of around 25°–65°/70°–20° will improve performance with little loss in low-speed flexibility. The wildest cam I would recommend for a road machine is what I call a semi-race cam, which would have a maximum duration of 290°; the timing would be 40°–70°/75°–35°. After this we enter the field of full race competition cams, the shorter durations of which are more suitable for high-speed closed stage rally cars, road circuit cars and quarter-mile dirt speedway machines, while the longer-duration (320–330°) cams would be used in 1-mile speedway cars and drag machines. Table 10.1 indicates the power range of various camshafts.

Table 10.1   Camshaft duration and power range

Cam type		Rocker arm ratio			
		1.7:1	*1.5:1*	*1.25:1*	*1:1*
'Sports'	duration	198–214°	202–218°	208–224°	215–232°
	overlap	–20° to –6°	–18° to –2°	–12° to 8°	–5 to 16°
	valve lift	.450–.470"	.430–.450"	.360–.370"	.380–.420"
	power range	0.4–1.05	0.4–1.05	0.4–1.05	0.4–1.05
'Semi-race'	duration	230–240°	235–245°	240–255°	245–260°
	overlap	10° to 25°	15° to 29°	20° to 40°	30° to 50°
	valve lift	.540–.560"	.510–.530"	.375–.400"	.410–.460"
	power range	0.6–1.1	0.6–1.1	0.6–1.1	0.6–1.1
'Full race'	duration	255–275°	260–280°	270–280°	270–285°
	overlap	43° to 65°	46° to 68°	54° to 73°	58° to 76°
	valve lift	.670–.850"	.600–.700"	.410–.430"	.430–.520"
	power range	0.8–1.1	0.8–1.1	0.8–1.1	0.8–1.1

Note: duration and overlap measured at .050in lobe lift.

Valve lift with zero tappet clearance.

To calculate approximate power range, refer back to Table 3.2 and formula in Chapter 3. Multiplying the rpm at which maximum hp is anticipated by the above figures will provide a guide as to the usable power range. For example, if the information in Chapter 3, pages 35 and 36 points to maximum power being produced at 7,000rpm and a semi-race cam is fitted, the power range should be about 0.6–1.1 x 7,000, or 4,200rpm to 7,700rpm.

The amount that the valves are lifted has a large bearing on the performance of an engine. Standard cams normally lift the valve about 23% of its diameter, while racing cams may increase this to 35% or more, even though flow in the inlet port may not increase, or even drop marginally when the valve is lifted more than about one third of its diameter.

Why then design a cam to lift the valve 35% of its diameter? It may sound silly lifting a valve so far, imposing higher loads on the valve train and making it necessary to use deeper valve cut-outs to clear the pistons, but this is how it works. Engine tuners have found that cams with quick opening and closing rates (high acceleration and high lift), but with relatively moderate duration and overlap, are a good way to get a broader torque curve. In other words, you pick up top-end power without sacrificing so much mid-range power. This occurs because the area under the lift or displacement curve increases (see displacement curve in Figure 10.7) which improves the total quantity of flow into or out of the cylinder.

When you think about it, if we are obtaining peak flow at 0.29–0.31 of inlet valve diameter, the idea should be to keep the valve open to that amount of lift for as many degrees as possible. Cam lobes are not square, so we would only hit that peak flow lift for an instant, literally 2–4°, if maximum lift was restricted to 0.29–0.31 of valve diameter. Therefore to maximise cylinder filling the valve lift is taken up to 0.37–0.40 (or even 0.43 in engines with huge cylinders but comparatively poor breathing like big-block Chev drag race engines taken out to over 600cu in) if reliability is not a worry and port flow does not drop off too much at these high lift figures.

LOBE SEPARATION ANGLE

While many tuners spend a good deal of time agonising over cam duration and lift figures, often little thought is given to the lobe separation angle. Many accept whatever the cam supplier has on offer because they do not understand how grinding it on different lobe centres affects the cam and how in turn this will influence the engine's power characteristics.

Simply stated, this angle fixes the actual position of the lobes on the camshaft and as such determines the opening and closing points of the inlet and exhaust valves, and the valve overlap period (Figure 10.2). For example, a cam lobe may have an advertised duration of, say, 310°, but it is the lobe separation angle that fixes the lobe phasing to produce a valve timing figure such as 53°–77°/77°–53°, or 50°–80°/80°–50°, or 47°–83°/83°–47°. The inlet and exhaust lobes all have 310° duration, but grinding the lobes on a different centre has resulted in the inlet and exhaust valves opening and closing at different angles of crankshaft rotation.

Assuming that this 310° lobe profile is of symmetrical design, the lobe centre, the peak of the lobe, must be at the halfway point, or 155° after the opening point. Thus if we subtract the inlet opening angle of 53° from 155°, we arrive at a lobe centre angle of 102°, which in turn means that the inlet valve will be at full lift 102° after TDC on the induction stroke. For the exhaust we subtract the closing angle, in the first

Figure 10.2 Cam lobe phasing.

Lobe separation angle.

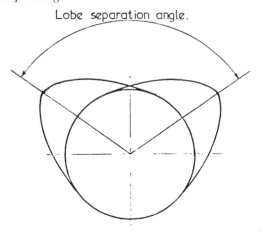

example 53°, from 155° and find the exhaust lobe centre to be at 102° before TDC. Hence this cam would be said to have 102° lobe separation. Following the same method you will find the other two examples have lobe centres of 105° and 108°.

On a small race engine of about 1.6 litres with good-size valves and ports and big carbs we might find that grinding the cam on 102° centres gives the best overall power spread. The inlet valve is closing sooner, reducing the amount of fuel/air mixture that will be pushed out of the cylinder by the rising piston (Figure 10.3). Thus cylinder filling will be better in the mid-range of the power band, which increases hp. Also the increased valve overlap period of 106° (as opposed to 100° and 94° for the cams on 105° and 108° centres) should, in conjunction with the engine's good breathing potential, ensure that exhaust gas momentum has ample time to pull additional fuel/air mixture in, which will give good cylinder filling at high rpm.

However, a late-closing exhaust valve can cause problems at lower rpm. Because the outgoing exhaust gases have less inertia, the downward movement of the piston will readily draw spent gases back into the cylinder. These hot gases occupy a lot of cylinder volume, which limits how much fresh fuel/air mixture can be drawn in; they will also slow combustion of that mixture, reducing hp output (Figure 10.4). If this was the case, a lobe separation of 105° may work better.

When an exhaust port that is flowing well is connected to a properly designed exhaust header, another problem can be encountered. At higher rpm the exhaust may over-scavenge the cylinder, drawing out not only all of the exhaust gas, but some fresh fuel/air mixture as well (Figure 10.5). The larger the cam overlap angle and the more efficient the exhaust port and header, the greater is the potential for this problem, which robs the engine of high rpm power and fuel economy. The solution could be a wider lobe separation angle or an exhaust lobe with shorter duration and/or less lift. Do not try to fix a problem like this by fitting a head with less efficient exhaust ports or a less efficient header. With a push rod engine you could swap the exhaust rockers to a lower ratio (say from 1.6:1 to 1.5:1).

Figure 10.3 Inlet reversion.

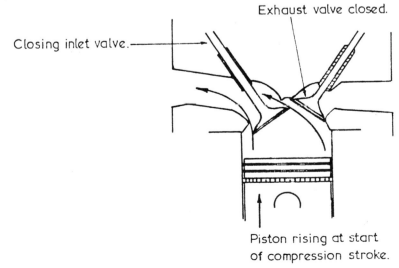

Closing inlet valve.

Exhaust valve closed.

Piston rising at start
of compression stroke.

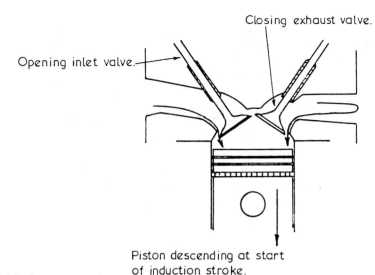

Figure 10.4 Exhaust reversion.

In a race class that limits the engine to just one small carburettor (or inlet restrictors) and insists on stock inlet and exhaust ports, a cam with wider lobe centres may work best. The small carb and inlet port will ensure high gas velocity in the inlet tract, which will improve mid-range hp because of improved cylinder filling. Increasing flow velocity down the inlet tract also resists reversion flow back past the inlet valve as the piston rises at the end of the inlet stroke. Then at higher rpm the late inlet closing allows more time for the fuel/air charge to complete the cylinder filling. On the exhaust side, opening the exhaust valve early gives the cylinder more time to expel burnt gas through the tight exhaust port. Consequently less engine power is used to push the gas out past the open valve as the piston rises on the exhaust stroke.

Figure 10.5 Over-scavenging.

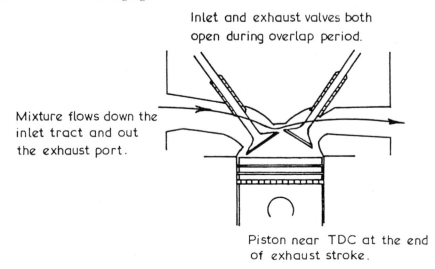

Summing up, a narrow lobe separation angle tends to improve mid-range power, but go too far and bottom-end power could be lost due to exhaust reversion, and top-end could be lost due to over-scavenging. Conversely, a wider separation angle favours top-end power at the expense of a drop in the mid-range due to inlet reversion.

When we look at it from the aspect of port flow characteristics, we see that a comparatively restrictive inlet and exhaust calls for a wider phase angle. An engine with excellent inlet and exhaust flow, and a good balance between the two, will run a medium lobe separation angle (about 104–106° for race engines, 108–110° for road engines). However, an engine with good inlet flow, but by comparison only average exhaust flow, will want a narrower phase angle.

Obviously just changing the lobe separation angle may not provide the inlet and exhaust flow characteristics desired. What may be called for is a cam with more duration and lift on the inlet lobes, or we may need more on the exhaust lobes to get the best hp and a wide power spread. With other engines such as the Mini we may grind race cams with different lobe centres and even different lobes on the centre cylinders. On others such as a Chev V8 race engine with just one carburettor we do the opposite, giving the four outer (corner) cylinders more lobe duration and lift, or alternatively higher-lift rockers.

CAM ADVANCE AND RETARD

Another useful strategy to 'tune' the cam to give the desired power characteristics is camshaft advance, or in a few instances camshaft retardation. When we advance a cam with 108° lobe centres and 47°–83°/83°–47° valve timing by 6° we in effect advance the inlet lobe centreline to 102° after TDC, and likewise the exhaust lobe centre moves to 114° before TDC. The valve timing changes to 53°–77°/89°–41°; the inlet and exhaust valve both open 6° earlier and they also close 6° earlier. Mid-range power rises because reversion in both the inlet and exhaust tracts is reduced. Usually maximum hp falls a little. However, if with split timing (ie both lobes on 108° centrelines) the engine was over-scavenging and drawing through the mixture, advancing the cam will reduce this problem, so maximum hp may improve a little (see Figure 10.12).

Basically, advancing a cam makes it work like one with narrower lobe separation, but without the disadvantages of the increased valve overlap and a late exhaust valve closing point. Thus a cam ground on 108° lobe centres and installed with 6° advance will perform in the mid-range like a cam with 104 or 105° lobe separation, and at high rpm will work similarly to a cam with 106 or 107° lobe centres.

Normally I do not install cams in the retarded position. Theory says that it causes the engine to lose mid-range power, but gain hp at maximum revs. I must have been doing it wrong all these years because any time I have tried retarding cams I lose power everywhere. In essence, retarding a cam, say, 4° will see the valves open 4° later, but more significantly they also close 4° later, which increases reversion in both the inlet and exhaust tracts and may also increase mixture draw-through on overlap.

A situation where we can take advantage of these normally unwanted characteristics is if the engine is detonating and the best fuel available is being used. For many tuners the first line of defence against detonation when the compression ratio has been made too high is to cut back on ignition advance. This is totally wrong – it kills performance. What we want is to reduce pressure in the cylinder. Cam retard helps in two ways: first it reduces cylinder filling at mid-range rpm with both inlet and exhaust reversion, and at higher rpm the late-closing exhaust valve may permit some over-scavenging, which also reduces cylinder filling. The second benefit is the result of exhaust reversion allowing spent gases back in to contaminate the fuel/air charge. This effectively slows combustion, therefore the combustion chamber, piston crown and valves all cool down, thus suppressing detonation.

Certainly cam retard will cause some hp to be lost, but nothing like the amount caused by reduced spark lead. The amount of retard necessary will depend on how much too high the compression ratio is, and the cam lobe separation angle. Whereas 2–3° retard may get you out of trouble with a cam ground on 108–110° lobe centres, a narrower angle like 104–105° may require 6° or more retard.

A reverse situation exists in race classes that require a low compression ratio down around 9:1. These classes also often limit inlet breathing with a small carburettor or air restrictor. With a low-compression engine we have to come down about 6–10° on lobe duration to get the torque back, so if a typical short dirt-track motor on a 12:1 compression works best with 254° duration we would cut back to around 244–248°. Then to achieve the best possible high-rpm cylinder filling, we would want a fairly wide lobe separation; usually about 110° with a two-barrel carb on a 350 V8; 108° with a small four-barrel on a V8. However, this introduces too much inlet reversion with a late-closing inlet valve killing mid-range power, so we dial in a lot of cam advance. With 110° separation this will mean up around 8° advance; a long-duration cam may need another degree or two. A cam with 108° lobe phasing will probably want 7° advance.

If the rules limit compression to 9:1 but have unrestricted breathing, allowing a big carb or fuel injection, the situation is a little different. Again we reduce lobe duration, but the cam lobe centres will be narrower at around 106° as the engine has an unrestricted inlet system. Then to pump up the mid-range the cam would be advanced probably 5°.

My experience over the years has been that regardless of whether the engine works best running a cam ground on 102° centres or 110° centres, all engines respond positively to some cam advance. Race engines like to have the cam moved forward such that the inlet lobe centre is at 100°–102° after TDC. There are exceptions to this, but I do not remember very many. Road engines run shorter lobe durations and have to get by with less fuel octane, so they typically give best overall performance with the inlet lobe centre around 104°–107° after TDC. However, if you run into detonation at 107° and the maximum ignition advance has already been backed off 3 or 4° less than stock, you will have to go back to perhaps 109°. I do not like dropping down further than this as it just kills the mid-range and leaves the engine really sluggish; fuel economy also suffers. If the engine is detonating with the inlet lobe at 109° and you have already pulled 3 or 4° off maximum ignition advance, you will have to lower the compression ratio or else increase the fuel octane.

What if your race engine performs best with the inlet lobe centre at 104–106° rather than the 100°–102° that I have suggested to be the ideal range? The conclusion to be drawn is that the engine wants the inlet to close later, so probably the lobe separation angle is tighter than ideal, therefore the separation should be widened by a couple of degrees. Alternatively the engine may want more lobe duration and lift on the current lobe separation angle. If it is a single-cam engine I would first try more duration and lift, but with twin cams it is easy and does not cost anything to swing the 311 separation angle apart. With the inlet in the 100–102° range, the engine should still make the same sort of mid-range hp and the top end will now be stronger.

The other possibility for the engine preferring the inlet lobe at 104–106° is that this is reducing cylinder pressure and thus getting the engine away from trace detonation. Consequently, with a more controlled burn you are seeing a power increase. If there is a bore scope on hand, take a careful look at all of the pistons, particularly around the edges, for evidence of sandblasting. The other option is to lift the head and check for signs of detonation. If the engine is running into detonation, lowering the compression ratio and running the cam at the correct angle, along with correct ignition timing and fuel mixture; will improve performance and engine reliability.

UNDERSTANDING CAM DURATION FIGURES

Referring back to Table 10.1, you will note that all the duration figures are measured at 0.050in lobe lift. This serves to avoid confusion as people tend to measure duration in all sorts of obscure ways. Typically, car manufacturers measure duration from the point where the lifter commences to move. Some cam grinders measure the duration as starting when the valve begins to move taking into account valve train flex and valve clearance. Such a system appears reasonable until you begin to appreciate that clearances change with engine temperature and engine speed, as do valve train flex and camshaft deflection. Moreover, consider how stiffer valve springs alter these latter two factors. Other cam manufacturers rate their cams on a sliding scale. Soft road cams show a duration spec at 0.004–0.006in lobe lift, semi-race at anything from 0.010–0.015in lobe lift, and race cams at 0.018–0.024in. All very confusing, I'm sure you will agree!

The solution has been to rate cams at 0.050in lobe lift. This is not perfect either, but it does give a better picture of what the duration number actually means and so gives some basis for comparing cams without actually testing every one. For example, looking at Table 10.2 you can see how dramatically advertised duration figures and figures at 0.006in vary from cam to cam. Cams No 1 and No 2 both measure up with the same duration at 0.006in, but at other lift points cam No 1 has 11–19° less duration! Comparing No 4 and No 5 the same picture emerges, with the duration of No 5 being 12–15° shorter. However, when we look at the 0.050 figures we easily see that cams Nos 1 and 5 are both extremely mild road cams. Nos 2 and 3 are a bit warmer and should provide similar performance. Likewise with Nos 4 and 6, which are both very close to each other and hotter than the other four.

Table 10.2   Camshaft duration comparison

	No 1	No 2	No 3	No 4	No 5	No 6
Advertised duration (°)	296	252	260	260	264	266
Lobe lift (in)			*Actual duration (°)*			
0.006	254	254	255	260	260	260
0.050	195	206	204	212	200	210
0.100	163	175	174	181	168	180
0.200	96	115	114	121	106	120
Maximum lift (in)	.260	.285	.284	.292	.272	.293

Table 10.3   Race cam duration comparison

	No 1	No 2	No 3	No 4	No 5	No 6
Advertised duration (°)	290	294	291	300	299	298
Lobe lift (in)			*Actual duration (°)*			
0.050	260	261	263	270	271	268
0.100	229	226	225	231	230	237
0.200	183	179	174	184	182	191
0.300	137	132	125	136	132	145
Maximum lift (in)	.430	.418	.393	.425	.395	.435

The ideal situation would be for the cam manufactures to provide more detailed information, such as that presented in Table 10.3. If we only had the 0.050 duration figures we could mistakenly conclude that cam Nos 1, 2 and 3 are pretty much the same. No 3 has more duration than the others but it has less lift, so that should balance things out, or so it would appear. When we look at the 0.100 number we see a clearer picture emerging: No 1 has a much more aggressive profile and this is borne out by the figures at 0.200 and 0.300in lift. The same could be said of Nos 4, 5 and 6. At the 0.050in lobe lift figure they are all around the 270° mark. No 5 has less lift but it has a few degrees more duration, but at 0.100in it shows itself to be a significantly milder cam.

Does this mean that if you were looking for a 260 or 270° cam, Nos 1 and 6 would get the nod? Well that depends – I would be worried about their more aggressive profiles killing the valve gear. That may not be a huge concern in a sprint-type engine used in hillclimbs, for example, but how about if we were running a distance endurance event? How long would the valve springs and rockers, not to mention the valves and valve seats, stand up under such a hammering?

VALVE BOUNCE AND TOSS

Added to these questions, all of which demand answers, it is sobering to remember that a more aggressive profile on paper may not in the event deliver in practice when installed in a race engine. Figure 10.6 illustrates what may actually be occurring at the valve at high engine speeds. One curve plots ideal valve motion with no cam or valve train flex and the lifter faithfully following the profile of the cam lobe, finally easing the valve down on to its seat. The other curve depicts actual valve motion: during the first 100° valve motion lags as the camshaft, push rods and rocker arms flex. Then, as the lobe attempts to decelerate the valve as it approaches the point of maximum lift, the valve train and valve mass overwhelm the valve springs and the lifter is tossed off the lobe. For the next 160° the valve continues to act independently of the cam lobe. At this point valve spring pressure and valve and valve train mass combine forces to slam the lifter back on to the face of the cam. This combined mass then causes the entire valve train to bend again, allowing the valve to crash on to the valve seat around 25° ahead of schedule. However, rather than remaining seated the valve bounces off the seat and does not reseat for another 80°, and finally settles after a further 130°.

For those yelling out 'fit stiffer valve springs and lighter valves and rockers', it is sobering to reflect on the fact that such moves may reduce the amount of 'toss', but the

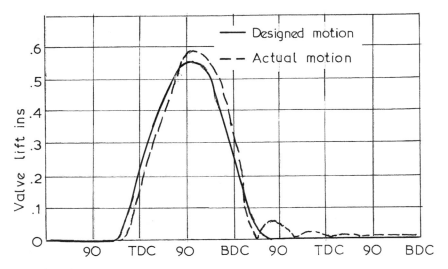

Figure 10.6 Valve motion curves.

bounce on to the seat may in fact worsen. The real solution may be a more gentle cam profile or a lower maximum engine speed.

It should be obvious that from a mechanical point of view valve bounce is to be avoided, but additionally it is something we must eliminate with respect to engine hp. Clearly if it is the exhaust valve that is bouncing off its seat, the intake charge will be contaminated by exhaust gas drawn back into the cylinder past the bouncing valve. Then, as the inlet valve bounces off its seat, fuel/air mixture is expelled by the piston rising on the compression stroke. This lowers cylinder pressure and shoots a massive reversion blast up the inlet tract, which in turn will disrupt the following inlet cycle.

Thus in the real world cam profiles Nos 2 and 4 may assist the engine to generate the highest hp because they maintain better control of valve train motion. However, cam Nos 3 and 5 may indeed be the ideal choice. They may be down a touch in the power stakes, but they could be much more gentle on the valve gear. Also, on the track they may prove to be faster because they will allow the engine to safely rev faster by, say, 300rpm without valve bounce.

Valve toss isn't always bad from the standpoint of max hp in some race engines. The specific exception is with regard to silly regulations limiting maximum valve lift. The original intent of such rules was no doubt noble, penned to keeps costs down and even out the competition. Racers are always looking for the winning edge so those with more money approached engine tuners looking for a legal way around this rule. The solution was to design the lobe and valve train to deliberately toss the lifter off the nose of the cam; effectively gaining valve lift, and thus more hp and rpm. This isn't kind to the valve train, but when valve motion is controlled so that they don't bounce on the seats, it provides a winning advantage.

CAM LOBE DYNAMICS

This leads us to what we call cam dynamics. Figure 10.7 shows a displacement curve, a graph of camshaft rotation in degrees relative to the motion of the cam follower. You

DISPLACEMENT CURVE

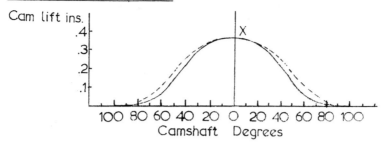

VELOCITY CURVE

ACCELERATION CURVE

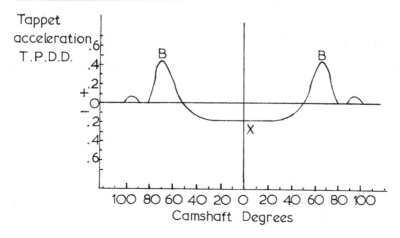

Figure 10.7 Cam lobe characteristic curves.

can readily see that just knowing the duration and lift of a cam will not give a true indication of its performance potential. The dotted line shows a cam of the same timing and lift but with quicker opening and closing times.

The velocity curve is the rate of lift expressed in thousandths of an inch per degree of rotation. The most significant parts of this diagram are the maximum velocity points. The maximum velocity of a cam occurs when the cam is contacting the follower nearest its edge. With a given tappet diameter, a maximum practical cam velocity can be used without the cam striking the sharp edge of the cam follower. Table 10.4 indicates the maximum velocity for various cam follower diameters. Most high-performance cams produce a velocity of 0.007in per degree (or 7 thousandths of an inch per degree), which is generally within limits, but some racing cams are running 0.009 and up to 0.012in per degree velocity, which is way above the safe limit for many engines. Once the safe limit is passed, high cam wear and follower breakage is imminent.

Table 10.4 Maximum safe cam and tappet velocity

Tappet diameter (in)	Cam/tappet velocity (TPD)	Engine application
0.780	6.63	
0.800	6.8	Ford Anglia/Cortina
0.812	6.9	Austin 'A' Series
0.842	7.16	Oldsmobile 260/455, Chevy 6 and V8, Holden 6
0.850	7.23	Cortina/Escort (Kent motor)
0.874	7.43	English Ford 3000 V6, American Ford 6 and V8
0.904	7.68	American Motors 6 and V8, Chrysler 6 and V8
0.921	7.83	Oldsmobile 1967 model 400/425
0.941	8.0	VW Type 4
0.960	8.16	Replacement Chevy mushroom tappet
0.980	8.33	
1.000	8.5	Replacement Ford V8 mushroom tappet
1.060	9.01	
1.100	9.35	
1.125	9.56	
1.155	9.82	VW
1.186	10.08	Morris 1,500 and 1,750 ohc
1.200	10.2	
1.300	11.05	
1.375	11.69	Lotus/Ford twin cam, Jaguar, Alfa Romeo dohc
1.400	11.9	

The acceleration curve shows us the rate of change of velocity in inches per degree, per degree. As will be explained when we deal with cam 'fingerprinting', this curve is critical in showing factors that affect reliability, as well as information concerning the maximum rpm attainable by the valve train. Negative acceleration determines this maximum rpm. This is the part of the valve train motion that is working against the valve spring, as the lifter is slowing down to go over the nose of the cam. As the engine turns faster and faster, a point is reached where the force generated by the mass of the valve train equals that generated by the valve spring in the valve open position. Any further increase in rpm would cause valve float. A cam profile with the lowest negative acceleration (or deceleration) will allow the highest rpm potential or allow the use of softer valve springs if that rpm potential is not going to be used. Ideally, negative acceleration should be less than –0.0002, but up to –0.00028 is tolerable (–0.2 to –0.28 thousandths of an inch per degree, per degree).

The two higher-positive acceleration peaks are significant in assessing the durability of a cam, since a heavy valve train combined with high acceleration will cause high cam loading and wear. Valve spring loads in this area are comparatively low, but stresses due to inertia are high. The two smaller positive acceleration peaks are the opening and closing ramps. Maximum positive acceleration may be as high as 0.0006–0.0007in per degree, per degree (0.6–0.7 thousandths of an inch per degree, per degree).

To help you understand what you are looking at, I have marked some points of significance on the three curves. Point 'X' is the nose of the cam, where full lift occurs. Point 'A' is where maximum velocity is reached, and 'B' indicates the point of maximum acceleration. 'A' is also where cam lobe contact is at its farthest from the centre of the tappet. We call this the point of maximum eccentricity.

MEASURING CAM CHARACTERISTICS AND ACCURACY

Quality and grinding accuracy are both very important considerations in buying a high-performance camshaft, but unfortunately they are not always found. An inaccurately ground cam will lose you a lot of power, cause tuning problems, inducing early valve float and causing premature lobe and lifter wear. Fortunately, there is a way of not only checking out the cam, but also delving into its actual profile, to produce the curves shown in Figure 10.7. All that is needed is to set up the cam in a lathe or rest it on a set of V-blocks. A 0.5in dial indicator is then attached to one of the lobes and a degree wheel bolted to the cam. I always check my racing cams on the two lobes in the middle, and also No 1 intake and exhaust lobe for comparison. If the cam is bent, or if it has been forced against the grinding wheel, this will show up more on the centre lobes. When I find a cam to be outside the tolerances mentioned, I return it to the grinder for replacement.

With the cam set up so that it can rotate between centres, and with the 360° degree wheel bolted up, set a fixed pointer next to the degree wheel and position the dial indicator to read off the desired lobe. It is best to make a fixture to hold the actual lifters you will use with that cam and set up the dial indicator to read off the lifter. For most purposes you can check the cam every 0.005–0.010in of lift.

It is very important to set up the dial indicator accurately and solidly. With this done, and the cam rotated so that the lifter is on the base circle, zero the dial indicator. Rotate the cam to lift and lower the cam follower at least six times to verify that the indicator returns to zero with the follower on the base circle. If it does not return to zero either the lifter is sticking or the indicator is not mounted solidly.

The first thing we want to check is the base circle run-out. This should be around 0.001in; certainly more than 0.002in is unacceptable. Next we check the actual timing and lift. The cam grinder should indicate how he arrives at his claimed timing figures. Some measure the duration as starting and finishing when lift is 0.020in, and others 317 measure a few degrees past the end of the clearance ramp, where lifter acceleration is positive. As already mentioned, many are now specifying a timing figure for 0.050in lift, which is better as we are well off the ramp at this stage, so the figures are more accurate. I work to a tolerance of ±1° of the stated opening and closing points, and ±0.002in of the rated lift. Remember that the cam duration is only half of the advertised duration, which is measured off the crankshaft.

After these basic checks we get down to the nitty-gritty of profile curves. As shown in Table 10.5, we record the cam angle for every 0.010in lift. Once we have a full set of figures for that lobe we can set about computing the velocity and acceleration figures. You will note that these figures are placed between the basic lift and angle reading. The third column will be the change in degrees for each 0.010in lift (Δ). The fourth column is lift velocity expressed in thousandths of an inch per degree of rotation (TPD). To find the TPD figures simply divide each Δ° into 10. The fifth column is the change in TPD (ΔTPD). This tells us the amount that the velocity of lift is changing for each 0.010in of lift. The final column is for acceleration, which we call TPDD or thousandths of an inch per degree, per degree, and is worked out using the following formula:

$$TPDD = \frac{\Delta TPD}{\Delta°}$$

The acceleration figures show us the accuracy of the profile. If the figures jump all over the place this may indicate grinding wheel chatter marks, or it may indicate polydyne correction in the cam design. The machine that grinds cam lobes traces the pattern from a larger master cam. The grinding wheel is controlled by a spring-loaded roller that rides on the master cam as it rotates. If the operator feeds the grinding wheel against the cam too rapidly, the roller can be forced off the master cam, resulting in a cam profile that does not conform to that of the master.

Table 10.5   Cam profile table (in part)

Cam lift (in)	Angle	Δ°	TPD	ΔTPD	TPDD
0.010	101.6°				
		7.6	1.32	0.90	0.118
0.020	109.2°				
		4.5	2.22	0.72	0.160
0.030	113.7°				
		3.4	2.94	0.51	0.150
0.040	117.1°				
		2.9	3.45	0.55	0.189
0.050	120.0°				
		2.5	4.00	0.76	0.304
0.060	122.5°				
		2.1	4.76	0.80	0.381
0.070	124.6°				
		1.8	5.56	0.69	0.383
0.080	126.4°				

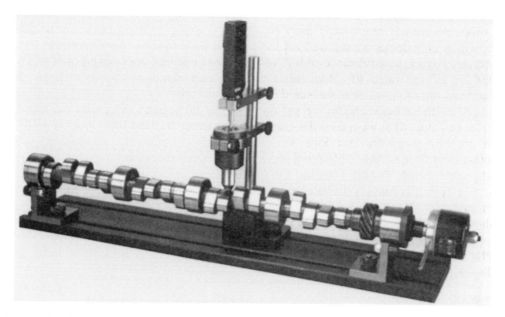

Cam lobe characteristics and camshaft accuracy can be assessed using fairly basic equipment. This takes more time than with more sophisticated gear that inputs directly to a computer, but is no less accurate.

Polydyne correction is quite different, and is a designed correction factor that has been planned to correct some valve train problem caused by the fact that most valve trains are not rigid enough (due to push rod flex, camshaft flex, etc). What this correction really does is to accelerate the lifter, then drop back, then accelerate again. This is done to give the valve train a chance to 'catch up' so that it is not overstressed. If you find your velocity and acceleration figures are regular and consistent with, say, four or six of these bumps in one full rotation, you can assume that the cam profile has polydyne corrections.

To help in determining this I always draw up an acceleration curve. This will help determine if the 'bumps' are to a set pattern. A golden rule of cam design is that the area inside the acceleration curve on the positive side must always equal the area inside the curve on the negative side. It is quite logical: if you are going to accelerate something a certain amount, the only way you are going to get it back to a standstill is to decelerate it by the same amount. If the cam does not conform to this rule, valve train problems will result.

The next problem takes some time to check as we must check each lobe to determine correct indexing. If the cam lobes are not phased (or indexed) at exactly the right angle to each other from cylinder to cylinder, the valve timing of the whole engine will be amiss. I have seen cams with lobes out of phase by up to 15°. When checking the phasing I also record the maximum lift for each lobe. As mentioned earlier, I would expect the lift to be within ±0.002in of the cam grinder's quoted figure, and all the lobe centres (full lift angle) should be in phase by ±1°.

This means that a four-cylinder engine will have all four inlet lobe centres 90°   319

(±1°) apart. Therefore if the firing order is 1–3–4–2 and No 1 lobe centre is at, say, 70° on the 360° degree wheel, No 3 should be at 70° + 90° = 160°; No 4 at 160° + 90° = 250°; and No 2 at 250° + 90° = 340°.

The four exhaust lobe centres should also be 90° apart, but to determine at what angle they should be in relation to the No 1 inlet lobe, we have to go back to the cam timing figures and do some calculations. If the cam had symmetrical timing of 30°–70°/70°–30° this would mean that the valve open period would be 30° + 180° + 70° = 280°, measured at the crankshaft, or 140° at the cam. Therefore the inlet lobe centre should be at

$$\frac{280}{2} - 30° = 110° \text{ ATDC (at the crankshaft)}$$

and the exhaust lobe centre should also be at

$$\frac{280}{2} - 30° = 110° \text{ BTDC (at the crankshaft)}$$

At the camshaft the No 1 exhaust lobe centre should be

$$\frac{110° + 110°}{2} = 110° \text{ ahead of the No 1 inlet lobe.}$$

This would mean, using the above example, that the lobe centre for No 1 exhaust would be at 70° – 110° = 320° (±1°) on the 360° wheel. No 3 would be at 320° + 90° = 50°; No 4 at 50° + 90°= 140°; and No 2 at 140° + 90° = 230°. It all looks very complicated on paper, but once you sit down and work it out with a cam and a degree wheel in front of you, it is no problem at all.

Note that there are exceptions where the lobe phasing and/or lobe profile may be deliberately altered on specific cylinders for certain engine types; as previously mentioned the 'A' and 'B' series Austin engines with 5 port head and push rod American V8s, running in demanding classes of competition. Obviously we want every cylinder to produce, ideally, identical hp. The obstacle to achieving this may be race rules limiting the type of cylinder head, inlet manifold and carburation permitted. Alternatively the engine may have a basic design limitation and competition is just so intense that we have to venture into ridiculously high engine speeds, aggressive lobe profiles and valve spring pressures to stand any sort of chance of being a winner that really weird things begin to occur with regard to actual valve motion. In push rod V8s the problem is a single camshaft confronted by massive valve spring loads from sixteen big heavy valves, being banged open perhaps 0.750in at engine speeds approaching 10,000rpm. In addition to the actual valve timing at the valve seat being muddled by flexing of the push rods and rockers, the camshaft will begin to wind up as engine rpm increases causing the lobes furthest from the drive sprocket to lag behind. The extent of valve train flex and lobe lag is checked in a Spintron at various rpm, and then, depending on where in the engine's rev range we need to pick up more power, the lobe phasing will be progressively advanced along the camshaft. Obviously this takes many experimental cams and a lot of dyno time to get right.

The Spintron is used to spin the engine at various rpm to enable checking of valve motion, valve train stability etc. with laser measuring devices. High speed video and still photography may also be employed.

THE CAM FOLLOWER

The next vital link in the valve train is the cam follower (also called tappet, lifter or bucket). This has the task of changing the rotating motion of the camshaft to an up-and-down motion. The contact point between the tappet and the cam lobe is the most heavily loaded spot in any engine; it can be as high as 300,000lb/in^2, which is one reason why cam followers require very special attention in a high-performance or racing engine.

Contrary to popular opinion, cam followers are not flat; in fact, they are ground with a spherical radius of 37–75in, which means that they are around 0.003in high in the centre. This spherical radius, along with a cam lobe angle of 3–16', and the tappet offset from the centre of the lobe, causes the tappet to rotate (Figure 10.8). The effect is to reduce cam and tappet wear; in fact, if the tappets do not rotate, this part of your trick engine is quite likely to self destruct in around 15 minutes. For this reason I always have the cam followers ground to the required spherical radius whether they are new or used. I have found many new followers to be flat, which, while not being as bad as old followers worn concave, means they are not up to the task of providing reliable service with a performance cam.

Before we take a look at roller tappets it might be as well to examine the basic types of flat tappets. You will note that I make no mention of the hydraulic lifter   321

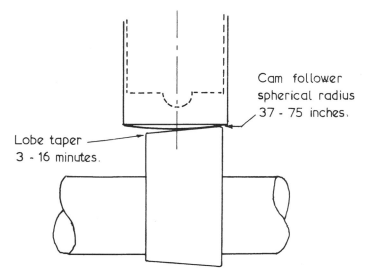

Figure 10.8 Cam lobe and tappet design.

because in function it is similar to a conventional flat tappet. The conventional bucket-type flat tappet used in most double-overhead-cam and a few single-overhead-cam engines has many advantages: light in weight, large in diameter, and with a small rocking moment. However, manufacturers and service mechanics do not like this simple arrangement because of the tedium of adjusting the valve clearance. This

Camshaft lobes that have been damaged by worn tappets.

adjustment is made by inserting shims of various thicknesses between the valve stem and bucket (Figure 10.9). This means that the cams have to be removed each time valve clearance adjustment is needed, then, on being refitted, they have to be re-timed.

Manufacturers have devised a couple of ways to get around this problem, but in doing this they have created others. Thirty five years ago the ohc Vauxhall and Chevy Vega both used an adjusting screw with a tapered flat on one side, which does the same job as the adjusting shim. Using an Allen key, the clearance is adjusted by turning the screw in or out. Adjustments must be made in full turns as the screw has a flat only on one side.

The system most often used has a shim recessed in the top of the tappet. To adjust the clearance, a special tool is used to compress the valve spring. The shim can then be flicked out of the recess and another shim of the required thickness fitted.

While both designs have simplified valve adjustment, the weight of the bucket tappet has in some cases been doubled, as compared with the conventional bucket tappet and shim. This is not such a problem on more mundane motors, but high-revving motorcycles and race engines are a different matter. The extra weight of the valve train imposes a higher load on the valve springs, and this lowers the valve float rpm drastically. To combat this, valve spring pressures must be increased; however, an increase in spring pressures soaks up power and increases valve train flex and wear. Another problem is that of missed gear changes or deceleration over-revving causing valve float. This then allows the adjusting shims to flick out of the buckets, with disastrous consequences. The only way around the problem, and it should only be a problem in competition engines, is to fit the lighter, conventional bucket tappet and

Figure 10.9 Bucket tappet clearance adjustment systems.

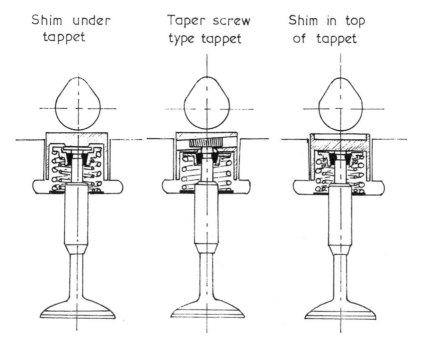

Shim under tappet   Taper screw type tappet   Shim in top of tappet

shim. When this is done, special valve spring retainers will be required to keep the shim in position between the valve stem and tappet.

This problem of the adjusting shim jumping out of position can also occur with the conventional bucket tappet and shim, but it is very unusual. In this instance valve float allows the shim to move out of the valve spring retainer recess and become wedged between the top of the spring retainer and the tappet. Instead of the valve closing, it is held open maybe 0.200in, whereupon the piston bangs into the valve and proceeds to destroy the motor. The more usual problem with the conventional bucket and shim is with shims that have been ground with faces that are not perfectly parallel. When this happens the shim rotates in an eccentric path, which wears away the top of the valve spring retainer. As a consequence the retainer collapses and allows the valve to drop into the piston. To ensure that this does not happen, measure all adjustment shims of this type with a micrometer, to ensure that their faces are parallel within 0.0003in. Also make sure that the shims are of almost the same diameter as the recess in the valve spring retainer.

The conventional flat tappet used in nearly all push-rod-type engines is losing ground to the mushroom tappet in competition where roller cams are banned. Earlier we discussed the relationship between cam velocity (and eccentricity) and tappet diameter. We are able to increase the eccentricity of a cam by increasing the tappet diameter. Unfortunately, most blocks cannot be enlarged to accept larger-diameter tappets, so the next best thing is to make the face of the tappet larger.

Enlarging the tappet diameter means that we can increase cam velocity, which results in a gain of around 15% in area under the displacement curve while retaining the same cam duration and lift. This means that we can improve performance due to the 15% flow improvement without the disadvantage of a loss of mid-range power if a hotter, long-duration, long-overlap cam were fitted to give us the same 15% increase. From Table 10.6 you will see what this means in actual performance. The motor in this instance is a 350 Chevy set up with good mid-range power in mind for road circuit racing. Each cam was chosen to give the best compromise between maximum power and mid-range power. The inlet rocker arms were changed to a 1.6:1 ratio to increase inlet valve acceleration. At 7,000rpm you will note that there is very little difference in maximum power between the three cams. However, down at 5,000rpm and below you can see the power margin widening. This is due to the difference in valve opening rates of each type of cam. Of course, if we had wanted more top-end power, while retaining the same bottom-end power as with the flat tappet cam, we could have achieved this too with the mushroom tappet and roller tappet cams. Many cam grinders are producing high-velocity cams for use with mushroom tappets, so take a good look at this performance route before resorting to the more expensive roller tappet set-up.

Overhead cam engines utilising bucket tappets can also gain a similar performance boost even when it may not be physically possible, or perhaps desirable, to increase the tappet diameter. In this situation we have the option of either going with an oval bucket design, or we can use a round bucket with a ramped face. For example, an oval bucket with a lobe contact face 30mm across by 35mm long replacing a round bucket tappet 30mm in diameter will be lighter than a round 35mm bucket, but offers the same increase – about 16% – in maximum safe cam and tappet velocity as the larger 35mm bucket. A round bucket tappet with a ramped face, to keep

Table 10.6   Engine dynamometer results with a 350 Chevy using flat tappet, mushroom tappet and roller tappet camshafts

Test 1 Flat tappet 0.842in diameter

rpm	hp	torque (lbf ft)
4,500	346	404
5,000	401	421
5,500	462	441
6,000	506	443
6,500	541	437
7,000	569	427
7,500	567	397

Test 2 Mushroom tappet 0.960in diameter

rpm	hp	torque (lbf ft)
4,500	362	423
5,000	415	436
5,500	471	450
6,000	515	451
6,500	547	442
7,000	572	429
7,500	570	399

Test 3 Roller tappet

rpm	hp	torque (lbf ft)
4,500	382	446
5,000	430	452
5,500	479	457
6,000	525	460
6,500	556	449
7,000	574	431
7,500	569	398

the edge of the tappet from being struck by the cam lobe, offers the potential for even higher cam and tappet velocity rates. Alternatively if minimising valve train weight is of greater importance than being able to run a more aggressive cam lobe then the tappet diameter can be dramatically reduced without any need to resort to a milder lobe profile. Porsche in fact went this route with their 3.6ltr GT3 24-hour endurance race engines, reducing bucket diameter from 35mm flat-faced to 28mm ramped-face. Apart from higher cost the downside with both oval and ramped face designs is that neither type is able to rotate (the ramped bucket is keyed to prevent rotation), so lobe and tappet face wear rates are higher. However, with diamond like coatings (DLC) applied to cam lobes and tappets this need not be an issue.

If your sport requires the use of more than 8,500rpm from a push-rod-type engine, or super low-end power, roller tappets are the trick set-up. More radical cams can be used since the cam velocity can be increased past that possible with flat or

The rev kit preloads the roller tappet against the cam lobe during the period when the valve is seated.

mushroom tappets. Because the roller, by its very nature, rolls over the cam, lobe scuffing is virtually eliminated, which leads to longer cam and tappet life. To gain full benefit from the roller tappet and cam's rev potential (10,000rpm for the small-block Chevy V8), greater valve spring pressures are required, so take care to follow the cam manufacturer's recommendations carefully. A 'rev kit' will be required to provide the proper tappet preload for high-rpm operation. The rev kit consists of an extra set of springs that fit between the tappet and the head, which load the tappet during the valve-closed period and keep it in contact with the cam. Additionally in a heavy duty or endurance race environment the rev kit functions as an engine saver by preventing a tappet coming out of the block in the event of a valve spring, rocker arm, or push rod failure. With all the lifters held in place in the block engine oil pressure is maintained, which may enable the engine to finish the race down one cylinder, or if that isn't possible at least prevent further engine damage.

PUSH RODS AND GUIDE PLATES

Two requirements for an efficient valve train in a high-performance engine are light weight and rigidity: light weight to allow an increase in operating rpm, and rigidity to ensure accurate valve operation to attain the desired rpm. Push rods and rockers require particular attention with regard to both of these important but conflicting ideals. Where possible, I always replace push rods with those made of aircraft-grade seamless 4130 chrome-moly steel tubing, heat treated to 120,000psi tensile strength. These must be of the correct length to maintain correct rocker arm geometry.

Basically, rocker arm geometry is correct when the centre of the rocker arm tip coincides exactly with the centre-line of the valve stem, with the valve lifted 40–50% of its total lift. If this is not the case, the valve guide will wear to an oval shape very quickly, due to the increased side thrust, which can cause valve seating and valve burning problems. Rocker arm geometry may be upset by the installation of a high-lift cam, or high-ratio rocker arms, but may also be changed by head and block deck milling.

When a good thing becomes too much

Something like 30 years ago the myth arose that all 'serious' cams for two-valve four-cylinder race engines had to have 0.500in lift or more. Anything less was a sure indication that a cam developer didn't know his stuff. When these engineers/tinkers/hobbyists could not convince 'engine tuners' that more lift/less duration is only good up to a point, to stay in the business of grinding cams they had to come up with something to fulfil customer expectations. Thus, going against their better judgement, a whole raft of these cams have appeared with the 'right' numbers. With what result? Engines like the Ford Pinto are wiping out cams and followers at an alarming rate. Engines like the VW Golf, Ford Crossflow and Ford CVH are down on top-end power and the mid-range has virtually disappeared.

Somehow 0.500in lift became a magic number, but personally I cannot remember seeing a Pinto work better with valve lifts more than about 0.475in. The Crossflow and CVH lose mid-range power with more than about 0.430–0.440in lift, and when you cut duration to regain mid-range the top-end goes away.

The same thing happened with a long-stroke 1.6 Golf being developed for an open-wheeler in a class requiring carbs and stock crank and an 8,500rpm rev limit. A bag-full of mega-lift cams in the 0.490–0.530in range were tried and the results were hopeless. On 50mm Webers the engine was only making the sort of power we were getting out of Golfs over 25 years ago on 45DCOEs. When a fairly ordinary cam was finally tried, power jumped to 189hp at 8,250 with a power band running all the way from 6,200 up to 8,500. The cam in question had a 0.418in lift and 284° duration!

Now I am not saying that high-lift cams do not work. What I am saying is that there are no 'magic numbers'. Some engines work best with high-lift cams, but there are many that do not. If an engine has an efficient intake and exhaust, and engine rpm is restricted either by mechanical considerations or by race regulations, massive valve lift may not be a good thing. Remember that it takes time to get a gas column moving down the inlet tract and past the valve into the cylinder. When the duration is shortened too much to compensate for increased valve lift, reduced cylinder filling can result because we have failed to get the fuel/air column moving quickly enough.

Another problem can be that with more area under the lift curve at TDC we may get good initial flow, but the mixture may go straight out past the exhaust valve, which may be 0.230in open, reducing cylinder filling. The secret is to obtain that desirable strong initial flow without sacrificing mixture loss through the exhaust. Of course lobe separation and cam advance (or retard) also have considerable influence in this respect, but if there is a lot of valve lift at TDC, as is usual with a short-duration/high-lift cam, a lot of development time can be wasted fiddling with lobe phasing for very little gain, as it is the duration/lift relationship that is wrong for the particular engine.

If I think an engine will work better with additional valve lift and there will be no mechanical problems such as broken valve springs, broken lobes or rockers and no reduced combustion efficiency (remember that more lift may mean deeper valve pockets in the pistons, which may in turn require that the top ring has to be lowered on the piston, which may upset combustion), I would reckon to decrease lobe duration by 1° for each 0.010–0.015in increase in lift.

Also to be considered at this point are push rod guide plates. If the standard plates have a history of breakage, replace them with plates of a better design or made of better material. Any motor that has ball-fulcrum-type rockers must be fitted with guide plates if reliability is to be maintained. As well as allowing up-and-down 327 motion, these rockers unfortunately engage in a side-to-side motion, which does a great job of wrecking the valve guides. The only way to curtail this sideways twist is to install push rod guide plates. Generally, I have found that standard motors not fitted with guide plates suffer twice as much valve guide wear in line with the cylinder head (180°) rather than across the head. It can be imagined how much more the valve is going to be pushed sideways when stiffer valve springs are fitted and cam acceleration rate increased, when there are already problems with the standard arrangement. Remember when you fit guide plates that hardened push rods will have to be fitted to prevent rapid push rod wear.

THE ROCKER ASSEMBLY

Next in line for scrutiny are the rocker arms. These transmit the tappet motion to the valve and may be pressed steel or forged items. Generally, stock forged rocker arms are reasonably rigid and will do a good job in a high-performance engine, with some modification. The rocker should be lightened with a view to retaining the vertical section while reducing the horizontal section. The rocker does most of its work directly in line with the push rod and valve stem centres, so in most instances material can be removed without weakening the component. The area over the valve stem must be left wide enough to give full valve stem contact. The shank of the rocker should be left alone except to remove 'dingle berries'. Shot peening is to be recommended in racing applications. Obviously there is no point in removing material close to the rocker shaft as this mass is of no consequence.

Most forged rockers are supported by a light steel rocker shaft and posts of steel or light alloy. The Austin Mini-type shaft and posts are about as rigid as possible in production form. However, the same cannot be said of the four-cylinder British Fords, which leave a lot to be desired in this department. If any modification is intended for one of these, no matter how mild, the alloy rocker posts must be discarded and replaced by more rigid steel posts. The use of a moderately hot cam will also make it

A shaft mounted rocker assembly provides a much better base for reliable valve train operation at high rpm with heavy valve spring pressures.

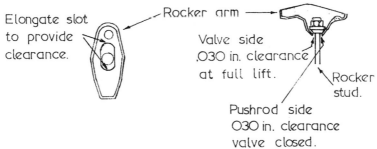

Figure 10.10 Rocker arm clearance check.

necessary to use a heavy-duty steel rocker shaft. The ultimate is without doubt the Piper integral rocker box, which supports the outer ends of the shaft very effectively.

The separation springs fitted between the rockers should be replaced by tubular sleeves made of steel. While doing this, pay attention to fitting sleeves of the correct length to centralise the rockers over the valves.

Pressed steel rocker arms are another story. While they have been used with some fairly warm cams, I do not like them, and I would not use them in any motor fitted with anything wilder than a sports cam. The alternative is expensive but well worth it. These are made of aircraft-quality, extruded high-density aluminium or forged steel, and are fitted with needle roller bearings and a roller tip. Assuming that your rocker geometry is correct, these roller rockers will reduce valve guide wear by 'rolling' over the valve stem as it pushes the valve open. Standard rockers scuff the valve to the side, which wears the stem and valve guide. Generally, I have found that roller rockers reduce the oil temperature of Chevys by up to 20°F, due to reduced friction, which means that we are picking up power as well.

Ball-type rockers require attention when high-lift cams are installed, to ensure adequate working clearance between the end of the slot in the rocker arm and the rocker stud. This clearance should be measured using a wire 0.030in thick (a paper clip is fine), with the valve closed and also at full lift (Figure 10.10).

Table 10.7   Replacement rocker arms

Engine	Standard ratio	Alternative ratio
American Motors 290–401	1.6:1	1.7:1
Austin 'A' series	1.25:1	1.4:1, 1.5:1
Buick V6	1.5:1	1.6:1, 1.7:1
Chevy: small-block and V6	1.5:1	1.6:1, 1.7:1*, 1.8:1**, 1.9:1**, 2.0:1**
Chevy: big-block	1.7:1	1.8:1, 2.0:1**
Ford Cleveland	1.73:1	1.63:1
Ford Windsor	1.6:1	1.7:1
Ford V6 (British)	1.4:1	1.5:1, 1.6:1*
Ford big-block 332–428	1.76:1	1.66:1
VW 1200–1500	1.23:1	1.45:1, 1.5:1, 1.6:1

*Requires offset studs

**Shaft-mounted rocker arms

When budget constraints put a shaft mount rocker arrangement out of reach the next best path is heavy rocker studs and a rocker stud girdle to spread the load.

An absolute must is to replace pressed-in rocker studs with screw-in studs, if a racing cam is to be fitted. Many push-in studs are marginally stable even with the standard cam and valve springs (eg English V6 Capri), so if the standard cam is being retained, or if a sports cam is being fitted, at the very least the push-in studs should be pinned. When screw-in studs are being fitted, seal them with gasket sealant to prevent water seepage if they break into the water jacket.

If possible, 3/8in rocker studs should be replaced with 7/16in studs, to improve rigidity. A rocker stud girdle is also a good investment as these brace all the rocker studs against each other. This reduces the load on each stud and consequently the amount of flex, as all studs share the load when a valve is opened. With canted valve heads it is not always possible to brace all the studs together using a single girdle, but generally two studs can be girdled together for load sharing. Some girdles use a single brace bar with 'U' bolts clamping the bar to each stud. This type does a reasonable job but I prefer a double brace bar girdle for added rigidity. With proper setting up, it is possible to make push-rod-type valve gear almost as rigid as single ohc valve gear employing rockers.

Generally, rocker arms have a ratio of 1.2–1.7:1. This means that rocker arms with a 1.5:1 ratio will lift the valve a theoretical 0.600in if the cam lift is 0.400in. Many racers get carried away by fitting rocker arms of a higher ratio than standard to increase maximum valve lift. This is not the purpose of the exercise at all. What we are after is to lift the valve off its seat faster in the initial stages of opening, to improve mixture flow and cylinder filling. The actual increase in maximum lift is of little consequence except to cause us more problems with valve spring coil bind, valve-to-piston clearance, etc.

High-ratio arms are different from their standard counterparts by having a shorter distance from the push rod centre to the rocker stud (or shaft). The distance between the rocker stud (or shaft) and the valve stem is fixed (unless the rocker studs are re-positioned or offset studs are fitted), so the only way that the rocker ratio can be increased is by decreasing the rocker arm length on the push rod side. For this reason, possibly the guide slots in the push rod guide plates, and also the holes in the rev kit bar, will require elongation to prevent push rod fouling.

Before fitting high-ratio rocker arms, check with your cam grinder regarding the changes that will have to be made in the valve train. Remember that the velocity and acceleration characteristics of the cam are being changed when the rocker arm ratio is changed, so will the cam, tappets and valve springs be able to handle the extra forces being imposed on them? Too many tuners, and cam grinders as well for that matter, feel that you can just go ahead and use any rocker arm ratio you wish. If this were the case, life would indeed be much easier. Unfortunately, modern-day camshaft profiles are often not designed for a specific engine with a specific valve train, so rocker arm ratio can be varied without major problems, but check with the cam grinder first. If all cams were designed as an integral part of one specific motor, with a certain specific amount of valve train flex, as they should be, a change in rocker arm ratio could mean something as drastic as a cam change as well.

Think carefully before changing standard rockers for high-ratio rockers. If you do not need more low-end and mid-range power, you will be wasting your time fitting them. Most performance cams give ample total valve lift without having to worry about fiddling with rocker ratios. If your valve train is already marginal in the reliability department, a change to high-ratio rockers will worsen the problem, so be careful.

VALVE SPRINGS

The valve springs have the unenviable task of keeping the whole act together and functioning smoothly. Therefore the cam grinder should be able to give you all the information you need to make that camshaft operate as designed in your engine. This must, of course, include the following vital details: recommended valve spring, installed height and on-seat pressure, and full lift pressure. Also a recommended safe rpm limit should be stated for a valve train correctly set-up.

Valve spring selection is especially critical in engines with aggressive cam lobe shapes, heavy valves and valve train components, running at high rpm for long periods. This basically means all large push rod race engines and endurance race engines without air restrictors. Buy the best quality springs you can find. They will be expensive because the purest, cleanest steel such as is produced by Kobe Steel (Kobe, Japan), and special drawing dies and winding techniques, along with precise heat treatments and shot peening, and many inspections during each phase of manufacture, doesn't come cheap. I prefer to source springs from suppliers with a consistently good product like Schmitthelm or Kurt Kauffmann, or in more recent times also Endura-Tech.

Regardless of where you source your springs, if you are competing in a tough environment such as described above, be prepared to devote a lot of time to carefully sorting through each new batch, weeding out those that aren't up to spec, and then properly finishing those that pass. First off inspect the wire for nicks, scratches, indentations, or deformity under a 4X magnifier. Next measure the height and spring rate. Then check for squareness by determining that the spring stands straight when placed on a flat plate – check this from both ends. All springs that pass these inspections should now be polished on both ends. You don't want any sharp edges anywhere on the spring that could lead to breakage, and you don't want any sharp ends nicking or wearing into the next coil as the spring compresses. Likewise you don't want sharp edges cutting into the spring retainers or spring seat.

Valve springs have to be heavy enough to keep the tappet in constant contact with the cam lobe and allow a possible over-rev from a missed gear change, yet also be light enough not to cause excessive cam and lifter wear and valve train flex, or rob us of power.

Valve spring surge can lead to erratic valve spring behaviour at certain rpm, caused by vibrations set up in the valve train. These vibrations excite the natural frequency characteristics of the spring, and when this happens a surge reduces the available valve spring tension, its force opposing the valve spring tension. This can lead to the tappet losing contact with the cam lobe, the possible end result being valve float, valve to piston contact and increased valve train wear.

To help overcome the problem, spring manufacturers have used several approaches to dampen surge. One takes the form of a damper coil of flat spring steel, which dampens by friction through contact with the inside of the coil spring. Another is the use of counter-wound inner springs, with coils wound in the opposite direction from the outer springs. Variable-pitch coil springs with a progressively smaller spacing between coils towards the bottom of the spring have also proved successful. Possibly the most common approach, in production engines at any rate, is to close up completely the coils at the bottom of the spring, and also sometimes at the top.

A more recent approach has been the adoption of beehive-shape springs in some applications that can get by with a single spring. GM used this type in the 5.7ltr V8 Chev LS1 released in 1996 and it is being used in NASCAR restrictor plate engines. The design has a number of advantages over the conventional shape valve spring. First, its reduced diameter at the top allows the use of a smaller and thus lighter, by about 5gm, valve spring retainer. Secondly, because this reduced diameter at the top cuts the amount of leverage trying to bend the valve stem, valves with a thinner stem – to improve air flow and reduce valve train weight – or lighter valves with a hollow stem can be fitted. Thirdly, it allows a spring pressure reduction at full lift of around 10%–20% without any reduction in safe engine speed and an on-seat pressure decrease of 15%–25%; cutting both parasitic losses due to friction, and valve seat wear. This is possible because of the beehive spring's superior harmonics. Each coil increases in diameter when compared with the coil above, so each coil has a different natural frequency which helps dampen spring surge.

Beehive-shaped valve springs help reduce spring harmonics and enable lighter springs to be used.

The natural frequency of the valve spring should be five times that of the engine rpm. Therefore if the engine speed is 7,500rpm the valve springs should have a natural frequency of around 37,500 cycles per minute. Interestingly, reducing the number of working coils (ie those not wound so close as to touch together) increases the natural frequency of the valve spring. This has another benefit to the racing spring manufacturer in that the reduction in working coils will also reduce the solid stack height of the spring. Therefore the spring can be compressed further before coil bind occurs.

Another development has been the use of ovate rather than round wire in the manufacture of springs. In cross-section such wire has a shape similar to a chicken egg. This means it has greater surface area, and thus greater strength than conventional round wire of the same thickness. Also the added surface area allows heat to be dissipated more easily, increasing spring durability and life. Round wire with the same spring characteristics would result in a valve spring that was heavier and taller. Then to stop coil bind a longer heavier valve may be required if the valve spring seats could not be cut deeper.

CHECKING FOR VALVE SPRING COIL BIND

Just how much clearance should there be between working coils at full valve lift? That depends on the spring design, but I always work to a minimum of 0.008in between working coils, although I like to aim for 0.010–0.012in. Some spring manufacturers specify figures as low as 0.005in and as high as 0.020in. If they specify a figure higher than my recommendation, follow their instructions. This safe working clearance between coils must always be maintained, otherwise the valve spring will stack solid with disastrous consequences.

Simply providing a safe working clearance between coils doesn't guarantee that the spring is performing at its best; nor does following the spring manufacturer's minimum installed height figure. What is the best installed height for that particular cam lobe, valve train and spring combination, from the aspects of spring life and engine performance, can only be assessed from extensive Spintron testing.

Because of an increase in valve lift, many heads will require modification to prevent coil-binding when a high-lift cam is installed. Others may not require the valve spring seat to be deepened but may require the valve guides to be slimmed down to permit the installation of inner springs. Either operation can be performed with a counterboring tool of the appropriate dimensions. To determine how much deeper the spring seats must be machined (if at all), it will be necessary to fit the valve and valve spring retainer and locks. Pull the retainer up tight and measure the distance between the spring seat and bottom face of the retainer. If the measurement is less than the valve-open or installed spring height specified by the cam grinder, it will be necessary to deepen the seat. This must be repeated for each valve, and repeated each time the valves are replaced or re-faced, or if the valve seats are re-cut.

If the valve springs are set up at the on-seat height specified (and they should be otherwise your full lift spring pressures will be all over the place, possibly allowing valve float), you should not have any problems maintaining the correct clearance between coils. However, check the clearance at full lift, using a feeler gauge to be sure, and do not forget to check the inner springs.

333

Pneumatic valve control

This term is quite a misnomer, for it seems to infer that rather than being controlled by a cam lobe the valves are being blasted open by compressed air, which is perhaps activated by a computer. That would be nice – infinitely variable cam timing providing just the ideal phasing, duration, lift and opening and closing rate to suit every engine speed. The reality is, in fact, much more basic.

For years now the bane of race engine builders have been valve springs and pistons. Both of these components are responsible for the majority of race engine failures, and many engines that do finish are running quite ragged and are way down on power due to valve springs that have weakened and lost tension. Additionally, we seem to be nearing the limit for naturally aspirated engines with bmeps (brake mean effective pressures) now around 240psi, so the only way more power is attainable is to raise engine speeds, but valve springs are blocking this path.

Enter pneumatic valve control, pioneered by Renault Sport under the direction of Jean-Pierre Boudy. In the early 1980s Boudy saw progress with Renault's 1.5-litre V6 Turbo Formula 1 engine being stymied by valve springs. Then, during 1986, they sat a car on the start grid without any valve springs. Six years later the Honda F1 engine also raced without valve springs, later followed by Cosworth, Ferrari, Yamaha and Ilmor (Mercedes). Since that time cars like the Mercedes running in the International Touring Car (ITC) Championship have also adopted pneumatic valve control systems, even though the 2.5-litre V6 engines are rev-limited to 12,000rpm. Obviously to be employed at these lower engine speeds (compared to F1 at 19,000rpm and CART Toyotas, Hondas and Cosworths at 17,000rpm, which are required to run valve springs) this expensive system must be permitting the use of some pretty impressive (radical?) cam lobe profiles, which would otherwise lead to valve train failure if valve springs were used.

Referring back to Figure 10.9, you can see how simply an ordinary purpose-built race engine valve train operates. The cam lobe runs directly on to an inverted bucket tappet with a clearance-adjusting shim between the tappet and valve stem. The valve spring holds the valve closed and, as the cam rotates, forces the tappet to maintain contact with the lobe. In the pneumatic system the valve springs are discarded and the valve is held closed by air or nitrogen compressed to relatively high pressures: the Cosworth system is at 14 bar (206psi); the Honda system runs at 6–8 bar; the Mercedes F1 at 8 bar; and the ITC at 9 bar. To maintain that pressure the tappet has been modified and has a seal much like a piston ring, which bears against the tappet bore as the tappet moves up and down to open and close the valve. The valve guide also carries a seal to prevent the compressed gas escaping down the valve stem. Obviously there is some leakage, so the system is topped up from a small pressure reservoir of about 0.5-litre volume. This canister contains gas at a pressure of 150–200 bar, and in turn may be topped up by a small pump.

Apart from obviating worries about weak or broken valve springs, the system allows for more accurate valve timing, with the follower faithfully tracking the cam lobe. With no spring surge the equivalent of soft valve spring pressures can be run, which reduces valve train wear, and also valve and valve seat wear.

On overhead cam motors using bucket-type cam followers it is not possible to check for coil bind by using a feeler gauge between the coils. What you must do in this instance is to count the number of working coils and multiply that by the required clearance between each coil. If this works out to be, say, 0.036in, insert a feeler gauge of this thickness between the cam lobe and follower and turn the cam over to full lift. The cam may lock up before full lift, which would indicate insufficient working clearance. To rectify this, the valve spring seat will have to be machined deeper. Just how much the seat will have to be machined can be found by inserting progressively thinner feeler blades until the cam will turn freely. If the cam turns with a 0.023in blade inserted, this means that the spring seat must be deepened by 0.036–0.023in = 0.013in. This procedure should be repeated for each valve spring.

While we are on the subject of bucket tappets, there is another very important clearance check that must be made. When high-lift cams are installed, it is possible for the tappet to run out of travel and bang into the head. To check for sufficient travel it will be necessary to fit just the cams and tappets to the head (leaving out the valves and springs). Turn the cam over by hand until you have a lobe in the full lift position and see if you can fit 0.060in of feeler strips between the nose of the cam lobe and the face of the cam follower; carry out this check on every tappet. If you can fit only 0.052in of feeler strips, you will need to remove 0.008in from the lower edge of the tappet; up to 0.015in can be removed, but if that is insufficient it is better to machine the head. Put a nice radius on the lower edge of the bucket after any machining is done.

VALVE SPRING PRESSURES

Remember that valve springs wear out. High rpm and excessive heat accelerate this natural fatigue process. We can't do much about high rpm, but we can spray the springs with a constant flow of oil to transport some heat away. On a competition motor this ageing process may cause the spring to break or it may lose tension and become weaker. If you are a racer, check the spring tension each time the head is removed. The pressure at the on-seat and full-open lengths should check out within a few pounds of new springs. If any are not up to specification they should all be replaced.

Many people are rather mystified by any reference to 'spring rate', so it might help to explain just what it is and how we work it out. Firstly, spring rate is defined as

Valve spring cooling is critical in endurance race engines and those operating big valves at high rpm. The simple solution is to locate an oil spray bar in the rocker cover to spray each spring, but this path adds weight and complexity with external oil pipes to each rocker cover. A better approach is to have an oil gallery in the rocker bed with a series of screw-in jets to meter oil onto each spring.

the amount of build-up in pressure when the spring is compressed. For example, if we had a spring with an on-seat pressure of 100lbs @ 1.625in, and a full lift pressure of 300lbs @ 1.125in, it would have a spring rate of 400lb per in, which would mean that we would require a load of 400lb to compress the spring 1 inch. In the above example, compressing the spring 0.5in (1.625 to 1.125in) resulted in the spring pressure increasing from 100lb to 300lb, an increase of 200lb. Therefore compressing the spring 1 inch would require a load of 400lb.

This should help you to appreciate the need to set up valve springs at the precise specified height. If the springs in the case quoted were set too high, the on-seat pressure might be reduced to, say, 70lb, so the full lift pressure would now be 270lb, or 10% less than it should have been. In terms of rpm reduction, if the valve float rpm with correctly installed springs was 7,500rpm, this would reduce it to 7,115rpm.

$$\sqrt{\frac{270}{300}} \times 7{,}500 = 7{,}115 \text{rpm}$$

When the on-seat height is more than specified, shims of the appropriate thickness must be installed under the valve spring, to compress the spring to the correct height. A superior method of achieving the required spring height is to use collets with locating tabs in three different positions: stock, +0.050in, −0.050in. The valve cap can then be raised or lowered by fitting the appropriate collets.

Sometimes it is possible, and desirable, to increase the rpm at which valve float will occur. Providing that the valve train and camshaft are capable of running a higher speed (check with your cam grinder), stronger valve springs will have to be installed. To find the required full lift pressure of the new springs, use the following formula:

$$NP = \frac{Nrpm^2 \times P}{rpm}$$

where NP = the new valve spring pressure required, P = the present valve spring pressure at full lift, Nrpm = new valve float rpm, and rpm = the present valve float rpm.

A decrease in effective valve train weight will also increase the valve float rpm limit. We can bring about this decrease by using light-weight, high-strength push rods, by tappet lightening, and by fitting light rocker arms or lightening the original rocker arms. Remember, however, that a decrease in rocker arm weight close to the pivot point does not effectively decrease the valve train weight. The intake and exhaust valves are also effectively lightened when modified to improve flow. However, using a titanium–aluminium–vanadium alloy allows us to lose 35% of the valve's weight. A cheaper alternative for exhaust valves is to use hollow-stem austenitic stainless steel items, which are around 20% lighter than their solid-stem counterparts. An effective decrease of 10% would increase the valve float rpm by the factor

$$\sqrt{\frac{100}{90}} = 1.054$$

Therefore if the old valve float speed was 7,500rpm, the new speed will be 7,500 x 1.054 = 7,900.

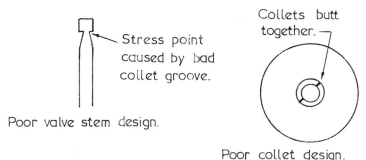

Figure 10.11 Bad valve and collet designs.

VALVE SPRING RETAINERS

Valve spring retainers and collets (or valve stem locks) require attention to maintain reliability. A valve stem and collet design that is to be avoided is that used in many Austin engines (Figure 10.11). This design is very bad, as the stress concentration at the square shoulder of the collet groove is sure to cause failure. Another problem design is that where the two collets actually butt together and allow the valve stem to lie loosely and float in the centre. This is done to allow the valve more freedom to rotate and clean the valve seat. What has to be done is to grind off the faces of the collets so that they clamp tightly on to the valve stem. When fitted, there must be a gap between both halves of the collet for this to be possible.

Standard spring retainers and stem locks will do a good job, but for ultimate reliability and a saving in weight, special pieces should be fitted. Titanium alloy retainers are the lightest/strongest available, while steel retainers of heat-treated 4140 bar stock are the next best, but heavier. I do not like aluminium retainers, and consequently do not recommend their use except in relatively unstressed conditions.

The next check that must be made is for interference between the bottom of the valve spring retainer and the top of the valve guide, in the simulated full valve lift condition. There must be at least 0.060in clearance at full lift, but I always aim for 0.100in. This clearance check can be done very easily without the heads being fitted to the motor. All that must be done is to set up a telescopic gauge or a snap gauge at the full open valve spring height, then fit the retainers to each valve and check out the

Figure 10.12 High lift cams can cause the valve spring retainer to hit the valve guide at full lift. The minimum clearance required is 0.060in.

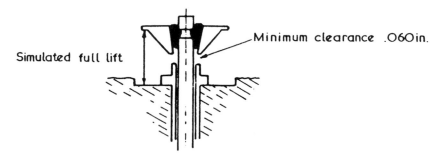

Dropped valves can result when valve stem locks butt together like this.

clearance between the retainer and valve guide when the snap gauge is fitted in between the retainer and valve spring seat. If there is less than 0.060in clearance, metal will have to be machined from the valve guide. (Figure 10.12)

CAM DRIVE ARRANGEMENTS

Returning to the camshaft, we require some accurate and reliable means of driving it. Several methods are in use, but none are without their problems. For many years cams have been driven by single-row chains. These have proved themselves reliable in very-high-speed racing engines, with open-valve spring pressures of 250lb, but chain and sprocket wear is a problem at high engine speeds. Double-row chains are more up to the job and can successfully handle open-valve spring pressures of around 420lb in excess of 8,000rpm. Note that we are talking about quality roller chains and steel sprockets, not the silent Morse chain running on fibre or nylon tooth sprockets. With a new chain and sprockets installed, the valve gear will normally retard the cam by $^{1}/_{2}$–1°, and as wear takes its toll this retarding will increase. Therefore chain-drive cams should be advanced in the initial set-up to compensate for this.

The toothed rubber belt also seems to be up to the task, having been Renault's choice for their 1.5ltr turbo Formula 1 engine running in excess of 11,000rpm almost 30 years ago. In more recent times many push rod American V8s in competition have converted to belt drive to provide more accurate valve and spark timing as a belt more effectively isolates crankshaft harmonics from the camshaft. However toothed belts are not completely problem free. First you need to be careful never to turn the engine over backwards or the belt may slip, altering the valve and maybe also the ignition timing. Worse, the valve timing can be so far off as to cause valve to piston contact, and also valve to valve contact in twin cam engines. Also when belts fail bad things happen inside the engine. With mild cam profiles the manufacturer's stock belt and normal replacement interval usually can be followed without problems. However, it is always smart to check with your cam grinder to be sure, and be careful to use a good quality belt from a reputable manufacturer like Gates. If a heavy duty belt is available it is wise to fit that. Remember too that the factory gets it wrong at times. Lancia recommended belt replacement on the Intergrale four-valve at 100,000km intervals, but many broke belts at only half that distance with standard cams – wrecking the head and valves, and pistons too at times. When fitting the belt be careful not to kink it, and if reusing the belt ensure that it will rotate in the same direction as when first fitted. To avoid this problem I always fit belts in such a way that when facing cylinder No.1 any lettering on the belt is correctly orientated. Stretch will also allow cam retarding with this type of drive, so allowances must be made when setting up the cam.

In some ways gear drive is the ideal system, but there are many complications. Align-boring (or tunnel-boring) the block will allow the crank gear to mesh tighter, so some system to adjust backlash and meshing depth must be provided. If you had the job of setting the gear mesh on a Formula 1 engine you certainly would not consider gear drive to be the ideal set-up. If you change from chain drive to gear drive, and use the simple two-gear system, it will be necessary to install a reverse-ground cam as it will now be turning backwards. A reverse distributor gear will also be required, to keep that component turning the correct way. However, in spite of all this, gear drive is the best set-up for a competition motor.

Many motors use gears in standard production form, but generally these are useless, and are not capable of reliable service, even if only a sports cam is fitted. Production-type gears are designed with silent operation in mind, so are made of such material as compressed fibre, or nylon-coated steel and aluminium. If you intend to

A toothed timing belt can provide reliable service only if handled and fitted properly, and is replaced at the intervals specified by the cam manufacturer.

Steel or alloy gears provide reliable drive to the cam.

extract any type of performance at all out of an engine with gear materials such as these, you are in for trouble. The only way around the problem is to use quality steel gears.

Remember accurate ignition timing and performance also has its beginning with a good cam drive arrangement that will keep the spark in step with piston motion. This is one reason why some ignition systems now work directly off the crankshaft and others use sensor-trigger magnets attached to the flywheel or harmonic balancer. As well as driving the distributor or magneto, the cam may also look after the chores of supplying drive for the oil pump and fuel pump, as well as mechanical fuel injection, if fitted.

CAM FITTING AND RUNNING-IN

Now that we have covered the theory of the camshaft and valve train, let us get down to the actual camshaft installation. At this stage we will assume that you have already read the chapter on block preparation and the cam is ready to drop in (if the motor has an overhead cam the same information covered in block preparation will apply, but in this instance to the head). You will note that the cam possibly has a black coating; this should not be removed except from the bearing journals. Freshly ground steel does not have any oil retention ability, and as lubrication of the high-performance cam is of the utmost importance during the first few minutes of engine operation when running in the cam, we give the cam a special treatment and coating. I also treat the tappet faces in the same way. This treatment is called Lubriting, Parkerising or Parko-Lubriting. Actually the last name best describes the treatment, albeit the reverse of the way in which we actually apply it. The cam bearing journals are taped and the cam is plunged into a high-temperature bath of phosphoric acid, which etches open the pores of the cam so that it may retain oil more effectively. This is the Lubriting part of the process. Next the cam receives a phosphate coating to aid the breaking-in process.

To assist lubrication even further, always coat the cams and lifters with a mixture of high-pressure Hypoid 90/140 gear oil and molydisulphide; alternatively, if the engine will be running on castor oil I use Castrol R40, as castor oil must not be contaminated by mineral or synthetic oils. The first 10–15 minutes is the critical running-in period, and during this time engine speed should be maintained at 2,000–2,500rpm, to ensure adequate oil flow to the cam and lifters. Some engines, notably the push rod and ohc Cortina/Pinto, require special care, and in their case high-performance cams should be run-in for around 25–30 minutes, and racing cams for 40–45 minutes. After this, the racing cam should be given more treatment, a 4,000–5,000rpm run for 10–15 minutes, but taking care not to let the engine overheat.

After the cam has been slid into place, fit the thrust plate (or thrust washers) and measure the end float. This should be 0.002in; more than 0.005in is unacceptable. If we do not control 'cam walk' within fine limits, we can upset the whole valve train. Remember that flat tappet cams have the lobes ground at an angle, which tends to push (or thrust) the camshaft as the lobes open and close the valves. This thrusting backwards and forwards also has a bad influence on the ignition timing, as the distributor is usually driven off the camshaft. When mushroom tappets are used, there is the possible problem of the tappets overlapping two cam lobes if cam walk is not precisely controlled.

SPLIT, ADVANCED AND RETARDED TIMING

The next thing we must do is to time the cam so that the opening and closing of the valves is in a special 'tuned' relationship with the up-and-down motion of the pistons. Unfortunately, many feel it is sufficient to line up the timing marks and leave the valve timing at that. With a sports cam that may be so, but you will not be able to achieve optimum performance. Due to manufacturing tolerances the cam may be several degrees advanced or retarded. This may be the result of timing marks, keyways or dowels being out, or in ohc designs could be due to surface grinding of either the head or block. Additionally the cam lobes can also be out in relation to the cam dowel or keyway due to grinding error.

Something else that must be taken into consideration is that even if the cam timing was spot-on according to the manufacturer's figures just by lining up the timing marks, would that necessarily be the best position for the cam for optimum overall performance? Figure 10.13 illustrates three timing diagrams that represent one complete cycle (two revolutions, or 720°) of the engine. The first diagram indicates that the cam has symmetric (or split) timing of 30°–70°/70°–30°. You will also note that the inlet valve is fully open (maximum lift) at 110° after TDC, and that the exhaust valve is fully open 110° before TDC. The second diagram shows that the cam has been advanced 6° from the manufacturer's recommendation to produce a timing of 36°–64°/76°–24°, with full lift occurring at the inlet 104° after TDC and at the exhaust 116° before TDC. In the third diagram the cam has been retarded 4°, with a timing of 26°–74°/66°–34°. Maximum lift will now be at 114° after TDC at the inlet and 106° before TDC at the exhaust valve.

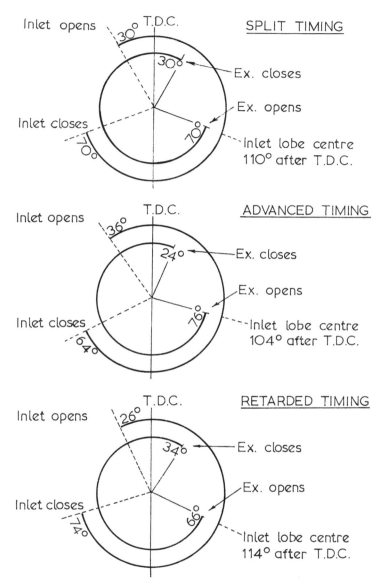

Figure 10.13 Camshaft timing diagrams.

You will note that in each instance the duration has remained 280°, the overlap 60°, and the lobe centres 220° apart. This being the case you are probably wondering why bother 'tuning' the cam timing if duration, overlap, lift and lobe centres stay the same? If you think about it, of course these figures must stay the same – we are not altering the physical shape of the cam. All we are doing is changing its position in relation to the crankshaft. There is an exception to this, and that is in the case of twin overhead cams, where we may advance the inlet cam, say, 5°, and advance the exhaust cam 9°, but more on that later.

342　　Basically, advancing the cam will improve bottom-end and mid-range power, while retarding it will decrease bottom-end and mid-range power but may very slightly increase the top end. Around 2° advance will have very little effect, but from 4° to 8° it will show a marked improvement in mid-range power, perhaps with some decrease in maximum power. The improvement in the mid-range comes about as a result of a decrease in the reverse pumping action, which raises cylinder pressure. Because the inlet valve is being closed earlier, there is less mixture being pushed back up the inlet port as the piston moves up. As the exhaust valve is also being closed earlier, there is less chance of the exhaust gas turning around and being drawn back into the cylinder as the piston descends. Generally, I prefer to run all road and rally engines with the cam 4° or 5° advanced. For track work, it depends on the nature of the engine. If it is an unrestricted engine I usually run 3–4° advance, but for small-carb restricted, or 9:1 engines 6–8° advance is typical.

I never advise cutting back on cam advance except in one circumstance, and that is when the machine is losing traction because of excessive torque in the low or mid-range. This will usually apply only to drag strip or speedway vehicles. On the strip, too much low-end may cause excessive wheelspin or rear-end location problems, while at the speedway an excess of power at a particular engine speed may be causing traction problems on the exit from a specific turn. Taking off 4 or 5° advance should help with either annoyance.

VALVE FOULING IN TWIN-CAM ENGINES

With twin-cam engines we have much more scope when it comes to cam tuning. Not only can we advance or retard both cams by the same angle relative to crankshaft rotation, but we can also alter the lobe separation angle between the inlet and exhaust cams without having to go back to our cam grinder and pay money for another cam. We can choose one lobe profile for the inlet cam and a different lobe for the exhaust cam. In fact, we may decide on an exhaust cam from one cam grinder and an inlet from another. However, caution is necessary to avoid valve-to-valve fouling during the overlap period, especially with the more radical race grinds.

When you start jiggling twin-cam timing, keep in mind the need to maintain a minimum of 0.060in clearance between the inlet and exhaust valves. I check this by drawing up the cam displacement curves for both the inlet and exhaust cams. But remember when you draw up the curves that the angles (see Table 10.5) for each 0.010in lift will all have to be multiplied by two, as the camshaft is turning at half the speed of the crankshaft. Therefore for each revolution (360°) the camshaft turns, the crankshaft turns twice (720°). As we set the cam up in relation to the crankshaft, we now have to know what its valve lift is relative to degrees of crankshaft rotation.

To save time I draw both curves on separate pieces of transparent drafting film, to the same scale. This way I can lay the curves over each other according to whatever lobe centre position I wish to check. To keep things accurate, a third piece of paper is required as a reference or standard, and this piece is placed under the two displacement curves. The reference paper will have just three vertical lines on it. The centre will indicate TDC, the first line will indicate the exhaust lobe centre (full lift position), and the third line will show the inlet lobe centre. These lines will be to the same horizontal scale as that of the displacement curve. The lobe centre (full lift)

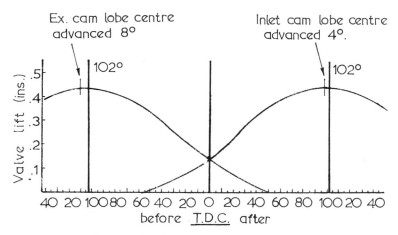

Figure 10.14 Valve interference checking curves.

positions will be marked in accordance with the cam timing figures given by the cam grinder (Figure 10.14).

If the cam grinder has given a lobe centre figure of 102°, this means that the cams should be set up such that the inlet valve is at full lift 102° after TDC and the exhaust valve is at full lift 102° before TDC. However, if no lobe centre angle is stated, you will have to work it out from the timing figures. Let us say that the timing is 53°–77°/82°–58° for the inlet and exhaust. This would mean that the cam had an inlet duration of 53° + 180° + 77° = 310°, and an exhaust duration of 82° + 58° + 180° = 320°. Therefore the lobe centres of the inlet and exhaust have to be 155° (310° ÷ 2) and 160° (320° ÷ 2) respectively after the opening point of each valve. If we subtract the inlet opening angle of 53° from 155°, we find that the full lift (or lobe centre) position will be 102° after TDC. For the exhaust we subtract the closing angle, 58°, from 160°, and find the exhaust lobe centre to be 102° before TDC.

Now that you know the lobe centre angles, draw these in as reference lines before and after the TDC line. If you decide to advance the exhaust cam 8°, lay the exhaust displacement curve on the reference sheet with the peak of the curve (the lobe centre) 8° before the exhaust reference line. Similarly, if the inlet is being advanced 4°, lay the inlet curve with the peak 4° ahead of the inlet reference line. It is only by moving the displacement curves around in relation to the reference lines that the next part of the operation can be accurate.

Looking at the curves it is obvious that the valves will come close to fouling during the overlap period, so what we have to do is make up a list to show us what the inlet and exhaust valve lift will be for each 2.5°. It is not necessary to record the lift over the entire overlap period; usually 30° on either side of the intersection point of the lift curves is enough. Once the list is made up, it is necessary physically to measure the clearance between the valves. If at, say, 10° after TDC the inlet valve has a lift of 0.180in, and the exhaust a lift of 0.156in at the same angle, accurately set the valves up in the head at those measurements and measure the clearance. As you can see, this involves quite a deal of work, but if you are after that last bit of power and you do not want a wrecked motor, it is a must. If it is an engine type you do a lot of work with you can skip a lot of this hassle by sacrificing an engine block and slicing off the rear cylinder. Then with the head fitted you can fairly easily get into the combustion chamber to physically measure valve head clearances with the cams timed to a variety of lobe centre angles. If you have a lot of faith in computer software you can also simulate this sort of thing, but I sleep a lot easier when I can actually measure things.

The procedure just outlined to check twin-cam engines for valve fouling can also be used if you are running a push rod canted-valve motor and you wish to increase the rocker arm ratio. Normally, the cam grinder should be able to tell you if you can use that particular cam with, say, 1.65:1 ratio arms instead of the standard 1.5:1 arms, without risk of the valves coming too close together. However, if he is not able to advise you on this, it will be necessary to work it all out as for a twin cam.

HOW TO TIME THE CAM

Now that you know why we advance or retard the cam, you are in a good position to set up your cam just where you want it. With the cam fitted, and the timing marks lined up, the next step is to see where the cam is in relation to the crankshaft. In other words, is it advanced or retarded? To check this you will need a degree wheel (8in is a good size) or a 360° protractor bolted to the nose of the crank. You will also need a dial gauge to measure the cam lift. You should fix a good solid pointer under a convenient bolt to lap over the face of the degree wheel.

The first thing we must do is accurately to find TDC, and for this we need another piece of equipment, a positive stop. If you are finding TDC with the heads fitted, the best positive stop is an old spark plug with the insulator removed and a piece of steel rod welded in so that it projects past the thread far enough to stop the piston reaching TDC.

An easier way to find TDC is when the head is removed. Then we merely need a piece of steel fixed across the top of the bore to prevent the piston reaching TDC. If the piston does not project out of the top of the bore at TDC it will be necessary to fit a bolt in the middle of the positive stop bar.

With the positive stop fitted, rotate the crank as far as it will go, taking care not to damage the piston as it contacts the stop. Take a note of the angle indicated by the pointer, and turn the crank in the opposite direction until it stops. Halfway between the two stop angles is TDC, so remove the positive stop and rotate the crank to TDC – the halfway point. Now very carefully loosen the degree wheel and turn it around to align the zero mark with the pointer, and lock it in place. To double-check, refit the positive stop and rotate the crank in both directions as before. When the degree wheel is in the correct position, the number of degrees before and after TDC will be identical when the crank stops.

After TDC is found, you can go ahead and check the cam phasing. It is a waste of time trying to set up a cam according to the cam grinder's timing figures. The best way is work out the full lift (or lobe centre) angle and see at what angle you are reaching full lift. If, for instance, the cam had a full lift angle of 110° after TDC, but maximum lift was occurring at 104° after TDC, it would mean that the cam in that position is advanced 6°.

The cam grinder may supply you with checking (or degreeing) timing figures for 0.050in lift. The cam timing may be 60°–88°/96°–52° and the timing at 0.050in lift 41°–69°/77°–33°. Set up the dial gauge on the lifter or push rod (not the rocker) and   345 record the angles for 0.050in lift. Your cam may check out 40°–70°/76°–34°, meaning it is retarded 1°.

Having determined where the cam is, you may decide to change its phasing, to tune it to your engine. The next problem is just how to do it. With some motors this is easy as they have vernier timing wheels (eg Jaguar and Alfa-Romeo) or taper fit wheels (Ford BDA). The majority, however, use either dowels or keys to locate the cam or crank sprocket positively.

Dowelled drives will need offset dowels fitted and, if more than a central bolt fixes the sprocket to the cam, the bolt holes will require elongation with a round file. The amount of offset required is minute. For example, with the push rod British Fords and Lotus Twin Cam, 0.006in offset (at the cam) represents 1° at the crank, so to change the cam position by 6° (at the crank) requires a dowel with 0.036in offset. Instead of supplying offset dowels, some cam manufacturers have a range of offset bushes that are fitted to the cam sprocket. Others are able to supply slotted cam sprockets, and many V8s have a range of crank drive sprockets available cut with three or more keyways to change the cam phasing.

If there is nothing available for your particular engine, you will have to make up the appropriate hardware. Keep in mind that the dowel or key does not require hardening in most instances as it does not actually transmit the driving force, which is taken by the friction between the sprocket and shaft (key-located) or by pressure between the sprocket and cam created by the fixing bolts (dowel-located). Incidently, these fixing bolts should be locked using Loctite.

It can be difficult to figure out just which way to move a cam and by how much to advance or retard it. To advance the cam in relation to the gear or sprocket attached to it we have to move the camshaft further forward in the same direction of rotation as illustrated in Figure 10.15. Conversely to retard the cam we move it backward in the opposite direction to the normal rotation of the cam timing gear.

Because the cam turns at half engine speed, it only moves through half the number of degrees relative to the crankshaft. Hence if the cam timing is retarded 6°

This crank timing sprocket has multiple keyways to simplify cam timing changes.

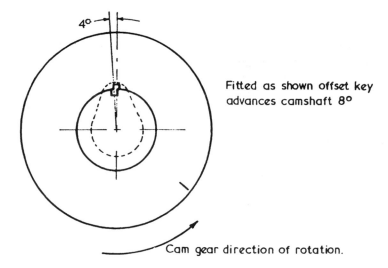

Fitted as shown offset key
advances camshaft 8°

4°

Cam gear direction of rotation.

Figure 10.15 To advance the cam it is moved forward relative to the cam gear's direction of rotation.

from what we want, then the cam must be advanced 6° measured at the crank, or only half that, 3°, at the camshaft. Therefore if we plan on making the adjustment at the cam and cam timing gear a 3° offset key/dowel will be used.

To calculate just how much the key or dowel must be offset to move the cam 3°, we need to accurately measure the radius between the cam centre and the centre of the key or dowel. Let's assume it measures 0.594in, which means that in one full rotation of 360° the key will move around in a circle with a radius of 0.594in and a circumference of 3.732in (2 x π x 0.594 = 3.732). Therefore to move the cam forward 3° within the timing gear the key must be offset 0.031in (3.732 x 3 ÷ 360 = 0.031),

Figure 10.16 When the valve timing is advanced at the crank timing gear, the gear has to be moved forward on the crank nose in the direction of normal engine rotation.

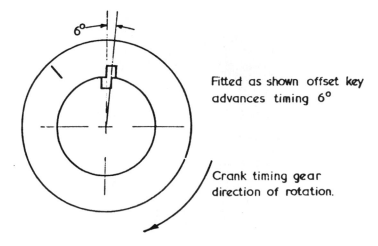

Fitted as shown offset key
advances timing 6°

6°

Crank timing gear
direction of rotation.

which will advance the cam 6° when measured on a degree wheel bolted to the crankshaft.

If the timing change is to be made by moving the gear fitted to the crankshaft the procedure is different. To advance the cam the crank timing sprocket has to be moved forward on the crank nose relative to the normal direction of engine rotation (Figure 10.16). To retard the timing move it backward. The amount the key has to be offset is calculated in exactly the same way as previously, but the offset has to be the full number of degrees, in this example 6°.

With ohc and twin-cam engines I prefer not to use slotted cam pulleys. I find it a hassle setting up a dial gauge and degree wheel when all I want to do is make a simple cam adjustment to see how the engine responds. Some tuners mark the inner and outer ring of slotted pulleys, but unless the cam is being moved something like 6–10° (measured at the crankshaft) this is very inaccurate and not good for repeatability during test sessions. To get around this problem I use multi-hole cam pulleys. If I have a pulley with eight holes each 'plus 1°' apart, once I have initially set the lobe centres using a dial gauge I know that moving the cam forward one hole will advance the cam 2°; likewise moving the cam back one hole will retard it 2°. So when the engine is assembled the cam pulley is positioned to give, say, 4° advance using the dial gauge and degree wheel. Later, during a dyno session, moving the cam forward one hole in the pulley gives exactly 6° advance. Conversely swinging the cam back one hole will retard the cam 2°. However, as it was initially set up 4° advanced, it is in reality 2° advanced.

It is quite simple to calculate where the dowel holes or keyways should be machined. If, for example, the pulley has 40 teeth, this means that each tooth, from centre to centre, is 9° apart (360 ÷ 40 = 9). The first dowel hole, the index hole, should be centred directly under the centre of a tooth. The next hole centre will be 5 teeth + 1°, or 46° clockwise from the index hole ([9 x 5] + 1 = 46). The third will be at 10 teeth + 2°, or 92°, the fourth at 15 teeth + 3°, or 138°, followed by the fifth, sixth, seventh and eighth at 184°, 230°, 276° and 322° respectively. Obviously a machine shop carrying out this work must be able to guarantee the accuracy of dowel hole or keyway placement.

ADJUSTING VALVE CLEARANCE

With the cam phasing sorted out, the next thing we have to think about is the valve clearance ('lash'). The cam grinder will supply a clearance for the intake and exhaust valve, and sometimes he will specify a different clearance for different types of valve material. If he gives a 'cold' clearance he means just that; the motor should not have been run in the previous 5 hours. The 'hot' clearance is for a motor at normal operating temperature, usually 70–88°C water temperature, 90–100° oil temperature. It is very important to maintain sufficient valve clearance to allow the valve to seat firmly and to remain on the seat long enough to transfer heat to the cooling medium. Running the valves tight to quieten them is a sure way to get valve burning in a performance engine.

Sometimes we can benefit by changing the valve clearance within reason and according to the type of competition involved. Note that we are talking about a competition motor here, not a road or rally motor. We have already pointed out that for serious competition the motor must be set up to suit the track or strip, but our best-laid

A cam drive sprocket with multiple dowel holes allows the cam to be advanced or retarded accurately.

plans can go astray. Suppose we have set our cam for a particular dirt speedway but as the night progresses the surface begins to break up or the weather turns foul. Obviously we are not going to have time to advance the cam, so the only way to pick up some bottom-end power in a hurry is to increase the valve lash. This will have the effect of shortening the duration by 3–4° for each 0.005in that the clearance is increased. There is a very definite limit to how far we can go, however, as this has the effect of shortening the opening and closing ramps, which could lead to serious shock loads in the valve train. Therefore the clearance should not be increased by more than 0.005in unless the cam grinder says otherwise. Keep in mind that the valve float limit will now be lowered, so be careful.

If, on the other hand, you find that you need more top-end power on the night, you can decrease the lash, but this is only feasible for short-distance events such as drags, hillclimbs or speedway sprints. Remember that decreasing the lash will increase valve temperatures, so always maintain 75% of the recommended clearance. Also, if you know that the valves and seats are getting a bit rough or the guides are shot, do not decrease the clearance at all – you could easily wreck the motor. An increase in valve temperatures, under competition conditions, could cause pre-ignition or detonation; both are piston and engine breakers.

With push rod type engines you must maintain a valve-to-piston clearance of 0.080in and 0.100in for the inlet and exhaust valves respectively. Therefore it will be necessary to set up the pistons with adequate valve cut-outs before you attempt to change the valve clearance or change the cam phasing.

It is surprising how many enthusiasts have little idea of setting valve clearances accurately. First, let me point out that it is impossible to do much of a job if the contact face of the rocker or valve stem tip has a dip worn into it. The feeler blade will be too wide to fit into the dip, so we will not be able to take this wear into account. When we measure the clearance we want to have the lifter fairly close to the centre of the base 349 circle. With most ohc engines it is possible to see when the lifter is on the base circle, but with other types we have to use another method.

The simplest method for in-line engines is visually to divide the engine in half. All the rockers in the front half we number from 1 to 4 (or 1 to 6 if it is a six-cylinder) and we do likewise for the rear half, but this time we start No 1 from the extreme rear of the engine. In this way we have both No 1 rockers at opposite ends of the head, and both No 4 (or No 6) rockers in the middle, alongside each other. As we turn the motor over we always adjust the valve that partners the one that is fully open. Therefore if No 1 at the rear of the motor is fully open, we adjust its partner No 1 at the front of the motor; if No 3 at the front is fully open, we adjust No 3 at the rear, and so on.

With flat and vee motors, the safest way is to turn the motor over and adjust the inlet and exhaust rockers for each cylinder together, midway between the inlet closing point and the exhaust opening point, ie with the piston at TDC at the end of the compression stroke. If you adjust each cylinder in turn according to the firing order, it will save turning the motor over unnecessarily.

When adjusting clearances on ohc motors, I have found it simpler and more accurate to adjust the clearance by inserting the feeler strip between the cam and rocker rather than at the valve stem. However, when using this method it is necessary to reduce the clearance because of the effect of the rocker arm ratio. Therefore if the clearance at the valve is normally 0.013in and the rocker arm ratio is 1.45:1, the clearance at the cam lobe will be $0.013 \div 1.45 = 0.009$in.

ADJUSTING VALVE CLEARANCE WITH HYDRAULIC TAPPETS

The majority of manufacturers recommend that a hydraulic valve train mechanism is adjusted hot, with the engine running. They suggest that each rocker is slackened off until it emits a distinctive 'clacking' sound, then the adjuster should be taken down one half turn. What I prefer is to carry out the adjustment with the engine stopped and either cold or warm. With the lifter on the cam base circle, slacken off the rocker to give a little clearance at the valve. Then rotate the push rod and tighten the rocker down at the same time. When you feel some resistance to turning the push rod, note the position of your spanner and tighten the adjusting nut a further quarter-turn.

Today, many manufacturers make no provision for the adjustment of hydraulic valve systems, so when you fit a cam with a smaller than standard base circle you will have to take special steps to obtain the correct adjustment. The simplest but most expensive way out is to fit adjustable push rods. A fairly effective and less expensive method is to machine the base of the rocker pedestals by an amount equal to half the difference of the base circle diameter of the standard and modified cam divided by the rocker ratio. For example, if the standard base circle diameter is 1.260in and modified it is 1.120in, and the rocker ratio is 1.5:1, the pedestals will require 0.047in milled off their bases ($1.260 - 1.120 = 0.140$, $0.140 \div 2 = 0.070$, $0.070 \div 1.5 = 0.0466$). Often, though, the head or block will have to be machined to increase the compression ratio, so this has to be taken into consideration. If in the above example 0.060in had been taken off the head, the pedestals would have to be shimmed up. The most accurate method to determine the required shim thickness is to tighten down each pedestal a quarter-turn past the position where resistance to turning the push rod is felt. Now measure the clearance under each pedestal and insert a shim of the same thickness.

Chapter 11

The Bottom End

Enthusiasts associate high performance with cams, carburettors and exhaust modifications. However, many hidden horsepower can be found by proper attention to blueprinting the bottom end of a motor. Remember that it is in the bottom end where we lose the most power to friction. Consequently everything we do to improve the accuracy and fit of components gives us back power that would otherwise have been burned up fighting friction. This is also the place where if we have the budget we can further minimise such losses by the application of the new high tech coatings. An additional consideration is the added reliability we can expect when things are done properly and to an exacting specification.

Logically, the place to start is the cylinder block, because it is the home for everything else in or on the engine. First, inspect the water passages for rust or scale. If any is present it will be necessary to have the block boiled and cleaned in a chemical bath. This should be done with all the welch plugs (freeze or core plugs) and oil gallery plugs removed.

A mildly dirty block can be steam cleaned or washed with solvent. At the same time the oilways should be carefully cleaned, using brushes designed for this task. Stud holes deserve the same treatment, particularly head and main bearing cap stud holes. Finally, high-pressure air must be used to clean and dry off everything. Even brand new (green) blocks should be cleaned as outlined, with particular attention to ensure that no casting sand has been left in the water passages.

INITIAL BLOCK PREPARATION AND CRACK TESTING

With the block perfectly dry, it can be visually inspected for cracks. A competition block should be pressure crack tested; really it is a waste of time and money if this is not done first. You can do a pressure test yourself as only very basic equipment is required. Preferably the head should be bolted to the block (it is acceptable to use an old head gasket for this test if it is not torn) and both head and block should be fully stripped, but with welch plugs in place. All water openings should be blocked off with steel plates. 351

One plate should have an air line fitting installed (or you may prefer a tubeless tyre valve). Connect to this your air line tap and pressure gauge (the use of an old oil pressure gauge is suitable). Now slowly open the air line valve and gradually let the air pressure come up to 40psi. Do not let pressure come up too quickly because if a welch plug is not in tight or if there is a weak spot in the block it could blow out and cause you injury.

If everything is holding satisfactorily, again open the air valve and let the pressure slowly build to 50psi. Some people advocate that you should check at 60psi, but this can be quite dangerous if there is a weak spot, and in any event most cracks will become evident at 45–50psi. (Note that heavy duty thick-wall race blocks cast with special chrome moly alloy iron can be tested up to 100psi.) It is really more a matter of how carefully you look for cracks as you slowly work your way over the block (check the head too, and inside the inlet and exhaust ports), rather than going to very high air pressure.

To make the cracks more clearly visible some prefer to spray over the entire outside, then the inside, of the block with a penetrating aerosol like WD-40, carefully covering just a small area at a time, while others choose to spray on water with a little added liquid detergent. Either way any cracks will be shown up by the presence of air bubbles.

Note that if you find a crack do not quickly discard the block unless it is obvious that it is not repairable either because the crack is too large or it is in a critical location. Some cracks can be inexpensively repaired, and a block that has been repaired may be just as strong as one that is not cracked. In fact, some engines routinely crack in certain areas, so if you are too fussy you may have to check out many second-hand blocks to find one that is not cracked, then after you race it a few times you may find that it too has cracked, whereas the block that was initially inspected and subsequently repaired may now be stronger in that particular spot and so not give any more trouble.

With the block crack-tested, next take a plug tap and clean the head stud and main bearing cap threads of dirt or burrs. This is important to get a true stud tension reading. Any stud holes that have not been chamfered should be, to prevent threads pulling up; a pulled head stud thread can cause head gasket sealing problems, while a pulled main bearing cap thread can allow a bearing to turn. Finally, check the depth of each hole to be certain that the stud will not bottom.

To avoid cuts to yourself and possible engine damage, carefully grind away any casting slag. The main area for concern is around the main bearing webs, the sump pan deck and, in vee motors, around the oil drain back holes and the rest of the valley area.

MAIN BEARING ALIGNMENT

The next operations involve 'squaring' the block. A check must be made to ensure that the main bearing bores are perfectly aligned, as any misalignment will wreck the bearings and possibly even the crank. It will also soak up a lot of power as the frictional losses are greater. I have found new blocks with up to 0.007in misalignment, so do not assume that the alignment is correct. Any misalignment can be corrected by line-boring. When main bearing caps are replaced by heavy-duty items, line-boring will also be necessary. To ensure that alignment is maintained, the main bearing caps should be numbered and have the front position marked. This will assist in fitting each cap in its correct location each time the motor is rebuilt.

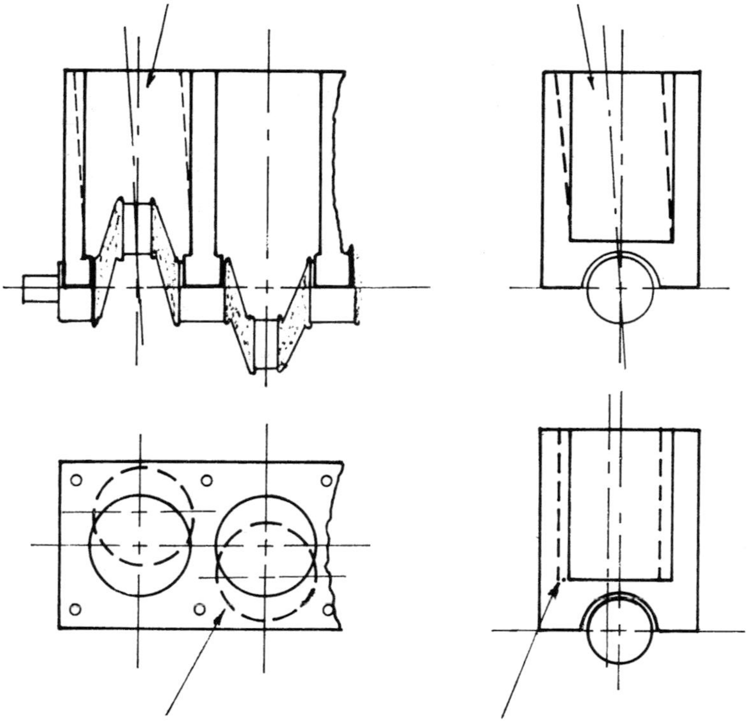

Cylinders should intersect crankshaft centre at 90°.

Cylinders should not be offset from crankshaft centre.

Figure 11.1 Cylinders must be accurately rebored.

With the main bearing bores true, the block should be checked at each corner to guarantee that the distances between the top of the block (the deck) and the crankshaft centreline are identical. If the block is out of true, milling will be required. Even if the deck is true, we may decide to have it decked to reduce the distance between the top of the piston and the top of the block, to reduce the squish clearance.

CYLINDER BORING

The cylinder bores must be true at 90° to the crank centreline (ie across the motor) to keep the frictional losses low and maintain good ring sealing. If the bore is canted slightly to the front or the rear, the piston pin will hammer out, so a check must also be made in line (ie at 180°) with the crank. There must not be any steps or taper from the top to the bottom of the bore (Figure 11.1).

Boring and honing should be carried out by a firm with precision equipment able to maintain a tolerance of 0.0003in. Forget about garages using small boring machines that bolt on to the block, as the tolerance can be as bad as 0.002in.

On a street engine the machinist sets up the boring bar centred on the existing cylinder bore. However, there is no guarantee that the existing bore centres are correctly located (indexed) in relation to the crank throws or the combustion chambers 353 in the cylinder head. Therefore in a race engine I prefer to see a bore index plate bolted to the block as a reference to locate the bore centres correctly. This ensures that all the cylinders are centred over the crank throws, and it also means that cylinder heads can be swapped between blocks with the certainty that combustion chambers will all be correctly located over the cylinders.

When a race engine is being bored I like to see only 0.010in taken out with each cut; with a road motor this can be increased to 0.015–0.020in. Thus while a 0.030 or 0.040in overbore could be achieved with one cut on a road engine I would want to see two cuts made on race blocks. This costs more because of the time involved, but the bores will be easier to hone accurately because the boring tool marks will not be so deep and rough.

CYLINDER WALL THICKNESS AND RING SEAL

There are definite limits as to how far a cylinder can be overbored. If the cylinder walls become too thin they will warp due to the pressure and heat, which will allow blow-by past the rings, resulting in lost power. Another problem not often recognised is also due to thin cylinder walls. In a racing motor, or when a long-stroke crank is used, the main bearing webs can actually break away from the bottom of the cylinders.

Generally, 0.060in oversize is about the limit. Some of the older design British motors will go to 0.150in oversize, but care must be exercised. Many American motors are limited to plus-0.030in due to thin wall casting techniques. It is possible to obtain special thick-wall racing blocks for some engines. As a bonus these are generally stronger and less prone to flexing, due to the use of a special grade of cast iron. However, there is a considerable weight penalty, about 40lb in a small-block Chev, for instance.

Motorcycle cylinders are restricted to 0.120–0.160in oversize, depending on the thickness of the steel liners. By boring out the original liners and pressing in new sleeves we can at times go to 0.400in. This, however, is limited by the bore centres and block rigidity.

Remember that there is no benefit to be gained if an increase in bore size will induce cylinder warping or block flexing. Both conditions will rob us of power and lead to reliability troubles. Also to be avoided is the practice of dry-sleeving cylinders to compensate for thin walls or to eliminate water seepage. What generally happens is that the sleeve shifts due to the very thin walls, which may allow water into the sump or result in a blown head gasket. Many tuners feel that sleeving is a good thing as the sleeve always has enough wall thickness not to warp, but they forget that the sleeve must be adequately supported.

It seems to me that many people do not understand just how little wall thickness there is even in a stock block that has not been re-bored. Today many cast-iron blocks have a designed cylinder wall thickness of only about 0.110–0.140in when finished with a standard bore diameter. However, during casting a core can very easily shift 0.040in. This means that the wall thickness can be down to 0.070–0.100in, and we are not talking high-grade alloy steel here; some manufacturers use some pretty ordinary 'soft' cast iron in their blocks. Obviously with today's race engines making about 65–95hp per cylinder, such thin walls, if overbored, will either crack or at best cut the power of the engine due to inadequate ring seal.

Basically for good ring seal I reckon that you need a cylinder wall thickness of 0.095–0.105in minimum for an engine expected to make 65–70hp per cylinder. This is most critical at the top half of the stroke because it is the top area of the cylinder where we require good ring seal, first to make compression, then, after ignition, to retain cylinder pressure to drive the piston down and make power. Toward the bottom of the cylinders we may be able to drop approximately 0.020in in wall thickness, but there are many other factors to consider such as operating rpm, crank stroke, main bearing web strength and whether the engine is ever likely to suffer detonation.

As the power levels increase, so does the need for thicker cylinder walls. At 75hp per cylinder I would be looking at a minimum wall of around 0.110–0.130in; at 85hp the wall should be 0.150–0.180in and at 100hp 0.220–0.250in. These latter two thicknesses for engines at power levels of 85 and 100hp per cylinder might appear excessive, but if you want a block to seal well and have a service life of up to 5,000 race miles at 8,500rpm, that is the sort of wall thickness you must be considering. I know that some race teams get away with less wall, but I also know that they are scrapping blocks with less than 300 miles on them. Considering the amount of time and money invested in a race block, this does not make much sense, and I wonder how often they lose an expensive crank because of the main bearing webs breaking away.

STRENGTHENING OPEN-DECK BLOCKS

A few engines though have problems that go well beyond cylinder wall thickness. Some for example have an open-deck design where the top of the cylinder is unsupported or only lightly braced by the top of the block. At low power levels this doesn't usually cause problems, but as the hp and rpm rise so does cylinder and block flexing. The solution for small Hondas is to fit a block guard. This is inserted into the water jacket to fit between the block and cylinder to add rigidity.

Inserting rods between the cylinders and block serves to brace the cylinders, reducing blow-by and head gasket leakage in high hp engines.

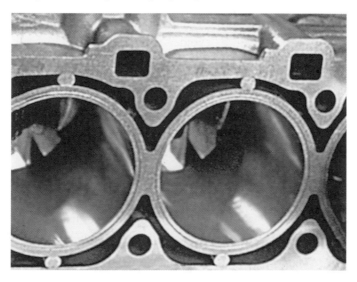

At times the fix can be more radical, and expensive. Some Subarus have an open-deck block. Upgrading to a closed-deck block means a big outlay. The K-series Rover 1800 engine has a different problem. As we approach 200hp the engine does nasty things like splitting the cylinder liners. The solution here is to shrink a steel sleeve around the outside of the liner up toward the top.

CHECKING CYLINDER WALL THICKNESS

Checking a block for wall thickness and core shift takes a lot of time and care. However, the reward is that the engine will produce more power and you will not be wasting money on machining a 'thin' block that you will have to scrap after just a few races. I have seen some people trying to figure out cylinder wall thickness in the strangest of ways in the hope of getting a massive overbore. Some apparently feel that they can simply measure the thickness of the web between adjacent cylinders. Then, with the welch plugs knocked out, they use a bunch of feeler gauge strips to measure the width of the water jacket between those cylinders, then calculate the wall thickness. Unfortunately, they forget that core shift makes such measurements pretty well meaningless.

Some race teams rely on sonic testing to provide reasonably accurate information on metal thickness. The main thing with sonic testing is for the operator to use care and good judgement, but it is also wise to recognise that a sonic test will not detect a

Measuring cylinder wall thickness has become easier in recent times with the availability of relatively inexpensive sonic testers.

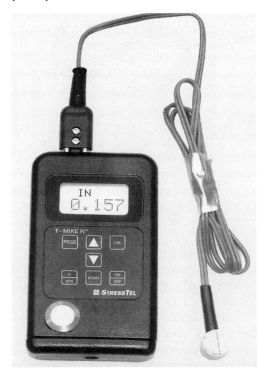

porous area in a block or an area of 'dirty' metal. Also, the actual metal thickness may be 0.020in less than the tester is indicating.

Therefore along with sonic testing it is vital to do a pressure crack test as discussed earlier, and it is wise to measure the block using basic measuring tools. In fact, this is what race engine builders had to do before cheap sonic testers became available. I do not know of any machinist's callipers that will do the job, so you will probably have to build your own. What you need is a pair of vernier callipers with a set of very long jaws. One jaw has to be the correct size and shape, and with just enough 'kick' in the leg to fit down through water jacket holes in the deck of the block. I've seen some people cut up a pair of 6 or 8in outside callipers and weld the legs to the jaws of their verniers, but I generally find that outside callipers have too much 'bow' in the legs to fit down into the water jacket.

What I prefer is to chop up two pairs of callipers, one an inside calliper and one an outside calliper, then bolt one leg of the outside calliper correctly orientated to one jaw of the vernier. Then I reverse one leg of the inside callipers and bolt it to the other jaw of the vernier. With a bit of grinding this leg will fit down into the water jacket through holes in the deck of the block, and it generally has enough kick to contact the outside wall of the cylinders. With these legs bolted, rather than welded, to the vernier callipers it is possible to swap them about or to pull them off for grinding to fit down into the water jackets of different blocks.

BIG CYLINDERS – EFFECT ON POWER

Even when an engine is not excessively overbored there is no guarantee that you will achieve a massive increase in power. I think most people understand that a 10% increase in cylinder displacement will not yield a corresponding rise of 10% in maximum horsepower. However, few tuners realise just how ill-advised large capacity increases can be in some situations. The point to be remembered is this: it is no use giving the engine big lungs if the induction system (ie carburettor, manifold, ports and valves) does not have the capability, or the potential capability, to flow sufficient air to fill those big lungs.

A situation like this is not really a problem if the engine is running in a street car, but in a road race vehicle, and particularly in a rally car, this type of over-modification must be avoided because of the disastrous effect it has of compressing the power band. True, the increase in mid-range power is a very important plus in favour of a displacement increase, but if the engine does not have the breathing ability to be able to rev as hard as previously, the increased number of gear changes now necessary may easily reduce the performance level of the car/engine/driver combination to what it was before the capacity jump.

In Table 11.1 you can see how the power range was affected on an ohc Vauxhall rally motor when the capacity was raised from 2,279cc to 2,496cc, about a 10% increase. The smaller motor makes good power between 4,500 and 7,500rpm, and if need be it can be lugged down to 4,000rpm, which gives a very nice 3,500rpm operating range. The 2.5-litre engine is working very well at 4,000rpm (15hp increase over the 2.3-litre engine), but it runs out of steam at around 6,500rpm, which means that the power band has been narrowed down by 1,000rpm. You will note too that there is only a difference of 1hp in maximum power between both engines.

Table 11.1   Dyno test of Vauxhall ohc rally engine

rpm	2,279cc engine		2,496cc engine	
	hp	torque (lbf ft)	hp	torque (lbf ft)
3,250	100	161.6	103	166.4
3,500	108	162.1	118	177.1
4,000	127	166.7	142	186.4
4,500	136	158.7	163	190.2
5,000	170	178.5	183	192.2
5,500	185	176.6	194	185.2
6,000	199	174.2	206	180.3
6,500	202	163.2	200	161.6
7,000	205	153.8	178	132.6
7,500	197	137.9		

Table 11.2   Dyno test of Vauxhall twin-cam 16-valve rally engine

rpm	2,279cc engine		2,496cc engine	
	hp	torque (lbf ft)	hp	torque (lbf ft)
4,250			139	171.8
4,500	144	156.4	154	179.7
5,000	173	181.7	195	204.8
5,500	188	179.5	212	202.4
6,000	216	189.1	236	206.8
6,500	231	186.6	251	202.8
7,000	240	180.1	244	183.1
7,500	244	170.8	234	164.2
8,000	248	156.2		
8,250	232	147.7		

In its present form the 2.5-litre motor would not be any better than the smaller engine in a rally car. However, with a lot of development the big motor proved to be marginally superior. A wilder camshaft raised maximum power to almost 209hp and enabled the motor to run to 7,000rpm (192hp), but the mid-range was so badly affected that the power band was narrowed to even worse than before.

After this a 16-valve Lotus head was tried to determine what effect better breathing would have (Table 11.2). The small engine has a 3,250rpm power range extending from 5,000 to 8,250rpm, while the 2.5-litre motor is best between 4,750 and 7,500rpm, a 2,750rpm spread. When a wilder inlet camshaft was fitted (no other changes) this motor ran much better at 7,500rpm (239hp) and made 230hp at 7,750rpm with just a small decrease in mid-range (190hp at 5,000rpm). Maximum power went up to 253hp.

Obviously in this instance the 2,496cc motor should be superior, but since that time some competition rules have outlawed the Lotus head and the 16-valve Vauxhall head will not perform anywhere near as well (ie 20hp less for the 2.3-litre motor).

Of course not every type of competition machine requires an engine with a good wide spread of power, so large increases in displacement can be made without adversely affecting performance. Therefore if you are involved in rallycross or quarter-mile dirt speedway, the 2.5-litre Vauxhall in either 8-valve or 16-valve form should prove superior. However, as you can see from both tables, there is no significant increase in maximum power, so to gain any benefit from the big motor the suspension will have to be capable of getting those extra 15–20 mid-range horsepower down on to the track to accelerate the car faster.

CYLINDER HONING

During cylinder honing operations, a 2in thick honing plate should be fitted, along with the head gasket, and tensioned to normal head stud tension. This operation is necessary on racing engines to guarantee perfect bores, as the pull of head studs always causes a certain degree of cylinder distortion. When a honing plate is fitted at the specified head tension, the block is distorted during the cylinder finishing procedure. Therefore the bores will be true when the head is fitted. The main bearing caps, when tensioned, also distort the cylinders, so these should be fitted as well.

When we say the bores will be true that is in a relative sense only. Measured at the same cylinder bore temperature and block temperature as when honed the bores will be true. However, once heated to normal race engine coolant temps the bores will no longer remain perfectly concentric. And the change will be more extreme in poor quality blocks, excessively overbored blocks, blocks lightened after being honed, and on blocks which were incorrectly honed using steel honing plates instead of aluminium (aluminium blocks and cast iron blocks which will be fitted with aluminium heads should be honed using aluminium hone plates). The only way we currently have of minimising this inaccuracy is to run hot coolant through the block

Honing with a honing plate in place improves cylinder trueness and ring seal.

In a correctly honed cylinder an even crosshatch pattern, without waviness or boring tool marks underneath, should be clearly visible.

during the honing process so that everything is at about 90°C (some prefer higher temperatures; up to 120°C). This isn't perfect either as we can't simulate bore distortion due to combustion pressures and vibration, but it does get us closer to what we are trying to achieve, and this shows in a small power gain of about 1%. Some tuners are finding closer to 2% but my feeling is that since going to hot honing they are now paying a good deal more attention to other aspects of cylinder trueness that were previously neglected, and that is where they are finding the additional hp. Looking at the gain from the aspect of actual blow-by you can expect a reduction of around 3cfm.

If you are preparing engines for a category of competition where a 1% power gain is important for a modest additional cost in time and equipment then here is how you need to do it. Apart from the obvious things like a hot water supply and fittings for the block you have to install a very good ventilation system to get rid of all the smoke, and you will do more consistent work using an infrared heat gun to monitor block and cylinder temps. Most cylinders grow 0.0035in when heated from room temp to 90°C so to avoid having the pistons stick in the bores when the engine is cold you first need to measure the bores cold and then after you have heated the block, before you start honing. Subtract the cold figures from the hot size, and add the result to the dial bore gauge finished size. If you find a cylinder that grows way out of line with the rest you probably have a dud block so don't waste time and money on it. Remember during all this to continually keep checking and adjusting your bore gauge. It will quickly pick up heat and expand. Finally, don't panic if after hot honing you find the bores are all over the shop with the block cold. Of course they will be, but once the block is heated they will again be nice and round.

I prefer to bore the cylinders to within 0.004in of the finished size, then hone each cylinder to fit a particular piston. In this way I can keep piston clearances to a tolerance of about 0.0003in.

The actual honing procedure varies a little from engine to engine, but a fairly standard method using the preferred Sunnen CK-10 automatic hone is as follows. First using 220 grit stones, about 0.003in of material is removed to bring the bore to 0.001in from its final size. Then another 0.0005in is taken out with 280 grit stones, and finally 400 grit stones are used to bring the bore to its final diameter. This results in a very accurate bore with a fine finish that requires very little break-in.

The cross-hatch pattern left by the hone on the cylinder walls is critical. It must be just right if the piston rings are to bed-in quickly and have a long life. I prefer a 45° cross-hatch with a finish of 10–12 micro-inches. This type of finish makes it necessary to run the rings in, but they last for a long time and seldom leak. A finish any smoother will not hold enough oil and will allow a glaze to form on the ring face and bore wall. Oil consumption will be a problem and power will be lost due to blow-by. A rougher finish will usually eliminate the need to bed in the rings; however, ring life is greatly reduced. Keep in mind too that glazing can again be a real problem, but not due to lack of lubrication; a rough finish acts like a file on the rings, and the added friction increases their temperature and allows glazing to form.

The upper and lower lip of each cylinder should be chamfered lightly to remove the sharp edge produced by boring. A smooth-cut half-round file will do the job, but take care not to let it slip and nick the cylinder wall. While you have the file at hand, lightly dress the sharp edges of the main bearing caps and webs.

SPECIALISED CYLINDER COATINGS

With increasing recognition of hp losses due to friction it is obvious that one of the major areas of friction within an engine – between the piston rings and cylinder wall – has to be carefully scrutinised. Originally, coatings were applied to provide a superior bore surface that improved ring seal and reduced bore and ring wear rates. Going back about 30 years Mahle began working with a superior electro-chemical plating called Nikasil. This plating was originally developed for Mercedes when they were building experimental Wankel rotary engines. Then Porsche began using Nikasil plated cylinders in the 630hp air cooled 917 model Le Mans racer. This engine later produced 1,100hp in turbocharged form for the Can-Am series. Today, Nikasil cylinders are in use on tens of thousands of chain saws and other industrial two-strokes throughout Europe. It has proved to be very successful in racing two-stroke engines as well. In time it began to be applied directly to the aluminium cylinders of four-strokes, initially as a better alternative to chrome plating of linerless bores, and later because of its ability to also reduce frictional losses.

The Nikasil coating is a nickel and silicon carbide matrix about 0.07mm thick. The nickel matrix is very hard, but it is comparatively ductile, whereas chrome is brittle. Dispersed through the nickel are particles of silicon carbide less than 4 microns in size. These extremely hard particles make up about 4% of the coating and form a multitude of adhesion spots on which oil can collect. So besides providing a very long-wearing surface for the piston and rings to bear against, the silicon carbide particles also contribute to long engine life by ensuring good cylinder lubrication.

Naturally other companies weren't going to sit back and let Mahle steal the market so they began to develop their own proprietary coatings. Consequently there are now many coatings available, even from within the same company, so there are numerous products/processes from which to choose.

A joint project of Perfect Bore Liners and Poeton Aptec is their ceramic coating, Apticote 2000. In regular use now since late 2000, it consists of a hard metal matrix packed with ultra-hard ceramic particles. The hard metal coating has a strong affinity for holding oil which allows for an extremely fine hone finishing of the cylinders; down to as low as 0.05Ra. This reduces ring and bore wear, improves gas seal and oil consumption, and cuts frictional losses. Some are reporting power improvements of as high as 1.5%, but I find a little under 1% to be a more realistic expectation. The reduction though in ring, piston and cylinder wear is remarkable, with bore wear cut to about 20% of what is typical in a race honed cast iron cylinder. Some engine builders say that another advantage of this product is that because of Perfect Bore's expertise with very thin, down to 0.75mm thick, dry aluminium liners – they also have steel and MMC available – engine blocks do not have to be shipped all over the world to be coated/recoated. Blocks can be prepared to Perfect Bore's specs and then have finished liners pressed into place. The disadvantage of doing it this way though is that you are never going to be able to achieve the quality of bore finish and accuracy that Perfect Bore can deliver when they do the work in their temperature controlled environment using the best honing and measuring gear available. While you will no doubt get similar wear improvements with the pressed in liners, I don't think it would be possible to arrive at the same precision seal between piston ring and bore, so I wouldn't expect an hp gain in a fresh engine over that possible with a careful hot hone of uncoated bores. However, at the half life stage I would expect it to show more power than an engine with uncoated cylinders.

FINAL BLOCK PREPARATION

Finally, check the mating faces on the back and front of the block; they should be square to the crankshaft centre-line.

Two more inspections are necessary for racing engines. The camshaft bearing bores must be in line and each tappet bore must be of the correct diameter and perpendicular to the centreline of the camshaft. A tappet tipped off centre may easily dig into the lobe of a racing cam, causing premature wear and/or breakage.

About the only other parts of the block to which we have to give consideration are the main bearing caps and studs. I use ARP studs when these are available. Standard production main bearing studs should not be re-used on racing engines, and the same applies to big-end bolts. Usually, the standard cast-iron main bearing caps fitted to modern engines are acceptable but some older engines, or very-high-hp race engines, may require steel caps for reliability. In the very hottest motors I sometimes use a main bearing support saddle. This is a one-piece device that supports all the main bearing caps, or it may take the place of the individual main bearing caps. Either way it often extends out to the oil pan deck and transfers the bearing load so that it is shared by the outside of the block as well as the main bearing webs.

After all the machining work has been completed, the block should be thoroughly washed with hot, soapy water. Be sure to get all traces of honing grit scrubbed out of the cylinders, using a bristle scrubbing brush. Blow the block dry using compressed air, and spray all the cylinders, tappet bores and bearing bores with a water dispersant such as WD-40.

Stock square-shoulder main bearing caps like these are generally very strong.

CRANKSHAFT SELECTION AND PREPARATION

With the block prepared we now turn our attention to the crankshaft. The majority of engines use cast nodular iron crankshafts, which generally give good service even in race engines if sensible rpm limits are observed and the rods and pistons are not too heavy. Some of these come from the factory with rolled fillets, which significantly increases their fatigue resistance and some may be heat-treated using a process such as Tuftriding. However, as the rpm limit is raised so the need for a better-quality forged steel crank becomes more apparent. In general the forged cranks fitted by Japanese and European car makers are very strong and suitable for high-rpm competition use; some will also feature rolled fillets, and a few will be heat-treated by the nitriding process.

   Not so good, however, are the forged steel crankshafts fitted by some American manufacturers. For example, the steel crank that Chev use in some of their small-block V8s is none too strong and cannot be recommended for use in competition engines, they are forged from fairly poor grade, and often 'dirty', 1053 steel. A nitrided version is also available, and while being a touch stronger they are production-machined without suitable big fillets. In fact, Chev's cast-iron crank, if ground with decent fillets, will last longer in a race engine when limited to about 7,000rpm and less than 500hp.

   Another worry with many production V8 cranks is the forging method employed. Typically they are forged 'flat', then the front and rear throws are 'twisted' 90° to give the required crankpin orientation. However, in production the throws will not be twisted exactly 90°, which means that not only the crankpins but also the counterweights will be 2 or 3° out. The raw forging has enough meat in it to enable the crankpins to be machined at 90° and the crank can still be balanced, but the incorrectly indexed counterweights will impose undesirably high bearing loads in a high-rpm competition engine. For this reason 'non-twisted' forged cranks, where all four rod journals are forged in place, are preferred for V8 race engines.

The sharp parting line on the web of this crank indicates that it is a cast-iron part.

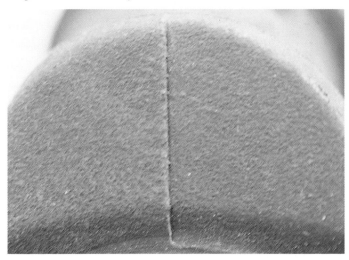

Left *This broad parting line indicates that it is a forged crank. In a competition engine the ball that has been staked in place to block off a cross-drilled oilway should be replaced by a threaded plug.*

Right *Rolled fillets improve crank fatigue strength by compressing the material in an area subject to very high loadings.*

Assuming that the standard crank is suitable, we must have it crack-tested before doing any work on it. If it is free from flaws, carefully and fully demagnetise it (the same applies to rods), as any residual magnetism after a Magnaflux crack test will attract ferrous metal particles to the area, which will soon wipe out the bearings. Next a check should be made to determine its straightness. Cranks can be straightened, but generally it is a waste of time as the pressures of combustion and inertia loads will reverse the straightening process. Because a bent crankshaft increases bearing load and parasitic losses, it must be machined undersize by 0.010in, or else discarded, if bent by more than 0.002in.

Next measure each main bearing and crank pin journal. Remembering that crank journals wear oval, measure the diameter at several angles around the journal. Also measure at each end and in the middle of every journal, as wear can vary along its length. Ovality and taper should be less than 0.0003in in a high-performance or racing crank. If the wear is greater than this, grinding the journals undersize will be necessary. However, grinding weakens the crankshaft, so a crank replacement may be necessary in high-horsepower and high-rpm engines. When the crankshaft is machined, instruct the grinder to pay close attention to maintaining the fillet radii specified by the manufacturer (Figure 11.2); any reduction here will weaken the crankshaft. On the other hand, an increased radius serves to strengthen the shaft;

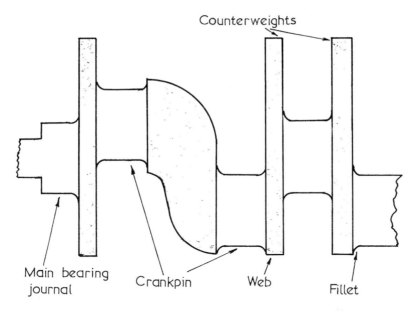

Figure 11.2 Austin Mini crankshaft.

however, this should not be overdone or we can arrive at a situation where the big-end or main bearings are locking on to the fillet. Narrower bearing shells, or bearings modified with a larger chamfer, can be fitted to avoid this problem.

Any casting slag should be ground off the crank and the area dressed. These slag spots can become a stress raiser or future failure point.

To assist in the smooth operation of the motor and to reduce bearing inertia loading, the crankshaft should be dynamically balanced; this will increase its life through a reduction in the shock loading and vibration that any imbalance would cause. Most manufacturers already do a reasonably good job of balancing their cranks, so unless the engine is going to spend a lot of time running in excess of 6,000rpm, it is probably not worth the expense of having the crankshaft re-balanced. An exception to this is in the case of V8 engines. If these are fitted with pistons or rods much heavier than standard, the crank has to be re-balanced regardless of whether it is to be used in a road engine or a race engine.

Some manufacturers list Tuftrided replacement crankshafts, which are excellent for high-performance road and rally engines. They can also be used in racing motors, but I would suggest that a strict eye be kept on rpm limits and that they be crack-tested each 300 miles.

THE TUFTRIDING PROCESS

Standard cast-iron cranks can be Tuftrided, but there is some risk involved. Any ferrous metal object can, in fact, be Tuftrided, but as the process requires immersion in a chemical bath at a temperature of 1,060°F for 180 minutes, internal stresses can lead to deformation. Cast-iron cranks are susceptible to bending and changes in journal diameter, so I feel that it is a better proposition to buy a pre-treated crank as they are 365 often not much more expensive than the standard item. However, do have the treated crank checked for straightness and phasing of the throws. Remember that cranks with rolled fillets should not be Tuftrided as this will destroy the pre-stressed condition of the fillets and weaken the crank.

There is a good deal of misunderstanding about the Tuftriding process, so I will explain the benefits that it will impart to a treated object. Contrary to popular opinion, it does not increase the core strength of the component. The Tuftride bath, composed primarily of cyanide and cyanate compounds, releases specific quantities of carbon and nitrogen in the presence of ferrous materials such as cast iron and alloy steel. Nitrogen is more soluble than carbon in these metals and diffuses into the component, while the carbon forms iron carbide particles at or near the surface. These particles act as nuclei, precipitating some of the diffused nitrogen to form a tough compound zone of carbon-bearing epsilon iron nitride.

The compound zone (0.0003–0.0005in deep in treated cast iron) is tough and very resistant to wear, galling, seizing and corrosion. The nitrogen diffusion zone (0.0008–0.014in deep in treated cast iron) underlying the tough compound zone is responsible for the improved fatigue properties. This fatigue resistance is the most important value of the Tuftride process in the racing engine. The nitrogen in solid solution prevents incipient cracks from becoming fatigue failures, so the endurance limit of a cast-iron crankshaft can be increased by 20–60%.

HIGH PERFORMANCE CRANKSHAFTS

Forged cranks are more suitable for higher-output rally and racing engines. Forging increases the density of the component as the metal is literally squeezed into the required shape and compacted, resulting in a stronger core and better fatigue resistance. However, it is really the type of steel and the heat treatment that it receives after being forged that determines the crank's suitability for use in a race engine. Because a crankshaft twists and bends with every power thrust, the steel must have a high tensile strength and high fatigue resistance. High tensile strength – the ability to resist breaking under high loads – is important, but the ability to endure repeated high bending and twisting loads – fatigue resistance – is also important in high-rpm race engines.

In the UK competition cranks are often forged from EN40B steel, while in the USA 4340 and 5140 steel (5140 is inferior to 4340) are preferred. At this point it is wise to realise that just because a crank is said to be 4340 steel, it is no guarantee of its quality or fatigue resistance. Technically all 4340 should be the same, but it is not. The steel may be 'dirty', containing many impurities, or the alloy may not be up to specification. Also there is the question of what heat treatment the part has received after the forging and machining operations, as this has a significant influence on the metal's strength and fatigue resistance. Some heat treatment imparts considerably more strength and fatigue resistance, but because there may be a greater risk of failure during the process, which may result in an entire batch of cranks being discarded, a crankshaft manufacturer could choose a cheaper and 'safer', albeit inferior, heat treatment. Obviously such a crank will be less expensive to manufacture, but as it will have less fatigue resistance and a correspondingly shorter 'life', it may not be any cheaper in the long run.

Another factor influencing the cost of a racing crank is its weight. Naturally, complex machining costs money; a 20% weight reduction could add considerably to the price of the crankshaft. However, any reduction in reciprocating mass will pay dividends in improving acceleration out of corners, and in reducing bearing loads.

The most expensive, and strongest, cranks are fully machined from a bar (billet) of high-grade steel that has been hammer forged. If the crank weight is to be kept to a minimum then a 'cleaner' and thus stronger double vacuum re-melt steel, produced using vacuum electromagnetic induction melting, and costing around ten times as much as normal EN40B, will be used. After being machined the billet crank is heat treated to further enhance its strength and fatigue resistance.

The cranks of very-high-rpm or endurance race engines should generally be fully counterbalanced. All crankshafts are counterbalanced overall, but not at each crankpin. As a result, the individual throws are subject to forces that, in combination, tend to make the crank whip and flex. Such increased loading at the bearings can wipe them out at high rpm, and in endurance engines fatigue failure of the crank could occur. The way to overcome these problems is therefore to counterbalance each throw. This does not change the overall crank balance, but achieves an internal balance for each throw. Obviously extra counterweights increase the crank's reciprocating mass and this in turn slows acceleration off the turns. Thus in sprint-type engines, where bearings can be replaced frequently and the crank is regularly crack-tested, a fully counterbalanced crank may be a liability.

However, to prevent main bearing failure or case stretching in the VW engine, always fit a fully counterbalanced crank. Even in a very mild state of tune this is good insurance against engine damage. The standard crank will whip and pound the case, allowing the centre main to turn and wreck the engine. If you cannot afford a fully counterweighted crank for your air-cooled VW, have weights welded on to the standard crank.

In the high-rpm engine, crankshaft oilway modifications are undertaken to prevent bearing failure due to lack of lubricant. Many feel this means that engines such as American V8s, which have only the upper main bearing grooved, should have the main bearing journals cross-drilled. This is a total waste of money for road engines and it may not even be necessary for race engines. Looking at Figure 11.3, you will see what can be done to improve the quality of lubrication at the big ends while at the same time reducing the amount of oil that is pumped away from the main bearings. With this system, when one crankpin hole is blocked off due to centrifugal loads on the rod, the other hole feeds oil to the crankpin bearing. When carrying out this modification, great care is necessary to ensure that the new holes break fully into the original oilway.

Thus far we have only considered the crankshaft from the aspect of engine reliability, but it can also affect overall engine performance. Theoretically, crank throws should be of equal length and correctly indexed (phased). Slight differences in the stroke from cylinder to cylinder will not have a profound effect on performance, but incorrect phasing will knock power. A four-cylinder engine should have a piston at top dead centre every 180°, a six every 120°, and an eight every 90° (180° with a single-plane crank). If any cylinder has a crank throw out of phase by 5° this will have the same effect on performance as an ignition or camshaft timing error of 5°. An expensive racing crank should have perfect phasing, but make a check to be sure.

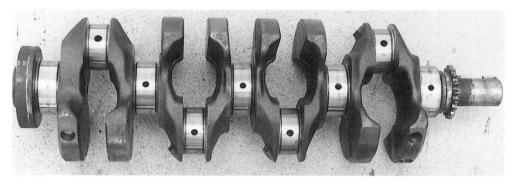

A fully counterbalanced crank has improved fatigue resistance and reduces bearing loads in a long-distance endurance engine, but the additional rotating mass will be a disadvantage, reducing acceleration.

Figure 11.3 Crankshaft oilway modification.

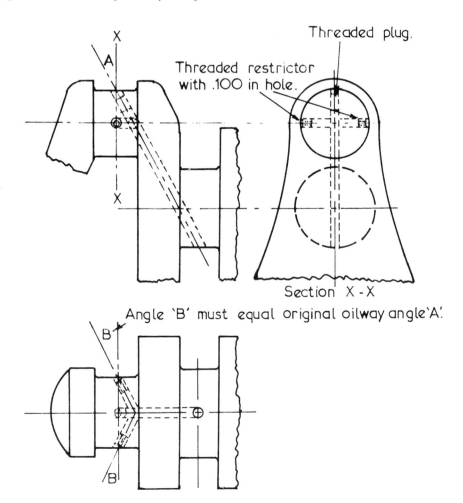

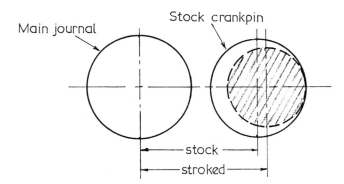

Figure 11.4 Crankshaft stroking by reducing the crankpin diameter.

STROKER CRANK CONSIDERATIONS

Welding to increase the stroke of a crankshaft is not a practice to be recommended. The welding of the crankpins will cause a structural change in the crystalline structure of the underlying steel, and the affected area then becomes a stress point, likely to fail. When the pin is ground on the new centre, much of the original core material is destroyed, further weakening the beam. Additional to these considerations, give some thought to the higher inertia loads generated by the longer throw.

At times, manufacturers increase the crankpin diameter in later-model engines and in these instances it is possible to gain a small increase in stroke by grinding the crankpin to the original small diameter on a different centre (Figure 11.4). This modification reduces the crank beam strength and increases bearing loads, but on the plus side a useful increase in engine capacity is gained, together with reduced frictional losses due to the reduced crankpin diameter. In lower-stressed engines for sprint-type speedway and hillclimb events, and moderate-duty road engines, this modification is useful, but there are definite limitations.

Specially manufactured billet-steel or forged cranks can be obtained with a stroke up to 1/2in more than stock. The strength of the crankshaft is not of primary concern here – it is block rigidity that matters. If the motor is to be used in sprint-type competition, a standard, crack-free block with heavy-duty main bearing caps and rods will be adequate. However, if the motor is expected to live for a minimum of 300 miles and more between rebuilds, a special heavy-duty racing block should be considered. At times, a stronger, more suitable block may be available from another model vehicle by the same manufacturer.

When a long-stroke crank is fitted, some grinding may be necessary inside the block for connecting rod clearance. The clearance slots at the bottom of the bores will probably require enlarging, and the camshaft may also need clearance slots, but do not machine the cam all the way around as this will weaken the shaft excessively and lead to flexing and inaccurate valve timing. Do not forget to check the sump pan clearance.

CON ROD SELECTION AND MATERIALS

The connecting rod provides the mechanical link between piston and crankshaft, and is subjected to alternating compression and tensile loads. It is true to say that the 369 connecting rods in an engine have a tougher job to do than any other component, so it is not surprising that a large number of failures in high-performance and racing engines are caused by the rods letting go.

The highest load is reached when the piston is at TDC on the exhaust stroke. This tension load can range from a few thousand pounds in a small low-rev engine to well over 15,000lb in larger high-rev engines. Interestingly, this maximum load occurs on the non-firing stroke and is caused by the inertia of the reciprocating assembly comprising the small end, piston and pin. At TDC the piston is suddenly stopped, then reversed, and it is this sudden change that produces the high tensile load.

On the compression stroke the load is not as high (up to 11,500lb) as compression builds up slowly, and soon after TDC, when combustion has finished, the load changes from tension to a light compression load.

It is not only the fact that stresses are high in a rod; more importantly, they are applied and reversed each time the engine completes a cycle. This pulsing is much worse than if the loads were constant and applied continually, and it is this that leads to eventual fatigue and failure. A rod has to survive millions of stress cycles during a lifetime so it has to be tough and thoroughly prepared.

Most rods are forged from carbon steel or more recently powdered metal, but they may also be made of cast iron, aluminium or titanium. Cast-iron rods have no place in a modified engine and should not be used. Titanium is prohibitively expensive and is used only in big-budget race engines. Aluminium rods are light and reasonably strong, but fatigue quickly, so they should be used only in drag race and sprint-type speedway engines where frequent replacement is possible. Some time ago Chevrolet released some information on connecting rod fatigue testing that they had carried out. Some aluminium rods failed after 150,000 cycles. The heavy-duty small-block rod, polished and shot-peened, survived 1–2 million cycles at the equivalent of 7,500rpm, while the Chevy Bow Tie rod survived a minimum of 10 million cycles at 8,000rpm. When it is considered that the average race engine is required to stay together for 300 to 500 miles between rebuilds, the equivalent of 1–1½ million cycles, it is evident that care is needed, first in selecting the correct rod, and second in regular crack testing and replacement.

Powder forged rods are just beginning to gain limited acceptance among tuners even though some manufacturers such as BMW have used them in fairly potent engines, the quad cam V8s for example, since 1992. The powdered rod is a forging – its correct name is not a powdered rod, but rather a 'precision powder forged' rod, abbreviated to PPF within the industry. Like any other forged rod the PPF rod's suitability is dependent on its design shape, the metal used, heat treatment and final machining. I guess the thought that compressed powder can be strong doesn't line up with what we observe with wood products. A tree with a definite grain structure and interwoven fibres is comparable to a forged bar of steel. It is strong and will withstand massive forces for centuries, even millenniums in the case of some trees in California and Australia. When ground to dust though and compressed, the same wood is relatively weak and easily damaged. I guess in the back of our brain we expect powdered metal products to display similar weakness. However the powdered rod is not a simply compressed mass of iron filings; it is a precision, high grade product that can be suitable in a number of competition engine environments. It has several advantages over a conventional forged rod: it is cheaper for a rod of equal strength; it is lighter usually, because of the method of manufacture; tolerances can be extremely

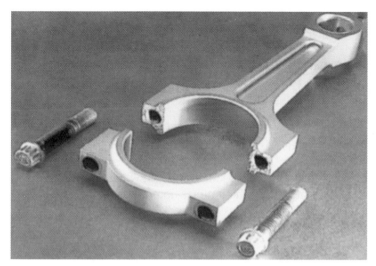

This is a stock BMW V8 precision powder forged rod. The fractured big end is clearly visible.

tightly controlled, so weights can be kept to ± 2gm; with fractured big-end caps the cap is virtually locked in position on the rod which cuts problems with cap to rod movement and fretting, and helps maintain a round big-end bore which almost eliminates problems with bearings being pinched due to cap spread under load.

The basic manufacturing process needs to be understood otherwise some tuners will continue to toss out stock rods that may be perfectly adequate for their needs, perhaps even replacing them with inferior old-style stock forged rods; others will perhaps try to get by with weak old-style stock forged rods purely because of uninformed prejudice, when a set of strong PPF rods were well within their budget.

The base powder may be a high grade metal like 4340 (or 4260 which is superior). To this will be added special alloying materials and perhaps a lubricant such as graphite. This is all thoroughly blended and then fed to a compaction die where two punches press the powder into the shape of the die; in this case a con rod. The next phase is sintering – applying heat to the compacted powder to force the alloying materials uniformly throughout the rod, without actually melting. Next in a controlled atmosphere the rods are quickly heated to 825°C and forged to bring them to full material density. They are then heat treated and finish-machined.

Connecting rods designed for the most stressful conditions are usually forged or machined from 4340 or E4340 steel. However, as with crankshafts the type of steel used is no guarantee of a quality rod. Many other factors such as steel purity, accuracy of machining, heat treatment, shot-peening, design and weight also enter the equation.

The standard rod is what we refer to as an 'I' beam rod because if you were to cut through the beam connecting the little and big ends the steel section would look like an 'I'. This style of rod can be very strong and manufacturers like Oliver, in particular, and Crower have proven that their 'I' beam rods hold up very well in high-rpm endurance engines.

Possibly the most respected manufacturer of con rods, Carrillo, use an 'H' beam design, which is a little stronger below the pin boss. However, the real secret to

Carrillo's superiority over other rods, at great expense I might add, is due to their tight control of the steel alloy (E4340) and similar tight adherence to their chosen heat treatment and shot-peening standards.

Many heavy-duty rods are more massive than the standard component, so there are a few things that must be considered during installation. As they are physically heavier, the crankshaft counterweighting will have to be re-balanced. Since the big end of the rod is larger, care must also be taken to verify that it, and the rod bolts, clear the block and camshaft.

PREPARATION OF STOCK CON RODS

If you intend to retain the standard con rods, they must be carefully, and individually, hand picked. Rods with any forging irregularities or indentations should be avoided. Bumps standing proud of the rod can be removed, but indentations are stress points, likely to cause failure. The little-end eye should be in the centre with an even thickness of material around it. Again the big end should be well formed and symmetrical. Select rods that are reasonably equal in weight; a heavy rod may be excessively weakened if material was ground off to balance it with the lighter rods. If they are not already numbered, number each rod and cap, using a number punch, to ensure that they are never mismatched.

Standard connecting rod preparation must always include a check to ensure that the rod is not twisted or bent, as either condition will wreck the piston and/or big-end bearings. Also necessary is re-sizing to bring the rods to an equal length. At the same time the big-end inside diameter should be checked for size and concentricity with the bearings fitted and the bolts torqued to specification. The little-end bush should be honed to give the correct piston pin fit.

The failure point for many rods is at the corner formed by the flat machined for the rod bolt and nut seat. These corners must be radiused to avoid stress concentration in this area. Every stock con rod will require some modification here (Figure 11.5).

These indentations are stress raisers, indicating that this stock rod should not be selected for use in a high output or high rev engine.

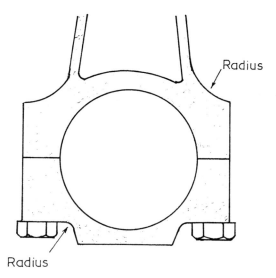

Figure 11.5 Connecting rod modification.

ROD POLISHING AND SHOT-PEENING

The tough skin formed on the con rod by forging gives the rod much of its strength and fatigue resistance, so it should never be polished unless it is followed by shot-peening, to create another work-toughened and compressed skin. It is a waste of time polishing the entire rod, then having it shot-peened. If you look at the shank of a rod you will see, along its edges, a rough band where metal appears to have been sawn away. That is where the excess metal, called flash, was squeezed out from between the forging dies when the rod was being made. Later, most of the flash is trimmed off, but a bead is left, as you can see. Of course, there is no hard skin along this ridge; in fact, its roughness is a stress raiser, so this ridge should be removed on a sanding belt. Give the entire beam a polish with fine emery cloth, then follow up with buffing and shot-peening.

The shot-peening process has a very useful place in connecting rod preparation. Fatigue failure almost always starts at the surface due to a combination of two things. First, under most forms of loading, maximum stress is at the surface, and second, surface imperfections are stress raisers. By bombarding the surface with steel shot the surface layer is compressed and unified. This means that when the component is under load, any tensile stresses at the surface will be reduced and any compressive stresses will be increased. However, because peening can seal over any surface cracks, all crack-testing must be done first. Also any straightening should be carried out before peening, or this will remove the effect of the peening. After peening, check the component dimensionally, as there will be some growth and, if the peening has been done incorrectly, bending may occur.

CON ROD LENGTH

The relationship between con rod length and the crankshaft stroke, called the con rod ratio (con rod length ÷ crank stroke = con rod ratio), is of importance in the high-performance and racing engine. Most rod ratios range from 1.5 to 2:1; 1.65 to 1.75 is average.

For a long time it was argued that the length of the rod directly affected the performance of an engine. Basically the idea was that a long rod would improve top-end performance and also reduce piston and cylinder wear, while a short rod would pick up bottom-end performance, but with increased cylinder wall loads, piston and cylinder wear would increase.

Obviously a long rod will cause the piston to dwell at TDC longer and to move away from TDC more slowly, so there will be a change in the way combustion of the fuel/air mixture occurs. However, this does not affect the power output of an engine with flat-top, or fairly low dome, pistons. It is really only in race engines with very high top pistons, which badly upset the combustion process, that we see this influence coming through with an increase in hp in the upper rpm range.

With short rods the effect is reversed. The short rod accelerates the piston rapidly to TDC where it dwells for a much shorter time, before accelerating rapidly down the bore. When high-top pistons are fitted this rapid movement to, then away from, TDC tends to counteract to some extent the way the piston lumps disrupt combustion and the end result is that we see an increase in hp at lower engine rpm. However, again in engines running flat-top or low-dome pistons this influence is not seen.

This does not mean that if our engine has flat-top pistons we can forget about connecting rod length. With shorter rods, engine wear is a problem with which we have to contend in endurance racing. While in high-rpm sprint engines this may not be a concern, the increased cylinder wall and piston loadings evident in short-rod engines certainly is, as any bowing of the cylinder reduces ring seal and the hp goes off. Hence I do not like rod ratios below about 1.65:1, and I would prefer it to be around 1.8:1. This is worth thinking about before you fit a long-stroke crank, as the tendency for the piston to rock in the bore is also increased as the rod-length-to-stroke ratio is reduced. Pistons with a reduced compression height and shorter skirt must be used with stroker cranks, otherwise the top would pop out of the cylinder and the skirt would contact the crank counterweights. This aggravates the wear and ring seal problem, as short pistons rock more than those of standard length.

CON ROD BOLTS AND CAP SCREWS

Rod cap bolts have to be designed to withstand a considerable force, to stop the cap from breaking away from the rod. At times it is necessary to fit bolts of a larger diameter than standard. Whatever the diameter, the tensile strength of the bolts should be 185,000psi minimum and it may be up to 270,000psi in extreme applications. However this is only part of the picture as to whether a particular bolt or cap screw will provide reliable long-term service in our competition engine. If it's an ARP (Automotive Racing Products) fastener you can be sure that it has been thoroughly tested to high loads for a million cycles, so will have excellent fatigue resistance. By comparison so called 'aircraft quality' fasteners are tested up to 45% load for only 100,000 cycles. What is worse for engine builders who think they are getting a better-than-normal bolt, because these have passed supposedly tough aeroplane standards, is that if all of the test samples endure only 85,000 cycles the entire batch is released for sale. In an average race engine that translates to a life of 25–45 miles. This isn't to imply that 'aircraft quality' bolts won't be reliable in your engine – they may be, but don't be lulled by those words into a false sense of security. Those magic words or some fancy AMS (Aerospace Material Specification) identification should not be the basis on which your bolts are selected.

Prior to assembly, carefully inspect every big-end bolt with about a 4X loupe, checking for any nicks or imperfections on the surface 'skin' of each bolt. There should not be a square shoulder where the shank meets the bolt head, but rather a generous radius. Note that stock big-end bolts should not be re-used, but high-quality boron steel bolts will generally not require replacement until after several rebuilds.

BEARING SELECTION AND CLEARANCE

Bearings in a high-power engine, as well as providing a low-friction wearing surface, also have to absorb tremendous shock loads. Therefore only top-quality trimetal bearings should be used for the mains and big ends, although white metal bearings are satisfactory for carrying the camshaft.

Correctly tensioning rod bolts

Frequently rod bolt failure can be traced back to incorrect tensioning techniques. If the bolts are over-tensioned they may fail at less than their designed rpm limit. On the other hand, when big end bolts are not sufficiently preloaded – stretched – they can loosen and fail.

There are three aspects to obtaining the correct bolt preload. First, use the specified lubricant and apply it not only to the bolt thread, but also to the thread of the rod (or the nut). Additionally, lube the underhead area of the bolt (or the base of the nut) where it bears against the con-rod cap. If the bolt manufacturer recommends engine oil and you apply hypoid diff oil, moly cam lube or moly rod bolt lube, the bolts could end up overstretched. All these lubricants will cut the friction between the bolt and the rod cap and between the threads more than engine oil, so a torque wrench reading of 45lb could be stretching the bolt to the equivalent of a 55lb reading. Conversely, if the bolt manufacturer specifies moly rod bolt lube and you apply engine oil, the bolts will also not be correctly preloaded, and they may loosen in service.

Second, stick to the bolt tension specified by the bolt manufacturer. Do not assume that because standard bolts are torqued to 45lb, the manufacturer of the high-grade bolts has made an error in stipulating a tension of, say, 38lb.

Third, use the correct tensioning procedure and an accurate tension wrench. This involves torquing up the bolts three times. After the first tensioning the bolts are backed off, then they are torqued a second time and backed off. These two operations polish the threads and the bolt head (or nut) and cap contact areas. On the third and final torquing the correct bolt preload will be obtained.

Naturally the techniques described above will be successful only when either new or within-spec bolts are fitted. If used bolts, which have been stretched beyond their design limit, are installed, bolt failure is inevitable. For this reason all new bolts must be accurately measured using a micrometer, and their length and the position where they are fitted must be recorded. Later, when the engine is dismantled, the lengths of all rod bolts can be checked and compared with their new length. Any bolt that has stretched more than 0.001in (check with the bolt manufacturer, as this will vary) must be discarded. A bolt that has yielded more than 0.001in has either been subjected to an over-rev or else it has been over-tensioned at the time of installation.

I use only Vandervell lead-indium and Clevite 77 bearings because of their special features, both types being able to stand up to the worst competition loads when correctly installed. These bearings are steel backed, with a copper-lead intermediate layer that gives the bearing good fatigue strength and load-carrying capacity, as well as resistance to hydraulic break-out. The running surface for the Vandervell bearing is a precision overlay of lead-indium, while the Clevite 77 overlay is lead-tin.

Correct bearing clearance is an obvious necessity. Excessive clearance will promote knocking and pounding and allow excessive oil throw off into the cylinder bores; this in turn will cause higher frictional losses in the cylinder and increase oil consumption. Excessive clearance at the big ends will lead to oil starvation at the main bearings, with resultant bearing failure. Insufficient clearance will cause rapid bearing deterioration as a result of the increased temperatures that come about due to insufficient oil flow or a thin oil film (Table 11.3). A good rule of thumb is 0.0009in clearance for each inch of shaft diameter for main bearings and 0.0012in clearance per inch of shaft diameter for rod bearings when running 15W-50 fully synthetic oil at 100–110°C. With a thinner oil such as 0W-30, bearing clearances can be a little tighter. Con rod side clearance (end-float) also affects bearing lubrication, so this should be checked on every big end to ensure proper oil control.

Table 11.3   Bearing clearances for trimetal copper lead bearings

Diameter of shaft (in)	Clearance between shaft and bearing	Side clearance
1.5	0.0012–0.0017	0.004–0.006
2.0	0.0015–0.002	0.005–0.007
2.25	0.0018–0.0025	0.005–0.007
2.5	0.0022–0.0027	0.005–0.007
2.75	0.0024–0.0028	0.006–0.008
3.0	0.0025–0.0028	0.007–0.009
3.25	0.0025–0.003	0.007–0.009

Note: in engines where two con rods share a common crankpin (eg a V8) multiply the side clearance by 3 for steel rods, and by 4 for aluminium rods.

A slightly different situation exists when an aluminium alloy block is used in a race engine. Because aluminium expands more than cast iron when heated, what were ideal main bearing clearances at room temperature could become excessive at race engine temperature. For example, a clearance of 0.002in cold will increase to at least 0.003in, and more probably 0.004in, when hot. To address this situation the engine should be assembled with tighter main bearing clearances, which will frequently be close to what the manufacturer quotes for stock engines. Thus if the race clearance with an iron block is normally set at 0.002in, I would probably be looking at 0.001–0.0013in main bearing clearance when running an alloy block. However, with such tight clearances the oil and water should be pre-heated prior to engine fire-up.

MAIN BEARING INSTALLATION

There are just a few simple rules to follow for correct bearing installation. Accurately measure and record the inside diameter of every main bearing and big-end housing without bearings fitted. Now do the same with the crankshaft main and crankpin journals. Unwrap all the bearings and carefully wash them in clean solvent to remove the protective film, but do not polish them with any sort of abrasive pad as the overlay is very thin and is easily damaged. Do not worry about any little 'peaks' in the overlay – they will soon flatten out when the engine is run. Next measure the bearing shell thickness and double the measurement as there is a shell on each side of the shaft. The difference between the shaft and housing diameters and the doubled shell measurement is the space left for the running clearance. When measuring the bearing shell thickness be sure to take the measurement well away from the parting line as race bearings typically taper down by 0.0005in and up to 0.0015in over the last $1/4$ to $1/2$in. This eccentricity is manufactured into race bearings because at very high rpm the connecting rod bore pinches in due to rod stretch.

Many Clevite 77 and Vandervell bearings are available with three levels of eccentricity, 0.0005in, 0.001in and 0.0015in. Ideally a bearing should show wear over about 65–75% of its surface. If it is showing contact almost up to the parting line, fit bearings with more eccentricity, but when the contact area is too short bearings with reduced eccentricity are called for.

When you have calculated the running clearances for each bearing you will probably find that some have a little more than you want, while others may be a touch tight. If the engine is a popular unit for competition use the bearing manufacturer may have special 0.001in undersize and oversize bearings available. Using just one half of such a bearing allows the clearance to be opened up or closed down by just 0.0005in. When mixing a 0.001in undersize shell with a standard size shell the recommended orientation is to fit the shell with the thickest wall in the upper position in big ends and in the lower position if it is a main bearing.

Trimetal bearings have a very thin overlay that should not be polished with abrasive scouring pads. These big-end shells are identical, but the mains are not; the upper shell is grooved to provide oil feed to the big ends, while the lower bearing is ungrooved to increase its load-carrying capacity.

After ensuring that all the bearing housings and bearing shells are perfectly clean and dry, fit the shells and check oil hole alignment; any misalignment should be corrected using a small round key file. After filing, carefully dress the steel back of the shell to remove any metal fraze. Next coat all the bearings with engine oil and fit the crankshaft (do not use a 50–50 mixture of oil and any substance like STP). Fit the main bearing caps in their correct order with arrows facing the front of the block and gradually tighten them down. Before final tightening, the crank should be tapped to each side with a soft hammer in order to line up the bearing caps. Now check the crankshaft end float: it should be within 0.004–0.006in with a cast-iron block. If the clearance is more than this, fit thicker thrust washers.

BIG END BEARING INSTALLATION

When it comes to fitting the big-end bearings follow the same procedure as for the fitting of the main bearings. There are still a few historic engines that use lock tabs on the big-end bolts. Throw these away, as they crush and give a false bolt tension reading. Use Loctite on the threads and you will have no problems with loose bolts.

Note that when the bearing shells are pushed into their respective housings they should feel 'springy', and 'snap' into place; this indicates good bearing crush. A lack of crush in new bearings indicates that either the bearing housing is distorted or that bearings with oversize shells are required to match housings that have been bored oversize. With used bearings a lack of crush usually indicates that the bearings have been hammered by detonation, but may also indicate a distorted bearing housing.

COATED BEARINGS

As well as going in for special oil additives, some tuners are advocating the use of products that must be baked on to bearings at very high temperatures for several hours; they are supposed to provide bearing protection when lubrication is inadequate. I do not recommend such products, as any time a bearing is heated in excess of 200°C for more than about an hour it will be ruined. This comes about due to the high temperature curing causing diffusion between the second and third layers of the bearing, which in turn weakens the overlay structure. Clevite 77 have produced a coated bearing, called TriArmor, using a lower temperature spray method to apply a 0.0003in polymer layer containing both molybdenum and graphite. This is intended to reduce friction, and in times of marginal lubrication when the bearing surface touches the crank scuffing is minimal.

PISTON SELECTION

Moving further up in the block, the next components for consideration are the pistons, piston rings and piston pin. First, you must decide whether the standard piston is up to the job. If the motor is in sports tune, it is quite probable that the standard cast and slotted pistons will be satisfactory. Higher states of tune will demand unslotted cast pistons, and in racing tune unslotted forged pistons will be necessary.

Most production engines use cast pistons, as they are easy to produce and shape as required. Some high-performance engines will be fitted with high-quality forged or cast pistons right from the factory. By looking inside the piston you will be able to see whether it is cast or forged: cast pistons have quite intricate under-crown shapes around the gudgeon pin boss, while forged pistons are smooth inside and lack intricate struts and braces.

The cast piston, either conventional or hypereutectic, has a relatively low material density. Whereas the ordinary cast piston is made from a low silicon (7–8%) aluminium alloy, the hypereutectic piston is cast from an alloy containing about twice as much silicon (usually 15–20%) and can withstand higher temperature and pressure. The additional silicon makes the piston harder, which increases wear and scuff resistance, and also reduces piston expansion when heated. Thus the hypereutectic piston will run tighter piston-to-cylinder-wall clearances, and as it can be cast with intricate underhead struts it can be made reasonably strong and generally lighter than a forged piston. For these reasons hypereutectic pistons are a good choice for very-high-performance road engines and budget race engines.

By comparison, forged pistons are much denser and consequently have a higher tensile strength. They are capable of withstanding higher pressure and heat loads than the cast piston, and due to their higher density thermal conductivity is improved such that a piston crown temperature reduction of 100°F is usual. Because of these beneficial features forged pistons are usually preferred over hypereutectics in maximum-effort race engines.

A less common piston, which some engine builders prefer, is the billet piston. These are fully machined from a billet of forged aluminium alloy to produce a lightweight and relatively strong piston. However, as they are quite expensive, and in my experience in no way superior to well-designed hypereutectic race pistons, I do not recommend them.

The worst feature of many production pistons is the slot for oil drainage behind the oil control ring. This usually extends almost from one boss around to the other, on both sides of the piston. To make the situation worse, expansion control slots cut into

Oil drain/expansion control slots seriously weaken the piston and make it prone to breakage in performance applications.

A slipper piston has much of the skirt cut away and often has a very short gudgeon pin. This piston is for a 12,500rpm race engine, which is why it has only one compression ring.

the piston skirt usually break into the oil drain slot. Slots weaken the piston considerably, allowing the skirt to break away from the top. In standard production engines this can be a problem, so you can imagine what you are up against if slotted pistons are retained in a high-performance unit. Pistons suitable for high-performance use (either cast or forged) do not have any slots for expansion control or oil drainback. Instead, small oil-drainage holes are drilled right the way around the oil control ring groove. Extra piston clearance and special design take care of expansion.

Racing pistons may be of either the full skirt or the slipper variety, and some may be a cross between both, with a skirt extending to below the pin boss, but cut back to the thrust faces below this point. The slipper designs are lighter but piston life can be as little as 250–300 miles at sustained high rpm. Also, depending on such things as rod length, crank stroke, piston diameter and piston clearances, piston ring sealing and oil control may not be as good as with a full skirt piston. Additional to these problems I sometimes find that I have to use a heavier gudgeon pin to reduce pin tower flex, and the heavier pin tends to offset the weight advantage of the slipper piston. Consequently I have a preference for the full skirt design. Together with a long taper-wall gudgeon pin (with a length at least 0.7 times the bore diameter), piston life will be anything from three to six times longer than an equivalent slipper type.

RING GROOVE ACCURACY

Apart from durability the next most important thing I look for in a piston is accurate machining of the ring grooves. Twenty years ago it wasn't such a big issue as ring manufacturers were struggling to supply us the best competition rings parallel and flat to within ±0.0005in. Today the flatness and parallelism of the best quality competition rings can be held to ±0.00005in; a tenfold improvement, fortunately there has not been a similar jump in price, but at this standard they are certainly not cheap! To take advantage of this advance, and avoid wasting money on accurate but expensive rings, we need to find pistons with a matching level of accuracy in the ring grooves. This has to be true of the piston not only when new out of the box, but also well into its service life. Obviously there is little to be gained if, because of metallurgical or structural design problems, the ring lands move soon after the you begin to work the engine hard. Mahle for example can supply their top of the line pistons with land flatness held to within a micron (0.00004in). Such pistons cost two to three times that of ordinary off-the-shelf forged competition pistons. In absolute peak hp terms such pistons and a matching ring package will be worth 1–1.5% on a newly built engine. As the engine nears the end of its service the gain will be about double those numbers, and lower in the rev range the improvement may be a bit higher.

We have always known that flat lands and flat rings seal better as the piston rises on the compression stroke, and then descends on the power stroke, by blocking gas from around the back of the ring escaping between the bottom of the ring and the land. Therefore it was always considered vital that the bottom of the ring and the lower side of the land never be scratched or damaged in any way. However in reality the same is true when it comes to the top of the ring and the top of the land. The seal here is just as important if we are going to make good power. We have to remember that in a naturally aspirated engine we rely solely on the vacuum created within the cylinder as the piston descends to drag in the air/fuel mixture. The bigger the vacuum the more power producing mixture we draw in. Therefore the better the rings seal, not only on the power stroke but also on the induction stroke when the vacuum is being developed, the more hp the engine will deliver. The only way we can pull the best vacuum is by using a piston/ring package that will seal efficiently on the down stroke. This means that the flatness of the top of the ring groove, and the top of the ring, is equally as important as that of the bottom side. Consequently we have to understand that that top side seal must not be compromised in any way. That means being careful not to scratch or nick any side of the ring groove or any side of the ring. It also means that a piston should not be machined anywhere after the grooves have been machined. Put another way – if you are looking to build a top performing race engine the very last operation on a piston should be the machining of the ring grooves.

RING GROOVE PLACEMENT

The actual placement of the rings is important to gain those last few hp. As shown in Figure 11.6 we want the rings as high up the piston as possible, but this is limited by the engine's hp potential and the heat load on the top ring. This means that in engines producing up to about 65hp per cylinder the top ring should be 0.180in from the crown and the second ring should be 0.0160in below the top ring, with the oil control ring a further 0.090in down; while at higher power levels the top ring will be at 0.240–0.300in. High ring placement brings a number of benefits. First, we can locate the piston pin higher in the piston which permits the use of longer con rods, which in turn lowers the piston skirt loadings, so there is less risk of scuffing and piston distortion; they also reduce piston rock at TDC, so ring seal is better and hp rises. Second, high placement of rings allows the piston crown to shed its heat load more rapidly and with the second ring also placed high it is able to play a much greater role in getting heat out of the top of the piston, rather than leaving this task to the top ring. In turn, with a greater burden of heat transfer being shared by the second ring it is now possible to reduce the width of the top ring, the benefits of which we will cover later.

Rapidly ridding the piston crown of heat increases piston durability, and a cooler piston top lessens the risk of detonation as the incoming fuel/air charge will not be

Figure 11.6 Piston ring placement.

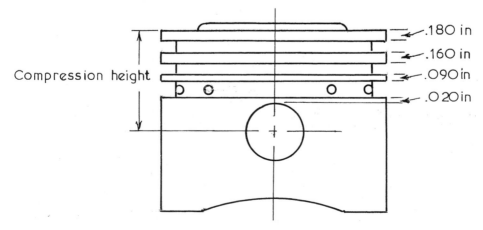

Compression height

.180 in
.160 in
.090 in
.020 in

This full skirt piston has been machined across the pin boss area to reduce its weight and cut friction, and to allow the use of a shorter and lighter pin. Note the 'H'-section con rod.

preheated to such an extent. This opens up the possibility of greater engine reliability, with the engine being able to run harder for longer in endurance events. Alternatively we may choose to sacrifice some reliability for more hp and so opt to bump up the compression ratio or the spark, or else lean the mixture off closer to full power lean.

PISTON-TO-CYLINDER CLEARANCE

We tend to think of pistons as being round, but actually the skirt is cam-ground an oval shape, and the piston also tapers from bottom to top; both features being necessary to prevent seizure. The top of the piston is almost twice as hot as the bottom of the skirt, so it expands more. Due to the extra metal around the pin bosses, more heat is directed to this area, elongating the piston across the piston pin axis. To compensate, the piston skirt is ground oval. Most pistons are from 0.005–0.012in less in diameter across the pin axis than across the thrust faces. Be careful to measure piston clearance only on the thrust faces, and either at the bottom of the skirt or up near the pin (check this with the piston manufacturer).

Accidentally dropping a piston may damage the skirt and lead to eventual seizure due to skirt distortion. Never bang a piston pin out with a hammer and drift: this is a sure way to push the skirt out of shape. If the pin will not push out easily, heat the piston in boiling water or oil, then gently tap it out with the con rod secured in a vice to prevent any pressure at all on the piston.

For better lubrication, and to allow for extra piston expansion, high-performance engines must have more piston-to-cylinder clearance than models off the showroom floor. It is best to consult the piston manufacturer on this, but in general I would be 382 looking at a minimum of 0.002in and preferably up around 0.003in clearance in road engines running cast pistons (including hypereutectic cast) with bore sizes in the 80–110mm range. In a race engine cast pistons would require a little more clearance, 0.0027in–0.004in. Road engines running forged pistons require about 0.0012–0.0015in clearance per inch of bore, while competition engines typically require around 0.0015–0.0018in per inch of bore. However, some forged pistons, for example some manufactured by JE, run only 0.003in clearance just like cast pistons. There should be a maximum of 0.0005in difference in clearance between the tightest and sloppiest cylinders. If the tolerance is greater than this, try swapping the pistons around in different cylinders. When it is finally decided which piston goes where, number each inside the skirt using a suitable marking pen. Do not mark the crown as this may be machined later to give the correct deck height.

VALVE-TO-PISTON CLEARANCE

As the majority of motors have heads with inclined or canted valves, some thought must be given to providing adequate valve-to-piston clearance. There should be a minimum of 0.060in vertical clearance, although for push rod engines, which in competition are more likely to suffer valve float, I prefer 0.080in for the inlets and 0.100in for the exhaust. The cut-out diameter for safety is 0.120in greater than the valve head diameter, but in race engines, where there is no build-up of carbon on the valves or pistons, this can be reduced to 0.050in.

There are two basic ways to go about checking the safe valve working clearance, but both methods involve quite a deal of work. Both techniques also require that the motor be almost totally assembled. The cam must be installed and accurately timed, and the head and head gasket need to be fitted.

The first way involves the use of a piece of modelling clay pressed down on the top of a piston. After the clay has been smoothed out, spray it and the valves in the cylinder that is being checked with a light coating of WD-40. This will help prevent the clay from sticking to the valves later, when the clearance check is made. Fit the head and head gasket, tension it down and adjust the valve clearances. Now very carefully turn the motor over two full turns to completely open and close both the inlet and exhaust valves. Remove the head and measure the thickness of the clay over both valve cut-outs. Next cut the clay, using a sharp, wet knife, to check the clearance around the periphery of the valve head.

The other method is accurate only if the valve cut-outs are central under the valve, as there is no provision for a check to be made on the clearance between the edge of the valve head and the edge of the cut-out. In this instance light checking springs need to be fitted instead of valve springs. First tension down the head and head gasket as before, and adjust the valve clearances. Next set up a dial gauge on the inlet valve and turn the motor over until the valve is fully open. Zero the dial gauge and push the valve open as far as it will go. The dial gauge reading gives the clearance. Measure the exhaust valve clearance similarly.

PISTON-TO-HEAD CLEARANCE

To assist in equalising compression and combustion pressures, the crown of every piston must rise to the same point in each cylinder; this is called the deck height of the 383 piston. Generally we would want to be running minimum deck clearance to assist cylinder scavenging, and to increase the compression ratio. A good solid motor with steel rods can run with a minimum of 0.040in clearance between the piston crown (not the compression lump) and the squish area of the head. Therefore if the head gasket is 0.030in thick when compressed, we could run a minimum deck clearance of 0.040 – 0.030 = 0.010in. This means that the pistons would all be machined so that they are 0.010in from the top of the block at TDC. If one piston is 0.015in down the bore, it will be necessary to machine all the other pistons so that they are also 0.015in from the block deck at TDC. To restore the compression we would then need to machine 0.015 – 0.010 = 0.005in from the block deck.

Aluminium connecting rods stretch more at high revs, and aluminium has a greater coefficient of expansion than steel, so we would need at least 0.070in piston-to-head clearance. Engines that have steel rods but suffer block flex or crankshaft whip, eg air-cooled VW, will require 0.060in clearance. Most American V8s are more rigid and can run 0.045in given the full treatment of steel crank and rods and heavy-duty block. If a standard block and crank are retained, increase the clearance to 0.050in.

DECK CLEARANCE AND SQUISH IN ROAD ENGINES

In road engines I like to keep the squish clearance between 0.035 and a maximum of 0.045in. Usually, to achieve this figure the top of the block will have to be milled. Note in a road engine that it is not essential for all pistons to rise to the same height in each cylinder; a variation of 0.005in is acceptable. The reason I like to build a good deal of squish into a road engine is this causes the piston to squish the fuel/air charge from the edges of the cylinder toward the spark plug. The fast moving gases meet the spark plug and quickly carry the combustion flame to the extremity of the combustion chamber, thus reducing the risk of detonation. This opens the way to use a higher compression ratio to enhance part throttle performance and fuel economy.

With the passing of time more benefits of building squish into the engine have come to light. The mixture being purged across the combustion chamber from the squish areas homogenises the fuel/air mixture more thoroughly and also mixes any residual exhaust gas still present with the fuel charge. This serves to speed up combustion by preventing stale gas pockets from forming. Such pockets slow down and in some instances can prevent, flame propagation. With improvements in combustion quality, performance is improved particularly at cruise. Consequently the engine is markedly more responsive, plus fuel consumption falls.

Turbulence caused by the squish effect also serves to enhance heat transfer at the spark-initiated flame front. Without proper heat transfer, jets of flame would tend to shoot out toward the edges of the combustion chamber, prematurely heating the surrounding gases to start off the cycle leading to detonation.

Whenever dished or reverse dome pistons are fitted to lower the compression, the outline of the dish should ideally be a mirror image of the outline of the combustion chamber. This means that the piston has a squish surface which exactly matches the cylinder head squish area. Unfortunately, pistons machined to mirror the combustion chamber tend to be much more expensive because of the intricate machine operations involved. Hence, car manufacturers tend to use lower cost pistons with a central dish and narrow squish band or an offset dish which places a large squish area

This piston has a squish area that matches the cylinder head squish area.

over to one side of the piston crown. When the piston squish band is as wide as the cylinder head area the required squish is produced. However, the squish band on some pistons is much narrower than the cylinder head squish area, and some tuners when lowering the compression ratio also machine the squish band too narrow.

SQUISH IN RACE ENGINES

The situation is different with competition engines. Here low speed combustion quality and cruise economy are not usually a concern. What we are after is the best hp over a range of about 35–45% engine revs at the top of the power band, usually on throttle openings wider than 60% open. Under such circumstances mixture density is quite high so there is a corresponding increase in mixture turbulence as the piston rises to TDC on the compression stroke. Therefore the squish area can be reduced or the squish clearance can be increased in many race engines without any power loss. Perhaps there may be a power gain.

I have experienced engines on the dyno that sounded good and sharp with wonderful throttle response, but with only average power output. Frequently opening up the squish clearance would see a nice power gain and much smoother running. The conclusion I reached was that tight squish was causing some sort of combustion instability, or possibly the very rapid compression as the piston squeezed the gases between the squish faces meant that the gases became the equivalent of solid matter, so in effect it was like the piston banging into the head.

While you digest that last thought keep in mind that engines literally can go solid, or 'hydraulic'. The problem is more often noted in nitro burning engines running pistons that are not dished, but I have also seen it in engines operating on very rich alcohol mixtures and also when crude water injection systems have been employed. What happens is that as the piston accelerates up the cylinder it collects all the 385 unvaporised fuel or water. Violent wind across the piston crown disperses this liquid away from the centre of the piston out toward the edges. If the clearance between piston and head is sufficient no harm is done as the piston comes up to top dead centre. If it is too close the engine goes solid as the piston attempts to compress the liquid against the head. There is no time for this liquid to be gently squeezed out of the squish gap into the combustion chamber as some suppose. Nor does fuel or water puddled into one area on the piston crown get 'flattened' or dispersed across the entire squish area. Basically the engine damage will range from distorted pistons through to a totally destroyed engine.

In two stroke engines the squish areas are extremely tight, down to 0.020in, but best combustion often results from squish areas that diverge toward the centre of the combustion chamber. Thus, while the squish clearance may be only 0.025in at the very edge of the piston, it may open up to 0.032in about 16mm from the edge. I have experimented with the same idea on four strokes and while it had the desired effect it did not appear to be superior to simply opening up the squish clearance a little, or reducing the squish area.

PISTON CROWN MODIFICATIONS TO AID COMBUSTION

As I mentioned right at the beginning of the book, the top of the piston is a part of the combustion chamber, and those high compression lumps on the top of your pistons can add to, or detract from, the complete combustion of fuel inducted into the engine. They may retard flame travel after ignition and upset complete cylinder scavenging during the exhaust cycle. On the intake stroke, the dome can restrict the critical initial air/fuel flow, then disrupt final mixture homogenisation before ignition.

To improve air flow into the cylinder at low valve lift, the intake valve pocket must be laid back to reduce valve shrouding (Figure 11.7). As the initial flow is along the floor of the port and around the short radius toward the squish area of the head, this modification will assist in cylinder filling. Many tuners worry about removing metal from the piston dome because of the slight drop in compression ratio; however, the improved flow and better combustion will far exceed the slight power losses due to the drop in compression ratio.

After ignition, we want the flame to travel smoothly across the piston dome and back towards the squish area. Any abrupt edge on the compression lump will disrupt the flame front as it moves across the piston, leaving pockets of mixture that are either unburned or only partially ignited. Rounding and smoothing the top and sides of the dome does much to reduce this problem.

The exhaust valve cut-out must not be laid back, as this is usually not advantageous. The sharpness of the exhaust valve pocket does cause some flame disruption, but exhaust flow and cylinder scavenging are usually superior when the exhaust valve is shrouded by the cut-out.

After the engine has been run for a time, a careful study should be made of piston dome coloration, which is a surprisingly accurate means of investigating combustion completeness. Keep in mind that combustion begins before the piston reaches TDC and continues well past TDC. If at any time something happens to cause the flame to stop, the piston colour will indicate where the dome is causing the cessation.

All motors with bath-tub or wedge-chamber heads will show an area of no carbon build-up on both the piston and cylinder head. This is in the squish (or quench)

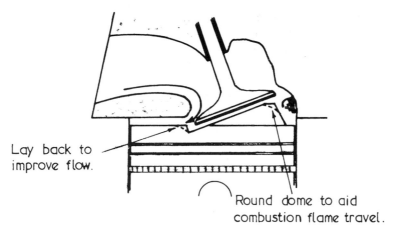

Lay back to improve flow.

Round dome to aid combustion flame travel.

Figure 11.7 Piston dome modification.

area where no combustion takes place due to the closeness of the flat face of the head and piston. Any other areas on the piston dome where there is little or no carbon build-up likewise indicate that the dome is coming too close to the combustion chamber and is retarding the ignition flame at and around TDC.

The solution is to machine the compression domes lightly until the carbon build-up is more even in quantity and colour. Because the flame moves from the spark plug out across the combustion chamber, you will need to keep in mind the direction of flame travel when you come to remove any metal from the dome. Generally, it will not be necessary to machine the entire uncoloured area as it is usually the area immediately in front of and around the beginning of the uncoloured area, relative to the direction of flame travel, where the dome is coming too close to the combustion chamber wall and creating a pocket of unburned fuel. The place of least flame activity is usually around the high side of the piston dome in the area of the intake valve cut-out, close to the cylinder wall. If you can modify the dome to colour evenly in this area, you are well on the way to achieving good combustion.

PISTON PIN AND PIN CLEARANCES

As mentioned previously, I prefer a long piston pin with a tapered bore to cut its weight. However, if we go too far we end up with a pin that is nice and light but which allows the piston to flex excessively. The end result will be cracking in the top of the piston where the pin towers join the crown. The ends of the pin should be chamfered to bear up into round wire circlips and the length should be such that when the pin retainers are fitted, pin end float is preferably 0–0.001in; more than 0.005in is unacceptable in a race engine.

When we add vacuum to the crankcase to reduce windage losses we begin to experience marginal lubrication in a number of areas; the piston pin being one such component. The fix may take several forms including a squirter nozzle in each cylinder to spray oil up into the piston crown/pin area to both lubricate the pin and cool the piston, or con rods with an oilway from the big end up to the little end to lubricate the pin. Another route is to fit pins with a Diamond Like Coating (DLC). 387

The big-end is grooved to provide continuous oil flow up the rod to the little-end.

As well as enabling the pin, piston and little end to perform very well with only limited lubrication, a pin with a proven DLC such as Casidiam from Anatech enables us to run rods with an unbushed little end. This then translates to a smaller, lighter rod that reduces bearing loads and may enable us to cut bearing size, reduce crank weight etc.

The piston pin is retained by a variety of means in the production engine, the most common being either an interference press fit in the connecting rod, or by flat circlips. If the latter are used, they should be coated with Loctite. Ensure that the circlip grooves are clean and undamaged so that each circlip can seat securely. The interference press fit (0.0015–0.0025in) is suitable for racing engines, but care must be taken to assemble and remove the piston from the rod without causing any piston damage.

As racing engine speeds are now moving past 8,000rpm, many engine builders are experiencing problems with circlips (either flat or round wire). At very high rpm or if the engine detonates they may close up, due to the forces exerted on them, and drop out of the piston into the bore. To overcome this it is necessary to employ another means of pin retention. Some have reverted to interference press fit, but generally I prefer to use double Spirolox. Never re-use old circlips or Spirolox retainers.

The fit of the pin in the piston exercises more control over piston dimension than is often appreciated. The additional clearance given to a piston by cam grinding is nullified if the piston is unable to expand correctly due to a tight pin. The pin clearance (pin-to-piston and pin-to-rod) in the high-performance and racing engine must be greater to compensate for forces that the standard production engine is unlikely to experience. At high engine speeds crankshaft whip and con rod distortion can severely load the piston pin, and if it has too tight a fit, piston-to-cylinder scuffing or seizure may result. In extreme instances the pin will push the side out of the piston.

For most engines I set a pin-to-rod clearance at 0.0008–0.0015in, and a pin-to-piston clearance a little tighter at 0.0005–0.0008in. This will alleviate any binding between rod and pin or between pin and piston that could lead to piston damage. However, no matter how free the pin is, any con rod misalignment could wreck the piston, so have the rods checked to ensure that they are not bent, twisted or offset.

Oil drain-back holes that break out below the bottom oil rail improve oil control and reduce parasitic losses. Note the lightweight taper-bore gudgeon pin.

THE PISTON RINGS

The piston ring, as it slides up and down the cylinder wall, has to function like a bearing, but also has to seal off the combustion chamber to keep the gases from escaping past the piston into the crankcase. Most engines use either two or three rings per piston.

The first or top ring is called the compression ring; its purpose is to contain the combustion pressure so that maximum power can be obtained. This ring also has the burden of dissipating most of the piston crown heat (about 80%) to the cylinder wall.

Some racing engines do not use a second compression ring, but if yours does, it has the task of backing up the top ring in sealing off the combustion charge and removing heat from the piston crown. However, its primary function is to support the oil ring in scraping excess oil off the cylinder wall.

The bottom ring is the oil scraper or oil control ring. Its job is to scrape oil from the cylinder wall, but ensure that enough oil remains behind to lubricate the upper rings and assist in sealing.

As indicated in Table 11.4, the oil control rings cause a good deal of engine friction, and we all know that friction costs hp. Therefore many manufacturers are able to supply oil rings in three grades of tension. Standard tension rings are those mostly fitted to ordinary road engines by car makers, but low-tension oil rings are now being fitted to some production cars and are the preferred option in competition engines as they usually provide oil control almost as good as standard tension rings, but with reduced parasitic losses. High-tension oil rings are rarely used, but may be necessary in some engines running at very high rpm with poor rod-length-to-stroke ratios.

Some engine builders have been dropping the second compression ring in the hope of gaining some reduction in parasitic losses. This appears to be an easy route to increased hp, but the power gains are only small, and then only at high rpm. In fact, it is very easy to lose power due to reduced oil control. When done properly I am finding power gains in the order of 0.7% at 8,500rpm, and the gains increase at higher engine speeds. Personally I would not run a two-ring piston in an engine that was running at less than 8,500rpm, and then only with crankcase vacuum applied. Frequently, at these lower engine speeds, the largest gains come from being able to run with a shorter, lighter piston. This can then permit a lighter rod, reduced big end width or diameter etc.

RING TENSION AND RING WIDTH

Let's take a closer look to see what goes on when the compression ring seals off the combustion chamber (Figure 11.8). Many feel that it is the ring's inherent radial tension that holds it against the cylinder wall. As the piston descends on the inlet stroke that is correct. If there was very little radial tension the piston would not be capable of pulling a good vacuum; so radial tension is critically important. However after ignition it is primarily gas pressure behind the back of the ring that forces the ring face against the cylinder wall to provide an effective seal.

Table 11.4   Comparison of piston ring function and friction

	Pressure sealing	Oil control	Frictional losses
Top ring	78%	5%*	30%
Second ring	22%	45%*	20%
Oil ring		70%	50%

* Top and second rings only assume such high levels of oil control when oil control rings are worn excessively or sticking.

A detrimental phenomenon that may occur in a high-rpm engine to reduce the ring's sealing ability is ring float or flutter. As the piston approaches TDC it is slowed down by the connecting rod, but the rings try to keep on moving, and if they have

Figure 11.8 Only the top ring is shown to illustrate how combustion pressure behind the ring forces it against the cylinder wall to effect a good seal. When ring mass causes it to swap sides in the groove, gas pressure is unable to get behind the ring.

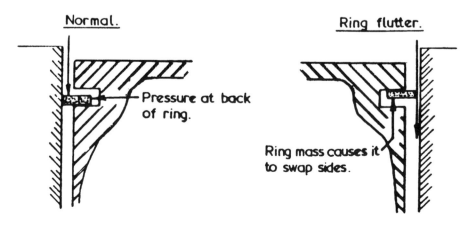

enough weight each will break contact with the lower side of its groove and bang into the top of the groove. When this happens, the ring seals off the gas pressure in the combustion chamber so that it cannot get behind the back of the ring and force it against the bore wall. Any gas pressure that may have been behind the ring quickly leaks into the crankcase, and combustion pressure forces the ring to collapse inwardly. Immediately the ring breaks contact with the bore wall, the combustion gases blow-by into the crankcase.

Radial tension in the ring is unable to prevent blow-by caused by ring flutter. However, a certain degree of radial tension is necessary for good sealing, otherwise the pressure at the back of the ring would only be equal to the pressure trying to force the ring off the cylinder wall. This would allow blow-by and it is this that we normally see occurring when the rings are old and have lost their tension.

Ring flutter allows blow-by, but it can also wreck engines. When the ring loses contact with the bore wall it is unable to transfer heat from the piston to the water jacket. The end result can be melted pistons or severe detonation, due to increased combustion temperature.

The narrower a ring for a given radial depth, the higher the rpm at which this effect commences. This has led many tuners to believe that they should use very narrow rings in all competition engines. However, narrow rings have a disadvantage: as was mentioned earlier, the compression rings are the primary heat transfer path for the pistons. Reducing the ring width will slow heat transfer, so the piston may overheat and soften. The top ring land may distort and jam the ring, which will result in the hp falling off, or worse the piston will melt.

The other negative aspect of narrow rings is their reduced service life. This may not be a concern in sprint engines if you have the time and cash to replace rings regularly. However, in an endurance engine rapid wear of the top ring could see a serious drop off in power before the race concludes, hence my recommendation to keep right away from narrow rings unless they are really necessary.

For the majority of high-performance road and competition engines running up to about 8,000rpm I recommend either 1/16in or 1.5mm top and second compression rings. Engines running up to 9,500rpm would run a 1.2mm or 0.043in top ring and either a 1/16in or 1.5mm second compression ring. Above 9,500rpm I would usually drop the second ring and retain a 1.2mm top ring, and only at 11,000rpm or higher would I go down to a 1mm ring. Note that when only one ring is used it may be necessary to move it to 0.260–0.300in from the piston crown to reduce the heat load on the ring. The oil ring should then be placed 0.220in below the compression ring.

With oil control rings the tendency also has been to go to very narrow three-piece rings and, surprisingly, no attempt is being made to use the space made available to move the gudgeon pin higher, which raises the question of why bother with narrow oil rings? If there is no problem with sufficient space between the piston pin and the top of the piston I prefer to run with a 3/16in or 4mm oil ring pack. Such a wide groove allows for four good size oil drain-back holes on both sides of the piston. Along with a full piston skirt with a square bottom edge to scrape oil off the cylinders, such good oil drain-back ensures that the top ring will seal effectively rather than 'aquaplaning' over a deep film of oil. A good top ring seal also means more hp, and less oil in the combustion chamber reduces the likelihood of power-sapping trace detonation. Only in very limited circumstances would I consider going down to a 1/8in or 3mm oil ring, and then I would insist on large 3.2mm oil drain holes that actually broke out of the bottom of the oil ring groove by around 1.2mm so as to drain oil from below the lower rail.

PISTON GAS PORTS

Apart from reducing the weight of the top ring, by reducing its width, there is something else we can do to help keep away from ring flutter in competition engines. By adding a series of lateral gas ports above the top ring we are able to maintain gas pressure behind the ring, even if the ring does swap sides as the piston moves past TDC. In effect these gas ports help an ordinary piston ring work like an 'L' section Dykes ring by ensuring that there is always an open path for gas pressure to get in behind the ring and push it out against the bore wall (Figure 11.9).

In earlier times builders of drag race engines routinely drilled many gas ports from the crown of the piston down through to the back of the ring groove. Unfortunately this practice exposed the piston and ring to a lot more heat, so component life was dramatically shortened. Lateral gas ports are nowhere near as aggressive, even so I recommend that no larger than a 2mm bit be used to mill a half round port to the full depth of the ring groove. The number of these ports will vary according to piston diameter. Below 83mm we should not exceed 6 ports, up to 93mm this would increase to a maximum of 7 and up to 105mm and 115mm we increase to no more than 8 ports and 9 ports respectively.

PISTON RING LIFTING

This brings us to another problem that many tuners do not appear to understand. As well as the top ring being thrown up to the top of the ring groove as the piston rapidly reverses its direction of travel at TDC, it can also be pushed up by pressure building up between the top ring and the second ring. What happens is that gas escaping past the

Figure 11.9 Lateral gas ports allow combustion pressure to get behind a ring that has swapped sides in the groove and force it against the bore wall.

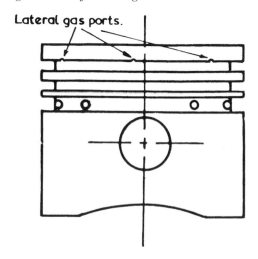

face of the top ring and through the gap between the ends of the top ring may not get past the second ring and into the crankcase as quickly as gas is building up in this area. This pressure will then work in opposition to combustion pressure which is pushing the top ring down onto the bottom face of the ring groove to effect a gas seal. Consequently the ring breaks full contact with the bottom face of the ring groove and combustion pressure then escapes under the top ring. That in turn increases the volume and pressure of gas trapped between both rings, further reducing the effectiveness of the seal between the lower surface of the top ring and the bottom face of the ring groove.

Clearly this scenario is going to cost us hp because gas pressure that should be driving the crankshaft is simply leaking into the sump. However that isn't the end of the story. That gas escaping down under the top ring then proceeds to give up some of its heat to the lower part of the piston. With this part of the piston now much hotter it is unable to act as a heat sink and pull some heat out of the top of the piston. Even more serious is the fact that the top-ring and piston are not making good contact for quite some time and as this is the piston's primary heat rejection path the piston overheats and in serious cases fails. Before that point is reached the engine will be down on power as the hot piston will heat the inlet mixture, and to keep out of detonation the spark advance will have to be reduced.

There are two things we can do to keep gas pressure from lifting the top ring. First up we must ensure that the second ring has sufficient end gap. Everyone frets about losing gas pressure through the ring gaps and into the sump. Therefore we have worked to bring the ring gaps down smaller, but we need to keep in mind that there is a limit to how far we can reasonably go. A race engine with thick, rigid cylinder walls should have a second ring gap at least as wide as the top ring. If the cylinders are prone to flexing a little then you need more gap in the second ring.

The second thing we can do is increase the space between the two rings to provide a larger reservoir for gas to escape into. In a race engine we gain a little extra volume anyway as we use a thicker ring land, but in addition to that we can machine a gas balance groove into the ring land. This groove may appear insignificant but it adds considerable volume to the area and as such reduces any tendency for pressure to build up and lift the top ring.

Never do we want the pressure to equalise above and below the top ring. If that happens we only have the weight of the ring to keep it sealing against the bottom of the ring groove, which isn't anything like sufficient. In fact this is part of the reason why when we add vacuum to the crankcase our horsepower rises. We cover this in more detail in the following chapter, but basically what we find is that when we keep crankcase pressure below zero by means of a scavenge pump drawing blow-by gas out, then we gain hp.

Part of this increase is because there is less friction. The low pressure environment means that we don't have a couple of litres of oil clinging to the crankshaft or suspended as droplets in the crankcase area for the crank and rod big-ends to smash into and thus cause drag. Additionally the vacuum literally pulls oil out of the cylinders. Therefore pistons and oil rings draw off less power scraping oil out of the bores. Because the oil rings have less work to do we may be able to drop the ring tension right off and cut parasitic losses even more.

The other portion of the power increase is due to the bigger pressure differential existing above and below the top ring increasing the effectiveness of the seal between 393 the face of the ring and the cylinder, and also between the bottom of the ring groove and the lower edge of the ring. A better seal means a bigger push on the crankshaft, plus it ensures best possible heat transfer out of the piston to the water jacket.

ZERO GAP SECOND RINGS

At this point some readers may be questioning how the above information can be accurate when zero gap second compression rings are held up by some race engine builders as being good for power. Clearly with no gap the second ring's escape route for blow-by gas is quite restricted and this must be causing the top ring to lift. However to my mind the merit of zero gap second rings relates more to how they help those engines operating at extremely rich air/fuel ratios achieve some semblance of engine life. These rich mixtures may be necessary to cool the engine internally, or they may be the product of crude injection systems forced on us by race regulations.

When we have an engine running very rich methanol or nitro mixtures cylinder lubrication is marginal. Added to that a huge volume of fuel can escape past the rings into the sump, severely diluting the lubricating oil and exposing the engine to wrecked big-end bearings and cam lobes/tappets in particular. When zero gap second rings are fitted they appear to do a better job of stemming the flow of this liquid fuel down past the rings. The rings and cylinder bore then bed-in much better and so effect a superior seal. Additionally because the lube oil is not diluted to such a degree the engine makes more power after a couple of hours' operation than an engine with conventional rings due to the cam lobes being closer to their new shape and the engine bearings being healthier. As well as keeping parasitic losses lower, bearings in good shape help to subdue crank harmonics and this in turn improves the accuracy of the valve timing events and ignition firing events.

Consequently while it may appear on the surface that zero gap second rings offer many benefits, such is not the case. Outside the areas I have just mentioned, ie when extremely rich alcohol or nitro mixtures are present, they are not recommended.

However do not assume that I am opposed to the idea of gapless top rings. Now that the technology is available to machine the two pieces, called the primary ring and the rail, to more exacting tolerances necessary in a top ring they can work very well in certain types of engines operating at up to about 8,000rpm. Some are claiming power gains as high as 5%; I think it is not above 2% at best, but any gain is a help at any time performance is not limited by traction.

RING END GAP

I have always accurately positioned the ring ends so as to reduce gas and oil leakage through the ring gap, even though some maintain this isn't necessary in a race engine. It has been proven that the rate of ring rotation to crank speed is about 1:1000. In other words an engine operating at 7,000rpm will have the compression rings rotating at 7rpm. Hence the idea that it's a waste of time staggering the gaps. However I still maintain that the ends of compression rings should be staggered 180°, and oil rails should have their ends staggered at least 90°.

Leakage through the ring gaps and blow-by (not flutter-induced blow-by) is more of a problem at low rpm, simply because there is more time for the gases to find

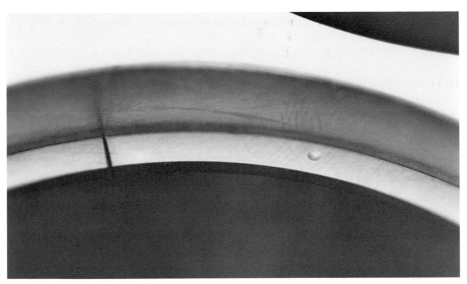

Running ring gaps too narrow is not wise in a high hp engine. Typically such engines put a lot more heat into the rings due to more time spent at wide open throttle; perhaps due also to the use of less conductive high silicon piston material and higher placement of the rings on the piston. The 'dimple' near the ring end indicates that this side of the piston ring faces up.

their way through the ring gaps. This is why high rev engines usually require only one compression ring, providing the oil control ring can look after oil control without the assistance of a second compression/scraper ring.

This in no way implies that we can simply unwrap a new set of rings and stick them straight onto pistons without first checking the end gaps. Actually the converse is true; we have to be extremely careful to fit each ring perfectly square in its bore and then measure the end gap and increase it if necessary by filing the ring ends. The minimum ring gap per inch of bore is as follows: air-cooled, turbo and supercharged engines, and engines burning alcohol or nitro, 0.006in. This is suitable also for light nitrous doses, but a competition nitrous engine will want this increased to 0.0065in per inch of bore. Oil ring rails must be at least 0.004in per inch of bore diameter, but a larger gap won't hurt. All other engines 0.005in top ring and second ring, and 0.004in oil ring rails. Engines with hypereutectic pistons put a lot more heat into the top ring, hence some manufacturers are recommending that the top ring gap be increased by 20% when these pistons are fitted. I find that this increase is about right for road engines but with race engines I reckon that you should start out with 35% more gap. Then when the engine is rebuilt if there is no sign of ring end polishing, indicating the ends are touching due to insufficient gap width, decrease the gap by 0.002in. Then if at the next rebuild there is still no indication of the ends touching reduce the gap another 0.002in.

Some people will no doubt question such large ring gaps but let me assure you that when the engine is actually running at full power the top ring gap will close up to around 50% due to the heat put into it. If the engine gets hot enough to detonate, the gaps will go close to closing right up. One way you can check if you have sufficient ring gap is by inspecting your old rings. If the ring ends are polished the ends are touching, therefore increase the gap by 0.002in. If you don't you could break the rings, severely score the bores or ruin the pistons!

In practice most blow-by is due to bore distortion and leakage past the ring faces rather than through the gaps, so be careful when it comes to setting the end gaps. Also keep in mind that once sonic velocity is achieved through the ring gap the flow volume will not rise with an increase in combustion pressure or supercharger boost. Therefore as we tune our engine to higher performance levels blow-by through the ring gaps will not increase. Overall blow-by though will worsen, but this is due to more bore distortion and increased leakage past the ring faces.

Some people will point to superior leak down test figures as evidence that zero gap second rings and smaller gaps, especially on the second rings, is the route to less blow-by and thus more hp. Let me assure you that in spite of what you may have previously been led to believe, there is virtually no relationship between extremely low leak down numbers and increased hp.

GROOVE CLEARANCE

These days ring breakage is rare and can usually be attributed to worn piston ring grooves that allow the ring to flop around and break, or excessive taper of the bore, causing radial flutter and subsequent ring breakage. If new rings are fitted to a worn bore, and a ridge is present at the top of the bore, the new rings will bang into the ridge

Figure 11.10 Before rings are fitted the back clearance and groove clearance should be checked. With used pistons carbon may build up in the groove, causing ring jamming and breakage. Excessively worn grooves allow the rings to twist and flop about, unable to seal effectively and likely to break.

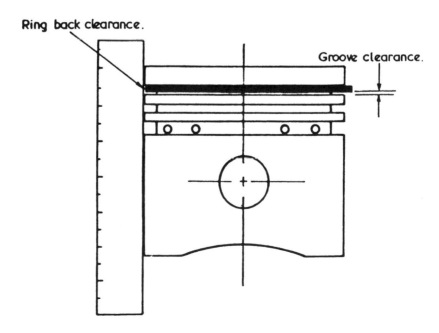

and break. Excessive piston-to-bore clearance can lead to ring failure due to the piston rocking and twisting the rings as it passes TDC.

Generally, a racing engine should be set up with very tight groove clearances of 0.001–0.0015in. Certainly there should not be more than 0.002in side clearance between the ring and ring groove. A road motor should ideally have the same groove clearance as a racing unit, but up to 0.0035in clearance is acceptable. If we have chosen a top-of-the-line premium race engine piston/ring package, we can go very tight on groove clearance. An unrestricted engine should be held at 0.001in ± 0.0002in, while a naturally aspirated inlet restricted engine can usually tighten up to 0.00065in ± 0.00015in, unless your supplier advises otherwise for your particular application.

Also check for ring back clearance as shown in Figure 11.10. This is vital if you are re-using a piston as you will very quickly find if a ring land has closed up and is jamming the ring anywhere. And what can appear to be just a light layer of carbon in the back of the groove may in fact be deeper than it appears and jam a new full depth ring hard against the bore wall.

RING DESIGN AND MATERIAL

In the past compression ring material was usually plain grey cast iron, either plain, chrome-plated or moly-filled. However, most top rings are now ductile nodular cast iron, which is much more durable and heat resistant, and less prone to detonation cracking than plain grey iron. There is nothing wrong, though, with using plain cast iron in the second ring position.

Generally for the top ring I prefer Sealed Power/Speed Pro moly-filled nodular cast iron rings. Nodular iron has almost three times the strength of conventional grey cast iron. It is ductile rather than brittle and can be bent without breaking. Molybdenum belongs to the same chemical family as chrome; however, it has a lower coefficient of friction and higher resistance to abrasion. Its thermal conductivity is several times greater than that of either cast iron or chrome-plated cast iron, and its porosity acts as an oil reservoir, reducing scuffing and cylinder wear.

For oil control I like the multi-piece pressure-back type. The idea is to keep frictional losses to the very minimum while at the same time maintaining adequate oil control. Therefore only low-tension-type oil control rings should be used for race engines. The Sealed Power/Speed Pro low-tension oil ring is excellent in this type of application. However if I'm using a top spec piston, usually from Mahle or JE, I will order a complete piston and ring package. Mahle, for example, source their rings not only from their own manufacturing facilities, but also from other European and Japanese manufacturers, so as to provide the best product for a particular application.

HOW TO FIT PISTON RINGS

When rings are being fitted, care is needed to avoid fitting them the wrong way up and to prevent damage by incorrect installation. Compression rings can be permanently twisted if they are fitted in the groove at one end and gradually screwed around until the entire ring is in place. Instead, they should be expanded sufficiently to fit over the piston, then allowed to drop into the groove. Special expander tools are available for 397

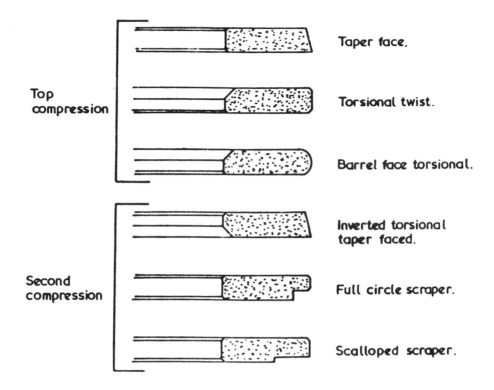

Figure 11.11 Rings must be fitted the correct way up to effect a good seal and maintain proper oil control.

this purpose, but I prefer two 0.015in feeler blades placed between the ring and piston. The blades provide a bearing surface and prevent the ring from digging into the piston.

Taper-face rings are marked 'TOP', or have a dimple mark, and should be fitted that side upwards, providing the greater diameter or contacting edge on the lower face of the ring (Figure 11.11).

The unbalanced section or torsional twist ring is fitted with the inner chamfered edge uppermost. This causes a slight dish in the ring face and provides the same characteristics as the taper-face ring, in that the lower edge makes a high-pressure contact with the cylinder wall. Whereas the taper-face ring eventually wears parallel, the torsional twist ring retains its characteristics.

The 'Multo-Seal' type second compression ring is fitted with the serrations in the ring face downwards.

All multi-piece oil control rings should be fitted in accordance with the packaged instructions. Always double check that the ends of the expander ring have not been lapped over.

Before fitting the assembled pistons in the engine, dip each entire piston in engine oil and oil the walls of each cylinder. Some feel that the oil should be fortified with some additive like STP; some even paint straight STP on to the cylinder walls and pistons. This is wrong. Piston rings are not designed to cut through an additive like this; the end result could be glazed rings and bores.

BEDDING-IN RINGS

The initial bed-in of rings is achieved by giving the car a full throttle burst for a few seconds, followed by snapping the throttle shut and coasting for a few more seconds. This should be repeated at least 12–15 times with the engine at normal operating temperature. Accelerate the vehicle in top gear from the slowest speed it will pull in that gear.

By giving the engine full power, the high gas pressures force the rings out against the bore wall. Snapping the throttle shut causes a vacuum in the cylinder, which draws up extra oil. This and a low engine speed minimises the risk of glazing and allows the ring face and cylinder wall to cool.

After the rings are initially bedded-in, the engine can be operated at up to 80% of its rev/power potential, but constantly vary the speed. If this is not done, the rings may still glaze. After about half an hour of this on the dyno or the race circuit, the rings can be considered as being run-in. A road engine with chrome rings should be run in for around 200 miles, preferably in one session. Again, constantly vary the engine speed and include heavy acceleration for short bursts as for initial bedding in. Avoid constant high speed until the engine has done 500–700 miles.

I prefer to break in my engines on the dyno, carefully controlling the engine speed and load to ensure long engine life and maximum power. This takes 1–1¹/₂ hours for most types of engine. When the engine cools, the tappets are adjusted and the head is re-tensioned. Then, following a warm-up to bring the water and oil up to temperature, full load power tests are made to determine ignition advance, fuel jet sizes, etc. By the end of the tests the engine is fully run-in (Table 11.5).

Table 11.5   Standard break-in procedure on an engine dyno

rpm	Engine load (torque lbf ft)	Time (mins)
3,500	40	10
4,000	50	5
4,500	70	10
5,000	85	15
5,500	100	20

Note: this is the procedure used for all race and rally Ford BDA engines of 1,600–2,000cc producing maximum torque of 135–165lbf ft. Other engines require a different run-in load according to their displacement and torque output.

Some feel that it is preferable to run an engine on the dyno from some external power source. Theoretically this should smooth out the differences in fit and surface finish, but this solves only part of the problem. Internal temperatures influence the fit and shape of parts, and to further complicate matters clearances will alter with mechanical loads as well as with temperatures. It follows then that the engine must be run-in under its own power, initially unloaded, then progressively loaded to produce the required running surface.

TESTING RING SEAL

When full power testing is being carried out, a blow-by gauge should be connected to the crankcase, which will give a quick overall indication of how well the rings are sealing.

With the amount of scavenge I usually run on the dry-sump pump I expect to see the blow-by gauge reading less than 1–1.5cfm. If the power is down and the gauge is reading higher than this, I can be pretty certain that there is a ring seal problem somewhere.

An alternative is to block off all the engine breathers except one, then connect a 'T' into the open breather hose. Connect one branch of the 'T' to a 'U'-tube water manometer, and to the other branch, which is vented to the atmosphere, connect a drilled restrictor plug. If the engine is dry sumped I would first try an 8mm vent hole. The idea is to use a restrictor small enough to produce a pressure reading of around 2in of water in a carefully built engine with excellent ring seal; then on another occasion it is very easy to quickly check on the ring seal. If, for example, the engine is down on power and the water gauge is showing a blow-by pressure of 9in with the same-size breather restrictor as previously used, you know that the ring seal is not good.

Obviously, for this latter method to be of any value, a leak-down test must be done first. Then, having established that all cylinders have an average leak-down of, say, 3%, you can be reasonably sure that you have excellent ring seal. Therefore your initial manometer 'calibration test' to establish what size of breather restrictor is required to produce a blow-by pressure of 2in of water will have real relevance. These days with special coatings on things like piston skirts and pins, and cylinders and with oil feed through the rod to the pin, we can be a lot more aggressive with the scavenge pumps. Consequently running a sealed crankcase I expect to see negative crankcase pressure, even at the end of endurance engine tests.

LEAK-DOWN TEST LIMITATIONS

The leak-down test is a much less accurate indicator of ring seal, so I prefer to use it only after I see an abnormal blow-by reading to isolate which cylinder(s) is causing the high blow-by reading. Obviously a static comparatively low pressure test like this cannot accurately reflect what the ring seal is actually like when the engine is operating; it can only point to where a problem may exist. Note that this test will also show up leaky valve seats, so you need to listen carefully for air leakage to determine in which area of the engine the problem lies.

The actual leak-down test is fairly straightforward. After bringing the engine up to temperature, pull all the spark plugs, then bring No 1 piston up to TDC on the compression stroke, connect the leak-down tester in the spark plug hole and connect the compressor air line to the tester. The leak-down tester will then display a percentage air loss reading. Ideally we want only 2–3% leakage, but 4% is acceptable. If it exceeded 5% I would look for problems in that cylinder. Every piston is brought up to TDC and tested in turn for leakage.

Really, any serious competitor should do a leak test at the race track as soon as a practice session is concluded, and likewise at the end of competition for the weekend. If the leak-down shows up a problem, look for it and fix it before your next race. Some foolishly haul a race car with a tired engine hundreds of miles to a race meet and spend the weekend frustrated because they are off the pace, or they even blow the engine because it so badly needs attention. What they should have done was to save their money for meals, accommodation, fuel, etc, and spent it to give the engine a light hone and a set of rings, and touched up the valve seats and perhaps replaced the valve springs and bearings.

HARMONIC BALANCER

The pulley or harmonic balancer attached to the nose of the crankshaft has its part to play in the durability of an engine, and the surrounding environment. Many four-cylinder engines use a pressed metal drive pulley, spot welded or riveted to a hub. At higher engine speeds, ie 6,000rpm-plus, a pulley of this construction is liable to fly apart, wrecking anything in its path. To avoid this, a cast or machined component should be used.

The harmonic balancer is fitted to dampen crankshaft torsional vibrations that could, if not controlled, wreck the crankshaft. At times the balancer and pulley may be in one piece, or a separate pulley may be bolted to the harmonic balancer. Again, if this pulley is a pressed metal component, scrap it to avoid problems.

The actual harmonic balancer is made of three parts bonded together. A rubber belt is bonded between the outer inertia ring and the hub. Failure is normally caused by the inertia ring losing its bond with the rubber. If this occurs at high engine speed you can be assured of spectacular and expensive results. To prevent this, the harmonic dampener must be carefully inspected on a regular basis. If you race, do it after each race meeting. To assist in your inspection you should mark a distinct, common line between the hub and inertia ring. If the two marks move out of line, it indicates that the ring is moving on the hub, so scrap it. Under no circumstances should you try to repair the balancer by bolting the inertia ring to the hub. This will wreck your crankshaft just as surely as running 2,000rpm over the limit. The inertia ring must be able to move, within limits, to dampen crankshaft vibration.

There is little that can be done to improve the reliability of the harmonic balancer except to check it for run-out before fitting. The other modification necessary, if a fully counterbalanced crank is fitted, is to machine away the counterweight cast as part of the hub.

Before you fit the harmonic balancer (or pulley) to the engine, paint it black. After fitting, accurately find TDC and file a good groove into it, to align with the TDC mark on the engine timing case. Paint the groove with silver or white paint. If you also paint black the area around the timing marks on the engine timing case, and the TDC and ignition timing marks or pointer silver, the ignition timing will be much easier to adjust later on. To adjust the timing accurately you must be able to see the timing marks easily, so anything that you can do to make them stand out must help.

FLYWHEEL

The flywheel is attached to the other end of the crankshaft. To ensure that it remains attached, two good dowels (³/₈in) and retaining bolts that have been coated with Loctite and correctly torqued provide good insurance. To cut costs, manufacturers seldom fit dowels, so it will be necessary to machine the flywheel and crank to fit these.

Over the years there has been a fair amount of controversy with regard to flywheel lightening. Some claimed that a lightweight flywheel improved acceleration due to reduced inertia, others stated that the only benefit was better crankshaft life because the twisting load on the end of the crank was reduced, and there was less risk of flywheel explosion due to the inertia load on the centre of the flywheel being lessened. At this time we can state and prove that any reductions in an engine's 401 reciprocating mass or rotating mass will improve acceleration. Thus lightweight pistons, rods, cranks, clutches and flywheels all benefit performance.

The problem previously was that we had no reliable means of measuring the performance advantages of light components. However, the situation changed when relatively inexpensive computerised engine dynos like the Superflow SF-800 became available. These dynos can accelerate an engine at a fixed rate and accurately record the horsepower. This means that we can programme the dyno to accelerate the engine at, say, 2,000rpm per second, and record the power levels every 250rpm. When such a test was carried out on a 388cu in Chev speedway engine, it recorded almost 25hp more when titanium rods and a light flywheel were fitted. The driver claimed that the car was quicker by about a half length out of turns, which backed up what the dyno had showed. Tested with a static load as we had to with the older dynos, the engine showed no difference in hp when the lightweight parts were fitted.

A very light flywheel is undesirable for a road vehicle as it can produce a lumpy engine idle. The reason manufacturers use a relatively heavy flywheel in the first place is to absorb the uneven torsional impulses coming through the crankshaft and keep the engine turning smoothly at low engine revs. A fairly hot engine with a relatively heavy flywheel is much more pleasant to drive on the road than one with an overly light one.

If you decide to use a lighter flywheel it is not always necessary to buy a new lightweight version or even have your old flywheel turned down. Some manufacturers have, over the years, built many engines of various capacities around the same basic design. Therefore the flywheel fitted in production to the 1,000cc version may also fit the 1,500cc derivative and save possibly 5–7lb; if you have the 1,500cc engine in mind for modification, you can use the lighter flywheel from the smaller engine.

Lightening should only be done near the outside of the flywheel. Removing metal from the centre is fatal and likely to lead to failure. When metal is removed from the outside it makes life easier on the centre of the flywheel as the inertia loads are reduced. This is important as some flywheels are none too strong. To prevent distortion from heat, do not machine away so much of the clutch side of the flywheel that there is only a thin ribbon of metal left, just wide enough to provide a seat for the clutch plate friction material. If the clutch is subjected to severe usage, that thin ribbon may distort, due to localised heating, and allow clutch slip.

A light flywheel improves acceleration on the track but can make street driving unpleasant.

Chapter 12

Lubrication

In the past the lubrication system was simply that – a means of pumping lubricating oil between vital engine components to prevent metal to metal contact, and premature wear or seizure. Today's engines, however, demand much more of the lubrication system as the lubricating fluid is called upon to perform a bigger role in cooling the bearings, pistons and valve springs. This is especially true of high output engines as there are clear limits on how much heat we can move out of the piston crown to the water jacket via the piston rings. The only alternative to this route is to utilise the lubricating oil, literally squirting it up into the top of the piston to transfer heat from the piston to the oil.

However, in performing the dual roles of lubricating and cooling, the oil ends up in large quantities in places where we don't want it. The reason we don't want it in certain places is because this increases parasitic losses – costs us horsepower and impedes engine acceleration. Additionally we don't want it in certain areas because while there the oil is whipped up, becoming aerated and thus unable to carry out its lubricating and cooling activities so effectively on its next pass through the engine. Consequently when we think of engine lubrication we have to extend our focus well beyond just the lubricating oil in isolation. We have to look at the entire delivery system, plus the oil return system and oil cooling system. Also we want to examine ways of enabling the oil to do its work more efficiently while winning back hp previously lost to parasitic losses.

Obviously stock or lightly modified engines will work quite well without any modification of the lubricating system. And as manufacturers take parasitic losses ever more seriously in their quest for higher hp and reduced fuel consumption, the opportunity for us to make gains in this area in road cars is becoming smaller. Therefore for some readers their prime concern will be the lubricating oil itself. They will be desirous of choosing an oil that minimises engine wear and provides a power gain by cutting friction and other parasitic losses.

Apart from its lubricating and cooling roles the engine oil has a number of other basic tasks that we most probably don't even think about. These are: provide a seal between piston rings and cylinder, permit easy engine starting from cold, keep the engine clean of sludge, minimise combustion chamber deposits, not 'poison' the lambda probe and catalytic converter, provide rust and corrosion protection, and resist foaming. To indicate just how well an oil performs in these areas, various test organisations around the world assign engine oil for street use a series of letters and/or numbers to tell us what tests the oil has passed. While there is a question mark over the validity of such tests, they do give the average consumer some idea of how well a particular oil does its job.

OIL TEST STANDARDS

For example the American Petroleum Institute (API) assigns petrol engine oils a service rating such as SD, SE, SF etc. Currently the toughest API rating is SM, and to carry that rating an oil must pass a series of tests with the engine running on an engine dyno. One test monitors the oil's ability to prevent valve train wear in an ohc 2.3-litre American Ford. Like its 2-litre European cousin this engine is notorious for valve train problems, in its early life being subject to a recall for abnormal cam lobe wear. Zinc is a great lifter/lobe anti-scuff agent, but unfortunately as it does nasty things to lambda probes and CATs it had to be removed from the oil additive package. An equivalent substitute has yet to be found, so all street oils now struggle with this test. (Race oil and some motorcycle oil formulations are superior in this regard. They don't have to meet car manufacturer's demands regarding lambda sensor and CAT life, so zinc can still be added by the oil companies.) Another test monitors the oil's capacity to prevent wear and resist oxidation in a 350cu in Oldsmobile run for 64 hours with the oil at 149°C sump temperature. Poor quality oils finish up as tar by the end of this test, but the better oils, usually full synthetics, will still look like oil at the finish of the 64 hours. In fact some oil companies now duplicate this test and extend it up to 128 hours to show how well their synthetic oils hold up. Consequently while the majority of oils available may achieve an SM rating, literally just scraping through to gain a pass, others will easily pass and a few will far exceed the test standard.

The oil packaging usually lists some of the test standards that the oil has passed.

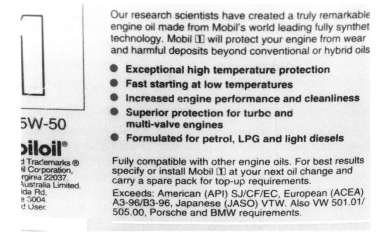

5W-50

oiloil®

d Trademarks ®
il Corporation,
rginia 22037.
Australia Limited.
Ida Rd.
e 3004.
d User.

Our research scientists have created a truly remarkable engine oil made from Mobil's world leading fully synthet technology. Mobil [1] will protect your engine from wear and harmful deposits beyond conventional or hybrid oils

- **Exceptional high temperature protection**
- **Fast starting at low temperatures**
- **Increased engine performance and cleanliness**
- **Superior protection for turbo and multi-valve engines**
- **Formulated for petrol, LPG and light diesels**

Fully compatible with other engine oils. For best results specify or install Mobil [1] at your next oil change and carry a spare pack for top-up requirements.

Exceeds: American (API) SJ/CF/EC, European (ACEA) A3-96/B3-96, Japanese (JASO) VTW. Also VW 501.01/ 505.00, Porsche and BMW requirements.

It is these latter oils in which we should be interested. Each will have its strengths and weaknesses. Others may not be outstanding in any particular area, but may be close to the top in a number of categories. Generally it would be just such an oil that I would choose. However for a special situation I may also select an oil with that particular attribute which I deemed to be absolutely essential.

VISCOSITY AND HORSEPOWER

For example, my usual oil of choice for road engines is Mobil 1, 5W-50 grade viscosity. It provides a very high level of engine protection first and foremost. There are one or two other oils about which are similar, or even marginally superior in this regard, but they are not so readily available and they are considerably more expensive. Also these are down on power and show increased fuel consumption. The horsepower king, while still providing adequate engine wear protection is the 0W-40 grade of Mobil 1. As you can see in Table 12.1 when tested against a large number of oils, including some with lower viscosities, it was a clear winner. In comparison with Mobil 1 5W-50 it has slight fuel economy benefits too, in the order of 1–1.5% under highway cruise conditions. Therefore when it is maximum hp that I am after 0W-40 tri-synthetic is the grade I choose. However it allows slightly more engine wear than 5W-50 and if the power advantage is to be maintained it has to be changed more frequently as it thickens up more rapidly due to a significantly higher evaporation rate.

Table 12.1 Synthetic oil horsepower homparison

Rpm	Mobil 1	Shell Ultra	Castrol R	Amsoil	Mobil 1	Royal	BP Visco	Castrol SLX
	5W-50	5W-40	10W-60	10W-40	0W-40	Purple*	5W-40	0W-30
3000	143.2	144.8	140.5	141.2	142.9	140.7	139.8	138.6
4000	202.9	201.3	203.6	203.2	202.4	202.5	202.3	201.2
5000	263.1	262.5	262.4	262.5	266.6	262.8	261.5	260.8
5700	290.4	290.0	293.3	290.7	297.4	294.0	289.9	289.7
6200	304.3	303.5	306.5	305.6	311.2	308.7	303.6	305.1
7000	280.7	278.9	282.7	281.4	288.1	284.5	279.1	282.4

*The Royal Purple used in this test did not have a viscosity rating specified, but lab testing shows it to be in the 0W-20 to 0W-30 range.

Note: Test engine was a slightly modified Subura Liberty RS turbo. Oil and water temperature were controlled at 95–97°C and 85–87°C respectively.

In recent times the idea has been that low viscosity oil, being thinner, will always help an engine make more hp. However, viscosity is only half of the picture – friction modifiers are the other half. You would think that a light oil would always guarantee a hp benefit, but as you can see when you compare the two Castrol products that isn't the case. The thicker 10W-60 Castrol R synthetic made more maximum power than most of the oils tested, while its thinner sibling was close to the bottom in overall hp. Clearly if we are looking to gain hp from a particular type of oil then there is more to it than simply choosing one with a very low viscosity.

UNDERSTANDING VISCOSITY AND VISCOSITY IMPROVERS

The viscosity of oil is a measure of its ability to flow through a graduated hole at an established temperature. High-viscosity oils are thick and offer more resistance to flow, while low-viscosity oils flow more easily and so offer less resistance to the engine turning over.

A viscous (high-viscosity) oil leaves a physically thicker oil film under any condition than a non-viscous (low-viscosity) oil. This fact influences both engine wear and blow-by. Obviously if an oil film is so thin that it cannot keep moving parts from contacting one another, wear results. Realising that gases in the combustion chamber are at a high pressure following ignition and that the oil film between rings, piston and cylinder wall is assisting in sealing, we know that the oil film must be viscous enough to withstand this pressure.

However, if too heavy an oil is selected, it will fail to get between closely fitting parts in sufficient quantity to lubricate or conduct heat away. Tests on viscous oils in the 60 and 70 grades have given poor results due to temperature build-up at the bearings and the inability of the oil to lubricate in tight areas. Added to this, these oils have been found to hold heat rather than dissipate it, and to trap air, so de-aeration is a problem.

Many drivers use a thick oil to give a good oil pressure reading, which apparently gives them some sense of confidence in the ability of the engine to hold together. However, the reluctance of the viscous oil to pass through the bearings creates a wiping action, which actually promotes wear, while the cranking and pumping resistance of a thick oil will give a substantial decrease in power.

All oils become thinner when hot and thicker when cold, but they do not all react to temperature changes in the same way. For example, two 40 grade oils that possess the same viscosity at 100°C may have radically different viscosities at higher and lower temperatures. The oil that thins the most at high temperatures will also thicken the most at low temperatures, so obviously it is the oil that shows the least change in viscosity that is the most desirable one to use. Such an oil is said to have a high viscosity index, while the one most affected is regarded as a 'low VI' oil. An oil with a high VI is most desirable for racing engines, providing that the high rating has not been obtained by using additives.

VI improvers, referred to as polymers, have enabled the development of multi-grade or multi-viscosity oils. Polymers are molecules that expand and thicken the oil as the temperature increases, and reduce in size and thin the oil as it cools. Therefore an oil such as 20W-50 will have the characteristics of 20W oil at low temperatures and of 50 SAE at high temperatures.

Large advances have been made in polymer chemistry, but these VI improvers are still not completely shear-stable at high loads. During shock periods they tend to lose their structure momentarily and collapse, so a 20W-50 oil would only be offering the protection of 20W oil under those conditions. This loss of structure is particularly likely to occur at heavily loaded areas such as at the bearings and the tappets. For this very reason you will find that most camshaft grinders recommend that their cams be run-in using a straight 30 or 40 grade oil.

BLENDED AND SYNTHETIC OILS

However, adding polymers or seeking out special mineral oil base stocks is not the only way of producing an oil with a high VI. Another route is to blend synthetic base stock with mineral oil base stock to produce a blended synthetic. Such an oil is Valvoline Duoblend (SynGuard), which combines mineral oil, synthetic and polymers to produce a high-grade, wide-viscosity oil suitable for use in both high-performance road and competition engines.

Taking the process a step further, we have so-called 100% synthetic oils. In reality they are not 100% synthetic, as a considerable portion of engine oil is taken up by an 'additive package' that is blended into the base stock. However, if the base stock is fully synthetic, without any mineral or vegetable oil blended in, it is said to be 100% synthetic. An example is Mobil 1, which is described as not containing polymer VI improvers; the wide viscosity range of OW-40 and 5W-50 being made possible by special refining processes.

While mineral oils are produced from petroleum crude oil after the distillation process has removed substances like tars, petrol, diesel, kerosene, etc, synthetics go considerably further in the refining process until the very basic components of the crude are separated. These base components are then combined into new man-made molecular structures to produce synthetic base fluid. Some synthetics may use components derived only from petroleum crude, but others may combine molecules from a variety of carbon sources: coal, natural gas, animal fat and bone marrow.

Synthetic oils offer many benefits in competition engines over even the very best mineral and vegetable oils. Because they are so thin when cold they lubricate better when an engine is first started. Then as the engine and oil come up to race temperature they do not thin out like mineral oil, thus reducing cam/lifter wear, bearing/crank wear, and piston ring/cylinder bore wear. Additionally, synthetics are more oxidation-resistant, so they are less stressed by high operating temperatures.

Some people are claiming big power increases due to reduced frictional losses when running synthetic. Yes, there are power increases, but I have never seen anything like the 2 and 3% some claim. I would say it is closer to 1%, or even a little less in some instances.

At this time my prime recommendation for all competition engines operating on petrol and high-performance road engines is Mobil 1. Personally I use 15W-50 in maximum output competition engines, but for road engines and less developed race engines running bmeps of less than 200psi I recommend either 0W-40 or 5W-50 grade Mobil 1.

Generally I do not use blended synthetic or synthetic fortified oil, but I know some who have tested Valvoline SynGuard (Duoblend) 10W-50 and find it very suitable for both highly stressed road and race engines. However, the one exception is for race engines burning methanol where my recommendation is Castrol R40 synthetic/castor oil.

I no longer recommend mineral oil for road engines; it just does not provide the cold-start protection and the oxidation resistance that I demand. However, in race engines that have frequent oil changes, and which in cold weather have the oil and water heated prior to engine start-up, Valvoline Racing 20W-50 will provide very high levels of lubrication.

OIL ADDITIVE PACKAGE

Earlier it was mentioned that a considerable part of engine oil is in fact an additive package. Beside polymers, oils also contain a number of other compounds. Some work as anti-oxidants, some as detergents, some as foam suppressants, and others are anti-wear additives that in total may constitute 20% of the oil.

These identical upper rod bearings have done the same competition distance in identical engines. The shell on the left, lubricated with competition mineral oil, has more than twice as much wear as the bearing on the right, which came from an engine lubricated with Mobil 1 synthetic.

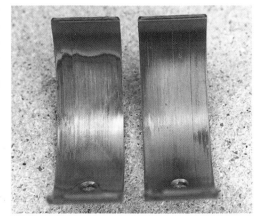

Oxidation occurs due to the presence of oxygen and combustion by-products in the oil and due to the temperature of the oil itself. As the oil temperature increases past 100°C, the rate of oxidation accelerates and the anti-oxidant becomes less effective.

The by-product of oxidation and combustion is known as sludge. To keep this in suspension, rather than allow a build-up inside the engine, detergent is added. Racing oils, however, may contain very little detergent, and for this reason they should only be

Mobil 1 synthetic 15W-50 is preferred for all maximum output competition engines, while 5W-50 (or 0W-40 tri-synthetic) is recommended for all other engines. In sprint events where oil does not get time to warm up and stays below 85°–90°C use 0W-30 to avoid power loss.

used in road vehicles when they carry an API rating such as SJ, SL, SM etc. or the European ACEA rating of A3 or A5.

To counter aeration, a foam suppressant is added, which will prevent the formation of foam under the conditions for which the oil is designed to be used, but it cannot eliminate the foam resulting from the presence of water in the oil or from air sucked into the lubrication system either through a fractured pick-up or due to oil surge that has allowed the oil pump to pump air.

Obviously this additive package eventually wears out, and when the anti-wear compounds are depleted engine wear accelerates rapidly; when the anti-oxidants and detergents break down, sludge begins to build up in the engine, and so forth. This situation should be avoided, and it can be if the oil is replaced while these various compounds are still working effectively.

HOW OFTEN THE OIL SHOULD BE CHANGED

How often the oil should be changed will largely depend on the air temperature and driving conditions. Stop-start driving and cold weather under 10°C/50°F are hardest on oil, while long distances between stops with little or no engine idling in warm weather (20°C/70°F) is very easy on today's oils. In the first instance I would be changing Mobil 1 every 4,000 miles or four months, whichever came first. In the latter situation Mobil 1 would provide good protection up to 12,000 miles or six months; however, I would change the filter at the midway point.

In race engines how often you change the oil will probably depend on your budget more than anything else. However there is no good reason to throw away synthetic oil after every race meeting. Obviously if you have just done a 24-hour event you would toss the oil, but for most engines there is probably no need to replace the oil any more frequently than when the engine is stripped for a rebuild. Really when you get your oil tested for the presence of metal and contaminants the report should state how the viscosity has changed and if the additive package has been depleted.

One major concern with oil in competition engines is fuel contamination. Rich mixtures wash off into the sump and even just a little methanol does nasty things to the oil. To get around this the oil can be drained after each competition meeting and gently heated at 90–100°C to boil off the fuel. In fact some barbecues see more use cooking fuel and water out of oil than cooking meat!

OIL TEMPERATURE AND OIL COOLERS

No matter how good your oil is, it must be maintained at the correct temperature to lubricate effectively. A good deal of engine wear takes place because engines are operated with cold oil and/or water. An engine should never be driven hard until the oil reaches 70°C, while the ideal operating temperature is 95–110°C. It can go as high as 130°C for short periods, but oil breakdown and excessive oxidation will take place above this temperature. In a race engine, bearing failure is a possibility any time the oil temperature goes past 130°, and generally hp is lost over 115°.

Years ago an early modification was to fit an oil cooler, but with advances in oil technology this is often no longer necessary for street engines, and also sprint type competition engines. An exception would be when we are limited in what we can do to 409 bring water cooling temperatures down without a large outlay of money and/or major re-engineering of the plumbing system. In such situations the simple addition of an oil cooler could help to get enough heat out of the engine that no change to the cooling system is needed.

At the completion of big events you at times see a podium finisher express his amazement in standing there due to a problem in the oil cooling system sending the oil temperature sky high for much of the race. After thanking the sponsors, which invariably includes an oil company, it is often difficult to determine if the tale of the high oil temperature was a free advertisement on national TV for the sponsor, or if it was for real. However, I know of a race car completing several hundred miles of an endurance event with the oil cooler bypassed after accident damage. Temperature in the oil tank went as high as 170°C but on strip down engine components did not appear to be in any worse condition than if temperatures had been normal. That was on full synthetic 15W-50 Mobil 1. However I have also seen full throttle 24-hour track endurance tests by manufacturers with the same mineral oil in their sump as their new vehicles in the showroom. During such tests sump oil temperatures of 150°C and higher, up to 180°C, for the entire test have been recorded. Yet subsequent engine teardown revealed that such high temperatures were not a problem. This is not an endorsement of very high oil temperatures, but they do show that at least for short periods a new engine, or one still with very good piston ring seal, and within spec bearing clearances, can operate at 120–130°C sump oil temperatures. I would only recommend an oil cooler if under hard driving conditions the oil is regularly in excess of 120°C. I base that recommendation on the fact that I have seen a number of highly stressed race engines lose bearings when the oil went past 130°C.

When an oil cooler is necessary there are several 'musts' which should be kept in mind. As already noted, cold oil wrecks engines and deteriorates quickly so in road vehicles either an oil thermostat will be required, or else the oil cooler should have a shutter or blind fitted which can be adjusted to suit driving conditions and the ambient temperature. The oil lines connecting the cooler into the system should be of at least $^1/_2$in bore, preferably $^5/_8$–$^3/_4$in, so as not to restrict flow. Additionally, if a take-off sandwich block fitting between the oil filter pad and oil filter is used, it must be of a non-restrictive design. Many such adapters are simply drilled with passages intersecting at 90°, severely restricting oil flow. The adapters you should select will have oil passages which are cast or CNC machined into the alloy block. They should be finished to look as though they were 'ported' to maximise oil flow. Oil coolers are impossible to clean out so do not purchase a used oil cooler. It could be full of dirt or bearing material. Also if your engine or turbo suffers bearing failure it is always prudent to replace the oil cooler, thus avoiding possible damage from pumping rubbish into your rebuilt engine and turbo.

After fitting the oil cooler, continue to monitor the engine oil temperature. While high oil temperatures may lead to inadequate lubrication, and subsequent failure of bearings, tappets and cam lobes, oil cooled below about 85°C is no good either. In a competition engine vast amounts of money are expended to pick up a few additional hp, but many fail to realise just how much power cold oil is costing them. I stumbled on this when I first began dyno testing my engines. I would shut the engine down to make some adjustment and maybe 15 or 20 minutes later do a dyno pull, and when I

did all the calculations (there were no computer print-outs then – we had to calculate

Top left: *If sump oil temperatures regularly exceed 120°C, an oil cooler will help engine bearing and oil life.*

Top right: *The bearings were ruined and the crank journals ended up worn like this, all due to a dirty oil cooler.*

Above: *Oil cooler take-off blocks must be cast or CNC machined without 90° internal passages. Also to be avoided are restrictive oil line fittings with 90° bends like these.*

everything manually) power would be down everywhere. I would quickly do another pull and the power would change. What was going on? During the short shut-down period the oil had lost heat, so when the engine was fired up again power was being consumed overcoming the increased oil drag, then when a number of dyno pulls were done in quick succession to double-check figures the oil temperature would rise, and with reduced losses the hp would go up. Basically I want 5W-50 or 15W-50 grade oil at 95–105°C; dropping it down to 85°C will cost at least 1% hp.

411

In hotter climates, high-performance road vehicles may also need an oil cooler. It is always a worry recommending an oil cooler for a road car or bike because for a good deal of the time the oil will be over-cooled, particularly during winter. Therefore before you decide on an oil cooler for a road machine, be sure that you really need one. Fit an oil temperature gauge and determine your oil operating temperature in midsummer. If under normal driving conditions your oil temperature is in excess of 140°C, fit an oil cooler. However, if it stays around 110–120°C when you run at full throttle for quite a few miles, you will be wasting your time and causing yourself unnecessary trouble by fitting an oil cooler.

OIL FILTRATION

The next requirement of an efficient lubrication system is adequately filtered oil. Any solid material in the oil will act as an abrasive, wearing away at bearings, crank journals, tappets, cam lobes, etc. The oil filter must remove the majority of this type of material from the oil. Very few lubrication systems are unfiltered these days, but if yours is one of them remember that long engine life is at least partly dependent on clean oil, so steps must be taken to install a filtering unit.

The term 'Micron Rating' is often misused in filtration technology. The important figure is the one that indicates the smallest particle totally removed by the filter. For example, a filter may have to stop all particles over 40 microns from passing through, but 5% of particles of 20–30 microns size are allowed through. A system suitable for a racing engine should remove all particles, but this ideal is not possible at present.

A micron is one millionth of a metre – a human hair is about 50 microns thick. The larger the particles circulating in an engine's oil, the more likelihood there will be of abrasive wear. The challenge facing filter manufacturers is to stop all of these abrasive particles with a filter that has an acceptable service life. You can do your part by changing the filter regularly, as specified by the manufacturer, and by re-installing

If possible choose a larger capacity oil filter. Both these filters have identical thread and gasket sizes, but one is much larger. This cuts flow restriction and provides more filtration area. If there is insufficient space in the stock location, consider installing a remote mount.

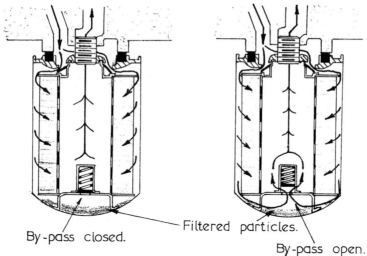

By-pass closed.

Filtered particles.

By-pass open.

Figure 12.1 Bypass-type spin-on oil filter.

the new filter correctly. If the type fitted to your engine has a replaceable element, be sure to remove all traces of sludge from inside the canister before fitting a new element.

A race or rally engine with thousands of dollars invested in it requires a higher level of filtration than that offered by over-the-counter spin-on or replaceable-element filters. The standard type of oil filter may have a bypass in case it becomes clogged with sludge and other material; this is done for the benefit of the motorist who does not bother to have his filter changed regularly, and also to prevent the filter element from rupturing when the oil is cold and viscous. Once the bypass opens, due to excessive pressure, unfiltered oil is allowed to circulate through the engine. It can easily be seen that the area where the bypass is located is where much of the sediment material from the oil collects. When the bypass opens this rubbish is flushed through the engine (Figure 12.1).

A racing oil filter must not contain any bypass and consequently must be burst-proof at oil pressures up to 200lb. It must also be fine enough to stop abrasive particles from circulating with the oil without reducing oil flow to a dangerous level, particularly during cold starting.

Many engine tuners cut open their oil filters to judge engine condition; however, I believe in a better system – oil analysis. For a small fee, specialised laboratories and oil companies will analyse oil for the presence of wear metals (indicating filtration effectiveness and/or engine wear), for dilution and sludge (indicating excessive blow-by, incorrect oil type or incorrect oil change period), and other potential problems.

OIL PUMP AND OIL PRESSURE

As engine tune is increased and bearing clearances become greater, the need to investigate the flow potential of an engine's oiling system grows in importance. In lower stages of tune the standard oil pump, if in good condition (check the manufacturer's specifications for gear clearances, etc) will usually be acceptable. It may be possible to increase the oil pressure and oil flow a small amount by fitting a 413 stronger relief valve spring or by fitting a spacer under the existing spring. A common modification with the four-cylinder British Fords is to increase oil pressure to 45lb with a spacer, or to 60lb by using a stronger spring.

Once the engine reaches semi-race tune, a higher-capacity oil pump, which utilises wider gears, will become necessary to keep sufficient oil passing through the engine. At times it may be necessary to change the oil pump drive due to the standard drive not being able to cope with the additional oil pump load.

Some engines suffer oil starvation because of restrictive oil passages. The German Capri V6 and Buick V6 are both good examples of this type of problem. The Capri has an oil passage in the block about 40% smaller than the oil pump outlet. In the very early stages of tune this passage must be enlarged to match the pump outlet if bearing failure is to be avoided.

In the V8 Chev the restriction in the main oil gallery is the result of a fundamental flaw in engine block machining. General Motors decided that it was simpler/less expensive to bore the passage from opposite ends of the block! Tunnels are put through mountains using this method all the time, with surveyors and engineers keeping the boring operations on course. The tip of an unguided long drill wanders off course, so when boring from both ends of the block the gallery area can be down to 50% where the two holes meet. This is usually not a problem in stock engines but as the power rises so the need to drill the main passage all the way with a very long drill increases.

The V6 Buick has a passage for oil pick-up running from the middle of the block to the oil pump located at the front of the engine. This passage is about 25% too small to flow enough oil for a racing engine. After the oil leaves the oil pump, it encounters another restriction, a 90° bend. Following this, the oil is fed into the right lifter gallery, which supplies the right bank lifters, the cam bearings and finally the mains and big ends. Additionally, the front cam journal bleeds off oil for the left lifter bank. All of this bleed-off to the valve gear, combined with the oilway restrictions, reduces the oil flow to the crankshaft bearings. An early modification in the development of this engine must include enlarging the pick-up gallery and eliminating the 90° bend after the oil pump. This engine is a good candidate for an external oil plumbing system that supplies oil directly to the main bearings.

Many engines, in fact, bleed too much oil for the lubrication of the cam and the lifters. To limit the bleed-off, restrictor plugs should be fitted. If you have switched from hydraulic to solid lifters, oil flow to these parts should be restricted by reaming the lifter bores and fitting a lifter sleeve kit.

Some tuners, in an endeavour to supply oil in sufficient quantities to the main bearings, increase oil pressure to 100–120psi. This should never be necessary if the lubrication system is properly modified. In fact, if an 8,000rpm race engine is experiencing any failures at 60–70psi, it usually indicates that work is required to open up oilways and/or restrict bleed-off to the cam and lifters. For example, the Cosworth DFV Formula 1 engine started life running a minimum oil pressure of 85psi. About ten years later after a major rework of passage sizes and angles the maximum pressure required was down to 60psi, and the engine was still reliable at 45psi. This in spite of the engine now running 1,500rpm faster and producing 17% more power. Current Formula 1 engines, producing 920hp and running to 19,000rpm operate at only 30psi. A stock block based competition engine operating above 8,500rpm may benefit if the oil pressure is raised to 80–85psi. The power required to pump oil through an engine is considerable, so do not increase the power drain to ancillary equipment by unnecessarily increasing the oil pressure.

PREVENTING OIL SURGE

Oil surge can be a serious problem, and hard to overcome in some engines (eg air-cooled VW). Any vehicle with a wet sump (ie an oil reservoir in the sump) will be prone to oil surge unless the manufacturer has taken preventative measures during production (very unusual). Oil surge is caused by braking, acceleration or cornering forces surging the oil away from the oil pick-up, allowing air to be pumped to the bearings. If allowed to go unchecked, bearing failure is imminent.

To reduce surge the trend is to fit vertical baffles in the sump, but these have little effect as the oil will rise over them during hard acceleration or braking. Instead a flat, horizontal baffle should be fitted in the sump about 1/4–1/2in above the full oil level, first checking that at this height the rods will not hit the baffle. The baffle should cover the entire oil reservoir area in the sump, and have a hole cut in it just large enough for the oil pick-up to fit through. Around the hole a 1/2–3/4in turned-down lip is required, to discourage oil from surging up through the hole. This hole will also take care of oil drain-back into the reservoir. Do not forget also to cut a hole for the dipstick (Figure 9.2).

The height of the oil pick-up above the floor of the sump must also be adjusted. If it is closer than 1/4in the oil flow into the engine will be restricted; more than 3/8in and the engine will gulp air with G forces around 0.8. Remember when measuring to include the thickness of the sump gasket.

In engines subjected to the full range of G forces – left and right turns and acceleration and braking – the pick-up should be located right in the middle of the sump's oil reservoir. However, in a drag race engine it would be offset toward the rear of the sump, and in a speedway machine running anticlockwise it should be off to the right side.

To ensure that the baffle is working and to keep a check on the oil pressure, a reliable capillary-type (not electric) oil pressure gauge is required. A sudden drop to zero will indicate surge or a low oil level; a small pressure decrease indicates bearing failure or a blocked oil filter.

When testing the effectiveness of sump baffling, gauge readings can be missed, particularly surge readings induced by cornering forces. For this reason I also fit an electric oil pressure switch, adjusted to operate at 30–45psi. I wire this switch to a 3in stop/tail light mounted on the dash and fitted with a 21-watt lamp. If the light flashes on, low oil pressure is indicated. A vehicle driven at night will also need a change-over

Figure 12.2 Wet sump anti-surge baffle.

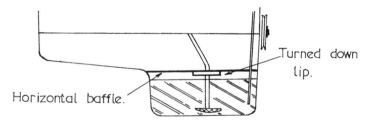

Turned down lip.

Horizontal baffle.

This oil pressure sender switch operates at 30psi and is useful when assessing sump baffles and sump oil fill levels.

switch to connect with a 5-watt lamp in the light, otherwise you could be momentarily blinded if the 21W lamp flashes on in the dark.

DRY SUMP SYSTEM

The dry sump system avoids many of the pitfalls of the wet sump, so is the preferred lubrication system in competition engines. Figure 12.3 shows a typical dry sump system. The oil is scavenged from the engine and is piped to an external oil tank, usually passing through the oil cooler en route. The oil pump will have at least two scavenge stages drawing oil, blow-by and also, if the engine is unsealed, air back to the oil tank. The oil tank is designed to not only store the oil, but also to de-aerate it effectively, for if aerated oil were pumped back into the engine, bearing failure could result. The pressure stage of the pump then draws this de-aerated oil from the oil tank and pumps it through the oil filter and into the engine.

The beneficial aspects of this type of system are obvious. The absence of oil surge helps to increase engine life and reduces the risk of bearing failure. The vehicle can be lower without the risk of sump damage, as a shallow oil pan without a reservoir is used. Oil leakage from the engine is reduced as the scavenge stages reduce pressure, caused by blow-by, within the crankcase. Depending on the scavenge pumps used, crankcase pressure should be less than a couple of inches of water at maximum engine speed and load in a race engine with good piston ring/cylinder seal. This reduced crankcase pressure contributes to a power rise of the order of 3–4%, in spite of the extra hp required to drive a big dry sump pump.

The disadvantages of the dry sump system mainly revolve around the expense and additional weight, but also a dry sump system can give many problems if not correctly engineered. The main areas where I see deficiencies are in the design and mounting of the oil tank, and also the size and routeing of the pressure and scavenge lines.

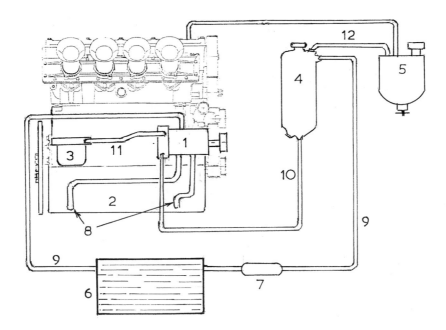

Figure 12.3 Dry sump oil system with two scavenge stages and one pressure stage. The components illustrated are: 1 scavenge/pressure oil pump; 2 dry sump oil pan; 3 oil filter; 4 oil tank; 5 breather catch tank; 6 oil cooler; 7 aircraft screen filter; 8 scavenge lines with inlet screen filters; 9 tank return lines; 10 suction line; 11 pressure line; 12 breather lines.

A dry sump system would have prevented the destruction of this engine, which occurred on a long high-speed turn. The sump baffling could not control oil surge and, with the oil flow interrupted, a rod bearing seized.

417

OIL TANK

The size of the oil tank will to some extent be dependent on the size of the engine and the quantity of oil being pumped into it, the effectiveness of the scraper/scavenge system in rapidly returning oil to the tank, the efficiency of the tank in quickly de-aerating the stored oil, and engine oil consumption and race distance.

The oil tank must not be filled more than two-thirds full. With that in mind a properly designed system used in sprint-type competition will use a tank of around 5½–11 litres, with smaller engines running a reservoir up to around 7 litres, V6s up to about 9 litres and V8s up to 11 litres. In distance events consideration must be given to engine oil consumption, not only in the early stages when the engine is 'fresh' and consuming, say, ½ litre/hr, but also in the later stages when consumption may triple. Also think about how long the car will be out on the circuit between pit stops, how time-consuming it will be to top up the oil, and if the regulations limit how much oil may be added. When these factors are weighed up it may be concluded that the sprint tank is suitable, or it could be that up to 30% additional capacity is required.

A tall round oil tank with the oil line entering the top of the tank at a tangent works best (Figure 12.4). With the oil entering at a tangent it will tend to swirl around the tank wall, which assists the air to separate out. To further aid de-aeration a horizontal baffle perforated with 4–5mm holes should be located about midway between the top of the oil and the oil inlet. Then, by keeping the height-to-diameter ratio of the tank greater than 2:1 – preferably around 2.5:1 – the oil will give up more air, reducing the air content from as much as 7% down to a round 2–3%. Also, by keeping the tank tall, and with the pump suction line drawing from the bottom of the tank's cone-shape floor, the pump will always be drawing oil into the engine regardless of the G forces being encountered.

Figure 12.4 Dry sump oil tank.

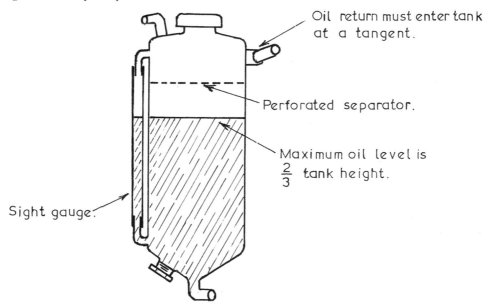

Oil return must enter tank at a tangent.

Perforated separator.

Maximum oil level is $\frac{2}{3}$ tank height.

Sight gauge.

It is a good idea to build the tank with a sight gauge consisting of a high-temp clear plastic tube. This is a quick check to see that the oil tank actually has been filled prior to firing the engine. Yes, I know everyone is supposed to know that standard start-up procedure is crank the engine until there is oil pressure, then go to 'ignition on', but with an engine that is a lazy starter and with limited battery capacity I have seen this overlooked. A sight gauge is also a good idea in distance race engines, as a minor engine problem can quickly accelerate oil consumption beyond what was anticipated, and a blown engine can result because nobody realised that an unscheduled top-up was needed.

However, it is during dyno development that a 'sighted' oil tank is invaluable. Here you can quickly see how effectively the scraper/scavenge system you have in place is working. In a 2-litre race engine I would expect the oil level to drop by about 0.5 litre, and certainly not more than 1 litre, as the engine is accelerated from idle up to maximum rpm. With a big V8 I would prefer to see the level drop by less than a litre, up to a maximum of 1³/4 litres. This should be followed up with an on-circuit test where G forces are involved to check on the suitability of your scavenge pick-up locations. Run the engine at full speed around the circuit and immediately cut the engine while simultaneously de-clutching. Coast back into the pits and drain the oil pan. If there is considerably more oil in the pan than the sight gauge drop during dyno testing, it indicates that the pick-ups are located incorrectly.

Mounting the oil tank in the engine compartment as close to the engine as possible cuts down the length of the various oil lines, and thus reduces flow losses. However, flow losses also occur when hoses are too small in diameter or are bent too tightly. The minimum radius of bends should be 2in; if you do not know what that looks like, take a length of 4in exhaust pipe. That has a 2in radius, so no bend should be tighter than that. The actual diameter of hoses will depend on oil flow rates through the engine and whether they are scavenge or pressure lines. A typical 2-litre race engine will have an oil flow rate of around 15 litres per minute, while a 6-litre V8 will be double that. Thus while a 2-litre could run ¹/2in bore pressure hoses and ⁵/8in bore scavenge and suction hoses, bigger V6s and V8s would need ⁵/8in pressure lines and ³/4in scavenge and suction lines.

ENGINE BREATHERS AND CRANKCASE VACUUM

With a dry sump system installed, large engine breathers are not required. With small engines a ³/8 or ¹/2in hose from the cam cover to the breather catch tank is ample, while for bigger V6 and V8 engines run two hoses. There are two schools of thought here: some tuners advocate running an 'open' breather, one that vents directly to the catch tank, while others prefer a 'closed' system, which incorporates a check valve between the engine and the catch tank. Personally I prefer a closed system as this allows the scavenge pumps to run down the crankcase pressure very low, perhaps below zero when there is minimal blow-by. With zero crankcase pressure hp rises a little and oil leaks around the crank and cam seals, for example, dry up. If the engine runs sour during a race and blow-by increases crankcase pressure beyond what the scavenge stages can handle, the breather pipe flapper valve opens to vent excess blow-by back to the catch tank. With an open breather, pressure in the crankcase will never drop down to zero because if the scavenge stages have excess pulling capacity beyond

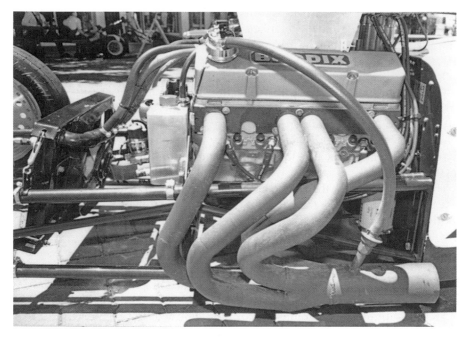

The pan evacuator system uses exhaust pulses to draw a vacuum on the crankcase. A good system will pull up to 36in water (2.65in Hg) vacuum, which is useful but a lot less than that possible with a vacuum pump or a dry sump scavenge pump. The pan evacuator cannot be used on turbo engines. The fitting into the exhaust pipe is an anti-backfire valve.

handling blow-by, they draw air into the engine via the breather pipe. In the closed system this cannot happen because the check valve allows only one-way flow in the breather pipe.

In recent years the lubrication system has been carefully scrutinised in the search for more power. It should be obvious that a crankshaft rotating at 8,000rpm and banging into the gallons of oil draining from the camshaft, lifters and rockers, etc, will be experiencing a certain degree of drag – maybe not as much as you experience when you drive into a puddle of water at high speed, but there will be drag none the less. This drag consumes a lot of power and results in oil frothing (aeration) and heating, due to the friction involved and energy being expended. 'V'-type push rod engines are the worst offenders in this respect as they dump all the oil from the cam and lifters on to the crankshaft.

You learned during school physics lessons that fast-moving air creates a low-pressure zone, which is why aeroplanes fly, etc. A crankshaft spinning at 8,000rpm is also moving the air at quite a speed, and this too creates a low-pressure region in the area in which the crank and rods are moving. The rest of the crankcase may be experiencing a pressure of 2–5psi depending on the effectiveness of the breathing system on your engine. Let us assume that there is a difference in pressure of 5psi between the high-pressure and low-pressure zones in this engine. What will tend to happen is that the oil pouring through the engine bearings will continue to cling to the crankshaft, because the centrifugal force of the crank is unable to overcome the pressure differential within the crankcase. Of course part of this mass of oil must continually be released, but in a big V8 there may be 3 pints of oil clinging to the crank, and being carried around by it to cause fluid drag additional to that being caused by oil drain-back from the cam and lifters.

An effective dry sump system can help with this problem in the following way. If large scavenge pumps are used, the air pressure in the sump pan can be brought to almost zero or close to equal the low-pressure zone surrounding the crankshaft. This will allow the force of gravity to have its way and pull a considerable amount of oil away from the crank. Basically, this explains one reason for the power increase shown in dry sump engines.

The other reason for the rise in hp is due to improved piston ring to cylinder wall seal. Whenever we increase the pressure differential existing above and below the top compression ring, we get a superior ring to cylinder wall seal. This comes about because the pressure above the ring improves the seal between the lower edge of the ring and the bottom of the ring groove. If we achieve zero leakage here more combustion pressure builds behind the ring forcing it hard against the bore to effect a more gas-tight seal. Obviously with added combustion pressure trapped above the piston a bigger shove is transferred to the crank, which we record as increased hp.

There are limits to the amount of vacuum desirable in the crankcase. First off it costs us power to drive a scavenge pump harder, so we reach a point of diminishing returns. Additionally we can run into quite a serious lubrication problem. The high vacuum can pull so much oil away that piston pins seize unless we pressure lube them using special rods with an oil passage from the big end to the little end. Exhaust valves also run dry and seize. Some have experienced serious cylinder lube problems, and scavenge pump reliability problems. Consequently my recommendation is not to exceed depressions of 10–12in for street engines. For competition engines start out at 14–15in vacuum and carefully inspect the engine before going further. Personally I don't think there is any gain above about 18in, but I understand some big money teams have been finding hp in the 22–25in area. In Formula 1, for example, the 3.5ltr V12 Honda RA122E/B started out running modest crankcase pressure of 64% of atmospheric. The vacuum was later increased to lower pressure to 30% of atmospheric, and maximum power rose by 16hp to 774hp at 14,000rpm!

SCREENS AND SCRAPERS

The dry sump system cannot get all the oil away from the crank and for this reason we need a system of screens and scrapers to assist (Figure 12.5). The screen should be of rigid 16–20 gauge steel mesh running the full length of the crankshaft and positioned, as shown, in close proximity with it. The idea is that the screen will prevent oil from splashing back on to the crank after it has been flung to the floor and sides of the oil pan; the screen effectively dissipates much of the oil's energy on the way through, so there is less energy available for splash-back when the oil hits the pan.

A rigid 22 gauge steel scraper positioned along the side of the oil pan deck will scrape oil from the crank and rods if machined to extend to within just a few thousandths of an inch of these.

To improve the oil drain off from the scraper, the side of the oil pan should be   421

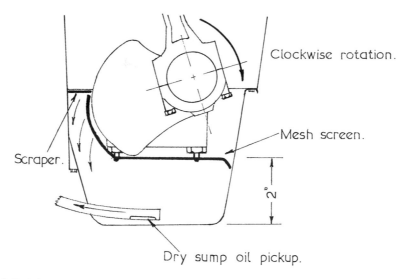

Figure 12.5 Oil screen and scraper.

extended out an inch if possible. With these modifications you can expect a further 3–4% power increase over and above that possible with dry sumping alone.

Do not despair if you cannot afford a dry sump system, because the screen and scraper set-up can be adapted to work almost as effectively with a wet sump. There are two ways to approach the problem. If ground clearance is not a consideration, deepen the sump to give $1\frac{1}{2}$in clearance between the screen and the horizontal anti-surge baffle. For improved oil drain from the scraper, move out the side of the sump 1in, the same as for the dry sump oil pan.

The windage tray and scraper strips oil off the crank and rods and prevent the low pressure area around the spinning crank from drawing oil up out of the sump.

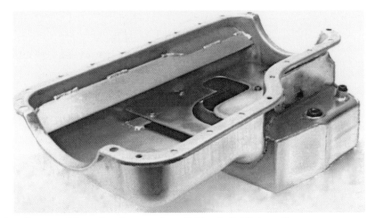

This sump has been widened to lower the oil level. Additionally, a scraper and both a horizontal and vertical baffle have been added.

If ground clearance is a problem, the only alternative is to widen the sump to lower the oil level. Again there should be 1½–2in clearance between the screen and the horizontal baffle.

OIL FILL LEVEL

Having considered the foregoing information it should be obvious that the sump should never be overfilled, otherwise you are sure to have the crank and rods dipping into the oil every revolution. If that is not bad enough, you will end up with a situation where too much oil is being thrown up the cylinders; the rings have to drag it off the walls and that consumes power. If the rings cannot cope with this additional oil load you will have combustion chamber and plug oiling problems, which will affect combustion and rob you of performance.

Personally I keep the oil level well below the full mark on the dipstick. First I check for oil surge with ½ litre less. Then if there is no surge problem I drop another ¼ litre and so on down to a maximum of 1 litre below full. With a complex baffling system involving several swinging trap doors and a swinging pick-up I have been able to drop to a 50% oil fill. This is dangerous territory though, and the hp gains are minimal. Lowered 1 litre some engines have shown maximum hp gains of around 2½%, but a little over 1½% is more usual. In road cars at cruise the gains are much greater, and this pays a nice fuel economy dividend.

CRANKCASE AIR PASSAGES

We may have an opportunity to go much further in our endeavours to reduce crankcase windage losses. For example in the upper echelons of motor sport, engines are built with the crankcase divided into separate compartments so as to limit air movement and subsequent frictional losses caused when a piston rapidly descends in its cylinder. Obviously if an engine has an individual cylinder capacity of 500cc each time a piston descends it has to push 500cc of air out of the way. If it is only a 4-cylinder engine working at 7,000rpm we are pushing the equivalent of 7,000 litres of air back and forth 423

To reduce parasitic losses, and avoid numerous other problems, never exceed the 'max' oil level mark. If possible run closer to the 'min' mark.

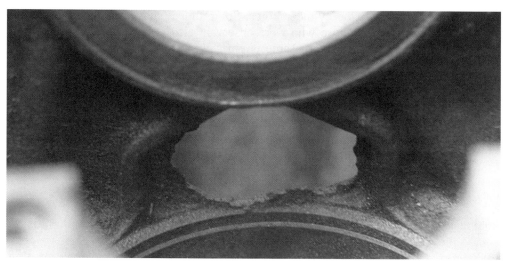

Above: *These passages between the cylinders and main bearings are supposed to allow the air below the pistons to easily shuttle back and forth as the pistons go up and down. Before being properly ground out they partly block flow and introduce stress raisers into the block.*

Below: *Using a grinder all corners are radiused to help prevent main bearing web cracking, plus air flow is improved, cutting parasitic losses.*

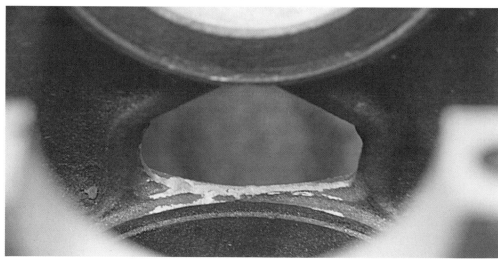

in the crankcase every minute! That costs us power even if we have a slight vacuum in there. Remember, normal air pressure is 14.7psi, so if we apply a vacuum of 15in, about 7.4psi, we are still moving a lot of air (about the equivalent of 3,480 litres). When we divide the crankcase into compartments we arrange things such that the air being displaced as the No 1 piston descends moves next door to fill the void created as the No 2 piston rises. In this manner air movement is restricted to a smaller area, windage losses decrease and hp rises.

Car engine manufacturers have done something similar. In the late '80s I noticed that some engines began appearing with a large passageway between the main bearing webs and the bottom of the cylinder bores. Some tuners suspected this was to save engine weight. However, those who were observant also noted that at the same time these passages appeared the very same engines were outfitted with windage trays which wrapped up close to the crankshaft. While these pressed metal trays did a reasonable job of pulling oil off the crank and rods, and prevented the hurricane being generated by the spinning crank from drawing oil up out of the sump, they created a secondary windage problem. There was now no easy path for the air to shuttle between cylinders as the pistons travelled up and down. The solution was to add these holes to interconnect the bottom of the cylinders. The resultant windage losses produced hp gains in the region of 2%, and in a few engines it was over $2^{1}/_{2}$%.

In some blocks these holes are machined, but generally they are cast. Either way they need some help to properly do their job, and at the same time we can partly get rid of a potential failure point in the block. We have to view these passages in a similar light as the inlet ports. They are expected to move the same gas volumes, but in considerably less time. Cast passages are usually quite large. However they are often partially blocked by casting slag. This stuff has to be ground out to improve flow capacity, and more importantly to get rid of a stress raiser which could end in the main bearing web breaking away from the bottom of the block. Machined passages are better in this respect, however, as they are quite small be sure to radius both ends of the hole to help flow.

WET SUMP BREATHERS

To vent crankcase pressure most engines in standard tune rely on a single $^{1}/_{2}$ or $^{5}/_{8}$in hose connected to the air filter or inlet manifold. Any wet sump competition engine should have at least a 1in hose connected into each rocker cover and another 1in hose connected into the block. Take care when connecting breathers into the motor that oil is not going to be splashed up the breather pipe by a rocker arm or a con rod. If such is the case, steps will have to be taken to fit a suitable deflector at the breather inlet.

The problem with these breather systems is that they fall far short of what we actually want to help us make more hp, and improve engine reliability. The stock breather system is required by law on road cars to cut pollution of the air we all breathe. We aren't allowed to simply dump blow-by gases into the atmosphere as is done on competition engines. Thus this gas, along with any oil mist that the oil/air separator in the cam cover has failed to remove, is recirculated into the inlet tract. Clearly this gas occupies volume and so reduces the power potential of the engine. The oil mist though can wreck engines by lowering the fuel octane and setting off detonation.

CRANKCASE VACUUM PUMP

How can we get around this and still do our part in not ruining the environment? In the past I have used the belt driven smog pump that was fitted on some engines back in the '70s and '80s to pump air into the exhaust so as to lower emissions. However, rather than have the pump draw in atmospheric air I connected it to suck blow-by gas out of an oil/air separator tank which I connected to the crankcase and cam cover. These pumps are quite reliable if not spun too fast and are protected from exhaust back-fires by a check valve. Rather than pump the blow-by gas into the exhaust manifold I connected a single stainless steel pipe into the exhaust at the exhaust header collector. Obviously in turbo engines these gases must be recirculated after the turbo, either into the dump pipe or just prior to the CAT.

The main problem with these smog pumps, properly called an AIR or Air Injection Reactor pump, is that they are big (5in dia x 3–4in long) and didn't pull a really good vacuum on the crankcase. However in more recent times Moroso have marketed two dedicated vacuum pumps which are very effective. The big 4 vane 22641 pump will pull over 15in vacuum while the smaller 3 vane 22640 pump will draw up to about 12in. The 3 vane is a better street pump, but is also useful in endurance events where you are required to run a wet sump. The 4 vane race pump will wear out fairly rapidly if spun faster than about 4,000rpm. The life of both pumps is enhanced if some oil mist is allowed to flow through them. This means that it is best to locate the oil/air separator after the pump, and in road cars with a connection into the exhaust the back-fire check valve is located after the separator. Street engines routinely show a 3–4% hp rise at 10–12in vacuum – over double of what I record with smog pumps.

On wet sump engines a Moroso vacuum pump can be used to improve piston ring sealing and thus reduce blow-by and oil contamination, plus gain hp.

Chapter 13

Cooling

Your engine may be air-cooled or water-cooled, but in both cases you rely directly or indirectly on a flow of air to stabilise the temperature of the cylinder head and the cylinders. The cooling system of every internal combustion engine performs a vital function: the dissipation of heat in order to maintain normal engine operation.

The heat engine relies on the conversion of fuel into heat, and then into mechanical energy to produce power at the crankshaft. Only about one-third of this heat is converted into power; another third is eliminated through the cooling system. Right away this should alert you to the load placed on your cooling system. Thus if our engine is generating 300hp we are also calling on the cooling system to get rid of the equivalent of 100hp of heat energy. Now if our stock engine produced 150hp the manufacturer obviously installed a cooling system capable of handling that heat load and not much more, so it would be foolish of us to think that the stock arrangement could cope with 300hp.

AIR-COOLING

If your engine is air-cooled, there is not a great deal that you can do to increase the engine-cooling capacity to cope with higher power outputs. Therefore it is essential to ensure that the cooling system provided by the vehicle's manufacturer is operating at 100% capacity.

Heat radiation from the cooling fins is retarded by the presence of oil and mud, so ensure that the fins are clear. Fins that are silver-coloured can have their radiating capacity improved by a coat of matt black paint.

Anything that is obstructing air flow on to the head and cylinders should, if possible, be moved to another location. I am amazed by the number of bikers who persist in fixing lights, air horns and oil coolers in front of the engine – the idea is to encourage air flow over the motor, not restrict it.

Air-cooled cars rely on a fan to circulate cooling air over the head and cylinder. Think carefully before you decide to modify a cooling system of this type, as there are several arrangements in service from the various manufacturers. Without a proper understanding of the system any modification could spell disaster for the engine.

The first consideration is whether the air inlet or outlet is ducted, because it is important to keep the inlet and outlet separated. If the inlet is taking in hot air that has just been expelled through the outlet, overheating and even a blow-up could result.

On the VW Beetle the outlet is ducted (Figure 13.1). The fan intake is open inside the engine compartment and the hot air is exhausted beneath the engine tray. The hot air from under the car must not be allowed to enter the engine compartment, so ensure that all the tinware is properly fitted and sealed with Silastic. Check the rubbers around the spark plug caps; hot air escaping through here will be re-circulated. Badly planned body modifications may also allow the entry of hot air into the engine compartment, so look into this as well.

Figure 13.1 VW cooling systems.

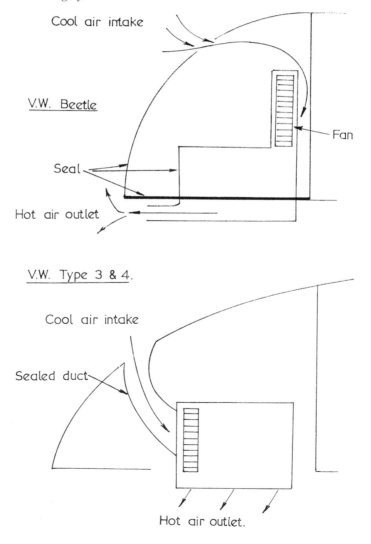

By contrast, the Type 3 and 4 VW use a ducted intake. The outlet is open and the space between the engine and body is not sealed. In this instance you must ensure that the inlet duct remains sealed and that any modifications do not bring the inlet and outlet so close that hot air will be re-circulated.

Most air-cooled cars have their air intake in an area of low air pressure, which reduces the amount of air available for cooling. Never fit a different pulley to slow the fan. Some claim that this gives better cooling because the fan is more efficient at lower speeds. Also they feel that because less power is being used to drive the fan, performance will increase. I have found the opposite to be true – slow up the fan and blow up the engine.

It may be possible to increase fan speed to increase air flow over the engine, but on the other hand the fan may already be moving all the air it is capable of moving and any increase in engine rpm or fan speed will only result in a marginal flow improvement. Frequently, increased cooling can be best cared for by thinking more in terms of massively increasing the size of oil coolers, and perhaps upping oil flow in the engine. Especially, there is a need for more flow volume up into the pistons and across the cylinder heads.

When Porsche added turbos to their 630hp 917 racer, increasing the output to 1,000hp and then later to 1,100hp, they successfully increased fan speed from a maximum of 7,400rpm up to 9,000rpm, a 22% increase. However cooling air flow rose from 2,400ltr/sec to 3,100ltr/sec indicating that the big fan on the 5ltr flat-12 (5.4ltr on later version) was more efficient at this higher speed. Also you should note that, due to the much higher hp, full throttle was used less frequently and for significantly shorter periods. As a result air flow per hp was dropped from 3.8ltr/sec in

Cooling of air-cooled engines can be improved by ensuring only cool air is being drawn in, also possibly by increasing fan speed, and by increased oil cooling, ie increasing oil flow to the pistons and cylinder heads and larger oil coolers.

the naturally aspirated engine to 2.8ltr/sec in the 1,100hp turbo engine without any problems with overheating.

MONITOR CYLINDER HEAD TEMPERATURE

Before you even think about modifying a fan-air-cooled engine, be sure to fit a cylinder head temperature gauge; it could save you a lot of money. The liquid surrounding the combustion chamber of a water-cooled motor tends to act as a heat sink and stabilises the combustion chamber temperature. An air-cooled head has very little in reserve to take away a sudden increase in heat, so the combustion chamber and piston temperature could take a sudden and unexpected rise, perhaps large enough to melt the pistons. For this reason the head temperature must be continually monitored when you are engaging in high-speed motoring.

What is the maximum safe head temperature? That depends on where you measure it and on the quality of the pistons. If pistons suitable for competition are being used and the temperature is being recorded from a thermocouple washer at the base of the spark plug, I would suggest throttling back once the temperature exceeds 220°C. If the thermocouple is attached elsewhere on the head, I would advise that the same action be taken at a 200°C read-out.

LIQUID-COOLED ENGINE, CORROSION AND FREEZE PROTECTION

Cooling by water or liquid is usually thought to be more straightforward than by air, and to a degree this is so. For instance, it is easy to accommodate a large power increase from a liquid-cooled motor and avoid overheating; you simply use a larger radiator. Other aspects of water cooling are, however, not so elementary.

The two major deterrents to proper heat transfer from the combustion chamber and cylinder to the cooling medium (usually water) are deposits and air in the cooling system.

Metallic oxides (eg iron oxide, or rust) are formed in the water passages. A deposit 12-thousandths of an inch thick will cut heat transfer by up to 40%. In order to maintain optimum heat transfer within the engine, the cooling system should be chemically cleaned in a bath when the engine is stripped down, and should contain an inhibitor that will keep water jacket surfaces clean and free of deposits.

There are two basic types of inhibitors: chromates and non-chromates. Sodium chromate and potassium dichromate are two of the best and most commonly used water-cooling system corrosion inhibitors. These chemicals are toxic, so handle them carefully.

Non-chromate inhibitors (borates, nitrates, nitrites) provide protection in either water only or water and permanent anti-freeze systems. Chromates must not be used in systems protected by anti-freeze.

When freeze protection is required, a permanent-type anti-freeze must be used. If a solution of 30% by volume anti-freeze is used, additional inhibitor protection will not be required, but solutions of less than 30% concentration do not provide sufficient corrosion protection, so a non-chromate-type inhibitor should be added. Concentrations over 50% adversely affect heat transfer and should not be used in high-performance or rally vehicles.

Ethylene glycol base anti-freeze is recommended for use in all high-performance engines, but methyl alcohol base anti-freeze should not be used because of its effect on

water pump seals and radiator hoses, and because of its low boiling point.

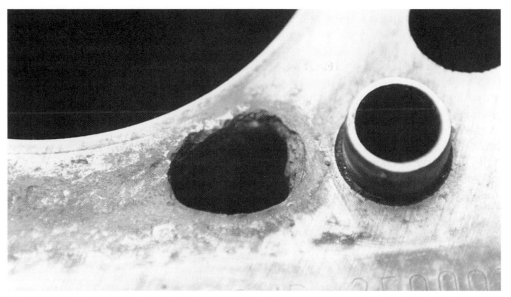

This engine blew a head gasket due to corroded water passages. The glycol coolant looked okay, but, because of a lack of cooling system maintenance, had in fact turned to acid.

To prevent corrosion and mineral build-up in water jackets, a mixture of distilled water and inhibitor or a mixture of distilled water and anti-freeze should be used, and regularly replaced as recommended.

Anti-freeze containing cooling system sealer additives must also not be used due to the possibility of the sealer plugging the radiator core tubes and various other areas in the cooling system. In fact, a sealer or stop-leak of any description is not to be recommended, except in an emergency to get you home or to finish the race. Then, as soon as possible, it should be flushed out of the cooling system by a cooling specialist using high-pressure air and water.

Petroleum-derived products such as soluble oil, often used as a water pump lubricant and rust inhibitor, should never be used in the cooling system. A 2% concentration of soluble oil will raise the cylinder head deck temperature by around 10%, due to the reduced heat transfer efficiency of the coolant. One popular radiator stop-leak contains a high proportion of soluble oil, which is another reason for keeping clear of radiator sealers. Soluble oil turns water a milky colour when added.

ELIMINATING AIR BUBBLES

The presence of air bubbles in the coolant reduces its heat transfer capacity and the efficiency of the water pump. Air can be sucked into the system through a leaking hose or gasket, and gas bubbles can form in the system due to localised boiling, or due to water pump cavitation.

In the first instance air can be kept out by ensuring that the system is free of air or water leaks, and by maintaining the coolant at the correct level. However, a good deal more is involved. At the very least take care to bleed the cooling system carefully whenever it is disturbed in any way to replace a hose, etc. You must ensure that there are no pockets of air trapped in the block and head, or, in the case of road cars, in the interior heater. Some engines will self-bleed fairly satisfactorily, while others may have to be bled through a factory-fitted bleed nipple. Others, however, require the addition of a bleeder nipple high up on the block right under the deck and/or a bleeder in a high point in the head.

After letting trapped air escape through the bleeders, do not assume that the cooling system is now free of air. With a race engine running a restrictor, start the engine and throttle it up and down for a couple of minutes. The vibration and water surge should get most air bubbles moving to the high spots, so then open the bleeders to release any air and top up the radiator.

A road car is a bit different as we also have to worry about getting air out of the heater and from under the thermostat. What we need to do after initially bleeding the system is to take the car for a run for about 15 minutes with the heater full on. The thermostat will open in this time and the combination of engine vibration and water surge in the passages should get any trapped air moving either into the high point in the head or into the radiator. At the end of the run, with the engine still running, carefully open the top bleeder to let any air escape. With that done, shut off the engine and allow it to cool. When down to ambient, check the coolant level and top up if necessary.

Even after all these steps, the cooling system will probably contain some pockets of trapped air that will only be eliminated by evacuating the system using a vacuum pump. People accept the fact that refrigeration and air-conditioning systems must be evacuated prior to being re-gassed, and in reality race car cooling systems deserve the same treatment. What is required is to pump all the air out of the cooling system and bring the vacuum down to around 25 inches of Hg. After turning the vacuum pump off, the vacuum should hold at that figure; if it does not there is a leak somewhere that has to be eliminated. With all leaks rectified the system can then be completely filled with coolant, free of any air pockets.

THE PRESSURISED COOLING SYSTEM

In the second instance gas bubbles or steam pockets can be prevented by pressurising the system to the degree necessary to prevent the coolant boiling. Many wonder why it is that we pressurise the cooling system. The boiling point of water is 100°C (at sea level), so why is it necessary to increase the boiling point by pressurising the system when most cars operate at around 90°C and most competition vehicles operate at an even lower temperature, usually 70°–75°C?

First, the system is pressurised to prevent boiling after the engine is turned off. Once the coolant stops circulating, its temperature climbs rapidly from its normal 90°C to something like 110°C, way past the boiling point of water at sea level pressure (14.7psi). If the water boiled each time the engine was stopped, a considerable amount of coolant would be lost, and if the system was not re-bled an air pocket would form.

Second, regardless of what the temperature gauge is reading, the temperature is very high in the water passage around the combustion chamber, particularly close to the exhaust valve. Remember that the temperature gauge is only giving a reading of the circulating water temperature, not the temperature of the water around the exhaust valve seat, where the temperature is well above the boiling point of water. To prevent the water around the combustion chamber from boiling and forming a steam pocket, the cooling system has to be pressurised. If the coolant were allowed to boil here, localised heating of the metal would occur, creating thermal stress points that would lead to cracking of the metal.

By pressuring the system using a 14psi radiator cap the boiling point is raised to approximately 125°C at sea level. As well as preventing boiling when the engine is switched off, the radiator pressure cap also serves to stop gas bubbles in a number of other situations. For example, a road engine may be given a lot of throttle at low engine speed, which will give rise to rapid heating of the combustion chamber, exhaust port and valve area. At low engine rpm the water pump is turning slowly so the water flow is limited and the water pump will not be creating any pressure in the block and head. It is only the radiator cap that stops this sort of localised boiling.

A similar sort of thing occurs when a race car pits. The top of the engine is extremely hot because of all the full-throttle driving out on the circuit, but now, with the engine idling while adjustments are carried out, tyres changed, etc, the engine would boil without a pressure radiator cap.

WATER PUMP CONSIDERATIONS

However, when water pump speed increases to the peak efficiency speed of 4,000–6,000rpm it is not the radiator cap that stops boiling but water pressure created by the water pump. Even many race engine tuners do not seem to understand that regardless of the radiator cap pressure a water pump spinning at maximum efficiency rpm will produce a pressure head of around 30–40psi in the engine block and head when water flow out of the head is limited by a thermostat or restrictor plate. This 433

An open back impeller is inefficient, and consequently this water pump has poor pumping capacity and a strong tendency to cavitate even at relatively low rpm. In fact what appears to be rust on the impeller is actually erosion due to cavitation.

A closed back impeller is much more efficient and far less prone to cavitate. The four holes promote coolant flow to cool and lubricate the seal.

pressure packs coolant around the top of the cylinders and around the combustion chambers to carry away combustion heat and stop an insulating blanket of gas bubbles forming in these areas.

In the third situation, gas bubbles due to water pump cavitation have to be tackled on two fronts: water pump design and water pump rotation speed. Even the best of pumps cavitate if you spin them fast enough, but some stock pumps begin to form bubbles at relatively low rpm due to both poor design and cost-cutting manufacturing techniques. In the past, water pump impellers were cast with a closed back, and clearance between the pump body and impeller was kept tight to ensure maximum flow volume. However, in modern times stock pump impellers tend to be pressed from light metal, which results in an open-back impeller often spaced well out from the pump body. This design will not only pump less volume, which also means reduced block pressure, but it will also begin to bubble the water at lower pump speeds.

Race pumps are available for some of the more popular engines; look for one that has a good close-fitting, closed-back, cast impeller. Some so-called race pumps merely feature a stronger bearing and large-diameter shaft, but with a poorly designed body and impeller flow volume and cavitation resistance may be no better than the stock pump.

If no good race pump is available you will have to modify the stock pump. It may be possible to modify a closed-back cast impeller from another pump, which may involve searching out old engines in scrapyards. An alternative is to close up the back of an open impeller by welding a backing plate on to it. Then, when the impeller is pressed back on to the pump shaft, press it on further to reduce the pump-body-to-impeller-vane clearance.

With that sorted out we now have to turn our attention to pump speed. In a well-designed pump, water flow will increase proportionally to pump rpm up to about 5,000rpm. Between 5,000 and 7,000rpm water flow continues to increase, but the rate

434

of increase begins to taper off rapidly as the water begins to bounce around off the impeller vanes and pump body. Thus past a pump speed of about 5,000rpm it is costing more hp to move proportionally less water. In a 650hp race engine a water pump spinning at 5,000rpm will be consuming around 15hp; increase the speed to 7,000rpm and the parasitic loss increases to 25hp for only a 15–20% increase in water flow.

As pump speed increases the pump will begin to cavitate, at which point not only does a lot of air get introduced into the system, but flow rates will also plunge by 20–25%. Apart from excessive pump speed and poor pump and impeller design, water temperature and block pressure also influence at what point cavitation will set in. As the average system temperature increases past about 85°C, the pump rpm at which cavitation begins decreases. Likewise with block pressure; less block pressure means that cavitation will occur at a lower pump speed. In a race engine this means that we must limit water pump speed and control engine block water pressure, and not concern ourselves only with water temperature.

First I would look at pump speed. While most pumps tend to work at peak efficiency at 5,000rpm, they do vary, so check with the pump manufacturer or do some flow testing yourself. If the pump peaks at 5,000rpm and the engine produces maximum hp at 7,750rpm, I would fit a big pulley to the pump to underdrive it to 65% of engine speed. Thus at 8,500rpm, the engine redline, the pump will be turning at around 5,500rpm, and down at 6,000rpm it will be running at 3,900rpm. Basically I am aiming to keep the pump in its maximum efficiency zone of 4,000–6,000rpm.

CONTROLLING COOLANT FLOW RATES

Next I would look at restrictor size to control the rate of water flow through the engine and radiator, and to get water pressure in the block up around 30psi. Let us say that a restrictor with a 16mm hole is fitted and the block pressure is where I want it but the water temperature is too cold. The options are to go to a smaller restrictor, or a lower pump speed, or a combination of both. If the testing was being carried out in hot weather I would go for less pump speed to reduce parasitic losses, but I would keep an eye on block pressure, as I would not want it to drop off. If the testing was during cold conditions a smaller restrictor would be fitted. If that brought the water temperature up, but there was a steep rise in block pressure to over 35psi, I would probably try a slightly slower pump speed combined with an intermediate-size restrictor hole.

However, what if the engine was too hot on the first test with a 16mm restrictor? If going to a 19mm hole did not bring the temperature down and we were losing block pressure, we would have three options: a larger radiator, more pump speed, or a combination of both. Assuming that it was a hot day test I would go for more pump speed with a limit of around 6,200rpm. However, if the temperature was way up on a cold day, more pump speed might not get you out of trouble when the weather warmed up. Therefore a larger radiator might be the way to go.

Some of course would just go for bigger and bigger restrictors, or discard the restrictor altogether. This is not a good move; certainly the temperature gauge may come down to where you want it, but consider what is happening inside the engine. With no outlet restriction, water pressure in the block and head will be right down. With lowered water pressure steam pockets will form in the hottest areas of the engine. The combustion chamber, exhaust valve and piston crown will then overheat, driving   435 the engine into detonation. At this point hp will fall, and if the situation continues the engine will be destroyed.

An old wives' tale states that if you discard the thermostat or the restrictor the engine is damaged because the water is flowing through it too quickly to draw off excess heat, or it is flowing through the radiator too fast to give up its heat. This is not so; what causes the engine damage is insufficient water pressure to pack the coolant in tight around hot spots in the engine. Then any water that hits these hot spots dances about like water droplets on a sizzling barbecue plate without drawing off any heat. As the water boils off, the size of the hot spot grows as a bigger and bigger steam pocket forms.

In reality we want reasonably rapid water flow through an engine, as this tends to reduce the incidence of stagnant high-temperature pools. Additionally the rapid flow will scrub off gas bubbles as they appear in the hottest parts of the engine before they have a chance to congregate into an impenetrable steam pocket. In fact, the solution to cooling problems is not so much a matter of moving more water through an engine, as moving less more rapidly. This will pay large dividends in more hp and better engine reliability.

COOLANT FLOW PATH

What we have to be thinking about is the accurate delivery of coolant at higher velocity to critical areas where hot spots are most likely to form – around combustion chambers, exhaust valves, spark plugs and the tops of the cylinders. Right away you can see that we have a problem with the way water travels through most stock engines. Typically the water pump forces all the coolant into the front of the engine block. Then, in theory at any rate, the water courses towards the back of the block, taking up heat as it goes. On reaching the rear of the block, the water moves up into the head through the large water passages interconnecting the cylinder block and the head. From here the coolant flows towards the front of the head, taking up heat from the combustion chambers and exhaust ports as it goes. The water then exits the engine through the thermostat or restrictor and enters the top of the radiator to be cooled.

However, the theory falls down because to prevent steam pockets around the tops of the cylinders we need a series of vent holes, usually 0.060in to 0.125in in diameter, drilled in the top of the block. While these holes are primarily to vent air and steam that would otherwise be trapped in the top of the block, they also allow the free passage of coolant from the block into the head. Also, as the spark plug bosses are often very close to the surface of the head, it is usual to find a series of holes in the block that direct water flow from the block up around the spark plugs. It should be obvious that all this coolant flow straight from the block to the head reduces the volume and slows down the flow velocity of coolant past the far-end cylinders and combustion chambers. The result is that the rear cylinders and combustion chambers run too hot, while those at the front run too cool. Thus to keep the back cylinders out of detonation we have to run the engine with a less than ideal compression ratio and reduced spark advance. All this costs us hp and engine efficiency.

Of course if we had the time and resources to experiment we could run each cylinder at a different compression ratio, higher at the front and progressively lower towards the back cylinder. If the race regulations permitted sequential fuel injection and ignition trim control we could trim the quantity of fuel injected into each cylinder, running the hot cylinders richer and the cool ones leaner, and likewise with the ignition we could increase advance on the cold cylinders and decrease it on the hot ones. All this effort would unleash additional hp and improve engine reliability, but the rewards are nowhere near as great as would be achieved by correcting the coolant flow problems.

To give you some idea of how much 'free hp' is available in a race engine when basic cooling deficiencies are cured, consider what we have seen in the small-block Chev. Twenty years ago a 6-litre engine tuned for road racing would give a peak of around 570hp. Today we are getting another 100hp with better reliability, fewer blown head gaskets and less detonation damage. Around 55hp has come from better cylinder heads with improved air flow and better combustion chambers, which have allowed us to run pistons with flatter tops. The other 45hp is the result of improved cooling. We have picked up 8–10hp because we can now run a slower water pump speed, and even with less pump speed water temperatures have come down from 90°C and more to about 75°C. This has allowed a compression boost from around 12.2:1 to 14:1, which has lifted torque and hp at all rpms, and given around 13–16hp at peak. In turn more compression has permitted more aggressive cam timing, while maintaining the previous torque on 12.2:1 compression, for a 15–18hp gain at the top end. More uniform cooling and the elimination of steam pockets has allowed full power lean mixtures and increased spark advance for another 5–7hp.

Basically what we have done is to equalise engine temperatures as much as possible from front to back, and top to bottom. This has meant rethinking how much water we direct into the block and heads, and taking care of specific danger areas that expose the engine to head gasket failure.

It should be obvious that as the combustion process takes place in the combustion chambers, which are located in the head, it is the head where we have to focus the cooling effort. Yes, the block does require some cooling, but because by comparison the cylinders have such a huge surface area to give up their heat to the coolant, cooling difficulties in this area are minor. Consequently in a race engine we want to move a lot more water through the head, to take excess heat away from that area. However, if we follow the conventional coolant flow path this also means circulating more water through the block, but as the cylinders are already overcooled this would not be a good idea.

The solution is to change the coolant flow path. Rather than all the water flow from the water pump being directed into the block, then up into the head, why not take the bulk of the flow straight from the pump to the head? Such a move reduces parasitic hp losses because we do not have to push bigger and bigger volumes of water through the engine, and frictional losses reduce as we allow cylinder wall temperatures to rise. Thus in a road race engine we would usually direct 65–80% of pump volume straight into the back of the cylinder head, and I understand that some tuners have gone to 90% without problems. Of course in a drag engine the block often gets no flow at all; the block has water in it and the water passages still match those in the head, but all flow goes into the back of the head. Even the stock V8 Jaguar has only half the pump output going into the front of the block, while the other half goes directly into the back of the heads.

In a distance road race Chev small-block, 35% is taken into the block and 65% straight to the heads. However, because of some cooling problems in localised areas there is a further splitting of flow to direct water to specific areas. For example, the centre exhaust ports are side by side, with the result that the head overheats in that area, which in turn reduces head gasket integrity. The solution is to tap off a fraction of the water being piped to the back of the heads and send it down a tiny 2.3mm hole drilled in the centre of the head below the exhaust ports. This reduces the head deck temperature and improves head gasket reliability. Down in the block, water flow pretty much goes to sleep around No 7 cylinder, and with reduced flow through the block that cylinder can begin to detonate. The solution is to run an external water line from the pump directly into the block at No 7. This provides a constant flow of cool water to mix with the stagnant, overheated fluid surrounding that cylinder.

One problem area with V6 and V8 engines is the manner in which coolant from the right and left heads comes together in the inlet manifold water passage before exiting through the thermostat or restrictor. Because flow is not the same in both banks – typically there is a 2–3% flow difference – water from the head with more flow will tend to reverse flow into the other head. This not only restricts coolant flow out of that head and causes it to overheat, but because there are two columns of water crashing head on into each other in the inlet manifold passage, there is a lot of flow turbulence. A few hp can therefore be wasted driving the water pump harder to force sufficient water volume through the engine to keep it cool. In a race engine the solution to this is to forget about bringing the water out through the inlet manifold, but instead to put a water outlet in the front of each head, if possible positioning it off-centre to favour flow along the exhaust side of the heads. Then coolant flow from the two heads can be brought together without turbulence through a pipe fabricated in the same style as two branches of an exhaust header blending together at the collector. The coolant flow restrictor or thermostat must be located in the system after the two pipes join.

Regardless of whether we follow the traditional pattern of cooling, with all of the coolant going into the block, then up into the head, or whether we use a split system with coolant diverging at the pump to both the block and head, we must concern ourselves with the size and number of coolant holes that interconnect the block and head. Obviously it is only at the rear of the block where we want volume flow of coolant going into the head. All other holes must only be as large as necessary to vent air and steam from under the deck of the block into the head, or to allow metered coolant flow from the block to a specific area in the head. Thus we may have flow

Take a few moments to study both blocks. The one on the left is the stock road car block while the other shows what BMW did to make it suitable for 1,000hp during the Formula 1 turbo era. The main change is the addition of coolant passages at the ends of the block and the elimination of six small steam holes between cylinders.

from the block to purge gas bubbles from certain areas such as from around the bosses for the head studs; we may have flow up around the spark plugs and the exhaust ports. Note here that we are talking metered flow, not bulk flow. Going back to the example of the small-block Chev mentioned earlier, that single 0.090in hole drilled below the centre exhaust ports feeds enough coolant to lower the cylinder head deck temperature in that region by 70°C!

However, what do we regularly find in production blocks and heads? Frequently these coolant transfer holes are around 1/2in in diameter, and at times larger. Usually they are so large not for the sake of coolant transfer, but to make it easier to get the core sand out at the end of the casting process. Naturally big holes in the top of the block and correspondingly big holes in the head mean that a lot of coolant entering the front of the block will flow straight up into the front of the head and only a small volume will course to the back of the block to cool and purge steam from around the end cylinders. Thus the rear cylinders will overheat and there will be reduced coolant transfer in this area from block to head to purge gas bubbles, cool spark plugs, etc.

HEAD GASKET COOLANT HOLES

Manufacturers attempt to rectify this undesirable situation by punching small holes in the head gasket where they desire only limited coolant transfer, and they punch larger holes where they want more flow. This works well enough on the road, but at the much higher flow rates in a competition engine there is usually an excessive amount of coolant transfer between the block and head, particularly at the front of the engine. Remember too that manufacturers have to make allowances for poor maintenance over a long period, so the holes may be larger than necessary to provide adequate flow even when partly blocked by rust and scale. Of course we do not see this sort of problem in a competition engine, so the transfer metering holes can be smaller.

It is at this point that we come up against a problem in that manufacturers of heavy-duty head gaskets generally punch their gaskets with the same hole size (or larger) as the original manufacturer. There are a number of ways to get round this problem. Preferably, if there are large round holes in the block, tap them out and screw

The six small white holes allow only limited water flow from the block into the head, thus ensuring that the majority of flow is through the three large white holes towards the rear of the block.

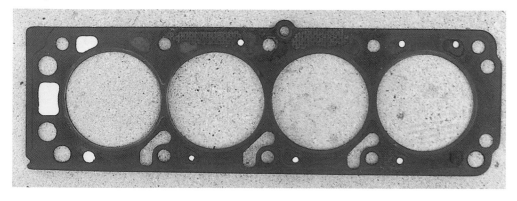

in soft aluminium pipe plugs. If the holes are smaller, gently knock in a short length of aluminium rod; obviously these plugs must not protrude above the block deck. After fitting them, drill the appropriate-size metering holes, which will usually be in the range of 0.060 to 0.125in. Note that in competition engines using a restrictor in place of a thermostat, the bypass hole is left completely blocked.

Where the transfer holes are an irregular shape they can be cleaned with a file or die grinder, then plugged with a silicone sealant such as Silastic. Coolant metering is taken care of by a length of aluminium rod, pre-drilled to the required size, being inserted into the silicone sealant. I prefer to run a drill through the sealant after it has cured, then force in the drilled rod, but some like to hold the pre-drilled rod in place, then pump sealant in around it to plug the core hole.

Clearly these small metering holes in the block must match the holes in the head gasket to allow the venting of air and the flow of coolant into the head. Some tuners just punch large holes in the head gasket, but this is a job that will have to be repeated every time the head gasket is replaced. What is preferable if solid plugs have been inserted into the block deck is to use the head gasket as a template and drill each plug to match with the corresponding hole in the gasket. Naturally where the deck has been plugged with sealant and a pre-drilled rod has been inserted, it may be necessary to punch a matching hole in the head gasket.

Because we want the bulk of coolant circulation from the block to the head to take place through the large holes at the rear of the engine, we do not want them restricted in any way. With this in mind it is a good idea to smooth them out and match them up using a die grinder or a file. In a conventional flow system this encourages

The coolant hole on the right is badly blocked by casting slag. This must be ground out to encourage coolant flow through the back of the block and up over the end combustion chamber and exhaust port.

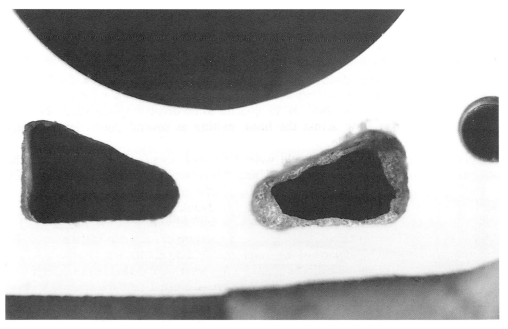

coolant flow right to the back of the engine, rather than flow short-cutting through transfer holes towards the front. With a split-flow system a good flow of coolant in this region is also important; first, to cool the top of the rear cylinder adequately, and second, so that the majority of the hot water from the block goes into the head at this point to mix with cooler water entering the back of the head, which has come straight from the water pump. This serves to balance out engine temperature front to rear.

COOLING HIGH OUTPUT ENGINES

While the modifications we have just discussed will provide adequate cooling in the majority of engines we have to accept that as we push production type engines to very high power levels it may be advisable to scrap the stock type cooling system. This means changing to an external competition water pump and completely altering the coolant flow path through the engine block and cylinder head. The aim being that coolant flow should be equally divided between cylinders, and then after cooling just that single cylinder the coolant is returned to the radiator.

How this is achieved will vary from engine to engine, so I will describe the basic concept for an inline engine with 4 to 6 cylinders and if you have a Vee or flat engine follow the same pattern, dealing with each bank as a separate engine. The simplest arrangement is to introduce all coolant flow from the water pump into one side of the block. When the cylinders are siamesed we would have only a single inlet in the centre of the block. However, as I will explain later, if the cylinders are not joined and we are unable to seal the water passages between them we will require two or three inlets respectively for 4-cylinder, and 5- or 6-cylinder engines. The main thing we want to do is get maximum water movement up close to the top of the block and we want to equalise cylinder to cylinder temperatures as much as possible. Generally we would knock out existing welch plugs and tap the holes to accept suitable water fittings. Obviously because we have got rid of the stock water pump we have to cover that hole in the front of the block. Also it will be necessary to fill the large coolant flow holes in the deck at the other end of the block.

Next we have to decide on a suitable flow path across the head. Note that we are not talking about coolant entering the head at one end and then exiting at the opposite end, after having flowed over every combustion chamber. No, what we want in a high output race engine is for the bulk of the coolant to be divided up and enter the head along one side then flow across the head, exiting at several points into a water manifold on the opposite side.

Some race engines actually split water flow with about 70–80% going into the head and 20–30% going into the block. Using this more complex arrangement, which is really only necessary when we exceed about 250hp per litre, a water manifold is attached to both sides of the head. An obvious advantage of such an arrangement is that if in a 4-cylinder engine we have a water manifold with four outlets, the size of those outlets can be adjusted to equalise the temperature of each combustion chamber. Additionally the individual ports of the water manifold do not have to terminate where they attach to the side of the cylinder head. Rather what we can do is extend each port right into the water jacket such that the coolant is blasted into the main hot spot, usually around the exhaust valve seats. From there the water will course over the combustion chamber, then exit the head into the exhaust water manifold.

441

AN ALTERNATIVE COOLING METHOD

When we opt for the simpler arrangement of flowing all water into the block and from there into the head we are not able to exercise such precise control of flow across each combustion chamber. Of course if we have an engine management system offering individual cylinder fuel and spark trim, small temperature differences between combustion chambers can be compensated for, but in an endurance race engine where fuel consumption is a concern, injecting additional fuel into a 'hot' cylinder isn't a satisfactory solution.

What we have to decide early on is on what side of the head do we want the water to exit? If we decide it should exit on the exhaust side then most flow, around 65–80%, should travel from the block into the head along the inlet side. This will ensure that for the most part, water will move from the block, straight up into the head, turn 90° and flow over the combustion chambers, then past the exhaust ports whereon it enters the water manifold and returns to the radiator (Figure 13.2).

To achieve that flow path we may not have to do much more than punch bigger holes in the head gasket along the inlet side. In all likelihood, coolant holes in the block and head will already be larger than necessary to achieve the flow rates required and we will have to balance flow across each combustion chamber by adjusting coolant hole sizes along the inlet side of the head gasket. This may sound simple enough but usually involves long dyno sessions with temperature probes stuck down onto the exhaust side of all combustion chambers, testing head gaskets with various

Figure 13.2 Revised coolant flow path for a high output engine.

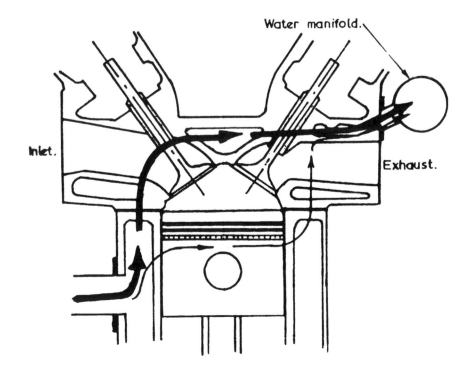

The Waggott TC-4V 2-litre produced 270hp. That was almost 40 years ago and much of what I learned early on about high output engines was as a result of my being befriended by Merv Waggott as he developed this engine, and its earlier siblings in 1,600 and 1,850cc sizes, to take on the then dominant Cosworth FVA and FVC. The water manifold above the exhaust ports ensured that the exhaust valves and seats were well cooled. For packaging reasons and because the actual cylinder block was cast iron with siamesed cylinders, which were a rarity then and pretty much an unknown in a race engine, Merv felt that he needed better cylinder cooling. Thus he chose to have coolant flow into the block on the left side, then around the end cylinders and up into the inlet side of the head rather than use the path I prefer as illustrated in Figure 13.2.

combinations of different hole sizes to even out the temperatures. We can do the same sort of thing with track testing, but that is even more tedious.

Some tuners choose to always, if possible, have the coolant exit on the exhaust side of the head. It is frequently more convenient to locate the water manifold on that side, but usually the reasoning is that inlet ports should be kept as cool as possible to maximise charge density, and flowing coolant from the exhaust side, across the combustion chambers, and out past the inlet ports gets the inlet hotter. While there is merit in that argument there are other issues which may, depending on the particular engine and its hp level, be a more pressing consideration. Another view is that it is at times possible to achieve more control on the direction and quality of flow around the exhaust valve seats by having the water enter the head on the exhaust side. Then, because the exhaust valves will be cooler, they will add less heat to the inlet charge. Also being cooler they are less likely to cause detonation after combustion has commenced.

443

However regardless of whether we settle on the coolant exiting on the exhaust or the inlet side, that decision will have a bearing on what side of the block the coolant should enter. The arrangement illustrated in Figure 13.2 with the inlet and outlet on the opposite side is correct, but we could still run into problems if the cylinders were non-siamesed. For example, if the engine had 4-cylinders and a single water inlet in the centre of the block there would be minimal water flow around the outside of the end cylinders – most flow would be through the three gaps between the cylinders. If we had two water inlets located at about quarter distance and three quarter distance, flow around the cylinders would be evened up, but there is a better way. Depending on where openings are located it is often possible to block the gaps between cylinders with silicone sealant. We don't want to convert the block to being siamesed. Rather leave the top of the gap open down to about 25% of engine stroke, and close the gap from there to the bottom of the cylinder. This forces flow around the end cylinders and the small gap helps cooling around the top of the bore. Distortion of the bore is reduced, ring seal is better and hp rises slightly.

Usually it is possible to block those gaps, even if you have to add a plastic extension hose (use 4–6mm id) to your silicone gun. What though if you can't? Well, as pointed, out two inlets would be the way to go (three inlets for 5- and 6-cylinder blocks). If we were to put additional inlets in the opposite side we would simply compound cooling problems around the end cylinders.

With a block that has siamesed cylinders we can improve cooling and reduce bore distortion, if the siamesed walls are sufficiently thick, by adding a small coolant hole in between cylinders. This is precision work so the block must be set up on a mill. Obviously, if the hole goes off course the block becomes scrap! Basically the web joining the cylinders has to be around 6mm or more wider. If it is 6mm you will be restricted to a 2mm hole. The idea is to set the mill up so as to leave a minimum wall of 2mm either side of the hole. First you drill bigger access holes through one side of the block. Later these will be tapped and plugged with small pipe plugs. The coolant hole will be located as high as possible up under the deck of the block. The idea of this is to get rid of any steam that may become trapped there as well as move a little coolant through that area which is the hottest part of the cylinder.

RADIATOR MAINTENANCE AND DESIGN

The actual heat exchange between the coolant and air takes place at the radiator. Bugs and debris that restrict air flow through the core should be cleaned out to maintain cooling efficiency. Cleaning out balls of rubber thrown up off the track is always a problem. The easiest method seems to be to soak the radiator, after plugging all openings, for a day or two in a tray of solvent. Then direct compressed air at the back of the radiator. Any balls that will not budge can be carefully picked out. A large tray of solvent is both a health and fire hazard so be very careful. Any fins which are bent must be straightened, as bent fins present as much impediment to air flow as trapped rubbish. The radiating efficiency will be improved further if the radiator is regularly repainted with matt black paint. This will also serve to increase the life of the core, by reducing the effects of external corrosion.

However, when it comes to a competition radiator many more factors are involved, such as whether it will be constructed of copper or aluminium, how many

rows of coolant tubes it will have, what fin count will be most suitable, etc.

Track debris and bent fins both restrict air flow through the radiator. Debris should be picked out and bent fins should be straightened using flat-blade tweezers.

For many people the decision between a copper or aluminium radiator is based on possible weight savings, but this is really a bit of a nonsense as most weight in a radiator is due to the volume of the coolant it contains! Copper conducts heat better, but in a crash aluminium will show more resistance to damage; in addition, it is less likely to be damaged by stones or debris thrown up off the track by other competitors.

Really the biggest difference between the two is their relative strength. Copper is fairly weak, so to avoid coolant tubes exploding due to water pressure, the tubes must be kept quite narrow. Aluminium, on the other hand, is much stronger, so the tubes can be twice as wide. At first glance this may not appear to be such an advantage, but if you take a look at Figure 13.3 you will understand where the gain lies. The water flow characteristics of a four-row copper radiator are pretty much the same as a two-row aluminium core. However, when we consider heat transfer area the aluminium tubes easily win to the tune of up to 20% gain. The fins, which transfer heat to the air passing through the radiator, only contact the flat sides of the tubes. The rounded ends 445

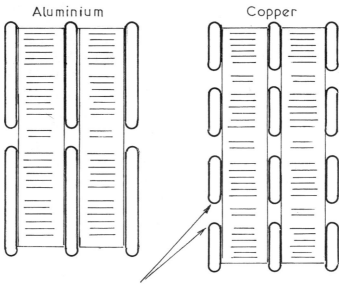

Aluminium   Copper

Tube ends do not transfer heat.

Figure 13.3 Aluminium radiator tubes are twice as wide as copper tubes.

of the tubes have no finning, so there is no heat transfer of any significance from this area. Thus with only half the number of tube ends, the aluminium radiator will give up more heat to the fins.

Another big difference between the radiators installed in road cars and race cars is with regard to their construction philosophy. Radiator tubes are much more expensive than fins, so road cars tend to skimp on the number of tubes and attempt to compensate with a very high fin count (Figure 13.4). At low speeds this presents no problem, but at race track speed all those closely spaced fins massively reduce air flow through the radiator. Even with good ducting, which should force the air entering the nose cone to flow through the radiator, a stand-off results: a high-pressure column of air builds up in front of the radiator, and some trickles through, but there is insufficient flow to take up heat rapidly enough from the radiator fins. It is a bit like pouring oil down a funnel. The rate of flow is controlled by the size of the hole in the bottom of the funnel; the size of the hole at the top and the amount you pour into the funnel, even to the point of overflowing, really does not change the rate of flow through the funnel by very much.

The only way around this is to construct a radiator with many more tubes – but not necessarily side by side, as this just adds to the air flow problems unless we can build the radiator wider or taller (depending on which direction the tubes run). What we usually need are more tubes placed one behind the other. The exceptions would be competition cars operating at speeds too low to force sufficient air through a thick radiator core.

Typically a road car will have a two-row or perhaps a three-row copper radiator, while a race car will perhaps have a radiator that is four or five rows deep, and to assist air flow the tubes may be spaced a little bit further apart across the front of the radiator. So, whereas a road radiator may have the tubes closely bunched at, say, 29

Louvres on the fins increase air turbulence across the surface of the fins, thus raising their heat shedding capacity. However, this also cuts air flow through the radiator, and so deeper radiators must have less fin density.

tubes per foot with a fin count as tight as 17 per inch, a competition radiator may space out the tubes to 22 per foot with a fin count opened up to 10–12 per inch, or even as low as 8 fins per inch in dirt-track cars where there is inadequate protection to prevent dirt getting in and blocking air flow.

If you have a close look at the fins you will better understand why a high fin count is so bad for good air flow through the radiator. Rather than having a smooth flat face, the fins are very finely louvred across their surface. These tiny louvres create turbulence to increase their radiating efficiency, and as they are packed more closely together it is this turbulence across their surface that cuts air flow through the radiator.

Figure 13.4 Competition radiator construction.

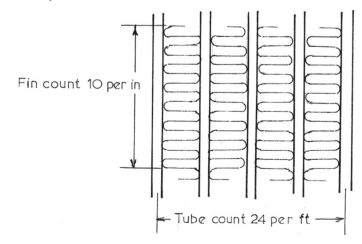

Fin count 10 per in

← Tube count 24 per ft →

When it comes to correcting a cooling problem racers often go about it the wrong way; they adopt the road car radiator mentality of closely bunched tubes and high fin counts. When that fails to work they may even exacerbate the problem by moving to an even higher fin count! Because the overheating just gets worse they drive the water pump faster, which in turn increases parasitic losses at best, or else runs the pump into cavitation. Alternatively they may throw out the restrictor, so water pressure in the block and head goes down (remember that we want about 30psi here), so big steam pockets develop, the engine detonates and loses power at best, or perhaps lunches a head gasket or piston.

Really what we want is a large number of radiator tubes but a low fin count. This costs more money, but you may save a great deal in the long run. If the radiator brings the temperature down too far, run the pump slower, but fit a restrictor with a smaller orifice to get block pressure back up to 30psi. Less pump rpm will cut parasitic losses, and reduced air flow resistance through the radiator may see a speed gain on fast straights.

DOUBLE-PASS RADIATOR

Another way we can increase the heat dumping ability of the radiator is to build it as a double-pass unit (Figure 13.5). As you can see when a splitter plate is welded in one tank the effect is to force all the coolant through half the number of tubes, but over twice the distance as the water flows from one side to the other side across the top half of the radiator, and then back again through the lower half. Providing the water pump is up to the task a two-pass radiator will dump 15–20% more heat than an otherwise identical conventional single-pass radiator.

This happens in spite of the flow rate through the tubes dropping 25–30% due to increased friction and water turbulence. What then accounts for the increase in efficiency? Obviously the water travels twice as far, giving up heat as it goes. However the real gain comes as a result of increased water turbulence in the tubes. At low flow rates the water clinging to the tube walls pretty much stalls, and in effect becomes an insulator which reduces how much heat is shed by the main body of

Figure 13.5 A double pass radiator halves the number of tubes and doubles their length improving radiator efficiency.

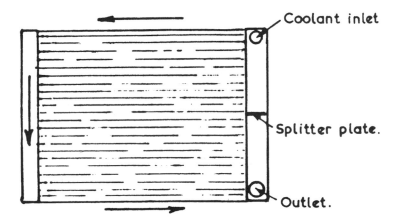

coolant flowing through the centre of the tube. When the flow rate is pushed up by effectively halving the number of tubes, water turbulence increases and this has the effect of breaking up and scrubbing away this stagnant insulating blanket clinging to the tube walls. This improves the heat transfer rate from the coolant to the radiator.

REGULATING COOLANT TEMPERATURE USING A THERMOSTAT

A high-temperature thermostat, which maintains the water temperature at 88–90°C, is usually fitted to production cars, but that is not the temperature for best power. The 88°C thermostat is fine if you want good heater efficiency in winter, and the higher temperature partly compensates for the stock manifold and carburettor being unable to vaporise the fuel properly, but apart from that there is no reason for its use.

Some feel that high engine coolant temperature in the range of 90–100°C is good for power. The theory is that anything lower just takes away heat energy, which we should be using to push the pistons down and produce more hp. To an extent this is true at low engine speeds and small throttle openings, but generally in a full-throttle, high-rpm dyno test an engine will make more power at coolant temperatures in the 70–80°C range. Only dyno testing will confirm what is ideal for a particular engine, but in my experience I rarely see an engine that makes more power running higher than 84°C or less than 68°C. I have seen engines gain 2–3% hp when the temperature was dropped from 90 to 70°; conversely I have seen gains when the temperature was pushed up from 65 to 80°C.

The water temperature in a road car can be lowered by fitting a cooler thermostat, providing that the radiator is large enough. Whenever a thermostat is replaced, use the correct type. Many modern engines use a dual-function bypass-type thermostat. When open to allow water flow out of the head into the radiator, this type of thermostat also closes off the engine bypass port. If an ordinary thermostat is fitted this port will be open, thus allowing a large volume of very hot water to circulate in a closed loop within the engine. This may lead to the engine overheating because of the volume of hot water from the bypass mixing with coolant from the radiator and significantly raising its temperature as it flows into the block.

A bypass-type thermostat improves cooling system efficiency by blocking off the bypass port when the thermostat opens. Never replace this type with a conventional thermostat.

RADIATOR COOLING FAN

The fan fitted to most cars consumes a good deal of power, which could otherwise be used beneficially to improve performance or reduce fuel consumption. Generally, a road speed of 25mph and above will provide sufficient moving air to cool the engine. Therefore a fan will not be required in competition vehicles. I have never had one fitted to my road car, although I would recommend that a fan be retained if you engage in peak-hour city driving.

If a fan is required it would be of benefit to fit an electric unit, which can be an engine-saver on rally and dirt speedway vehicles. You never know when you are likely to be bogged or when you are going to come up against a greasy half-mile climb in a rally; either occurrence would probably cause coolant boiling in the absence of a cooling fan. Speedway cars are sometimes required to circulate at a crawl under yellow lights for what seems like an eternity, another ideal situation for coolant boiling and engine damage.

Liquid-cooled vehicles with rear-mounted radiators (eg Imp and Renault) or side-mounted radiators (eg Mini) will, if modified for more performance, almost certainly require a larger cooling fan and also a separate expansion tank connected to the radiator. Some engines have a tendency to overheat if the radiator header tank is not completely full to give proper water flow down through the radiator core; an expansion tank ensures that the top tank is always full.

If a front-mounted radiator is installed, the fan can be removed and you can be sure of maintaining the correct coolant temperature under competition conditions. This is a simple modification on the Mini, particularly if of the Clubman body design.

Whenever an electric fan is fitted it should be mounted behind the radiator to avoid blocking off air flow into the radiator. Also remember that the fan may have a current draw of around 10 amps, so be sure that the alternator can handle the additional load; modern race engines place a heavy demand on the electrical system, so do not just assume that everything will be fine. I have seen engines shut down when the fan was switched on because the ECU could not handle the electrical surge. I have also seen engines lose a lot of power and come close to a meltdown because the fuel pump slowed and fuel pressure at the injectors dropped.

Some drivers run the electric fan all the time to get sufficient cooling, but this often just indicates that a bigger radiator with better air flow is needed. An exception is for speedway cars running with a grill closed off either to avoid a radiator blocked with mud and dirt, or in the case of super speedways, to improve the car's aerodynamics. Others use a thermostat control to switch on the fan at a pre-set temperature. Personally I feel that this just complicates things. I prefer to see the driver operate a simple switch to bring the fan into operation only when it is required. Then if he is given instructions such as 'fan on on long boggy hills', 'fan on under yellow', 'fan on into the pits', etc, he will not have to worry about studying the temperature gauge in such situations and make a decision as to when the fan should go on.

HELPING FLOW THROUGH THE RADIATOR

Another situation where an electric fan will provide an improvement in cooling is when air flow through the radiator is poor due to excessive pressure build-up in the engine bay. Really we need to work to exhaust air out of the engine bay to get air

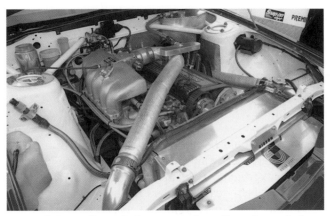

Building a duct around the radiator helps more air to flow through the core, improving cooling.

pressure down as low as possible behind the radiator. However, while a solution is being found an electric fan may provide a short-term fix. Reducing air flow under the front of the car will help, as will opening holes into the wheel tub area. At times the problem can be traced back to an inappropriate bonnet air scoop, which may be providing good air flow into the engine air intake, or cooling air flow over the turbocharger, but which is 'over stuffing' the engine bay with air.

Of course every effort must be made to ensure that all the air entering at the front of the car actually passes through the radiator; we do not want any air bypassing it by going over, under or around it. This means blocking off any openings around the radiator or else constructing a duct from the front of the car that seals up against the radiator's edges.

THE BENEFITS

To some, no doubt, all of this discussion and concern over cooling may appear to be over the top. However let me remind those folk that during the Formula 1 turbo era the major problem confronting teams, even allowing for their vast resources both monetarily and technically, frequently related to engine cooling. While readers may not be pushing the boundaries to the same extent as the F1 crowd, the fact remains that when we generate very high hp levels out of relatively small mass produced stock based road engines we are moving a considerable distance away from what the manufacturer's powertrain engineers ever envisaged, or made provision for. Consequently if we are to attain such power outputs with relative reliability we have to spend much in the way of time and resources to take care of engine cooling.

The other aspect is, if we are ever going to attain big hp then to some extent that outcome will be attainable only when we equalise, as much as practicable, combustion chamber and cylinder temperatures. Until that is achieved there will always be at least one cylinder giving less than 100%. And if we don't have individual cylinder engine management capabilities the situation is even more depressing as the cylinder that is the detonator will dictate just how much compression, fuel and spark we give all the other cylinders.

Chapter 14

Power Measurement
and Tuning

M any racers spend vast amounts of money building an engine, but never concern
themselves with fine tuning on an engine dynamometer. No matter how much
we may try to fool ourselves, there is no way that an engine can make top performance
tuned by ear and/or experience. Even when you build a number of engines to identical
specifications, each one will have to be set up differently for best power. I have found
that I pick up at least 5% more horsepower by fine tuning on the dyno. If it is a motor
with which I have not had a lot of experience, more often than not I gain something
like 10%.

ROLLING ROAD DYNO

There are two basic types of dynamometers, the engine dyno and the rolling road or
chassis dyno. The rolling road is very convenient as you just drive the car on to a set of
rollers and run the engine to find the power and torque output. However, rolling road
dynos can be a total waste of time for engine development or fine tuning. It all
depends on the skill and understanding levels of the operator, and the type of rolling
road. The dyno may be either an inertia type or a brake type and the latter can be
further categorised as being either a water brake or an eddy current brake.

   The inertia dyno employs a large diameter drum which is accelerated by the
vehicle's driving wheels. A large diameter drum has more inertia than a smaller drum
of the same weight. That extra inertia requires more torque to accelerate. The dyno
manufacturer knows the inertia value so when the wheels accelerate the drum the
torque can be computed. Accurately measuring this acceleration over a small time
frame gives a torque figure from which the hp is calculated. Consequently the inertia
dyno is of little use to us. All you will determine is if the engine is developing good
power. For example, if a car fully developed for rally work usually produces around
145–150hp at the wheels and yours is turning out 148hp then you are on a good thing.
On the other hand if it showed 135hp then you can be sure something is amiss.

Above: *Under the control of a competent operator, the eddy current type rolling road has much in its favour.*

Right: *This is the eddy current brake unit. The lever on the right connects to the strain gauge and the signal is taken back to the dyno computer software to calculate engine output. What appears to be a brake rotor actually directs cooling air through the brake.*

A much more useful rolling road is the brake type. This utilises some form of brake, or varying load, connected to the rollers that the wheels turn. Years ago most brakes were water type employing hydraulics to load the wheels. These are still around and are quite useful but an eddy current brake is much more user friendly. The actual eddy current brake unit looks like a large alternator. Applying electricity to the brake provides the load to resist wheel rotation. The force is measured by a strain gauge and computed into torque, and then into hp. Because a constant load can be applied the eddy current rolling road is excellent for mapping of the ignition and fuel injection.

The power outputs computed by inertia and brake rolling roads puts them at quite significant odds with each other. While an inertia type like the Dynojet might record something like 120hp, an eddy current road will most likely indicate closer to 102–104hp, something like a 14 or 15% difference, and as the power increases the difference is magnified.

THE ENGINE DYNO

The engine dyno is very sensitive and will give a clear indication of precisely what size of carburettor jets and ignition timing the engine prefers for best power. We can also check the effect of a change in the dwell angle, or a change in spark plug gap. The cam can be advanced or retarded and the change in power noted. We can note the results of any changes in carburettor venturi size or air horn design. In fact, anything that it is possible to twiddle with should be twiddled and the results accurately recorded so that you will know exactly how to set up the engine to perform at its best on any circuit. This all takes time, but at the end of the session you will know exactly what to do to get the best low-end power when you need it. You will know what combination gives best overall power, and if you need maximum power you will know what magic to perform to achieve that too. Remember to keep accurate notes – do not leave anything to memory.

Now don't get me wrong – engine dynos are definitely not the 'be all and end all' of engine tuning. There are clearly definable limits to the usefulness of most engine dynos due to the static nature of the load applied to the engine. Only on computerised dynos like the Superflow SF-800 and its more recent siblings can you check how crisply an engine will accelerate, or what its throttle response will be like.

Usually the areas where you will get caught out are those of carburation and ignition timing. There are many combinations of different brands of manifolds and carburettors that, on the dyno, give seemingly identical performances, but on the race circuit there will generally be one set-up that is superior to the rest, allowing improved lap times or maybe better performance in race traffic if you have to drive through the field, as in speedway racing.

LIMITS TO RELIABILITY OF HORSEPOWER FIGURES

There are several types of engine dynos in use, and while all do a good job in enabling a motor to be set up correctly, do not take a lot of notice of the power figures – variations of up to 10% from one dyno to another are not uncommon. The reason for this is that tuning companies do not have the money to outlay on the latest, most accurate dynos. Instead, in many cases they make do with older or new, less sophisticated types. This in itself is not such a bad thing providing that all the tuning is done on the same dyno. Otherwise you may try out some new trick part and find that it gives you 8% more power on a dyno on the other side of town, when in fact you had lost power with that trick. It was just that the dyno was reading higher than the one on which the motor was originally tuned (Table 14.1).

Another trap may also result from the use of these older dynos. Within the trade it is generally well known whose dyno gives the highest, most distorted power outputs. To sell an engine or even go-quicker bits, some have resorted to testing their motor or equipment on such a dyno to make it appear from the dyno test sheets that the motor is much hotter than it really is. Before you buy a motor or equipment on the pretext of it being more powerful, or more something, be sure that you know on which dyno it was tested and make enquiries as to the fidelity of its power readings. Also ensure that the engine number is quoted on the dyno sheet and check that it corresponds with the motor you are buying, otherwise you could be taken for a ride at considerable expense.

Table 14.1   Dynamometer comparison using 350cu in Chevy test engine

	Dyno A		Dyno B	
rpm	*hp*	*torque (lbf ft)*	*hp*	*torque (lbf ft)*
5,500	472	450.7	477.7	456.2
6,000	505.3	442.3	532.7	466.3
6,500	567.6	458.6	560.5	452.9
7,000	601.4	451.2	582	436.7
7,250	606.3	439.2	582.8	422.2
7,500	611.8	428.4	584.8	409.5
7,750	622	421.5	551.4	373.7

Note: this motor was not altered in any way between tests. The hp and torque figures have been corrected to compensate for changes in air density.

While we are on the subject, keep in mind that there is no guarantee that a company does top-quality work just because some big names use their engines or equipment. What you buy and what the top name buys (or is given) are not necessarily of the same standard. This is unfortunate, but it is a fact of life. Power figures get thrown around rather carelessly by some firms; I refer to them as 'paper horsepower'..

To cite an instance of this, I remember a top engine builder advertising that his particular engine produced in excess of 200hp. This was surprising as most comparative engines were producing around 15hp less. A couple of these trick engines were bought for evaluation and one produced 186hp and the other 193hp. Now these were guaranteed to produce a minimum of 200hp. About the same time a top-name driver ran two engines identical to these, and on the same dyno they did indeed produce in excess of 200hp. The two dud engines were stripped and the deck heights were found to be all over the place; combustion chamber volumes had not been equalised, the valve seats were not concentric or of equal width, and inlet ports were not of the same configuration. A pair of replica engines were built up using the same design features, but with everything done correctly, and these produced 208 and 209hp. That must prove something about doing things the correct way. It also proves that you do not get the best just because you pay for it. To get the best in many instances you will have to tidy up the loose ends.

Top firms have their problems with outside suppliers too, so it is not always entirely the fault of the engine builder when things go wrong. Obviously he must bear some responsibility if he has not made an adequate check to ensure that the outside work is up to standard. Just a few years back a Formula 1 engine constructor was having a series of crankshaft problems. When an investigation was made, it was found that the supplier had made a machining error during manufacture, due to an improperly dressed grinding wheel. A whole batch of cranks was affected and those that had not been used were scrapped. You can appreciate how much harder it is for a private individual to get top-quality work when a World Championship engine constructor cannot always get it.

PERFORMING A STANDARDISED TEST

Even if you are using the newest, most sophisticated engine dyno, the performance figures obtained will be pretty much meaningless, except for perhaps some sort of shallow bragging rights, unless you do all you can to perform a 'standardised test'.

Left: *Tuning using an A/F ratio lambda meter while running on a dyno enables the operator to tune the engine for best power output with little risk of engine damage from going too lean. However, if the atmosphere has not been controlled, the whole exercise may have been a total waste of time and money.*

Below: *This dirt track sprint car engine is being tested with the same exhaust and inlet systems as run when installed in the car, even going as far as having a good coating of bull-ring clay on the headers! The induction atmosphere is dyno cell air, which the operator reasoned was OK as there was a good flow of cool air into the room, and anyway, the methanol mechanical fuel injection system is not exactly a precision metering device. However, as the atmosphere changed over the several days that cam comparisons were being done, how was he going to see exactly what cam was really the most suitable?*

By this I mean you have to carry out your testing in a controlled environment as much as possible so that the engine being tested today will produce an identical set of numbers tomorrow, next month, or next year. That may sound like a tall order but in the higher forms of engine development where we consider gains of 3% exceptional, and 0.7–1.0% the norm, we have to do all possible to determine if we are making real headway with development.

There are three areas of concern. First, the atmosphere influences power so we need a standardised atmosphere in our dyno room. True, we can apply correction factors to compensate for variables in temperature, pressure and humidity, but while being useful in ordinary testing such corrections are not a good idea for intensive development. They can also lull a dyno operator into believing that the test atmosphere doesn't matter; he can simply compensate and correct any deficiency! The big problems that can be easily rectified revolve around the source and availability of intake air for the engine. It is pointless testing with the engine dragging in hot air from within the dyno room; that's pretty obvious, but it is no better for it to be pulling in air from outside contaminated by exhaust gas, or by water spray from the air conditioning tower on the roof, or by solvents from the paint shop or parts washer room.

Equally important as the quality of air available for the engine is the volume of air available. Obviously we don't want the engine drawing a vacuum and gasping for air; equally we don't want the air supply pressurised either. Therefore the air supply system, whether it be unconditioned outside air or air from a conditioning unit, must supply at normal atmospheric pressure at all engine loads. If different engines are being developed this can be very easily overlooked if it is not your normal practice to measure the atmospheric pressure in the air supply ducting where it connects to the engine's inlet.

Operators of wheel dynos have many more problems in this area. The best thing you can do is have a good exhaust extractor fan drawing on an oversize flex pipe connected to the exhaust. If you find that your eyes water when testing cars running race fuel or methanol the extractor fan isn't doing its job, so the engine will be drawing in exhaust gas as well. Air supply quantity can be an issue too as noise regulations often dictate that the garage doors be closed so be sure to install a big fan to blow air into the garage.

Second, engine variables must be eliminated. This means testing with the complete air inlet system and full exhaust exactly as it will be in the car. If the engine uses an ignition system affected by battery voltage then the car's battery and charging system, together with any other high current draw components need to be connected. In the past we were content to hold water and oil temps within 5°C. That's still okay for ordinary development, but in tightly controlled classes where we are constantly looking for tiny gains we have to keep to ±1°C. And at this level we maintain water temp in the brake to ±3°C.

Also we have to test with a 'known' fuel. The fact that a fuel has a certain label doesn't mean that it's identical to another drum with the same label. Ideally we want fuel from the same batch and that has been stored under the same conditions. This can mean buying in sufficient fuel to meet your test needs for an entire race season. Then at the beginning of the new season back to back tests would be done to compare performance with the 'old' and 'new' fuels.

The third variable is the dyno operator's test methodology. To get consistency in the numbers, the dyno operator has to be consistent in how he goes about his work. 457

Things like engine geometry on the test stand may not seem hugely important, but if the engine is misaligned, that can affect windage losses in the crankcase, and fuel preparation in the inlet manifold, plus losses in the brake coupling. Then there is the actual test procedure. The operator has to establish a set test sequence and not deviate.

ROLLING ROAD PITFALLS

It is when working with a rolling road that the operator must be even more diligent not to unwittingly introduce erroneous test methodologies. There are just so many areas where what may seem a minor oversight can make the power graph a complete farce. Then of course there are the unscrupulous operators who prey on the unwary, producing a fudged dyno printout to prove their impressive skills in being able to extract more hp, when in reality their only talent is for extracting wads of money for a very basic tune-up.

The main problem centres on the fact that the rolling road relies on consistent contact between tyres and rollers to arrive at an hp number. Since there is no direct connection between the engine and rollers, we have to understand that if at any stage there is a change in tyre/roller contact or tyre circumference, or if the operator has made an error in the information he has input to the dyno's computer software then the power figures will be unreliable, and unrepeatable.

The rolling road is dumb; it doesn't know anything about your car. Consequently it relies on a smart operator to provide factual input to enable it to give an honest power graph. The usual procedure is to run the vehicle at 100kph and 'tell' the dyno software the engine revs that correspond to this speed. The dyno has no knowledge of what gear the car is in; it doesn't know the tyre circumference; how much slip is occurring between tyres and rollers etc. Therefore it is imperative that the dyno knows exactly how many rpm the engine is turning at 100kph road speed, and it is imperative that the pressure between tyres and rollers is not changed at any time during the run otherwise the tyre circumference will change.

At this point you should be beginning to see glaring problems. If the measuring line – and as far as the dyno is concerned that is all the tyre is – keeps changing length according to how much pressure is pushing it down between the rollers, then what are the chances for accuracy? Additionally what if the dyno operator is inputting the rpm at 100kph based on eyeballing a tacho mounted in front of the steering wheel? And what if that tacho is not only inaccurate but regularly changes its mind as to how many rpm equals 100kph?

This last problem can be overcome if the dyno software is hooked up so as to directly measure engine rpm straight off the engine. This way we are taking the operator's eyesight and the accuracy of the car's tacho out of the loop.

Tyre circumference is a different problem, and to minimise its influence on the power graph we have to rely heavily on the operator being completely on the ball. Many people involved with cars know that tyres grow due to centrifugal force as their rotational speed increases, ie the tyre gets longer. However tyre circumference decreases when we add more weight to the vehicle, or reduce speed. In this situation the tyre gets shorter. Therefore anytime we add weight to minimise wheelspin on the rollers, or change tyre rotational speed from 100kph, the road speed to engine rpm relationship that has been programmed into the dyno software will be incorrect. In computer speak 'garbage in equals garbage out'. Therefore the operator needs to warm the tyres on the rollers to bring them up to pressure, and then set the software to read the rpm for 100kph. If there is a wheelspin problem and the car has to be weighted down he will have to go back and reset the software at 100kph.

You, as the individual having your car dynoed, also have to be on the ball. What adds to the problem on a rolling road is that we have each drive tyre wedged down between two rollers, so with each revolution the tyre is compressed twice. As rotation speed increases so does the number of tyre compressions. Consequently tyre pressure, tyre construction, tread width, tread depth etc will all be influencing frictional losses and distorting the power graph. Therefore ideally for utmost consistency you should have a dedicated set of drive tyres that you use only for dyno tests. If you decide on taking this path your dyno tyres need to be sealed in plastic bags and stored out of light so as to maintain their original characteristics as much as possible. You don't need new tyres, in fact the less tread the better. Obviously you need to correctly pressure the tyres to identical pressure for each dyno test, and in this regard nitrogen is a more reliable gas than compressed air loaded with water vapour.

Over the years all sorts of ideas have been put forward to 'convert' hp at the wheels to hp at the flywheel. Some have the idea you can simply add a certain percentage – 15% is a popular number – to account for losses in the gearbox, driveshafts, diff and tyres. Others prefer to add 20 or 30hp to the wheel hp numbers to make up for these losses. All such theories are dead wrong, but don't despair because with a modern eddy current rolling road equipped with a bi-directional strain gauge we can arrive at a pretty accurate figure – providing the methodology is correct.

What the operator has to do at the end of the power run is pull the car out of gear

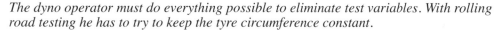

The dyno operator must do everything possible to eliminate test variables. With rolling road testing he has to try to keep the tyre circumference constant.

and let it run-down. Then by measuring the run-down rolling losses and adding them to the power graph we arrive at a graph that will come close to mirroring that from an engine dyno. However there are two provisos: first the operator has to select an acceleration rate to match the engine; and secondly, he has to ensure that there is no change in the load over the drive wheels between that applied during the power run and the run-down. If you doubt the reliability of this method, try doing a series of runs in three different gears and overlay the graphs with run-down losses added, and you will find that they match up pretty well. Measured in the conventional way the graphs would have been all over the shop. Generally the lower the gear the higher the wheel hp. This is due to there being lower rolling losses as there is greatly reduced friction because of less tyre rotations during the power run. The run will also take less time so with less opportunity to put a lot of heat into the combustion chamber the engine may make more power.

At this point you may be wondering if an eddy current rolling road is so accurate when power runs are done properly, why are engine dynos the development tool of choice? Basically it all gets down to consistency and repeatability from one test to the next. With an engine dyno the test environment can be carefully controlled. This enables test results with variations of no worse than 1%, and in the very best engine shops working for well funded teams their back to back test consistency is closer to 0.5%. Even when you do all you can to eliminate variables, you can't do better than about 3% with a rolling road, although at certain points on the power curve it can be less than 2%. That's perfectly acceptable in many forms of motorsport, but when we are looking for small gains we need greater accuracy. There's also the aspect of convenience. With an engine dyno there is no time wasted installing the engine in a car prior to testing each new modification. And with the engine reasonably accessible while attached to the dyno many bits can be changed and tested quite quickly.

WHAT THE NUMBERS MEAN

Getting back to horsepower figures again, few realise that they do not tell the whole story about engine performance or even how well a motor has been modified. Of much greater value are the torque and brake mean effective pressure (bmep) figures. These indicate much more to us and show where we are heading with our modifications.

Torque is a measure of the twisting force at the crankshaft expressed as pounds-foot force (lbf ft, commonly called foot pounds). For example, if an engine is producing torque of 100lbf ft it means that it will lift a load of 100lb with a lever 1ft long connected to the crankshaft. If the engine moves this load through one revolution, work is being done; in this instance 628ft/lb (twisting force x revolutions x lever length x 2π). Power is the rate at which this work is being done, hence

$$\text{Power} = \text{work} \frac{(\text{torque x revolutions})}{\text{time}}$$

In the Imperial system, power is measured in pounds/feet per minute. However, these units are very small, so the unit we know as horsepower (hp) is the one used today. One horsepower equals 33,000lb/ft per minute. This was calculated as a result of experiments carried out by James Watt, using strong dray horses. It is obvious, realising that power is the rate at which work is done, that two motors both producing 100lbf ft torque could have differing power outputs. In fact, if one motor lifted its 100lb load twice as quickly as the other, then it must be twice as powerful or have double the horsepower. Engine speed is measured in revolutions per minute and this is the time unit we use in calculating horsepower, so

$$hp = \frac{torque \times rpm}{5252}$$

Also

$$hp = \frac{bmep \times L \times rpm}{13,000}$$

where L = engine capacity in litres.

Earlier, I mentioned that high horsepower figures can be misleading. We can end up with a big power figure because the motor turns a lot of rpm, but unless it produces a higher torque output over a wide rpm range, lap times could be slower due to poorer acceleration or an increase in the number of gear changes required.

For this reason we have the measure of brake mean effective pressure (bmep), which gives a true indication of how effectively the motor is operating regardless of its capacity or its operating rpm. It is, in fact, a measure of the average cylinder pressures generated during all four engine strokes. We calculate bmep using the following formula:

$$bmep = \frac{hp \times 13,000}{L \times rpm}$$

or

$$bmep = \frac{lbf\ ft \times 2.475}{L}$$

where L = engine capacity in litres.

The highest bmep will occur at the point of maximum torque. In fact, this formula gives the true bmep only at that point. At other places on the horsepower or torque curves it is very close but not exactly true, but do not let this worry you.

The average motor runs at a bmep of around 140–165psi. A good road motor should run at 165–190psi. Rally engines will generally be in the 185–205 bracket and racing motors from 205–230psi. A few exceptional motors will run up to 240psi, naturally aspirated.

In standard form, motors such as the Alfa Romeo double overhead cam, the Lotus/Ford Twin Cam and the Ford BDA operate at around 170psi. Many motorcycles operate at a figure of about 165–180psi and superbikes are showing bmeps of 195psi, with a few nudging 200psi.

On paper, 175hp from a 1,300cc Ford BDA looks impressive, but when you work it all out it is rather less so. This motor was a fully modified racing unit using two 45 DCOE Weber carbs and Cosworth Formula 1 cams. It produced 102lbf ft torque at 7,200rpm and 175hp at 9,500rpm; the rev limit was 10,500rpm. The bmep was 194psi. A properly modified motor should have produced 207–210psi considering that it had four valves per cylinder, good porting, good combustion chambers for a proper burn, etc. In fact, a well-tuned Mini 1300 using the old five-port head will run a 195psi brake mean effective pressure, and the 355cu in NASCAR speedway V8 motors pump 205psi – and on a single four-barrel carburettor at that.

Another measure we use to analyse combustion efficiency is called brake specific fuel (bsf). This is worked out by dividing the engine's fuel flow (lb of fuel per hour) by its horsepower output. If the engine is consuming 174lb of fuel per hour at 5,000rpm and the power output at that rpm is 424hp, the bsf would be 174 ÷ 424 = 0.410. Obviously the less fuel the engine is using for each horsepower produced, the more efficient combustion must be. As the numerical value of the bsf decreases, combustion efficiency improves, up to the point where subsequent reduction in the bsf causes reductions in horsepower.

GEARING'S INFLUENCE ON PERFORMANCE

With the dyno session over and all the twiddling completed, do not go home and file the dyno sheets. The next thing you must do is work out if your gear set is suitable for the torque characteristics of your engine, and when you decide on a gear set work out your gear change points for maximum acceleration. In Table 14.2 I have listed the results of a 1600 Ford BDA dyno test. This is a strictly limited-budget club-level engine, a wet sump unit with a heat-treated cast-iron crank and stock rods that have been polished along the beams and shot-peened, and fitted with Cosworth Sierra bolts. Although this engine would be more competitive running to 8,500rpm, it should not be regularly buzzed beyond 7,750rpm out of regard for the crank and rods; however, an occasional run to 8,000rpm is acceptable. You will note that this engine makes a big jump in torque from 6,000rpm, so we would not want to drop below this engine speed if possible.

Table 14.3 shows one method that can be used to check the suitability of various

Table 14.2   Dyno test of 1600cc Ford BDA

rpm	hp	torque (lbf ft)	bmep (psi)
4,500	94.4	110.2	170.5
5,000	111.3	116.9	180.8
5,500	130.4	124.5	192.6
6,000	154.5	135.2	209.2
6,500	169.2	136.7	211.5
7,000	178.9	134.2	207.6
7,500	190.1	133.1	205.9
7,750	190.9	129.4	200.2
8,000	183.2	120.3	186.1

gear sets. By calculating the 'step' between gears it is a simple matter to calculate what the engine rpm will be when you slot into the next gear. Then you can determine if the engine will be dropping out of the power band between gears. The T5 box and 'Rocket' gear set are very popular at club level, but how suitable are they? With the T5 the change from second to third gear with an 8,000rpm change point is going to see engine revs fall to about 5,500rpm, which is 500rpm out of the power band, but even worse, using a 7,750rpm redline puts the engine 700rpm out of the power band. The gap from third to fourth appears to be less of a problem, with a rev drop of around 2,000rpm, putting the engine 250rpm out of the power band. However, at this higher speed the car's frontal area and aerodynamic attachments are creating a lot more drag so the gap may be more of a problem than that between second and third. The Rocket set is more suitable, with the second-to-third change dropping engine rpm by about 1,900rpm, and the third-to-fourth change is dropping engine speed by 1,600rpm. By comparison, gearboxes used by racers with fat wallets, such as the ZF and Hollinger, appear to be an overkill, with the upchange in most gears dropping engine rpm by only 1,000–1,300rpm.

However, this assumption merely indicates just how inadequate a simple chart like Table 14.3 really is. A lot of people use charts like this, but I do not think that they

Table 14.3   Gearbox gear step and rpm step comparison

	Gear ratio	Gear step	rpm drop at redline rpm					
			6500	7000	7500	8000	8500	9000
T5	1st 2.95							
	2nd 1.94	+34.2%	2223	2394	2565	2736	2907	3078
	3rd 1.34	+30.9%	2008	2163	2318	2472	2627	2781
	4th 1.00	+25.4%	1651	1778	1905	2034	2159	2286
	5th .80	+20%	1300	1400	1500	1600	1700	1800
Rocket	1st 2.54							
	2nd 1.67	+34.3%	2230	2401	2573	2744	2916	3087
	3rd 1.26	+24.5%	1593	1715	1838	1960	2083	2205
	4th 1.00	+20.6%	1339	1442	1545	1648	1751	1854
ZF	1st 2.3							
	2nd 1.6	+30.4%	1976	2128	2280	2432	2584	2736
	3rd 1.36	+15.0%	975	1050	1125	1200	1275	1350
	4th 1.14	+16.2%	1053	1134	1215	1296	1377	1458
	5th 1.00	+12.3%	800	861	923	984	1046	1107
Hollinger	1st 2.57							
	2nd 1.99	+22.6%	1469	1582	1695	1808	1921	2034
	3rd 1.61	+19.1%	1242	1337	1433	1528	1624	1719
	4th 1.35	+16.1%	1047	1127	1208	1288	1369	1449
	5th 1.14	+15.6%	1014	1092	1170	1248	1326	1404
	6th 1.00	+12.3%	800	861	923	984	1046	1107

really tell us anything much about the suitability of a gearbox. Looking at gearing from the aspect of remaining within the engine's power band is all right for a road car, but for track work there are many other considerations. To some extent this illustrates why many racers look at tuning the engine to produce more hp when the opposition is showing them a clean pair of heels, when in reality there may be a lot more performance gain for money spent in areas such as brakes, suspension, weight, aerodynamics and gearing.

Certainly, more power will accelerate a car faster, but power is not the only factor in the equation. Vehicle weight obviously also figures prominently, as does gearing. Gearing is all about torque multiplication. If we have 100lbf ft torque at the crankshaft and 10:1 gearing, the twisting force at the axles will be 1,000lbf ft. That will cause the car to accelerate harder than an engine producing 10% more torque but with 8:1 gearing, or 880lbf ft (110 x 8 = 880) at the axles.

Looking at Tables 14.4 to 14.7 will help you to get a clearer idea of a frequently overlooked truth. Even though you are probably not interested in road speed in a race car, gearing figures need to be given a third dimension so that they can be related to the real world, and the only way that we can get the idea of what we are looking for in a gear set is to consider axle torque, road speed and engine speed together. Axle torque is found by multiplying engine torque by the overall gear ratio, while road speed can be worked out using this formula:

$$\text{Road speed} = \frac{\text{rpm x tc}}{\text{gr x 1050}}$$

Where tc = tyre circumference in inches (πd), and gr = overall gear ratio.

Checking Table 14.4 you can see the problem with the T5 gear set for this particular BDA engine. On the change from second to third we are dropping axle torque by

Table 14.4   Rear-axle torque and road speed with 5.14 differential and T5 gearbox

	1st 15.16		2nd 9.97		3rd 6.89		4th 5.14		5th 4.13	
rpm	*torque*	*speed*	*torque*	*speed*	*torque*	*speed*	*torque*	*speed*	*torque*	*speed*
4,500	1671	21	1099	32	759	47	566	63	455	78
5,000	1772	24	1165	36	805	52	601	70	483	87
5,500	1887	26	1241	40	858	57	640	77	514	96
6,000	2050	28	1348	43	932	63	695	84	558	104
6,500	2072	31	1363	47	942	68	703	91	565	113
7,000	2034	33	1338	50	925	73	690	98	554	122
7,500	2018	36	1327	54	917	78	684	105	550	130
7,750	1962	37	1290	56	892	81	665	108	534	135
8,000	1824	38	1199	58	829	83	618	112	497	139
Torque drop*	40.6%		34.1%		24.6%		15.0%			

*Approximate torque drop at 7,750rpm redline

around 34% – from 1,290 at 7,750rpm in second down to about 850 at a little under 5,500rpm in third gear. In the higher gears the torque drop is less dramatic, but wind drag will contribute to slowing the rate of acceleration as road speed increases, so the figures are even less healthy than they appear on paper.

Table 14.5   Rear-axle torque and road speed with 4.7 differential and Rocket gearbox

	1st 11.94		2nd 7.83		3rd 5.90		4th 4.7	
rpm	*torque*	*speed*	*torque*	*speed*	*torque*	*speed*	*torque*	*speed*
4,500	1316	27	863	41	650	55	518	69
5,000	1396	30	915	46	690	61	549	76
5,500	1487	33	975	50	735	67	585	84
6,000	1614	36	1059	55	798	73	635	92
6,500	1632	39	1070	60	807	79	642	99
7,000	1602	42	1051	64	792	85	631	107
7,500	1589	45	1042	69	785	91	626	115
7,750	1545	47	1013	71	763	94	608	118
8,000	1436	48	942	73	710	97	565	122
Torque drop*	40.8%		24.0%		16.1%			

*Approximate torque drop at 7,750rpm redline

Table 14.6   Rear-axle torque and road speed with 4.7 differential and ZF gearbox

	1st 10.81		2nd 7.52		3rd 6.39		4th 5.36		5th 4.7	
rpm	*torque*	*speed*	*torque*	*speed*	*torque*	*speed*	*torque*	*speed*	*torque*	*speed*
4,500	1191	30	829	43	704	51	591	60	518	69
5,000	1264	33	879	48	747	56	627	67	549	76
5,500	1346	37	936	53	796	62	667	74	585	84
6,000	1462	40	1017	57	864	67	725	80	635	92
6,500	1478	43	1028	62	874	73	733	87	642	99
7,000	1451	47	1009	67	858	79	719	94	631	107
7,500	1439	50	1001	72	851	84	713	100	626	115
7,750	1399	52	973	74	827	87	694	104	608	118
8,000	1300	53	905	76	769	90	645	107	565	122
Torque drop*	34.2%		10.2%		11.4%		8.5%			

*Approximate torque drop at 7,750rpm redline

We see the same sort of problem with the Rocket gear set; big slumps in axle torque that, while not dropping the engine out of the power band, will handicap engine performance on the race circuit by not permitting the car to accelerate as quickly as is possible with a better selection of gears. However, when we look at the ZF and Hollinger boxes we see a quite different situation. With both gear sets there is only a slight drop in axle torque – about 10% – between gears.

Table 14.7   Rear-axle torque and road speed with 4.7 differential and Hollinger gearbox

	1st 12.08		2nd 9.35		3rd 7.57		4th 6.35		5th 5.36		6th 4.7	
rpm	*torq*	*spd*	*torq*	*spd*	*torq*	*spd*	*torq*	*spd*	*torq*	*spd*	*torq*	*spd*
4,500	1331	27	1030	35	834	43	700	51	591	60	518	69
5,000	1412	30	1093	38	885	48	742	57	627	67	549	76
5,500	1504	33	1164	42	942	53	791	62	667	74	585	84
6,000	1633	36	1264	46	1023	57	858	68	725	80	635	92
6,500	1651	39	1278	50	1035	62	868	74	733	87	642	99
7,000	1621	42	1255	54	1016	67	852	79	719	94	631	107
7,500	1608	45	1245	58	1008	72	845	85	713	100	626	115
7,750	1563	46	1210	60	980	74	822	88	694	104	608	118
8,000	1453	48	1125	61	911	76	764	90	645	107	565	122
Torque drop*	19.1%		14.9%		11.4%		10.8%		8.5%			

*Approximate torque drop at 7,750rpm redline

All of these tables highlight the need to accelerate out of turns in the correct gear to ensure maximum speed on to the following straight. For example, using the ZF box to illustrate the point you could exit an 80mph corner in either third, fourth or fifth gear, but there would be significantly different vehicle speeds attainable on the following straight because of varying rates of acceleration in each respective gear. Exiting in third gear, the twisting force on the axles would be about 855lbf ft, but if either fourth or fifth were used this would decline to 725 and around 565lbf ft respectively, resulting in reduced speed along the straight. Remember that being in the correct gear is even more important on higher-speed turns because here the wings and car frontal area are sapping considerably more 'accelerative power'.

The charts also accentuate another aspect of gear set selection that is frequently overlooked: that of having available a suitable gear for every corner on a circuit. Drivers do not want to be on the redline through a corner, neither do they want to be lugging the engine at the bottom of the power band. Usually it is easier to 'steer' the car on the throttle around the middle of the power band, which is the 6,500–7,000rpm area with this Ford BDA. Based on this assumption, and driver preferences do vary, the T5 box, when mated with a 5.14 axle, really only has a gear for 50mph, 70mph and 90mph turns. With a 4.7 axle the Rocket box has a gear for 40, 60, 80 and 100mph corners. It is when we get to the ZF and Hollinger that we see their clear advantage in this area. The ZF cogs suit 45, 65, 75, 90 and 100mph corners, and the Hollinger has gears for 40, 50, 65, 75, 90 and 100mph turns.

On the subject of gearing, some tuners have the mistaken belief that an engine tuned to produce hp at very high rpm and running short gears will be quicker, due to better acceleration from the big gear numbers, than an engine producing the same hp at lower rpm and with taller gearing. This was the reasoning given by some for Cosworth's dominance in Indy racing a few years ago. The Buick V6 was making the same hp as the Cosworth, about 750, but whereas the Buick was producing its maximum at 8,500rpm the Cossie was doing its thing at 12,500rpm. Hence the theory that the Cosworth-equipped cars were quicker because the shorter gearing was getting them up to speed more rapidly off the turns.

When calculated out the theory does not hold up. At 8,500rpm the Buick is making 463.41lbf ft torque. Running a 3:1 axle, this becomes 1,390lbf ft at the axles. The Cosworth on the other hand is making 315.1lbf ft torque at 12,500rpm. Geared to run the same top speed as the Buick, the Cosworth will have to run a 4:41 axle (12,500 ÷ 8,500 x 3 = 4.41) which results in the same axle torque of 1,390lbf ft. Obviously lower gearing does not give the Cosworth an advantage.

It really gets back to engine design. At high rpm the Buick with rocker arms and push rods is struggling for reliability so it has to be geared so as to keep the engine together for a full 500 miles, which may mean limiting the rpm to 8,500 under race, as opposed to practice, conditions. The Cosworth on the other hand has no long-distance reliability problem with twin cams and small lightweight valves, so even when racing 500 miles it can be safely geared to run out to 13,000rpm. Clearly it is engine design, which allows the Cosworth to safely rev past maximum hp revs, together with the slightly shorter gearing that this permits, that gives the Cossie some advantage.

ASSESSING THE BMEP CURVE

This statement should not, however, be confused with the idea of making more power at high rpm. The problem for tuners is when a lot of rpm is being turned, but no more power is being gained. The 1,300cc Ford BDA mentioned earlier making 175hp at 9,500rpm is a good example of what I am getting at. This is an output that should have been achieved at 8,500rpm or perhaps 8,800 at the most. At 9,500rpm a 1,300 BDA should be showing 190–195hp. Why run an engine faster for no power gain when component life and reliability are reduced?

The time to run an engine harder is when you are at max bmep and you want more hp. For example, a 2-litre Opel running a bmep of 225psi at 8,000rpm is making 277hp. If it can be tuned to produce the same bmep at 8,250rpm, the power will go up to 286hp. This again illustrates why looking at bmep is so important; ordinary hp at dizzy rpm levels is a lot of pain for absolutely no gain.

Additionally, when we get the engine running at high bmep we want to tune it to give a flat bmep curve over a wide power band. Thus a four-cylinder, four-valve, 2-litre motor running in a class rev-limited to 8,500rpm would be expected to pump close to 230psi at about 7,000 or 7,250rpm and not dip below 220psi all the way from 6,000 to 8,500rpm. Basically we do not want the bmep to fall more than 3–5% from maximum over a 2,500rpm range. Obviously to develop an engine to this level involves considerable expenditure of both time and money, but even with engines in a lesser state of tune the aim should always be to produce a nice broad and flat bmep curve. Therefore if engine design or budget restricts you to a realistic bmep of, say, 205psi, aim for that figure 1,200–1,500rpm lower than the maximum engine speed at which you can afford to operate and keep the bmep within 5% of 205psi, ie more than 194.7psi, over a 2,500rpm spread. For example, if maximum safe rpm is 7,500, try for a bmep peak at 6,000–6,250rpm with a bmep number over 195psi starting at 5,000 and going to 7,500rpm, or starting at 4,750 and going to 7,250rpm. Future development of the engine, if the rpm limit was to stay at

7,500, would centre around raising the bmep at the lower and upper ends of the curve to within 3% of the peak; thus we would be looking for a figure over 199psi. Such an improvement would see a power increase in a 2-litre engine of about 4hp between 5,000 and 7,500rpm.

In some types of competition, rallying for example, an even broader power band is desirable, and here the bmep curve will be different. Assuming a four-cylinder, four-valve, 2-litre engine with a rev limit of 8,500rpm, we would want the torque peak at an engine speed at least 2,500rpm and preferably 3,000rpm below this. This means the bmep peaking at around 5,500rpm with a pressure approaching 220psi. Then we would be looking for a bmep figure within 7–10% of this over a 3,000–3,250rpm range, say from 4,750rpm up to the hp peak at around 7,750–8,000rpm. In reality a good strong road engine should have a curve very similar to this, but with a bmep peak of something like 190psi at 4,500–5,000rpm and an hp peak at 7,000rpm.

GET AN ACCURATE TACHO

Obviously to get gear change points right and to avoid engine damage you need an accurate, easy-to-read tacho. The car manufacturer's stock unit is useless for competition, and many aftermarket units are not a whole lot superior. Unfortunately, many people have been led to believe that a tacho reading is infallible, but stock units are frequently 500–700rpm in error. This can, and should, be corrected by having the unit recalibrated. Aircraft instrument repairers can rectify such a problem, which will probably mean that the tacho is then suitable for a road car. However, there will be other problems that render it useless for competition, as we shall see.

Because we are running short gears, powerful engines and lightweight bodies, a race car tacho must have a needle that swings around with lightning speed without overshooting the mark; for example, we do not want the needle zinging around to 9,000, then dropping back to a correct 8,300. Neither do we want it lagging behind true engine speed. Years ago drivers regularly had to guess gear changes in the lower gears because of needle lag. Thus if the rev limit was 8,500 the driver would change up at 8,000 going out of first gear and 8,200 on the change from second to third, and so on. With cheaper tachos the manufacturers reduce needle lag by reducing damping, but this of course increases needle flicker in stiffly sprung race cars; then needle bounce and overshooting the true rpm and dropping back become bigger problems.

A good-quality (expensive) race tacho will have these kinds of problems engineered out. Some, like the Stack and Racetech units, use a stepper motor to drive the needle, and both are highly recommended for those who can afford the best. They incorporate a tell-tale and a shift light. A little more affordable are the Auto Meter range of Pro-Comp tachos. These have an air-core movement and a huge 5in dial. The Pro-Comp 2 has a tell-tale but no shift light. The Auto Meter 6841 has a tell-tale that records highest and lowest rpm, which can be useful in setting up with the correct axle ratio. Both these tachos are easy to read and have a fast, flicker-free needle. The only budget tacho that I can recommend (one-third of the price of a Stack, and half that of an Auto Meter) is the Elliott Clubman. It is a no-frills unit with no tell-tale or shift light, but the needle is fairly fast and flicker-free; however, get it checked for accuracy as I have seen a few 100–200rpm slow.

SAFE ENGINE RPM

You are probably wondering just how fast it is safe to rev a motor, but of course there is no definite answer. The number of variables involved means that you must use an educated guess, or what is generally known as a rule of thumb. You must remember that engine wear increases dramatically at higher rpm, so a road motor should not be subjected to peak rpm operation continuously, unless you have the time and money for a rebuild every 7,000–10,000 miles.

The same type of reasoning applies in the case of the other types of motors where the rpm limit rule is applied. A rally motor operating at, or close to, the limit will require a rebuild at 1,200–4,000 miles; a road race engine every 300–1,500 miles; and a drag race motor every 1–4 meetings. The rebuild must include not only the replacement of worn parts, but also careful crack testing of components likely to suffer fatigue failure.

The rule of thumb we work to revolves around the mean piston speed in feet per minute. Many people feel that piston speed is of no consequence because of the large advances that have been made in modern-day metallurgy. In years gone by, this figure was used as a measure of an engine's likely wear rate – the higher the piston speed the faster the engine would wear out. I have found that working to an engine's piston speed is a surprisingly accurate means of avoiding blow-ups and general unreliability.

Mean piston speed is calculated using the following formula:

$$\text{Piston speed} = \frac{\text{stroke mm x rpm}}{153} \quad \text{or} \quad \frac{\text{stroke inches x rpm}}{6.024}$$

After you have calculated the rpm limit from Table 14.8 and the above formula, you may find that the limit imposed by the valve gear is lower. If this is the case, do not exceed the rpm limit of the valve train.

Table 14.8   Mean piston speed (fpm)

	Road	Rally	Road race	Drags
Standard cast iron crank and rods	3500	3500	3650	3800(B)
Standard forged crank and rods (A)	3800	4000	4200	4800(B)
Standard cast iron crank, special rods and heavy-duty main bearing caps	3800	4200	4350	4500(B)
Special forged crank, heavy-duty rods and main bearing caps (C)	3800	4200	4600	5500
	–4000	–4400	–4800	–6500

Note: (A) applies to some standard high-performance American V8 engines and many standard European and Japanese engines.

(B) applies to street machines used for occasional drag racing.

(C) most standard motorcycle engines also fit into this category due to the use of heavy-duty components in standard tune.

It is assumed that the engines in every category have balanced crank, rods and pistons and that either forged or top-quality unslotted cast pistons are fitted.

Appendix

Table of Useful Equivalents

1 inch = 25.4mm

1 cubic inch = 16.387cc

1 horsepower = 0.7457 kilowatts
    or 1.0139 PS

1 pound foot torque = 1.3558 Newton metres
    or 0.13824 kg m

1 pound inch torque = 0.11298 Newton metres

1 psi = 6.89476 kilopascals
    or 68.95 millibars
    or 2.0345 inches of Mercury (Hg)
    or 27.67 inches of water

°F = 1.8 x (°C + 32)

1 gallon (Imperial) = 160 fluid oz
    or 4.546 litres

1 gallon (US) = 128 fluid oz
    or 3.785 litres

1mm = 0.03937in

1 litre = 61.024cu in or 1,000cc

1 kilowatt = 1.341hp

1PS = 0.9863 horsepower

1 Newton metre = 0.7376 pound foot

1 kg m = 7.2336 pound foot

1kPA = 0.14504 psi

1 Bar = 14.5038 psi
    or 100kPA

°C = (°F – 32) x 1.8

1 fluid oz (Imperial) = 28.4cc

1 fluid oz (US) = 29.57cc

Index

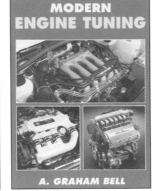